Slutsk and Vicinity Memorial Book (Belarus)

Translation of
Pinkas Slutsk u-benoteha

Original Book Edited by:
N. Chinitz, Sh. Nachmani, Yizkor Book Committee

Originally published in Tel Aviv, 1962

Volume II

JewishGen
מרכז עולמי לגנאלוגיה יהודית
The Global Home for Jewish Genealogy

A Publication of JewishGen
Edmond J. Safra Plaza, 36 Battery Place, New York, NY 10280
646.494.2972 | info@JewishGen.org | www.jewishgen.org

MUSEUM OF
JEWISH HERITAGE
A LIVING MEMORIAL
TO THE HOLOCAUST

Slutsk and Vicinity Memorial Book (Belarus)
Translation of *Pinkas Slutsk u-benoteha*

Volume II

Copyright © 2025 by JewishGen. All rights reserved.
First Printing: February 2025, Shevat, 5785
Editor of Original Yizkor Book: N. Chinitz, Sh. Nachmani, Yizkor Book Committee
Project Coordinator Emerita: Margot Tutun
Cover Design: Irv Osterer
Layout and formatting: Jonathan Wind
Indexing: Stefanie Holzman

Library of Congress Control Number (LCCN): 2024949233

ISBN: 978-1-962054-20-1 (hard cover: 622 pages, alk. paper)

About JewishGen.org

JewishGen, is a Genealogical Research Division of the Museum of Jewish Heritage - A Living Memorial to the Holocaust, serves as the global home for Jewish genealogy.

Featuring unparalleled access to 30+ million records, it offers unique search tools, along with opportunities for researchers to connect with others who share similar interests. Award winning resources such as the Family Finder, Discussion Groups, and ViewMate, are relied upon by thousands each day.

In addition, JewishGen's extensive informational, educational and historical offerings, such as the Jewish Communities Database, Yizkor Book translations, InfoFiles, Family Tree of the Jewish People, and KehilaLinks, provide critical insights, first-hand accounts, and context about Jewish communal and familial life throughout the world.

Offered as a free resource, JewishGen.org has facilitated thousands of family connections and success stories, and is currently engaged in an intensive expansion effort that will bring many more records, tools, and resources to its collections.

Please visit https://www.jewishgen.org/ to learn more.

Vice President for JewishGen: Avraham Groll

About the JewishGen Yizkor Book Project

Yizkor Books (Memorial Books) were traditionally written to memorialize the names of departed family and martyrs during holiday services in the synagogue (a practice that still exists in many synagogues today).

Over the centuries, as a result of countless persecutions and horrific atrocities committed against the Jews, Yizkor Books (Sefer Zikaron in Hebrew) were expanded to include more historical information, such as biographical sketches of famous personalities and descriptions of daily town life.

Following the Holocaust, the idea of remembrance and learning took on an urgent and crucial importance. Survivors of the Holocaust sought out other surviving residents of their former towns to memorialize and document the names and way of life of those who were ruthlessly murdered by the Nazis. These remembrances were documented in Yizkor Books, hundreds of which were published in the first decades after the Holocaust.

Most of these books were published privately, or through *Landsmanshaftn* (social organizations comprised of members originating from the same European town or region) that still existed, and were often distributed free of charge. The languages used to document these crucial histories and links to our past were mostly Yiddish and Hebrew. JewishGen has undertaken the sacred responsibility of translating these books into English so that the culture and way of life of these communities will be preserved and transmitted to future generations.

In 1986, a group of farsighted JewishGenners started a project to pool their efforts together in groups based upon their ancestors' towns and donate funds to translate the Yizkor books of their ancestral towns into English. As the translated material became available, it was made accessible for free at https://www.JewishGen.org/Yizkor . Hardcover copies can be purchased by visiting https://www.jewishgen.org/Yizkor/ybip.html (see below).

It is our hope that the translation of these books into English (and other languages) will assist the countless Jewish family researchers who are so desperately seeking to forge a connection with their heritage.

Director of JewishGen Yizkor Book Project: Lance Ackerfeld

About JewishGen Press

JewishGen Press (formerly the Yizkor Books-in-Print Project) is the publishing division of JewishGen.org, and provides a venue for the publication of non-fiction books pertaining to Jewish genealogy, history, culture, and heritage.

In addition to the Yizkor Book category, publications in the Other Non-Fiction category include Shoah memoirs and research, genealogical research, collections of genealogical and historical materials, biographies, diaries and letters, studies of Jewish experience and cultural life in the past, academic theses, and other books of interest to the Jewish community.

Please visit https://www.jewishgen.org/Yizkor/ybip.html to learn more.

Director of JewishGen Press: Joel Alpert
Managing Editor - Jessica Feinstein
Publications Manager - Susan Rosin

Notes to the Reader

The images in the original book were reproduced from photographs from the time of the first edition. These reproductions were already of poor quality, being pre-war and at least 60 or more years old. As a result, the images in the book are the best achievable.

A reader can view the original scans of the book on the websites listed below.

The original book can be seen online at the Yiddish Book Center website:

https://www.yiddishbookcenter.org/collections/yizkor-books/yzk-nybc314001/nachmani-samson-chinitz-pinkas-slutsk-u-venoteha

OR

at the New York Public Library Digital Collections website:

https://digitalcollections.nypl.org/items/f6dfc840-74eb-0133-bf27-00505686d14e

To obtain a list of Shoah victims from **Slutsk (Belarus),** the reader should access the Yad Vashem web site listed below; one can also search for specific family names using family name option. These lists are continually updated by Yad Vashem, so it is worthwhile to periodically search them.

There is more valuable information (including the Pages of Testimony, etc.) available on this website: https://yvng.yadvashem.org/

A list of all books available from JewishGen Press along with prices is available at: https://www.jewishgen.org/Yizkor/ybip.html

Additional Information is available at: https://kehilalinks.jewishgen.org/slutsk/slutsk.html

Cover Photo Credits

Cover Design by: Irv Osterer

Front Cover:

Yitzhak Katznelson in Slutsk
Photo From the Collection of Y. D. Berkowitz
From right to left: Hillel Dobrov, Yitzhak Katznelson, Avraham Epstein, Y.D. Berkowitz
[Page 163]

Back Cover:

First Row (left to right):
Rabbi Avraham Aharon Peshin [Page 185, Rabbi Chaim Kabalkin [Page 211], Faigel Sperling [Page 42]

Second Row (left to right):
Reb Kuti Isaac Goldhas [Page 155], Rav Moshe Yakov Mendelowitz [Page 192], Rabbi Yosha Ber Soloveitchik [Page 37]

Third Row (left to right):
Pesach Karon [Page 158], Rabbi Joseph Dov Ber Efron [Page 74], Itke Efron [Page 74]

Fourth Row (left to right):
The Gaon Reb Aharon Kotler [Page 111], Rabbi Yossele Peimer [Page 38], Rabbi Zechariah Finkelstein [Page 46]

Geopolitical Information

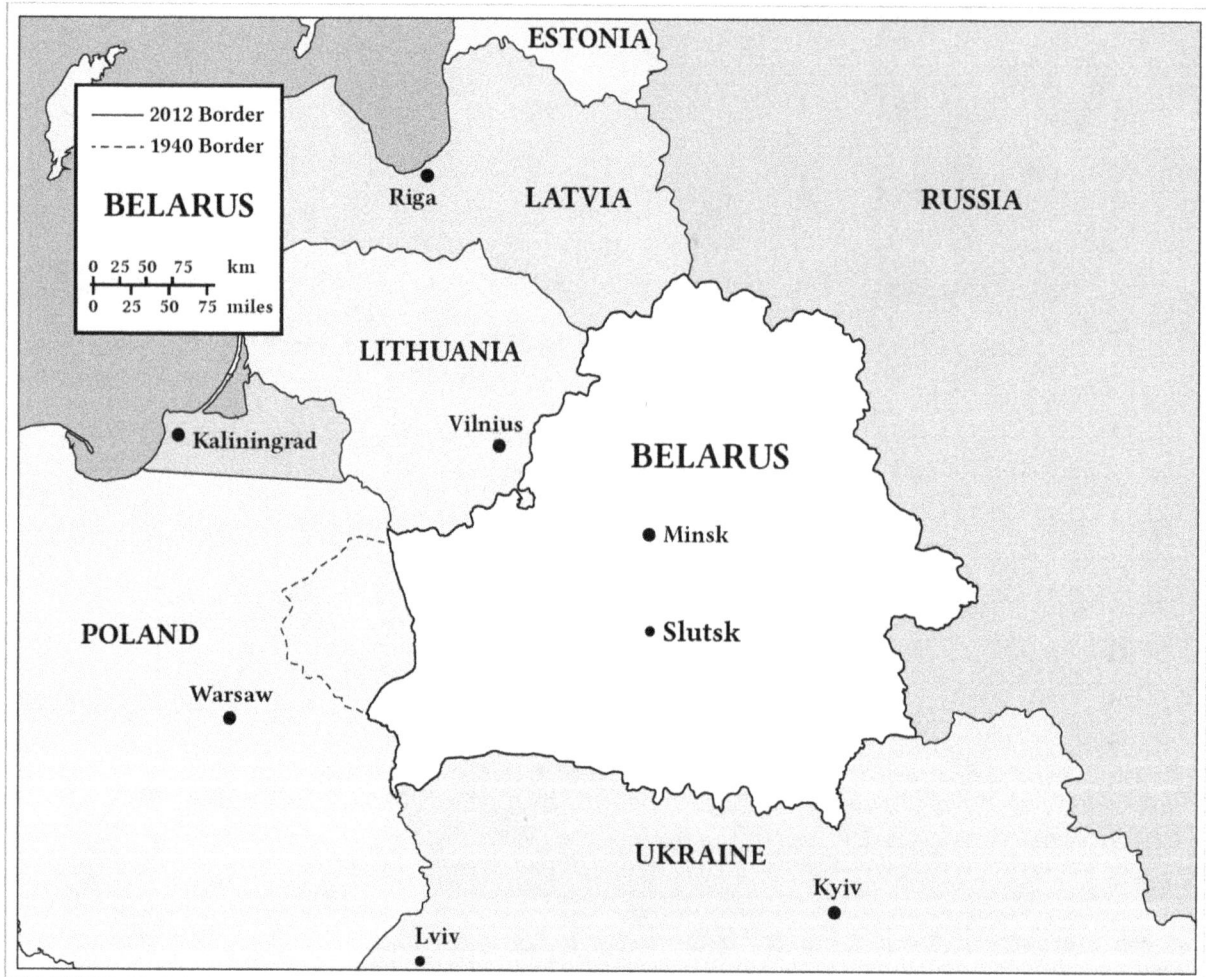

Map of Belarus showing the location of **Slutsk**

Slutsk

Slutsk, Belarus is located at 53°02' N 27°34' E 60 miles S of Minsk

	Town	District	Province	Country
Before WWI (c. 1900):	Slutsk	Slutsk	Minsk	Russian Empire
Between the wars (c. 1930):	Slutsk	Minsk	Belarus SSR	Soviet Union
After WWII (c. 1950):	Slutsk			Soviet Union
Today (c. 2000):	Slutsk			Belarus

Alternate Names for the Town:

Slutsk [Bel, Rus], Słuck [Pol], Slutzk [Yid], Sluzk [Ger], Słucak

Nearby Jewish Communities:

Gresk 10 miles NNW
Pahost 13 miles SSE
Grozovo 13 miles NW
Lenino 14 miles W
Urechcha 15 miles ESE
Chyrvonaya Slabada 21 miles SW
Kapyl 21 miles WNW
Starobin 21 miles S
Lyuban 24 miles SE
Tsimkavichy 24 miles W
Shatsk 27 miles N
Losha 27 miles NNW
Staryya Darohi 29 miles E

Jewish Population: 10,264 (in 1897), 8,358 (in1926)

Table of Contents

English Section

End Volume II

Slutsk and Vicinity Memorial Book (Belarus)
Volume II

53°01' / 27°33'

Translation of *Pinkas Slutsk u-benoteha*

Edited by: N. Chinitz, Sh. Nachmani, Yizkor Book Committee

Published in Tel-Aviv, 1962

Acknowledgments

Project Coordinator:

Emerita Coordinator: Margot Tutun

Our sincere appreciation to Chaim I. Waxman for permission
to put this material on the JewishGen web site.

With grateful thanks to Stefanie Holzman for obtaining the pictures appearing in this translation
project.

This is a translation from: *Pinkas Slutsk u-benoteha* (Slutsk and vicinity memorial book),
Editors: N. Chinitz, Sh. Nachmani, Tel Aviv, Yizkor-Book Committee, 1962 (H, Y, E, 450 pages).

Note: The original book can be seen online at the NY Public Library site: Slutsk

---

[Page 2]

Preface

by the Committee

Translated by Jerrold Landau

When we began to collect the material on Slutsk, and to organize and edit it, some things came to our view, whether factual or popular legends, that were hidden in the treasury of ancient literature and in the memories of the elders of the community. Indeed, the annals of this city throughout the latter four centuries testify clearly, according to documents and historical sources, about its greatness in the distant past, and its essence as a Jewish center in the recent past. Slutsk served throughout the generations as a host to Torah, Haskalah, Zionist activity, and the dissemination of Hebrew culture.

Similarly, our city gave forth famous personalities, great rabbis, famous writers and poets, and communal activists of stature. We find many prominent people in the towns around Slutsk as well, and material and spiritual influence existed among them.

Various images from the past stand before our eyes: images of simple folk, various tradespeople, porters, wagon drivers, good for nothings, leaders of parties, and counselors of youth.

Where are they all? Indeed, during the Holocaust, the Nazis wiped out virtually the entire community of Slutsk, as they wiped out all the Jewish communities.

We, the survivors of Slutsk and its environs, found today in Israel and the United States, bear in our hearts the memory of our city, in which we lived during our childhood. Unforgettable images of our brothers and sisters who perished at the hands of the wild beasts in the form of humans, flutter before our eyes.

So that the memory of Slutsk will not leave us for generation after generation, we took council and decided to establish a memorial monument in the form of this book, presented in Hebrew, Yiddish and English, for the readers who are natives of Slutsk and its environs, and for their descendants in Israel and the Diaspora.

* * *

Our thanks are extended to all those who helped materially and spiritually to actualize the desire of our souls.

[Page 3]

Editors:
Shimshon Nachmani Nachum Chinitz

Editorial Committee:

Tzvi Hagivati
Rabbi Nisan Wachsman
Tzvi Assaf

Printed in Israel
Etchings: Land of Israel Zincography
Publisher: Achdut Cooperative Co., Tel Aviv

[Page 261]

Yiddish Section

Pinkas Slutsk and its environs

Published by the Yizkor Book committee in New York and in Tel Aviv.

Editors: Nachum Chinitz, Shimshon Nachmani

Editorial members: Rabbi Nissan Wachsman, Tvi Assaf.

[Page 262]

The officers of the Yizkor Book committee in New York

First row standing (from right to left): Shmuel Rachlin and his wife, Aharon Rolnik, Chaika Meisel, and Alex Reichman
Second row, sitting: Rabbi Nissan Wachsman, Avraham Meisel, Eliyahu Altman

Members of the Slutsk Council in Israel

Sitting (from right to left): Aryeh Shapiro, Tzvi Hagivati, Sh. Nachmani, Nachum Chinitz, Baruch
Domnitsh
Standing: Lipa Kikayon, Tzvi Assaf, Shimon Maharshak

[Page 263]

Pinkas Slutsk
and its Environs

Uretshe

Horka

Hlusk

Hrozova

Hresk

Vizne

Verchutin

Timkovich

Lyuban

Starobin

Stary-Dorogy

Pahost

Kopylia

Romanova

Shemezeve

[Page 264]

[See Hebrew translation of Heavenly Slutsk]

[Page 265]

Slutsk in Eternity

Translated by Hershl Hartman

This was Slutsk–an old Jewish town in Russia, on the border of Poland... surrounded by thick forests and swampy fields...with green gardens and rich orchards...traversed in its length and breadth by the deep yet narrow, swiftly flowing *Slutsh* River...secured by its old, wooden, yet solid homes and stores... enriched and respected for its varied Houses of Study, prayer gatherings and synagogues...all sorts of large and small *yeshivas*, drawing young boys from nearby *shtetlekh* and towns to study Torah...settled and populated by old-time, pious and well-learnéd Jews...tradesmen and craftsmen, almost all schooled in the holy books, Talmudic experts among them...famous egotists...sharp minds and sharp tongues, among whom pedigree was based not on wealth, nor even on ancestral glory, but on the merit of Torah...where a drayman would enter the House of Study with his whip under his arm to study a chapter of Talmud –a real Slutsk that disappeared from the Earth long ago.

It began to crack and crumble soon after the First World War, with the outbreak of the Russian Revolution, when Polish bandits invaded that district, attacked towns and villages and pogromized, murdered and robbed the defenseless Jewish population. This was followed by Bolshevik rule which, in addition to the hunger and poverty it brought to the [economically] displaced Jews, brutally destroyed, ostensibly for ideological reasons, the Jewish spirituality which had inspired and elevated the Jewish people over generations, tearing out by the roots the enshrined Jewish soul. What miraculously remained of Jews and Judaism in that area was destroyed by that beast of gentile humanity, the most horrendous criminal of all generations, may his name and memory be obliterated.

Now Slutsk, the living Jewish Slutsk that we knew, from which we originate, along with all the thousands of other Jewish communities in Eastern Europe, has been totally wiped off the face of the earth,

[Page 266]

so that not even a sign of it has remained for us, its children, as well as for the Jewish world that knew its name.

So we must direct our view and our hearts to that old, former Slutsk that still lives in our memories as the good, warm nest of our childhood years and that serves us now as a sort of "Slutsk in Eternity." It is no longer on Earth, but it floats high above us...in our minds...in our yearning dreams...providing us with a rich heritage for our spirits...the foundation of our Jewish spirituality.

"Know from whence you came"–this commandment in its higher meaning must serve as a signpost not only in a general sense for the children of an entire people, but also in a narrower sense for the children of a specific location. They must remember for themselves and transmit to future generations that they were not born from a stone, that they had parents, that they came from a loving, lofty home which one may embrace and from which one may benefit and may learn something for the future. – Y. D. B.

[Page 267]

From Historic Sources

From the Jewish-Russian Encyclopedia Brokhauz – Efron

Translated by Hershl Hartman

Slutsk was the residence of the Duchy of Slutsk.

The first references to Jews in Slutsk date to the year 1583.

A Jewish community was already in existence in Slutsk at the beginning of the 17th century and, according to the minutes of the Lithuanian Va'ad [rabbinic council] in 1623, Slutsk was under the influence of the Brisk Va'ad.

However, in 1691, the leaders of the Va'ad gave autonomy to Slutsk and other major communities, recognizing the large Jewish population of Slutsk and its greatly honored learnéd men and Talmudic experts. The meeting of the last Va'ad took place in Slutsk in 1761.

In 1655, when the Moscow military occupied Lithuania, there was a panic in Slutsk and most Jews took refuge in Vilna [Vilnius]. Slutsk again became one of the major trading towns in Lithuania when the military unrest died down.

The Radziwills, to whom Slutsk belonged as their property, aided in the redevelopment of the town and related to its Jews in a friendlier fashion than to the other inhabitants. This explains the accusation against Lord Radziwill by the Slutsk archimandrite [Eastern Orthodox Church cleric] in 1660. In 1754, the Orthodox Church in Slutsk complained to the commissar of the Slutsk Duchy that, ever since

[Page 268]

Jews had been appointed tax-farmers [collectors on commission] of the meat tax, the Russian Church had lost all its income.

The Jewish population of Slutsk and its surrounding region in 1776 came to 1,577 individuals. (*Pinkus kehiles Lite*–record of the Lithuanian Jewish communities and according to Bershadsky.) According to the *pinkusim* [records] of 1800 there were three Christian traders in Slutsk and 47 Jewish traders. Christian citizens–641; Jews–1,537. A survey of 1847 counted 5,897 Jews; in the Kapulye community–1,824.

The census of 1897 showed the total population of the Slutsk region to be over 260,000, of which 40,906 were Jews.

Town/Village	Total Pop.	Jewish Pop.
Slutsk	14,349	10,264
Vizne	1,593	532
Hresk	1,674	207
Hrazave	928	765

Kapulye	4,463	2,671
Fahast	863	685
Romanove	1,535	494
Semzheve	2,538	2,881
Starobin	2,315	1,494
Timkovitsh	2,393	1.523

Slutsk in the Period of the "Council of the Four Lands"

There is a very strong tendency in the historiography of Jewish life-styles in the post-exilic period to emphasize the striving toward communal autonomy in the spiritual and social sense. Such striving was realized in olden times from the Babylonian to the Hispanic exiles. This review will not dwell needlessly on the details of that period.

A "Va'ad of the Land" was organized in Poland in the 15th century. The famous "Council of the Four Lands" was established in the 16th century (1580-1), which included the Jewish communities of Great Poland, Little Poland, Russia [Eastern Galicia] and Volhynia.

The Jewish communities of Lithuania joined that Council in 1588. The records of that year refer to "five lands" (Great Poland, Little Poland, Russia [Eastern Galicia], Volhynia and Lithuania). The main communities were: Posen, Krakow, Lemberg and Brisk.

The Lithuanian communities, headed by the one in Brisk, participated in the "Council of the Four Lands" over the course of many years.

In the year 1623, when the Lithuanian Jewish communities had achieved a high level of spiritual and economic development, a gathering of all of them was held and the "Council of the Land of Lithuania"[1] was proclaimed. At the beginning, participating delegates represented Brisk, Grodno and Pinsk.

In 1652, at a meeting of the "Council of the Land," it was decided to admit a representative of the Vilna community. The Slutsk community was independent of the Brisk community in all matters during that entire period. Finally, it was in 1691 that the Slutsk community attained equal standing in the "Council of the Land" with the above-cited communities.

The gatherings of the Councils took place during the "market-fair days" in various central cities, including Slutsk, where important issues of the day were dealt with:

1. Relations with central and local power-organs [governments and church powers].

2. Determining amounts of taxes due the governments and collecting them.

3. Regulating the internal life of the communities: selecting communal heads, judges, synagogue heads, sextons, etc.

4. Religious and education matters: *yeshivas*, Talmud-Torah [schools], etc.

5.   Economic concerns: leaseholds[2], internal taxes[3], etc.

The meeting of the "Council of the Land of Lithuania" in Brisk in 1623 passed an all-embracing statute regarding the lifestyle of the Jewish communities. The rules discuss and determine the duties of each community to the government, inner-relations among community members themselves as well as intercommunity relations. Details on the role of the Slutsk Jewish community as recorded in rabbinic literature of that period will be found in the Hebrew section of this volume.

Translator's footnotes:

1.   Generally referred to as "Council of the Principal Communities of the Province of Lithuania."
2.   "Jews were permitted to rent not only estates but even entire villages from the feudal landowners." – Nathan Ausubel, *A Pictorial History of the Jewish People*, 1953.
3.   Taxes on such necessities as candles and meat were to cause great inner friction in later centuries.

[Page 269]

Documents

Translated by Hershl Hartman

Our respected fellow-townsman, Prof. Tsvi Razran of New York, sent us an article on "Slutsk of Old and in the Recent Past," accompanied by important historical documents in Russian. We found it necessary to translate the documents into Yiddish for publication in our records [pinkes]. We believe that these documents reflect the history of the Slutsk Jewish population over the course of centuries.

The Editors

1583

297   No. 642

Feb. 23 – Elia Lifshits and Merkl Novakhovitsh may export from Slutsk to Lublin this merchandise: goat skins; local, ordinary animal skins such as fox, wolf, etc.

This merchandise is free of duties in Orsha, in Tsetsersk, in Mistislav[1] and Bobruisk. Part of the merchandise is for shipment to Lublin and the balance to the market-fair in Gnezensk on April 15.

1622

766

A complaint by a Slutsk Jew against a Christian for failure to appear at the Koful court on a charge of suspicion of theft of various items.

Avrom Aranovitsh, a Slutsk Jew, accuses Meshtsanka Yoroshevitsaya, of Slutsk, of hiding her son Karp who had stolen several items from Aron. Karp was jailed pending further investigation. On advice of her elder son, Stefan (a foe of Jews), Yoroshevitsaya brought a charge against Aron, accusing him of arresting Karp without authority and of robbing her home; it was found that his action was in accordance with the law, with permission of the court, and that nothing was robbed.

Acts of Vil. Arch. Com. B XVIII, p. 258

1622

768–"Kofus," an investigation in the matter of a theft. The matter of a theft by Karp Yaroshovitsh from the Jew Aron. Karp did not appear, and his brother and mother, under subpoena, stated that Karp is not under their control, and as an independent businessman he is never at home during the day.

Karp was declared guilty of failure to appear at the appointed time.

Acts of Vilna Archive, B, XVIII, page 257

1623

700   17th November

Report by Ilya Leskovitsh about blows struck by Mikhl Moshkevitsh, who also jailed the former. He was freed by the "Kofna" court.

Ilya Leskovitsh accused Mikhl Moshkevitsh, a Jew, in the following: leaving his work in Ratskovitsh, where he was employed by Mr. Yitskhak Moshkevitsh, Mikhl's brother, he, Leskovitsh, came to Slutsk; there he met Mikhl, who invited him to come home with him. At home, at the beginning he tried to convince him to return to his [Mikhl's] employ. When he refused, Mikhl began to curse at and beat him. At the same time, Leskovitsh's belt tore, from which money fell that Mikhl took for himself. Noticing later that Leskovitsh was consulting with friends as to what to do next, Mikhl had him put in jail, from which he had him released after a week, in order to accuse him before the court in Kopnish and to set fire to his brother's courtyard.

The court declared Leskovitsh innocent. Vizh testified that he had seen the wounds caused to Leskovitsh. At his demand, it was recorded in the books.

Vil. Act. B XVIII, page 266

1623

771   18th November

Protest by the *zhid* [sheenie, i.e., Jew] Mikhl Moshkevitsh against Ilya Leskovitsh's accusation dealt with in Kope. The Slutsk Jew, Mikhl Moshkevitsh, reported the following to the Slutsk government's high official: Ilya Leskovitsh, heroic [*sic*. read: loyal] servant of his brother Yitskhak Moshkevitsh, also a Slutsk Jew, participated in a robbery and was punished; then he began to threaten that he would escape, and he finally did voluntarily leave his employment. The next day he set fire to Yitskhak's grain barn. Yitska[2] asked his brother to sue in court and, if possible – to detain him.

[Page 270]

Mikhl asked that his brother's charge be recorded in the books and, happening upon Leskovitsh in Slutsk, he ordered that the latter be arrested and extradited to Ratskovitsh, in order to make it possible for his brother to bring him before the court (Kofo) to investigate the matter of arson.

Kofo freed Leskovitsh pending further investigation. Leskovitsh charged Mikhl with beating and robbing him.

All of this, Mikhl avers, is no more than a lie, invented through envy to avoid punishment. Mikhl Moshkovitsh guarantees that he will be able to prove the correctness of his charges and asks that his testimony be recorded in the books. This was granted.

Vil. Ac. Arch. Kom. B XVIII, page 261

1654[3]

953   8th August

A letter from Vilna (writer unknown), describing the unrest in Vilna due to the absence of the [Cossack] Chief and the advance of the Moscow [Russian] troops. It reports, in addition: "In Slutsk there is also a great uproar of the Cossacks. The *zhides* [sheenies, i.e., Jews] are running off to Vilna."

Vitebskaya Starina, B. IV, part 2, page 358

1659

972   17 April

A letter of the Protopop [Cardinal] Jan Bakatsish, on behalf of all the [Russian Orthodox] clergy, to the Lithuanian Prince Boguslow Radziwill. Jan Bakatsish informs Duke Radziwill that criminal acts are occurring among the Jews of Slutsk. A Jew from Sloboda Krolevets, on the estate of Lord Panyatovski, had converted to Christianity along with his wife and children. He had always shown envy of the Christian faith and, after the death of his first wife, having married again, being a Christian for ten years, he came on a visit to Slutsk. The Slutsk rabbis convinced him to return to Judaism with his Christian-born wife and children. Seeing this as an insult to the Church, Bakatsish complains to the Prince in the name of all the clergy, reminding him thereby that the Christian boy they [the Jews] had murdered ten years ago in Doktorovits had still not been buried.

Archeog. VII, page 112

1660

976   18 March

A letter from the Kaydan constable, Oborski, to Prince Radziwill in Konigsberg. Sending the letter via a Jew, Oborski reports that the Jew came from Slutsk to Kaydan at the risk of his life and that he will be a "living letter." The Jew, according to Oborski's words, "was shackled in chains by the [Ukrainian?] Prince Khovanski, was in Novogrodek, also endured Russian whipping. He saw the enemy military" and can report on all of it. Oborski recommends giving the Jew verbally or in writing everything that is needed to enable him to penetrate the enemy's camp: "He speaks like a native-born Russian, his demeanor is purely Russian and he has done this more than once."

Archeogr. Coll. B. VIII, page 3–3

1666

1045   24 March

The letter of the Slutsk archimandrite [Eastern Orthodox Church cleric] Feodosy Vasilevitsh to the Lithuanian Prince Boguslaw Radziwill:[4]

Certainly reports, circulating through Lithuania and Poland, have by now reached the Prince that the Slutsk Jew Yakub Davidovitsh dared to use sharp, piercing words against holy praise and against Vasilevitsh's honor and that he had attacked him with a knife.

Arresting Davidovitsh, Vasilevitsh brought him the castle and charged him with heresy, insulting the Prince as the defender of all the churches and monasteries, as well as for insulting the Metropolitan and clergy in the person of Vasilevitsh. The Assizes Court sided with Davidovitsh – not by legality, but due to the special respect shown to Jews.

"More than once, the Jews of Slutsk have attacked holy houses, graves, clergy, and now it appears that the unbelieving *zhides* have become believers. I am a Christian and (as I have been informed) the subject is known to be a nonbeliever. The court has often condemned Christians to death because of Jews, but for insulting God himself, His houses of prayer and his holy ones, for disrespect of the Prince, of the Metropolitan, of the clergy, there is refusal to establish the same precedent of abolishing the death penalty for Jews – because of Christians."

[Page 271]

At the end Vasilevitsh asks the Prince to condemn the Jew to death. He admits that he is not blood-thirsty and would not insist on carrying out the death sentence, but would be satisfied with whatever punishment might be meted out to Jews. But everyone must know of the guilt of the Jews. Because he is shamed before all the clergy when the Jews of Slutsk attack him.

Archeo. Ac. Coll. B. VII, page 31

1669

1071   11 April

A letter, from the Slutsk archimandrite Feodosy Vasilevitsh to Prince Boguslaw Radziwill:

Inter alia, he complains that the Plotsk court refuses to take up his complaints against Jews; for five years he has lost the deposit of his assigned sum of 100 silver *grivenyes*; since the court official refuses to deal with his issues, he asks the Prince to turn the matter over the Slutsk commissars.

Archeograph. Collection B. VII, page 146

1669

1079   4 October

A letter from the Slutsk archimandrite Feodosy Vasilevitsh to Prince Boguslaw Radziwill:

Inter alia, he says: he is unable to cease complaining about the Slutsk Jews until he obtains the return of his deposited sum of 120 *grivenyes*; though he, the archimandrite, trusted the Prince's promise, it was not fulfilled. True, the honorable commissars wanted to deal with the matter. However, the Jews have delayed it all until now and have issued only promises. He will have to go to Krakow, where he, the archimandrite, will be forced to legally prove their guilt. He pleads with the Prince to deal with him, at least, with as much good will as he shows to the Jews; would that he were not to defend the Jews as he does not defend the archimandrite from their damages and insult.

Archeogr. Collection VII, page 148

1734

1765   26 February

Complaint of the Slutsk clergy to the Tshernigov commissar about the "estates" of the Slutsk nobility:

About the fact that, as the Slutsk Jews have received the lease over meat, all the freedoms granted to the clergy have been abrogated. They do not receive meat from the leasehold, nor the 16 pounds of wax-income for the Slutsk churches.

The Jews do not pay tariffs on wax, food products, wood.

Imports to Slutsk are free. The clergy has received a new prescript from Princess Radziwill; but the leaseholders have not yet provided any wax. They stop wagon-loads of food stuffs and wood and demand tariff payments. In addition, on February 21, 1734, the same leaseholders with the aid of soldiers of the Slutsk garrison, attacked the home of the priest Roman Kazyulitsh while he was baptizing a child, driving off the guests at the celebratory meal, frightening with noise and banging the priest's sick wife, the children and all the house-residents, confiscating clothes, oxen and two barrels of beer – and all this was done to oppress the clergy.

In view of all this, the clergy requests: requiring the leaseholders under threat from the garrison to hand over the wax, restoring their independence, forcing the return of the stolen goods and punishment of the guilty in accordance with the law.

Archeo. collection VII, page 178

1741

1875   1 August

Protest by householder Saveli Korda against the chief treasurer, Kritsevsk constable of Prince Yefonim Radziwill, the *zhid* Shmula Itskovitsh, for an unnecessary investigation of his land.

In his own name and in that of his relatives, he complains that the chief treasurer and Kritsevsk constable Shmula Itskovitsh, with the aid of an armed mob, forcefully conducted an investigation of the land-seekers in the villages of Patuze, Leshtsanke, Ushaki, all in the Mistislav district, and levied inventory taxes that are paid only by Christian serfs, on the lands of the seekers and Yaskevitsh. Saveli asks that, in the event of resistance, the criminals be arrested and sentenced to the Slutsk prison, and their lands settled by others. In carrying out this order, he promises all benefits and protection to his neighbors.

Hist. Jurid. Mater. Sasonovas, Edition XVII, page 280

1754

2036   27 September

A letter from Mikhael Kozatsinski, Slutsk archimandrite, to Prince Yefonim Radziwill:

[Page 272]

He complains against several Slutsk Jews. By demand of the Jews, last July there was proclaimed, by a beating drum, that any kind of trade is forbidden in the area around the Slutsk Troyitsk Monastery. There has never been any kind of trade there, neither now nor since Slutsk has been in existence. This is probably over some minor debt for an eighth [of a kilo] of bread or a stalk of hay.

This was the first result of the Jewish complaints.

The next time, the beating drum proclaimed that no one might enter the monastery's inn, in which liquor has not been sold for scores of years. No one drank beer there, fearing punishment by knightly blows at the stocks of shame. To carry out this [order], three soldiers were sent into the inn by the Slutsk commander on market days. Thus, people were not even allowed to rest in that place.

But as the Slutsk archimandrite, on the basis of the tariff established in 1690 under oath, was to pay 160 *gulden* per year to the *"retsi pospolitoy"* [?] – the question arises: where did they get the money if even a glass of beer was forbidden there? This was the second [result of] Jewish informing. In the end, the leaseholder of the monastery's inn pays all possible taxes to his [Jewish] community, and all the craftsmen who live in the vicinity of the Troyitsk monastery carry out all their craftsmen's guild responsibilities; even those who bring things to town for sale or who buy whatever they need – they always pay the required tax. One might ask: what do the Jews lack? Perhaps but one thing: to oppress the Christians.

Archeogr, Collection B. VII, page 249

Translator's footnotes:

1. Subsequently spelled in various ways.
2. Disrespectful diminutive of Yitskhak.
3. The unrest briefly described here refers to the Khmelnitsky uprising of Cossack and Ukrainian peasants against their Polish overlords that was deflected into a terrible slaughter of scores of thousands of Jews.
4. Here and further, the apparent pro-Jewish prejudice of Radziwill and other Polish and Lithuanian nobles, also reflects their antagonism as Catholics toward the Eastern Orthodox Church.

Rabbis, Judges and *shuln* of Slutsk

Translated by Hershl Hartman

1. Rabbi R'[1] Yekhiel Lurye, the father of R' Shloyme Lurye, known by the name of "Maharshal," [Our Teacher Sh. L.], *nifter*[2] 12 Kislev, [common year] 1574.

2. Rabbi R' Nakhum of Slutsk Katzenelenboygn, Chief of Rabbinic Court in 5415 (1655). *Nifter* in 5446 (1686).

3. R' Moyshe, son of Peysakh son of Tanakhum of Cracow, rabbi and head of *yeshiva* in the small study house (1664), *nifter* in 5446, 12 Nissan 1686.

4. Rabbi R' Benyomin Volf (Master of the House of Benjamin), *nifter* 28 Kheshvan 5446 (1686).

5. Rabbi R' Naftoli Herts Gintsburg, came to Slutsk as rabbi in 5430 (1670), *nifter* 22 Tammuz 5447 (1687).

6. Rabbi R' Yitskhak Mayer Tumim (1693).

7. Rabbi R' Arye Leyb Epshteyn, son of the Gaon [genius] Yudl of Kavle (he was called R' Leyb the rabbi's son). 5457 (1697). He was previously the rabbi of Smolovitsh.

8. R' Moyshe of Radom 5460 (1700).

9. R' Shloyme of Zalkava (R' Shloyme the Bright), son of the Gaon R' Elkhanon. *Nifter* 25 Tammuz 5466 (1706).

10. R' Yehuda Leyb, son of Asher Enzil 5482 (1722).

11. Rabbi R' Betsalel, son of Shloyme of Slutsk (R' Betsalel the Preacher), 12 Nissan 5482 (1722).

12. Rabbi R' Arye Leyb, son of rabbi R' Nosin Note, *nifter* 29 Nissan 5489 (1729).

13. Rabbi R' Yitskhak Yosif Tumim 5505 (1745).

14. Rabbi R' Avrom Katzenelenboygn 5512 (1752).

15. Rabbi R' Isakhar Ber 5521 (1761)

16. Rabbi R' Chaim HaKohen [the High Priest] Rapoport. Arrived as rabbi in Slutsk 5490 (1730). *Nifter* 17 Tammuz 5531 (1771).

17. Rabbi Chaim Zeldes (it is reported that he was in Slutsk a short time after Rabbi Rapoport.

18. Rabbi R' Shloyme Zalman Lifshits 5531 (1771).

19. Rabbi R' Yosif, son of the Gaon R' Menakhem Mendl of Slutsk 5532 (1772).

20. Rabbi R' Yehude Yudl, son of Avrom Halevi [the Priest] Hurvitsh, 7 Tevet 5534 (1774).

21. Rabbi R' Shloyme Zalman Monish 5558 (1798).

22. Rabbi R' Simkhe Bunim, *nifter* 5584 (1824).

23. Rabbi R' Yosele Faymer. Sat in the rabbinic chair of Slutsk for 35 years. *Nifter* 5624 (1864).

24. R' Yoshe-Ber Soloveytshik, rabbi in Slutsk (1865-1875). *Nifter* in Brisk 5652 (1892).

25. Slutsk Rabbi R' Mayer Faymer, who brought to Slutsk Rabbi R' Yankif Dovid, son of Zev Vilovski in 1899.

26. Rabbi R' Yankif Dovid son of Zev Vilovski, Slutsk rabbi from 5654 to 5660 (1894-1900).

27. Rabbi R' Iser Zalmen Meltser, from 1901 to 1920.

28. Rabbi R' Yosele, son of Mayer Faymer, Slutsk rabbi until 1920.

29. Rabbi R' Yekheskl Abramski 1924-1927.

30. Rabbi R' Yitskhak Hakhmark – last Slutsk rabbi 1928-1930.

[Page 273]

Names of the last Slutsk *dayanim* (judges of rabbinic court)

- Peyshe the judge
- R' Mayer, son of Peyshe
- The Salanter (R' Yehude Dov, our judge)
- R' Leyb Naymark

Names of the *shuln* [synagogues] and *bote-midroshim* [study houses] in [Yiddish] alphabetical order

1. Ostrover *shul*
2. R' Iserke's *shul*
3. Bogodelner *shul*
4. *Balebatishe* [for the well-off] *shul*
5. *Bes-medrish* [house of study]
6. Vigoder [benefits] *shul*
7. Zaretser *shul*
8. Khafashker *shul* (the old one)
9. Khafashker *shul* (the new one)
10. Yeshive *shul*

11. The Muravankes

12. Mishne *shul*

13. Butchers' *shul*

14. Cold *shul*

15. Furriers' *shul*

16. *kloyz* [small study house]

17. Cobblers' *shul*

18. Investors' *shul*

19. Tailors' *shul*

20. Blacksmiths' *shul*

Translator's footnotes*:*

1. Abbr. for Reb: term of respect similar to Mister.
2. Died: used to describe the passing of a highly respected person.

Slutsk

by M. L. Gorin, New York

Translated by Hershl Hartman

In its hundreds of years of existence, Slutsk experienced good times as well as bitter, difficult periods of war, plagues, fires and epidemics.

There was an ongoing struggle for existence in all aspects of life. The region saw strife between Poles and Russians, Russians and Germans. Slutsk was often devastated.

The Jews of Slutsk, as all Jews in the "Pale of Settlement,"[1] occupied the middle classes, mostly as petit-bourgeois such as storekeepers, traders and craftsmen like tailors, cobblers, smiths, tanners, commission-agents and draymen.

For the most part, the stores and workshops were their own private property and their earned income came from their labor, alone or with the aid of family members.

The more prosperous storekeepers or craftsmen had aides, employees or apprentices. These workers, insignificant in number, constituted the working class, the proletariat in the Marxist lexicon. The upper and lower classes of Slutsk – a major regional city of the former province of Minsk – were composed of the Belorussian, Polish, Christian population, with a mix of Poles [*sic*; read: Ukrainians] and Great Russians. The nobles, the estate-owners and a small group of capitalists owned the greater part of the lands and the small number of minor industrial factories. The peasant masses were the underclass.

In a modest but important sense, Slutsk served as the spiritual and cultural center [of the region] for generations.

The children [*i.e.,* sons] of poor parents had but one goal: to study Torah and achieve higher levels of piety. They studied in large and small *yeshivas* [schools of advanced religious studies]. The wealthier studied to become doctors, pharmacists, dentists; they took entrance exams for the Slutsk *gymnasia* [secular high schools] and often failed. A small percentage of them studied in the *gymnasia*, commercial, and liberal arts schools.

The greatest part of poor young men had to earn their bit of bread quite early in life as apprentices at various crafts, assisting tailors, cobblers, tinsmiths, iron forgers, carpenters, etc. or as clerks in stores and trading houses. The latter earned more and had opportunities to work themselves up and, in time, to own their own businesses.

The more intelligent – who absorbed Jewish knowledge in the *khedorim* [elementary religious schools] and *yeshivas* and who excelled in Hebrew, Bible, Talmud and a bit of Russian, besides – became teachers, *melamdim* [instructors in the *khedorim*], while some of them would be hired by the semester to teach the children of *yeshuvnikes* [isolated Jewish settlers] in rural villages or smaller communities in the Slutsk area.

The practical term for this type of pedagogy was "a condition." A poor *yeshiva* student would save a few rubles toward studying or marriage, go off to the village to teach and would return home at *peysakh* or *sukis*[2] with a hundred rubles and sometimes even more.

Slutsk was truly a genuinely Jewish center for many centuries–first under Polish rule, then at the end of the 18th century, under the Russians. According to historical records, Slutsk figured significantly in medieval times in the famed "Council of the Four Lands"

[Page 274]

of the regions in the Polish state. Its customs and spokesmen had great influence there. Thus the name of Slutsk was famous in the Jewish world, not only for its born aristocrats, the rich, leading families, but more importantly for its learnéd householders. Almost every tradesman and many poor Jews and workers knew well the holy books. There were Jews who were learnéd and experts in the Talmud and its later interpretations.

There was a commonly-told joke that, when a Slutsk Jew would travel to another area and the subject of his *yikhes* [patrimony] would arise, he would hold out his hand and begin to count on his fingers, bending the pinky and declaring: "Well, first of all, I'm from Slutsk."

Slutsk had a large *yeshiva*, small *yeshivas*, [traditional] *khedorim*, modern *khedorim*, genius-rabbis such as R' Yosele, R' Yoshe Ber Soloveytshik, R' Mayerke Feymer, R' Yankef Dovid, R' Iser Zalman Meltser, R' Yekheskl Abramski, R' Yosele Feymer the Second. Famous judges, such as Peyshe and R' Mayer, R' Leyb Naymark of Salant. *Yeshiva* heads: R' Nekhemye, R' Yoshe Tritsaner, R' Peysekh, R' Berl Gribenshtsik.

In Yiddish literature, the character of *Mirele Efros*, whom Jacob Gordon immortalized in his famous play [of that name], was a type taken from the reality of Slutsk. Such an aristocratic heiress, highly privileged, actually represented the class position and psychology of those times.

Such inter-class struggles between the upper and lower societal groups went on then not only between the rich and poor, but there were also disputes within the rabbinate.

Slutsk was divided into two camps. The battles persisted for many years between R' Mayerke and R' Yankif Dovid, until the latter left and finally settled and was *nifter* in Safed [Palestine, now Israel].

The rise of the *haskala*[3] produced literary figures and personalities whose birthplace was in Slutsk or its surrounding areas. The "*zeyde*" Mendele[4] came from Kapulye, about 20 *vyorst* from Slutsk. He studied, "ate days"[5] in Slutsk. He describes it in his [autobiographical] novel, *Shloyme reb Chaim's* [Shloyme, son of Chaim]. In [his novel] *di klyatshe* [The Old Horse] he depicts types and characters taken from reality. *Kaptsansk* and *Gluptsk*[6] are *shtetlekh* [Jewish hamlets] identifiable as being in the Slutsk area and relecting that sort of lifestyle.

The philosopher Solomon Maimon, from Nezvizh, studied and lived in Slutsk.[7] Too, Prof. Raphael Cohen, of [New York's] City College, preeminent in modern philosophy, comes from the Slutsk area.

Among the famous modern writers is I. D. Berkowitz [son-in-law and chronicler of Sholem Aleichem], Slutsk-born. Also the well-known poet A. A. Lisitski and Zamye [Zalman] Wendrof, once characterized as the Yiddish Chekhov for his sketches and humorous tales, who lives in old age in Moscow.[8] Prof. Mayer Vaksman came from Slutsk and studied at the Slutsk *yeshiva*.

The late Yehuda Grazovski came from the Slutsk area, from the *shtetl* of Fahast. Rabbi Prof. Sh. Asaf comes from Lyuban, Slutsk region, as well as the two famous writers, the brothers Zalman and Yitskhok Epshteyn. The writer Rokhl Faygenberg (Amri) is from Lyuban. The historian Dr. Y. N. Shimkhoni is a son of the famous Slutsk scholar and leader Shimkhovits.

The famous pedagog and writer Avrom Epshteyn (Aba Arikha) was from Slutsk; the poets Yakov Kahn and Barukh Katsnelson are Slutsk-born. These well-known teachers (now in Israel) and others are from Slutsk: Shimshon Nakhmani, Yarkoni, Nakhum Khinits.

Folklore

by M. L. Gorin

Translated by Hershl Hartman

Slutsk nicknames:

    1.   Reb Nekhamye Imerman, the famous Head of *Yeshiva* in Reb Iserke's *shul* [synagogue], was a strictly observant Jew with red hair and with a flaming red beard. Because he wouldn't allow them to smoke cigarettes in *shul*, the older *yeshiva* students called him the "Red Cow."[9] –

    2.   Khashke the *rebetsin* [rabbi's wife], who taught Jewish girls to pray and read the women's prayers, limped. When she walked carrying the evening prayer-book under her arm, her head would bob up and down. So they called her: "Khashke, a bob up, a bob down."[10] –

    3.   One of the congregants in the *Vigoder* [benefits] synagogue was called "the hunchback." One can't recall any other name for him. Once someone called to him from behind, "Reb Hunchback!" and he turned and replied without rancor: "Are you calling me?" The amazing part is that he was not hunchbacked. His back was as straight as those of the others in that synagogue.–

    4.   There was a pelt-trader on Zaryetsher Street who was short and had a great red beard. His wife was twice his size. So the folks in Slutsk called them: "Short Friday and the Great Sabbath."

Translator's footnotes:

1. Beginning in 1772, a vast section of Southwestern Russia and Ukraine, Eastern Poland, and Lithuania, established as the sole area of the Russian Empire in which Jews were permitted to reside.
2. Passover and Succoth, the eight-day festivals that mark, respectively, the onset of spring and autumn. They also denoted the breaks between teaching semesters.
3. Enlightenment, which brought modern scientific and cultural ideas into the Pale of Settlement.

4. Sholom Yankif Abramovitsh (1836?-1917), regarded as the *zeyde* – grandfather (patriarch) – of both modern Yiddish and modern Hebrew literature. He assumed the pen-name *Mendele moykher-sforim* – Mendele the Bookseller – in 1863 because writing in Yiddish was then regarded as shameful or degraded.
5. Custom whereby poor *yeshiva* students would take supper one day a week each at a series of well-to-do homes.
6. Respectively, "Poortown" and "Idiotville," among Mendele's pseudonyms for Jewish hamlets.
7. 18th century prominent German philosopher and critic of Immanuel Kant, Maimon became a rabbi in Lithuania at an early age but rebelled and fled the ghetto to Germany, where ten years later he rose to fame in his new role.
8. Wendrof lived in the U.S. for a few years after the failed 1905 revolution, returning to Russia as a correspondent for American Yiddish journals. Arrested and jailed for ten years during Stalin's 1948-1952 purge of Yiddish writers and cultural leaders, he was released at age 80. His 90th birthday was marked by the publication of his works in Yiddish in Moscow and celebrated worldwide. (See Sol Liptzin, *A Literature*, 1972.)*History of Yiddish*
9. Biblically designated to be sacrificed, burnt, and its ashes used to cleanse impurities. In Yiddish folkspeech: naive fool.
10. In original, a bi-lingual play on words: Yiddish *kop* (head) and Russian *kopek* (penny).

[Page 275]

The Cold *Shul* and Its Courtyard

by M. L Gorin, New York

Translated by Hershl Hartman

From the distance of the surrounding fields and highways, a tower appeared: the famous, attractive, walled-in, white-plastered Cold *Shul* [Synagogue] with its sloped, green-tinted tin roof. Handsome, symmetrically-built in the Gothic style with balancing, architecturally straight lines, ledges, cornices, tall windows with panes colored blue, green, red, etc., the impressive building produced both respect and divine inspiration.

Little birds would fly through the multi-colored little panes, chirping and squeaking, marching back and forth, singing their avian hymns. The building was tall, drawing everyone's attention, and rested on large, thickly-rounded interior columns. It appeared that the great pillars held and supported the building, symbolically representing the Slutsk community, itself supported by its age and great ancient pedigree. Even in winter, crowds would come to pray in the Cold *Shul*, wrapped in furs or thick, warm coats. Teeth would chatter, but neither the common folk nor the elite paid attention. The prayer leader's voice echoed and bellowed; one felt hurriedness, scrambling to get it over with.

The Torah-reading was cold, as was the cry of "rise up" [*yamoyd*–to read a portion]! There was no standing: it was too cold. The *mi-shevorakh* [blessing of the reader] and the prayer of holy contribution were rushed, as well.

Prayers were said while strolling through the large, spacious building. No one sat in one place: people moved like whirlwinds, their prayer-shawls draped over long coats. murmuring, reading, praying.

In 1908 a rumor spread like lightening: there would be a women's gallery built on two sides of the Cold *Shul*. So the jokes and witticisms began: let the women, too, know the meaning of cold.

But in summertime, the congregants cheered up and enjoyed the coolness and comfort–almost a Garden of Eden. Prayers then were far different.

Famous cantors would appear in paid performances at the Cold *Shul*. Gershon Sirota, Mayer Lider, Leybe Uzder and many other cantors would cause a great stir in town. People would express their opinions, relishing bits of successful cantorial skill. Many Jews stood outside, listening to the cantillations and becoming ecstatic: "Ay, did he pray! Such sweetness deserves having every body-part kissed!"

The Slutsk [volunteer] fire brigade would hold training at the Cold *Shul* during the summer months. Almost every Thursday evening a fireman in uniform and a brass hat would drive through town in a horse-drawn cab, blowing a trumpet, alerting his fellows

The Kalte [Cold] Shul

[Page 276]

to that night's exercises at the Shasen—a large, empty square near the marketplace, where they stored the fire wagons, the pumps and water barrels, stalls for the horses as well as a residence for the guards who stood watch around the clock in the event of a fire alarm.

The Slutsk fire brigade was headed by Yisroyl Baron, a shrewd Jew, and the nobleman Kuratsevitsh who lived on his estate, a handsome building at the closed end of the boulevard.

The firemen, in neat uniforms, would march in straight rows, like military squads, led by an orchestra whose notes and sounds would draw the boys from the *khedorim* [religious primary schools] and ordinary ne'er-do-wells, good-for-nothings for whom this was a useful spectacle for time-wasting.

Standing in the courtyard, near the bath-house, they would place their ladders against the walls of the Cold *Shul* and climb on its slanted roof. A contest developed among the lads to see who could climb faster than the others and show off their training in the craft. Music would play as the hoses, plugged into the barrels, would pour streams of water far and wide into the air.

Little boys would volunteer to work the pumps with the firemen, to draw water from the nearby wells.

These fire drills were, in their display, both useful to the community and a good pastime for the volunteers and for the bands of boys, and the onlooking townsfolk who were curious about such things. The firemen would then relax at the taverns where they would enjoy Slutsk's tasty dishes: fish, goslings, cracklings, *blintses*, layer cakes, sponge cakes, and then wash them down with genuine 90 proof vodka.

During "chart days" [Czarist government holidays] the students of the [secular] "Hebrew Day School," of the *gymnazye* [public high school] and the commercial school would march into the Cold *Shul* in their parade uniforms like well-trained troops. They would be seated in the pews around the *bime* [platform] at the center, and [government-appointed] Rabbiner Eshman, dressed in his black robe with a chain around his neck, would deliver a patriotic speech for them in Russian about the importance of the event. He would center his sermons on current events: the birthday of the Czar or other personages of the Romanov dynasty.

After the ceremony, reading from the 21st Psalm [21:2], "Lord, the king rejoices in Your strength," he would end with a call to be good and pious and to obey the Czar. After the prayer for deliverance and "Lord our Czar," they would disperse.

The induction oath was also administered in the Cold *Shul* to the young Jewish draftees into military service. Embittered, disheveled, eyes ablaze, they murmured with compressed lips the oath that Rabbiner Eshman proclaimed in poor Russian, demanding loyalty and devotion to the Russian Czar. His words rang out wildly and echoed ironically in the empty *shul* in the presence of military and civilian officials. Sometimes, there would appear here the commander, the German Shtriker, a hefty blonde man. He commanded 25 policemen and a squad of soldiers who lived in the barracks. Their parade grounds was near the Catholic church.

He had secret agents in the Cold *Shul* who would, in disguise, visit the synagogues.

He was not generally a bad person. Everyone knew him. He would stroll

First row: from right to left — Yaakov Kimayevich, Aninski, Zalman Rubinstein
Second row: Epstein, Lipa Leinovich
Third row: Prochovnik, Sperling, Winograd, Jachedov

[Page 277]

the streets dressed in his grey uniform with epaulettes on the shoulders and bright brass buttons and smile at the passers-by.

He was, however, cruel to young people guilty of membership in freedom movements and to "sitsialists" [socialists].

In March of 1905, his 15 year-old son, a *gymnazye* student, after an argument with his father, grabbed the latter's revolver and shot himself. He was leftist inclined and could not stand his father's actions.

This caused a great furor in Slutsk. It happened just a week before Passover. The funeral was held in the Lutheran church, on the boulevard, and he was buried on the *mohilkes* [?].

There were five synagogues on the *shul* square: the Cold *Shul* on the east side; to the west, the *bes-medrish* [house of study]; at the north, the *kloyz* [small study house] and the *karanim* [investors'] *shul*; and at the south, the *shnayderishe* [tailors'] *shul*.

In the middle [of the square] there was a significant open space. which could accommodate hundreds of people. It was here that *khupes* [wedding canopies] were erected under open skies, where *klezmer* [musicians] would play. If Eyzl the *klezmer's* group or Shimon Leyb's music was heard in the streets, it was a sign that a wedding procession was headed for the *shul* square.

It was on the *shul* square near the *kloyz* that orations for the worthy departed would be given. The final funeral ceremony would be held here, among the walls of the nearby houses of prayer. Members of the *khevre-kedishe* [burial society] would bring the corpse and place the coffin near the *kloyz*. On a table resting on a study stand, the orator–the rabbi or Reb Leybe Naymark, the *dayan* [religious judge]–would relate the good qualities of the departed, that he was a son of Torah and a fine Jew. The assembled crowd, men and women, would dissolve into bitter tears.

The mournful *nign* [melody] and the funeral participants threw a pale over the *shul* square. *Kheyder* boys would follow the black bier singing "justice shall follow you all the days of your life [?]." The town sexton R' Fayvl would shake the collection box, intoning: "charity rescues from death." This was how the sorrowful processions went forth in summer heat, in autumn's mud, in winter's snows, carrying the biers on their shoulders–exhausted Jews with measured tread, in still, respectful silence, other than the sound of coins in the charity box, until they arrived at the cemetery near the river, at the end of Zaretser street, which was fenced-in by a stone wall.

One would often hear from the synagogues the cries of women who, with possessed shrieking at the Holy Ark, would plead with the Master of the Universe to take pity and preserve the honor of a seriously-ill person who was at death's door.

Often, one would hear unusual sobbing and cries from bitter hearts at the opened Holy Ark. If a pregnant woman was having a difficult delivery, her mother or grandmother would plead with the Master of the Universe not to withdraw His grace but to help everything to turn out well.

Folklore

When a Slutsk Jew would talk about his town with good-humored, homey scorn, he would call it "Slutshizne."

"*slutsker krupnik*–A Slutsk stew"–an ordinary dish of water and barley in Slutsk homes among both rich and poor. This also meant: "An ordinary, run-of- the-mill guy," "A common man."

"*slutsker flodn*–Slutsk fruit layer cake" —A sort of sweet, hard-baked tart, homemade, filled with honeyed dough-balls, that served as the best treat at a cake-and-whisky event, as well as an export item beyond Slutsk. Day-old cake could be chopped with an ax. This also represented the nature of Slutsk people: hard on the outside but sweet within.

"*slutsker beres*–Slutsk pears" –Large, heavy pears from Slutsk's famous orchards. They would be stored until late winter when they would finally grow ripe, soft and sweet. In certain cities they were sold in large fruit stores. This, too, represented the nature of Slutsk people: it would take a long time until one could uncover their real nature.

[Page 278]

At Home and On the Street

My Memories of Slutsk

by Eliyahu Shulman (New York)

Translated by Paul Pascal

Eliyahu Shulman

General Overview

White Russia, or Byelorussia ["Raissn" in Yiddish] was frequently depicted in Jewish literature: Avrom Reisen, Dovid Einhorn, Moishe Kohlbach, Leib Naidus, H. Leivick, and the "grandfather', Mendele Moikher-Sforim, portrayed the landscape the fields, and the forests with their little white birch trees. Somehow a delicate, quiet sadness enveloped this countryside. The sadness could be felt in the folksongs of the White Russian peasants, and in the descriptions found in Jewish literature.

But you could not say that White Russia was entirely poor and drab. Slutsk was a lively town, full of activity and of wonderfully energetic Jews. The town was a regional seat, an "oyezdne gorod," – the center of economic and cultural life for a large district. In the surrounding *shtetlach* (Jewish villages) as well, creative activity bubbled over. Slutsk is noted in the chronicles of Chmielnitski's [Cossack] uprising. It is believed that Jewish Slutsk is 400 years old.

I remember Slutsk as a Jewish town, although many Christians also lived there. All the government appointees, the teachers in all the Russian schools and *gimnazias* (high schools) were non-Jews. In Slutsk there also lived Lutherans; on Broad Street *(Breiter Gass* or *Shirokoi Ulitsa)* near the Boulevard, there was a Lutheran church. Many Poles lived in town as well. In 1918, a Polish *gimnazia* was founded, which had many students. Christians lived on Tritshan Street near the monastery, on Broad Street, on Yuryev Street near the *Zemstva* (District Administration), on New Street, on Ostrava, and on some side streets. However, the largest part of the population was Jewish.

Slutsk Jews absorbed themselves in commerce and labor. I can recall only a few non-Jewish stores in Slutsk, such as Mukhin Bros. Co., Gorokhovich, and a few others. Almost all the other stores on the Chaussee (main street) and on the streets near the Chaussee were Jewish. Besides running stores, Jews were also skilled. workers of various kinds. The town was full of Jewish tailors, cobblers, quilt-makers, bricklayers, dyers, carpenters, comb-makers, potters, cutters, wig-makers, and so on.

Slutsk was a true intermediary between city and country. From every direction, each Sunday peasants would arrive in town with their produce. Jewish men and women would buy up corn, wheat, barley, eggs, potatoes, chickens, and cows, from the peasants. Sunday until noon the businesses would stay closed, because that was the time for the Christians to be in church, but after twelve o'clock all the stores would open and the peasants would

[Page 279]

buy whatever they needed.

The countryside around Slutsk produced a lot of grain and the Slutsk merchants would purchase the grain and ship it all over the Russian empire. In Slutsk there were three steam-run mills: Fainberg's, Gutzait's, and Mishelev's. Their flour was sent to the most far-flung places. Jews would also buy up pigs' hair and even export it abroad.

In the hardest times of the First World War or the Bolshevik period of December 1918 to August 1919 (after which the Poles occupied Slutsk) – even when all of Russia was starving – Slutsk had enough bread not only for its own needs but also for export. During this period, so-called *meshotshnikes* would arrive in Slutsk daily, people with sacks come to buy up broad. Every day, thousands of pounds of flour would be taken out of Slutsk, whether by train or by wagon.

Slutsk had an abundance of orchards and gardens, both in the town proper and in the outskirts, and the well known. "Slutsk berries" were packed in cases shipped deep into Russia. Slutsk also produced a fine goose- *schmaltz*, which was famous everywhere. In general you could say that the town was truly alive, industrious, and creative.

Slutsk was full of Jewishness. Among her residents were real Jewish scholars and students. In every synagogue, between afternoon and evening prayers, people would pore over the religious books such as *Ein Yaankev*, *Hayei Odem*, and the Talmud. After dinner on the day of the Sabbath the synagogues were packed.

At the entrance to the agricultural exhibition in Wigoda in 1905

Slutsk had 18 synagogues and study-houses. In the *Shul Heif* (Synagogue Courtyard) alone there were five: the splendid and truly magnificent *Kalteh Shul* (Cold Synagogue), the extremely old *Kloiz*, the *Beis-Medresh Ha-Godl* (the Great Synagogue), the *Karnayim* Shul (Horns Synagogue), and the *Schnaidersheh* Shul (Tailors' Synagogue).

Not far from the *Shul Heif* were the *Katsovisheh Shul* (Butchers' Synagogue), Reb Isserkeh's Shul, and the *Mishnayes* (Talmud-study) *Shul*, In the *Kalteh Shul* were two little houses of prayer –

the *Moirevankes* [or *Muraveinikes*: the Yiddish spelling seems to allow for two pronunciations, and therefore -two meanings – in Yiddish, "The God-Fearers"; in Russian, "The Ant-hill"!]; and the *Vatikin Shtibl*, (Sages' or seasoned One's House of Prayer) was situated in the *Beis-Medrash Ha-Godl*.

In the *Mishnayes Shul* was the only Hassidic house of prayer. Besides those, there were other shuls: the. *Kapulyer Shul*, the *Bal Ha-batisheh* (Well-to-do) Shul, the *Kirzhner* (Furriers' or Hatters') *Shul*, the *Zaretser Shul*, the *Vigoder Shul*, the *Ostrover Shul*, the *Shmidesheh* (Blacksmiths') *Shul*, and the New and Old Shuls on Khapashker Street.

The town was filled with one-room Jewish schools (*kheders*), small schools of higher Jewish learning (*yeshivahs*), and one big *yeshivah,* two community-supported Jewish schools for the poor, and a modern Jewish school. The great Slutsk Yeshivah was respected throughout Russia. Yeshivah boys came there from the most distant places. The Yeshivah published a periodical, *"Yogdil Teireh"* ("God Makes the Torah Great"). In the Yeshivah an on-going battle raged between the *Muserniks* (followers of a nineteenth century religious movement which stressed moral strictness) and their opponents. Slutsk was totally absorbed in Jewishness.

But the spirit of modernity also infiltrated the town. Slutsk had many Russian schools: the classical Men's *Gimnazia*, the Women's *Gimnazia*, the Commerce School, the *Pension* (Boarding School), several *pro-gimnazias* [preparing the student for *gimnazia*], the government-run Jewish school *(Yevreiskoye Utshilishtshe)*, the municipal school (the *"Gorodskoye"*). Near the monastery there was the Greek Orthodox religious school (the *"Dukhovnoye Utshilishtshe"* or "Spiritual School"). In the *gimnazias* a certain percent were non-Jews, but many Jewish children studied there. In addition, the "Realist" School arrived in 1917, as well as the White Russian *gimnazia*and a technical school.

Slutsk was truly a cultural center, and the town was filled with scholars from the surrounding villages and hamlets. They needed textbooks and so consequently there were a number of booksellers in town: Greenwald's, Rubinstein's, Tomashov's, Feitlson's, and a number of others. In the Byelorussian and secular bookstores you could also buy Jewish and Hebrew books, newspapers, and periodicals.

The town's community library had a significant place as well. It was founded at the beginning of this century by the Zionists. It held a large collection of Russian, Hebrew, and Yiddish books. At one time,

[Page 280]

The gymnasja for girls

it was located on Khapashker Street or Vilensky Street [on next page author confirms it was Khapashker]. After the great fire of 1915, it was moved to another location, on a side street near the Exchequer *(kazna-tshestva)*. Later it relocated in the one-time home of the government- run Jewish school. Among the librarians were Elyeh Charny, Afelsin, Zoluskin, Bunin, and Aaron Rolnik. It's amazing that such a small, out-of-the-way town should contain so many Jewish and general cultural institutions.

As mentioned earlier, Russians, White Russians, and Poles also lived in Slutsk, her surroundings, and her estates. These were landowning families, but even together they would not have been able to sustain any post- elementary schools without the help of the Jewish population.

Another phenomenon in Slutsk were touring theater troupes, both Jewish and Russian, as well as amateur groups. Theater was staged at Soloveitchik's Hall in the "Squires' Club" (later called the Democratic Hall), and in the auditoriums of the Commerce School and the *Gimnazia*.

My Family

The writer of these lines left Slutsk in October 1920, during the time the Polish army occupied Slutsk for a second time. I was then just a young fellow, but I clearly remember our town, before the First World War, during the Revolution, during the German and Polish occupations, and during the early Bolshevik regime from November 1917 until the Germans came in January 1918. The Bolsheviks took Slutsk a second time and ruled from December 1918 until August 1919. The third time was from July 1920 to October 1920.

My father left Slutsk when I was four years old, consequently I spent a lot of time in the home of my grandfather, Yossl Barhan. He lived on Khapashker Street, where he had a grocery store. Other Barhans lived on the property as well. The oldest, Shaia-Yoba Barhan, an uncle of my grandfather, was a retired soldier of Nikolai's army. In the army he learned shoemaking, so he took this up when he came back home. His wife Riva worked with medicinal suction cups, leeches for bloodletting, and so on, and for that reason she was known as the *"doktorsheh."*

Shaia-Yoba's oldest son was Isroel Barhan, a well-known personality in town – the head of the town's volunteer fire brigade, *(gorodskaya pozharna)*, a friend of all the police officials, of the *Marshallek* (chief of police), and of the landowners, and a frequenter of the Squires' Club. A story is told of how Isroel traveled once to the governor in Minsk on a mission for the *Marshallek* but took the opportunity to bring back revolvers for the Jewish self-defense group [against pogroms]. Isroel Barhan did many favors for Jews. As a confidant of every regime, be was successful in freeing [falsely-] arrested Jews.

My grandfather Yossi Barhan, the boilermaker, had been to America a number of times – the first time

[Page 281]

in 1892 – and lived in Odessa and Ekaterinoslav for a period of time. An enlightened man, a reader of [current] Jewish literature, he would lend and trade books with the Hebrew tutor Pesach Ezra (Pesach Karon), who had a private library. Along with Dovid Nisenson and Itsheh, the official Torah chanter, he subscribed to Jewish newspapers. On the same property, right by the river, lived Isroel Barhan. That's where the orchestra of the "Firefighters Commando" would rehearse.

The Zionist library was in Finkelstein's house on Khapashker Street until 1915. The owner of a furniture business and its cabinet-maker, Borukh Postov, was active in the Zionists' charity fund, or as it was officially called, the *"Tshaina"* (teahouse), because at the beginning of the Zionist movement a teahouse-Zionist club existed there.

On Khapashker Street a wealthy man, Ostrovsky, lived in a two-story house. His sons, students, would come home during vacations, wearing their student uniforms. The happiest house on Khapashker Street was Zelig Maniuk's. Zelig was a tailor. A large sign with a blue background and big gold letters announced that this was the location of a "tailor of military and civilian clothing." Military men and nobility would bring their finery to Zelig. Besides himself, there were his sons, Yonkl, Araleh (killed at the front in the First World War), Elkana-Neyakh and his young son Velvl, and Chaim helped out. Several associates also worked with him. Zelig had daughters in America, and they sent home *plastinkas* (phonograph records) with songs from the Yiddish theater. The gramophone played all day long, and everyone sang along. In particular I remember one song, "Look, God, See For Yourself" *("Gott, zeh allein")*.

Two synagogues were on Khapashker Street: the Old and the New. The Old was a wooden affair containing a beautifully carved holy ark, a fine Torah-reading platform with polished railing, and heavy brass chandeliers. My great grandfather, Itzik-Mikhl Barhan, was the assistant *shammes* (sexton) in the Old Shul. The New Shul was a brick building, whitewashed, and much bigger than the Old Shul. Rich influential people *davvened* (prayed) in the New Shul. All the Barhans *davvened* in the Old Shul except my grandfather, who had a reserved seat in the New Shul.

Like all synagogues everywhere, the New Shul on Khapashker would be decorated in honor of *Simkhes Teireh* (Simhat Torah). Around the reading platform and throughout the whole shul wires were strung on which there hung colorful paper lanterns. Red apples were fitted into the chandeliers with candles stuck in them. People lit fireworks shot from little rifles. The older, established folk would object, but in retrospect, I think they were also envious.

On the eve of *Tisha B'Ov* (a solemn day of fasting and mourning), young boys would gather pinecones and, during the dirges, fling them into the thick beards of the important people, and inside their collars. On *Yom Kippur* at *Kol Nidre* time, the rich folk would bring big, thick, wax candles, and set them into small boxes filled with sand the candles would burn the entire twenty-four hours.

Purim was very joyful in shul, except for youngsters who were crippled. We would arrive with big sticks and beat up on *Homen* (Haman) with all our might. Epstein the dentist passed out money to the kids who were toughest on the legendary villain.

The Streets of Slutsk

Khapashker Street was connected to the *Chausee* by a number of side streets. One street started next to the New Shul – Sadover (Orchard) Street. A number of very beautiful wooden houses existed on that street. In one of them lived the wealthy Evin family. In another lived Migdal, an agent for an insurance company. Across the street was Krainess' Hotel, where gentile landowners would lodge. A little further along was Soloveitchik's Theater – and in the garden was the "Summer Theater." Russian and Jewish troupes would perform at Soloveitchik's. Kids from the street were taken for roles in the Jewish productions. This is how I "performed" a few times in the Jewish theater.

A second street, linking Khapashker Street with the *Chausee*, started opposite Tshiptshin's Pharmacy. On that street you could find Vitkin's brick house, Shaia-Mendl Dretshin's large haberdashery, the Bristol *Gastinitsa* (Hotel), and at the very end, the home of Epstein the dentist. Opposite Epstein lived Bronstein the pharmacist, whose son was the *Kazyoner* rabbi.

A third street began next to the little wooden church [on Khapashker]. It went toward Tritshan. Mainly Christians lived on this street, but the lawyer Tshiptin [sic; Tshiptshtin or Chipchin had his house there. The same street went through *Drai Bedli Klatkess* (a narrow footbridge over the river) and connected to Krivisolka Street and the [Jewish] cemetery. Khapashker Street -stretched past the monastery, but the second section of the street, closer to the monastery, was referred to as Tritshan Street.

The monastery grounds were surrounded by a thick brick wall. Inside were a number of churches, a residence for monks, for priests, and the tombs (*mohilhas*) of the Christian aristocracy. There were beautiful pictures inside the monastery. Boys would often

[Page 282]

View of Kolonia over the bridge

go into the monastery to play on the huge grounds there and watch how the gentiles pray. Sundays and on Christian festivals great numbers of gentiles would make their way through Khapashker Street toward the monastery.

The children of Khapashker Street were not very taken with Jewish learning. They played in barrels, swam in the river, marched around in imitation of the volunteer fire brigade, and spent a lot of time playing with pigeons. On our block there also lived a Christian family – Petryl and Shakloita. Their children went to the Greek Orthodox religious school, but they spoke a good Yiddish and chummed around with Jewish children

In the summer of 1915, a great fire broke out. Everything on Khapashker Street was burned down, including both shuls, the library, and Tshiptshin's pharmacy. Our family resettled on Bobruisk Street, near Leizer Vilensky, the *shammes* of the Great Synagogue and of the *Linness Ha-Tsedek* (hostel for the poor). This new location was a complete change – a narrow, crowded street, with no river and no trees – but we got used to it. It was a new neighborhood with new faces.

Leizer Vilensky, otherwise known as Leizer the *Shammes*, had two daughters – Khasheh-Reizl and Riva. Khasheh-Reizl gave private lessons in Russian and arithmetic. She was a Zionist, and when Zionists would get together at the Vilensky house she would read out various literary pieces, sing, and recite Hebrew and Yiddish poetry. Among the visitors to the house were Avrom-Itsheh Shpilkin, Nokhum Chinitz [one of the editors of this book], Shmuel-Neyakh Goldberg, Shmaryohu Barhan, Feigl Tucker, Kaminsky, and other Zionists. Khasheh-Reizl was also friendly with a number of very intelligent girls such as Feigl Lisbaran, Dona Epstein, and Raitseh Katzenelson. Raitseh Katzenelson would often take a Russian book and read it aloud directly in Yiddish. Leizer's younger daughter Riva was a student of the *gimnazia*. Riva Vilenskaia and Gabai would present Zionist lectures in Russian.

Besides the comings and goings of Vilensky's daughters and their friends, many other people also came to the house to learn accounting with Leizer's wife.

Messl [Moishe] Immerman and his family lived in the second house next to us. His wife was a baker. In that same house lived Henya, whose occupation it was to stuff tobacco into paper cigarette-tubes *(papirosn)*. It was always cheerful in that household. You could come and buy baked goods and unpackaged cigarettes. At the end of the street lived a family whose name I recall as "Coffee" *("Kaveh")*. Coffee's son Eliohu-Borukh was a Bundist (follower of a leftist Jewish diaspora-centered nationalism movement) from as early as 1905. He would often visit us and carry on discussions about Zionism and Bundism; he found no lack of people interested in discussing those topics.

The daughter of Yabrov the carpenter was a Bundist. Yabrov's son, Neyakh, was one of the first members of the Jewish Communist Party of White Russia, which existed for but a short time. Later he was a high-ranking officer in the Red Army.

Right next to us lived my uncle, Chaim-Leib the *seifer* (i.e. – *soifer or sofer* – scribe). Chaim-Leib would ship Torah scrolls,

[Page 283]

The modern Cheder
From right to left, between the children, the teachers:
Yarkoni (Grynfeld), M. Chazanovich, Avraham Epstein, Kagan

mezuzahs, and *tfilin* (phylacteries) all over Russia and even to America. Scribes would sit in his house and do their calligraphy. Right in the house they would turn raw skins into parchment. I was there, dragging the wet pelts to and from; my dream was to become a parchment maker.

Chaim-Loib took an interest in the welfare of yeshivah students. He would arrange free accommodation for them, and help get up a community rotation of free meals (*essn teg,* lit. "eating days"). His sons, Eliohu and Binyomin, were scribes. Eliohu also studied Talmud with the congregation at the Great Synagogue.

A third son was the well-known *maggid* (preacher), "Meisheh Yidaber", author of the interpretive religious works, *Meisheh Yidaber* [note that the author's name is derived from his book, not vice versa; lit. "Thus Spoke Moses"], and *Face of the Sun*. He was a son-in-law of Reb Nekhemya, the head of the Yeshivah. Reb Nekhemya's daughters were learned girls, *Folkistkehs*. [Followers of the *Folkistn* Movement asserted that Jews as a group were not members of the proletariat, as the socialists believed, but of the middle class.], and teachers at Slutsk's first Jewish Secular School. Later one daughter became a doctor.

Also situated on Bobruisk Street was the Shelter for Poor Wanderers *(Hakhnosses Orkhim)*. Later the Jewish Assistance Committee ("Yekapa" or E. K. P.) opened a soup kitchen there. The Landes family had a fine house with an orchard not far from the "beetshak" [meaning unknown]. They had a dry goods business. Their oldest son was the bead of the Zionist Youth, the middle son was active in the Bund, and the youngest was a member of the Jewish Socialist Workers' Party. They had two lovely daughters, one a dentist and the other a teacher in the White Russian *gimnazia*. At the end of the block in a brick house lived the family of Yossl Harkavi, who produced cheese. His daughter, Musya, was a passionate Zionist. She left for Palestine, got married, but died young. Harkavi had sons, students, who were also Zionists. At a large Zionist demonstration at the *Shul Heif* (main Synagogue Courtyard), following the February 1917 revolution, one of the sons gave a fiery speech, declaring that Jews must be able to defend themselves.

At the end of the street was the new Yeshivah building and next to that lived my teacher, M. Hazanovich, of the Jewish "Modern School".

When I turned six, I began the Moriah Modern School. It was different from the old-fashioned *kheders*. First of all, school went only till 3 p.m., instead of 8 p.m., as the *kheders* did. Secondly, the 'Modern School was divided into classes. Students didn't sit at long tables but at separate desks. However, these are only the formal distinctions. The Modern School differed in more important details. The learning style was more progressive, using modern readers, teaching Hebrew grammar and Bible study, Jewish history, geography of the Land of Israel. In a short time the students were speaking Hebrew.

[Page 284]

The building of the old Commerce School

Soirees would frequently be held in the evening where slides would be shown, Hebrew poems recited, and songs sung. During my time there, Russian and mathematics were not taught, but in comparison to the old *kheder,* the Modern School was a progressive phenomenon.

When I left the Modern School, my grandfather sent me to a regular *kheder*, to Avremeleh the *Melamed* (Avremeleh Zaturensky, the Hebrew tutor). Why, I don't know. I was already well versed in Bible and Scripture, and here I was sitting, in an old-fashioned *kheder*, studying Genesis. "In the beginning…" from the beginning. After a term there, I spent a second term learning with Stifakov, a follower of the *Haskalah* (Jewish Enlightenment Movement). His method of teaching was pretty outdated, though we did learn Hebrew as a living language, and we did write essays.

By that time, the Moriah Modern School no longer existed. But Gutzait opened a private school, at the home of Ben-Tsion Shpilkin, together with Avrom-Itsheh Shpilkin. I was a student there until I went to the Commerce School in 1917.

After the February 1917 revolution, Jewish children flocked to the Russian schools. The quota system, which restricted Jewish attendance, had been abolished. A Jew no longer had to pay tuition for a number of gentile children in order that his own child would be able get around the quota. The traditional kheders closed down one after the other. In order to stem the tide to Russian schools, even Agudas Isroel (a very traditional institution) opened a modernized religious middle school. I, however, opted to wear "the hat with the green trim", the uniform with green stripes at the collar, and prepare myself for government exams.

Riva Vilenskaia tutored me, and very soon I was sitting for the exam. In September 1917, 1 entered. the Slutsk School of Commerce – the Commerce School. It was headed. by the liberal director, Dmitri Ivanovich Ivanov. The students in the higher grades were evenly divided, Jews and Christians. In the lower grades most of the students were Jews. The Jewish students spoke Yiddish among themselves – not only during recesses, but also in class proper. Most of the teachers were Russian women. The physical education instructor was a Pole, who, later under the Polish occupation, became the warden of the Slutsk Prison. Another teacher was the well-known Bundist, Leib Mishkovsky. The Commerce School, in contrast to the old *kheder*, was a real academy. Frequently, dances and pageants were held at the school. I was a student there for three years.

In spring of 1920, the Polish *gendarmerie* discovered a communist cell at the school, and the school was shut down. A short time later, the Poles evacuated, but not before burning down the Commerce School, among others. By the fall of 1920, the Commerce School had opened again, in the

[Page 285]

building of the former Men's Gimnazia. As for me, it was already the eve of my departure for America.

In the course of just three years, the Commerce School had accomplished a great deal. During the German occupation, the occupiers had not interfered. As long as the German language was taught from the earliest grade on, they were happy. During the Polish occupation, there was a course in Polish language and history. When the Bolsheviks returned (December 1918 to August 1919), definite reforms were carried out: homework was abolished; nature walks were instituted on the estates and in the countryside; lectures on the history of the Revolutionary Movement were held; tuition fees were eliminated.

The three years at the Commerce School were interesting and important for young people. At the same time, however, I was continuing my studies of Hebrew and Hebrew literature. That was around the time of the founding of the evening courses at "Tarbess" ("Tarbut" or "Culture"). The evening classes took place in the building of the old Jewish community school (the "Talmud-Teireh"). My teachers were Hazanovich, Chinitz, and Nekritsh.

A Story About Gabriel

In 1912 the Jewish population of Slutsk was fearing a pogrom, in connection with the proposed transfer of the Holy Gabriel's bones from the Suprasl Monastery to the Slutsk Monastery.

This is how it happened: "And it came to pass..." the head priest of the Slutsk Monastery one day stood up and told his congregants that the Holy Gabriel came to him in a dream and requested that his bones be transferred back to Slutsk's holy "Tritshan Monastery". A new church was built on the grounds of the Slutsk Monastery as a tomb for Gabriel's bones. For weeks prior, people were housecleaning and washing the town. Slutsk had never been as clean and tidy. The inmates of the Slutsk Prison, in their jail-frocks and round hats, swept and cleaned the main streets, painted the houses and the fences.

The police were outfitted in new uniforms. As if anticipating a pogrom, police were brought in from Minsk and Bobruisk, and the local firefighters were mobilized. A few days before the ceremony, important guests started arriving: the governor of Minsk *guberniya,* the archbishop, bishops from Moscow and Kiev, and high-ranking military officers. There were fears of disturbances.

The great holy day began quite early. Tens of thousands of people came to Slutsk. The procession streamed through Khapashker Street. Holy pictures and flags were hold aloft. The White Russian peasants remained quite peaceful. Since you couldn't buy liquor on that day, even the drunkards couldn't make trouble. For the entire morning, the Jews stayed in their homes. By noon., however, they ventured out into the streets, and mixed with the guests. On this occasion, the police actually did keep order, and everything transpired peaceably.

« *Editor's Note*: The story of the Holy Gabriel is mentioned in "Sketches" Volume I, by H. Boyarsky, and we present it here translated from the Hebrew:

In 1690, an accusation of ritual murder was dreamt up against the Jews of Bialystok and Zabludove, alleging that they had killed a Christian boy named Gabriel. In time he was made a saint. His bones were interred in Slutsk's Greek Orthodox (*Provoslaz*) Monastery. The blood-libel was commemorated a number of times in the Russian Duma (Czarist era parliament) and also at Beilis's trial [an influential blood-libel trial in Kiev, 1911]. In 1908, in accordance with a decree from the Orthodox Church, Gabriel's coffin was moved from the Slutsk Monastery near Bialystok, to the Suprasl Monastery near Bialystok. There a huge procession of priests and ever-increasing crowds took place. At that time, also, they circulated a newly printed Russian brochure entitled 'The Young Gabriel." »

1914-1920

In the summer of 1914, a general mobilization was called. The First World War was beginning. The town was filled with mobilized soldiers. Inasmuch as Slutsk had no train in 1914, the soldiers would go on foot to the nearest train station – Uretsheh. Each day, whenever a group – Christians and Jews – would prepare to leave, terrible shrieks and cries broke out. Men gave their wives a *tnai-get* (a conditional divorce that frees the wife to re-marry if her husband does not return from war). Wives were left without the means to get by.

It so happened that at that time in Slutsk there were a number of Jewish actors so benefit performances were staged. A huge concert was arranged in the Cold Shul, starring the famous actor Lensky.

The war was creating tremendous tension. People would grab any newspapers from Minsk, Moscow, and Petersburg. The printer Tomashov put out a daily bulletin, and a large crowd would continually stand by the print shop and wait. Since the Slutsk *Chaussee* led directly to Brest-Litovsk, large baggage transports streamed daily along that road toward the front. The town became full of soldiers on their march to the war. They would be billeted overnight in private homes.

In no time, masses of White-Russian refugees began appearing, coming from Grodno and Suvalki *guberniyas*. They had abandoned their farms and were fleeing into the Russian interior. They trudged along in covered wagons. As a result of all this hardship

[Page 286]

and suffering, sickness accompanied them; many of their young children died. The *Ziemtsva* (District Administration) helped them a little, then sent them on.

Very soon Jewish refugees, as well, began appearing, running from the Polish towns around the German border. These refugees, Polish Jews with long beards and *peyess* (religiously mandated sidelocks), long kaftans, and deep Polish accents, brought out a sense of wonder in us. The Jewish Assistance Committee (E. K. P.) immediately took them under its care.

Overall, in fact, the refugees were warmly received. They were billeted in private homes and in synagogues. Kitchens were open to them. Most of them eventually traveled more deeply into Russia. Refugees also arrived from Baranovich, Brisk, Lekhevich, Sinyavka – villages that were close to the front. A special school was opened for the children of the refugees. This was a Jewish Secular School, with Yiddish as the language of instruction and Hebrew as a subject. Later, in 1917, this school became part of the [new] school system operated by the [post-Czarist] Educational Committee of Slutsk.

The front was drawing closer. Soon the highest-ranking staff of the Third Army arrived in Slutsk. The whole town was transformed into a military camp. Officers and soldiers were quartered in private homes and in public buildings. Synagogues and houses of study were confiscated and occupied by soldiers. Military hospitals were opened.

Wherever you walked and wherever you stood, all you would see were soldiers and officers. Large warehouses with provisions were set up. Transports headed to the front daily, and always returned with wounded. It was during this period that the railway line was extended to Slutsk [for the first time], from Uretsheh. Because of the overcrowding, epidemics broke out in town: cholera, typhus, dysentery. I myself was sick at this time.

Thanks to the stationing in Slutsk of the Third Army, the town became rich. Suddenly the town had new moguls, new entrepreneurs who had been able to stock the army with its needed supplies. They bought up corn and wheat and sent it deep into the interior of the country. Abundance creates new rich people, but it also creates new poor people who cannot adjust to the new circumstances.

Life in our town was accelerating rapidly. Theater and movies had come to Slutsk, balls and military parades were taking place. Army Cossacks showed off fancy tricks, riding on their adorned horses. But you couldn't say that the Jewish youth showed enthusiasm for fighting on behalf of Nikolai. They tried finding ways around having to go serve. Bribes would be given to the *Marshallek* and other members of the [military] "Presence" *("Prisutstva")*. In the "Presence" at that time was a Jewish doctor named Marakhovsky. (He married Ora Zindel's daughter.) Since the whole "Presence" was mixed up with graft, he was made into the sacrificial lamb. He was arrested, and his colleagues had him poisoned in prison.

The Revolution

In February 1917 rumors spread that uprisings against the regime were occurring in Petrograd and Moscow. Within a day, students appeared in Slutsk streets proclaiming, "Down with Self-rule" and "Down with the Monarchy". They marched down the *Chaussee*. The police and military command were nonchalant about it. It became clear that Russia had been liberated from its monarchy. There were daily assemblies and meetings. A town election was set, and huge election rallies were held. Political parties developed all kinds of activities.

On the Jewish streets, activists appeared as if out of nowhere: Zionist Youth, Labor Zionists, Mizrakhi (Religious Zionists), Agudas Isroel (Religious Non-Zionists), Bundists, the United Jewish Socialist Workers' Party *(Sionistsheskikh Sotsialsti or "S. S.")* the *Volkspartei*. In addition there were other active groups in town: the "Cadets" (Constitutional Democratic Party, which favored an interim constitutional monarchy leading to a republic sometime in the indefinite future), the Socialist-Revolutionaries, the Mensheviks, the Bolsheviks. There was constant excitement and discussion. The parties opened clubs and reading rooms.

One morning, my sister ran into the house with great enthusiasm: there was a Jewish announcement – a poster had been put up in Yiddish. I went straight out into the street and saw a large notice in Yiddish about a Sholem Aleichem evening in Soloveitchik's Theater. Very soon a Yiddish theater was indeed created. All the actors were amateurs. The principal actors were the Tsimering sisters from Lekhevich. They performed Hirschbein, Kabrin, Sholem Aleikhem, Gordin, and Andreyev. Another of the principals was Salap.

At that time, in the group, which called itself "The Disseminators of [Jewish] Enlightenment" *(Mfitsei Haskoleh)*, there was great discussion on the pros and cons of Yiddish versus Hebrew. The proponents of each side brought in speakers from Minsk and Bobruisk. An animated political and cultural revival was going on. Our neighbors, the Byelorussians, had begun their own cultural revival of the Byelorussian language. Theater presentations were given in Byelorussian, White Russian books and newspapers were published. Ostrovski, one of

[Page 287]

their key activists, opened the White Russian *gimnazia*.

(After the Bolsheviks consolidated their power in White Russia, Ostrovski fled to Vilna, from where he pursued his campaign for an independent White Russia. In Vilna, he was director of a White Russian *gymnasia*. Later he cooperated with the Germans in trying to create a Nazi-controlled White Russia. In Smolensk he issued anti-Semitic appeals).

The war with the Germans continued, even after Kerenski's unsuccessful military offensive. [Kerenski held positions of power in Russia's Provisional Government, after the start of the revolutionary process but before the accession of the Bolsheviks]. A terrible demoralization spread throughout the Russian army. Each day soldiers from the Slutsk garrison turned back home. The Bolsheviks became active in Slutsk. They held huge meetings in the hall of the Democratic Club, where they prepared the public for new developments. Newspapers from Petrograd and Moscow were quickly snapped up; something was expected to happen.

But in the meantime, people were getting ready for the elections of the Constituent Assembly and for the All-Russias Jewish Convention. Agitators for various political streams arrived in town – Zionists, Agudas, Isroel, Bundists, United Jewish Socialists. Jewish newspapers from Petrograd also found their way to Slutsk – the great Zionist paper *"Togblat"* ('Daily Bulletin") from Minsk; the Bundist *"Vecker"* ("Alarm"); *"Der Yiclff"* and from faraway Kiev, the United Jewish Socialists' newspaper, *"Di Nayeh Tsait"* ('The New Times").

In October 1917 the Bolshevik Revolution [i.e., the second of the two 1917 Russian revolutions] took place. In Slutsk, the *soviet* (people's council) of workers/peasants and soldiers/deputies made it known that the reins of power had been transferred to the *soviets*. At the very same time, the Zionists put on a huge celebration in the Great Synagogue – in honor of the Balfour Declaration [recognizing Jewish aspirations in Palestine].

Before the Bolsheviks could fortify themselves, Slutsk was occupied by the Germans in January 1918. Suddenly – in the middle of the day – in rolled trucks full of German soldiers, accompanied by cheers. The Germans stayed until December 1918. Many local opponents of Bolshevism were happy with the occupation. Those eleven months were tranquil ones. True, the Germans shipped out food and other things. They took the entire stockpile of iron that the Kerenski regime had collected on "Iron Day." And they also had people do forced labor. You could "buy" your way out if you supplied someone else to take your place.

Since there were so many unemployed in town, the richer townspeople would hire unemployed to work for them. Contact was lost with America, and many wives whose husbands were in America suffered greatly, and needed to find some way of surviving. But, for that reason, links were established with Warsaw, Vilna and Berlin. In Hirsch Getzav's store on the *Chausee* the Germans had opened a book dealership, and Jewish newspapers from Lodz, Warsaw and Vilna would be sold from there. The Germans didn't concern themselves too much with the affairs of the town, as long as they could appropriate food. And the streets had to be kept clean.

They began to build a power station [the town's first]. Every day a military orchestra would play next to the commandant's office. Jewish prisoners of war in Germany would come home. The authorities also permitted political parties to function. Around October 1918, rumors were afoot that the Germans were about to surrender. The German revolution had broken out. This first expressed itself when [German] soldiers at a military bureau hung out a red flag. Soon after armistice, the Germans prepared to leave Slutsk.

Who would replace them in Slutsk? No one knew. Would it be the Polish legionnaires or the Bolsheviks? The White Russian newspaper "Rodne Krei" imagined that it would be the Poles. In only one night, the Germans vanished. The authorities undertook the administration; their hats were those of the Firefighters. After a few days, the Bolsheviks moved in. This was now December.1918.

The Bolsheviks began by a mobilization into the Red Army, with contributions and confiscations. The *Cheka* (counter-revolutionary secret police) had begun its work. Because of a famine in Russia, every day *mesholshnikes* ("sack-carriers") would come to town wanting to buy up food. Slutsk had a lot of flour, so a great deal would be shipped out to other towns. But the scarcity was encroaching.

It was at that point that the poor compelled the rabbis to carry out a *herem* (religious ostracization, excommunication) against anyone who exported flour from town. The *herem* was executed in the Cold Shul. Both rabbis came. Black candles were lit, the *faareh-bret* (board on which dead bodies are ritually cleansed before burial) was brought out, and those who dared to ship out food from Slutsk were cursed [literally]. The *herem* had a huge impact.

In the meantime, the undeclared. war between Poland and Russia had broken out. Poland took Vilna and Baranovich – and were marching on Minsk and Slutsk. The Bund and the Labor Zionists mobilized their members for war. The Jewish Communist Party of White Russia, which had been founded at that time, also mobilized her members. (This was the only time the Bolsheviks permitted an independent Jewish communist party, as distinct from a sub-group of the broader party. The Jewish Communist Party lasted about one year.)

Berger, a Labor Zionist, and son of the Hebrew teacher Berger, was killed near Minsk, as were Yosseleh Krainess and Maisheh Barhan. My uncle Alter Barhan was wounded. Shleimekeh Granat saved my uncle's life, by carrying him for miles on his shoulders.

Although business was still permitted at that time, co-operatives were opened with privileges for workers. The entire school system was made Communist, and

[Page 288]

the students had to vote as to which teachers should be allowed to continue teaching. Two theaters were opened, a Russian one and a Jewish one. Lectures, meetings, and parades were staged. In the market square, a rostrum was set up, and agitators made speeches. One of the main organizers in the *soviet* was Tivin although the head of the *soviet*, the boss of the town, was chosen from above.

The Jewish parties were all rendered Communist. The Bund opened a large club under the name of [a late Polish Bundist leader] Bronislav Grosser, in Marder's brick house where. there had once been a bank. The Labor Zionists opened a club in the hall of the former government-run Jewish school (Yevreiskoye Utshilishishe). All the while, the fighting went on between the Bolsheviks and the Poles-and in August 1919, the Poles occupied Slutsk.

The Poles came in with a great deal of fire and explosiveness. For the first few days, the soldiers looted a bit, but slowly order was restored. During this period of Polish occupation, America opened up again – letters and money arrived. Two delegates from New York visited, Naiburg and Tsurkov and brought a lot of help. The "Joint" [American Jewish Joint Distribution Committee, or JDC, founded in 1914 to relieve Jewish overseas war sufferers] sent support. The Jewish Assistance Committee (E. K. P.) was revived. A soup kitchen was opened. Assistance was apportioned.

The Poles ruled with an iron hand. Elections for town council were indeed held, but since the majority elected were Jews, the council was never convened. A town head ("galava") was appointed, but it was the military authorities and police who kept the reins of power. The anti-Semitism was undisguised, although it never got to the point of pogroms. Zionist Youth, the "HeHalutz" (the "Pioneer"), began to function again, while the Bund had its cooperative, "Einikait" ("Unity"). In the schools, the study of Polish and Polish history was instituted.

The arrest of a group of Communists in the nearby countryside caused a great stir. They were convicted of waging guerrilla warfare. On a Sunday when the town was packed with peasants come to market, eleven partisans were marched through the streets in chains in the direction of the tombs where they were shot. The peasants murmured: "Those communists must be *Zhids* (Jews) since it's our people who are doing the executing."

When the Polish army took Kiev in spring of 1920, the authorities in Slutsk riskily undertook to put on a military parade on the Boulevard. But soon afterwards, the Red Army defeated the Poles, and the Bolsheviks began their Great March. The battered Polish army, which was streaming through the Slutsk *Chaussee*, had for several weeks in a row been terrorizing the populace, beating them up and pillaging. On the last day, the Poles set fire to the town and tore up the bridges. The fire was put out. However, the beautiful structure housing our Commerce School was burned to the ground, as well as a number of houses in the Colonia section of town.

The first thing the victorious Bolsheviks did was to have a celebration in Tsvirki's garden in honor of the "liberation". Speeches were given by representatives of the "political prisoners," Labor Zionists and Communists. The *Cheka* became active again, and shot more than twenty people that they had arrested. Every day, masses of soldiers passed through Slutsk asking, "How far to Warsaw?"

This round, the Bolsheviks stayed in Slutsk but a short time. The Red Army had suffered a huge defeat near Warsaw and later near Brest-Litovsk, and the great retreat had begun. But prior to that, the Bolsheviks had, with great fanfare, exhumed the bodies of the executed partisans and re-interred them in a collective grave in Colonia. In Krainess' Club (formerly the Democratic/Squires' Club) public courts-martial were conducted against deserters and civilian counter -revolutionaries. They were sentenced to death.

The arrival and discharging of the train bringing back the Red Army was completely orderly. Tens of thousands of soldiers filled the *Chaussee*. The *soviet* had put up posters warning Poles that for every Communist or worker [that came to harm], the Bolsheviks would shoot a Polish bourgeois. The Bolsheviks also arrested a number of Jews as "hostages" and. led them out of town. Among them were Isroel Barhan, Tshiptshin the pharmacist, and others.

After a battle in town, which lasted several days, the Poles recaptured Slutsk. This was now September 1920. Several townspeople were killed in the fighting. Soloveitchik's Theater was burned down, as well as Rozovsky's brick house, where the Jewish community offices were located. This time the Poles remained surprisingly subdued.

Before long everyone was anticipating that Slutsk would again pass into the hands of the Bolsheviks. A large part of the population left Slutsk. Some remained in Poland – in Slonim, Niesvizh, Baranovich, and Kletsk. Others went to Palestine and America.

I visited Slutsk in 1936. It was no longer the Slutsk of 1917 or 1920. Of all the synagogues, only the Tailors' Shul remained. A Jewish folk school still existed. But signs of the spiritual devastation were visible everywhere. A small Jewish presence remained until the Nazis came and ravaged it, erasing it altogether.

[Page 289]

In the House and In the Street
Vigoda

by Y. D. B.

Translated from Yiddish by Judie Ostroff Goldstein

Our street *Vigoda*[1], where the city of Slutsk began, had probably been named for its topography and character. If one does not take into consideration the autumn mud in which the street was sunk before the cobblestones were laid, whether in summer or winter the street appeared very free and airy. It was surrounded on two sides with the deep, clean flowing Slutch River, hugged by wide fields, large, green gardens and orchards. During summer weekdays young and old from the "city" (this is how people on Vigoda referred to all the other Slutsker streets) came to bathe in the "Yatsever River". There were three beaches: "first beach" for women, "second beach" for *heder*[2] boys and non-swimmers and "third beach", which was the deepest, for swimmers. *Shabes* (the Sabbath) afternoons, most of the young people, walked in the "Mayovka" – a sort of open park behind the Vigoda orchards.

Entering town from the south side

Vigoda began at the first city-bridge and ended at the second, at Zaryetcher Street. This was a quiet, cozy, sparsely built street with wooden one-story houses. The inhabitants were mainly from poor, Jewish families of gardeners, fruit growers, field overseers, grain merchants, some tavern keepers, *melamdin* [3], scribes, also several artisans (craftsmen) and wagon drivers. There were also some gentiles on Vigoda: the

Polish nobleman Salyuta, who lived on an estate in the middle of the Vigoda fields and was very friendly with his Jewish neighbors. (Later for his part in the Polish rebellion, the Russian government confiscated his property and gave it to a Russianized Polish general). A second Polish noble, who owned "Gorki" behind the Vigoda bridge, leased out his fields to the Slabodskis, a wealthy Jewish family with a lot of sons, large and small, who came from somewhere else. They were busy in the Vigoda *shul* (synagogue) and had a place of honor at the Holy Ark and every *Shabes* and *Yontif* (Heb. Yom Tov, holy day) were given the honor of reading the *maftir* [4]. The Greek Orthodox priest, a rich man from Minsk, owned the largest orchard on Vigoda and he rented it to Jews. His son, a hunch-backed, epileptic, gentile was infected with revolutionary godlessness and secretly was friends with Jewish boys his age. There were more ignorant men: Simon and his sons, Poles who had converted to Greek Orthodoxy, the *Shabes-goy* [5] Vasil, took care of the lights in the *shul* on Yom Kippur and in honor of the holy Jewish day shaved his beard once a year.

[Page 290]

And there was the *Shabes-goy* [5] Stanislavikhe, a drunk, would take down the candlesticks in Jewish houses, therefore a religious fanatic, and milked the cows before they went to pasture.

In the middle of the block, as is customary, was the Vigoda synagogue, in which in olden days the voices of Torah students rang out clearly from the windows. In the last years it stood empty the entire day except for morning and evening prayers. When old Mota *"kapulshchik"*, did not sit there over a *gemore* [6] and study from morning until late at night, it would be locked. But for prayers, mainly on *shabes*, the *shul* was always full, with young and old, and here the Vigoders displayed their peculiarities and their wrinkles. To describe them properly would take too much space so I will describe a few Vigoda Jews who will serve as models for all the others.

First of all, there were the Vigodskis. Because of their surname alone they had a place of honor on Vigoda. This was a sizable family of brothers, with children and children's children who all settled in the outermost houses at the bridge and were grain merchants. They were called the *"sons of David"*… in total seven small Jews with big beards. The oldest and the richest of them was *Elia David's*, a former tavern keeper and later when the government had monopolized the liquor trade for itself, he became a grain merchant. He became a rich man, went slowly, never ran like his extremely busy, poor brothers the small grain merchants, he only "walked" as he called it, gave his children an education and sent them out into the world. His oldest son started a large factory in Minsk and one of his granddaughters, Clara, a revolutionary, lead the Slutsker youth in the Russian Revolution.

There goes Mota Ayolo, from the Slutsker *maskilisher* [7] family Ayolo. But Mota was not a *maskil* [7] and because of military conscription he chose a different surname: Rozenzweig. He was a simple Vigoda Jew with a large yellow beard and a sizable household, over ten sons and daughters. *Yom Kippur* [8], his gang of youngsters would bring a full sack of hard-boiled eggs from home and when the adults were in the middle of fasting, the small children peeled the eggs. Those around them who were fasting swallowed saliva and turned their heads away in order not to waken the desire to eat. He lived in a fine house with large storehouses, far behind the Vigoda Bridge, opposite the Gorki Estate. He was a large grain merchant, exported wagon loads, was by nature a quiet, reticent man and nevertheless he lead, through his eldest son, a relentless struggle with the "Sons of David", especially with Chaim David's son, competed in buying peasant wagon loads of grain from the others' hands. Once it went even as far as a fight and a quarrel in the synagogue *Yontif* during prayers. At the Vigoda *heder* [2] where boys learned *tanakh* (Jewish Bible), Shmuel B. described a verse: Hebrew word the war Hebrew word sons of the House of Saul and sons of the House of David"…

Then comes Yusef Shmuel Neikrug, a heavy Jew from outside (not born in Slutsk), of fine character. He was a mix of scholar and commoner, ranging from a charitable person to a wild miser, always ready to help a neighbor with an interest free loan and at the same time told clumsy stories to save a *groschen* (a penny). He dressed very commonly in a worn out *kapote* [9] with sleeves too short and heavy, dried out, warped "boots". When he would walk, his head would go to the right and to the left and it seemed as if he was going and going but he stayed in one place. The Vigoders talked a lot about his stinginess and his poor attire that were incompatible with his wealthy circumstances. In his house one ate bread and onions. He was also a humorist: "How do I make tea? I drink a quart of cold water and lie on my stomach at the oven – then I have tea". He owned, through an inheritance, two large vacant lots on both sides of the street, a small one that he sold to the neighbors and a larger one that he converted into a brickyard. People dug and made bricks, fired them in a lime kiln and on a half-starved horse, with his youngest son using the whip, drove the bricks to Slutsker homes to make ovens. The work in the brickyard was primitive and was done by a peasant, or poor Jews (often it was even a half-crazy person from among the well-known Slutsker crazies) for pennies. Men dug, kneaded, laid out the wet brick in a wooden mold, later put the half-dried bricks in the sun and then took them to the kiln. Yosef Shmuel used Vigoda schoolboys for the lighter work. The older ones were paid cash – a kopeck and the younger ones were paid with something valuable - with a ride across the street in his shaky wagon with the half-dead horse and one day it ended in catastrophe.

[Page 291]

Once when the wagon was loaded with small children it turned over at the lime kiln and the children fell into the fire, barely escaping with their lives. Vigoda then went into motion.

Yosef Shmuel played an exalted role. He was very often the *gabe* (synagogue trustee, Hebrew gabbai), *Shabes* and *Yontif* he prayed at the pulpit (most people were not happy about this because his voice cracked). *Shabes* in the evening, in the dark, he lead the people in *"Ashrei Tamimi Derekh"* (a prayer) which he recited by heart. During the week, during *mincha-maariv* (afternoon and evening prayers), at the large table behind the oven, he said *"Ein Yankev"* (a story from the Talmud) for the ordinary Jews.

By nature he was a compassionate man and listened to everyone's troubles with good, deep worried eyes and was always prepared to help. Often he would take a red kerchief and go into the street with it "to take up a collection" of several florins for a needy neighbor. Overall, his reputation on Vigoda Street was that of a good, religious Jew.

Judel *"der zeidener"* also occupied a respected place in the Vigoda *shul*. He was called *"der zeidener"* because he came from a silk family – he was an Eizenstat. He was a big-bellied Jew, worldly, not a great scholar, but not ignorant either and lived therefore as the only Jewish representative on the city council. According to the Jews, he took himself for a Jewish *"starosta"* (governor). But he was not officially the governor, only one of the writers who copied papers. He wore a *yarmulke* (skullcap) in council and kept a low profile in regard to the gentile officials, who persecuted him, even flattered a young gentile, a writer, who he called *"panochek"* (young squire). In return he was very haughty with poor Jews who would need to come to him for a favor. In the Vigoda synagogue he conducted himself as if he was the representative of the authorities, never said a bad word about the Russian government. But he was fundamentally a good person and an honest Jew, a religious man who loved to serve the Almighty, prayed the additional service on Shabes and *Yontif* and was also a strong competitor of Yosef Shmuel.

Jankiel *"der Koyen"* [10] was a gardener who rented a nobleman's fields on Vigoda where he grew cucumbers and grain. The work was done by day laborers, peasants from the neighboring villages, under the supervision of his sons and daughters. Jankel *"der Koyen"* [11] was a good boss, a *gabe* in the *shul*, often the prayer reader at the pulpit, led the grandeur of *Heshayne Rabe* [11] on Vigoda and at night distributed apples from a sack to the *heder* [2] boys who said Psalms in *shul*. On *Simchas Torah* [12] he invited everybody to his house for a reception (at which alcoholic drinks were served) and he was the leader of the revelers. When the priestly benediction was performed in *shul* with the Vigoda *Koyenim* [10], his singing resounded louder than all the others. For all of these things he was known on Vigoda as *"der Koyen Godl "* [13] even though he was not a great scholar. *Shabes* at *musaf* (additional service), singing from the pulpit *"Tikhns Shabes"* (a prayer) he would always say *"Vitzibanu haShem Elokainu"* instead of *"vitzivanu"*. And when one would tell him that in the *sidur* (daily and Shabes prayer book) it states expressly *"vitzivanu"*, he would answer with a rebuke: "Of what use is the *sidur*? My father, *olevasholem* [14], also prayed from the pulpit and also said *"vitzibanu"* – that for me is the holiest!"…

Mota the *kapulshchik* came from Kapulia. As a young boy he studied in a *besmedresh* [15] with Sholem-Yakov, Rav Moishe's, who later became famous, among Jews, as *Mendele Mokher-Sforim* [16]. In his younger years he was a flax merchant. He bought flax and traveled to the villages to sell it. When he was older he settled in Slutsk, on Vigoda and was greatly respected by his son who was also a flax merchant. He sat day and night in the Vigoda *shul* studying *gemore*[6] with *Rashi* [17] and *toysefes* [18]. He went through the entire *Shas* [19] in a year and *erev* (the eve of) *Yonkipper* [8] celebrated the conclusion. Thanks to him the Vigoda *shul* always stood open and the voice of Torah was never silenced there.

The old Vigoda *shul* was a strong brick building with thick walls. It had an old Holy Ark full of Torah scrolls, ancient curtains, a colorful, embellished pulpit and two dark coal ovens. Behind the ovens were two cases with well-bound *Sforim* (holy books), old and new: all kinds of *shasn* [19], *medrashim* [20], *yori-deah's* [21], *sheiless un tshuves* [22], even philosophical books such as *"moyre-nevukhim"* [23], the *"Kuzri"* [24]. The *shul* stood alone in a corner of the green gardens and grain fields. It overlooked a large pond where frogs croaked during the summer and when it froze during the winter served as a good *"katok"* (skating rink) where urchins could skate. How did a pond come to be at a *besmedresh* [15]? *Heder* [2] boys used to tell this story: A long time ago when Vigoda Jews decided to build the *shul*, the nobleman of the street decided to build a church exactly opposite. However the Jews thought this was wrong – and G-d performed a miracle, the church sunk one night and in its place was a river. This frightened the noble and he begged the pardon of the Vigoda Jews and sent from his brickyard well-fired bricks for the new *besmedresh* [15]. And so the walls of the synagogue were thick.

[Page 292]

Once, during a hot summer the pond dried up and people saw the tip of the sunken church. This happened only once.

What has become of the Vigoda *shul* with the pond now that Jewish life has been eradicated from all of Slutsk, together with Vigoda and has been seized by today's rulers? It is difficult to find out, but one thing is clear: today there are no more miracles.

Translator's footnotes:

1. Vigoda - (Polish) comfortable, cozy.
2. Heder – religious grade school for boys only.
3. Melamdin, pl. of melamed - teacher of children in a heder
4. Maftir – reading of the haphtarah (lesson from the Prophets) in the synagogue.
5. Shabes-Goy – gentile hired to perform domestic chores forbidden to Jews on the Sabbath, e.g. lighting a fire.
6. Gemore – Hebrew Gemara, that part of the Talmud [25] which comments on the Mishnah (post-biblical laws and rabbinical discussions of the 2nd century B.C.E.)
7. Maskil, adj. Maskilisher – An adherent of the Haskalah (enlightenment movement.
8. Yonkipper – (Hebrew, Yom Kippur) the Day of Atonement the most solemn Jewish holiday and fast day, when every person's fate for the coming year is to be decided.
9. Kapote - kaftan, gabardine, long black coat traditionally worn by observant Jews.
10. Der Koyen - pl. Koyenim priest in ancient Palestine; descendant of the priests, accorded certain privileges and obligations by Jewish religion.
11. Heshayne Rabe - Hebrew Hoshanah Raba (lit. great hosanna) The seventh day of Sukkos (Tabernacles) on which seven circuits are made around the synagogue reciting a prayer with the refrain, "Hoshanah!" (Please save us!"). Every person's fate for the coming year is irrevocably sealed in Heaven on this day.

12. Simchas Torah - Hebrew, "rejoicing with the Torah". A festival that celebrates the conclusion of the annual reading cycle of the Torah.
13. Der Koyen Godl - High Priest in ancient Palestine.
14. Olevasholom – rest in peace.
15. Besmedresh – prayer and study house; small synagogue, also used for meetings.
16. Mendele Mokher-Sforim – the father of Yiddish literature.
17. Rashi – Rabbi Shlomo Yitzhaki (1040-1105) Torah scholar unequaled in his commentaries. Best-known for his commentary on the Torah.
18. Toysefes – important commentaries on the *Talmud* [25] written between the 12th and 14th centuries.
19. Shas - pl. Shasn abbreviation of *shishe sedorim* meaning six books. The six parts that make up one Mishnah and one Talmud; the Talmud
20. Medresh, pl. Medroshim – commentaries on the Hebrew Bible, as well as legends and fables compiled in the Talmudic and post-Talmudic era
21. Yori-Deah's – second part of the Shulkhan Arukh put together by Joseph Caro 16th century as a compilation of Jewish ritual law.
22. Sheiles Un Tshuves – books written by Rabbis expressing their analysis of certain questions regarding Jewish religious law.
23. "Moyre-Nevukhim" – title of a well-known philosophical work by the Rambam.
24. "Kuzri" - title of an important philosophical book by Yehuda Halevi.
25. Talmud – there are two Talmuds: one known as *Bavli* Babylonian is the most famous, completed about the 5th century; the second is Jerusalem, edited around early 4th century. The core of both is the *Mishnah* [26] and *Gemore* [6] (Heb. Gemara); has become term used for Talmud.
26. Mishnah – the collection of post-biblical laws and rabbinical discussions of the 2nd century B.C.E, forming part of the *Talmud*

Crumbs of Memory

by Moishe Strugatch – New York

Translated from Yiddish by Judie Ostroff Goldstein

Fifty years, a half-century! When one has been torn from a city, and one's childhood was spent in the neighboring area, it is natural that a lot would be forgotten, erased from memory, even though it was my hometown. The names of people and streets have disappeared, and the little that remains is shrouded in a thick veil.

Only small incidents remain in memory. Perhaps this will give everyone a picture of the once existing and now destroyed Jewish Slutsk.

* * *

It is understood; I am a Slutsker, born on Vigoda at the home of my *zayde* [grandfather], Reb Szaia Zhitkowitcher. I remember that opposite our house was an empty field, on which was later built a wooden city jail for petty criminals.

The *"smotritel"* or supervisor of the jail tormented the Jews unmercifully, but he more or less tolerated my *zayde* as a neighbor. This *"smotritel"* had two sons, *gymnazia* [Polish high school] students, tall gentiles with honest faces and naturally just as cunning as their father. It occurred to my *zayde* to ask them to teach me Russian. We both went to see them. The two gentiles took us into one of the empty cells. They sat down on the cot and they left my *zayde* standing. There was only one other piece of "furniture" to be found in the room: a wooden pail used as a stool by the prisoner.

The chat lasted a long time and my *zayde* found it difficult to stand, but neither one asked him to sit down, so he sat on the "stool."

This incident has such an impression on me that when we had left I said to my *zayde:* "Under no circumstances will I study with such anti-Semites!"

* * *

I started going to *heder* when I was 5 years old. My first *melamed* was Hirshel Berl – an emaciated Jew, who simultaneously was also the *shamas* [beadle] in the Vigoda *shul.* As I recall, the *heder* was built directly on the ground, and the front door just cleared the ground. The house next door to the *heder* belonged to Y.D. Berkowitsh's parents – just higher and somewhat roomier in comparison to the *rebbe's* (teacher's) house.

Now an episode from my second *heder* – also on Vigoda, close to the cemetery:

One autumn morning somebody ran in to tell the *rebbe* that the *nadizatel* [superintendent] was going around to all the houses demanding *nalog* [taxes]. The *rebbe* should not have been afraid because he rented the space for the *heder* and the house was not his; but in any case, a *melamed* needed to have a "certificate" that cost three rubles and this he did not have. The *rebbe* yelled to the children that they should run. The children ran out onto Vigoda.

I, along with another boy, ran to the Yatzeva, far behind the *shul* and sat there hungry the entire day. When it began to get dark, we decided that we could return home. But not feeling entirely safe, we hid behind the *shul* and looked out around the corner to see if one could go into the street and go home without meeting up with the superintendent.

When I came into the house, my mother was very upset. She did not know where else to look for me and she was taking out all her evil nightmares on the *rebbe's* head.

* * *

I would like to mention an interesting fact about the police. A new bridge was being built over the river on Zaretzer Street. Only the support poles for the new bridge had been put in place, and boards were laid over the poles providing two narrow passageways over the bridge. By chance my mother and I were crossing the bridge when suddenly we noticed that from Zaretzer Street, on the road to the market,

[Page 293]

soldiers were running, their faces exasperated and impatient. And of course we, along with the others who were crossing the bridge, were in their way. They said nothing and did not harm us. But their running had worried my mother and we turned back.

It turned out that the soldiers were running to the market place to carry out a pogrom. They managed to beat a number of Jews who were not able to run away and hide. But the strange thing was that they had not bothered anybody on the bridge. With very little effort they could have thrown a dozen people from the small boards into the river. But they had been told that the pogrom had to start in the market place and as the bridge was before the market place, this was not part of their mission.

* * *

I would also like to mention my third *heder.* It was located opposite the Zaretzer *shul.* The *melamed's* name was Itshe Note's, from his father-in-law's name, Note Tomback, the well-known educator and Hebrew writer who was also the uncle of Yehuda Grodzovski. He was different from all the other *melamdin* I knew, intelligent and well-read, and he read Hebrew newspapers as well as Hebrew books. I do not remember if he did this for everyone, but when he taught me grammar, he never stopped me from bringing reading books to *heder.* He even translated for me the difficult words when I didn't understand their meaning. (His wife Tille was known in Tel-Aviv for philanthropic activities).

At that time there was another event. There was not a legal library in Slutsk! There was only an illegal one in the house of the Khapashker *shul*. This library had to be open two or three times a week in the evening. It had to open at 8 o'clock, but the librarians were not in any hurry and would arrive at 9 o'clock.

At that time I was 8 years old and was caught up in reading Y. Levner's *"Kol Agodas Yisroyel"* [All the Israel Legends] – 36 books. I would get the books at the library.

I remember that I would leave *heder*, in the winter, at 6 o'clock in the evening, I would go to the library, and the room would be locked. Only the anteroom of the *shul* was open. I would stand there in the dark and cold until the library opened. And as soon as it opened, all the young boys and girls would come to get books, or simply to meet and enjoy oneself for a while. Naturally the librarians would meet girls there and a small boy standing quietly off to the side, was never noticed. Only when they had to close the library would they notice that a young boy stood waiting for a book and give it to him.

I had to go home late. I walked with the book, lifting the hem of my coat through the dark streets. Many times walking over pieces of wood, laid out over muddy or wet places instead of a footbridge, my heart would tremble from fright on hearing the barking dogs and the drunken voices of the gentiles who often came from the opposite side.

* * *

Another incident that was characteristic of that time:

I was then 6 years old and I was sick. My mother took me to Dr. Bildrzhikevitsh, a Pole. I remember that his apartment was on Shausayne Street on a corner opposite Folke the tailor. (Later the lawyer Rep lived in that house). The doctor wanted to see how I digested food, so he ordered the servant to bring a glass of milk and a piece of black bread for me to eat while I sat in the waiting room. But I said to him, "A gentile calls this food?"

Therefore they got me ready for the second order of the doctor – to go to a *datcha* [cottage].

* * *

In the Khorker forest it was very gloomy. Aside from us there was only one other cottager, a consumptive and my mother wanted to avoid sitting close to him. Mainly we would go to an isolated corner and sit by ourselves. But once we encountered an unexpected visitor, Iser the crazy man. Iser was a wild crazy man, and it was dangerous for me to be alone with him. He was a Slutsker, had brothers there and one of them was on Shausayne Street opposite Haim Mikhel's mill. But the brothers had sent him away to Khorki and he became a resident there. He walked around with long, uncut hair, a disheveled beard, and a bag that he never took off. From time to time he would remember his brothers, and he would make a pilgrimage to Slutsk and create a tumult there until his brothers would send him back.

And there I sit with my mother in the forest – and Iser arrived. He was not just passing through;

[Page 294]

he came and sat down near us. Our blood turned cold from fear. What should we do? Should we get up and leave? Would it be more dangerous? So we sat scared to death until he got up and left. But before he did, I had to say that in the morning I would repair his bag.

The next day, he arrived early in the morning, and I can still picture it today – how I sat on the ground with Iser next to me and I sewed up his sack. (Going outside to meet Iser, I knew I made sure to see where my mother was) My mother did not take her eyes off us the entire time.

We never went into the forest again and returned home.

* * *

Neither the doctor nor the *datcha* helped me. But I got well nevertheless.

My mother had a relative in Starobin, who was known as a big "charmer." I can still see him in front of my eyes: a tall, older man, with a gray beard, rings under his eyes and the forehead of a wise man.

People had to watch out for him when he came to town to buy merchandise and simply "catch" him. When he would come to town, he would go to ten market fairs. At the inn he would grab [food] and put away all the packages in a minute and run out to continue.

To be sure that one could "catch" him, we would go to the inn at 6 o'clock in the morning, when he was just getting up. He heard my mother, and she said that she must see him alone before he prayed and drove away two hours later.

What did she have to do now? She had to get a new knife from a store that nobody had ever used and a fresh apple. Well, a knife is a knife. My mother went to wake a storekeeper in order to buy the knife. But where could one get an apple since it was still early in the season and there were not any apples:

My mother had to search for one, and she had to pay fifty kopecks for the apple, but she had found the things and ran back to the inn.

The charmer took the knife and cut the whole alphabet around and around the apple. He handed it to me to eat. He ordered me to bite letter after letter, beginning with the *"tof"* [last letter of Hebrew alphabet] and ending back at the *"aleph"* [letter "A" in Hebrew alphabet].

I obeyed him and did it, as he ordered. And – believe it or not – in a very short time I was healthy again.

* * *

Yet another *melamed* lived on Ostrover Street, where he "taught." But such teaching this was that he charged thirty rubles a school term, and this was considered a good term. But for the most part he only took in around twenty rubles – or three rubles per child – for he never took enough children.

Possibly because of this, he had only one day a week to be with his children. This was *Shabes*. He had two old-maid daughters who worked all week in a workshop as dressmakers. *Shabes* was the only day that the two could expect to look decent and perhaps meet a young man. But how could one expect to look respectable when one must not use a comb?

Blood would pour every day in the house. Two young women who wanted to look decent had only one day a week when it was possible, but on *Shabes*, one had to go around with uncombed hair, which they did, because they were not strong enough to go against the iron will of their father.

I remember another Jew from Ostrover Street – Yonah the shadkhan [marriage broker], a tall, dried up fellow, always with an umbrella. He had a daughter, an old maid, and a dried up son who later died of consumption. People would life at him and tease him to his face – that he should be able to at least manage a *shidukh* [a match] for his own daughter.

* * *

There was another person once in Slutsk who should be remembered, Aliotke the thief. He looked fine, respectable and had a beard.

I did not know him. My mother told me what her mother had told her about a personal experience.

This happened during a winter night. The winter was a terrible one, with very cold temperatures and storms and blizzard. My *bobe* [grandmother] was lying in bed and heard something scratching in the stable and the goat, the only possession that she had of substance, was restless and bleated loudly. It occurred to her that there must a wolf. The house was at the edge of the city. Probably a wolf got lost

[Page 295]

and detected the smell of the animal. She did not think long, did not wake anybody, grabbed her shoes and an old garment, found a stick and ran out – to drive off the wolf and to save the animal.

She was not able to find the animal in the stable, and she did not see a wolf. So she raced out over the white field, to see if she could find a clue. Not a small thing for a poor person to have an animal!

Who know what my *bobe* wanted to find that night. As luck would have it, a thought came to her: what was she doing, the wolf would throw away the animal and catch her too?

She went back.

The entire night, understand, afterwards she did not sleep and with the gray light of morning she went with my *zayde* to the stable. There was no sign or a clue that they could find – the snow had covered everything.

My *bobe* then figured that it could not have been a wolf because there was no sign of blood in the stable. What then? It was likely Aliotke the thief… and she quickly dressed and went to see Aliotke.

"What do you mean, Reb Aliotke?" she demanded of him him: "How could you do this to me? There was not a richer person to go to, only to <u>me</u>?"

At first Aliotke played innocent, denying everything: "Who me?" He did not know what to say. Only when my *bobe* would not give up he said, "So, *nu*, Dina-Keila, you will give me ten rubles to get the animal back. Someone else would not give it back for under twenty-five rubles; indeed such an animal could not be bought for fifty rubles!

"But you are an honest Jewess, so for you I will give it back for a tenner. What do you say? For all my pain and trouble on such a cold winter night?"

The main thing was, they bargained and bargained until she had bargained him down to five rubles. She gave him the five rubles and brought the animal back to the stable.

(Remarks from the editorial board: According to older Slutskers in Israel, he repented in his old age and led a respectable life).

* * *

A couple of words about my mother who was from a poor house but a proud family – the Rakhmilievitshes (her maiden name was Leah Rakhmilievitsh). She was never bitter, never thought of herself, and always shared her last penny with others.

She had only one brother, Itshe, a son-in-law of Reb Zacharia.the *paloshnik*, who was also a scholar and a man of knowledge. In his twenties he had already written for *"HaMelitz."* My mother was their sister's landlord, the one he taught to read and write and learn vocabulary. My mother was the intelligent one in her family, and from the beginning sought to teach me Yiddish and worldly knowledge.

She died in New York.

* * *

The law profession, which properly meant writing petitions, seemed to be well represented in Slutsk. I can count the following names:

Ratner, Perkal, Rep, Tshiptshin, Bakaliar and Salop (The "Writer" – actually more of a card player than "writer")

* * *

Seldom did anyone have only given name in Slutsk. Just about everybody was known by a nickname. I remember the following:

Judel *"der zaidener"* [from a silk family] – served in the "uprava" and lived on Vigoda.

Shimon *"der trif'er"* (has a variety of meanings) – was assistant sexton in the house at the Zaretzer *shul*.

Itche-Niek (Yelin) – teacher in the "Evreiskoye Utshilishche." Hardly large than a dwarf.

Matrenka *"der shuster"* [the shoemaker] – later had a son, a doctor.

Yoshe Gon (Gaon *)* *"der shneider"* [the tailor].

Hershl Tzitzke – a *"rimizshnik"* [perhaps harness-maker – lived on Ostrova.

* * *

There were Hebrew speaking families in Slutsk by the name of: Aliashev [Alishib], Migdal, Ayolo, Yelkut, Gabai, Hofetz, Shur, Ofres, Efrun, Yorkhe (Yorkha), Mas (Mo's), Berkut, Minker.

[Page 296]

Nishke Kvasnik's Street

by Pesya Shapiro-Michanik

Translated from Yiddish by Judie Ostroff Goldstein

Slutsk was a well-known, old city with street and lanes, mostly wooden houses. On the main street were brick houses of one and two stories. The children would walk up and down the long streets: Zaretzer, Chapashker, Shosajne, Kapulier, and Ostrover. They left their tracks as long as the Jewish exile on the still clean, cobblestones. There was constant noise from the wagons and their drivers and from the carriages and their *eazvoshtshikes* [coachmen]. The town was bursting with life and comings and goings of the gentiles who flocked in from the surrounding villages to trade with the Slutsker Jews. Our street was short and narrow. In Russian it was called Soborny Pereaulok and but we Jews knew it as Nishke Kvasnik's Street.

Nishke Kvasnik was once a tavern keeper whose formal name was Nisen Ratner. He was an enlightened Jew and a Lover of Zion. His children were raised with the love of Israel and the Hebrew language. After his death, his sons opened a restaurant. They were well known Zionists, Moshe and Isik Ratner, and they had a sister Henie Ratner who was very fluent in Hebrew.

On one side of the street was a high hill with large trees behind which stood the large "Sobor Church." My mother would tell me that on that spot once a church sank, so the gentiles built the "Sobor Church" in the same place The church made the Jews tremble from fear with the constant ringing of the large bells. The gentiles would come to church and then get drunk, and the residents of the street would shake in terror. Our house was not far from the long bridge.

From right to left: Feigl (daughter), Tuvia Mechanik [Tevia, the carpenter], Pesia, Chana Chaia (mother), Milkha and Dvosia (daughters)

I remember our Jewish neighbors on the street, such as: Leib the *Tzadik* [pious man], Grinvald the bookseller and owner of a private library, and Podlipski Mordchai, the *shtumer* [mute].

[Page 297]

Also, Feiwel Zelda's, (the Russian soldier); Nechama, the hardware storekeeper; Sholem, the *melamed* [teacher]; Zelik Klotz the *kirzshner* [cap-maker]; Nachum Dan Baron, the yeshiva dean; and Sara Kushes.

Nishke Kvasnik's brick house was the only two-story building and because of it brought prestige to our little street, and so it was named for him and we did not call it "Soborny Pereaulok." My father, Tuvia Mechanik, [Tevia, the carpenter], employed six workers. He made furniture: benches and chairs for schools and government institutions in Slutsk. His relationship towards his workers was that of a father; he gave charity generously and gave loans without interest to those in need. Never once did he fail to pay what he owed. My mother, Chana Chaia, collected money to give a Torah scroll to the yeshiva. I remember the celebration for the Torah and my mother's joy on that occasion. Who was as honest as she?

Our house was a large one. In the courtyard my father planted trees and raised hens and turkeys. There was a pond with fish and in the stable a cow with a calf. In one word – my father was a *mensch* [good person]. During the summer we rented boats to row on the river.

My father was of the opinion that the real exile would happen with the coming of the Messiah, and yet he longed for Israel so much so that he pushed his sister to go Israel and sent her ten rubles a month. My mother loved Israel body and soul. For her the *pushke* [charity box] for *Keren Kayemet* [Jewish National Fund] was as noble as the *pushke* for Reb Meier Bal-HaNes [money collected for Orthodox scholars living in Palestine]. With trembling hands she would put money in all the charity boxes. Her lips would quiver as she choked on her tears: Because of *Shabes* and the Land of Israel Jews should help. She understood

Josef Mechanik
(died 1931 in New York)

When we became members of *Tseirei-Zion* [one of the many Zionist Youth movements], my mother would say, "You should be worthy of living and building our Holy Land." My brother Josef *olevasholem* [may he rest in peace] who died in America, was from the first year of this century [twentieth] an activist and devoted Zionist in Slutsk and belonged to "Kdima."

My mother's prayer was fulfilled. We earned enough merit so that some of us could live in Israel.

[Page 297]

A Fire in Slutsk

by M. L. Gorin

Translated from Yiddish by Judie Ostroff Goldstein

I remember the fire, when I was a child of 6.

It was a week before Passover, during a nice, clear, starry night. The weather was clear and dry. My mother, may she rest in peace, woke me around 2 o'clock in the morning.

"Look, see, it is burning!"

Through the window I saw how red the sky was. Sparks were flying in the air, falling on the roof of our house. My mother, brothers and sisters were busy gathering together the bedding, household goods and taking them out to the street. I got dressed and went outside. Panic reigned. All the neighbors were busy packing, dragging large pots, chests and bundles into the open field. The women sent up a lament, and we were screaming, the children were crying, and the men were busy trying to save everything possible, grabbing a look from time to time at the red flames whose hot breath could be heard coming closer and closer.

Neighboring houses had burned quickly and soon our house also began to burn. The children were sent away far from the street to a courtyard. From there I saw the terrifying tragedy: "Slutsk is burning!"

When the sun rose the fire

[Page 298]

had calmed down. That afternoon when I went with my older sister to see our street, it was enveloped in flames and smoke. The house was no longer there, had burned to the ground, and our family had to stay at a relative's house. This lasted for months.

There was enormous crowding. Three or four families lived in a house with five or six rooms. A lot of families remained homeless. They took corners in the anteroom of the *shul* – the walls of the *Kalteshul* [Cold Shul] sheltered about fifty families with their children and bundles for a long time.

After The Fire

With great difficulty and with help from America and other cities and countries, the city little by little was rebuilt. Instead of low, detached houses, new row houses were put up. Many brick and steel buildings of two or three stories were built and even reached the center, to Slutsk's poor people – "America" Street.

"After a fire people get rich," joked the graying Artshik, the tavernkeeper. A Jew, a scholar, with a handsome face and a long, well-groomed beard, he also had a brick house built where his had burned. It had a deep cellar and modern arrangements.

It cost my mother, a widow, a lot of trouble, sweat, and heartache until our new house was ready and we could move.

During reconstruction the streets were widened and paved with cobblestones; new, better wells were dug and the mud was done away with. In short this part of newly built Slutsk had a new, nicer look

It's Burning!

by Yehudes Simval

I do not remember the year. "*Pozhar*! *Pozhar*!" [Fire! Fire!] – the screams carried over the entire city. I was very small then. I was taken by the hand to run away from the fire. When I awoke and opened my eyes I saw flames through the shutters – a sign that the fire was close to us. My mother and father had already gathered the children and counted them – 4, 5, 6. My mother was very confused. She looked for the other children, where is Reizel, where is Henie? Mama! I am here – yelled all the children. The small children were taken by the hand, the older ones helped my mother with the clothes because all the children were still small. And when we were leaving the house my mother yelled to my father: run to the stable, tie up the animal and drag her out!

When we were out of the house, I remember a red world. The air was filled with smoke. We went to the field. The street was full of people who had come to help save something from the fire, and one after the other they ran with a pail of water to help the firemen put out the fire. Others ran with children into the field, as did my parents. Some good people saved some cushions and curtains from our house and brought them to us in the field. Half the city had been burned. We were left naked, without a roof over our heads. Early in the morning we were taken to the *shul* that had not burned. Every family had a corner between two benches. Food was sent from the city and from surrounding villages. I remember that at noon cooking was done in a large kettle; a *krupnik* [dish of groats] from large pearl barley and a few pieces of fat were floating in it. We stayed for a couple of days until my parents rented an apartment on Zaretzer Street.

Folklore

Rabbi Yakov David [RIDBaZ, abbreviation for Reb Jankev Vilovsky] came to Slutsk to visit Rabbi Yitzhak Yakov Raynes, the founder of *"Mizrahi"* [Orthodox Zionist movement] and stayed with him. A delegation of young Slutsk Zionists (among them Hillel Dubrow and Y.D. Berkovitsh went to pay their respects, welcoming him and speaking to him in Hebrew. Rabbi Yakov David jumped out from a side room and in a red silk dressing gown and as a playful prank screamed: "Impudent fellows, *govoritye po-Russki!"* This means: Impudent fellows, speak Russian…then he stood up and repeated a Zionist lecture that he gave in Chicago during his trip to America. The lecture began with the sentence: "I sing of barren women, not of giving birth,"

[Page 299]

Movements and Parties

The Zionist Movement in Slutsk

by Sh. Menachem

During the time of *"Hoveivi Zion"* [Lovers of Zion], before the founding of the Zionist movement by Dr. Herzl, there were some people in Slutsk who were interested in the subject of the community in Israel. Among them was the well-known grammar *melamed* and librarian, Pesakh Karan [Pesakh Ezra's]. Every *erev* [eve of] *Yon kipper* he would put *keiros* [collection plates for Jews living in Israel] in the synagogues and *boteimedrashim* [for the settlements in Israel.]

After the first Zionist Congress in 1897, he founded the association *"Bnei Zion"* [Sons of Zion] in Slutsk. The head of the association was a certain Dr. Meltzer who practiced for a short time in Slutsk. The goal of this association was only to sell shares of the Colonial Bank, and later to market *"Keren-Kayemet"* [JNF].

Executive Committee of "Bnei Zion" in 1900

Sitting from right to left: 1) Zabin, 2) Unknown, 3) Eizyk Ratner, 4) Dr. Meltzer 5) Shmerek Bailin, 6) Layer Ratner, 7) Shaikevitsh, 8)... Standing: 1) Abraham Kadish-Ber Epstein's son, teacher and writer, 2) Leib Sadovski, 3) Dr. Z???? 4) Moshe Ratner, 5)... 6) Hillel Dubrow, 7) Abraham, Moshe Yechil Epstein's son, 8) Feinberg

The Zionist youth, also a part of the above-mentioned association, were not too pleased with the limited activity. They wanted to spread Jewish culture and Hebrew, so they founded a club and a library. In 1900, there was a schism in the association and a more progressive association was founded under the name *"Kdima"* [Zionist Youth group], headed by the well-known Hebrew teacher, Hillel Dubrow. Those who stood with him were the young, talented speaker Aaron Singalowski (at that time he was known as the

President of "ORT"), Y.D. Berkovitsh, Abraham Epstein, Meier Waksman (later a famous author) and others.

Through the initiative of the *"Kdima"* Association, *the "Tshaine"* was founded, a well-known Zionist club and reading room, and thereby the first community library in Slutsk with books in Hebrew, Russian and Yiddish. They also started evening classes for young yeshiva students to learn Hebrew and Russian.

The Zionist youth (of both sexes) distinguished themselves with their persistent activities and ideals. After the Kishinev pogrom, thanks to the initiative of the Zionist youth, a self-defense organization was formed that had representatives from all segments of the Slutsker Jewish population.

At that time *"Poalei Zion"* was also founded in Slutsk under the "Minsk system." Both sides of the road were busy during the evening, *Shabes* (the Sabbath) and *Yontoyvim* (high holidays) with the masses of the Slutsker Jewish proletariat.

On one side was the "Bund" SDSR and on the other side was *"Poalei Zion"*, S.S (Zionist Youth group). There were meetings and debates that often ended in quarrels and fights. Both enemy camps very often organized strikes among the workers.

Afterwards, when Zionism was officially forbidden by the Czarist government the Zionist *"Tshaine"* closed, but the library continued to function for a long time.

After the failure of the first Russian revolution in 1905-1906, youth community activities were generally weakened, especially Zionist activities. And Slutsk did not stand down from the general stream that was influenced by the new tendency in Russian literature,

[Page 300]

"Tzeirei-Zion" in 1917

First row (on the ground) from right to left: 1) Sholem Shpilkin, 2) Eliahu Altman, 3) Dov Sheftel,
4) Eshke Lew
Second row (sitting): Chevra Aranbaum, Abraham Tshernikow, 3) Abraham Yitzhak Shpilkin, 4)
Mlinski, 5) Moshe Harkavy, 6) Mutye Paimer-Melamed
Third row (standing): 1) Lipe "Yontif gabe", 2) Chaia Rachel Sarasova, 3) Mutye Harkovy
Katzenelson, 4)... 5) Chaim Moshe Apelsin, 6) Shmuel Neach Goldberg, 7) David Zeymark, 8)
Shmeryahu Baron, 9) Fanye Krepf?

especially from Artzibashev's "Sonin" and others. The youth were devoted to worldly pleasures. Solomiak's confectionery was always jam packed with Trampatel circles, live life! This lasted several years until the youngsters grew up and became more idealistic, more or less. Then a new movement began among the General Zionists and the young people grouped around the new movement, *"Tzerei-Zion."*

The head of the General Zionists in Slutsk was the wealthy and great community worker, Leibish Gutzeit. Their activity was to distribute collection plates for the settlements in Israel, selling secret???? to Zionist congresses, and leading debates and lectures about national and Zionist problems. Those who were well known General Zionists were: the *shochet* (ritual slaughterer) Mr. Alter Mahrshek; the Hebrew teacher Hazanovitsh; Shvaydl; Gutzeit; Berger; Tshiptshin the pharmacist; old Itshe Feinberg; the drugstore owner Shayevitsh; Kermin and others.

Zerei-Zion led cultural and political activities. Mainly they organized clubs among the students in middle school and taught them Zionism and Hebrew. Abraham Yitzhak Shpilkin was one of the main leaders. His parents' house served as the center for secret activities. Besides him there were others who were active such as Epstein; the dentist's son, Sowa; the daughter Danye; Shmuel Neah Goldberg; Tzvi Razran (now a professor in New York); Apelsin; Lande; Chinitz; Mosie Harkavy and two brothers; Mlinski; Leibish Guzteit's son, Yoshe; Gabai; and Abraham Tshernikov.

From right to left: 1) Ezriel Nekritsh, 2) Boruch Lipshitz, 3) Yehuda Skokolski, 4) Krayne Maharshak, 5) Tzvi Hazanovitsh

Difficult times arrived for the Slutsk residents during the First World War, in 1915 when the city was close to the front and was inundated with military personnel.

Jewish soldiers in the Russian military came from Zionist roots, and they would search for meetings. To the all Russian Zionist conference in St. Petersburg, Slutsk sent five delegates.

During the election for the municipal council there was a struggle between the Zionists and the *Bund*, that had then united S. D. and S. R. Twenty-three Jews were selected among them seven Zionists and six Bundists, ten neutral Jews, and eight Christians.

At that time a part of the extremely orthodox founded *"Agudas Israel"* (Orthodox Jewish group against Zionism).

When a division of *"AZE"* (health care for children) opened in the city, the Bundists were against it, stating that the aim of the community was to take care of cultural affairs, but in general affairs, it united the entire community without differentiating between beliefs.

After Kerenski's revolution, the city in general was divided. Demonstrations by *Zerei-Zion* (Zionist Youth group) centered on a Jewish soldier in whose hand fluttered a blue and white banner with Russian and Hebrew writing: "Land and Freedom."

Also after the German occupation, Zionist gatherings were hindered.

After the Polish occupation Zionist activities were strongly limited, and then a Hebrew school opened in the city called *"Tarbut"*.

[Page 301]

In the room of this school various gatherings occurred.

In 1920 a group of Slutsker youth made *aliyah* [return] to Israel.

Because of the government agreement, the Polish military left Slutsk, and so a group from *Tzerei-Zion* succeeded in leaving the city. Some went to Israel and some immigrated to America.

Under the Soviet government beginning in 1920, an underground youth organization was founded. Hazanovitsh writes full details about this in Hebrew.

On March 12, 1923, five Zionists were arrested in Slutsk, four from *"HaNoar"*, *"Kdima"*, the fifth – the propagandist among the young – E. Nekritsh.

Their trial took place in 1923 in the city's theater.

The court decided to free the youngest. One was sentenced to a month under arrest and the fifth to a year in prison.

Details about them are written in the Hebrew section.

[Page 301]

The Rise and Fall of the Bund

Moshe Tulman, New York

In the last years of the previous century (19th) Slutsk became a very isolated city. Separated from the world and without train service, Slutsk had a weak perspective on developing its economy. The population, mostly Jewish, lived from small stores. There were also small workshops in the city that produced what was needed for the residents. Many of the workshops employed workers. A lot of people had immigrated to America and took their small and grown children with them. Those left behind had great difficulty adjusting.

The workers' children and generally the children of poor families learned a trade and became workers in the city workshops. They labored in very difficult conditions and naturally were not inspired by their situation.

Children of non-workers went into business, but most of the young people turned to studying and searched for an education hoping to do better this way.

The yeshiva drew those searching for a religious education or career. Some even studied Hebrew, i.e. Abraham Epstein, Hillel Dubrow, Y.D. Berkovitsh, and others, thereby agitating for travel to Palestine.

But the majority of the youngster studied Russian and secular subjects. The government school for Jewish children and the *gymnazia* [high school] were full and helped the youngsters prepared for their goal. People learned and thought about personal and general Jewish interests.

Moshe Tulman

The better educated traveled to the large, Russian cities. But they never forgot about Slutsk and very often they would visit Slutsk and make contact with the languishing youngsters. Thus, we received visits at one time or another from Merke Ratner, Berl Rabinovitsh; Rubke; one of the *melamed's* (teacher) sons, Zama Vengrov – a town *shochet's* (ritual slaughterer) son; Bronstein (mentioned by me – late – the Crown Rabbi of Slutsk); and a non-Jew Ochapovski, a child from a very liberal family in Slutsk, whose father was a judge in the city.

All of them had been students in Slutsk who had spread out over the Russian universities in Moscow and St. Petersburg. Visiting their hometown,

[Page 302]

they would contact us, the more or less educated, and inform us about life in the large cities. They would tell us about the efforts and struggles of the revolutionaries and of the various catch phrases of freedom and equal rights.

The Revolutionary Committee in Slutsk in 1905

From right to left: (sitting) - Grisha, the student Zhizmer and Boris
From right to left: (standing) - A. Ravitsh and Getzaf

They were members of the Social Democratic group. With great enthusiasm they gave us their party program that spoke about economic problems. They enlightened us about Socialism and Marxism and gave us illegal literature that answered all our questions.

Their speeches made a great impression on us Jewish children whose knowledge was limited by our "provincialism." Their propaganda had an enormous effect.

"Why are we thinking about going to Palestine for a future that Zionist fantasists predict, when our way is the practical one to solve the Jewish question?"

"Socialism can answer all the economic questions, and the new order can end all Jewish troubles."

At that time (around 1901 or 1902) the famous Jewish revolutionary, A. Litvak, (pseudonym of Chaim Yankel Helfand) came to Slutsk. He was a Jew from Vilna who was registered in Slutsk. He explained that the Social Democratic Party had a special committee that was active among the Jewish workers and spoke Yiddish. As most of them did not know Russian, the propaganda written in Yiddish had a great effect on the Jewish workers.

Litvak had called a small meeting at which several non-worker, educated people, and also a small number of Jewish workers were invited, people whom we knew and trusted. Among them was also a tailor from Bobrusk (I do not remember his name), who had settled in Slutsk and was very involved in revolutionary activities. Litvak influenced us to attract the Slutsker Jewish workers to the revolutionary movement. He told us he would send illegal Yiddish literature, proclamations revolutionary songs and also professional revolutionaries and speakers from time to time. We got down to work and organized a small circle of Jewish workers.

At the meetings we had with them, we spoke and interested them in the revolutionary movement and mainly in political-economic questions. Somewhat later we introduced them to the Social-Democratic program, their problems and efforts. Our lectures, discussions, and literature that arrived from Minsk had the right effect. The number of participants began to grow. When the organization through small strikes had begun to better the economic circumstances of the members, the majority of the city's Jewish workers decided to join our movement. A couple of years later, the Social-Democratic Party was faced with the question of "Jewish cultural autonomy" in the future liberated Russia. The Jewish group or the *"jargonishe"* as it was called until then, had endured and became an independent party under the name *"Bund."* [Ideologically, the Bund was against Zionism and thought anti-Semitism was the result of capitalism and would disappear with the rise of Socialism]. The *Bund* and our Slutsker organization immediately became a part of the new party.

Leaders of the *"Bund"* visited us and also spoke at our meetings. With time the movement had a strong effect on all our members and our supporters. The main principle of Socialism and Marxism stated that the working class would carry through the political and economical changes and would set up rights for everyone. This strengthened their hopes

[Page 303]

for the future and also made many of them proud of their lives. Our organization also had a hand in fighting against anti-Semitism, and this made us popular and brought us prestige.

A revolutionary demonstration in Slutsk in 1905
The leader in front is Yechiel Ravitsh (Chai'ke Meizel's brother)

The constant threat of pogroms made us decide to create a special group of strong and courageous men, workers or non-workers, for defense purposes. The Russian hooligans in the city always tried to incite the peasants from the surrounding villages against the Jews, during the fairs. They would call for a fight to start the pogrom. Our defense group warned them that we would settle with them if they persisted with these tactics. During the fairs, the members of our group would keep watch. I remember an episode that especially raised the level of respect for our group among the city's Jews. Accidentally a Cossack division stopped in Slutsk overnight. When it was dark some of them went for a "walk" around the city, in groups of two or three without weapons, and they fell on every Jew they met, beat them and took whatever they found on them. They also broke into Jewish houses and took whatever they wanted. From everywhere in the city, one could hear Jewish voices screaming.

Our defense group immediately armed themselves with iron tools, sticks and stones; quietly fell on the small Cossack groups, and took care of them until it became quiet in the city. Then Cossacks arrived on horses to search for us and revenge "Cossack honor." We ran away and they stayed to search, but the beating of Jews stopped.

In the morning when the Cossacks left the city a lot of them had beautiful marks from the beating they had taken. Two of them even had to – poor things! – stay in the city hospital "for several days of vacations." Also the police, who had done nothing when the Cossacks beat and robbed the Jews, suddenly were watching and searching for the participants.

When the Jews stood up to the Cossacks and gave them a beating, it was a new phenomenon in Slutsk and we were rewarded with respect.

[Page 304]

When Russia went to war with Japan in 1904, the situation created a lot of discontent in the country. The revolutionaries took advantage of the mood with the goal of unseating the government. They called for strikes, gave speeches throughout the country, and organized demonstrations and uprisings. But despite all this, it did not succeed because the army remained "loyal" to the government. Therefore the revolution failed. But the Czarist government wanted somewhat to reward the population. They allowed the selection of people's representatives for the parliament, the *Duma*, whose obligation it was to advise the government what it had to do. As the government did not like the advice from the Duma, they dismissed the first Duma and ordered that a second be chosen.

The Slutsk *Bund* took an active part in the elections. In the city and the surrounding towns and villages, candidates were chosen who supported the *Bund*. All those chosen later did what the party in Minsk told them to do. The government, however, was not patient and the second Duma was also quickly forced out. Many of the deputies were arrested. After that, the authorities went after the Revolutionary parties, their leaders and members. A lot of Slutskers who were active in the Bund had to run away to America, and the majority who remained were removed from the organization.

The last chapter of the Slutsk Bund played out when the police discovered the Bundist library and the small number of arms we possessed. The police then decided to arrest four of the leaders of the organizations committee. Three of them were found in Slutsk and immediately put in jail until they could find the fourth, so they would be judged together as a group.

The three were:

1. Rolnik, who years later came to America and there died soon after from tuberculosis that he had contracted while lying neglected in various prisons.

2. Lyata Bunin returned to Russia after the Russian Revolution.

3. I have forgotten his name and do not know what happened to him.

Not being able to find out from the three about the fourth, the police decided to be patient and to wait until he was found.

Meanwhile the fourth was hiding out in Stary Dorogy where he was a teacher. It happened that one of Bunin's sisters came to visit him in jail. Bunin put a letter into her breast that was addressed to the fourth. In the letter Bunin told the fourth all about what had happened to them also, (because the fourth was the manager of the finances for the organization), asked for an exact accounting of the two hundred rubles that he had taken from party funds before he was arrested.

The prison guard had noticed Bunin give the letter to his sister. The police sent a warrant to arrest the addressee. I was the fourth and I went alone to get the letter. What a warm welcome I received! I was immediately sent to Bobruisk.

Finally after many months of going from one prison to another we were brought to trial in Minsk and were sent to Siberia.

We trudged through various Russian prisons for long months until we came to Yenisaysk--the coldest part of Siberia. After about seven months I ran away to China and Japan until I finally arrived in America in 1910, where I remain all these years to live and tell this history.

What happened to the workers and non-workers who were influenced by the Slutsk Bund?

Many of them who emigrated to America took an active part in the Jewish workers' movement here in this country. Those who stayed in Russia lead underground activities and, after the fall of the Czarist regime in 1917, they revived the Bund in Slutsk.

When the Bolsheviks took over the government, they outlawed the existence of the Bund. Some of the members joined the Communist Party, but the majority was not able to adjust to Communist dictatorship.

When I visited Russia in 1929, I met with a lot of comrades from the Bund. They were exactly like most Jews there, beaten down and disappointed. "Is this what comes from the ideals for which we struggled and yearned for such a long time? Is this the reward for beautiful dreams?" Having observed everything that took place there, I returned to America a broken man. It was difficult to leave my relatives, friends, and former comrades to the Holocaust that ruled in every corner of the country.

[Page 305]

Personalities

Reb Refoel Yossel

by N. Chinitz

Translated from Yiddish by Judie Ostroff Goldstein

A.

Something amazing occurred in Slutsk. Refoel Yossel, the tailor, a young man had suddenly given up tailoring. When Chava, Chava, the broad bean seller, brought her husband's kapote to be repaired, the tailor was not in his house. And it was made clear to her that he had not been around for a couple of days.

Where was he sleeping? Everybody was interested in this question. The whole town was agitated and various opinions were given. One person said that he had gone to buy a house. Others said that the tailor had gone to the villages to work for the gentiles. A poor man, he tried to make a living for his wife and children. An honest young man, not a great scholar, but he had a good heart and worked hard. Now he had suddenly disappeared, not saying how long he would be gone or where he was going.

In "*vtikin shtibl*" [prayer house] the *shamas* [synagogue beadle] was found sitting engrossed in an "*Ein Jankev*" [a story from the *Talmud*] and told the tailor's wife that her husband was in *shul*. On no account did he want to go home. There was privacy there so he could study Torah and serve God.

Everybody came by and implored and made clear that he should go home. For what reason would a man suddenly leave his wife and children to sit and study? He was just being stubborn. Sitting in *shul* he will waste his few years, far from everything, carefree, far from worldly pleasures and demands-he should be so lucky!

"He will sit there a few days, then he will get hungry and he will long for home. The exile of the Jews should last as long as the time he will waste in the prayer house," – that is what people said.

But not Reb Refoel Yossel. Body and soul, he gave himself to studying Torah, went through the *Mishnah,* bit by bit the *Gemore*. He labored arduously. Eat, not eat, what's the difference? If his wife brought food, good. If not, it was also all right. Until late at night he studied. When he was tired he grabbed a nap on a hard bench. He did not go home, a waste of time! It would be contemptuous of the Torah! Better to go through another couple of pages of *Gemore*.

During the day he asked questions unashamedly and studied diligently, and at night, when all around was quiet, he sat by a small lamp, a Jew with a sweet, thin voice singing, poring over a large Gemore, peering deep into a difficult passage. People wondered how a simple tailor could reach such a level. Scholars were surprised by his great proficiency and deep understanding and were taken aback by his sharp mind. Nobody dared to call him "Refoel Yossel, the tailor" any more and with holiness on the lips of the Slutskers, the name "*Reb* Refoel-Yossel" made the rounds.

The city Jews made it their duty to care for his family and to provide them with food.

Reb Refoel Yossel would often fast, very rarely leaving the prayer house even for a couple of minutes. Years passed while he studied the law. He became pale, had sunken cheeks and long, silken *payos* [earlocks]. He had black eyes that expressed a deep sorrow and a love of the whole world. He charmed everyone, and he was known throughout the entire region as a pious man.

If something terrible happened, people would come to Reb Refoel Yossel. He would stand bent over and bitterly sigh with tears in his eyes-"What can I do to help, my child? I am a simple man, a tailor. Go home and he who lives in heaven will help you. The main thing is to believe in our Father in Heaven, He is the Almighty."

When somebody came to speak to him about studying, he answered, discussed with him, but other than that he was silent.

A Jewish woman came to ask a question concerning religious law and he said: "My daughter! Go to the Rabbi!"

"But, *rebbe,*" she said, "You are more

[Page 306]

like a rabbi!"

The *dayan* [judge in Jewish court] asked, "Are you are a "rabbi?"

"Go, daughter! I am Refoel Yossel, the tailor."

He would get up in the middle of the night and put ashes on his head. His voice trembling, full of anguish, rang out: "When will you have pity on Zion, our Father? Oy, great is the need and the necessity of your people Israel. Great are the worries of the Jews and they have no more patience. That is the marvel, Sweet Father! It is not their fault. This is a most bitter exile, full of troubles and sorrows. Please have pity, Great Father and help-the water is up to their necks!"

When he was older, he became ill. When they wanted to take him to a residence, he would not agree to it. How had he earned it?

The elite of the city took him to Warsaw. When he was served a quarter fowl and found out that it cost fifty kopecks, he did not want to stay in Warsaw any longer. "I do not want to be a burden to the community, they are spending too much money on me. I am going back to my city, Slutsk." And that same day he left Warsaw.

A worker came to the *Vtikin shtibl* and complained to Reb Refoel Yossel that he was disgusted with tailoring.

"My child! Do something else and God will bless you as one who has great knowledge and you will be lucky."

"I did not mean that, rebbe! I want to leave tailoring to sit and study."

"My child! Work as a tailor and serve the Almighty and this will be counted as if you were studying Torah."

"Rebbe, excuse me, you were also a tailor and today, you are a pious man and a rabbi."

"My child! First of all, I am scarcely a saint and far from being a rabbi. Secondly, there was no profession for me to leave, because I was not a good tailor, just a lowly patcher of clothes! But you, my child, you are an excellent tailor. Go back to your trade, recite a few Psalms each day, go regularly to synagogue, learn from "*Ein Jankev.*" Throw yourself into your work, and don't leave your wife and children [for Torah]. Oy! "For thou shalt eat of the labor of thine hands; happy shalt thou be, and it shall be well with thee." [Phonetically: "Y'giya kapeykha ki tokhal, ashreykha v'tov lakh." Psalm 128:2]

Then tears choked off his speech.

Entire days and nights Reb Refoel Yossel would study and console his visitors.

Few saw him when, little by little, he lost, his strength and died with an honored name.

With trembling and reverence the name "Reb Refoel Yossel" will be remembered.

In " *Vtiktin shtibl* " people would indicate: "That is where the "*Tzadik* " (pious man) sat".

Nobody else ever sat in that place.

There are hundred of things and stories about the greatness of a person who had earned merit to such a high degree.

B.

As told by Reb Chaim Zaydes:

I

Reb Refoel Yossel was a bungler of a tailor. Once he brought somebody a piece of work that was not perfect and this person hit him. So his friend Reb Yasha the Gaon [eminent rabbinical scholar, genius] who was already a master tailor told him: "You will never be a tailor. Sit and study."

Refoel Yossel asked, "Is it possible? I am an ignorant person who can only pray and have the responsibility of a wife and children."

Reb Yasha answered him, "Start with *Chumash* [the 5 books of Moses] with Yiddish translations until you are a scholar. About making a living, do not worry. I will set up your wife to make loaves of bread for which the rich housewives pay three kopeks a loaf. This will be a good living."

Refoel Yossel sat and studied in *Vtikin Shtibl* and went home only on Friday night. At that time kerosene was very expensive, so he burned a half candle between his fingers while studying, until his fingers would burn. The Slutsk Rabbi, Reb Yasha-Ber Soloveichik, befriended him, encouraged him and supported him. From the entire area, people would turn to Reb Refoel Yossel. Women called on him to interpret dreams. He never took money from anybody. He only took a candle so he could study.

II

When the *RIDBaZ* [acronym for Reb Jankev Dovid Vilovksy] came to visit for a Purim feast, he yelled to those sitting at the table:

"A tailor sits in *Vtikin-shtibl* and women go to him to interpret dreams, and soon they will ask the tailor questions about religious law. Let us go and ascertain if he is an ignorant person."

Arriving there, the *RIDBaZ* saw Reb Refoel Yossel studying. The *RIDBaZ* asked him difficult questions, but Reb Refoel Yossel answered and quoted the source. The *RIDBaZ* was surprised by his knowledge and said, "Until today I thought I was the only scholar in Slutsk. Now I see another sitting in the shtibl."

[Page 307]

III

A wooden monument stood over Reb Refoel-Yossel's grave for many years. Leybe Yoikh the blacksmith took the large rock that lay near the Kalter Shul and constructed a gravestone for Reb Refoel-Yossel's grave.

C.

Reb Refoel-Yossel stated his piece about women's fashions of his time.

The in-laws were fighting at a wedding. The groom did not want to go to the *chuppah* unless they gave him the promised rotunda, which was missing from the bride's wedding garb.

They sent for Reb Refoel-Yossel and asked him to make peace between the sides.

Reb Refoel-Yossel came and first asked what a rotunda was. They explained to him very clearly that it was a women's garment without sleeves.

Reb Refoel-Yossel sat down near the groom and asked him very seriously and sincerely:

"My child, you are fighting over a pair of sleeves before going to the *chuppah*. Does one make such serious laughter over a pair of sleeves?"

The groom smiled heartily. His parents also smiled.

Reb Refoel-Yossel continued his words to the groom:

"G-d willing, after the wedding, G-d will help you, and you will sew sleeves on your young wife's clothing on your own account. And perhaps in the merit of the pair of sleeves that are now missing on the garment, you will be blessed with abundant livelihood for your entire life.

The battling groom's side stopped smiling. The son and parents thanked Reb Refoel-Yossel for his blessings and hastened to arrange the *chuppah* in a good and fortuitous time.

Esther Malka Shpilkin
(Reb Refoel-Yossel's daughter)

Transcribed in Slutsk by R. P.

Portraits

by Mordchai Lipa Goren, New York

Translated from Yiddish by Judie Ostroff Goldstein

Dainov, Tsvi Hirsh (1832 - 21 Adar 1877)

[Tsvi Hirsh Dainov] was born in Slutsk and was a prominent man known by the name "The Slutsk *Maggid*" [preacher]. He was one of the first modern Yiddish orators to use simple Yiddish, without the traditional melody, without gesticulations and without frightening people with hell. With the strength of his words, he would make a great impression on his listeners. Inspired by the ideals of *Haskalah* [enlightenment movement], he described for the people the humiliating economic and spiritual condition of the masses. He spoke out against false pride, against idlers, about the government's need to help fight poverty, the necessity of education and the need to send [Jewish] children to public schools.

The members of the *Haskalah* movement sent him out on their behalf to Jewish towns and villages to give speeches to the people. His strength of expression against fanaticism and superstition, such as not being too rigorous in interpreting the law and keeping certain commandments, made the Orthodox Jews come out against him.

He also had a lot of enemies among the older generation. The Russian administration (to which he would turn for help) protected him.

In many towns people had closed the doors of the *besmedresh* to him. "*Hamagid*" and "*Hamelitz*" [Jewish newspapers] would often publish laments about the persecution that he endured from the opponents of *Haskalah*. Thanks to the endeavors of his friend YL'G, the community "Ein Jankov" invited Dainov as an orator in 1874. These were Russian-Polish Jews in London where he was very popular and well liked, even by the leader of the Jewish community, Rabbi Nathan Adler.

Characteristic of his relationship with the Yiddish language; in one of his letters to the "*Chevra Mfitze Haskolah*" in 1873, he drew the society's

[Page 308]

attention to the need to publish Jewish books, through which one could have an effect on the Jewish masses. He told them how useful the Yiddish writings of Michal Gordon, Linetsky, Axenfeld and others were. Dainov left a lot of manuscripts.

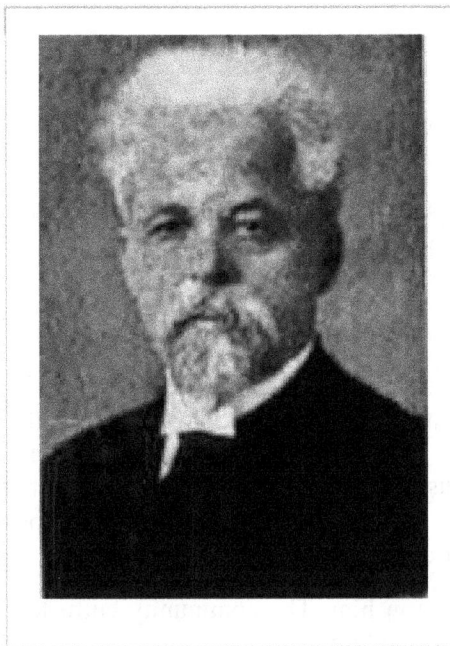

Reb Tsvi Hirsh Masliansky
The famous public speaker

Reb Tsvi Hirsh Masliansky was born in Slutsk, 3 Sivan 1856 in a middle class family and received a traditional education. Even as a child he showed his aptitude for learning. At seven he knew the *Tanakh* [Five Books of Moses] by heart. At 10 he would wrap himself in a tablecloth and would give his friends a lecture about the destruction of the Temple that moved them to tears.

He studied at the yeshiva in Mir, then settled in Pinsk, Karlin, where he became a Hebrew teacher, private as well as in the Talmud Torahs. At around 14, after the pogroms of 1881, he was drawn to the "Lovers of Zion" movement and began to agitate for them in schools and synagogues. Showing a great talent, he undertook a speaking tour in Southern Russia, Lithuania, Zamet, and Courland, propagandizing for the movement and Jewish nationalism. He inspired both Orthodox and assimilated Jews.

Due to police interference, he left for America where for the first four years he traveled to different cities as a speaker. He settled in New York and in 1898 he was appointed as "orator" in the "Educational Alliance." He participated in the Yiddish and Hebrew press. He published a book entitled "Droshes: [lectures] Memories of a Public Speaker."

(From Rayzin's Lexicon)

Reb Shmuel Sinknovitsch

The rich grain merchant, Reb Shmuel Simkhoivitsh, was a famous Slutsk personality and distinguished himself in many ways. He was smart, educated in both Jewish and worldly subjects, and was fluent in several languages. He was an international businessman, traded stock on the London stock exchange, and subscribed to Hebrew, Russian, German and English newspapers. From time to time he would write to the St. Petersburg German newspaper "Petersburger Herald."

In 1894 he was invited by the Russian government to take part in the Rabbinate commission.

Reb Mair Soloveichik

A Jew with a stately appearance, an experienced merchant Soloveichik had the talent to skillfully combine worldly problems with Jewishness and learning.

He had one of the sharpest minds in town. In his large, elegant house that stood in a beautiful garden was his large and rich library of rabbinical and worldly literature.

Chaim Michal Gutzeit

The most influential person in city affairs was the rich and powerful Chaim Michal Gutzeit. It was said that he had influence only because he had money. His fortune was thought to have a value, by those in Slutsk, of more than a hundred thousand rubles, which at that time was a legendary amount. He was a short, corpulent man, with a red face and dark brown hair. He was a good businessman, very decisive. Parents would come to him to deposit their daughters' dowries.

People had enormous confidence in him. The community entrusted him with orphans', widows' and divorced women's inheritances, and wedding pledge money, etc.

He created work for a lot of families in his sawmill and his large grain mill that was powered by a steam engine. Also a lot of workers made their living from his large undertakings and estates in the surrounding area.

Reb Yitzhak Hochmark

[Hochmark] had a multi-faceted personality due to being acquainted with the world at large as a delegate for community institutions and yeshivas. He visited the United States and also South America. Rabbi Reb Yhezkel Abramski was the last Slutsk rabbi of the council.

[Page 309]

Dr. Lyova Shildkroyt

Dr. Shildkroyt was renown in Slutsk and surroundings. Everybody knew him. He had an imposing personality. His white face and broad shoulders made quite an impression on everyone. He had studied medicine at Moscow University. His mother, who was poor, helped with all her might. He was a liberal man. To him everybody was the same - rich or poor. If somebody was fatally ill, he never complained about being tired, day or night.

Therefore Shildkroyt acquired renown among all classes of the population as a simple man and learned doctor. He had a phenomenal memory. He only had to meet a person once, and he remembered his given and family name, even after a long time. If he could not find a droshky, he went on foot to see his patients.

During the First World War (1915-1917), when Slutsk was full of refugees, Polish Jews who had run away, he was one of the ones who organized a relief committee for those who were suffering. He dedicated all his energy and used his own money to help the needy and save lives.

There were other doctors in Slutsk beside Dr. Shildkroyt. They were Drs. Melzer, Feinberg and the Christian doctors Wecher and Yanushkevitsh. Among the barber-surgeons, Grayew was very popular. The Jewish doctors served the one charity hospital and old peoples' home.

The well-loved young doctor Sinayski tragically perished as a young man. He was murdered in his house together with his beautiful young daughter. The murderer was his Christian coachman. Sentimental songs were written about this tragedy.

Eliyahu (Elia) Tsharni

Eliyahu Tsharni was known in Slutsk as a wit, a lover of literature. He was an editor for the "*SlutskerError! Bookmark not defined. Sheigetz*" that appeared in 1911.

A slim man, with a long pale face, he had penetrating gray eyes that accentuated his paleness.

He became an orphan very young, and his mother, the widow, had the task of maintaining and nourishing her two sons, Eliyahu and Pinye Tsharni. She owned a property with a house on the market place that had two stores, from which she derived her living. Both brothers were born weak and sickly. Pinye inherited consumption from his father, who had died young.

Sh. Nachmoni [Nachmanovitsh] and Elia Tsharni

Eliyahu studied with *melamdim* who would come to the house to teach him. His brother Pinye became a dentist and had an office in Stary-Dorogy. Eliyahu in his free time pursued his love for reading. He loved Yiddish and Russian literature. He had a sense of humor and a sharp memory. He was able to describe features in minute detail, a piece by a writer, a poet or an artist.

His mother Paya treated him lovingly and watched over him because of his weak health. This had a psychological effect on the old bachelor, so much so that he never sought employment. Most of the time he lay about in bed from meal to meal. Only late in the evening he would walk alone or with friends. He dedicated one hour a week to the Zionist library. This was his life as an old bachelor.

I knew him when I was 11 years old and visiting the reading room and library.

He always wanted to publish a humorist journal about the daily life of Slutsk and specific types. His dream came true with the *Slutsker Sheigetz .*

[Page 310]

Translated by Jerrold Landau

The title page of Slutsker Sheigetz, 1911

Der Slutzker Sheigetz
A literary-humor collection

Contents-Catalog

In 1928, I came to Slutsk as an American tourist. Jewish life in Slutsk, both spiritual and economic, was dying. Tsharni had aged. He was grey and thin, however, his eyes shone with deep understanding and intelligence, as previously.

"Oy, we have endured terrible tribulations from the awaited revolution! Nothing was left from our former dreamy years of youth," he complained to me.

"And what is with your health? How do you survive?" I asked him.

"We toil, everyone must work. In my old age, I have started to repair old, torn galoshes. That way I can say that I earn my livelihood. Sometimes I receive something from America, from former Slutsk friends; Altman, Meisel, and others. I also receive a few English pounds from Ch. Nachmanovich and others in Palestine. However, it is not sufficient for water and kasha…"

Even now, it was interesting to chat with him.

I visited Slutsk once again in 1935, and spent two weeks there. Both of us, Tsharni and I, strolled through the empty market, along the highways, and through the synagogue courtyard with the appropriated synagogues. We also visited government businesses, Artel cooperatives, and small stalls. Everything appeared gloomy, wretched, and non-homelike. The only Jewish cultural center was the Communist club, which contained a few Marxist books and newspapers. It was located in the building of the former Slutsk Yeshiva.

Sh. Nachmani relates:

At one time, Elya Tsharni decided to go to America, but since he had poor luck, he did not go and remained in Switzerland for a certain period of time. From there, he would write postcards as he strolled along the cold Jungfrau (the highest mountain of the Swiss Alps).

When Nachmani went to Slutsk on vacation

[Page 311]

he found Tsharni near his mother who was lying in bed. In response to the question as to why he had come there, he responded that he has discovered that the earth is round. One wanders and wanders about, and one comes back to the same place.

Tsharni whispered in my ear, "Comrade Goren, our life is completely new: revolution, the shops have been taken over, workers work on the side, one gets sick, one coughs, and the stomach is empty. They hate us, and not from today. What is going on, indeed?"

An echo of a hidden complaint emanates from a poem that he sent to Ch. Nachmani in 1934.

The Wind

What does the wind want, it roars so wildly,
It disturbs my weak sleep,
During my sleep, I see a pretty picture
It disturbs me, and I must wake up.

I do not want to go where it blows,
Where heavy clouds move:
Sleeping, dreaming – it does not allow,
Looking like blossoming flowers.

One wants to sleep, dream for a long time,
Seeing only lovely images,
But it disturbs, a malicious statement,
The bad wind, the wild.

With his warm soul and love of Jewish creativity, Elya Tsharni felt the malicious winds and dark clouds. The malicious words disturbed Jewish life, and he was murdered with the Jews of Slutsk.

Honor to his memory!

Folklore

Binyamin the fool, with his thick, dirty beard, was the most famous of the famous Slutsk fools – with his [words of] Torah and his statements. Once, when the were building the Butcher's Synagogue in Slutsk and people stopped to look, someone said to Binyamin, "So Binyamin, tell us something about this!" Binyamin said, "What use are some words for you? It is an explicit verse in *Al Ken Nekaveh*[3]: 'And all humanity shall call in Your Name'."

Once, someone encountered Binyamin pacing behind the city on the Slutsk highway, with a lit pipe in his mouth. He asked him, "Binyamin, where are you going?" Binyamin said, "To Hrozeve." "What do you need in Hrozeve?" Binyamin said, "To smoke the pipe." "Is there no fire in Slutsk?" Binyamin said angrily, "Slutsk fire is too cold for me."

* * *

The world would say that Slutsk Jews are known to be stuck up, that they go about with bent fingers. Why? If one asks a Slutsker, "Who are you?" He would answer with pride and bend his finger, "Who Am I? First of all I am a Slutsker…" When he has nothing more to boast about, he would remain with a bent finger.

Yaakov Dinezon, the well-known author of *Der Schvartzer Yungmanchik* [The Dark Young Man] and *Yossele*, had a different theory regarding this: A Slutsker always goes about with a hole in his heart because he beats his chest with his finger and claims: "I am, you should know, a Slutsker!" He does this so much that he bores a hole in his heart.

* * *

In Slutsk, they would joke about the nearby town of Romanova: "Romanover god" (in honor of the large idol that hung on the border between the Jewish town of Romanova and the gentile village with the same name). They would also say: "Romanova is nearly empty." What is the meaning of this – I no longer remember.

Translator's footnotes:

1. I did not translate (or transliterate) the author's names in the newspaper, as they are mainly obscure pseudonyms, some from various parts of the prayer service or from Talmudic references. E.g. for #5, it is *Melech Evyon* [Impoverished king] a reference to a Rosh Hashanah hymn. For number 9, it is *Kulam Ahuvim* [All are beloved] from the benedictions prior to the morning *Shema*.
2. A literary device of a reverse alphabetic code. The word itself is an acronym of the final four letters of the Aleph-Beit.
3. The second paragraph of the *Aleinu* prayer.

[Page 312]

Sextons in Slutsk

by Rabbi Nissan Waxman, New York

Translated from Yiddish by Judie Ostroff Goldstein

Slutsk excelled in its "clergy." Rabbis of Slutsk had been renown for generations in the world of the Torah. Even sextons of Slutsk were interesting characters.

Fayvl the Town Sexton

Fayvl Harakh [Charach] was born a sexton. His father Reb Aaron, the Jewish Court of Justice sexton, died young and left his widow, Esther Frume, with four small children, and the community, in respect for him, turned over the position of sexton to Fayvl. He was then only fourteen years old. He had a good head for studying, but he had no desire to take over as sexton. But this was the only way to feed his mother and the small orphans. So Fayvl, at fourteen, became the Court of Justice sexton and also "assistant sexton" for the *Kalter shul*. Several years later, when Reb Hirschl, the "head sexton" of the *Kalter shul*, left for America, Fayvl became the head sexton. Nevertheless Fayvl was very busy with city affairs, so he was never separated from his holy books, knew the *Tanach*, and was well versed in " *Ein Jankev.* "

As sexton for the Court of Justice, he usually managed to spend a large amount of his time around the rabbi. The rabbi, Rabbi Iser Zelman, would turn to him with questions: "Where is this verse or that tractate of our Sages of Blessed Memory to be found?"

When Liate, the sexton from the Butchers' *shul,* died, Fayvl immediately began to say *"Ein Jankev"* there between afternoon prayers and evening services, but not for money, God forbid.

Fayvl was a smart Jew and always happy. He had a good heart and everyone respected him. In the 1920s when the Bolsheviks had already naturally requisitioned all the synagogues and did not have any place for sextons, Fayvl purchased a horse and wagon and drove loads around town and once in a while took a passenger to the train station. But his livelihood was mainly derived from bringing kegs of water and selling it to the Soviet restaurants, even though the leaders were aware of his "bourgeois past" as sexton.

In 1930, after Trotsky's downfall, when the "*Cheka*" [Soviet secret police] made up stories to get rid of anyone on whom there fell the least bit of "Trotskyism," a certain Jewish Communist, a Trotskyist, was arrested in Slutsk. There was little to remind people of him but he left behind a young wife with several small children.

Reb Liate, sexton in the Butchers' and
Kalter Synagogues

Fear filled the entire atmosphere. People shook even when speaking to their families. But on a cold winter day at dawn, Fayvl put on his fur coat and left the city and stayed in "Otshered" for a couple of hours. There he acquired several bundles of wood, drove them back to the home of the wife of the "Trotskyite" and left them without any explanation.

When Fayvl arrived home late that night half-frozen, his wife asked him, "What did you earn?"

Chava! Blessed be His name, I earned a lot today."

In 1942 at the age of sixty, Reb Fayvl was murdered in Slutsk by the Nazis, may their names be erased. May the Lord avenge his blood and may his soul be bound up in the bond of eternal life.

(This article is based mainly on information from prominent people who prefer to remain anonymous. N.W.)

Reb Shlomo Demburg from the Tailor's Synagogue

Reb Shlomo Demburg was a scholarly Jew, a good speaker with a wonderful appearance and a pleasant face. Politeness and kindness exuded from him. He was cheerful Jew, full of joy. Even though a pauper, responsible for eight children who would wait every day for the couple of *groschen* their father earned as sexton in the Tailors' synagogue, Reb Shlomo still derived comfort from doing his work honestly, in good faith. For him it was not enough just to worry about poor people, the widows

[Page 313]

and orphans one would always see in the street. Reb Shlomo would go around with bags full of clothes or food and give them to these poor souls.

His goodness was renown in Slutsk. During the First World War Shlomo Demburg was a soldier. Soldiers lay in the trenches and shot, except Shlomo. 'What does it mean to shoot or be shot at?' he thought. One can still, G-d forbid, really meet a bullet!

Shlomo lay and sang Psalms when the shooting started. The division commander was told about it and he came and shouted: "Demburg, why don't you shoot?" Shlomo knew that "this meant trouble" and he took courage and lifted the rifle high in the air and shot three times until the officer left. Then he lay down the rifle and busied himself with Psalms again. Because of this he survived.

At the beginning of the 1920s, when the Red government had requisitioned the yeshiva buildings, most of the students from the yeshiva ran away with their leaders to Kletsk. Individual yeshiva students stayed, however, and continued their studies in the Tailors' *shul*.

As you know, the Tailors' shul had very nice benches. The bosses became angry with the yeshiva students who used too many benches and book stands. For appearance's sake, Reb Shlomo would scream: "Mischievous fellows, that is what you are! You are destroying the synagogue, breaking the benches, the book stands – they cannot endure your treatment!"

But as soon as the bosses left he would go to the yeshiva students and say: "The bosses are simpletons. If not for studying, then what are the benches and synagogue together for? Use them in good health. Just study, Torah children!"

Reb Shlomo was also the official speaker in the Tailors' *shul*. He never prepared a speech. But what strength there was in his speeches! *Shabes* during the day it would often happen that he would be angry, and with his sad melodies would bring tears to the eyes of many.

The Nazis, may their names be erased, murdered Reb Shlomo in Slutsk.

Reb Shmuel, the Sexton from the Kloyz [House of Worship or Study]

The *Kloyz* was the oldest synagogue in Slutsk and it looked more like a fortress than a synagogue. The walls were thicker than other buildings. As strong as walls of the *Kloyz* were, stronger still was the Jewish spirit that ruled inside the walls. In the *Kloyz* the Rabbi and the esteemed men of the community customarily prayed. Always after evening prayers, a daily page of *Gemore* [part of the Talmud commenting on the *Mishnah*] was read at a table, around which were seated two-three Jewish *minions* [ten men needed to make a prayer quorum].

There were a lot of holy books in the *Kloyz,* old ones from ancient scholars and also new sets of the six books of the Talmud and the *Rambam's* [Rabbi Moishe, son of Maimon, Maimonides] digest of Talmudic law, from Vilna. Reb Yehezkel Abramski, the last Slutsker rabbi, would say that the word *Kloyz* came from Hebrew "*kol eoz,*" the strong voice of the Torah that was called "eoz" [h' eoz lemo otn in Hebrew]. Slutsker Jewishness was strongly felt in the *Kloyz*.

The sexton Reb Shmuel Vendrov embodied a segment of Jewish Slutsk. In the course of his entire life he never left Slutsk, not even to travel. He saw Slutsk in its entire beauty and brightness, when Slutsk was thought to be second, after Vilna, in the dynasty of Lithuanian Jewry.

Reb Shmuel was the sexton during the time when Reb Yoshe-Ber Soloveitchik was the Slutsker rabbi (Reb Yoshe-Ber was the Rabbi in Slutsk from 1862-1870 5622-5630, also with Reb Yakov David and Reb Isser Zelman Meltzer. And he lived to be the sexton with Reb Yehezkel Abramski).

Shmuel was versed in *Talmud* [the *Mishnah* and *Gemore*] and very knowledgeable in *Midrash* [commentary on the scriptures]. He was always sitting and studying. This, however, did not stop him from fulfilling his duties as sexton in the synagogue. Mainly, he was in love with the *Kloyz's* holy books, and he watched over them as one would a treasure. It was very difficult to get a holy book from him, and as soon as he saw a *gemore* lying on a stand, he would immediately put it back in the bookcase and close it. Rabbi Abramski would joke: "Reb Shmuel had already barred and locked it in the bookcase, so men had to fulfill the "redemption of prisoners."

Because of his age and his closeness to the certain great Slutsker rabbis, he looked at the young rabbis and the newly ordained that always came to the *Kloyz* with contempt. "They are of no consequence, these 'made by machine' rabbis, what do they know-they are at present little boys-of Reb Yoshe-Ber's sagacity or Reb Yakov David's knowledge?" he would say.

But he referred to the young Rabbi of the city with great respect, even when he had something against him. Rabbi Abramski would stay in the synagogue after praying and studying wearing a *talis* [prayer shawl] and *tefillin* [phylacteries]. Once Reb Shmuel remarked that rabbi's *tefillin* " *shel rosh* " [the one of the phylacteries placed on the forehead] was something he would not take off, even though he should have. But it took courage to correct the rabbi.

[Page 314]

Shmuel did not leave the problem alone but went to the rabbi with a story, "You know Rabbi, I remember how Reb Yoshe-Ber would smooth down his hair when he took off the 'shel-rosh' so that there would not be a part." Rabbi Abramski looked at him and said, "So, I do not do this?"

Meanwhile he automatically brought his right hand up to the *tefilin shel-rosh* and immediately took it off. Reb Shmuel smiled as he had not, G-d forbid, offended the honor of the rabbi.

Reb always looked sullen, an angry Jew, but he possessed warmth and goodness without measure. Three of his daughters, G-d preserve us, died during his lifetime from diabetes, leaving behind small orphans. Reb Shmuel always claimed that each person received whatever was his fate, no more and no less. Of confirmation of this, he said, that he sees it clearly himself. He suffered a lot from life, but no toothaches. After all he had already lost almost all of his teeth, so he would never know the pain of a toothache, because it was not his to have this grief.

In 1925 the Soviet municipal government put out an order that all the synagogues may be open only for prayer, but not for studying, therefore they must be closed from nine o'clock in the morning until five o'clock in the evening. The one remaining yeshiva student would go and open the *Kloyz* through the back door and study there.

The Soviet attendants uncovered this and made a big fuss about it. The bosses of the Kloyz yelled at Reb Shmuel that he did not know what was going on in the Kloyz and he was frightened and became angry with the "criminal" who dared jeopardize the synagogue's existence. But shortly after when he had time to think about it, he went and apologized to the student for his hasty remarks against him. After all he, the student, had put himself in greater danger so that he could study.

In his last years Reb Shmuel gave over the position of sexton to his son-in-law, Reb Hillel the Scribe. He gave his attention to the Torah scrolls so they would always be ready at the place where one must read and also that each Torah scroll should be used one after the other, so that one would not remain unused for a long time. He kept this job because it was too holy to entrust to somebody else.

It happened that Reb Shmuel had prepared a Torah scroll and as usual, laid it on the edge of the table while he went to get somebody and together they would put it back the Holy Ark. Meanwhile the Torah scroll had rolled and fallen off the table. Reb Shmuel stood there trembling with fear. In his long career as sexton in the *Kloyz,* such a thing had never happened. He immediately said that this must be the end, that it would not be long before he left this nonsensical world.

So it was. In a short time Reb Shmuel died and so after his death his "kingdom" fell. The Soviet government soon closed the *Kloyz,* as well as all the Slutsker synagogues.

Reb Nathan Fishkin-Horn - Karni'im-shul

The "*Karni'im-shul*" was exactly the same as the Butchers' and Tailors' synagogues, a remembrance of past years when all of Jewish life centered around the shul for praying and to meet with colleagues. The comb-makers Society prayed in the *Karni'im shul,* and there were a considerable number of them in Slutsk. Therefore the synagogue was called *Karni'im* – made of horn. In the last years there were already fewer comb-makers, but the name *Karni'im-Shul* remained as a remembrance of this beautiful period in Jewish life.

The last sexton of the *Karni'im-shul* was Reb Nathan Fishkin-Horn. He took the additional name of Horn himself, as he was proud of the synagogue's name. Reb Nathan was a man of average height, skinny, sickly, always on a diet, and trembled from the thought of taking an extra morsel. Looking at him you could not understand how he managed to stay on his feet, and, G-d preserve us, not fall down. He seemed barely there, but as he stood at the cantor's desk as the prayer reader, he was immediately transformed into another being.

When Reb Nathan prayed before the congregation, they knew for certain that there stood a strong man with an iron chest. His praying conveyed an immense gusto, a religious ecstasy, and sharp longing. He read the Torah with a rare intensity and clarity. Even his treatment of a thing as simple as *Kiddush* (prayer recited over wine) every Friday evening in shul rang like a bell and was heard in several streets.

But mostly Reb Nathan excelled as he glorified *Shabes* right before nightfall when in the *shul* it was almost dark. Only one lamp burnt at the table. Then Reb Nathan went to the cantor's desk and, in a tenderly sad, and melancholy plaint, canted the penetrating melody of the *Ashrei Temimei Derech* [Psalm 1]. Several Jews pushed towards the lamp in order to read from small Books of Psalms, but the majority of the congregation repeated after Reb Nathan, verse by verse, by heart. With each verse, his ardor rose, so that one clearly felt the quiet lament from the walls of the *shul*. Even the devilish little youngsters, coming back

[Page 315]

from the third meal, were awed by Reb Nathan's *Shabes* night Psalms reading and did not move from the synagogue until after evening prayers.

Reb Nathan was a pauper; only his stature was affluent. His expenses soon exhausted his small salary as sexton, so he took small jobs such as helping a *shatkhn* (marriage broker) complete a *shidekh* (a proposed match), or helping a broker sell a house. He made his name as an expert in the house business, mainly as a great trustee to whom one could entrust great wealth on his word. Therefore a lot of people signed over their houses in his name. An old father who was close to dying was afraid that the children would fight over the inheritance, signed over his house to Reb Nathan, and he was able to die in peace because Reb Nathan would see to it that everything was satisfactory. A son ran away from military conscription and the father was afraid that the government would put a large sum of money as a fine, against his house. He signed his house over to Reb Nathan.

With his first wife of many years, Reb Nathan had no children. His love of children remained strong, however, during all this time. Later, his first wife died and he had a child with his second wife. The children also loved him a lot, and he spent time with them talking about their studies in *heder* and helping them with their studies.

Reb Nathan would give orphans in marriage and helped a lot of poor people. The poor always knew that if worse came to worse they could go to the *Karni'im shul* – "Reb Nathan, the sexton, would find a way and would not let a Jew leave with empty hands." Everyone in Slutsk knew that Reb Nathan was always ready to help. It mattered not what the issue. He would help write a letter for a widow to her relatives in America. He would assist a poor couple in making a nice *bris* [circumcision ceremony]. He would speak a little with a Jew, an embittered soul, who was anxious to talk about what was bothering him. Sometimes he was also able to play the idiot as if he could not count to two.

In 1923, when the Soviet municipal government had already closed all the *hederim* and forbidden teaching Jewish children Torah, a Jew hung a notice proclaiming in all the synagogues that Jews should give their lives to teach their children. The *yevsekes* [police] knew who it was and brought a sexton to court for permitting such a "crime." *Erev Tishebov* [9 Av – destruction of the Temple] 5683-1923, a trial began that shocked the religious elements of the city. When the Procurer screamed, why had they allowed such a call to be hung in the synagogue, Reb Nathan made like a *golem* [dummy] and said that he did not know what was written there. "Who cares that a notes hangs in the synagogue?"

His speech had excited even more the expectations of the *yevsekes* because they well knew that he was not as unworldly as he made out. The procurer became agitated: "Do expect us to believe you are so naïve when you work at brokering houses?"

But Reb Nathan looked them right in the eye and stroked his beard as if they did not mean him.

After that as all the synagogues were closed, Reb Nathan worked to keep a minion and some remnant of a meaningful Jewish life. Every day the situation became more difficult. The eyes of the *yevsekes* penetrated all the hiding places and sought to root out every remembrance of Jews and Jewishness.

Reb Nathan was murdered together with all the Jews from Slutsk. May the Lord avenge his blood and may his soul be bound up in the bond of eternal life.

Reb Isserke's Kloyz and its Later Sexton, Reb Israel Feller

Reb Isserke's *shul* was the only one in Slutsk that was named for a person. The name itself embodied a piece of Slutsk's history that went back hundreds of years.

The Isserlin, [Isserson], family, had supplied a lot of sages and learned men and were descended from the *Gaon* [sage] Reb Moshe Isserlesh who was famous as "the RM'A" (1520-1579). Members of the family had lived in Slutsk for many generations. They were buried only in prominent places in the Slutsk cemetery (see "Daas KA'doyshim" *The knowledge of holy people,* Section "Yisroyn Daas" which translated means *the benefit of knowledge,* page 25).

Reb Abraham, Reb Isserke's Isserlin, lived in Slutsk at the beginning of the 19th century. Because of his great lineage, the fact that he was a great Torah scholar and very well to do, his wife Rivka built a synagogue that was called "Rivka Reb Isserke's *Kloyz.*" Their son Yonah enhanced it. Reb Yonah Isserlin married Deborah, the daughter of the very respectable Reb Yoel Sirkin, and all his businesses went well. His wealth was estimated at approximately six hundred thousand rubles, a colossal sum in those years in Slutsk.

To the Slutskers, Reb Yonah was a great philanthropist. He provided for everyone who requested *challah* and meat for *Shabes*. One of Reb Yonah's daughters was the bride of the young Gaon Reb Tzvi Hirsh Ornstein who later became the Rabbi in Brisk and Lemberg. Old Slutskers say that the match had great repercussions and created ripples in the Jewish world because the groom due to his greatness in Torah, came from the greatest *gaonim* and lineage from Lemberg, and along came a wealthy man from Lithuania who caught such a rare son-in-law.

[Page 316]

Due to the great match, Reb Yonah even consented to allowing the wedding to take place, not as a normal Jewish wedding would in the bride's hometown, but in the groom's city. Reb Yonah had even advised his rabbi, the old *Gaon* Reb Yosele Peimer, that he would have to travel to the wedding as far as Lemberg.

Reb Yosele's name was famous in the entire Jewish world and the *gaonim* from Lemberg impatiently waited to welcome him and to hear something great from his mouth.

Reb Yosele came to the wedding but only to perform the marriage under the *chuppah* (marriage canopy) and not one more word did he say. The other rabbis, as usual, wanted to study near Reb Yosele and sought all means to approach him and engage him in talking about the Torah. Some even began to doubt his greatness: "No matter what, in Lithuania people can spread the word around."

They decided to arrange a small bit of fruit on a plate and put it near Reb Yosele so he would be maneuvered to eat something and have to say a blessing first.

Reb Yosele "stopped the examination." He looked over the rabbis. "As you are aware, a Litvak knows about the small letter, yes. Around here he is silent!"

Endlessly they came to stand with him and question the reason for his silence. Reb Yosele answered cold-bloodedly that he never said anything about Torah, not even what he heard from his rabbi, Reb Chaim Volozhiner.

But the match did not succeed. The difference between the two worlds was too great for this couple, and about one year later they divorced and Reb Yonah's daughter came home to Slutsk.

A short time later she married Shmuel Simchovitz from Minsk. He was "a jewel," a "rarity," a Jew with all the necessary qualities: a Torah scholar of high standards with a great brain and a big Jewish heart.

Reb Shmuel Simchovitz was known as a wise man and a worker for social justice, beyond the area of Slutsk and even the Province of Minsk. The Russian Tsar had set up the "Ravinski Commission" in which the greatest rabbinical leaders such as Reb Yitzhak Elhanan Spektor and Reb Yoshe-Ber Soloveitchik took part. The idea was to discuss with them from time to time Jewish questions. Reb Shmuel Simhonwitz was also a member of the council.

Rabbi, Gaon Reb Yosele Peimer

Error! Bookmark not defined.

A man of great wealth, Reb Yonah Isserlin liked religious book and students of Judaism. He created a vast library made up of a very large collection of Jewish religious books. He brought ten students of Judaism to his mother's *Kloyz* who were supported by him and they studied Torah without any worries. They were referred to then as "asore batlonim" ["Ten Idlers"]. (See Tractate Megilla 5a: "What can be called a big city? Any one in which there are ten idlers.").

Old Slutsk jokers told about one episode that reflected the poverty and the paupers' conception of those years. Reb Yonah had *yahrzeit* [anniversary of the death of a close relative] for his father and he came to his *minion* and said: "I beg of you, tomorrow night sit all night and study with devotion in memory of my father, of blessed memory. For your trouble I will also reward in the morning with a meal according to each one's desire."

The society fulfilled his desire and studied the entire night. In the morning when he asked them what they desired for the feast they answered that they had already deliberated and unanimously chosen beet leaves with milk and buckwheat porridge cooked with butter.

[Page 317]

In 1868 the synagogue burned down together with a large part of the city Slutsk and also, for the most part, Reb Yonah's religious books were destroyed (Z. Halbnitz, from a periodical, The Lebanon, Year 5, Number 27).

Reb Yonah Isserlin rebuilt the *shul* and put his *minion* back to studying. From then on it became known as a family thing, "Reb Isserke's *Kloyz* or *Shul* " where men always studied. Years later the shul was also the home of Reb Nechemia's *Meykhina* Yeshiva until it united with Reb Berl and Reb Yoshe Tritzaner and together they formed the " *Meykhina* " and remained until the beginning of the 1920s.

The last sexton of Reb Isserke's Shul was Reb Israel Feller. Feller was born in Orla and studied with Reb Boruch Ber in Slobodka. During the First World War he came to Slutsk with his parents as war refugees and remained there.

Reb Israel married one of Rabbi Yitzhak Yakov Sheynboim's daughters, who was called in Slutsk the " *Harazaver* messenger."

He was a Jew, a firebrand and when he gave a sermon it was like a volcano. Jokingly, he was called "the tool from hell."

After his marriage, Reb Israel Feller made an attempt at business but failed and he became a poultry *shochet* [kosher ritual slaughterer]. Meanwhile he taught *Mishnah* to men in the *Karni'im shul* and also said a page of *Gemore* in Reb Isserke's *Shul* where his father-in-law prayed.

In 1924 the municipal government took the main part of Reb Isserke's Shul and left only the women's section open for prayer. Then Reb Israel took over as sexton more in the way of a good deed than for the income. So this synagogue was almost the only one still open through all the years until the great doom. Both his occupations as *shochet* and sexton truly were more acts of self-sacrifice than anything else.

During the last years of the 1920s with the government's dreadful repression, people sat in prison until they would give outlandish confessions. This is what people called the "Dollars Inquisition." Reb Israel Feller was put in prison: The *Cheka* agents tortured him thinking he would be the one to tell them whom one can "squeeze" and "extort" dollars.

But Reb Israel outlasted all the suffering and never betrayed anyone. Furthermore, even sitting in prison together with many others, he comported himself so well that his arrest earned him respect from everyone in prison with him. He impressed even the heartless *Cheka* agents. During his entire life, everyone was convinced that his word could be trusted and they believed him. On his word alone were those arrested set free and the preparations for further arrests were stopped.

As mentioned he was sexton until the last destruction and also worked as poultry slaughterer together with Rabbi Reb Simcha Rishin (son-in-law of Reb Chaim Ber, a well-known respectable man in Slutsk who was also the trustee of the *Karni'im-Shul*).

Those two were the last ritual slaughterers in Slutsk. After Rabbi Reb Yehezkel Abramski ran away from Slutsk to a foreign country, Rabbi Reb Yitzhak Hochmark, who married Yihumaner Rebetzin [a rabbi's wife] Yerusalimski, daughter of the RIDBaZ and mother-in-law of Rabbi Abramski, stayed only for one year afterwards.

The last schochet and sexton in Slutsk, Reb Israel Feller with his family (murdered in the ghetto)

These were the last of the Mohicans in the long, glorious period of religious institutions in Slutsk.

At the end of the list permit me to write several personal memories from one born in Starobin, for whom Slutsk was the first gate into the large outside world.

When Starobin burnt, we decided to stay in a village. Destiny took us to Michavitz that was about sixteen Russian *versts* from Starobin and four *versts* from Pohost. In this village

[Page 318]

a few Jewish families lived. An *eruv* had to be put up in the village of Seltz so that on *Shabes* people could go to pray in the Pohost *besmedresh* [synagogue, study house and meeting hall]. [On Shabes according to the law, people must not go outside town on *Shabes* more like a "Sabbath limit" that was almost two versts long unless there was an *eruv*].

The grandfather of Rabbi Waxman,
Berl Chashes (Rivin)

This went on in the beautiful early morning of summer and also in the snow and cold of the White Russian winter. Also for the Days of Awe (High Holidays) we would travel there and stay in Pohost. The first time I went to the *besmedresh,* adorned with large lamps, the rabbi taught *Chumash* on *Shabes* before praying and Reb Hirshl Aydli's hearty additional services on the Days of Awe left a deep impression on me. But going daily to Pohost to attend *heder* was impossible. Therefore, my grandfather had to teach me the first couple of years (my father was already in America).

My grandfather, Berl Choshes, *olev hasholem* [peace be with him], was a typical product of his time. Broken from squalor and a life of troubles, still he remained confident and naturally proud. Despite his angry demeanor, his smart eyes were mild and warm, a fact I took advantage of at every opportunity. His learning marked him as what one would call "a *mishnayes* Jew." He knew Psalms by heart, the entire *Chumash* with *Rashi, Tanakh* until *Yesheya* and the entire *Mishnah* (with the additional holidays) almost by heart, but no Gemore. He also knew a few other "small things" like *Ein Yankev* [16th century book with stories from the Talmud], *Midrash* and a little *Zohar* [Kabbalist "Book of Splendor"], in which he dabbled every Shabes at daybreak.

He taught me until I was six or seven. Then there was a question of where to study, in Starobin or Slutsk. Slutsk was chosen because his eldest daughter lived there and there would not be any problem about lodgings for me.

In Slutsk Reb Berl, the Yeshiva Dean, listened to me and said to *Zeyde*: "A good boy, only a drop too young. He should still go to Lipa Shiniovker for a year."

So I was left to stay with my aunt, Rashe the butcheress, who lived in the meat market brick building and I studied at Reb Lipe's. He was already knowledgeable in *Gemore* and the entire *Tanakh*. One studied the entire day and each summer I studied preparing *Tanakh* with my grandfather with whom simple meant "to break one's teeth." This did not stop me from running from *heder* into the Butchers' synagogue to listen to Reb Liate the sexton say "*Ein Yankev*" every day between afternoon and evening prayers and *Shabes* afternoon the sermon of Reb Leibe Neymark in the Tailors' *shul*.

Afterwards, all we youngsters would run around on the field at the new yeshiva. Usually people would encounter the rabbi's brother-in-law, Reb Sheptil Kremer, the yeshiva *mashgiach* [supervisor of dietary laws in institutional kitchen], going for a walk with his daughter (now Rabbi Feygl Ruderman in Baltimore).

When Starobin was rebuilt, our family moved back home. For several years I studied in Starobin and after that studied further in Slutsk. During the war, many people from Poland ran to Galicia. But the calm did not last, and it was the beginning of the end. The yeshiva building was requisitioned. The yeshiva moved back to the Tailors' *shul*. When the Reds arrived, Slutsk began to burn out, a long agony. Over twenty years, bit by bit, Slutsk died. It was a sad last breath…

[Page 319]

Torah and Wisdom

My Youth in Slutsk

by Yakov Patt – New York

Translated from Yiddish by Judie Ostroff Goldstein

The city of Slutsk stands before my eyes exactly as I saw it in my young years when I studied in the Slutsk *Musar* [moral] -Yeshiva, where the great *Gaon* Reb Jakov-David was the yeshiva dean. Now I do not have any material, no notes at hand and I will limit myself to a couple of crumbs dug up from my memory. I am grateful to the editors of "*Sefer* Slutsk" who moved me to search the long ago past.

How I traveled to Slutsk

Reb Jakov David Slutsker, who founded a *Musar –* Yeshiva in Slutsk depended on how much I remembered from the yeshiva dean from the Slobodker *Musar –* Yeshiva. He had to send students to the Slutsker Yeshiva in order to help them with it and to establish the yeshiva.

Although I was only young then, I had already studied one year in the Slobodker Yeshiva and was even famous – it is really not nice to talk about it now – as the "Bialystoker genius." Therefore when the request came from the Slutsker rabbi, the *mashgiach* Reb Note Hirsch, who was the big boss in the yeshiva, called me and he told me a secret. He was thinking of sending a group of his best students in the yeshiva, but he had also thought of sending with them a couple of young boys who he believed would help establish the yeshiva there. He wanted me to be one of them.

His speech greatly inspired me, and I was the youngest of the Slobodker group to be sent to Slutsk.

A journey of a day and a night took us as far as Baranovici. We sat there on the train to Lyakhovichi where we arrived early in the morning. It was late autumn. The fields were sunk in mud. A large stagecoach pulled by two horses, not heroes, took us from Lyakhovichi to Slutsk.

Yakov Patt

The journey lasted about ten to twelve hours, if not more – a long trip. The passengers who filled the stagecoach were for the most part Jews. It was a cold night so people were wrapped in fur coats with lambskin hats on their heads. In our area these hats were called "*kutshmes*." The highway was narrow and wound between fields and forests throughout the entire gloomy road. We also went through villages. The dress of the peasants was White Russian – colorful scarves on the wives' heads and the men wore large coats of coarse cloth. All of them went around in bast shoes, tied around and laced up the foot.

I see the road and the stagecoach before my eyes. Jewish merchants, storekeepers, are traveling. They talk about leather and about oats and among them, a young boy traveling to study Torah in far-away Slutsk. I was at the time around Bar-Mitzvah age. From traveling and shaking so long one becomes bored. One wants some fresh air. The driver knew this. From time to time

[Page 320]

he stops the horses. They will drink and also must be given oats. Meanwhile he let his passengers out on the highway to freshen up a little, to breathe. Everyone takes a rest and then, back on the stagecoach and we travel further until we have, thank G-d, arrived in Slutsk.

Der Ridvaz — Rabbi Reb Jakov David
Willowvski

In Slutsk, as in all the *Musar* – Yeshivas, the students did not have any "days" without eating. It was against the doctrine of the *Musarniks*. They stuck me in a room with another young boy at Raubke, the grain merchant's son. My roommate was a younger boy called Layzerke Telzer. His parents were poor and they would send him a couple of rubles a month for his rent and for *Krupnik* [barley soup] with potatoes. In Slutsk this was called "fish-potatoes."

I was listened to by the yeshiva dean and immediately accepted. My studies began at the yeshiva.

I cannot forget this. When I move my eyes and look in the distance, I see the large *Musar* – Yeshiva in Slutsk. There were two or three hundred students. All the benches were used; each student was at his bookstand, from the Eastern wall to the anteroom of the synagogue and the water-barrel, each one over a *Gemore*. Each one was studying out loud, and each one was studying something different, but the voices poured together. One did not see the time go, from the early hours of the morning to noon, from noon to evening and it is already soon time for evening prayers. One grabbed a bite to eat in between-a piece of bread with yogurt or with a glass of water. Then one rocked some more, sang and with others at the table, studied from the *tannaim* [teachers and scholars who contributed to the Mishnah, etc.], the *amoraim* [Rabbinic Jewish teachers -3rd and 4th centuries - produced the Gemore for the Talmuds]. Some were studying *Tosefos* [Talmud commentaries-12th and 14th century], some *Rashi* [Torah scholar unequaled in commentaries]. Each one sang a different melody, yelled his *Gemore* differently, asked his questions out loud, found the answers alone and screamed them out.

The yeshiva dean arrives and runs through the rows of students, between the benches, stops at a bookstand, looks at what the boy is studying. He gives a report with a question, waits for an answer. If the answer is good, a pinch of the cheek, a slap on the shoulder, and he runs further. The Torah, *gemore*, *pilpul* [subtle argumentation] – the genius, the Slutsker Rabbi, chased among the benches of the yeshiva students.

Once a week Reb Jakov David gave a lesson for the yeshiva students. He stood at his bookstand or on the *bima* [pulpit]. The yeshiva students stood around and listened and swallowed the Torah that came out of his mouth. A difficult Torah, a difficult Talmud debate, but it all becomes clear, it becomes easier, understandable. At the end he turns to the students, saying: "And now ask questions, whoever has a question, should ask." The questions fly from all sides, one after the other and the yeshiva dean grabs them all together. Then as if they are in a sack, he takes them back out one at a time, question after question, and answer after answer, and the heart feels better, one becomes smarter and the world seems nicer...

It was a wonderful time. So it appears now from afar, beyond the mass of years. A *mishmar* [all night study session] in the Slutsker Musar-Yeshiva. It is night; all the yeshiva students are already asleep in their quarters. Only a part-ten assiduous yeshiva students – studies at night a *mishmar*. All around the yeshiva it is quiet and dark. Only in the yeshiva, over some of the bookstands, burns a light and by this light a *Gemore* and over the *Gemore* a student.

And so one rocked, one studied and one sang. It was difficult to understand, one was quiet, absorbed in thought, and then one came up with answer and banged the table in joy and one rocked some more...

And I hear my own voice –

[Page 321]

intertwining the language of the *Gemore* with Yiddish, combining together the melody with a soulful yell. And not only were the students bewitched, but it often happened that a Slutsker boss would be in the yeshiva. He was drawn there because he wanted to see how the young boys studied in his yeshiva. The boss would stand still between the benches, looking at the religious boys, at the faces of the students. He stroked a head, a shoulder, smiled, was pleased, pulled out of a large pocket an apple, a pear and gave it as a gift and said, with his Slutsker pronunciation: "Child, refresh yourself, take a little."

There are no more Slutsk bosses. No more deep pockets with half-frozen apples. No more voice saying: "Child refresh yourself..."

Still I remember the resonance, the echo. Once there was and is no more.

As I already said, I lived with the grain merchant Raubke. There it was another world, other images, another life. Around Raubke's grain barns stood large, long, wide stalls. The peasants from the White Russian villages would drive in there when they brought sacks of grain to sell to Raubke. The peasants with sacks stood at the scales. The grain was weighed, measured, calculated. The men bargained, fought and slapped each on the back as if all of White Russia wanted to come here. They had no time to wait; they clapped their hands around a monopole bottle to test it. They said "*l'chaim*." The gentiles drank and – it hurt my eyes – they ate fatty pieces of pork. Then it seemed that the entire world would be impure from the peasants' pork.

The peasants would leave their wagons in Raubke's courtyard and come into the large rooms of Raubke's house. They sat on the floor and on chairs. Large samovars of tea were there and they ate and drank. Half-undressed, they were smeared with a salve, because every second one of them was sick. Raubke's large "hall" had turned into a hospital.

They hit the ornament of the samovar; the village gentiles drank glass after glass of tea, wiping away sweat with a handkerchief, which ran down their faces. And already half-drunk, they sang and yelled, and it became noisy and joyous in the rooms of Raubke, the grain merchant.

By haggling with the yeshiva dean, I obtained residence with the Jewish landowner, Turov, whose large estate was in back of the city. He had large orchards and fields. In his old age, sitting in his large house with the fruit trees, he did a good deed – he allowed his rooms to be used by a couple of yeshiva students and did not charge them rent. It was my luck to live in Turov's house. The garden and the trees full of fruit, the river in the middle of the orchard – all this I see in my memory. The respected Turov with his gray beard with two points, one on each side – an emperor's beard – sat on his chair, with a cushion at his back, and asked his lodger, the yeshiva student, if he would teach him a little Torah.

"Whether I understand or not," he would say, "In any case it is a great pleasure to hear Torah."

The Zionist "Tchaina"

From time to time at the threshold of the yeshiva would come two kinds of "missionaries," one from Socialism and one from Zionism. They would keep an eye on one of the yeshiva students, make his acquaintance, engage him in conversation and win his soul. Over the years I saw these people not only on the doorstep of the Slutsk yeshiva, but also at other yeshivas – Slobodka, Telz, Volozhin. These were good meeting places to agitate for the two Jewish movements, Socialism and Zionism.

From time to time, from the doorstep of the yeshiva, the road led to the Zionist "Tchaina." I do not remember the name of the street in Slutsk (Hafashker Street, maybe) where the Zionist "Tchaina" was located. But I see it in detail before my eyes, a wooden house. One could not go into the "Tchaina" from the street but from an inside hallway. The first time I went to the "Tchaina" it was as if I had stepped into another world. It seemed to me that it was very bright. Flashlights were on. The rooms-a large one and a couple of smaller one-were full of people, mostly young men and women, and for a yeshiva student at that time, it was a bizarre thing, women and men together. And they talked and yelled and laughed and had fun – how different this was from the Musar-yeshiva!

In the evenings the yeshiva became quiet and gloomy. The *Musar* melody, the piece "*Khoves-halvoves*" [The Duties of the Hearts] that we sang and the large, wide, long room, only deepened the sorrow. But here in "Tchaina" there was no *musar*, no sadness. One did not rock at a bookstand. One yelled, had fun. One laughed and sang Hebrew songs. I heard it the first time. I heard a song, immediately picked it up, hummed it and sang the tune with them,

[Page 322]

and the words brought me into the Zionist world.

I also did not resist Socialist agitation. Someone pointed out the student, the Socialist agitator. I asked that he come to see me and he did. He even came to see me at home. He accompanied me to and from the yeshiva and told me a lot of wonderful things: People were going to make over the world. People were going to overthrow the Tsar and strike down the "Cherto." Jews would have rights and there would not be any pogroms. There would not be any poor and rich, everybody would be equal.

The echoes of the names from that time swim around me, what the student, the Socialist had told me, and one name was above them all: Sofia Ferovskaya. It grew to a fantastic, holy status by men being sent to the gallows.

And since then I heard more. I heard the repercussions from the cities, Bobruisk and Minsk. In Bobruisk, a large Jewish library was made. A yeshiva student by the name of Kirschner built it. The number of books sounded fantastic, three thousand, four thousand, five thousand books! And I would have to read all of them. It took us an entire winter, an entire summer to learn one *Gemore*. And imagine thousands of books in the new library in Brobruisk!

From Minsk there was also fantastic news. There were already strikes by the workers. There, people were already demonstrating in the streets. Russian revolutionaries were coming to meet with them-and the entire world will burn!

I left my yeshiva bench and went to Minsk.

I write these words now and feel once again the wonderful spirit of that time. It was a time when ideologies struggled in the minds and hearts of the yeshiva students in Slutsk, together with everyone throughout Russia.

From the Zionist "Tchaina" they were drawn to another road-to the banks of the Slutsk River. There one bathed, swam in the river, played in boats. Entire groups would be there. I learned to swim and float. I swam until late in the evening, exhilarated and encouraged. Yes, it was good, it was worthwhile living in the world!

There was no wealth, no comfort, no prosperity. It was either the bookstands in the yeshiva, or the tables in "Tchaina," or a walk through the streets, or swimming in the Slutsk River. Youthful days in Slutsk-whoever had them has also lost them!

As luck would have it, Russia's revolution wrenched me from the yeshiva. I left the Slutsk Yeshiva and returned home to Bialystok, my hometown. No more *Gemore*, no more Torah, no more *Musar* and *Musar* melodies. "One must work for the revolution. One must overturn the world. One must make a new Jewish life."

I remember an interesting detail from those years. I was already in Bialystok. The old sexton from "*grinem*" *besmedresh* came to me and said that I should come to the *besmedresh* as I was needed. "For what"? I asked. He did not answer. It was an order: "Ask no questions and come."

I went. I did not know who had sent for me. When I arrived I was taken to a table with holy books on it. I saw Reb Yakov David Slutsker. How did he get to Bialystok? What was he doing here? What does he want with me? The questions were churning in my mind. I had thought that the *Gaon* Reb Yakov David was now a long way from here, but there he was, staying a couple of days in Bialystok.

I went to the *Gaon* and I acknowledged him. My heart was pounding. Every limb was trembling.

"*Shalom Aleichem*, Rabbi," I said.

He did not answer me immediately, nor stretch out his hand right away, only looked at me, and I still see the sorrow in his eyes. He did not ask me what I was doing, if I was studying or not. He only looked at me for a long time, shook his head and in the end said a couple of words.

"Jankel, you still have time to repent."

He did have to say what repentance he meant. I had understood. When men sit in the "*grinem*" *besmedresh* at the long table with religious books and Reb Yakov David Slutsker was speaking to you, and he calls to you to repent, you know what kind of repentance he means.

I left the table and did not repent, in any case not the kind of repentance that the *Gaon* Reb Yakov David wanted.

Now when I write these words, I still hear the echo of Reb Yakov David's words:

"You still have time to repent."

[Page 323]

My Memory of Slutsk

by H. Lang – Los Angeles

Translated by Tamara Selden z"l with missing gaps filled in by Jerrold Landau

My First Meeting

From the shtetl of Skud in Lithuania by the border of Kurland and eastern Germany, I, a young boy, on a certain day at the very beginning of the year 1900, took a distant journey to the city of Slutsk in Jewish White Russia. My trip was made in high spirits for a certain reason. First, in comparison to my birth village of Skud, Slutsk was considered to be a large city. Second, I would study in a Yeshiva side by side with older boys from various cities and neighboring areas and wanted to know what these larger places were like. Most important I would meet the great Rabbinic Peimer family, which had made Slutsk shine for many generations, and with whom my father had direct family ties. He used to tell me stories about them; nice stories which made me curious and anxious to meet them.

After a long trip by train to Baranavichi, and then by coach, I saw for the first time on a foggy Autumn night, which hung like a white mantle of thin feathers, the city of Slutsk. The flickering lights from street lamps and fireplaces in houses created an outstanding panorama. It impressed my childish soul as a magical moment. It was symbolic of Slutsker of old ways and learning. This image has remained in my heart until this very day.

On the first day, with my father's letter in hand, I went to see the Peimer family. I wanted to see with my own eyes the learning passion which made them world renowned. Waiting was my first disappointment in Slutsk. It was not possible for them to see me then. I walked around and noticed an impoverished house, which made me see the tragedy of that which always lays between the generation ascending and the generation descending.

The prominence that shone on Slutsk at that time was derived from the presence of the Gaon Rabbi Yaakov Willowsky, or as he was known by the shortened name Ridba'z.

On my first Slutsker day, a strong urge to see all the houses of study overcame me and I went to the Court school. There I saw the imposing figure of Ridba'z, dressed in a holiday *kaputa*, trimmed with purple feathers and golden threads. On his head he wore a fur hat. He held a large open book in his hands and his eyes were engrossed in its words. He stood by a legendary stone. I looked at him with great curiosity, and he sensed that someone was nearby. He closed his book and called to me.

H. Lang

He wanted to know who I was; not much more than a young boy. When he heard I was coming to Slutsk to study in the Yeshiva, so far from Skud, then he spoke to me as a grownup. His words have always remained with me. His serious demeanor lightened and he spoke to me with ease. He spoke from the heart to a strange boy. The words seemed like a lamentation. He had not been in Slutsk for two years. He had traveled to America and now there was nothing for him to do in Slutsk. He would soon return to America.

He had been in America twice: The first time to receive help with publishing his book on the commentaries of the Jerusalem Talmud; the second time with the goal to remain in the new world. The outcome was quite different and he was torn between the two places.

For ten years he had been the rabbi in Slutsk and the name the Slutsker rabbi gave him a great reputation. An entire folklore grew about him but he became the adversary of the Peimer family of that city.

[Page 324]

Mr. Gaon Rabbi Isser Zalman Meltzer

Certainly a philosophic difference existed on the face of it, but there was also a personal bitterness: the old conflict between the House of Shahmy and the House of Hillel.

The Ridba'z favored the House of Shammai. It was compatible with his character: strict, unbending, difficult, and aggressive.

The House of Peimer's custom was to follow Hillel: light, soft, interpretive, not punishing or angry, with good conversation and stories.

As for a fighter in a war situation, the whole world was a battlefield. And so it was with him. The fate of the Slutskers was discussed in far away America with the Ridba'z. A conference of aristocratic, important scholars assembled in Philadelphia to hear him speak, with the hope that he would bring order to the Jewish home in the New World.

However, strong opponents were against him. The same conflicts that existed in Slutsk had traveled to America. Soon he found a position in Chicago. His philosophy of learning was also rejected there and he went from place to place. He wanted to establish something similar to what he had had in Lithuania and Slutsk. Finally he decided to end his travail and go to Israel. There he would continue writing his commentaries on the Talmud Yerushalmi.

Destiny brought me to him once more in an unexpected meeting in America.

It was the year 1905, on East Broadway in New York City. Each day thousands of Jewish children from Russia arrived, many from Yeshivas in Lithuania. It reminded me of my Slutsker Yeshiva generation, and as if in a magical story, I suddenly saw the Ridba'z. He was dressed in the same holiday clothing, a satin *kaputa* trimmed with gold and feathers. He wore a fur hat and had an open book in his hand. He was standing near Seward Park, as he had stood near the stone in Slutsk. I felt as if I were in a dream. I approached him, reminded him of Slutsk, and he remembered me. Ridba'z spoke with cutting words. In America he was a leftover. He was an exile in the New World. He claimed that soon he would gather the Slutsker fighters and take leave with new energy.

The Yeshiva Head

The Yeshiva was housed in Ostrove, between gardens and meadows. It was a world of its own for young travelers from Lithuania, White Russia, and also from towns in Poland, as far as the border of the Ukraine. The head of the Yeshiva was Rabbi Isser Zalman Meltzer, who the Ridba'z himself brought from Slobodka to Slutsk, and was fated to become the teacher of an entire generation of children. They then were dispersed over all the seas in many directions.

Warmed by the rare inner charm of Rabbi Isser Zalman Meltzer's personality, the unique character of the Slutsker Yeshiva gleamed. Students even came from cities which had their own larger and sometimes more historic Yeshivas, and these usually went by the name of the town. In Slutsk there were also many different Yeshivas, but without a doubt the Yeshiva of Rabbi Meltzer was the most outstanding in the city.

Rabbi Meltzer possessed three blessed attributes:

First, love, plain love of the entire generation of young Jews, as much as the love of his own children; love with concern that nothing bad should happen to them; love with a Talmudic tension, from which they will receive great pleasure. Rabbi Meltzer often said: when you learn you are surrounded by the *Shechinah* [Editor's note: defined as the glory or radiance of God or God's presence] and the melody of learning. Then the Jewish heart sings. Can there be greater joy?

[Page 325]

Second, a rare belief in the psychological strength of the student of the *Gemara*. This student can be trusted. He will not desert the holy tradition of his people. He will protect it with his life. It is not necessary to stand over him with an iron discipline, and constantly threaten him with punishment. He must be encouraged to look into each book and he alone will select what is significant, although he may be suspected of not choosing properly. Rabbi Meltzer was the greatest defender of this approach. He was an outstanding figure for the entire young generation and hopeful that they would learn what was morally relevant.

Third, his modesty, his holy indefinability, his pattern for teachers that they not be boastful. He believed that those who are able to and those who are willing to teach are equals.

These characteristics of Rabbi Isser Zalman Meltzer became the hallmark of the Yeshiva in evolutionary development, which did not follow the path of the other Yeshivas.

In the Yeshiva there were three levels of study; those students with rabbinical training who are ready to become rabbis; those deep into Talmudic law and custom, who already have a specific direction; and those who study Gemara. Each studied by himself, and each is engrossed in his own choice and has his own melody. Complete dedication of the heart is required. Their inner being bursts and sings and the voices join together as a choir of philosophic dialogue. In that way the students intertwine their spirituality. It is a dramatic experience.

The Yeshiva is not a static place. The students mingle around the lectern on the platform. One passes on to the other what he has learned. They move about in friendship and speak and learn; the older with the younger. Questions and answers fly back and forth, and the teacher must deal with many naive questions of the new students who want to draw from his wealth of knowledge. It is a loving spiritual dialogue.

All generations are united by Rabbi Meltzer. Then there are general battles with those who challenge him. Before he comes to a point in his thinking, they question him and he immediately answers. They ask again and then the battle is between the questioners. They go back and forth to see who is more humorous, foolish, ironic, clever with satire and who sings out his questions. Rabbi Meltzer battles with everyone and calms those who question with great heat. They are very dear to him.

Slutsk followed the tradition of Volozhin, so that the voice of Torah will never leave the Yeshiva, and learning will continue for twenty four hours; day and night, it should be filled with learning. Slutsk did not use this system immediately. First it began with one session on Thursday night each week. Next three days and nights, summer and winter. Those who did not study properly did not have a spiritual enlightenment. Those who did were alone in the Yeshiva. Each sat at their Gemara and there was only enough light to allow reading. Each sang his own melody in the dim light, full of feeling, as if the Shechinah herself was crying somewhere in the shadows. Some students became silent as they listened to the various melodies of their fellow students.

It is summer. The night is ending and the sky grows lighter. The starlight is slowly extinguished. Soon it will be daytime. The windows are open and a cool breeze wafts through the room. It feels as if the grasses are secretly seeding. Each blade has had a night of rest and soon the sun will shine and the grass will grow in return. In the heart of each student there is no smile. Loneliness gnaws at him. Sadness pervades him. His melody must always bring a tear from the *Shechinah*.

Winter is the image which follows such sober thought. In the long winter nights the soul is a glowing ember and recollection. The Yeshiva, with a light coming through the window stands in heavy snow. The snow continues to pile up continuously.

[Page 326]

The wind banged on the windows. It was barely warm in the Yeshiva. The three students gathered close to the oven. Their melody soared higher and deafened the sounds of the nighttime winds. The air drafts from the frosty snow wrapped itself in a white friendship. There was a noise somewhere in the nighttime sky. The students clung to the Gemara in awe and outcry, and their melody begged to be heard. It was Jewish learning in full majesty.

The majesty had a crown which belonged to Jewish learning.

We Learn Ethics

An absolute must for every Slutsker at the Yeshiva is to steep himself in ethics. It did not always happen. Whoever felt the subject was irrelevant would sit silently during the lesson with another book. The class was rarely overfilled. Sometimes Rabbi Isser Zalman Meltzer would teach the lesson. He would put on his prayer shawl and a spiritual mood would pervade the room. One sensed that there would be excitement, exceptional learning, and special melody in use which was different than the usual teachers. He taught that which was required in learning: to make the point over and over and over again until it became a fire in the blood.

Others remembered the teaching of ethics in the dusk of the Sabbath evening when powerful poetic images were unfolded. Afterwards some would meet in Ostrove and take a Sabbath walk. They were nicely dressed but some did not wear their fringes. They did not have long sideburns. They were the young students and wore a variety of hats. This reflected changing times. The older people stared at them. They walked from Ostrove to the broader streets and from there to the home of Rabbi Meltzer. They went in pairs or groups of three and four in a line—a march of beauty to honor the Sabbath. The setting sun and the sky were different and so was the earth. The students went to Rabbi Meltzer's house with respect and reverence.

When he left to go to the House of Prayer, they followed him. They would hear his stories and poems and this stirred their emotions and created an inner excitement.

The melody of ethics began very softly, then rose higher and higher until it almost was a scream of pleasure of the heart of each one to the Father of mercy.

With their faces to the wall they often broke down in tears. Some had a tremor in their voice and some a lament. Each one had his own ethic in accordance with his own concerns and quandaries.

When it was dark, Rabbi Meltzer stood facing everyone and the students knew that he was going to give a special lesson in ethics. Each Sabbath he presented a different point from ethical philosophy accompanied by a poetic and visionary Torah portion. He told a story about a Cabalistic mystic or a founder of Ethics—life stories with wonderful examples in them to unite the Cabala and Ethics. Rabbi Meltzer paced the floor with spiritual elegance. The students sensed in themselves an elite soul and they prayed. Afterwards a new week of learning began during the day and in the quiet of the night

At that time a light of brotherhood (1902-1904) pervaded the Slutsker Yeshiva like a flaming soul. Such spirit rarely came into the lives of the students. It was called "Light of Shabbat" and concerned providing a Sabbath table for the commuting students, one that would be available for the entire semester and even the entire year.

The local students had to get grants and family support for meals so as not to stand at a different door each night like a beggar asking for food. They needed to have pride in themselves and not feel poor and hungry. Most of them came from poor homes where there was barely enough to eat. Their mothers and fathers made many sacrifices to feed their sons whose Yeshiva attendance was a source of great family pride.

[Page 327]

Sometimes they sent packages to the them with things they were able to afford; tea, a sack of sugar. A dear beloved sister helped a great deal, fulfilling the historic role of young Jewish daughters who assisted the students of the Torah.

Daughters were the first to leave their parents and go to England and America. From time to time, the student would receive a letter with some money from his weary traveling sister, often younger than he. His job was to study and be a joy to their mother and father. The entire money account for the Yeshiva student's life revolved around *kopecks* for housing, a day's food, etc. Usually four Yeshiva students were in one room, and the places were called stations. The owners themselves were poor mothers living in a bitter slum. They cooked for the students making a heavy Slutsker barley soup, or radishes with chicken fat. The rest of the week they often lived on bread and tea, except for the Sabbath. The Sabbath had to be different. It was the Queen, the bride, the entire beauty of Jewish life. On the Sabbath they must be at a table with a *challah*, wine, and a piece of meat. They would sing hymns together. A group known as the "Lights of Sabbath" found families in town to provide this dinner for the students. There had to be spirituality at the Sabbath table. The Yeshiva man was the representative of the Jewish world.

It was an exciting time for the entire city. At the Sabbath table of so many Slutsker homes, a few hundred Yeshiva students discussed the higher meaning of the Sabbath. There was a special atmosphere in Slutsk that gave the discussion a great historic character.

Slutsk also had a Russian gymnasja, which brought students from Minsk and other communities. Among them were children from well-to-do Jewish homes who wanted to go there to study certain subjects. Others never went to the gymnasja because they were poor Jews and could not pass the examinations. They did, however, remain in Slutsk and were taught by private tutors who helped them prepare for the examinations for four subjects, one of which was pharmacy. Slutsk was filled with students who either chose the Yeshiva or, if they could, went to the gymnasja.

A rumor began that anyone interested in the Yeshiva was a foolish person and that the spiritual life had no future. "The Yeshiva student has no ambition for modern civilization and world culture. He is an impractical person and clung to the old ways."

Others disagreed and felt that Yiddish studies would provide a good life for world Jewry.

Moments and People

Wonderful moments in the city and the Yeshiva remain in my memory with great clarity. They must be noted for all the Pinskers in our generation.

Once, right after the Kishinev pogrom, we said prayers for the murdered Jews. This was really a protest against the terrible darkness that befell Jewish life in Czarist Russia for many generations. It was known that on that day students from the gymnasja came, as well as from the Yeshiva. It was a rare scene. A city advocate stood near the Torah and talked about the pogrom, and stated that the entire world rang with it. One of the Yeshiva students recited the *Kaddish*. Another recited a famous poem written by H.N. Bialik called "City Massacre." The poem was printed in a small booklet which was distributed throughout Slutsk. During the reading a woeful cry broke out. We were so struck by this poem, frozen to the spot. Our eyes burned and teeth chattered.

Another moment—later that summer. Again an unforgettable scene.

Dr. Theodore Herzl came to Russia to talk about Zionism. When he was in Vilna at that historic time a rumor reached us that he had been shot. When this news arrived all the Jews assembled in the town at the Post Office on the broad street. People often went there to hear world news each day. It was said that at the Post Office one learned everything. Jews ran there in the middle of the day to hear about Dr. Herzl. They left their stores, workers left their jobs and students ceased studying.

[Page 328]

And a third memory: Stirring Peoplehood

A plea for help came to Slutsk; there was a great fire in the nearby city of Bobruisk. Entire streets were destroyed. The city of Slutsk immediately went to their aid. Bread, clothing and bedding were gathered. The Yeshiva students covered the town collecting things. Horses and wagons were brought to the broad street in order to transport the items to Bobruisk. The wagons left one at a time and behind them the Yeshiva students followed on foot singing prayers. They traveled slowly in order to avoid accidents on the journey. People came out of their houses to watch the procession.

More memories: from the later life of our generation

After the historic Zionist conference, which was held in 1902 in Minsk, a dramatic chapter in the history of Russian Zionism occurred. The conflict emerged between the Zionism of Dr. Herzl and the Zionism of *Echad Ha'ad*. Ahad Ha'am certainly participated in the conference. The most significant Jewish intellectuals, who supported the concept of Zionism, were present. Also present were young rabbis from various places in Russia. They were involved in the Eastern movement, created and run by Yitzchak Yaakov Reines from Lida, and he was also there.

After the conference, groups of delegates came to visit Slutsk on their way home. They had heard about the young Jews who gathered in Slutsk at the Yeshiva and gymnasja and wanted to observe. Every day there were guests in the Yeshiva. The guests did not participate in Russian Jewish life. I remember the great crowd that came to hear a sermon given by Yitzchak Reines in the great synagogue of Slutsk. Many students also came. He had a reputation as a modern rabbi. The Orthodox Jews had a dim view of him. However, a rabbi is a rabbi, so even the very religious came to hear him with great respect. He was held in high esteem and considered an outstanding speaker.

Because of the guests that sought out Slutsk, the Yeshiva people became interested in every aspect of Zionism. More information was needed and sought in the town library, where books in Yiddish and Hebrew were available. In addition, they had the journal *"Hashluach"* which published writings by Ahad Ha'am. Afterwards the teachers at the Yeshiva discussed him and also Dr. Harold Klausner and Dr. Simon Bernfeld, who were among the most important writers in the journal.

The library became a significant place in the city. It was the center for leaders of the Enlightenment and Hebrew teachers. There were young writers who later became well known; novelists, dramatists and translators of Sholem Aleichem into Hebrew. I.D. Berkowitz, a young looking teacher with olive skin and large round eyes, intelligence beaming from them, was a favorite with the students for the literature he taught. After he left Slutsk they heard of his large literary following and his wonderful storytelling. The story *Moshe'kele Khazir* created a holiday, a worldly atmosphere for the Yeshiva population. For the Slutsker students he opened a door to modern Yiddish literature, which let them wander in its garden. They would grow along with all that bloomed there.

At the same time I believe there was the beginning of the explosion of writers who described Jewish cultural life. Many of them were born in Slutsk. Meyer Waxman was one who wrote in English about Hebrew and Yiddish literature, thinking, and ethics with a glowing sagacity.

Also many crafts were developed in our generation at that time.

An accident with a magical content

A Slutsker winter evening, snow, frost, wind. We are secluded and there are only two of us, my friend who is a Chasid and I. We study the same Gemara melody, but his is different—my friend sings with a higher melody, almost a scream. He sings to the sky and to himself alone. Footsteps are heard at the door.

[Page 329]

A young man dressed in a gray student's coat with shiny buttons and a cape over his shoulders appears in the doorway. He wears a round white hat and resembles a military officer. He had been passing by and heard our voices so late on such a night that he decided to take a look. Could he talk to us? His name is Aaron Singalovski.

The future Doctor Singalovski, talented speaker for Jewish socialist groups on an international level, is an excellent representative for European Jewry.

A dialogue between us ensues. He is a stranger to Slutsk; a traveler with the hope of entering the gymnasja. What are you and your friend studying? He asks many questions; do you know about ethics, and who were the great Talmudic philosophers? Do you know about the Gaonim and the Cabalists? We are not intimidated by all these questions. We speak of the people from the time of the Gemara and their greatness and humanity. We speak of the difficult lives of those who received the mystical tradition. Some were rabbis, blacksmiths, shoemakers, woodcutters, upholsterers, and at the same time teachers and poets. Our guest is impressed with our knowledge of the mystical rabbi Shlomo Alkabetz, poet of the Sabbath song *"L'cha Dode"*. Rabbi Isser Zalman Meltzer had translated it for us. He is the forerunner of *Mussar.* Singalovski likes what he hears. He sits with us until the morning and comes a second and third time.

Later he is to found an organization in Slutsk for students and teachers, Sons of Judah. It will be a society whose purpose is getting together to learn from one another through discourse about morals and ethics, Gemara images, world ideas, and Socialism. We will learn about the Bund and Hersh *Lekert*, in Vilna and Minsk as well as Zionism. In a drop of water we will see the ocean and all of G-d's rainfall. In the Slutsker Sons of Judah we will see the future for our generation.

Slutsk of that time enchanted all of us who had her in our blood, and we took her away with us over all the seas. She took us to diverse political and social movements; some in cultural occupations, literature, journalism, and some in science

Hillel Dobrow and Aharon Singolovski

and college life in the free world.

On some of my journeys, my experience with meeting people, and seeing one phenomenal land after another, Slutsk stood out on my world map. In 1933 I came to Slutsk during the Soviet terror and year of hunger. Earlier I had had an opportunity to once again appreciate Slutsk. I had been in Israel and was a Sabbath guest in the Jerusalem home of Rabbi Meltzer. He was at that time the great Torah scholar there. I became weak seeing his beautiful new home. I met another famous Slutsker, I.D. Berkavitch, well known for the Hebrew literature which was to become part of the new state of Israel. I recalled the excellent

Slutsker library and visited the Ridba'z's grave site in Safed. Slutsk was ever present everywhere I traveled
.

I arrived in Slutsk from Bobruisk. The Soviet police power had cut her to pieces. They said I could go no further. Everything was controlled by the military. I was close to the city. If my automobile could go five more minutes more, I would be at Ostrove where the Yeshiva

[Page 330]

was located. I know the way and carried a map showing all the places I had ever been. The Soviet soldier was friendly. He took my papers and said he would help me. He took me to a military post and asked if there were Jews in Slutsk? One soldier carried a club and had a rope tied around him. He looked me over. One remarked that the Slutsk that once was is no more. That Slutsk died long ago.

I thought to myself that it died at the hands of this enemy.

Is the synagogue still there in the middle of the town? Is the stone still there?

The soldier with the rope around him said Slutsk is a military camp. Everywhere there were stalls with military horses. I felt as if my heart tore. So this was the end of our long ago Slutsk which now only remains in memory.

The Yevrehiskaye School

by R. Berkavitch

Translated by Tamara Selden z"l with missing gaps filled in by Jerrold Landau

There was a State school with Russian studies for Jewish boys in Slutsk. Officially it was considered to be a government school. It was supervised by the Vilna education system. If this was regulated by the government, I do not remember. The teachers held diplomas from the Vilna Teacher's Institute, and wore uniforms with decorative buttons and hats with ribbons. The students wore black *rubashkes* [gowns] and hats that had a shiny point. The school was comprised of four classes, plus a special preparation class. The courses were: Russian language, arithmetic, Russian history and geography. Later around 1903 they added algebra, geometry and eventually Jewish religion. We then also had singing: Russian patriotic songs, children's folk songs. A non-orthodox rabbi would speak to the students about patriotic Russian concepts.

Originally the school was in the beautiful home of the Soloveitchiks on Sadavah Street. Later it was moved to another place which belonged to a German whose name was Gerleh, near Ostrove Street, not far from a house with a cloister. There were five classrooms with benches for the students. In each room there were pictures of the Kaiser and Kaiserina on the walls. In addition, there was a teacher's room, a library, and a private office for the Principal. The school had a courtyard, where the students did gymnastics under the supervision of an instructor in an unusual uniform—an amazing sight for former cheder boys from Slutsk.

Most of the students came from comfortable homes and were students who did not show the ability to study in the Yeshiva. There were those who had the ambition to become Russian teachers or externs to supervise examinations in the Slutsker gymnasja.

As I went into the school, after finishing my usual Jewish studies, a new remarkable world opened up for me. The official language had to be Russian. My skill in this language was very limited. All I knew was the White Russian language of the peasants, which I picked up in the streets. At first I was laughed at, but it did not take long for me to improve and speak as well as my friends.

Speaking Russian disciplined the former Yeshiva students and kept them in good order. They were respectful of their teachers in their uniforms , and worked hard at their studies. However, among the students there were free souls, brats, mockers, who sneakily ridiculed the teachers and gave them nicknames in Yiddish. Thus, the teacher Rosenthal was called "rabbit" because he was short and round. Another was called "hunchback nose," and other such names. Even the other students found this amusing.

[Page 331]

These were the days of the "first revolution" in Russia (1904-1905). The *buntarisher* spirit captured the entire land and even blundered into our Yevrehiskaye school, particularly in our last class. When the gymnasts from the town gymnasja went out on strike, because nine friends had been locked out for revolutionary leanings, we joined them in sympathy with all the other organized revolutionary groups. We marched to the doors of the gymnasja and tried to bring those who had been driven out back inside. In the end soldiers with guns were posted at the doors. One of us was wounded and ran to us all bloodied.

When the demonstration ended we all went our separate ways. The school was closed. Some of the students resumed their studies in other places. Some followed the example of their fathers and went to work. Most left for America with the great Jewish immigration tide, after the October pogroms in 1905. In America I met several friends from the school.

Finally, we were reminded of the good things in the school. Mr. Levinson, who was the teacher of our last class, and was called by the bratty students, "The Old One" because he wore a beard, was a man of fine spirit. He was strongly attentive to each of his students who showed great curiosity and interest in higher learning. He concerned himself with their ability to look beyond the borders of the school. He gave them books to read from his private library that were part of classic Russian literature.

Slutsk, My Second Home

by Dr. L. Fogelman

Translated by Tamara Selden z"l with missing gaps filled in by Jerrold Landau

Dr. L. Eliezer Fogelman

I always remember Slutsk as my second home. I was born in Niesvizh, and I spent my childhood years as well as part of my youth there. However, I became bound to Slutsk with different strands, more spiritual and emotional.

My older sister Sara Kremer lives in Slutsk with her husband and children. My aunt Henya, who treated me like her own child, also lived there. I used to spend several consecutive months a year there in connection with my studies, which were connected with the Slutsk Gymnasja.

This was an important chapter in my life. It was a chapter that should be presented in greater detail, as it also reflects on the life of the studying Jewish youth in White Russia at the beginning of the 20th century.

There was no gymnasja at that time in Niesvizh (in later years, Niesvizh also had its own gymnasja). When I started obtaining worldly education, and that took place very early, at my Bar Mitzvah year, I had to go to Slutsk, which already had a government gymnasja with a significant number of students. Since Slutsk was a larger city that Niesvizh, its gymnasja became an educational center not only for Slutsk, but also for the surrounding small towns.

Therefore, Jewish youth from the surrounding cities or towns came to Slutsk to obtain secular education, just as students streamed to Slutsk to study in the Slutsk Yeshiva. There was no contact between the Slutsk Gymnasja and the Slutsk Yeshiva, for they were in two separate worlds.

[Page 332]

The fact was that in later years, when I was already grown up and on the broad road to an independent life, I met friends and yeshiva students who had studied in Slutsk in the same year as I had. In the past there had been little opportunity for those of us from the gymnasja to get acquainted with those who attended the yeshiva.

I will never forget another time in my life, which I call the Slutsker period. It was tightly bound up with a strong and even dramatic time in my early years. It was the first time I tasted the experience of being a young Jewish man from old Czarist Russia who tried to take himself forward along the difficult path of gaining worldly knowledge. At that time it was extremely difficult for a young Jewish man to attend a Russian gymnasja.

In order to clearly prepare for the difficult path, I recall that in Russia the "quota system" existed for Jews attending the gymnasja. This referred to the number of Jews as compared to the number of non-Jews attending the government gymnasjas or other institutions.

In the government gymnasja they took Jewish students of wealthier parents, who by various means and tricks and paid protection were accepted.

Sholem Aleichem, as we know, exposed this tragic-comedy about such Jewish parents and the various procedures of getting their children into the gymnasja in Czarist Russia. I experienced the bitter taste of these procedures in my first attempt to become a student there.

I was not a child of wealthy parents, who had the luxury of giving money in order for me to be accepted at the gymnasja. I had to take another, more difficult path. I became an "extern."

At that time everyone knew what it meant to be an "extern." However, it was so long ago that it seems proper to set forth here the peculiar Yiddish phenomenon which explains the term. It is useful for coming generations and for history as well, to understand, even though it has been written about before. Therefore, I am prepared to explain this Jewish student situation which was known as "extern."

The Jewish youths who did not have the possibility of attending a Russian gymnasja could study privately elsewhere. An examination was held every year at the gymnasja, which they were unable to take because of the anti-Semitic percentage norm. So they established this special category of "extern." I belonged to this G-d forsaken category. Why I describe it as G-d forsaken is not hard to figure out, if you knew every hardship, worry, and nervous tension which each of us experienced in trying to get a gymnasja diploma or a *"zrelasti"* as it was called in Russian.

Slutsk Gymnasja

[Page 333]

The Russian students of the gymnasja looked askance at the Jewish education seekers, who used to haunt the place in the summer months from May to June in order to take examinations. Some teachers were blatantly anti-Semitic and they made the examinations extremely difficult.

There was an accepted concept that the "extern" must know a great deal more than the usual gymnast in order to pass the exam. The cramming of all the facts in order to remember them well and to be outstanding truly was a torment, which only bright, patient, youthful minds could endure.

It often occurred that the work of an entire year was thrown away because of this. From one exam and one point of view, the examiner could fail the student—sometimes for a small detail because his memory failed in a critical moment of the examination, either in written or oral questions. The examiner claimed he had to hold the examination the next year including all the material, even though the student had passed certain sections.

In this way I also began the final stage of an "extern" at the Slutsker gymnasja in the years 1900 to 1905; and crept through several exams until the year 1906. I finally, through a miracle, completed the seventh class of the second Warsaw gymnasja on Navcalipkey Street with a medal. I was then able to become a member of the law faculty at Warsaw University, which I completed in four years.

When I completed Law School, I had a great deal of difficulty entering the legal profession because a Jew had to have a year of work as a "help advocate," and did not have full rights in the profession.

The anti-Semitic restrictions in Czarist Russia placed the Jews in lower class ranks which had many handicaps and restraints.

However, I remember Slutsk with warm feeling and gratitude and loss; it was there I gained

The Boulevard on the broad street

my first opportunity to enter into life with knowledgeable preparation. Later it opened a broad path to higher development in a profession with quality and status work. I am grateful to Slutsk for her contribution to my spiritual unveiling. I miss her especially because of the good experiences that made my younger years memorable and full of warmth.

Until the present day I think of my friends of those years, how I met different types of Jews. The scenes and pictures of Slutsker life are forever imprinted in my memory.

I remember several Jewish families because of my friendship with their sons and daughters.

[Page 334]

I became very close to two Slutsker families; private advocates Dotner and Karfman. I also remember other Slutsker families: Witkin, owner of the pharmacy, and the families Kantorvitch and Getsav, the externs and their sons who were bright young people. Some of these young people completed all eight classes at the gymnasja for examinations.

Besides these close families, I also remember those who played a special role in Slutsk; for example, the very popular Jewish physician, Dr. Schildkraut. He drove through the streets in a wagon dispensing medical help and was married to a beautiful young woman from Nesvizh from the family Shvershinski. Their children were my good friends.

Until this very day, I still think of those large businesses which appeared to me to be great, rich and luxurious stores.

The marketplace was full of noise. It was called the "Chausee" [main street] and had the feel of constant hoo-hah. Poor men and women dealt with cheaper items in order to earn a living.

I recall the breezy beautiful days of May and June when the boys and girls went for walks through the streets near the Slutsker "Chausee." We talked easily and the flirting was warm and friendly. Our hearts fluttered, our eyes were full of fire, and there was never an end to walking. We never got tired. At night we had to prepare for our examinations.

Whomever got tired at that time in our youth? Who ever thought about what was healthy? We were young, strong, capable, and hot blood raced quickly in our veins.

Where have you gone, my distant beloved Slutsker years? Now it is as if it had been a dream. How far away are the years with my young proud friends, dressed in their gymnasja uniforms, and all the beautiful daughters, full of charm and teasing ways! They awoke love in us, passion and tenderness. I also remember the elderly Slutsker Jews, who rested in the evening after a long hard day of work.

After a number of years I departed from Slutsk, my second home. Later, destiny sent me back, but in another role. This would be my last and final sad departure from Slutsk.

It was several years after the Bolshevik Revolution. In the year 1921 many Jews were sent to various cities and towns, and I was sent to Slutsk to be a teacher. This was a big change from the previous experience of my youth. I was assigned by the Soviet educational commission to teach in the same gymnasja where I had once in the summer months, with trembling heart, taken the examination to become an "extern."

For me it was a strange experience, standing in the same great rooms and teaching only Soviet students. They had come there without limitations or difficulties.

During my classes I would remember those terrible times I had in this place all those years ago. What would my present students know about how I suffered in this gymnasja?

I saw my role in Slutsk as a whimsical play about my life. There had been a bloody world war and after that a bloody revolution, in order for me, the Nesvizh Jew, to be here in a new role in this same place. In a way I felt that it was "historic justice" playing itself out before my eyes.

At that time in Soviet Russia the Commissariat decreed that mathematics be taught, despite the fact that we teachers had no time to prepare to teach it. My pre-Revolution education was centered in Russian language and literature. Those were the subjects I had taught in Petrograd.

There was a terrible shortage of teachers but the Government was not concerned about their ability to teach mathematics. The main concern was to fill the positions. How different this was compared to those earlier times when to become a teacher in a gymnasja in a specific subject required many years of intense dedication.

[Page 335]

The situation was so different now. The Russians recruited every intellectual, every person with education, in order to further the work in various government institutions. The most intellectual people did not have any desire to become part of this system. But they had no other choice because they could not find work that was compatible with their education elsewhere. Everything was centrally controlled.

In the Soviet gymnasja I met some of my old teachers who had given me the examinations in my younger year as an "extern." I sometimes reminded them of the miserable time the Jewish students had had with those examinations. Now we could feel equal. Now the examinations were the same for everyone. We were no longer excluded from the educational system.

However, there was not one bit of discipline in the gymnasja; just the opposite from the years of the Czarist government. The teachers had no control and work requirements were ignored by the students. Later the government introduced strict measures, but I had already left Russia.

Soviet Slutsk threw itself into the new world and a new life with great exuberance.

The memories of the past hung heavily on my shoulders and woke in me restlessness and negative thoughts. I felt dread for Jewish life in the cities and towns.

I did not find people I had known earlier. I felt lonesome and solitary in the same city which had played such a large role in my youth. It seemed empty and unfriendly. A strange feeling of loss overwhelmed me, but I could not foresee the terrible events of the Nazi era and the tragic loss of the Jews, who would become martyrs at the hands of the murdering Nazis. Yet, although this was before the time of Hitler's assault on Europe, I already felt something about the coming destruction.

Life in general deteriorated in Slutsk. The city was almost unrecognizable. The stores were empty of goods. The sidewalks, houses, and the marketplace were sad to see. People stood in line to buy various products. They looked old, worried, and gray.

Slutsk had achieved a different appearance after the tragic beginning of the war and revolution, and I felt as if I was a stranger in Slutsk, a place that had been such a meaningful part of my life.

My sister was already a widow and had great difficulty providing the bare necessities for her three daughters. There was only fear and worry in her cheerless home.

I left Slutsk with mixed feelings of worry, pain, and sadness. With a constricted heart my wife and I wandered even further from my birth city of Nesvizh, through Kletsk where my other two sisters lived with their families. There was an established Polish regime in charge.

There, as in Slutsk, I felt the suffocating sense of fear and impending doom.

An atmosphere pervaded the place which prevented people from living a normal life.

As I left Slutsk an important piece of my life was gone: a chapter full of drama and meaningful experiences

Now, after so many years of parting, I feel a deep longing for her. The name of Slutsk awakes in me a whole symphony of my past.

[Page 336]

Memories

Rabbi Yossele Peimer
(Grandson of the first Reb Yossele)

by H.A. Peimer – New York

Translated by Tamara Selden z"l with missing gaps filled in by Jerrold Landau

My father, Reb Yossele, Slutsker Rabbi "of blessed memory," was known by rabbis and gaonim. He possessed rare qualities and virtues, and had an intimate relationship with the great personalities of his generation.

His library was the most impressive in Czarist White Russia and contained antique books, some handwritten in Hebrew and Yiddish. There were newspapers, journals and periodicals which he collected over many years. The library was the greatest treasure he possessed. It was in the most spacious and beautiful room in our house. The books were bound and arranged in categories. He would often browse among them with great joy. He dusted and straightened, and took great pride in their breadth and beauty. It was characteristic of him to be the sole handler of the books. Whenever he bought a book he felt he had gotten a great bargain although he had paid a high price. The book dealers knew that with Reb Yossele they had to charge a high price because, if not, it would aggravate him to think that G-d forbid he had cheated them. He rarely forgot anything. His memory was phenomenal, except when he was insulted. He seemed to forget, but actually retained the insult and even wrote it down.

There were times when Father had vast sums of holdings: money, jewelry and securities. Every single item was registered by Father in this manner: day, month, year, chapter of the Torah...belongs to Mr.__, so many hundreds, two tens, and so on. Each one received his possession back exactly as he had given it to Father. Regarding the words of the Torah, if someone asked him something, he wrote down the question, the name of the questioner and the answer.

Reb Yossele (the second) Peimer

What pertained to the word or translation of the word of G-d was no problem for him. Before he answered, he immersed himself in the words of the law. He answered questions from the educated and the ordinary people, on mundane matters or even dreams. He would refer to the author, commentator on Jewish texts, and preachers. His energy had no limits and no boundaries. There was another Rabbi in Slutsk, but Father was the responsible authority in the city and he carried this heavy burden.

[Page 337]

He was the spokesman for every power and new regime; the ethical soul for our entire congregation and each individual. In addition, there was no European language that Father did not speak and understand.

It is interesting to note here how Father, in his playful manner, spoke to various groups. With the Russians, he spoke a cooked up German, and with the Germans a murdered Polish, and with the Poles a mishmash of all three languages. At this point we should honor the enlightened thinking of five esteemedmen of Slutsk; Gutseit, Chernikov, the two Feinbergs, and Dr. Schildkraut, who were estranged from religious Judaism, but were father's dearest, constant and devoted companions in all his various activities.

The Russian military, located in Teliekhen near Pinsk, decided to drive out the entire Jewish community. The Jews were ordered to line up. The rabbi led the way, followed by important businessmen and all the other Jews. Suddenly a crazy Jewish woman broke from the line and ran over to a soldier. She grabbed him by the ear and pointed to the Rabbi and the other important people. The soldiers decided to put the Jews in chains and march them to Slutsk. Most of the Jews did not have the good fortune that the Rabbi had. His family eventually rescued him from certain death and got him out of prison.

Once a military herald ordered Father to come immediately to the commander. Father called for Mr. Feinberg and they went together. The commander shouted, stamped his feet, and threatened to thrash the Jews and send them to Siberia, especially Slutsker Jews who sold liquor. The drunken, disorderly soldiers often attacked and robbed the Jews and destroyed their property. The commander asked Mr. Feinberg what he thought should be done. Father intervened and said he would try an old Jewish ritual of excommunication. He truly had compassion for the worthy Feinberg, who would have to clarify and explain this ritual. The commander laughed at this foolish, ridiculous idea that was meant to stop the illegal selling of whiskey. However, he left it to father of "blessed memory" to see what he could do together with the second rabbi in town.

On Thursday afternoon in the cold shul [kalte shul], the rabbis stood on the pulpit in white linen robes and wrapped in prayer shawls. Next to them were the assistants, sextons, and *shofar* blowers. On a table lay a parchment with a version of the excommunication ritual. A large black candle burned brightly on the lectern. On one side there was the ritual cleansing board used for the dead and on the other side a stretcher.

The tense congregation looked on with baited breath. The *shofar* blowers blew their ram's horns. The chief assistant proclaimed, in the name of the rabbi and other dignitaries and in a trembling voice, that if an unknown person or son of an unknown person would venture to violate the edict against producing or selling whiskey, may all the curses fall upon him. No one shall have any business dealings or contact with him because he is excommunicated.

In the dead stillness of delivering the curse, we heard the choking sounds of the women and the withheld breath of the men. The appalling ancient ritual closed with a weekday prayer. The clergy on the pulpit were gaunt and prostrate. Father of "blessed memory," who was a young man, had the appearance of a very old man. This was a deeply painful experience for him.

After that Father became an exceptional yet humble contact for the commander. He was chosen to inform the storekeepers whenever the military had to pass through the city. Then the Jews would be warned in time. This was of great importance because when soldiers unexpectedly came, the Jewish community was often devastated, especially on the Sabbath and Holidays. The soldiers would break down the doors and steal everything in sight. Now my father could give the warning in time. The rabbi would try to give the bakers time to prepare the baked goods that were required for the Sabbath.

One time when the Jewish New Year fell on the Sabbath, Father was told that the soldiers would be arriving soon. He and the other rabbi sent a decree to all the synagogues that the bakeries must stay open to prepare the challah, despite the danger. It is not difficult to imagine the broken hearts and beaten spirits that greeted the New Year.

[Page 338]

Men and women dressed in their best Sabbath and holiday clothes, were downcast with their prayer books in hand.

There was a well-known landowner who lived in Slutsk. His name was Bullhock, a significant person in the local Polish population. The Bolsheviks arrested him. They were prepared to break into his palace one night and arrest his wife also.

Someone informed Reb Yossele about this and late in the evening he sent a message to warn her. He told her not to sleep at home for several nights. Near Bullhock's palace lived a Jew. Between his house and the palace there was a fence with thin stakes. Reb Yossele instructed her to pull out a few of the stakes, go through the fence and replace the stakes afterwards. She was told that the Jew was expecting her. She did exactly as she was told and was spared arrest. In a short time, the city went from the Russians to the Poles and Bullhock was freed. His wife told him what had occurred, and he thought well of the Jews for what they had done.

Father's timely sense of responsibility and his well-run rabbinate benefited the Jews during the Bolshevik Revolution, until the German occupation and the Polish *"faznantshikes" and "Khalertsherkes"* destroyed the greatest part of Slutsk including our home. It not only destroyed our belongings but also our chosen spiritual life and incredible library.

One Friday we were thinking about possibly leaving the city as the Red Army was drawing closer. The commander of the Polish Army called for Father and told him that it was only right for the Jews of Slutsk to be proper hosts and collect a sum of money for their retreat by the Sabbath afternoon. If not, he would let his soldiers do whatever pleased them. When Father heard this decree, he did not lose his courage, but went home and put on his Sabbath clothes. Accompanied by the worthy Dr. Schildkraut they went to the houses of the prominent Slutsker Jews to accomplish the difficult task that had been assigned. In this manner the money was collected and given in time to the Polish commander who took it with a brutal cynicism. He then had a good laugh and left the Jews to the mercy of the Polish beasts.

Father went to the morning service at the synagogue. Three armed Polish hooligans appeared with packages of loot under their arms. Seeing father all dressed up with a top hat and his beautiful patriarchal beard, one of them pulled out a pack of matches, lit it and threw it towards his beard. Another had a knife which he could use to cut off the beard and the third simply tried to grab it with his non-kosher paw. Father gave his hand a slap with his entire strength. The contemptible man grabbed a stick and moved to hit Father, but Father took hold of the tip of the stick and averted the injury. One of the hooligans tried to kick him, but once again he fought back. He flung the stick at the perpetrator and it struck him in the face.

The hooligan quickly recovered, stood up, took out his sword, and struck Father on the head with murderous fury. The Sabbath top hat was a life saver. It lay on the ground trampled and squashed, but it had saved Father from serious injury.

The Jews outside, hearing the tumult and seeing their rabbi surrounded by three well known Polish bullies, attacked them with their bare hands and rescued Father from further harm. The hooligans did not wait long and fled.

The Sabbath service was transformed into a tribute for the Creator of the World and the miracle that had occurred. The eyes of the congregation were glued to Father throughout the entire time of praying. When the service ended they waited to hear their rabbi tell what happened in his own words.

For twenty years more Father continued to be the rabbi in Slutsk, and in 1920 he went to Baranovichi, tired, broken, old, and depleted. He had no books, limited funds, and thousands of letters from Slutsker Jews to their relatives in America from whom they begged for help. The letters had never been mailed.

[Page 339]

At that stormy time the Polish hordes filled up the trains. A Jew, a rabbi with a patriarchal beard, was an exceptional person. Seeing that Father struggled to climb aboard the freight wagon, the Poles assisted him and finally pulled him on with his baggage. He was surrounded by men with knives, bayonets, and burning matches. There was a wounded Jewish officer on the same wagon and had it not been for him, Father would not have survived the trip. The journey was made in peace all the way to Warsaw.

At that time Father's two sisters, two well-known dentists, lived in Warsaw and had their offices at Marszalkowska 81. Among their patients were generals, professors, and important government officials. Both sisters lived comfortably, even graciously, for that time in Poland. They wanted their brother to remain with them to rest and recover from the dreadful things that had happened to him.

By no means would he even discuss this with them. He wanted to do something worthwhile to help the poor, suffering people in Slutsk and its neighboring communities. He realized that he alone could not do the job or diminish the anti-Semitism and bloody persecution. Father contacted a Jewish woman who had a good relationship with the highest Catholic clergyman of that time, Cardinal Krakowski. Father met with him and was treated with courtesy and warmth. The Cardinal listened to Father's description of the violence against helpless Jews. He then wrote a letter to the commander of the military garrison in Baranovichi, Riks Shmigli. He appealed to the commander to show great regard, friendliness, and assistance to Rabbi Peimer of Slutsk.

At the same time Father knew that the influential Prince Bullhock was in Baranovichi. He appealed to him and Bullhock gave him necessary documents and papers and also a letter to a colleague, a well-known Polish leader, telling him to consider what the Rabbi told him as being Holy. The papers accomplished wonders. Arriving in Baranovichi, Father threw himself into his work of rescue, aid, and ransoming at the infamous internment quarantine camp.

The Cardinal's letter to the chief commander of the Polish troops helped to open the iron door to the tragic internment camp, and a ray of hope and trust brought relief to the devastated Jews in the camp. They felt that they had not been abandoned, and that someone cared about them.

Returning to the city, very alarmed, Father contacted the Jewish community and told them of the tragic conditions in the camp. He proclaimed that they must immediately provide food and clothing and medicine for the pitiable Jews in the camp. It might save their lives. It is important here to note that two intimates of father, Fein and Malinski, who were by chance also in Baranovichi, were able to help the Slutsker rabbi with his mission.

Father established a committee of which he was the director and whose main function was to provide for the needs of the suffering people. He immediately got in touch with the renowned Advocate and Sejm Deputy, Noach Prilutski. He requested that Prilutski send a Jewish advocate from Warsaw who could handle legal options.

A famous advocate from Warsaw came to Baranovichi. He dealt with various issues and requested that the Poles immediately send documents about the legitimate rights of the camp Jews to Polish cities and towns. The Poles responded by making all documents null and void which the camp Jews had from the Polish government representative in Soviet Russia and also from the Polish border official officer. They announced that all Jews are Bolsheviks and should be sent back to their Bolshevik communities.

Father suggested with his usual devotion and concern for his people that the camp Jews be given prayer shawls, phylacteries, books, either ordinary or in Jewish, candlesticks, bible books with stories for women, or a prayer book. These items certainly are not for Bolsheviks. He would be responsible for these Jews. It is worthwhile to note that from the other side of the border, they made use of the honesty of Father of blessed memory

[Page 340]

for saving lives, and smuggled from their side a significant number of party activists and propagandists, equipped with the genuine Jewish clerical garb against which the Yevseksia mercilessly fought at that time.

A rare demonstration of the honor of Torah and sanctification of the Divine name took place on that day in Baranovich with the arrival (from Russia) of the world famous *Gaon* of the generation, the Chofetz Chaim of blessed memory. Father of blessed memory not only worked for the Polish military office in Baranovich as the spiritual giant, so that his ten Yeshiva students should not have to endure the seven levels of Hell in the dismal, famous "Yur," but his official documents, which were published legitimately, and the like, were already prepared for him before he had to be at the train. My father arranged an exceptional welcome for the important guest, in which the entire Baranovich community participated. The impressive portion of that exceptional demonstration was when Father of blessed memory received a permit from the military authorities that a group of freed Jewish soldiers could take part in the reception for the Chofetz Chaim as an honor guard. The Gaon of the generation blessed them all and wished them that they should be able to return to their homes in peace. The impression was boundless when the Jewish soldiers literally led the great *Gaon* by his hands from the train car to his host. The thick Russian heads could not at all understand the scene that the Jews were making over the short, thin, emaciated Jew, the "Chlofetz Chaim."…

During those stormy days when Baranovich was flooded with thousands of Jews, returning and escaping, and some who were trying to run away both from Russia and Poland and were setting out to wherever their eyes would take them, came Moneh Katz, the great, famous Jewish artist, who wanted to rescue himself in France. However, he went ahead and set out for Paris while the Poles wanted to send Jews back to Russia. He went to Father, who in his usual manner, made efforts to obtain the papers he needed to leave Poland. The artist was very thankful to Father for his great help. He decided to perpetuate Father's personage in a large oil portrait. However, go try to produce a portrait of a Jew completely immersed in Jewish worries and tribulations, without even a free moment to breathe, and furthermore in Father's tiny room where it was impossible to sit and draw. However, M. K. the artist did not pay attention to this. He brought his canvas, paint, and paint brushes, and started the work with exceptional energy, consistency, and love. The great artist wanted to capture Father's character traits and splendid countenance on canvas in vivid colors and shades. However, it was probably predestined that this artistic work would remain unfinished. In the middle of the effort, M. K. received an order to leave Poland. The important painter hoped to have the possibility to complete the painting at a later time, and he quickly left all his paraphernalia, his mixed paints, the prepared paint brush, and the canvass with the incomplete portrait in Father's home.

Years later, when Father of blessed memory was already a New York resident, and Maneh Katz was with A. Liessin of blessed memory, he mentioned Father favorably, saying that he had helped him greatly to save himself from the Polish and Bolshevik persecutors. It is possible that the artist had forgotten Rabbi Yossele the rabbi… It is indeed a shame that a portrait painted by such a fine Jewish painter was never completed…

In connection with the aforementioned, it is important to note that during the time when Father of blessed memory was the only official representative of Slutsk and its environs, thousands of dollars of cash, clothing, food, and medications went through his hands, but Father did not derive benefit from any of it.

Father became acclimatized to America easily. He endured no challenges and had to make no compromises, for he was not a rabbi here. He lived in America for twelve year and the positive traits of America impressed him greatly. However, he could in no way bear the overly easy and vulgar freedom that many Jews took advantage of, casting off religious, national, and traditional duties. He considered this a travesty.

Jews were able to lead an intensive Jewish life in a free land, and if they do not do so, it is the fault of their leaders. That is the manner in which Father lived his middle years, quiet, inwardly turned, and alone. He gave up his pure soul after terrible suffering on 1 Kislev 5699 (November 25, 1938). Providence had it that Father's funeral would also be symbolic. An unusual storm took place during the funeral. The thick snow made it impossible for a large number of people to give him is last respects. The adage "He lived quietly and died quietly" was certainly fulfilled with him. May his soul be bound in the bonds of eternal life.

[Page 341]

The Rabbi's Wife

My mother Alter-Elke was raised by her father Reb Reuven Shachravit in Kovno, where he was a prominent businessman, respected and wise in Haskala and Talmud. For him Torah came first. His beautiful daughter's upbringing was both worldly and traditional. My mother received instruction in the Holy language, Russian, Polish, German, and Yiddish. Because of her personal charm, she was well known in her youth, and before she achieved maturity, her parents had notified the matchmakers of her eligibility. They then flooded the threshold of her father's house.

However, as it turned out—it seemed inevitable—mother would be a Rabbi's wife. This destiny fell on my father, who had been one of the best Slobodka Yeshiva students and who also knew many languages. He became a rabbi at the young age of twenty one. Although my parents were quite different in many ways, they were united in their love of Israel and their self-sacrifice for individuals as well as for the community at large.

For my mother, a new and exceptional chapter began in her short, difficult, and fruitful life. This rare beautiful woman quickly became one of the most famous rabbi's wife in all of White Russia.

Thanks to her intelligence and tact our house became a true center in the city. There was not one subject in which mother did not participate. It was a wonder that she had the energy to organize and to be active in so many undertakings. She was a nurse in the house when we were sick, and sometimes in hospitals. She did not consider any work which helped people as ugly or hard. Each thing mattered, was important, and was done with much enthusiasm. Our house was spacious on one of the most beautiful streets in town and had a lovely garden. The doors were open to all who came: rabbis, people with worthy causes, preachers, relatives, random visitors.

The house was public domain and everyone felt free to come and go as he wanted. It was clean, tidy and in excellent order.

At the outbreak of the First World War hundreds of young Jewish men were mobilized and had to leave their beloved wives and children. It was the custom to give them a divorce document. This was done to prevent the following: If a Jewish soldier was captured or missing in action or died, his wife became an *agunah* [a woman whose marital status remains unclear]. She could not remarry ever. Therefore she was given a conditional divorce document, stating that if her husband did not return from battle by this and this date, she was automatically divorced from the date of the conditional document. Reb Mordechai Jacob, the scroll writer, and Reb Shimon wrote these documents.

Alter (Elke) Peimer

Our town was packed with men, women, fathers, mothers, sisters. The weeping and lamentations split the sky. My mother and dear sister Motieh became nurses and comforters trying to help the weeping women. One fainted, another needed her head rubbed. Some needed a drink. In this way they were busy for weeks with the results of the terrible divorce process.

My mother and sister also became involved in preparing meals. The Jewish soldiers in the Russian Army could not carry much food with them and were living on bread and water. In the beginning there were only a few, but after a while there were many more. My mother and sister cooked and the numbers steadily increased. It became impossible to accommodate all of them in a private home. Mother turned to the Slutsker youth, composed of Yeshiva boys, other students, teachers, workers, and asked for their help. A committee was organized to prepare several places in the synagogue for the soldiers. A large modern kitchen was needed so they could prepare large amounts of food for soldiers leaving or returning home.

[Page 342]

They needed hearty and fresh meals. Of course none of this was easy. How do make something from nothing? How do you build a facility without funds or materials and products? My mother's iron will with the help of the Slutsker community was able to accomplish it. They not only built the kitchen with a dining area, but other much needed buildings as well. The news of this traveled so far that one of Czar Nicholas' daughters, who concerned herself with similar work, communicated with the Slutsker committee. Mother became well known for her packages of food that were sent to the front. In the evening, in our home, a large blitz lamp threw a warm yellow glow on the people that wrapped the packages of food, also cigarettes, chocolates, sugar, paper, envelopes, needles, thread, buttons, and other necessary items such as sweaters and canvas sacks. They then roped them up for shipping. The canvas sacks, a very important article for soldiers, were filled with sand to protect their heads when shooting from the trenches. In addition notes with heartfelt words hoping for their safety and return home were added as well.

The youngsters in the community addressed the packages and mailed them.

At that time epidemics had raged in Slutsk. My mother and sister went to help those affected despite the danger. Seeing their example encouraged others to do likewise. I, an only son who was full of devilish tricks, became completely changed and now only wanted to help. In this way my bad behavior changed and perfecting the necessary work was my goal.

My friends and I felt that it would be a good distraction to put on a play.

I no longer remember the artistic aspect of the performance, but I know it was a colossal success. The show was called The Sacrifice of Isaac, with costumes, make-up, and decorations, which, as you can imagine, also created a terrible mess. The animal we used had to be watched carefully until it was needed at the end of the last act. I do not remember if our parents and the nearby neighbors were pleased with our nonsense, fun, and noise, but my mother began to have hope for me. She did not give up and believed I would turn out well.

The house continued to swell with crowds of people. Days would pass and we would not even see our parents. I would catch a glimpse of my mother when she could no longer stand on her feet. Then I had to be her nurse/caretaker. One evening she came home burdened with packages and said she wanted me to come somewhere with her. We went to a house, knocked on a door and went inside. She laid down her packages, went into another room and came out with a child. She kissed and fondled it with great care. Mother laughed and talked to him with a very loving voice. Many years later I learned who this child was. This was not the only child that Mother had nurtured. These children had been abandoned and she had established a place for them and got them into families who would raise them as good Jews.

In the Slutsker jail Mother was a frequent visitor. She brought food, took away dirty clothes, and brought them back clean. She treated these criminals as if they were rabbis or Yeshiva students and workers. Some of their crimes were minimal. Last but not least, she knew how to save them from being sent to Siberia.

I will never forget Berele, a ten year old whom the Czarist government had charged with espionage. He was arrested and was in various jails until he came to Slutsk. Who knows what would have happened to him were it not for Mother? After much toil and intercession, she found a way to save him. On a certain Purim she sent the officer of the prison a lovely gift and pleaded that he save the boy from going to Siberia. Miraculously, he complied.

Frequently Mother would be informed about some prisoners who were being sent to Siberia. She would provide warm clothes, packages, and bolsters. She even helped non-Jews in the hope that it would please the other Christian prisoners and they would not harass the Jews. On one occasion she gave a Christian prisoner a Jewish name in order to help him avoid going to Siberia. She had a rare influence on the government officials.

Generally speaking Mother was rich in "pride" at that time. She was the first one to requisition some of the many synagogues in Slutsk and turn them into orphanages and old age homes.

[Page 343]

To those Jews who wanted to know why the Rabbi's wife was desecrating the house of prayer, she explained that while the synagogue was a place to pray, it seemed proper to use it also for the homeless, elderly, and sick, when necessary. If this was a sin, she would take it upon herself.

Mother made it possible for many Slutsker children, ill or orphaned, to have a good life. She did this for many children throughout Poland.

I remember when our family lived together with several other families who had suffered great losses. In our dwelling lived *Tavarishtch* [Comrade] Balashav with his "soldier attendant" Vanya. From our old house all that remained were grandfather's portrait and a few books. Now the house looked like an office for the Red Commander, where commissars and Red Army personnel continuously came and went. In this environment I felt like a fish out of water even though Balashav and Vanya were good hearted people. Even Pesheh, who vehemently cursed the Bolsheviks, liked them and cooked for them, and even prepared a *cholent* for them on the Sabbath.

At first when the brigade commander Balashav came to requisition a room, Pesheh sat in the kitchen on the oven and did three things at the same time; talked to herself, prayed, and cursed. As soon as she saw the commander, she would shout, "Hey, do you hear? Take the pitcher and bring water!" The commander would lay aside his briefcase, take the water pitcher, go outside and fill it, and with a smile say, "Here, little mother, is your water."

I became good friends with Vanya and the commander, rode their horses, wore their uniforms, and received tickets for concerts and theater performances. Everything would have been good and fine except Rabbi Ber Efton with whom I studied did not approve and was a heavy stone in my path. When Vanya would disclose information about various kinds of arms, I could hear the Rabbi's hoarse voice calling me. It is a good time to study the *Tanach* and learn something. He would say that Vanya could also listen... it will not hurt him. After the lesson he would tell me to put the books away and get dressed. "We cannot lose a minute because it is time to collect money for charitable causes." The great Rabbi Ber and his wild son would go around the city and do this good deed.

Now it was my turn. We went from one part of the city to another, from Astraveh to Tritsan, from the city gate to the cemetery. The rabbi took very long strides and I had to run to keep up with him. Coming to a dark house with closed shutters Rabbi Ber banged on the door. "Who is it?" The rabbi would respond by saying that we were Jewish robbers. The light went on and the door was opened by a sleepy angry Jew. "Is there not another time to do this?" The Rabbi calmed him and told him not to aggravate himself. "You should be satisfied that the holy one does not neglect you and favors you with the possibility of doing good deeds even when you are asleep. Do you know who this young man is? This is Reb Yossele's son and without him I would never do this".

It was inevitable that my mother would wear herself out. Her journey over the Polish border to Baranovichi to visit Father was like walking in the valley of death. There were members of the underground operating at all times (underworld people who smuggled things across the border with the approval of the Bolshevik regime because they furnished Communist literature to the Polish side and other contraband from Poland to Russia). My mother was with the underground and was forced to smuggle as well. When a border patrol stopped her party, the men ran away and left my sick, weak mother in God's custody. There she was, alone on a desolate, unpaved road covered with a burning frost, with stacks of packages of Communist literature lying at her feet.

Two soldiers with guns arrived and seeing what was going on wanted to shoot her, but a third soldier stopped him. He said not to take it out on this old Jewish woman. My mother was forty one years at that time. After a brief discussion they left her in the white blizzard in the middle of a field. In the bitter cold she dozed off.

A Jewish group of people saw her and placed her on their sleigh, half dead and frozen. She recovered at their house. They felt it was a privilege to help this forsaken woman from Slutsk.

[Page 344]

The wife in that family moved heaven and earth to help Mother recover her strength.

My sister and I remained in Slutsk. As soon as Mother was able, she returned home exhausted, gaunt, and worn out. Our home had been transformed into headquarters for undercover agents. Who knows how this would have ended without our neighbor, the good brigade commander, Balashav of the Red Army? He was not able to bear the abuse my mother had suffered nor her anguish. He went to *Tsheka* and told the authorities that there must be an end to all persecution. If it were true that Mother had ties with the Polish defensive and committed treason against the Soviet regime, he would be the first one to turn her over to the tribunal.

However, it was decided that it was time for us to leave Slutsk. My mother and sister were our main concern. The only money we had was earned by my sister and was barely enough to feed us.

One cold winter night we stole away with a few bundles. The only people we said goodbye to were the dead in the cemetery. The living must not know that we were leaving. After an arduous trip we arrived in Baranovichi where our father was. We were weary and had little energy. We found our father in a cramped single room. He had been unable to find a big enough place for us. We searched and finally found two rooms in Atvatsk filled with broken furniture.

My dear Mutie undertook all the work despite the fact that she was still a child. She was outstanding in lobbying the regime for visas in order for us to leave the country. We thought that since Father was a rabbi it would be easy to get a visa for him. He was well known and descended from many generations of rabbis, but it did not seem to matter.

Surprisingly, my sister was able to help one Jew who was a turpentine shopkeeper. He wanted to go to America. He grew a beard and put on a kaftan, a coat usually worn by orthodox Jews. She was able to get the necessary papers for visas for him and his family. How ironic.

Finally, through the lobbying of Luey Marshall, Abraham Lesin, and William Green, my father obtained the American Visa. My sister went to Israel and Mother and I to Poland.

After quite a while my mother and I finally went to New York. I felt safe and secure at last. My mother, although tired and ill, was glad to be in America. We celebrated Passover with Father. In the end she went to the hospital for some surgery. She spoke to us, saying that we should never lose hope and to always remain calm in all situations. She was destined to suffer for many weeks. Her beautiful soul was in a strange place and she died in the month of Tevet in the year 5689 (Dec/Jan 1929).

May Her Soul Be Bound in Eternal Rest.

Our father inscribed the following on her tombstone: "Many Daughters Have Amassed Accomplishments, But You have Risen Above Them."

[Page 345]

Summer of 1919 in Slutsk

by Nathan Kantoravitch

Translated by Tamara Selden z"l with missing gaps filled in by Jerrold Landau

In the summer of 1919, I received orders from the authorities in Minsk to travel to Slutsk and take the job of assistant to the "Peoples Controller." It was a time when the intellectuals in Russia did not want to work with the new council regime. They said that they had overtaken the government in an illegal usurpation through a bloody overthrow and dispelled the "establishment assembly" in all of Russia, which had been elected on a democratic basis.

At that time the council regime mobilized the necessary professionals and intelligentsia among the unfriendly population. The order that came to Minsk stated that all persons with greater education and students in institutions of higher learning must report to the council regime. As a young student at the

Moscow Technical High School and one year at the Riga Polytechnic Institute, which had been exiled to Moscow during the First World War, I was highly eligible.

A second reason was that the People's Controller was a non-political branch of the government. Therefore, it was allowed to take civilians who were not on good terms with the regime and opposition groups, which pertained to the Bolsheviks. The entire "People's Controller" in Minsk, as far as I can remember, was composed of non-Bolshevik professionals. The only Bolshevik was the cabinet maker Khadash—a Jew, who was incidentally weak in speaking Russian, and was the Bolshevik commissar. He supervised the Kashruth from the government standpoint.

This man Khadash was the only Jew remembered in the large book about the history of Minsk, which was distributed by the White Russian Scientific Academy a few years ago. This book does not say one word about the Jews of Minsk or the history of the destruction of the Jewish community brought about by the Nazis. Perhaps they were mentioned once or twice in order to tell the reader that the Jewish Bund was against the Bolshevik overthrow. It was not told that there was a Jewish section at the White Russian Pedagogical Institute, and a Yiddish newspaper "*The Actiaber*." Furthermore, there was a Jewish publishing company which produced many publications. Several other things connected with Jews were omitted. For Khadash an exception was made. However it was not written that he was an ordinary Jew, a plain cabinet maker, who was a little lame.

I was not displeased with the order to go to Slutsk. I had recently suffered the greatest tragedy of my life: the death of my mother. I was anxious to get away. The salary I would get did not exist in Minsk. It was known that in the town of Slutsk there was a store with much better food. There was not the great scarcity of green vegetables. The government did not requisition a large amount of food and life was easier.

Another thing that pleased me was the possibility of having a hook-up with the Zion Council in Slutsk. There was a struggle between the socialist and non-socialist elements. Siding with the first, I hoped that I would be able to strengthen the socialistic branch of the Zion Council.

I arrived in Slutsk at the either the end of May or the beginning of June. With the help of friends from the Zion Council, who greeted me warmly, I found a place to live in the house of Mr. Harkavi. This was located on the corner of one of the central streets in the city. The father and brothers Harkavi came from exile somewhere deep in Russia, I believe, in Rostov on the Don. Their employment was making cheese. There was also a daughter, Musia, and her husband. The house was filled with Zionist spirit. Later, after the Russian Polish War, I heard that they had gone to Israel. Musia died in Tel Aviv.

[Page 346]

When I arrived in Slutsk I had to report to *"Natshalsva."* It appeared that the entire pitiful "People's Controller" was located in a small house and the administrator of the entire operation was a man named Salaviav, a Jew from Bobruisk.

The work in the institution was very meager. Salaviav had a big mouth and one sermon about the benefits and good points of the Bolsheviks and the new regime. He did not demonstrate any great intelligence. The work he did was slovenly. It was likely that he did not know exactly what he was supposed to do.

However, he was aware of Minske Khadash. The previous administrator had told him about his popularity and good nature. I am not sure that Salaviav even spoke Yiddish, while it was the only language that Khadash could speak to express his plain, primitive common sense and thoughts. When he was in Minsk, one thing he liked to do as to tell jokes and use risqué words. He was only able to address these jokes to a few Jews who worked at the "People's Controller."

It should be noted that Russians, Poles, and other non-Jews prefer a non-political institution. A Jew rarely felt good there due to hateful glances from the *goyishe* [gentile] people. The Jews alone had a "White

Guard", a known Czarist, who taunted me constantly. He repeatedly asked me what I was doing there and saying I should be outspoken since Jews were well known Bolsheviks. The opponents of the Council Regime favored Trotsky and complained that Jews and Bolsheviks were one and the same. The Czarist officer and the Poles in the People's Controller were waiting for the regime in Minsk to fall. Then they would grab power and have a reckoning with the Bolshevik Jews.

Life in Slutsk continued in the customary way. It was a nice summer. The orchards bloomed with plentiful fruit. The best crop was the small *sapazhankes.* Someone told me that the genus originated in Slutsk. They were honey sweet pears which literally melted in your mouth. The name was derived from Count Safieha who first cultivated them.

Another delicious item that originated in Slutsk was called Slutsker cake. It was difficult for me to understand what the queer, bizarre, strange word cake meant. Where did this word come from? It shone and there was no word comparable to it. For us in Minsk, it would be called a *bapkeh* with cheese. If it was now called cake it must mean that it had an extraordinary taste. I did not know what kind of special baking method brought out such a taste. After all, this has nothing to do with Jewish studies. It remained a puzzle for me until this very day. Maybe others, true Slutskers, will explain it to me some time.

The cake soon left my mind. Scarcity began to mount in Slutsk. Products needed for simple living became very expensive. Everyone had difficulty, but for me, an outsider, with a very limited salary, it was even harder. I remember now, with gratitude, how the people in the house where I lived assisted me and one of my friends from the Zion Council.

The Zion Council had a committee under the leadership of F. Meltzer, the younger son of a Rabbi, and one other. Their discussions mostly involved the future programs of the Zion Council in connection with a Socialist-Zionist organization. Among the Slutsker Zion Council the differences were so strongly crystallized, compared to the Zion Council in Minsk, where the sharp discussions created a great division between the yes and no socialists. The strongest voice among the Slutskers was pro socialist. The writers of the times were adherents of the People's Revolutionaries, "Slutsker Socialists," and different from Marxist class conflict socialists, which had dominated the Russian Labor Zionists, and drove many away from Zionism.

[Page 347]

It was not long before we were destined to have the discussions in the "Zion Council." We had meetings once a week but sometimes less often, particularly when things became heated. Meanwhile the mood in town, which had generally been peaceful, also changed for the worse. From the *Bolshevistisher* press it was not possible to learn what was happening in the wider world, even in neighboring Poland, where the government set a goal to extend Poland from "sea to sea." That meant from her historic borders and the so called "Eastern crescent" and part of the Ukraine.

With the Poles

Close to the month of *Av* things began to stir in town. Refugees from the West arrived from the areas that the Polish legions had already taken. We were afraid to utter a word. Suddenly, there was a great tumult in the town as the government institutions began to evacuate. I was unable to learn anything. However, I observed that things were irregular, and once, going to buy food, I did not encounter anyone. Also, letters to be mailed were lying on the table.

I understood that I had to return home with my basket. I went to the train hoping to get as far as Asipovitch where you could get the train to Minsk.

As it turned out I did not get to Asipovitch because it became known that the trains from there were not going to Minsk. Asipovitch had already been taken by the Poles. I therefore went back to Slutsk, but the memory of that experience remains strong in my mind.

At the train station in Slutsk there was a huge crowd of people who had run away from the town. They were waiting for the train to be permitted to go to Asipovitch. Meanwhile a group of Cossacks arrived: cavalry who tied their horses to the trees and went to the station building. Suddenly in the nearby woods we heard shooting. The frightened crowd thought that the shooting was from the approaching Poles. There was an indescribable commotion. The crowd of Jews and Christians decided in haste to go back to town. They used fire wagons and horses and many went on foot. The word Pole was like a "scarecrow" and it was no wonder that it caused a panic and a wild race. In the meantime the horses that were tied to the trees tore away from their bridles and ran in an elemental gallop over the wooden slats near the station building.

The scene became unbelievable; young and old were running on the highway, which was, as far as the eye could see, overfilled with screaming and scared people.

I did not allow myself to join the hysterical throng immediately since the shooting had stopped. Now I understood that I had no reason to run back to Slutsk, when I had to go in an opposite direction.

Suddenly I saw someone running along with the mob; my basket in his hand. A sudden uncontrollable urge made me rise from my place and join the running crowd back to Slutsk. It did not take more than a second that I became part of the human lava which flowed, as if from a hot volcano eruption, over the highway to Slutsk.

And so I returned to Slutsk and waited with the entire Jewish population for the arrival of the Poles.

A few years later I was a student at the Free Polish University in Warsaw, where I attended a seminar on socialism by a well-known sociologist Ludwik Kosziwicki. It brought to mind the energy of the group at the train station, where its "herd force" affected my entire individual attitude about that experience. All this remains from that distant time but is strongly imbedded in my memory.

From all the examples of which were presented by Professor L. Kosziwicki about group feelings, my experience had the greatest impact on him.

The arrival of the Poles in Slutsk immediately brought a pogrom and robberies. In the city, fear ruled. The newly arrived Polish legionnaires and the local Poles both were guilty of these robberies and also White Russians who gave way to their brutish instincts.

[Page 348]

When things quieted down a little, the Jews were still afraid to show themselves in the streets and at night they just sat locked in their houses.

The bandits really liked to go at night, and what could the helpless Jews do against these night robbers? They used their common sense. As soon as a robber attacked a house where Jews lived, a great shriek arose from the residents. The shrieks slowly carried over to the neighboring houses and eventually to the entire street, then to the second street and the third street; a chorus of shrieks and screams to the heavens for help.

The result of these shrieks and screams was to drive away the attackers and this way the Jews escaped robbery and often death. It was told that when a delegation from the Jewish community protested to the Polish regime, the agent had to confess that he was helpless in the fight against the *saldatstva* which raged over the city. The shrieks and outcry in the night from the Jewish homes and streets were able to do what the Polish commander could not accomplish.

It is interesting that a year later when I was in various places in Vilna, I once again heard the shrieks, screams, and moans from the homes and courtyards, as a means to scare and expel the Polish attackers.

Vilna, at that time, was taken by General Zeligowski legionnaires, and again there were pogroms, assaults, and robberies of the unprotected Jewish community. The old technique of shrieks, moans, screams of the helpless Jewish was used as a means of self-protection.

From that time I also remember how a group of Polish soldiers once broke in through the kitchen in the house of the Harkavis. All they did, to our joy, was to scare us.

A few weeks later I went by wagon at dawn to Hrudi. I used this opportunity to travel this way in order to get to Minsk. We traveled the entire day. It was an exceptionally nice day, beginning of autumn, but we were taken aback by the numbers of people walking along way. At one point we were stopped by a Polish convoy and searched. It was a miracle that I remembered earlier to get rid of some incriminating items. I wore my student jacket with the shiny buttons. One of the convoy leaders asked me where I was going and said it was good to study in Warsaw.

Late in the evening we arrived in Timkovichi. Again we were overcome with the dead silence in the town. Soon a Jew arrived who took us to the rabbi. There we found a crowd of frightened Jews, who had pleasure at hearing our story of how we traveled an entire day from Slutsk and nothing happened to us.

Finally we arrived at Nesvizh. There I looked for a friend from the Zion Council by the name of Litvin, and we went to the train station to go to Minsk. On the train I already met new and not frightened Jews, who were carrying material from Warsaw. They ate white bread smeared with butter, which was for me a great wonder. In Minsk my friends met me with outstretched arms.

[Page 349]

Hasidim in Slutsk

Translated by Tamara Selden z"l with missing gaps filled in by Jerrold Landau

> Hasidim in Slutsk according to Dubnow's book "The History of Hasidism"
> A story of Slutsk from the book The Jewish Community of Hasidism"
> The preacher Reb Israel Laybe and his fight against Hasidism.
> Reb Zalman's responses to the question of Rabbi Avigdor.

The beginning of Hasidim of Slutsk in the 20th century

Two rich brothers who came from Galicia lived in Slutsk. They were in charge of leasing all the estates of the Polish Duke Radziwill. These two men were known to Shlomo Myman by the Polish name of Diershavtsi. They ruled over many town Jews who had leased taverns and stores from them. The influential brothers kept track of their activities in the leased places. From time to time they raised the rents, not concerning themselves with their tenants' complaints. Some became poverty stricken. People called the brothers tyrants.

A Hasidisher legend tells: Once the wife of one of the brothers invited her landsman, the *Bal Shem Tov,* to come to visit their sumptuous home for Chanukah. It was designed by a famous architect. The wise man stayed for three weeks, but felt that the *Litvitsher* community viewed him with suspicion and did not believe in his miraculous signs. When he was leaving the wife asked him how long would the good fortune of the family endure? His answer was: twenty-two years. It came to pass that after twenty-two years the Duke's wrath became so great that he threw them in jail.

Fragment translated from Dubnow's - The History of the Hasidim

The Besh't in Slutsk

There was a merchant, Reb Shmuel Slutsker, who traveled around to various places in Poland. When he was in Mezibozh he met the Besh't, who was a holy woman. Reb Shmuel followed him everywhere and became an intimate. When he came home he told his wife of the greatness of this man. She asked him to invite the Besh't to Slutsk. He did so, and arranged for someone to bring him to Slutsk.

Reb Shmuel had been in Kiev and could not get back in time. The Besh't immediately asked that the butcher should bring his ritual slaughtering knife in order to see if it was kosher. Reb Shmuel wife's Tybele sent for the butcher. The Besh't looked at him and seemed pleased. However, the butcher became resentful when the Besh't continued to look at him. He decided that he would play a joke on him and would see if the Besh't understood or not. He left to get the knife and rubbed it against his dirty rubber belt. Then he took two witnesses to watch him slaughter and inspect an animal for impurities and make it kosher. The witnesses had not seen what he had done with the knife before the demonstration. When Friday evening came, all the people gathered at the table with the Besh't. The butcher was also present. They ate fish and then were served meat broth. The Besh't took a little on his spoon and smelled it. He said it smelled bad and put it aside. They had no meat the entire Sabbath. The people regretted this very much. On the third Sabbath of his visit he tasted some meat and declared it not kosher and that the ritual slaughter was unfit.

[Page 350]

The butcher presented his witnesses who said that all had been properly done. There was a commotion, and everyone was embarrassed. The witnesses, although innocent, were afraid of the holy man, so they went to the *Docseh* and pleaded with her to give them some special power. She said she would, but only for one day. She gave them a lock for the door where the Besh't was staying and they posted guards at all the other doors. They did not allow anyone to go in or out. After *Havdalah* was over, the Besh't told his servant to bring his horse which was in a barn attached to the house, and he got on. When they came to the door, it lifted off the ground with the posts, and they rode away. The guards did not see or hear anything, and the Besh't rode from there traveling a great distance by occult means. He was home the next day. He told Reb Laybe to go to Slutsk and tell the people certain things. First he was to tell them he was a great preacher and would give a fine sermon. This pleased the people in Slutsk very much and they gave him thirty pieces of gold. He stayed for three Sabbaths and gave a different sermon each time. He was highly praised.

When the fourth Sabbath came, the people were gathered in the shul. He asked them to clap their hands, which they did. He then raised his eyes and asked where the butcher was and why he had not come to hear his sermon. Reb Laybe would not speak until he arrived. Two sextons went to get him, but when they arrived they saw that the windows and doors were closed. They banged on the door, but there was no answer. Returning to the shul the men told Reb Laybe that no one answered. He then told them to go and break down the door to see what was happening inside the house. He instructed the sextons to search the house thoroughly, and so they did. They found him laying with his daughter and dragged him to the shul. The sextons told what they had discovered. The townspeople were shocked. He never appeared to be a sinner. Reb Laybe began to scream: "Sinner, confess what you did when the Besh't was here." He confessed that he had made the slaughter knife unkosher. The meat was not pure. Now everyone knew that the Besh't had spoken the truth. Reb Laybe said that wise men knew one sin led to another and now the butcher was guilty of two sins. The merits of wise men remind us that we should beware of doing evil Amen!

(The Jewish community of Hasidim)

The preacher Reb Israel Laybe and his battle against Hasidism

Between the 18th and early 19th centuries the opponents of Hasidism journeyed through *Liteh, Raysin, Galicia,* Poland and Germany, let by Reb Israel Laybe . He preached his sermons with a sparkling spirit and read from many books.

Reb Israel son of Yehudah Laybe was, as it turned out, a Slutsker. He was the author of the book *Zamir Aritzim* 1795. His followers called him by the name Reb Israel Slutsker. Until the year 1892 he took the place of preacher in *Mohilev-Raysin.* Afterwards he was *Dyan* and Preacher in *Novaridak.*

His opposition to the Hasidim was frightening. You could see how great his influence was on young people.

He went to see Reb Zalman, who favored the Hasidim, to debate with him. Reb Laybe felt that the Hasidim would harm Jewry and the principles of discipline. His feeling was that the gentile world would recognize and be grateful to the rabbis who uncover the superficial activity in a minority of their people; that the Hasidim were complainers, money lovers, and spread superstition. Reb Zalman was greatly angered at these remarks.

Then Reb Laybe wrote *Sefer Vicoah* against the Hasidim and went to Warsaw to have it published. This was the year 1797, after which the *Vilna Gaon* came out with his famous protest against the Hasidim. The Gaon's envoy Reb Sedeha, who was the spokesman for the Misnagdim, had permitted the Lithuanian preacher to speak against the group and gave his approval to print the book in Sivan (May/June) 1797.

In the month of *Av* (July/Aug) Reb Israel traveled through Slutsk and received approval from the the community. He distributed his book and a brochure "*Tavit Tsadikim*" by Reb Israel Laybe, Warsaw 1798.

The Hasidim bought many of the books and tore them apart until nothing was left of them.

[Page 351]

It was told that fanatics awaited the preacher Reb Israel Laybe. They screamed and cursed him on the streets of Warsaw and in other towns. Supporters told of the opposition of his book "Zamir Aritim". It showed the excellence of the writing of Reb Israel. It was without rivalry and he was a zealot for the heavenly host. The cursed Hasidim spilled his blood like water-threw stones, tore his books, stamped on him as if he were the clay of the streets, and called him preacher of foolishness.

* * *

The Russian government was unwilling to intercede in this battle between the Misnagdim and the Hasidim in 1800-1801.

Of Reb Zalman's responses to the questions of Rabbi Avigdor, only two were noted in the government newspapers. The responses to the 18th and 19th questions were that the holy religious community of Slutsk was the enemy of the Hasidim. They committed great persecutions of the Lubavitsher Hasidim. When the crime became known a regulation was issued by the Minsker court to protect the Hasidim.

(These were the illusions of the Hasidim regarding persecution by the Slutsker Misnagdim. The leader of the Hasidim was Mordechai Liachawiter).

* * *

A Hasidic legend tells: When the Besh't came out of exile he went to Slutsk. However the Slutsker residents did not welcome him at first.

He warned the townspeople not ever to allow the Hasidim to come there. The warning was heeded, and Slutsk remained one of four known towns where Hasidism did not want to put down one foot. The other three towns were Kosove, Ruzhany, Pruzhany. The townspeople did not wish to live to hear the first morning prayer according to Nusah Sefard. Many generations passed and the Nusah Sefard was not heard in Slutsk.

* * *

In the beginning of the twentieth century there were a small group of Hasidim in Slutsk and their leader was Reb Pincus Pinye Kantaravitsh. They did not have a place to gather for prayer. After the residents of Slutsk had built the *Mishnayos* synagogue, they gave the small house where they used to pray to the Hasidim.

The Hasidim were very pleased and included their enemies in their prayers for a *yahrzeit (*prayer for the dead), *L'shem Tikon,* a prayer said at midnight. Then they would have a shot of whiskey. The Hasidisher house was always full on the night of the festival of *Shmini Atzeret.* They always carried the Torahs in procession on that night instead, of on the festival of *Simchat Torah,* as the Misnagdim did. Afterwards they celebrated this great moment with liquor, feeling it was quite appropriate.

And it was told that every time someone passed the house, day or night, the Hasidim pleaded with them to come inside because they needed to complete the minyon.

Regarding this request people wondered why the Hasidim waited for another person to complete the required number. One of them explained: It took a few Misnagdim to take the place of a tenth man who was a Hasid.

* * *

It was told that two Hasidim from *Retsitseh* met in Slutsk in an Inn. It was on the 19th of Kislev (Nov./Dec.) and they wanted to pray together and celebrate the feast in memory of the liberation of the Rebbe, the author of The Tanya. To get a minyon of Hasidim in Slutsk was not always easy, so they put a bottle of liquor on the table and desserts to lure some guests, and it did work. It was almost midnight when they finished praying and they burst into wild celebration and frightened one of the Jews who had just arrived. He asked where the doctor was, but instead of answering they offered him another drink. The doctor was also in the room. and joined in the drinking. Soon they were all very drunk.

This celebration was beyond estimation. They had completed their prayers and let themselves go wild. The wife of the Jew, who had asked for the doctor, was waiting for him to bring him to see their sick child. She waited and waited and finally decided to go look for him.

On her way she heard singing and clapping. She looked through the window of the Inn and saw that her husband was among the dancers. Angrily she went inside and fell upon him. " I sit alone and worry. Our child is ill and burns like fire and you dance!" Her drunken husband staggered and yelled, calling her a foolish woman. "The night is still young and it does the heart good to dance."

* * *

Slutsk was and remained a purely Misnagdic Lithuanian town. Slutsker Jews remained faithful to the school of thought of the Vilne Gaon, a Misnaged. They were strongly against Hasidism, which had spread widely in the Ukraine and Poland in the 1800s. They often joked : When there was a minyon of Hasidim in Slutsk and a rabbi, then the Messiah will come. That is the way it was and remained until the Soviet Messiah and the Nazi destruction.

[Page 352]

Folklore

Rabbis

Translated by Tamara Selden z"l with missing gaps filled in by Jerrold Landau

In his youth Reb Israel, son of Reb Yossele Slutsker, wanted to become a Hasid. He ran away from Slutsk, from his father, a traditionalist to *Kydenov* and sought out a rabbi. There he attached himself to Hasidim and became one of their number. The Hasidim thought very well of him because Reb Israel was a prodigy. He was very hot-headed but his father was a traditionalist. He did not remain there long. The Hasidim did not really care for someone from a Misnaged root.

During that short period with the Hasidim Reb Israel recited a Torah portion on the "Splendor of the Sabbath", which was very deep and difficult to understand or explain. The crowd of Hasidim did not understand it. After *Havdalah* several men went over to the Rabbi to ask him to explain the Torah portion.

Yes, said Reb Israel, I will explain. He directed them to the window. He pointed to a hole and asked them; What do you see there? A hole, they answered. – right said Reb Israel. Today I will take a tool and make another hole in it. What will that be called? – A hole in a hole. – A Hasid seized the idea.

Ah! So this is meaning of the "Splendor of the Sabbath."

* * *

Reb Mendele Slutsker was a Gaon of the people. However, he had never been a rabbi, and never wanted to be one. For many years he was in Reb Iserke's school. He ran a Yeshiva and was occupied with Torah *"Tsvelftl":* The twelve subjects that the rich Iserlen felt were imperative. Reb Mendele's custom was to go every day with his students to the house of Iserlin for a drink. Reb Mendele often made merry. There was tea for everyone, as much as they wanted. When they were finished he would then have his.

Once an emissary came to Slutsk and went to see the rich man. He saw a group of Jews sitting at a table drinking tea, and a small Jew invited everyone who came in to join them at the table. The emissary thought he certainly was a servant of the rich man. He sat down with the people and asked for a glass of tea. As he was an avid tea drinker, he asked for glass after glass. He spoke to Reb Mendele as if he were indeed a servant. The people stared at him but no one said a word.

Sabbath morning, after praying, it was the custom to go again to the house of the rich man for the *Kiddush.* When everyone was seated around the table Iserlin and Reb Mendele would arrive. Everyone would stand up and wish the rich man and the head of the yeshiva a good Sabbath. The emissary had gone there with the people and he saw that the rich man was with the little Jew. Then to his surprise everyone stood up to wish him a good Sabbath.

He then became very curious.

Who, he asks, is that Jew?

He is, several answered, Reb Mendele.

It becomes dark before his eyes. He had treated Reb Mendele as a servant. He ran immediately to Reb Mendele.

Please forgive me, I have no excuse. I did not know....

What offense have you made? Reb Mendele. asked.

I did not know who you were, said the emissary. I did not treat you properly.

I do not understand, said Reb Mendele with humility. How have you sinned against me that you ask my pardon. You asked me for a glass of tea, so I gave you one. On the contrary I have to thank you. I had the opportunity to do a good deed.

[Page 353]

Reb Yoshe-Ber as Slutsker Rabbi

by Chaykil Lunski

Translated by Tamara Selden z"l with missing gaps filled in by Jerrold Landau

The publisher of the writing was the librarian of the well-known Strashan Library in Vilna.

The grandchild of the great Gaon Reb Mordechay'le Ashmener, or Slonimer was he himself a great student and wise man. Lunski had the opportunity to study with him and familiarize himself with Judaism, Jewish Gaonim and prominent people. Chaykil Lunski gave out the following work *Toldot Hagaon, Rabbi Mordechai Veizel*(Hebrew), Vilna 5677, *Tipusim Vetzelilim MehaGhetto HaVilnai*, Vilna 5681: Gaonim and Prominent People from the Near Past, Vilna 5691. He put an entire series in the newspapers about this. He also did a series on the same subject in the religious weekly paper, "The Word" which gave the chapter from the holy text about the era of Reb Yoshe-Ber in Slutsk. In the thirty years that Mr. Peretz Wernick was the chief editor of the New York Morning Journal, he was strongly interested in publishing the series in his newspaper. The arrangements were made through the writer of these lines, a personal friend of the two great men, who incidentally did not know each other personally.

Mr. Wernick respected his Vilna colleague and his treasure of Yiddish folklore. Unfortunately, Mr. Peretz Wernick died and the matter became null and void.

There should be a moment for the noble soul of Mr. Chaykil Lunski which came together with the heart-felt and Yiddish Vilna.

Introduction

When the beloved Slutsker rabbi, the Goan Reb Yossele Peimer, died in 1864 the community began to look for a rabbi for Slutsk. This was easier to say than to accomplish. A rabbi in Slutsk had to be a worldly Gaon, because almost all the earlier rabbis were like that. Furthermore he had to possess other great talents and above all cleverness.

The leaders of the community had an eye on the Rabbi Yosef Dov the son of Rabbi Yitzchak Zeev Halevi. He was not a rabbi but rather the chief of a Yeshiva in Volozhin, and because of this his name rang all over the Yiddish world.

Exactly one year before he had an argument with the most important person in the chief yeshiva in Volozhin, Reb Hersh Laybe, or as they called him the *Netzi'v.* This had caused a feud. which spread from the town to the *Litvisher* Torah-world. The feud became so strongly felt that the entire issue was given over to a rabbinical court, in which the Gaon participated: Reb Yossele Slutsker together with Gaonim Reb David Tebl Minsker, Reb Velvele, the Vilna city preacher, and the youngest off the group rabbi Yitzchak Elchanan, who was then rabbi in Novhorodok.

Despite the greatness of the rabbinical court and the confidence which both saintly men had in it, Reb Yoshe-Ber still felt that their judgment was only a compromise and he was not pleased.

As a grandchild of Reb Chaim Volozhiner, and himself a great Gaon, clever and outstanding with an excellent character, the Slutsker leaders considered if he was a proper candidate for their rabbi and sent to him a "letter" inviting him to come to Slutsk.

N.VV

After the argument Reb Yoshe-Ber did not want to be head of the Yeshiva in Volozhin. Moreover, since he had later received a "Rabbinic License" from Slutsk, he took the job and became rabbi in the year 1868.

In Slutsk he became very beloved., despite the fact that he was a leader with a very strong hand. He befriended the poor and above all the bright students.

At that time an evil decree was issued from the recruiter. It was understood that they would take mostly children from the poor families, because the rich would pay many hundred ruble to save their children. Reb Yoshe-Ber put all his efforts into helping the poor and good students, He never rested and day and night he ran around collecting money in order to rescue the poor from military service.

They tell: once the recruiters grabbed a Yeshiva boy, but he escaped from them and he ran into a synagogue and hid himself under Reb Yoshe-Ber's prayer shawl. Reb Yoshe-Ber was afraid they would punish him for allowing this. He told the young man to hide elsewhere and later he would buy him a receipt to keep him out of the army. The Yeshiva boy was afraid to go away, so the rabbi told him to go hide in his house.

[Page 354]

The recruiters knew about this and went to Reb Yoshe-Ber's house. Their leader went in with a brazen attitude to convince the Rabbi to hand over the young man.

When the rabbi heard this, he called out to his son to get a stick. I will show this young man what comes from running away The Rabbi's anger and the raised stick somehow affected the leader, so he opened the door and shouted to the others: No one is here. From now on we will know that a scholar is wise in many ways.

* * *

I also heard that once a young man came to Reb Yoshe-Ber who was not too bright. He began to cry and begged the rabbi to save him from the military service. Reb Yoshe-Ber immediately ran to a rich man and borrowed money from him. Later the rich man came to him with complaints: The young man is supposed to go in the army. Reb Yoshe-Ber answered:-- If I wanted to make him a rabbi, then you could complain that he is too stupid to learn. Instead I made him a non-soldier and you could complain that he would not make a very good soldier either.

Reb Yoshe-Ber devoted himself, not only to ransoming, but also to generally assisting the poor. He literally would give away his last mouthful of food.

* * *

It was told[1]: Once a wagon driver, who was a resident of Slutsk, came to Rabbi Yoshe-Ber before Passover. He wept with bitter tears, "A misfortune has occurred, Rabbi! I was idle an entire winter, not earning a groszy. Now, before Passover, when people need to travel and one can earn something for the festival, my horse has fallen down."

"Go to my barn," R Yoshe-Ber told him, "Take my cow, go to the market, and exchange it for a horse."

The eyes of the wagon driver lit up. He did not hesitate. He went to the barn, took the rabbi's cow, and set out with it. A while later, the Rebbetzin entered the barn to milk the cow, but it was not there. She ran into the house and cried, "Yoshe-Ber, our cow has been stolen!"

"It was not stolen," responded Rabbi Yoshe-Ber innocently, "It is here."

"Where is it?" she asked.

"If the Jew has not yet exchanged it, it is with the Jew," responded Rabbi Yoshe-Ber. She looked at him, "What Jew? What exchange?"

Rabbi Yoshe-Ber explained the entire story to her, that he had given the animal to a poor Jew, so he can earn his bread. She continued on with her complaints:

"Tell me, we had one cow. Where will we get a drop of milk?"

"See," responded Rabbi Yoshe-Ber, "You have bread, you also want milk, while the poor Jew, unfortunately also has no bread? Is that proper?"

Later, the Slutsk tax collector sent him a cow with milk.

Several weeks later, the tax collector came to Rabbi Yoshe-Ber with a request that he issue a ban on meat slaughtered from the outside. Rabbi Yoshe-Ber did not agree. He immediately called the Rebbetzin and said, "Send the animal back to the tax collector immediately, and pay him for the time that you milked it…."

* * *

Once, a Slutsk wagon driver came to Rabbi Yoshe-Ber and cried, "Rabbi! My horse died, what shall I do?" Rabbi Yoshe-Ber asked him, "How much does a horse cost?" he responded, "Fifty rubles." Rabbi Yoshe-Ber called out, I have fifty rubles of salary with me. Take it and purchase a horse. When the people of the city found out that he had given away his entire salary and had nothing with which to live, they began to pay his salary to the Rebbetzin.

* * *

Once before Passover, a Jew came to Rabbi Yoshe-Ber with the following question, "Rabbi, can I fulfil the commandment of the four cups with milk?"

"Are you perhaps sick?" asked Rabbi Yoshe-Ber to the Jew.

"I am healthy, blessed be G-d," responded the Jew. "Wine, however," he said with a half mouth, "Is far too expensive for me."

Rabbi Yoshe-Ber called in the Rebbetzin and told her to give twenty-five rubles to the Jew. Naturally, at first the Jew did not want to take this money. He had come to ask a question, and not, Heaven forbid, to beg. Rabbi Yoshe-Ber, however, urged him strongly and said that the was giving this as a loan. When the Blessed G-d will help him, he can return the loan. Then he took the money.

When the Jew left, the Rebbetzin asked him, "Why did you give him a full twenty-five rubes, when one can purchase wine for the four cups for two or three rubles."

"What do you not understand?," responded Rabbi Yoshe-Ber, "You heard that the Jew asked whether he could fulfil the commandment of the four cups with milk. If he had

[Page 355]

provisions for Passover like other people, with fish and meat, he would not be able to drink milk at the Seder. This was a sign that he was unable to make Passover, so I gave him twenty-five rubles for Passover.

* * *

The following story was told about Rabbi Yoshe-Ber's generosity.

Once, Rabbi Yoshe-Ber was traveling from Slutsk to Volozhin. They had sent the town *shamash* with him with fifteen rubles for expenses, for they did not trust him with money, as he was liable to give it all away for charity.

Along the way, as they were in the wagon, the *shamash* noticed that Rabbi Yoshe-Ber was looking at an old Jew with great joy, giving him great honor and calling him rebbe. The *shamash* asked him who this rabbi was. Rabbi Yoshe-Ber responded, "That is the rabbi who taught me the *alef-beit*. He came to me asking that I help him. He has to marry off a daughter. Therefore, give him the money for expenses, so that I can fulfil the mitzvah of *hachnasas kalla* [providing for poor brides].

The *shamash* called out, "Rabbi, from where will I get money for expenses?" Rabbi Yoshe-Ber responded, "We will borrow." The *shamash* asked further, "Who will lend to us along the way."

When Rabbi Yoshe-Ber saw that the *shamash* wanted to thwart him, he said to him, "I order you to give my rebbe fifty rubles…"

* * *

Once, Rabbi Yoshe-Ber spent the Sabbath in an inn while on a journey. In the inn, the two loaves of bread for the third Sabbath meal [*shalosh seudos*] were not there for Rabbi Yoshe-Ber. They hurried to purchase bread. Rabbi Yoshe-Ber sat and waited. "Rabbi," one of the guests called out, "We know that one can fulfil the commandment of the third Sabbath meal with words of Torah, as well. What is the commotion today? Tell us some words of Torah. You will fulfil the third Sabbath meal, and we will hear a good piece of Torah." "You are correct," said Rabbi Yoshe-Ber. "However, I am afraid that my Torah words will be diverted, and I will remain both without Torah and without the third Sabbath meal…"

The Difference Between Hasidim and Misnagdim

Rabbi Yoshe-Ber used to give the following explanation about why *Misnagdim* fast on the day of yahrzeit, and Hasidim make a feast with a *lechayim*.

Before the giving of the Torah, when Jews did not know how to learn, and they saw that Moses our Teacher was late, they surmised that he had passed away, and they made a feast: "And the people sat down to eat" [Exodus 32:6]. Year later, when Moses our Teacher indeed passed away, it was already after the giving of the Torah. Jews knew how to learn, and they did not make a feast. They only observed mourning, as it states in the verse: "And the Children of Israel wept over Moses." [Deuteronomy 34:8].

Who is Crazy?

Rabbi Yoshe-Ber was not always of the same mind as the Slutsker tycoons. Once, a women came to him weeping, "Rabbi, have mercy. I had a dream that my only son had gone crazy."

"Do not cry, my daughter. This is a sign that he will become a tycoon… Because all the tycoons are crazy."

The rabbi said this about the tycoons of Slutsk. At that time, he remarked about the tycoons:

"You, wealthy people of Slusk, interpret the dream of the woman. Tell her that her son will become a rabbi... Because you believe that the rabbi is crazy..."

* * *

Aside from being a genius and a philanthropist, Rabbi Yoshe-Ber was a wonderful Tzadik, holy and pure – so much so that he was considered to be a miracle worker. Various stories were told about this.

Rabbi Yoshe-Ber was also awesome in his exactitude in fulfilling the commandments. He was a wonderful Tzadik. For example, it is told that he used to harvest the *shmura* wheat[2] himself, and grind it with a hand grinder. Then he would put it [i.e. the matzos] in the oven for such a long time that it would be half burnt. He would eat no more than a few *kezayits*[3]. Incidentally, he also had the custom, stemming from his great-grandfather Rabbi Chaim Volozhiner, of dipping a *kezayit* of matzo into wine at the Seder and eating it, in order to demonstrate that moistened matzo is permitted[4], in accordance with the custom of the Vilna Gaon. Not only did Rabbi Yoshe-Ber occupy himself with mitzvot himself, but he also searched out others to merit them with mitzvot.

* * *

It is told: Once an emissary [for charity] came to Rabbi Yoshe-Ber on the eve of the Sabbath. Rabbi Yoshe-Ber invited him to stay with him for the Sabbath. On Friday before candle lighting, Rabbi Yoshe-Ber said to his guest: "You should forgive me, I am asking for five kopecks from my guest." On Saturday night after *Havdalah*, Rabbi Yoshe-Ber gave the emissary the five kopecks. The guest recognized that this was the same coin that he had given to the rabbi. He said, "Do not be offended, Rabbi, if I ask: Why did you borrow the five kopecks from me? I see that you did not even use it." Rabbi Yoshe-Ber answered, "You are certainly a travelling man. You always travel around,

[Page 356]

when can you fulfil the commandment of giving charity? When does a Jew ask you for a loan? I wanted to grant you the merit of that mitzvah..."

* * *

Reb Yoshe-Ber once came to Minsk for a visit. The Minsker scholars came to welcome him. They wanted to discuss the Torah. Among the scholars there was a young man, a Minsker shopkeeper, who once was his student. When he heard that his Rebbi was in the city, he immediately came to see him. Reb Yoshe-Ber befriended him and they sat together.

– How are you? – He asked him, – I live well and have not much to complain about. I am healthy and make a good living.

They sat and talked with the other people.

A little while later Reb Yoshe-Ber asked the young man again:

– How are you? – Blessed be the Lord. – The young man answered again that he was healthy, made a living, and they talked further. Several minutes later, the Rebbi asks the young man how he is for the third time.

– I have no problem answered the young man, a little annoyed that he was asked the same question three times. I told you that I am healthy and make a good living.

– No! said Reb Yoshe-Ber – You answer me only about practical matters. I asked you how you are and you tell me you are healthy and have enough money. What I want to know is do you give charity?. Do you study Torah? Are you involved in Yiddishkeit?

There was a rich contractor in Slutsk and he was very religious, but also very stingy. He sometimes went to the Rebbi's study house to pray, reciting his prayers. Only donations were difficult for him to give. Reb Yoshe-Ber knew him well, but not one time did he make a donation because of his stinginess.

"Kol Nidre" when most of the people went home and only a small group of earnest Jews remained in the shul for an entire night, the rich man stayed also. He said the hymn of the unity of G-d with the people. He recited with the people a few daily assignments of psalms and made sure that Reb Yoshe-Ber should hear this.

Before morning while the people rested up a little, in order to get ready for the morning prayers, he went over to the Rabbi and called out: – What do you say Rebbi? It is hard to be here up a whole night and stand on our feet.

Listen – said Reb Yoshe-Ber. You are a contractor and work with the government quite a bit. You have knowledge about the military and the way it works. I will ask you a question. There are a variety of sections. There are horsemen and artillery. Each has its own job and each its own place. So I will ask you what happens if one soldier does the job that is not his. For instance, if a horseman decides to become one of the foot soldiers?

This soldier receives severe punishment – replied the Jew. He broke discipline. Why do you ask Rabbi?

– Because this applies to you. We know that the Kingdom of earth has its counterpart in the Kingdom of Heaven. The Rabbis of the people also have different tasks: to teach Torah, Service and Charity. You had been given control over wealth and your job was to give charity. Your job was to give generously to help poor people and follow the law of the Torah. Otherwise you could not lie in your soft bed and sleep. Saying prayers and learning is for the poor people who become soldiers in the mastery of Torah. What did you do? You went away from the job of charity to stay with the poor Jews an entire night. It was preposterous, unheard of. You did not hear what it was that you should do on their behalf. So what do you think is coming to you?

One time the tax collector fell in on Reb Yoshe-Ber with great shouting. – Rabbi they are bringing meat from another place into the city. What is all the commotion about? asked the Rabbi.

– Let us not have any anger smiled Reb Yoshe-Ber According to the logic of a minori ad majus (an inference from minor to major). It is quite understandable (with sarcasm) since we eat the meat of the slaughterers we know, we surely are permitted to eat the meat from slaughterers we do not know.

Reb Yoshe-Ber did not approve of the excessively religious people. One time he saw that one of them had washed before eating and threw away two full quarts of water.

– A pity on this Jew, smiled Reb Yoshe.

– He throws he entire reverence for G-d out with the slops.

[Page 357]

What is the novelty in this? – asked Reb Yoshe-Ber. The truth always wins out! – Rabbi, what are you talking about?, asked the members of the congregation who were observing him. You call heresy the Truth!!! – "Please understand me," responded Reb Yoshe-Ber, "the heretics are truly heretics and that is why they are successful, but the honest Jews are not truly honest."

While Reb Yoshe-Ber was rabbi in Slutsk, there was in Minsk a great Cantor, who sometimes gave lessons for the students. Reb Yoshe-Ber thought very well of him. He always praised him, saying he was a rarity, a distinguished teacher.

One time the Cantor said to Reb Yoshe-Ber, with a smile:

– You know Rabbi, when you praise my teaching, you actually do me a disservice, but not on purpose. – For instance? – asked Reb Yoshe-Ber. The people, – said the Cantor, always hear your praise of my teaching. Therefore, my cantorial singing is not worthy of praise?

– If this is so, said the Rabbi, then I must consult some experts about your cantorial singing. If I am caught in a lie regarding your cantorial singing, then they also will not believe what I say about your teaching.

* * *

Reb Yoshe's second wife died in Slutsk. It was told that when his wife died Reb Yoshe-Ber began to examine his actions. Perhaps he was very stressed out. Maybe he should do something to honor Reb Hersh Laybe after the quarrel in the Volozhin Yeshiva. He decided that he wanted to give something special to Reb Hersh Laybe, in order that he would forgive him.

As Reb Hersh Laybe knew that Reb Yoshe -Ber was in great pain. he came to Slutsk to comfort the mourner. Reb Yoshe-Ber told him what would like to give him whatever he wanted, in the hope that he would forgive him.

Reb Hersh Lab answered, give me your son Reb Chaim for a son-in-law. So Reb Chaim became the son-in-law of Reb Refael – Reb Hersh Layb's son-in-law.

Later Reb Yoshe-Ber was married for the third time to a woman from Warsaw.

In 1875 Reb Yoshe-Ber left Slutsk and went to Warsaw, where his third wife lived.

There he received great respect and they immediately wanted him to serve as Rabbi. However, since he had not been born in Poland he could not become their Rabbi. It was simply not possible. Instead he became the head of the Yeshiva of the Talmud Society, where for three years he gave a lessons in the study house. and all the great and honored people from Warsaw came to listen to his Torah discussion .

* * *

It is told that a Warsaw rich man, a Hasid traveled to visit a Rabbi in another town. Conversationally the Rabbi said to the rich man: Do you know that now there is a Great Gaon in Warsaw? The rich man asked who he was. The Rabbi answered that it was the Slutsker Rabbi....

When the rich man was in Warsaw he sent a message to Reb Yoshe -Beer that from that day on he wanted the honor of paying the salary he needed to live. Reb Yoshe-Ber did not want to take this money. It did not seem right to do so.

* * *

It was told that while he was in Warsaw without salary or a rabbinate, he once met a Jew on the train from that good city Brisk. Since Brisk was searching for a Rabbi, the man began to discuss it with R 'Yoshe-Ber asking him to consider taking the job as the Brisker Rabbi.

First, some years ago when Reb Yehosha Laybe left Brisk, a delegation of Brisker Jews came to Reb Yoshe-Ber with deliberation to become their Rabbi.

When this was heard in Warsaw, there was a great to do, and by no means did they want to lose the great Gaon the Gerer Rabbi. The Gerer Rabbi was also called the *Sfas Emes* which was the name of his writings. All the rich and prominent people of Warsaw organized to ensure that Reb Yoshe-Ber remained in Warsaw. A delegation of these people went to plead with Reb Yoshe-Ber not to leave Warsaw and go to Brisk. A feud began between Warsaw and Brisk regarding the Slutsker Rabbi. When the Brisker people saw that Reb Yoshe-Ber began to waver about coming to them, they said to him: Rebbe, thirty thousand Jews are waiting for you.!

Hearing these words, he put on his coat: Thirty thousand Jews waiting for me!

In the year 1878 he became the Rabbi in Brisk.

* * *

After Reb Yoshe-Ber left Slutsk and Reb Jacob David came there, they happen to meet traveling in the same wagon. They, of course, talked about the Torah.

[Page 358]

They both argued, and Reb Jacob left the wagon and sat on the coach box. next to the driver and this is the way they arrived in town. The townspeople were astonished: Two rabbis on a trip and one sits in the coach and the other sits on the coach box.

They said shalom to the one who sat on the coach box. Shalom Aleichem Rabbi. Where do you come from and who is the Rabbi sitting in the coach? – I am -- Reb Yoshe-Ber Brisker**Error! Bookmark not defined.** who sits in the wagon. and it is not according to his status for Reb Jacob David that I should sit with him, so I sit with the coachman.

Don't believe him – Reb Yoshe-Ber sticks out his head and yells, I am Reb Yoshe-Ber and he is Reb Jacob David!

– Rebbi – says Reb Jacob David, it will not help you. They know your modest person.

Reb Jacob David

While Rebbi Jacob David was rabbi in Slutsk, he was always arguing with the town that they did not hold him in esteem, and the shopkeepers always caused him trouble!

Once the townspeople asked him – Why are you sitting in Slutsk? Why don't you look for another rabbinate?

I will tell you – answers Reb Jacob David – In Hell there are seven divisions. Why are there seven? Is there not enough suffering with torture for evildoers with one division in hell? The answer is this. When the sinner become used to his

division of Hell, he ceased to suffer so much. So he is sent to another division of Hell with other kinds of torture and suffering.

Slutsk is really Hell for me. However, I am already used to it. A new town will be a new Hell for me with new suffering. –

Reb Meyer Slutsker

He was a people's Gaon and a totally good man. He was the rabbi in Slutsk for a few years.

When his grandchild, a girl, began going to gymnasium, Reb Meyer, said to the rabbis. – If I could not – he said – be a teacher in the right moral way with my own children, how can I be a teacher to an entire community of Jews.

Reb Isser Zalman Meltzer

The Slutsker rabbi was a very hospitable man. His home was open to everyone. A guest came to Slutsk: a rabbi. a preacher, an emissary, who had to stay with Reb Meltzer. Meanwhile the Bolsheviks overtook the government, and closed the Slutsker Yeshiva. Reb Isser Zalman Meltzer did not notice and continued to teach Torah quietly.

One time before Shabbat two Red soldiers arrived. and arrested Reb Meltzer.

As they are taking him to the market he saw the Nesvizsher emissary.

He asks the soldiers to stop for a while to call over that old Jew. He wants to say something to him. The soldiers granted his request.

As the emissary came over, Reb Meltzer**Error! Bookmark not defined.** said to him: – Reb Abraham Yitzhock, I beg you, do me favor and celebrate Shabbat in my home for me.

Translator's (Jerrold Landau) footnotes:

1. This story is essentially the same as the Hebrew version on page 128.
2. For the baking of matzo *shmura* for fulfilling the commandment of eating matzo on Passover.
3. A *kezayit* [olive size] is a halachic volume that defines how much matzo must be eaten to fulfil the commandment at the Seder.
4. Matzo *sheruya* (*gebrochts* in Yiddish) is matzo that has been in contact with water. Some people, especially in the Hassidic communities, feel that such matzo is forbidden on Passover, other than on the eighth day.

[Page 358]

Rabbinical Judges, Preachers

by Chaim Zaydes

Translated by Tamara Selden z"l with missing gaps filled in by Jerrold Landau

Better to have a clear rabbinical judgment with the Rem'a

In Slutsk there was a rabbi, Reb Abraham, who was also a great judge but he often turned over the more difficult cases to his assistant.

One time, before Pesach an animal became unkosher. The town was without meat and the poor town's butchers suffered a great loss.

Reb Abraham was forced to find permissibility to kosher the ox.

He found a leniency from a liberal person of the law to gather five persons on the court and together to make the ox kosher.

The assistant rabbi agreed that this could be done even against the authority of Rem'a who openly said such a case was not permitted.

Regarding this Reb Abraham Sharfzinik stated:

I believe that it can be made kosher even against Rem'a. When we come to the other world to the heavenly court, the ox will call us to a lawsuit in a rabbinical court. Why we prohibit his meat over which Jews wanted to make a blessing: The butchers will complain that they had damage and a great loss. It is already more reasonable to go to a rabbinical court with Rem'a than with an ox and butchers. With Rem'a we would sooner be able to come to terms.

[Page 359]

In Slutsk, there were a lot of scribes who wrote Torah scrolls and *Mezuzahs*. The Rabbi of the city had his own scribe, Reb Mordechai Jacob, who was an expert in writing divorces and was a true G-d fearing person. The day came that Reb Mordechy was sick, so they brought a Jew who was a scribe with the name Velvel. He was not a scribe that made a living from it. So, he also became a baker.

When it came to write a divorce decree, the Slutsker Rabbi did not want the scribe to do it.

– Why rabbi? – they asked him. – He is a good scribe!

The Rabbi answered: For a divorce paper there must be two witnesses. If one says in the daytime "written by me" and one says in the evening "written by me, the divorce decree is invalid. By day he is a scribe but at night he is a baker and that invalidates the divorce decree.

* * *

One time an overdressed merchant came to the Slutsker preacher, The Rabbi Reb Laybe Nymark, and wanted to get some advice from him about buying a wooded area. He said that with his business spin, which is not any direct thievery, he could make a big business deal.

The Rabbi Reb Nymark who was a clever man simply told him the verse of the Torah quoting the Ten Commandments.

What does this have to do with my issue, asked the merchant?

It has a great bearing on the issue replied the Rabbi. – " Thou shall not steal; can be understood in two ways. It remains the same transgression. Whether straightforward or with tricks. and spinning.,,

* * *

They wanted to enlarge the City Talmud Torah, and Reb Laybe Nymark encouraged the people with his sermon. Then, when it came to money, the people became uncomfortable. So Reb Laybe recited the weekly Torah portion (Vayakhel) which always perplexed him. First it says, "All the Children of Israel left," and then it says "Everyone whose heart moved them came."

Now the issue has become clear to me. Everyone came to the sermon, only when it dealt with money, the numbers of people diminished.

* * *

In Slutsk there was a very rich man, a cheapskate, a wildly stingy man, who did not want to give any money for charity Often he bragged about his lineage and claimed to be descended from the "Protector of Abraham."

A Slutsker emissary came to him asking for a donation, and as usual he told the Jew, with great pride that he derives his lineage from Abraham.

The emissary strongly resented this story. Being a clever Jew he said to the rich man :

Reb Jew I have great doubt in your lineage, because whoever wants to learn the laws of The Protector of Abraham must first read the commentary, which is an explanation of the Protector of Abraham. Unfortunately, I see you have not read or studied it.

He collects money for a widow with orphans

In Slutsk there was a rich man, Reb Moshe Shusterman was his name. However, he called himself Moshe Yedaber after Masliansky Yedaber the preacher and orator in New York. Moshe Yedaber and Masliansky Yedaber were both from Slutsk.

Jews liked the sermons of Reb Moshe Yedaber and in the synagogue there was an announcement that Reb Moshe Yedaber would preach a sermon. All the Jews ran to hear his sermon which was as if pearls fell from his mouth. The people cried and laughed together. He captured the audience with his moving stories.

Although he was so very good his wife never attended. In the morning she went out into the world and left him with two orphans.

In addition to this problem, the Bolsheviks took over the government after World War One and Reb Moshe Yedaber no longer could make a living. The Reds did not allow him to give sermons and moralize the people. He became very bitter. And then he married a second time and had a few more children. There was no bread and they went hungry.

A short time passed by and Reb Moshe Yedaber left Slutsk. He went to Poland and traveled to big and little cities and gave sermons,. And in order for the people to give him money he told in all his sermons a story of a wretched widow, who with the orphans traveled in order to get money. In this way he drew a picture of their house and how the orphans come to the to the widow to ask for bread, but she had none to give them.

And here comes one orphan and cries, he needs shoes. And his sister cries that she needs a dress like her friends have. But the widow has only one answer for everything – tears, what should she do? Other children have a father. He buys his children things.

[Page 360]

Everywhere Reb Moshe's sermons so moved the people that they gave him money. They gave what they could and sometimes even more.

So this was good. Once in a small shtetl, after Reb Moshe had given his sermon, a trustee of the synagogue asked him:

"Reb Moshe, who is this widow? Maybe you could tell us where she lives?"

Reb Moshe stood very still, as if they accused him of something. Quickly he recovered and answered:

"You want to know? Good, I will tell you. - she is my wife."

"Your wife!" The trustee looked at him and asked "how can this be, you are still alive, so how can she be a widow?"

" Well, do you mind if I am alive?" asked Reb Moshe Yedaber. "If I had died would it have been better?"

" You" And Not "I"

Reb Moshe Yedaber, the well-known preacher and publisher of books once came to a town to give a sermon. He was a Jew, stocky, heavy and with a countenance!

A well-known prankster and impudent man came to him and called out: – Rebbi, I barely believe that you implemented the idea of [you should eat bread and salt, and drink water, with a measure, and sleep on the hard ground, and a live a torturous life). It does not appear so on your face.

Reb Moshe Yedaber, who was a clever man, immediately, sharply answered the prankster:

– It does not state that I should eat bread with salt, etc. The language is thus, "you should implement all these things , "you" not "I".

* * *

Reb Moshe was a Jew with lots of troubles, had a good looking face, dressed nicely and looked like a rabbi.

Once he was riding on a train that was packed with Jews. There was not even enough room to stand. As he entered, the Jews began to murmur....a rabbi, a rabbi.

The crowds pressed together in order to make a path for him.

One who sat, got up and wanted to give him his seat. :

"Sit rabbi".

The preacher sat down.

People begin to talk to him:

"Where are you going rabbi?"

"Where you from?"

"Where do you stand on the Rabbinate?

"I am not a rabbi" – replied Moshe, "I am a Slutsker preacher, "As he spoke, the Jew who given him his seat went to him and said.

" Reb Jew that seat is taken. The preacher got up and stood on his feet all the way.

The Common People

In Slutsk there was a householder, who gave interest free loans, a great philanthropist

, Reb Isr'l was his name. Whenever anyone needed an interest free loan, they went to him. You could have the loan for many months. He did not charge any percent of interest. G-d forbid, he took nothing.

And in his time, in the town, there was an old butcher Reb Izik Tumanik.

He was not a rich man. There were times when he was old that he needed to get an interest free loan in order to buy meat for Shabbat or the Holidays. And if the officials said the animals were kosher, the butcher immediately, before blessing the candles, ran and returned the interest free loan. In his house it was very cheerful. He and his family had a good Sabbath. However, if the animal, G-d forbid became unkosher, it was a bitter moment.

It happened that Reb Izik brought meat to the slaughter house and it became unkosher. The butcher rushed around all mixed up. He could not pay any debts and could not get a new loan.

Reb Isik ran to Reb Isr'l in the spice store and and wanted to ask Reb Isr'l to wait for the interest free loan that he owed him until the holy one will help him.

As Reb Isr'l saw the butcher coming, he went inside and hid behind the oil cask. He was afraid that he would transgress one of the laws of the Torah, which says you must not be, to someone that you loan money, a percentnik.

[Page 361]

In the meantime a Jewish woman came in and asked for a quart of kerosene.

The store owner went to the barrel and saw that her husband hid behind the barrel. She became frightened and thought that G-d forbid something has happened to him. The store owner told him to come out.

"No", he said to his wife. Only I saw the butcher coming and he does not know from where he will get the money for the interest free loan.

Once again an animal has become non-kosher with him, and I do not want to transgress the the rules of Torah. That we should not be to a left side as a percentnik.

In the meantime the butcher came in and heard what Reb Isr'l said: He said:

G-d forbid, Reb Isr. I purposely came to you to ask you to wait another week."

"Certainly" answered Reb Isr'l. When I gave you the interest free loan, it certainly was my intention not to give you the money for only one week but for several weeks. Do not worry Reb Isaac said. The Holy One will help and when you are ready to pay me back you will return the loan".

Reb Meyer Rozovski used to say: Water and Fire are at war with each other and until the day they make peace. Unfortunately it becomes very black.

* * *

Dalhunike the *zugerin* used to shock people at the cemetery with her monolog and petitions to the dead that they should understand her suffering.

The first question was to the searcher of the graveside. "With tears or without tears ?"

* * *

A cemetery man went up to his daughter: "God will give me a corpse and I will give you a "groom."

Slutsker wives cursed in the meat stand when buying meat.

One said "May my enemies all have eighteen stomach aches. A second person calls out, why exactly eighteen? The first one answered, because chay (yud chet = 18) is to life...

Two Letters to the Land of Israel

by S. L. Beker

Translated by Tamara Selden z"l with missing gaps filled in by Jerrold Landau

Aharon Baruch Beker

Aaron Baruch Becker, who worked in the Slutsker Zionist Hall came to Israel in the year 1904. The first time he worked for the committee of Rishon le-Tsiyon and afterwards worked in a technical school called Hador-Ha-Karmel in Haifa.

He died in 1932 in Tel Aviv.

The fragments of the parents letters from Slutsk to Israel to their son Aaron Baruch are interesting. He is named for his grandfather the well-known Slutsker. He was the head of the Yeshiva, where Mendele Moker Seforim studied.

In them are reflected the father's interest in Zionism. His language was half Yiddish and Hebrew.

Slutsk 1914

We sang all the songs, ate a good meal and asked G-d who brought us all that is good. We finished with tea. Khile and Sarah are in the store, and Shaeah Lazer went into the street asking the merchants (those who are traveling to buy old clothes.) I remained in the house with the weaker mother. She begs me to write you a letter.

Dear son Aaron Baruch, clippings from Ussishkin (the leader of Chovevei Zion) are posted in the shul. He asks that we send donations to buy land in Israel. Also posted on the wall is a request from Rabbi Abraham Kook, the Jaffa rabbi with higher holier words. He points out that Jews have begun to have one thought for the holy land of Israel with the Jewish settlement. I read in the paper about the parade for the old Jewish patriot Rothchild, who gave millions for the settlement of the Land of Israel. Streams of tears flowed from my eyes. Wet with tears for I was like someone bound up – my pocketbook does not allow me to travel. –

[Page 362]

Do not forget, two in the Russian folk in the hands[1], and one has to send them money. Shaya Leizer is weak. Help him. He is toiling. He needs comforts, healthy food, scrambled eggs.

I, with my weak energies, must toil. Bound to a horse, and therefore I must bother – to send the merchandise to the train to where it is more expensive than in Slutsk. I must collect an entire wagon of bones that I send to Stari-Dorani. The wagon costs money for Velvele and Lechovitch, and the transaction is also larger than selling slowly.

An iron wagon is one thousand pod [a unit of measure], and it is about fifty rubles more expensive. One must have patience to obtain a wagon for half a year, travel to the city, hear Muzycza, the dirty talk of the anti-Semite. He laughs and shouts. If the Eternal gives me strength to bear this, I would have nothing with which to sin.

I would be very happy if I could meet you. Your thoughts are far from mine, although you are the practical one. By not following the Ashmener Rabbi, you have not carried out anything.

Nu, be true to your thoughts, and the Eternal should lead you further to a better and happier way than it is here. – – –

Your father who is solicitous about your wellbeing, Sh. L. Beker.

Slutsk, the eve of the first Intermediate Day of Sukkot

Greetings to you my dear son Aharon Baruch.

Today, the second day of Sukkot, while I was walking to the Vilner Beis Midrash, I received your letter, and it was raining. It rained strongly and I did not read it until I came home. I showed your letter through the window, and your young sister ran outside and received your letter with joy and gladness. A letter arrived from your brother Nachum in the second post. He writes that he has heard that he will go tomorrow to the battlefield, and he asks that we pray for him. Your brother Berl is currently in Moscow. When he went to the battlefield and sat upon the chariot and the horses galloped quickly, he fell to the ground. He lay alone on the ground, for the wheel of the chariot squeezed his foot. His battalion journeyed to the war, and they did not pay attention to him. A volley of arrows flew above his head. He raised his eyes and saw a pit. He lay there. He got up and ran four verst [an old Russian unit of distance] back to the camp.

The pain in his foot got worse, and he went to a field hospital. He was brought to five different cities, until he was finally brought to Moscow. They made *"fareviazkes"*[2] for him. He has been lying there for more than a month.

We have found out that the Russians have lost two brigades, and your brother was there. We went about depressed, with our hands bound.

News – weakness – news that is not happy:

The Russians ran and escaped in a disorderly fashion. They fled 150 verst. On the eve of Rosh Hashanah, we received a letter from your brother stating that he had not eaten for five days, not drunk for ten days and not changed his clothes for six weeks. He was awaiting the bitter Angel of Death, and he remained alive in the merit of his ancestors. The Germans are strong, and what time will do will not be comprehensible. In Austrian Galicia they perpetrated destruction in the wake of their victory, and have taken many prisoners. The marauding Cossacks pillaged, and robbed in accordance with the ways of war. Their hand was in everything – in Jewish property and goods. – – – and I, if I perish, I perish[3]. – We work and we keep busy as is appropriate. Be strong!

Your father who is solicitous about your wellbeing, Sh. L. Beker.

Sh. L. Beker' family

Translator's (Jerrold Landau) footnotes:

1. This idiom is unclear, as are some other phrases in this letter.
2. I could not find a meaning for this word, but it is evidently some sort of a crutch.
3. Esther 4:16.

[Page 363]

People's Character

by Chaim Zeides, New York

Translated by Tamara Selden z"l with missing gaps filled in by Jerrold Landau

Reb Chaim Zeides

A (Alef)

During the first world war there were many merchants in Slutsk who in their youth studied in Volozhin. In addition to running large businesses they were well-versed in Torah. Each day they went to the synagogue and studied a page of *Gemara*. And a merchant like *Yeshaya Mendel,* a large wholesaler, would study a page of Gemara with his son after praying, and then he would go to his store to attend to business.

Yeshaya Mendel Deretsin was well-known in the Minsk community. His home was a place of trade and charity, Thirty Yeshiva boys ate there every Tuesday. Yeshaya was active and generous in all charity organizations. A certain Jew whose name was Zelig the comb maker, was dedicated to collecting money for widows and orphans and others for studying Torah. He very often passed Yeshaya Mendel's house and saw thirty Yeshiva boys eating each Tuesday. He said to Yeshaya Mendel, "Very nice of you that you feed thirty Yeshiva boys one day a week. However, you know that the week has seven days and many other Yeshiva boys need to have eating days...What can you do for them?"

Yeshaya answered him, "Come to me at night and tell me the amount of charity money you collected in the course of a day, and I will give you my share."

This gave Zelig great courage and he tried to collect even more because he knew that Yeshaya would give a large matching portion. He told this to his valorous wife Rifke and she said to her husband, "Today I had a good day in the butcher shop, so I am giving you five rubles and you will have an impressive amount."

(Late at night Rabbi Zelig brought the money to Yeshaya Mendel and counted it before him. Yeshaya Mendel kept his word and matched the amount. Rabbi Zelig, who made combs, left Yeshaya Mendel in a very happy state. He wished that there would be individuals like Yeshaya Mendel in the thousands,

[Page 364]

summer in the heat, winter in the cold and snowstorms, Chaim Dovid did his work conscientiously. Many times it happened that because he always wanted to offer a Sabbath meal that he would eat Friday night at midnight. He was elderly, but ran like a young soldier from shul to shul organizing for every Yeshiva student a place to eat on Shabbat.

Not one time did anyone remain without a place, but if he did, he invited them as his guest.

B (Bet)

The school was not far from the market. There were over one hundred children who studied. Chaim Beryl Alshansky the Kohen, Leybe Yoikh the blacksmith, and Zelig the comb maker built a nice park on the place where the old bath had stood. The best teachers who taught from ABC to a page of the Gemorrah were there.

In Slutsk there was a hospice for the poor, who took care of the sick people, with a doctor and medicine. And every night two people came to care for the sick as nurses would.

All types of utensils that the sick were in need of were given by the hospice to the poor for free, and sometimes they did give money to the sick to get the patient on his or her feet. The Slutsker charities were under the leadership of Dr. Shildkraut and other doctors. They worked each day for free and did not ask once to be paid. The hospice was also for the Jews from around the area of Slutsk.

The old age home which bordered the hospice was also for the Jews in the entire Slutsker area. In the Yeshiva which was the largest in all of Russia, most of the students were concerned with "days" for eating. and a place to sleep. Even every poor Jew had to have several charity boxes. Every week the money was collected by people from the land of Israel and other places.

It was in Slutsk that a woman with the name Leah from Horki, a woman with little education, only with a good heart, had a Yeshiva student each day to eat. Many times she brought food to the Yeshiva for the students. She complained: maybe poor students were ashamed of this system, but they did not want to ignore learning the Torah. So she brought them food at the Yeshiva. She asked who needed food or to have their clothes washed? She said she would do this for free. She did not G-d forbid want to humiliate anyone. With different excuses she gave charity to fallen people. They should not be ashamed. For example, I remember that she alone brought wood in the wintertime to the poor families. and said to them that she had too much wood but next year they could bring some for her. Many a time she brought a pound of farfel. She was a very clever and active person. and a great house manager, and her words were: You know my Chaim"ke only wants lockshen not farfel. So take a sack of farfel and next year you will bring me some lockshen. This was her manner of charity, giving quietly. She gave every poor person charity with cordiality. She would tell him to wash and then eat whatever she had available. She did not have a machine to make sacks. but with four poles she made all sorts of sacks for Yeshiva students and brides especially for Shavuoth. She had a mother-in-law Pesele who had a reputation in town. She had a loud mouth but Leah did things quietly, did not look for honor, only begged G-d that she should have children that study Torah and were G-d fearing.

She often gave her own food to a poor man. She did not have esteem for her health, only of others. If someone asked her – : Doesn't the world say you come first? Her answer was with a smile: I am satisfied and pleased when I make the hungry full and give them clothes.

G (Gimmel)

In the year 1899, after the great fire, many were left with only the shirt of their back.

A certain Reb Mordechy Yonah, rebuilt his house and let it be known that he would only takes one room for himself and the rest of the house he gave away for a town hospice. He made regulations, that every guest has the right to eat two meals and sleep there one night. All the poor Talmud Torah children ate there two days a week and two days a week the Yeshiva boys who studied in Slutsker Yeshivas ate there.

The Rabbi's wife, Hinde Bayla, the wife of the Goan Meltzer called on the hospice committee every day. Shakhna the beadle of the shul, was the collector for the committee and Mendel, a *Nikalaievsker* soldier was the watchman over the building.

It was the custom in Slutsk, after shul, to take a guest home for the Sabbath to eat and have a place to sleep.

[Page 365]

D (Daled)

Leybe Yoikh

Leybe Yoikh was a blacksmith. He stood in the forge and banged with his hammer and blew with the bellows. The blacksmith, with so much work to do, was also concerned with the poor people, even the poor yeshive boys. Before Passover he began to worry whether the poor people in town had matzohs, potatoes or other necessary things for the great holiday.

For himself he required very little. He was not a particularly fastidious person with his attire. He wore an old worn-out fur coat the entire winter; a pair of torn boots and a hat, which was at least ten years old, and maybe more. The *kaftan* was patched and greasy. In such clothing he searched out all the rich men for money. Everyone knew him and it was very difficult to refuse to give him charity money. Everyone knew that Leybe Yoikh the blacksmith does not take one *grushen* from the charity donations. He gives it all away to the poor people.

When someone did not want to give a proper amount of charity, Leybe Yoikh usually accepted this. He could never even shame a very rich man, with the largest amount of silver.

However, in a certain year the income of the Jews in Slutsk was scarce. An entire winter the storekeepers sat and waited for customers, and workers sat without a bit of work. There was great concern because Passover would soon be there.

But Leybe had courage and chanted: G-d is a father. He will help me to aid his children. Going with his torn boots in the muddy streets from house to house, he did not collect as much as he asked for because things had been so bad. Then it happened that one rich man from *Zaretze* Street only gave him a small donation for buying matzoh for the poor; not one more coin. Leybe said to him.: "You are a dog's dog.: He explained what he meant:" When a dog gets a bone he keeps it for himself. You are the same with your money."

After saying this to the rich man, he left the house, and there was anger between Leybe and the rich man. However when Rosh Hashanah came, Leybe wanted to make up with him The rich man did not want to forgive him. Leybe was aggravated. He went to Reb Laybeeh Nymark the assistant rabbi and told him his problem. Reb Nymark who was a wise man calmed him down and said. "You did not insult him for your sake, but for the sake of collecting charity. If he will not forgive you, he is in the wrong.

But Leybe Yoikh the blacksmith felt he was to blame for calling a Jew a dog. He had to ask his forgiveness, so he waited for an opportunity.

Leybe, as poor as he was, wanted to observe all Jewish good deeds. When Purim came he sent every one Purim presents and even the rich man, that he called a dog, received a Purim present. When the rich man saw the lovely present he was softened in his attitude to Leybe and he felt remorse that he had given very little for charity when things were so bad in town. The rich man took the Purim gift from the saucer and placed five ruble with a note which said the following: "Reb Leyve here is five ruble and you can do what you want with it. ...I am very sorry that I did not want to be forgiving. When you want a charity donation, come to me. I will never refuse. I wish you well",

H (Hey)

The Wedding Dress

Shimon the porter, although he had a house with girls , he was a satisfied person. Most girls at that time worked for a rich man and each and every one of them had a nice dowry, Jonah the matchmaker was the mediator for all the Jewish daughters in Slutsk and vicinity.

Shimon's daughter Rachel, was a pretty girl with a nice figure. The groom was a very handy boy from the town of Krivits, not far from Starobin. The dowry was written in the engagement contract for two hundred ruble.

The wedding was supposed to be a week after *Shavuoth*. Rachel did not have a mother. Her stepmother was good to her. The wardrobe was made by the best tailor, *Yusel Ayrkhe* , from *Ayrenser* Street. When Yusel brought her wedding dress, Rachel washed her hands with soap, not to soil the ribbons on the dress.

and when she tried on the dress her step mother said: "See Rachel your good fortune should shine the way you shine in your wedding dress."

All her friends were impressed with the beautiful material and fine workmanship of Yusel the tailor.

[Page 366]

The magnificent wedding dress with frills cost fifty rubles of dowry. She had thought that her groom was a lad from the village, and he would be happy with 150 for the dowry instead of the agreed-upon 200 rubles.

Neighbors and porters from the market were invited to the wedding. Pesele the butcher woman, who always enjoyed bringing gladness to a bride and groom, especially when the bride is an orphan was there , as was Leybe Yoikh the blacksmith.

Now the bride was sitting on her chair and waiting to be led to the *chuppah* [marriage canopy]. Yankel the musician played the fiddle, Eliyahu played the pipes, and Chaim David played the large bandura. Then a commotion started. The groom's mother, a woman "with an earring," shouted that she wants to have to entire 200 rubles as dowry, not less!... Just as it was written in the *tenaim* [pre-marital agreement]. Shimon the porter talked to the groom's mother amicably, "See, dear *machateniste* [in-law], my daughter makes very fine dresses, all for your son if it pleases him. She will give fifty rubles... See, do not be shamed... Let us go to the *chuppah*... "

However, Doba, the groom's mother, responded, "It should have been written in the *tenaim*. If there is no dowry, there is no wedding!..."

The bride had been fasting an entire day, and she was weak. She fainted from the shouting of the groom's mother. They barely were able to revive her. And now it was almost the Sabbath, from where will one get such a large sum of money, an entire fifty rubles?

Leybe Yoikh said to Pesele, "Pesele, you know that I keep my word. Give your pearls with your diamond earrings to the groom's mother as a security pledge. I guarantee to you that in a week I will provide the fifty rubles... You will get your pearls with your earrings back..."

Pesele took of hear earrings with her pearls and gave them to the groom's mother. Then the musicians began to play a *freilach* [joyous song], and they set out to the synagogue courtyard for the *chuppah*.

Young and old were present at the *chuppah*. They all wondered: Shimon the porter's daughter is wearing such a magnificent wedding dress!?

It did not take more than two weeks for Leybe Yoikh to collect in the city more than the sum of fifty rubles for the bride, and he retrieved Pesele's jewelry. He told her, "You see, Pesele, I still have a few rubles left for a second poor bride... The wealthy people of Slutsk are stingy about giving charity, but I, Leybe Yoikh, know how to talk to them, and they give more, unwillingly..."

Leybe Yoikh the Blacksmith

by Rabbi Moyshe Goldberg

Translated by Hershl Hartman

Leybe Yoikh the blacksmith was still alive during my childhood years. I would often see him walking through the streets of town at a heavy but joyful pace. And when I would hear in the distance the pounding of iron *"podkoves"*[1] on the cobbled pavement, I would understand that Leybe the blacksmith was coming. It was his habit to drag along only on the cobbles rather than on the sidewalk with all the other people.

His imposing appearance, you may believe me on my solemn word, was not that of a smith. His thick white beard was more suitable to someone of the clergy, or to a well-to-do proprietor. But as he had it, it remained his and was put to good use at times, because a Jew with a white beard merits different respect though he is a smith...

When Leybe gave up working at the forge and began to earn a place in the World to Come, he acquired the nickname *leybe bal-mitsve'nik* [Leybe, master of the commandments]. People could not believe that such an ordinary smith who struggles three times a day over reading the prayers and who is, thanks be to God, sound of all limbs, should suddenly, out of nowhere, give up working and devote himself to the commandments and to doing good deeds. But Leybe paid little attention to what people said of him. As a smith who was used to everything, he welcomed his nickname lovingly, though he was well aware that it was meant in jest.

So he went his way: in his right hand he would hold a red kerchief, one corner of which always hung down. He would collect money for various causes in the red kerchief and use the hanging corner to wipe his nose...thus he would proceed through the whole town several times a week.

When his energetic work was noted, people began to respect him somewhat. The poor would regard him as a goodhearted father; his home became like a charitable institution. Any poor widow, a forlorn orphan, a penniless bride or a Jew who could not provide for *shabes* [sabbath], any person in need—turned to Leybe, and Leybe, who empathized and sympathized with his clients,

[Page 367]

went out like the honored head of a community with his red shawl in hand to collect a few coins.

But just as Leybe was the provider for the poor folk, he was seen as an avaricious worm in the eyes of the rich. He gave the rich no lick of honey…He was a hard man, not affected by cursing and most of all, may no woman be so afflicted, he had a clever mouth and a smooth tongue and knew the craft of blackmail…

When he would meet with a stubborn rich man with whom it was difficult to come to an agreement, he would say: "You can't send Leybe away with empty hands. You want to be rid of me, so hand something over. If not—I'll remain here in your house. You hear? You will have to give me food and a place to sleep, d'you hear?" The rich man, hearing such talk, had to, sadly, open his purse and contribute whatever Leybe demanded. The rich man had no other alternative. Could he throw him out? In the first place, how does one dare to throw out a Jew with a white beard? And secondly, if he tried to do so, he would antagonize the other smiths…who would come to defend Leybe's honor.

It happened once that Leybe entered a rich man's home wearing muddy boots. When he found no one in the kitchen, he went into the dining room, from there to the bedroom and from there to the salon where the rich man's wife sat on a soft sofa, reading a book. As soon as the woman saw Leybe's mud-covered boots she intoned "*vaytsaku*" [and they screamed]: "Get out of here, beggar! You've made a pigsty out of all my floors with your muddy boots!" Leybe replied calmly: "Hush, be still, don't get excited, lady of mine; we will both lie one day under the same "*perene*" [featherbed] at the cemetery."

Words were exchanged and when the rich man's wife saw that Leybe's tongue worked better and faster than hers, she gave him alms sadly and thanked God that the outcome wasn't any worse…From that point on she knew that she had to treat Leybe as a "*gentleman.*"

At the time of the "*priziv*" [forced military draft] he knew of all the draftees and asked them for alms in exchange for blessings that the virtue of their charity would free them. He would visit the inns where the small-town draftees would stay [awaiting induction]. He would take small change from them, as well, and bless them for freedom. When a draftee was freed from military service, Leybe would go off to him and say: "You see, little brother, my blessing came to pass. Now give me more alms and God will help you."

Most of all, Leybe was used for deeply confidential charity. If the rabbi needed a certain amount of money for an upstanding poor man, he would send for Leybe and say: "Reb Leyb, I am in need today of a twenty-fiver [25 ruble note]." Leybe would then reply: "Rabbi, I will contribute a fiver." The rabbi would then urge him to give more. Leybe would reply that he needed the money for others in need. So they would bargain until striking a deal.

Leybe attended every wedding and every *bris* with his red kerchief. It is interesting that he would not wet his lips. People would beg him: "Reb Leyb, *makht leChaim* [make a toast] in honor of the celebrant," but to no avail. He did want to cause suspicion that his main motivation for coming was to partake of the alcohol and cake, and besides, he did not want to enjoy himself, lest it be thought that he was benefiting in this life from his good deeds.

Translator's footnote:

1.   Lit., horseshoes. Used here humorously to describe the blacksmith's iron-clad boot heels.

Memories of the Old Home

by Yehudit Simval

Translated by Tamara Selden z"l with missing gaps filled in by Jerrold Landau

Our Slutsker relatives, friends, neighbors near and far in America and Israel and all over the world , who will look into the corner, will look back many years.

It will remind them of many things of sadness and joy and of the many years in our beloved birth town Slutsk.

It is fifty years already since we left Slutsk, but Slutsk is not forgotten. Above all, the honesty and goodness of everyone who was poor and often hungry.

Slutsker holidays, Slutsker foods, Slutsker weddings, brisn; oh how I long for my mother's butter cookies. Thursday mama used to bake Challah, cookies all night for her husband and nine children. The smell filled the entire house. For each girl there was a roll. For the boys a small Challah. For lunch on Friday each child received a small roll with a bowl of barley soup had a holiday smell. Before Passover we aired and cleaned the house. On Friday each child received a roll and a plate of soup. Everything had a holiday smell. Each child had their own goblet, one green, one blue, one white. The largest goblet was for *Elijah the prophet.* And for each child a new pair of shoes.

[Page 368]

Now I will tell you about a well-known character:

Itze Barker

Itze Barker with his wife *Tsira* were our neighbors. They were bread bakers. Itze was a tall handsome Jew with a long white beard. His wife Tsira was short and both were quiet good people. They did not have any children. so they adopted an orphan who was a relative. Her name was Rayzele, brought her up, made her wedding and took in their son-in-law Nathan, the scribe, into their home for *kest* (room and board so he could study). They gave them the best room and they slept in a dark room behind the oven. In the kitchen there was a table with a long bench where they laid out the bread straight from the oven.(In their house there was a large white cat with black specks. This was not just a cat that ran around looking for mice. Her work was to walk among the warm loaves of bread, lick and smell, and slap with her tail and from time to time lay down between the warm loaves of bread.)

The customers G-d forbid never complained about this. If Itze's cat has to do this then that is probably the way it was supposed to be.

Khava the Bean Carrier

Khava the crushed pea carrier. Who was she? Whether she had a husband and children I do not know. But, I do remember her very well. She was a tall and heavy Jewish woman with a nice happy face. All week she carried yellow chick peas around, well cooked and mashed and covered. It should G-d forbid get cold. The smell and the flavor permeated all limbs. She carried her wares in a big pot. Her measure was a heated cup which she sold for a *grushen* (penny, small coin).

To this day I do not understand how she was able to carry such a burden on her stomach. Friday, in honor of the Sabbath she would sell warm beans, She was proclaimed by all the tailors, shoemakers, and other tradesmen who bought with pleasure of their soul for a penny,

Hooray Khava, Hooray Khava ! The taste of the dark large beans with the warm yellow chick peas today still remains in my memory.

My grandfather Elyeh Flayshtsik

He was a Jew who liked to do good deeds. He was a "musician" and like a "musician" in those times earned very little. For Passover he would work in a matzoh factory. However this was not enough to provide for his large family. So grandmother Hashke baked biscuits at night and early in the morning sold them to the taverns and stores They worked hard and from their income were neither very rich or very poor, yet it did not obstruct them from raising someone else's children. It sometimes happened that someone had to get free of a illegitimate child. They would sometimes drown it in a tub or abandon it in the shul. However they knew that my grandfather would usually take it: Bring it home and grandmother Khashke , a naturally good person, would raise it like her own child. I recall three such children. With one, grandfather had a problem. When they grew older they would then go to learn a trade, but the problem one was very intelligent and fell in love with one of his daughters. He was a nice boy and she wanted to marry him. Grandfather did not approve and made the boy leave. Grandfather's word was holy.

My aunt Sara-Rayzel

My Aunt Sara-Rayzel was my grandfather's oldest daughter. She was a widow with two small children. She used to take two large baskets and would go to the market to do some business. She lived on America Street in a small town. She would stay up half the night and bake potatoes, cook a huge pot of barley soup for herself and the children. By nature she was a good woman, but the hard life made her nervous and she would curse and scream at every opportunity. Aunt Sara-Rayzel picked feathers for the daughter to fill two large cushions, a small one, an even smaller one, another tiny one. No one was allowed to sleep on the cushions.

From left to right (the second): Shimon Laybe Flayshtsik the musician

[Page 369]

Her husband was a musician and like a musician at that time earned little money. At night he lay down on a cot and in the morning when he awoke he saw a crook had snuck in and stolen the cushions. The aunt's sorrow and pain was indescribable.

Elye Fyfyel-Flayshtik

My aunt Khana Hinde

My aunt Khana Hinde was one of grandfather's daughters. The sad thing was that she was a young widow with two small children. Her husband Velvel went to the Golden Land America searching for a good living. Many Slutsker Jews at that time did that. In a short time, he and a friend suffocated in their sleep forgetting to shut the gas off. Grandfather's family came together and decided to open a small store for the widow. Those who had more and those who had less donated what they could and bought merchandise for her. In this way my aunt became a storekeeper. A Jewish woman came to buy a pint of cereal – My aunt would always add a cup to the amount ordered and said: You should be well. What will you do with a pint of cereal for an entire family? When children came with their mothers to the store she would give the children sugar cookies. In the evening everyone would gather at Khana Hinde's store and she would honor everyone with various things and eventually gave away all that she had earned. So, little by little the shelves emptied. My aunt's family once again gathered and bought her a store that sold material. However the same story repeated itself and the shelves were soon left empty. The third conference of the family decided that she must get married. Good people looked for a Jew from *Uretshe*. She took the daughter with her. The boy stayed with the grandfather. When grandfather died, the orphan was taken in by my father. And he grew up with us, every Jewish child should be so lucky. Today he is called Abraham Gafnee from *Khfar Ganyim*..

Khashke Flayshtik

My father Shimon Laybe Flayshtik

My father took after my grandfather. He was also a musician. He had nine children. He liked to do favors for people, just like grandfather Elyeh Fyfil.--They called him Fyfil because he played on a flute. What didn't my mother do to make the children well provided for. She dealt with orchard keepers, with and gardeners, had hens, rendered chicken fat and sold it to the tradesmen from a large city.

She had cows and sold milk, churned butter and made cheese, and kept Yeshiva students for *kest*. When the children grew up she said that she did not wish her children to spread themselves all over the world, which was then the custom in Slutsk. The children did not want to struggle like their parents, so they ran away from them into the big world. Most went to America. My mother thought they should go to Israel if anywhere. They should buy land and work it and live together. She did not live to see this. She died of a lung infection in 1910.

[Page 370]

We arrived in the Land of Israel without our mother in 1912. My father died on Passover in the year 1940 at 79 years old.

My mother's wish was that all her children should live in one place and it did indeed happen. All of us came together to Israel.

Going to Israel

We traveled on a old dirty ship called the Kirilaf. On the ship we carried many Arabs. The heat was strong. We came out onto the streets of Jaffa. We then traveled on a stage coach from Gaff to Ayin Ganim where Uncle Mordechai-Nisan prepared an apartment for us: A room with a small terrace, a small kitchen in a wooden house. The vacant walls of the room with vacant fields surrounding the house made an awful impression. It cast a terrible sadness in the house and surroundings. The furniture consisted of two beds, a large one and a small one. The items in the packed boxes earned us a table and chairs. The several hundred rubles that father received for his house in Slutsk enabled us to buy bathtubs, a closet in which to hang clothes and large and small benches, which today are with my brother under a tree at his house. We all worked very hard. There was a lot of illness and daily visits of doctors with medicine, but few hospitals. There were steady accidents at work.

My father's house was open for every Slutsker arrival. and their first stop was at our house. We children used to work and father was in charge. When guests came the barley soup was a little thicker. We gave our beds with an easy heart to the guests and we slept on the floor. During World War 1 of 1914 between the Turks and the English our home was destroyed. Later we built a new house.

In the middle Shimon Laybe (the klezmer) with his family in honor of his 75th year celebration in *Ptakh -Takvah*

[Page 371]

Under Soviet Rule

Economic and Spiritual Decline

by Mordecai Lipe Gorin

Translated by Hershl Hartman

The first time I visited Slutsk as an American citizen in 1927-28, Slutsk had already been under Bolshevik rule for ten years. The communist upheaval was to be seen and felt everywhere.

Gone was Czarist rule, represented by the drunken, bribe-taking constable, the city cop, the bailiff. There was no longer authority, respect for religion and older people, for the rabbi or for the old, well-off householders. The new government apparatus functioned through the Communist Party whose membership consisted mainly of young people. Discipline was iron-clad. The party line, determined and issued by the Central Committee in Moscow, was the sole moral and political commandment for the local population, to be upheld and followed as the Torah of Moses, may they not be compared.

I found Jewish life in Slutsk, as in all Soviet cities, to be in the worst of conditions. As mainly traders, merchants and small handicraftsmen in their economic lives, they were considered declassed under the new "Set Table."[1] Almost all of them were as if suspended in mid-air, having lost the earning-ground beneath them. The situation was miserable, tragic, because Bolshevism, as a new, fanatical religion, was mercilessly horrible. Its hand sliced through the formerly stable, conservative classes.

Most of the stores in Slutsk stood empty because private trade was destined for liquidation. Merchandise was in the hands of the government, which established cooperative stores. Private trade, under the burden of heavy taxation, was unable to compete and had to be liquidated.

Householders and *luftmentshn* [those who "starved by their wits"] were arrested on suspicion of dealing in foreign exchange, in black-market merchandise. Their fate was bitter and dark. There is no income because they are not fit for labor. And though the family's mouths need food, it is not available. Leaving Russia is impossible because the iron curtain had been lowered – no one leaves and no one enters[2].

Almost all the synagogues, houses of study, were converted into amusement places, theaters, movie houses or warehouses for grain and merchandise. The [main] House of Study, the Investors' Synagogue, as well as the Tailors' Synagogue, the large, beautiful Cold Synagogue – all became military storehouses for army supplies.

The same happened to churches. The smaller ones were signed over to the State after the costly items – icons, gold serving pieces, works of art – were removed and sent to the Religious Cult Ministry – in Minsk.

Along with all the *yeshives* and *khedorim* [respectively: schools of higher Judaic learning, and of elementary subjects], the Greek Orthodox Christian seminary, the hundred year-old monastery with its monks and nuns, were abolished.

Only a few synagogues and the large "Mikola Cloister" remained open for the few aged people who came to pray. The young people no longer came to synagogue to pray. Those few synagogues lacked a prayer-quorum [ten adult males].

The decline of the middle class

"If not for the packages, the aid from limited American dollars that are sent by our relatives, may they be blessed, we and many others of our fellow-Jews would perish from hunger. We cannot emigrate, because it is forbidden here, and America does not permit us entry, so it has become a closed world – no one leaves and no one enters. This shows that worse times will apparently arrive. First of all let there be peace – but war is in the air; Germany is sharpening its slaughter-knife against 'red' Ivan and also against us

[Page 372]

Jews – I hope that I'm lying." So said my observant and observing sister, as a tear fell from her pain-ridden heart.

"In addition, our children are being taken from us. They want nothing to do with their parents. Serving communism – the Party – and they don't need their parents," sobbed *reb* Leyzer Zalman, the abandoned former rabbi of Timkowicz, now a [private] teacher of small children.

"I myself expect to be arrested any day, because I teach children. One teaches them a bit of the Torah and Rashi's commentaries and how to say a blessing."

Leybush Gutsayt, the richest man in Slutsk, a capitalist-industrialist, managed to emerge slightly better. True, the government confiscated, took away all his estates, factories, cash, which had provided the family with a rich life, carefree and luxurious. But as he was familiar with banking matters as a financier, he was given employment.

"It's bad, brother," he told me. "I envy you for being an American. If only you could take and stuff me into your luggage. I would gladly travel along. Chaim Mikhl the-rich-man's-son must now struggle to make a living. I am at the mercy of the new rulers."

Leybush Gutsayt

Translator's footnotes:

1. Satiric reference to the Orthodox legal code, *Shulkhan Arukh*, compiled by Joseph Caro (1488-1575).
2. Hebrew-Yiddish expression: *eyn yoytse v'eyn bo.*

From Teaching to Cobbling

by N. Kh.

Translated by Hershl Hartman

In memory of Avrom Yitskhok Shpilkin, a grandchild of the famous holy man, Reb Rafoyl-Yosl.

Sitting at the workbench with a shoe in his hand, he hums a monotonous tune: "Little hammer, little hammer, beat, beat stronger!" There is no bread in the house; one's heart shakes and shivers. The surroundings – bitterly poor. His wife ill, hungry children are ragged.

When someone brings in a pair of shoes for repair – lively, he begins joyfully to sing in a lonely voice: "You are again our bread-giver, oh little hammer, little hammer!" ...Driving a nail after a brad, his youth flashes before his eyes: a deeply committed Zionist, illegal activities, a reader of all sorts of Hebrew newspapers and publications, a founder of [local branches of] *"khoveve sfas eyver"* [Lovers of the Hebrew Language], *"duvrey ivris"* [Hebrew Speakers]. Not wanting to make teaching his goal and future in life, he became employed as a *soyfer* [calligrapher] writing Torah Scrolls.

With the outbreak of the World War, when there was no market for Torah Scrolls and a large number of teachers were mobilized, Avrom Yitskhok Shpilkin decided to become a teacher of Hebrew. He feels that he is temporarily responsible to make sure that everything is in complete order until the true masters of the house have returned.

What did he derive from life? He did not think much of himself, always under-valuing his "I." When those greater than he were in town, he had no spirit and no pride to challenge, to compare himself with the true *maskilim* [enlighteners][1] and Hebrew teachers.

As a bachelor during the World War he was not mobilized but became a leader.

At the outbreak of the Russian revolution, he had become a well-known social activist, a Hebrew teacher whose name was familiar.

Married to Keyle, *reb* Yosif Aronzon's daughter (*reb* Yosif Rikiner). Happily content. It appeared that he was still a young little boy. Dedicated himself with fiery devotion to education and societal work.

Under the Bolsheviks, he was expelled from Jewish schools, though they recognized his abilities as educator and artisan. He, a Zionist, was not trusted to educate the proletarian communist generation. He tried to organize secret, illegal groups for the study of Hebrew. At first the Bolshevik powers paid no attention, but suddenly things became strict and private lessons were not permitted.

Pains, troubles...a sick wife, little children

[Page 373]

yearning for a piece of bread. Bitter cold penetrates one's bones...

Caught teaching little children, he is jailed for several months. He left prison with head bowed and a broken heart. He thought, struggled with himself: should he sell out his ideals? Should he go to the *yevseksye*[2] to ask for employment as a teacher? To bypass, to deny everything dear and sacred to him for the sake of a bit of bread? The life of the *"anusim,"*[3] outwardly a communist but inwardly a Zionist?

His associates resisted the regime – exiled to Siberia. There they die of hunger and cold, while he dies here for a bit of bread. But they fought, protesting, and he wants to sell himself as a *"nozer edoshim"* [group hermit]?...No. He will become a proletarian, a common worker. Once, as a bright, talented boy he would buy soles, bits of thongs, and repair shoes, just as a real cobbler.

So he sits at the little table. Tugs at the cobbler's thread, beats at the nails. Years tug by, the heart beats.

It is snowing outdoors, storm winds howl. Within the little house it is dim and dark. Loneliness is expressed in a quiet, monotonous tune: "Oh, little hammer, little hammer! You are truly our only provider. Little hammer, beat! Beat stronger!"

Livelier raises the hand of one who is satisfied with becoming a proletarian, who hasn't sold his soul. Life goes as it may, with a clear conscience. In truth, he suffers. "Labor is our life!" he sings quietly – "It saves us from all troubles" – He finds calm in the sounds; condolence, hope…

Two decades then pass. He wandered to Armenia, barely saving his life.[4] Slutsk is ruins beyond ruins in a firestorm, his wife and a son lost. More wanderings – with his son, he dragged himself across the Mountains of Darkness. Lost spirit. All lost.

Again the little hammer beats, weaker, more spiritlessly. The years drag by, clouded among strangers. Abandoned, alone. "There arose a new generation that knew not Joseph," he murmurs. "Who knows me? My son? Another language – other hopes. 'And the whole generation died' – Everything has died."

Translator's footnotes:

1. Followers and advocates of the Haskalah, Jewish enlightenment, who used Hebrew before turning to Yiddish to reach the masses of Eastern Europe.
2. Combined form of *yevreyskaya sektsye*, Jewish Section of the Communist Party.
3. Forced converts, term usually used to describe the *conversos* (Maranos) in 15th century Spain and Portugal.
4. Over 1.5 million Jews were evacuated beyond the Urals when the Nazis invaded in 1941.

Fighters and Martyrs

by M. L. G.

Translated by Hershl Hartman

The teacher Nokhem [Nahum] Molodetski, born in Slutsk, was highly educated. His father was a merchant and liberally inclined. The pogroms on Jews had a devastating effect on the young teacher and his young blood boiled without cease. He decided to sacrifice his life for the coming social revolution and carried out a terroristic attack on the Interior Minister, Melikov.[1] The latter was only wounded, and Molodetski was condemned to death by hanging.

He mounted the scaffold heroically, his light-blue eyes staring at awful death. He was only 23 years old at the time.

The heroism of Molodetski, the Slutsk Jewish youth, recorded in a printed underground revolutionary journal, is on display at the "Museum of the Revolution" in Leningrad, in the former Czarist Winter Palace.

This was the fate of a young Jewish teacher from Slutsk, to be a martyr for the revolution, for his ideals as a fighter for justice throughout the world.

The following Slutsk Jews played significant roles in the October Revolution:

I.

Velvl Krinski, the youngest son of the attorney Krinski, a student at an educational institute in Peterburg, fell in battle at the storming of the Winter Palace that overthrew the Kerenski regime.[2] It is said that he was an accomplished speaker and leader among the revolutionaries, as well as a favorite of Lenin's and his trusted representative. A street in Slutsk and judicial institutions were named in his honor.

II.

Another Slutsker was Yudl Kalmanovitsh, a high-ranking commissar in the Moscow government. He occupied important posts as an expert in agricultural matters. He was an agronomist by profession.

III.

A third was Yankif [Jacob] Goldberg, a tailor by trade, from a very poor family. He had a good head and was an autodidact. Dynamic, strong-willed, with a thirst for knowledge, primarily in socio-political problems. At first he was a Bundist[3] and later joined the communists. He rose rapidly. At the beginning he worked as a "yevsek" [cf. footnote 4]. He then became chairman of the Slutsk "Gorsovet" [city council]. This hump-backed Yankif Goldberg, a loyal servant of the dictatorship of the proletariat, suffered the same

[Page 374]

tragic end as all the Bolshevik old guard. During the Party purges of 1936-1937, he was arrested on suspicion of being a Trotskyite[4] – a former Bundist – he was thrown into the sorrowful Slutsk prison.

He had created many enemies by strictly enforcing high taxes to assure the success of industrialization. He was accused of wasting great sums of municipal funds and of diverting them to his personal purposes.

He suffered a couple of years of imprisonment and, due to ill health, died there, abandoned, forgotten…

Translator's footnotes:

1. Count Mikhail Tarielovich Loris-Melikov (1826-1888), appointed August, 1880. See http://en.wikipedia.org/wiki/Mikhail_Loris-Melikov.
2. Installed after the March, 1917, overthrow of the Czar, supplanted by the Bolsheviks in the October (November 7, current calendar) Revolution.
3. Member of the General Jewish Workers' Alliance (Bund) of Russia, Poland and Lithuania, a socialist organization whose withdrawal from the Russian Social Democratic Workers' Party left V.I. Lenin's group as the majority (Bolshevik) fraction.
4. Follower of Leon Trotsky (1879-1940), an associate of Lenin who lost the succession struggle to Josef Stalin and was driven out of the Soviet Union in 1929. A Jew, he was born Lev Davidovitsh Bronshteyn.

Between Both World Wars

Translated by Hershl Hartman

I left Slutsk with the Red Army on June 29, 1941.

I was born in Slutsk in 1914 and had lived all that time in Slutsk. I attended Yiddish School Number Five where Yiddish was the language of instruction, except for some subjects in Russian. We were also taught German starting in the 5th grade, as well as drawing. There were 20 teachers at the school and the student body reached around 400 in ages 8-16.

I remember one teacher's name: it was Lobus. Our school was near the former girls' *gimnaziyum* [high school].

The words *erets yisroyl* [Land of Israel] dared not be mentioned at school, where praise was constantly heaped on the great accomplishments of the October Revolution.

In 1925, huge taxes were imposed on the city's inhabitants and small shopkeepers could not survive, slowly liquidating their stores. Jewish cobblers, tailors, carpenters lived as self-employed craftsmen, but they had to obtain permits and to join the guilds. Everyone had to turn over his tools to the guild. Draymen had to turn over their carts and horses and join the guilds.

Everyone had to repair and improve his own dwelling at his own expense. The government was not concerned with building private dwellings, but built social institutions, as well as Jewish and Russian schools.

Jewish schools teaching Yiddish and Russian existed in Slutsk until 1935.

By 1935, most Jewish parents had stopped sending their children to Jewish schools, preferring to send them to Russian high schools. Many were concerned about their children's futures and many had begun to assimilate.

Kosher meat was obtainable until 1927. Butchers would buy cows and a *shoykhet* [ordained ritual slaughterer] would do the slaughtering.

In 1927 a decree was issued against [kosher] slaughtering and the butchers had to join a collective farm. Butchers who defied the decree, and their associates, were exiled to Siberia.

The population at the time consisted of three categories: *kulaks, bednyaks, srednyaks* [landed peasants ("fists"), upper class, middle class]. The owner of a certain amount of acreage was exiled as a *kulak*. A *srednyak* – a person of the middle class – joined a *kolkhoz* [collective farm]. Until 1928 such a person was neither dead nor alive – but they kept an eye on him.

A clubroom for self-employed craftsmen was established in the building of the [former] Slutsk *yeshive.*

The economic situation of Slutsk Jews was dire and strained. Every minor offense – for instance, if one sinned by selling a garment, a pair of trousers, a sack of flour – resulted in Siberian exile. Convoys filled with "sinners" would often leave Slutsk, followed by fearful gazes. Taxes were levied on garden fruits, on a couple of cows, and the weight was too hard for a Slutsk Jew. Slutsk was only about 10 percent Christian and 90 percent of the city's population consisted of Jews.

In 1929 the government abolished the old marketplace and converted the space into a handsome square, planted with flowers and partially paved with asphalt. All the booths and stores were torn down and in mid-square they erected a statue of Lenin. The entire beautiful square was enclosed in an attractive fence.

The market was transferred to where the *plushtshadke* [brookside?] had been. A government-run restaurant was opened in Solomyak's [former] *konditori* [pastry/coffee house].

Government-run general stores were also opened for workers and government employees. No anti-Semitism was noticeable, at least not in public.

Religious elementary schools did not exist. Stealthily, teachers and *yeshive* students would privately visit parents who still taught their children [biblical] Hebrew and portions of the Prophets. The Slutsk Cold Synagogue was converted into an arms warehouse, surrounded by barbed wire, and armed guards protected the armory around the clock. Synagogues

[Page 375]

were requisitioned, as well as – not to be mentioned together – the famous Slutsk monastery and many churches.

Summer Seminar for Teachers in Slutsk Yiddish Schools. 1924

First row, crouching, from right to left: The second is a daughter of *reb* Nekhamye, the yeshiva-head; the third – Malke Borukhovitsh

Second row, seated: The teacher Leybovitsh; the fourth is the noted Zionist Klara Mironovna Mishkovski; the fifth – Moyshe Efron; seventh – Maysl Baranovitsh

Third row: The sixth – teacher Brevda (inspector of the Yiddish schools); the ninth – Shimon Maharshak

Fourth row – above: The second is a[nother] daughter of *reb* Nekhamye, the yeshiva-head; the third is the teacher Shor, the fourth – Nekhame Shpilkin-Biler; the last is Karlin

In 1928, Slutsk Jews began to be accused of [spreading] Zionist propaganda. Anyone suspected of a relationship with Zionism was exiled. Even in the few prayer-quorums that remained, participants would fearfully, in haste, rush through the prayers and quickly leave the place.

Having a radio at home was forbidden, and if someone was caught with a small radio, he was jailed as a spy. Only ear-phones were permitted on payment of 15 rubles per year; through them, one might hear news and Soviet programs. Government news was also broadcast on the streets: programs and propaganda about Soviet wonders and unemployment abroad.

In 1932-33 the peasants in the Slutsk area did not plant their fields, unwilling to cede to the government their labor – the grain. They sold some of their hidden grain illegally and consumed part themselves. They paid dearly for this: hunger swept Russia then. Hunger was not felt as much in Slutsk because, in one way or another, the peasants sold part of their grain in secret.

There was not actual starvation in Slutsk. but one had to stand in line almost all day or all night to obtain a *kilo* of bread and, often, upon reaching the entrance they would announce: there is no more bread to distribute.

When a couple of *kilos* of flour [*sic.* context indicates "grain"] were distributed, religious Jews would have *peysekh* [Passover] in mind and, each month, they would save and put aside some flour for *matse* [matzo, unleavened bread]. Potatoes replaced bread in order to avoid eating *khomets* [hamatz, Passover-forbidden food].

Since all mills were under government control, the bit of saved grain was hidden. Over a year, a number of families, together, managed to save some 38 *kilos* of wheat for *peysekh*. A drayman came and told them that he was driving to Uretshe, where

[Page 376]

it could be ground at a private mill. A list of those who owned the grain was drawn up. Enroute, the grain was confiscated by the police. Going by the list, the individuals were called into an investigation. Since it was intended for *matse*, 16 *kilos* were returned and the balance was confiscated.

Bad times continued for Slutsk's Jews. Merchants, petty traders, brokers were exiled for the slightest reasons. By 1928, ritual slaughtering could not be done privately, but at the slaughter house near the mill on Kapulye Street at the little stream.

Peasants would hide reproductive cows. Calves were for raising and a young bull to be sold. A peasant would bring it before dawn [on a wagon], hidden under straw and hay, to a Jewish butcher, rap at the door and sell it to him in secret. Slaughtered in a stall, the rear [non-kosher] quarters were taken back by the peasant, and thus young-bull meat served to nourish pious Jews – their only kosher meat. It was permitted to buy fowls, but they could only be slaughtered at the [public] slaughter house.

Everyone obtained bread and sugar by means of ration cards. Brokers did not receive cards or [internal] passports, so that their children could not even attend school.

In general, fear raged in the home and on the street; when four people stood conversing, no one could be sure whether one of them was a spy. School children, unwittingly, would innocently expose their parents. Fear of one's own children was pervasive; one guarded against unwonted words in their presence.

Generally, one thought at home more about eating than speaking. During summertime one only thought about preparing 2 or 3 cubes [cubic meters] of wood for the winter, because [otherwise] water would freeze at home. Hoarding, or even preparing 10 *kilos* of flour, was punishable by 5 years imprisonment. Sewing up woolens or warm trousers was accompanied by hearts racing in fear. There was a saying among the Jews: the day is hard; may the night be calm, at least.

1934-36

A "golden age" began in 1934-36 for those who had gold coins. Jewish workers, smiths, carpenters, accepted no other coins but gold from their peasant clients. Bitter times developed for those Jews suspected of owning gold.

There was a case where a Jew was held in jail four times and gold was demanded of him. He surrendered the coins four times, but on the fifth jailing, after severe torture, lacking any more gold, he died. Another admitted under torture that his wife had left him 25 gold coins, specifying in her will that they were for erection of a tombstone. He was tortured for three weeks and put in jail among law-breakers and violent criminals.

He was rescued by the fact that a distant relative, a prominent communist, put in a good word for him.

He was taken home accompanied by secret [police] agents and, in their presence, a small part of an oven was broken open and they took away the gold.

Jews listed as having relatives in America were invited to sign [statements] that they had demanded dollars from their relatives. The government confiscated the dollars.

If someone refused to sign, he was put into prison.

This had bad results, because American Jews understood and knew the meaning of the decree and often failed to provide what the Bolsheviks were hoping and waiting for: a flood of dollars. Life grew easier with the opening of the *torgsin* [foreign exchange] stores; one could buy everything there with dollars. And that was how those with American relatives were helped.

1941

On the 22nd of June someone came up to me and said: the war with Germany has begun. I ran to the market-square and bought a sack of potatoes, took it home and then reported for duty to my [reserve] military unit. At 4:00 AM there were rumors that German paratroops had been caught around the city.

At 6:00 PM the Germans bombed the railroad station. People ran around like madmen all night long, not knowing where to turn.

On the morning of June 23 a squadron of 15 airplanes appeared and bombed along Zaretse Street to Vigoda. People carrying pillows and food ran toward the Siolke fields. The noise, tumult and clamor was indescribable. Children wandered about, lost. Huge panic reigned.

On June 24-25, all the roads were clogged by the homeless who were wandering toward Bobruysk and from Bobruysk in the direction of Minsk.

Airplanes appeared on the 26th of June

[Page 377]

and kept on bombing continuously. All of Zaretse Street was engulfed in flames.

The doors of our house were locked, the streets were dark, not a living soul to be seen. Everyone was out in the fields. Nothing had been moved from their places in their houses. It was apparent that only food had been taken along.

There were no Russian troops remaining in Slutsk by the 27th-28th of June. The town was afire and lines of communication with Minsk were down. There were rumors that German spies had concentrated all the retreating automobiles and buses and had bombed them. A bomb fell on the hospital near the commerce-school and hundreds of patients were killed. Surviving patients were led and dragged about, not knowing from where or how they might obtain medical help. Those remaining in town were the firefighters, doctors and prison guards.

By July 29th, 1941, the Germans were 15 kilometers around Slutsk. At 6:00 PM the last [Soviet] military unit left Slutsk, heading for Minsk.

The roads were packed with refugees who blocked each other's way and only chaos ruled.

As reported by a Slutsker

The Highway [Main] Street

[Page 378]

The Nazi Upheaval

Slutsk After the Destruction
(Seen with My Own Eyes)

by Maurice Hindus, New York

Translated by Pamela Russ

Maurice Hindus, the author of this article, is a famous writer and journalist. In 1944, he was actually the first American Jew who was permitted, as a correspondent, to accompany the Red Army as they entered Slutsk after the Nazi retreat from the city. At the same time, he published his observations and reviews in a series of articles in the newspaper "The New York Herald Tribune."

This article was written by Mr. Hindus especially for the Slutsk book.

In the middle of November 1944, I rode in an old, very used Ford, from Minsk to Slutsk. Several Minsker Soviet officials who knew Slutsk, accompanied me on this trip. We drove through desolate areas. On both sides of the road, there were clearly visible black chimneys, broken parts, everything that remained from the formerly populated towns and villages.

With their retreat, the Germans burned and destroyed everything that was in their path. Hours passed and still we did not see Slutsk.

Those with me kept on saying that we would arrive there soon, we would not be able to mistake it. Slutsk was a large city and even though the road signs were destroyed, they were certain that we would see the signs strewn at the sides of the road. But we did not see Slutsk. Unknowingly, we had passed it long before. Only when we asked an old peasant woman, who was bent over under a load of firewood, how far we were from Slutsk, did we find out that we were ten kilometers past it.

I mention this fact because as we rode by, we did not recognize the city because the Slutsker ruins were the most horrific that I had seen in war–torn Russia, and I even saw Stalingrad!

We went in the direction of Gutzeit's mill. The entire way to the market, I only saw a few buildings. The market, as I remember it, that buzzed with trade during the fall season, was now literally abandoned. There was no sign of birds, animals, hogs, or agricultural products that were a natural appearance in the Slutsker market! There was no memory of farmers with sacks and baskets filled with apples and pears with which Slutsk and the surrounding regions were famous.

I cannot describe the shock that I felt while walking down the wide street. I could not recognize the most beautiful and beloved street in town. The boulevard disappeared. With a bloodthirst and rage, the Germans tore down the beautiful trees, and only the chopped up stumps remained, overgrown with wild grass. Almost all the houses, the most beautiful in the city, were broken and destroyed. The Lutheran church with its pointed turrets and old city clock, one of the oldest, most famous architectural antiques in Slutsk, was cracked and just about ready to fall apart. The once beautiful recreation and relaxation places in Slutsk, were now a wild, tragic devastation.

Kopulye Street now must be renamed "Slaughter Street." Truthfully, it was no longer a street, because all the houses were destroyed down to the foundation. On the street, Jews were herded together behind steel fences and barbed wire, and then murdered. No one was able to tell me how many Jews had died as victims of the German machine guns. All that I found out was that from a population of 20,000, of which two–thirds were Jews, not many were saved from slaughter. The twisted and rusted barbed wire, which they did not yet have time to

[Page 379]

Maurice Hindus addressing a "*Yizkor*" gathering (in New York)
in memory of the Slutsk holy martyrs (Feb. 1952)

Seated from right to left: HaRav Tzvi Yehuda Meltzer, Binyomin Simon, Mali Epstein, Prof. Feivel Meltzer, and Dr. Avrohom L. Buni

clean away, were silent witnesses of the great pogrom.

The Germans captured Slutsk three days after the outbreak of the war. A few Jews fled the moment they heard the German airplanes flying high over the city on the morning of the first day of the war. Because trains, cars, and other transportation means were paralyzed or mobilized by the Soviet army, the only means left to save yourself was going on foot. Three of my nephews: Refoel, Gershon, and Shlomo Gindelewycz, gathered together their families and went on foot deep into Russia. Gershon reached a village on the Volga, and settled there. Refoel and Shlomo, members of a Slutsker *kolkhoz* [collective farm], reached a village in the province of Kastroma and joined up with a *kolkhoz* there. Their fleeing saved them from certain death. According to information from Soviet party officials, not more than a hundred Jewish families left the city and went on foot, and reached a shelter deep in the country. Who they were and where they settled no one could tell me. The rest of the Jews remained in Slutsk. They could not imagine nor believe that the Germans could be so evil and murderous as they had been informed. They could not imagine that the Germans would slaughter elderly men, women, and young children, without mercy. This was the most tragic error that our brothers made not only in Russia, but also in all of White Russia. Also, the Germans did not demonstrate any open signs of hatred when they captured the city. They asked the Jewish community to select officials who would represent them in front of the German commandant. The lawyer Tzifcin was elected for this position.

Within a few weeks, it was thought that he was successful with his new hosts from Slutsk. But when the pressures began, he protested more than once. One day, the Germans called a mass meeting with the Jews, seemingly to give them an opportunity to present their complaints openly. Tzifcin was the first speaker. He didn't have time to even say a few words when a German officer pulled out his gun and shot him. He was the first Jewish victim. The Jewish community was terrified. For the first time, they saw and felt the devil was even blacker than they had painted him. They felt helpless, as if in prison. Only a few were able to flee.

[Page 380]

A woman by the name of Mishelov risked her life and fled the city with her two children with the aid of a false passport. Her blond hair and blue eyes helped her escape the Nazi hands. The older people – the Najmark brothers also managed to successfully reach the Russian posts. A few others were also fortunate to escape, but no one was able to give me their names.

Slutsk was surrounded by a strong partisan army and the Germans were so afraid of the partisans that they rarely dared to go a distance from the main roads. I visited villages around Slutsk and was convinced that the Germans did not even touch the peasants' geese. The Germans left alone the villages that lay far from the roads. They didn't risk going to snatch any geese, which was really a much loved food for them.

A few young Jews in Slutsk were able to join the partisans. Why did the Jewish youth not tear themselves away and join up with the partisans? With the partisans, it was reasonable to think that they would be more secure with their lives, unless they would be murdered or shot by an anti–Semitic partisan. But according to the claims of those who remained there were many deaths from anti–Semitic partisans.

As the mayor of Slutsk, who was the chief commander of the partisan garrisons, related to me, Jews under his command seldom suffered anti–Semitism. He dealt strictly with those anti–Semites. Aside from that, the Jewish partisans were armed as well as the non–Jewish partisans and could well protect themselves against attacks. It is a fact that not only in Slutsk but in the entire White Russia relatively few Jews joined up with the partisans. Meyer Hendler, a fellow correspondent of the United Press in Moscow traveled through Pinsk at the same time that I went to Slutsk. When he returned, we compared notes. He brought the same tragic story from Pinsk as I did from Minsk, Slutsk, Pohost, and other communities in White Russia. Only a few Jews fused their fate with the partisans. Why, really?

I met a carpenter by the name of Popov. He told me that one evening during the time of the Occupation, the wife of a Jewish barber by the name of Melnik, ran into his house and begged him to save her children. Popov accompanied her to her house and took her three children home to his house. He kept them for a week. Once it became dangerous for him to keep them any longer, the mother came and said she would take them back to her house. Popov begged her to run away with her children to the partisans. He was one of their "secret" agents in Slutsk and he offered to help her find a way to get to the partisans. The mother replied, "If I were alone," she said, "then I would try this. But with the children I will not be able to accomplish this, and I won't go without them."

Despite Popov's arguments and pleas, she declined. And soon afterward, she and her children were killed.

There were many other incidents with mothers, fathers, sons, and daughters would have been able to save themselves by joining up with the partisans, but they did not want to separate. That's how mothers and fathers remained with their children, sons and daughters with their parents. The German terror created strong commitment and tightly bound families together.

If you cannot live together it is better to die together.

They all ended their lives behind the barbed wire of Kopulyer Street.

[Page 381]

Slutsk Under German Occupation

Translated by Hershl Hartman

Reported by David Mladinov, 17, born and raised in Slutsk; son of local cobbler Benjamin Mladinov. Escaped from Slutsk on the day of the liquidation action, hiding around Slutsk as a Russian. Crossed front lines via Bialystok.

There were about 12,000 Jews in Slutsk, Bobruysk Region, at the start of the war, among them refugees from Poland who came in 1939.

The German occupation of Slutsk began on May 7, 1941 [actually, June 26]. Rumors immediately began to spread and the Germans themselves began to say that all Jews would be annihilated. There were also some cases of Germans shooting Jews who had said something that displeased them. Jews lived in their own homes in town for the first seven months. The Germans forced them to perform all sorts of hard labor, such as building German homes, road paving, etc. While working, they were tortured and beaten with knouts (whips) and gun butts. The tombstones of the Jewish cemetery were uprooted to provide the foundations for four large German homes.

On a Sunday around November, 1941, a Lithuanian military detachment arrived to carry out an "action"[1] against the Jews. During the day, squads encircled the city while the others went from house to house seeking out Jews. Those caught at home or on the streets were shot on the spot, their belongings stolen. Some 500 Jews were killed that day in the course of a few hours. The others managed to hide. The Lithuanian detachment was withdrawn after the action. The Slutsk Jews were locked into two ghettoes in January, 1942. One ghetto, outside town, enclosed no more than 1,000 children, the agéd, sick, handicapped, single, common laborers. Some 40 houses in the center of town constituted the second ghetto, in which were crammed some 5,000 families.

Both ghettoes were surrounded by triple-rowed, electrified barbed wire.

The ghetto of the common laborers was liquidated in May, 1942. The Germans suddenly surrounded the ghetto. All the Jews were loaded into trucks and taken outside of town where they were all shot, according to reports gathered from the local population. The exact location of the slaughter is unknown to the reporter.

The second ghetto was liquidated a half-year later, around Nov. 8, 1942. An augmented Lithuanian guard force had encircled the ghetto on November 7, allowing no one to leave. On the morning of the 8th, the Lithuanians began taking truckloads of Jews outside of town. They harassed the Jews in many horrible ways: tearing children from their hiding mothers, shooting them on the spot; small children thrown to the ground and killed, etc. At that time, some ten armed Jews opened fire on the Germans. Wishing to avoid further resistance, the Germans decided to burn down

[Page 382]

the entire ghetto and its Jews.

Benzene was spread on all the houses and ignited. The greatest part of the Jews perished in the flames. The others were shot outside of town, where graves had been dug in "the bogs."

A small number of Jews, some 25 men, managed to escape through the fence at the time of the second action. Most joined the partisan bands[2] around Slutsk. Among the survivors are Galanson (son), 18 years old, Galanson (mother), 35 years old.

Signature of eyewitness Mladinov. Bialystok, May 31, 1945. Transcribed: Chair of the Regional Historical Commission (Yad Vashem Archive, Num. 1317/M11). Bialystok, May 31, 1945 Transcribed by Sh. Shteynman.

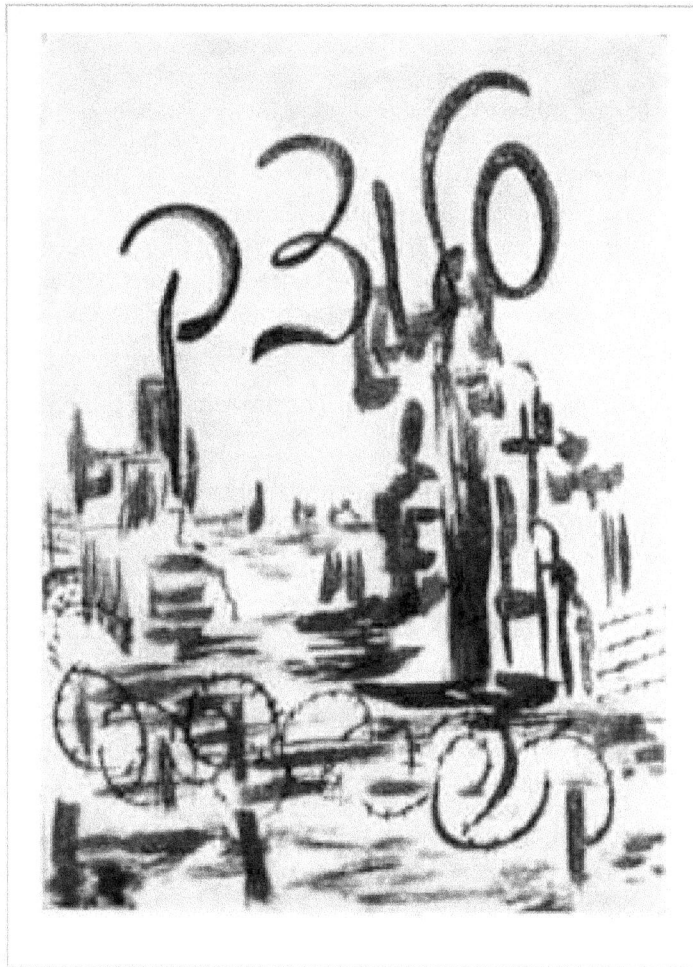

Drawn by the surviving boy from Slutsk,
Chaim Rusak, who now lives in Israel
[The cursive Yiddish letters in the drawing read: Slutsk]

Translator's footnotes:

1. German term for attack on Jews, adapted into Yiddish by the victims as *aktsiye*.
2. Guerrillas operating under Soviet military command.

[Page 382]

Letters From The Slutsk Ghetto

Translated by Hershl Hartman

A

Dear Brother Ezriel,

You want to know the circumstances of our mother's death. I was not in Slutsk at the time. I returned to Slutsk two months later. I was told that she lived with the family of a girl I was to marry, had the war not destroyed our plans. In addition to her parents, the girl had three brothers. They supported our mother quite honorably despite their own desperate condition. People have told me that often a day's food was a potato's peeling. Mostly, they starved to death.

This was Monday, October 12, 1941. When the word "Monday" was heard by a Slutsk Jew, a shudder would assail him because several horrible Mondays ensued before the final annihilation. There were many naive people who believed that they would be spared. Many Jews in Slutsk were executed for alleged reasons: for refusing an order, on an informant's word, etc. There were many varied orders: 1) Jews were not allowed to trade in the market square or with each other; 2) walking on the sidewalk was forbidden; 3) Jews had to have their hair close-cropped; 4) hats to be doffed before every German; 5) one's coat had to have sewn-on, front and back, a yellow patch in the shape of the Star of David; 6) Jews were not to speak to any non-Jews. Who can count the many other ridiculous orders?

Failure to obey such orders meant a death sentence. There was no ghetto in Slutsk until "that Monday." Jews and non-Jews had lived wherever they wanted.

There were large barracks past Vigoda Street where, pre-war, our military forces were housed. The Nazis settled many Jews into them, including Hannah and her children (two girls and a boy). Our mother and the family were on Monakhov Street (where the prison is).

Mother's health condition was never quite good. How could she feel in those bitter days? On the Friday before "that Monday," Hannah came running, sobbing. Her elder daughter, Khaye, had bought an apple at the market and was caught in that "crime"…The next day, on the Sabbath, our mother was told that all the Jews in the barracks (of course, including Hannah and the children) had been taken off somewhere. It was no secret to anyone that they had been slaughtered. Such "good news" confined mother more firmly in her sick bed.

On Monday, October 27, 1941, when Jews awakened before dawn, they learned that the entire city was surrounded by Germans, armed with heavy and light machine guns. When the sun was well up, large trucks pulled up into which Jews were tossed. The panic was indescribable. People scurried about like mice. The chase after Jews was on. Anyone trying to escape was fired upon.

Blood flowed in the streets. The trucks laden with Jews were driven out of town toward the Baranovitsh Road. Mass graves were waiting there. The Jews were machine-gunned, the ground torn up by grenades, victims buried, even those who were only wounded. This went on until mid-day. The so-called Regional Commissar arrived and ordered that Jews were not to be taken out of town, but killed right there in the barracks on Vigoda Street.

The family with which mother had been staying fell apart and was dispersed. A girl hid atop the heating oven, covered in rags, while mother lay helpless in bed. A Nazi soldier burst in, tugged at mother and ordered her to walk. Seeing that she really couldn't move,

[Page 383]

he brought in a Jew whom he ordered to carry her to the truck.

(This was related by the girl who lay hidden on the oven.)

Thus the Jews were brought to the barracks. Mother tossed all night on the floor, coughing and near death. There wasn't any water to wet her parched lips. I was told this by Leah, the *shveznerin* [*shvegerin* – sister-in-law?] who had survived until then and who in time was killed with her daughters and sons-in-law.

The next morning, October 28, a commission arrived and began sorting people into two groups, to the right and to the left – right to live and left, to die.

Our mother was ordered to the left. The condemned were taken out of town.

B

Dear brother:

I promised to describe what I lived through during our tragedy.

Writing about it is impossible, yet I try to toss some words on paper.

The war began on the 22nd of June and by nine o'clock that night the enemy was bombing Slutsk. The border [with Nazi-occupied Poland] was only 30 kilometers from town and on the 23rd to the 25th of June 1939 [should read: 1941] the Germans bombarded Slutsk day and night. Every corner of the city burned. Zaretse Street was aflame. The flames had not yet reached our street. Our mother said that our little street would not burn because a great holy man had predicted that no fire would ever afflict our street. Our mother and many other Slutsk Jews believed in this. Communications by radio, telephone, rail, and the electrical grid had been severed by the enemy.

During the first days we had no idea what was happening in the world; one only sought shelter from the bombs. People ran out into the fields, to the nearby surrounding villages. No one yet thought of leaving Slutsk entirely. No one expected the Germans to be this close to town. On the last day, when the situation became much clearer, the exodus began, some toward Bobruysk, some toward Minsk.

The Germans, however, outdistanced them, and most returned. Our mother and I were out in the fields on the first days. Mother was a sick woman, so living in the fields was difficult for her, so she asked to die, at least, in her own bed in her own home.

When we returned home, the house was in ruins. The bomb explosions had caused the window frames to fly out; pieces of the walls hung as if by threads. Mother said: in the end, one is somehow at home, not on bare ground. I could hand her a glass of warm tea to relieve her cough.

At 5:00 A.M. on June 26, upon leaving the house, I heard heavy gunfire coming from the railroad station. Dead silence ruled over the town. I told mother that the Germans were in town and that I had to escape because they would kill me. Mother asked, "And what will happen to me?" I replied that they would not harm women and children. I really believed that.

I could not stay with mother. She suffered from shortness of breath and had to stop to rest every three steps. It was terrible for me, but I had no alternative but to leave her with an old woman, a neighbor on our street, who was also ill. I went off to find other neighbors and a girl I knew, asking them to care for mother and not to desert her.

With a pained heart I decided to head toward Mozir through fields and forests, rather than along the roads which the enemy was bombarding day and night. His tanks and machine guns cut off all traffic to Bobruysk and Minsk. I arrived at Lyuban at 3:00 AM and could see the flames devouring Slutsk, Uretsha, Stari-Doroga and many other villages and towns. I made it to Kapatkevitsh after another 24 hours. Everything there was still in order. Trains were running. the civilian population had been evacuated. I reported to a mobilization point, from which I was sent to an artillery division.

We fought a two-month defensive action at Pinsk, though Minsk, Slutsk, Bobruysk, Smolensk and Homel had fallen. We were ordered to retreat to avoid the danger of encirclement. German bombardment dogged our every step. People fell like flies and our detachments were surrounded.

In a Ukrainian village I exchanged my uniform for old, tattered civilian clothes and decided to cross enemy lines to our side.

[Page 384]

German tanks around Slutsk. The town is immersed in flames and columns of smoke.
(A radio-photo from the "New York Times," Tuesday, July 22nd, 1941.)

I wandered across Ukraine for ten weeks. On foot, I crossed the districts of Tshernigov, Poltava, Dniestr-Petrovsk. I would cover 30, 40, 50 kilometers per day in hunger, cold and lice. A mishmash ruled: people wandering about, some trying to cross the front lines to get home. I would go through fields and villages that the Germans had settled.

I appeared everywhere as a Christian, because harboring Jews was a capital offense. The Germans had organized police forces in the towns, manned by Russian traitors, yet I had to go through them to get food to survive.

Once I was followed through a town by police. What could I do? I saw a wide river ahead of me! I was able to leap and dance from one to another of the river's ice floes, falling to my knees more than once, but reaching the opposite bank. My trackers were not that anxious to risk their lives.

Another time I was held by police and as they were taking me to the German commandant, I bought my freedom with my watch and the bit of money I still possessed, thereby saving myself from certain death.

I tried again to find some way to beat a path back home. After another three weeks of wandering the roads – not spending a night where I'd been by day, risking my life daily, plus suffering from hunger and cold – I was caught again. I was taken to a prisoner-of-war camp in Kanatop: an open field surrounded by barbed wire, guarded by Germans with machine guns. Thousands of people languished there without water or food. Each morning some of the dead bodies were removed. In many cases, soft tissue had been cut out, indicating the possibility of cannibalism. I somehow managed to tear an exit through the barbed wire and escaped during a dark, rainy night.

Ten days later I was captured again and taken to a prison in Rugatshov.

I managed to escape from that hell-hole, as well. This was in mid-December. I was almost completely naked: torn galoshes on my feet, trousers and jacket torn and completely lice-ridden. Life had become deadly. My only hope was to make it to the Belorussian forests

[Page 385]

to join a partisan brigade. I headed toward Slutsk.

Somehow, after much pain and little joy, I reached Slutsk.

I could not find our mother. There were many Jews in town. There were many dear friends who helped me. Some gave me shoes; others, underwear, a jacket, pants, etc. Starving, they shared their last morsel.

Most Jews then were still not in the ghetto. It was being set up when I returned to Slutsk. Large numbers of Jews were gathered into the area where the synagogues had been. The area was fenced-in by boards topped with barbed wire. Armed police stood guard in a watch tower. Every Jew was required to have a passport issued by the German authorities. Since I didn't have such a passport, people feared letting me spend the night in their homes. I had to sleep in the streets for some ten nights.

By then it was early January, 1940 [should read: 1942]. I obtained the passport of a Jew who had been killed and lived all that time with it.

At the time there were two ghettoes in Slutsk: one for skilled workers, the second for ordinary Jews. It was believed that the first was for living, the other for dying. I thought that, in the end, all the Jews would be annihilated. So I tried to rest a bit and regain my strength after my long stroll through Russia. I sought work that would at least save me from hunger. By great good fortune I got a job in a German restaurant. I feared staying – that is, sleeping – in the ghetto, because I knew it was a death chamber. There was an order posted everywhere that if a Jew were to be caught outside the ghetto, he would be hanged. Still, I did not go into the ghetto. There was a ruined, water-filled cellar at the restaurant where I worked, so I chose a spot that was somewhat dry and fit it out with boards and straw. When it was time to go home, i.e., to the ghetto, I would seize a moment when, sight unseen, I could duck into the cellar to spend the night. At dawn, I would crawl out, again seen by no one. The Germans with whom I worked believed that I slept in the ghetto.

Thus I slept in the cellar throughout the winter. When it grew warmer I slept in an attic over a horse stall near the restaurant. I was the only Jew who worked there. The others were Christians. Outdoors, men would saw and chop wood and, indoors, women would peel potatoes, cook, bake, clean the floors.

The restaurant owners were German Red Cross workers. My work consisted of stoking the oven fires, warming the kettles, seeing to it that wood and water were on hand. I was fully trusted. Not only was I sated, but I was able to provide food for many friends. Most especially, the family with whom mother had stayed. They had a large family of six. The Germans would supply a laborer with 200 grams of bread per day. If I had not helped the family they would have starved to death.

There were two radios in the restaurant. At 5:00 AM I would quietly tune in the latest news from Moscow and pass it on to the ghetto. It was dangerous but it needed to be done. The Germans were spreading rumors that Moscow and Leningrad had fallen and the Bolsheviks were *kaput.*

In 1942 the partisans let themselves be heard and I sought a connection with them in order to escape to the forests. I did not succeed. The restaurant was located on Proletarsk Highway, where there had once been the Kraynes Club, and the restaurant controlled a *"liyednik"*[1] [ice house?] on Kafashke Street. The *"liyednik"* was covered by a roof that formed an attic three-quarters of a meter high. There was no access to the attic. The keys to the *"liyednik"* were always in my care. I raised a plank in the ceiling of the *"liyednik"* as a means of entrance and began to store food there: about four kilos of sugar, four kilos of margarine, four kilos of preserves, four bottles of 100-proof rum, four kilos of rice. I did not have any opportunity to store bread. It was summertime. I endeavored to establish contact with the partisans but I did not succeed, and so the summer passed.

I worked at the restaurant exactly a year's time, from February 1942 to February 1943.

On February 8, 1943, I followed my usual procedure, leaving my secret abode and starting to stoke the ovens and the kettles. The Russian women who worked with me arrived with the news that German forces had surrounded the ghetto. It was clear to me that the last Slutsk Jews were to be annihilated.

The ghetto of the non-productive Jews had been annihilated and slaughtered in the winter of 1942. I did not give it a second thought, grabbed from the restaurant's pantry ten loaves of bread, each 1-1/2 kilos,

[Page 386]

and escaped into my hiding place. The monsters set fire to the ghetto on all sides and those who weren't incinerated were shot by machine guns. Armed Germans stood for ten days to make sure that there weren't any Jews who might have hidden somewhere. Anyone who showed himself did not emerge alive. Despite the fact that I was born in Slutsk, I did not know even the nearest surrounding villages and did not know how to make my way through the nearby woods. It was dangerous to walk on the roads. The only alternative was to wait until the weather turned warmer. So I stayed in my hiding place in the attic until April 15, almost 24 [should read: 4] months. No living person knew where I was. I cut the bread into tiny slices. At first, I would eat somewhat more, then reduced it to 50 grams per day, a spoonful of sugar, a spoonful of preserves, and a bit of margarine.

During the extreme cold I would take a bit of rum. For water, I would take a bit of ice from the *"liyednik,"* cut it up and sucked on it as it dissolved in my mouth. The cold was so severe that the skin on my feet peeled off. Fortunately, I had stored straw and a cotton coat that kept me somewhat warm, but when I tried to walk, I could hardly drag my feet. One could only sit or lie in that little attic.

For the first month I would only sit or lie. It then occurred to me that, in time, I would be unable to walk. I would let myself down into the *"liyednik"* at night and stamp my feet here and there for about half an hour. The situation was dangerous, because this was right in the center of town. If I emerged, I would surely be caught. I feared I might go mad in my solitude. To pass the time, I carved a chess game out of little boards (I just happened to have a penknife) and I would play chess with myself for five or six hours a day. Luckily, I also had a copy of Tolstoy's "War and Peace." I determined a quota of pages I would read each day, reading slowly, word by word, quietly. When I finished the book, I started over again. I had no pencil, so I used the penknife to mark the days and dates of the month.

I crawled out of my hiding place on April 15th. I decided to emerge during the day, because there was a curfew at night and I would surely be shot. I thought I would not be recognized because I had grown a terribly large beard, like a sixty year-old man, but many did recognize me. A Christian woman ran off to the gendarmerie to announce that a Jew had appeared in town. They searched from me in every corner of town, but I was sitting in the municipal park for three hours, trying to figure out where I might go. It was this that saved me. I went off wherever my eyes would lead me.

I walked for four nights until I came into a forest. I ate the rice that I had stored in the attic. I cooked the cereal in a preserves can. I had all of three matches and, when they ran out, I found a little stone on the path, made a wick from my cotton coat. I struck a fire with my steel penknife.

I wandered in the forest for five days until by chance I came across a small group of seven partisans.

My heart rejoiced at being among my own, free people. Together, we marched, ate, dreamt, joined a partisan detachment.

Now I want to live, to take revenge on the murderers.

I lived through so much! Was it possible? Is this the bitter truth? The Slutsk community is wiped out. Where are the Jews of Slutsk?

* * *

On the Fourth of April, 1942, a group of more than 20 people, led by Israel Lapidus, left the Minsk ghetto and went off to the woods near Slutsk.

Felye Vaynberg of Lodz escaped in January of 1943 from a slave-labor camp in Svyerzhani and joined the "Zhukov" partisan division in the Slutsk area. Several times she entered Slutsk, disguised and dressed as a peasant-woman, reconnoitering and familiarizing herself with the possibility of blowing up the large sawmill that provided building materials for the battlefront.

She completed her task outstandingly, bringing back an accurate map of the entire area and of the factory.

In May, 1943, she volunteered to blow up the Slutsk electrical station and the sawmill.

She again dressed as a peasant-woman, hiding a revolver in her basket, and placing a loaf of bread containing a mine among various vegetables.

[Page 387]

When she was five km. from the village of Gresk, a peasant recognized her and turned her over to the Germans.

After suffering great pain and torture, she was publicly hanged in Slutsk.

* * *

Misha Oytser of Ostrog (Volhynia), commander of a group in the "Zhukov" division, captured Germans on the Slutsk-Minsk highway and killed them on the spot. (As reported in the book by M. Kahanovitsh, "Jewish Participation in the Partisan Movement.")

Two Germans Confess to Slaughter of Jews in Slutsk

Kassel, West Germany, Aug. 10, 1960 – Two former German policemen, arrested several months ago, today admitted their role in the murder of about 700 Jews in the town of Slutsk.

"The Jews were slaughtered like cattle in the Slutsk blood-bath" on October 27, 1941, prosecutor Robert Hoppke declared.

The accused are: Franz Lechtroller, 69 years old, and Willi Papenkort, 51 years old.

Both declared that, under pressure of orders, they participated as part of two German police detachments and a Lithuanian detachment.

The prosecutor reported that the Lithuanians shot the Jews – men, women and children – while the German police prevented anyone from escaping.

The accused Papenkort claimed that he had stopped the slaughter because he could not bear seeing it anymore.

* * *

A Letter from Slutsk

Slutsk, February 19. 1946

Honored unknown friends,

Your letter of last May arrived in February…We have done what you asked. My husband and I did not know your relatives, but with [the information in] your letter we inquired among others, Jews who knew your family.

Your brother and his family escaped from Slutsk – so they are alive. They asked acquaintances for help in obtaining permission to return to Slutsk. But since it is wintertime and there is a housing shortage in Slutsk, permission to return has been delayed until May… Your sister and her husband and their children sadly perished. They survived until February 8, 1943, when all the Slutsk Jews perished.

Your sister's husband was an expert tailor. Such Jews were used until the final pogrom.

One Jew escaped the slaughter, Berl Kolbasnik, also a tailor. He reports that he worked with your brother-in-law until the final moment. I live a solitary existence, almost the only survivor of a large family.

Recently, I discovered another bereaved brother who lost his wife and five children, a daughter-in-law and two grandchildren.

He lives 40 kilometers from here. We often meet and mourn together.

I beg you to speak with my relatives and tell them not to forget me and to write to me from time to time.

That is our only consolation and hope: to hear a good word from afar.

With thanks in advance,
    Leah Sheyfer

Editorial note: The following [should read: preceding] letter is one of the first to relate the destruction of Slutsk. An uncle of the writer, in New York, had the letter (from Slutsk) published in New York Yiddish newspapers. On that basis, Avrom Mayzl wrote to the woman, inquiring about his relatives in Slutsk. The letter is the reply to his inquiry.

W O E !

by Sonya Rakhlin

Without a shroud and without a prayer,
Lacking even a grave.
Not covered, not buried –
Our ashes, strewn by the winds.

Goethe, Schiller, Schopenhauer,
Come and see the great fire
Of bones burned to ash.
You, the folk of art and knowledge,
See the bloody rivers flowing,
And sympathy from no one?
Words, words, lovely letters.
Desolate sounds are curses.
Woe! Our faith annihilated
And the grave – our exile.

Translator's footnote:

1.   Here and following, this word appears in the original as shown, italicized and in quotation marks.

[Page 388]

Writers of Slutsk and Vicinity

Translated by Hershl Hartman

Abramovitsh, Sholem Ya'akov (Mendele Mokher Seforim)
(2/1/1836 – 12/8/1917)

Born as the seventh child in Kopulye, Minsk region. The exact date of his birth is questionable: family tradition gives it as December 20 (old style calendar), 1836. However, his 75th birthday was observed on December 20, 1917.[1] His father, reb Chaim Moyshe Broyde (Mendele adopted the family name Abramovitsh later for reasons that are bound up with the spurious "granting of civil rights to Jews" and, it is said, after Limping Avreml[2], was one of the most prominent householders in the *shtetl.*[3]

– By the age of 14, Abr.[amovitsh] was well-learnéd in Talmud and rabbinic literature; however, the Tanakh [Hebrew bible], which he knew by heart by the age of nine, held a special place in his fantasies. His father died when he was but 14 and his relatives sent him off to study, first in Timkevitsh, a small hamlet near Kapulye, then to Slutsk, where he barely subsisted for two years.

For a certain time he studied in Vilna, in Rameyle's *yeshiva* and in the Gaon's[4] House of Study.

– Returning to Kapulye he took up studies in the *besmedrish* [house of study]. At that time there arrived in Kapulye a certain itinerant beggar, Limping Avreml (the prototype for *fishke der krumer* [Fishke the Lame, one of Mendele's novels]). His marvelous tales and wonders about prosperity in Volin [Volihynia] in southern Russia fired up the fantasy of the 17 year-old Abr., who decided to follow this Avreml into the wide world. They wandered through towns and villages, through Lithuania and the entire southwestern area of Russia, through Volin, Ukraine and Podolye, spending nights in the alms-houses or houses of study and begging from door to door. This journey in the broken down wagon drawn by a scrawny horse laid the foundation for Mendele Mokher Seforim's *di klyatshe* [The Old Mare], with which he travels through the entire Jewish pale [of settlement], in its length and breadth.

– In Kamenets he begins to visit with the Hebrew and Yiddish author Avrom-Ber Gottlober [1811-1899], whose daughters teach him Russian, German and mathematics. He passes the examination for teachers, and in 1856 he was appointed as a teacher in the Kamenets [secular] Jewish government school.

His first literary work [in Hebrew] is published without his knowledge by Gottlober in "*hamagid*"[5] in 5617 [1857], *A Letter on the Subject of Education*. He then moves to Berditshev, where he publishes a collection of articles under the title *mishpat shalom*[6] and another collection, *eyn mishpat* [? not recorded among Mendele's works]. His Hebrew novel *Fathers and Sons* was translated into Russian by Leyb Binshtok in 1867; the Yiddish translation, by B. Eplboym, did not appear until 1923.

The second period of Abr.'s creativity began with his writings in Yiddish under the later popular and beloved name, Mendele Moykher Sforim [Mendele the Bookseller].

– Abr. occupies first place in Yiddish literature. He is not only the first great Yiddish writer who drew from the deepest sources – from folk-life, folk-culture and nature – but is generally the first great artist to create in Yiddish. To the extent that Yiddish literature existed prior to Abr., it – with unimportant exceptions – had mainly religious and didactic purposes. He finally overcame those tendencies of his generation and raised Yiddish literature from its primitive state to a high level of purely artistic creation.

Papirna, Avraham Ya'akov
Born in Kapulye, 2 Elul 1840-1918

On his father's side, a great-grandson of the wealthy man and court-pleader R' Yisroyl Shershever; on his mother's, a grandson of the Kapulye Rabbi r' Suskind, under whose supervision he was raised. Under the influence of the *haskala*[7] P[apirna], already married, left for Zhitomir, completed the [royal government] Rabbiner School in Vilna. He taught at the [secular] Jewish school in Zakrotshin for a few years and in 1870-1909 taught religion in the *gymnazyes* [public high schools]

[Page 389]

in Plotsk and was principal of the local Jewish school. One of the most prominent representatives of the *haskala* movement in Russia, a fine stylist in Hebrew. Starting in 1862, participated in the Hebrew and Russian-Jewish press, publishing poetry, articles, historical essays. Of particular interest is his satirical poem *mishley ha'zman* [Proverbs of the Time] (1893). He wrote textbooks in Hebrew and Russian. His *zikhranot* [Memories] are among the best works in Jewish memoir-literature.

His collected writings, *kol ksavi* [all the writings of] *Avraham Ya'akov Papirna* were published in Hebrew.

Yehuda Gravovski [Gur]

Born 2/28/1862 in Fahast. His father Yeheshayu Reuven was a trader.

Studied in *kheyder* [elementary religious school] and in the Volozhne *yeshiva*. Among the first *hovevey tsiyon* [Lovers of Zion – pre-Zionist settlers], came to the Land of Israel in 1887. Was a laborer in Rishon L'Tsiyon and an employee in Danin's store.

From 1889 – a teacher in Ekron and from 1891 – in Zikron Yakov.

Among the first to teach Hebrew in Hebrew. Among the founders of the first teachers' organization. One of the overseers of the Anglo-Palestine Bank.

Published many newspaper articles, wrote textbooks, such as *beys seyfer ivri* [House of the Hebrew Book] (three parts), translations from world literature (Dickens, Jules Verne, Mark Twain, [Hans Christian] Anderson). Published dictionaries (with the participation of Prof. Kloyzner), 1903, with the participation of D. Yelin, 1920; Dictionary of the Hebrew Language, 1934-5. Died in Tel Aviv 1937.

Avrom Zinger
(1864-1920)

Born in Kapulye. Orphaned at age 10, studied in Minsk, Slutsk, Pinsk, Nesvizh, "ate days" [see footnote 5, pp. 273-274), devoted himself to the Enlightenment in his free time. Starting in 1885, published stories and articles in [Hebrew] "*hamelits*," [The Defender] "*ha'asif*," [Harvest-time] "*kneses yisroyl*," [Jewish People] etc. Also critiques, among them one against Y[itskhok] L[eybush] Perets.[8] Later also wrote stories and articles in [Yiddish] "*der yud*," [The Jew], "*der tog*," [The Day], "*undzer lebn*" [Our Life]. From 1888, lived in Warsaw, where he was a teacher of Hebrew.

When the city was evacuated by the Russians [during World War I], he returned to Kapulye.

Died in Bobruisk.

Avraham Epshteyn (Aba Arikha)

Born in Slutsk 1877. Wrote for [Hebrew] "*hatsofa*," [The Observer] "*hatsfira*," [The Dawn] "*hamelits*," [The Defender] "*hazman*" [The Time].

In Slutsk, edited the "*slutsk sheygets*," [Slutsk Wiseguy] (a humorous publication). One of the best Hebrew teachers. A teacher at the Slutsk "*kheyder mesukn*," [modern religious school] for a short time.

A teacher in Alterman's and Yekhiyel Halperin's Froebel [early childhood education] courses[9]. Lived in Warsaw and Odessa. Published feuilletons, stories and children's poems. An outstanding critic. He attained his proper place in literature in America, where he lived for 30 years. His articles and essays came out in [Hebrew] book-form, titled "*sofrim evrim b'amerike*," [Jewish Writers in .America] published by "*dvir*" [Holy of Holies] in Tel Aviv, two volumes

Died in New York, 1953.

Zalman Epshteyn (Shlomo Halkushi)

Writer since 1879. Born in Lyuban on the eve of *Rosh Hashana*, 5621 (1860), died in 1936.

Studied in *kheyder*, in the Volozhin *yeshiva* in 1875. Bookkeeper in Odessa, 1870-1904.

One of the founders of "*bney moshe*" [Sons of Moses] and secretary of its Odessa committee.

[Lived in] Peterburg 1904 – 1914 – 1916 – 1919.

Active in educational matters; a delegate to the 11th Zionist Congress.

In *erets-yisroyl* [Land of Israel] from 1925. Died in Tel Aviv in 1937. Involved as a publicist in the Hebrew press and published descriptions and memoirs in "*hamelits*," [The Defender], "*hatsfira*," [The Dawn], "*hashluakh*," [The Emissary], "*ha'arets*" [The Land].

Also wrote in Yiddish from time to time.

Published a collection of his writing in 1905; "*azkorot yitskhak*" [In Memory of Isaac], dedicated to his murdered son, Isaac, in 1927; Lilenblum's monograph in 1934.

Z. Vendorf
(5.1.1879 –)

Pseudonym of Zalman Vendrovski. Born in Slutsk into the family of a ritual slaughterers. Until the age of 13 studied in *kheyder* and *yeshiva*, and, with private tutors, Hebrew and Russian. At the age of 18 went to Lodz, worked in a kerchief factory

[Page 390]

while studying dentistry and attempting to write poems and stories. In 1900, he published in [Yiddish] "*der yud*" [The Jew] a few letters about Jewish social matters in Lodz, but soon left for England, was a laborer on a cattle boat, worked at a small soda-water factory, learned English quickly in his free time and became acquainted with English literature, peddling sheet music all over England and Scotland. Wrote for the Glasgow "*yidishe tsaytung*" [Yiddish Newspaper] and the London "*yidisher ekspres*" [Yiddish Express]; published stories in "*der arbayter fraynd*" [The Worker's Friend] and in the Labor Zionist weekly "*der vanderer*" [The Vagabond]. Earned his living at countless jobs, from that of a teacher at a *talmud-*

toyre [modern elementary religious school] to a tour guide in London; from a librarian to a porter at an exhibition, from a peddler in the villages to a typesetter in a printshop. In June 1905 arrived illegally in Moscow [after the failed revolution] and earned a living teaching English, then left for America. Engaged in all sorts of trades. Settled in New York on the staff of the [Yiddish] "*morgn zhurnal*" [Morning Journal – orthodox daily] and "*amerikaner*" [The American]. Wrote for the *F. A. S.* [*fraye arbeter shtime* – Voice of Free Labor – anarchist weekly]; invited to join the staff of "*haynt*" [Today] and "*yidisher tageblat*" [Yiddish Daily Newspaper] and lived in Warsaw from 1908 until June, 1915.

In "*haynt*" he edited the section called "Jewish towns and *shtetlakh*," wrote feuilletons, stories, contributed to various newspapers and journals.

Left Warsaw in June. 1915, worked as a director of the Committee for Aid to Jews dislocated by the war, participated in the Society to Spread Enlightenment, and "Aza," the Jewish Historical-Ethnographic Society. After the March [1917] revolution, invited to join the editorial staff of the newspaper of the Jewish People's Party in Petersburg. The newspaper never appeared, due to disagreements.

As a representative of "*yekofo*" [acronym of above-mentioned aid committee], made a three-month journey to the Urals and Siberia to investigate the situation of the Galician Jews who were exiled by the Czarist army as spies [during world War I]. He returned to Moscow from Irkutsk after the October revolution, becoming an official of the commissariat of the "*natsmindn*" [abbr. for the Commisssion for National Minorities] and, later, director of its division for press and literature for communication. At the same time, wrote for several Russian publications. Published correspondence and reports first for "*der tog*" in New York, later for "*forverts*" [Forward – largest Yiddish daily in the U.S.], the London "*tsayt*," [Time], for the Warsaw "*moment*" [Moment]. In book form, published "Humoresques and Stories," Warsaw, 1911. Two volumes, "*pravozhitelstvo*" [Permission] (Yehuda publishers, 1912), "Laughter Through Tears." His stories and humoresques were translated into many languages.

Shloyme Rabinovitsh

Born in Uretshe. At age four, moved with his parents to Minsk where his father, an Enlightener and a free-thinker, was a railroad expediter. He was arrested in 1899 by Zubatov for his activity in the Bund, served a year in Moscow prisons and then exiled to Olyakminski in the Yakut region [Siberia] from which he returned in 1904.[10] He was active in Minsk as an official of the Russian Social Democratic Party ("*iskra*") [the spark]. In 1907 he escaped the gendarmerie and went to America.

He began to write in Avrom Reyzin's [leading American-Yiddish poet] "*dos fraye land*" [the Free Land], then contributed to "*tsukunft*," "*fraynd*," "*veker*" [respectively: Future, Friend, Awakener – all radical Yiddish journals]. Published skits in the English [Socialist] newspaper, Sunday Call.

Yakov Kahan

Born in 1881 in Slutsk. Lived in Zgerzh, Lodz, Moscow, Warsaw. Obtained his PhD from Bern University [Switzerland]. Edited "The New Hebrew," "Anchor" [?], "Thorn Bush," "The Era." Came to *Erets-Yisroyl* in 1934. Edited "Gathering." Translated Goethe's writings.

His collected works, in 12 volumes, were published by Masada.

Awarded prizes in the names of: Byalik, Tshernikhovski, Israel, Paris. Died in Tel Aviv on *shabes*, 29 Heshvan, 5721, 1960.

Roza Simkhovitsh

Born in Slutsk into an aristocratic wealthy family. Her father, Shmuel, was one of the greatest scholars in Lithuania, in addition to being a great Enlightener, knowledgeable in general [non-Jewish] literature. He left after his death some manuscripts on *halakha* [rabbinic law], wrote many articles in the "Petersburg Herald." In 1894 he was a member of the rabbinic commission in Petersburg and was invited to sit on the rabbinic councils of Vienna and Warsaw. However, he did not wish to make of his learning "a spade with which to dig".[11]

Her brother was the famous Hebraist and historian Dr. Y. N. Simkhoni (1884-1926) and she received a good Jewish and general education in her parents' home, learning Hebrew and other languages.

After her father's death in 1896, she and her family moved to Minsk, where she joined the Socialist movement at a young age. She was arrested at 16. Thanks to her relatives' many connections,

[Page 391]

she was freed on condition that she go abroad. She studied in Geneva at the Jean Jacques Rousseau Pedagogical Institute and also at the university's philosophy department.

In 1919 she was director of the Froebel [kindergarten] courses in Vilna (of the Central Yiddish Education Committee, "aza" and "yekofo" [see above]). In 1921 she directed the established Yiddish Teachers' Seminary, played a major role in the modern [secular] Jewish school movement, delivered lectures on pedagogical and humanist themes. Her literary activity is associated with her co-editing of the pedagogical monthly, "The New [Yiddish] School," where, in 1921 she published several articles, such as: [on] Jan Amos Kaminski and others. She led the section on "German Pedagogical Journals." Was co-editor of the parents' journal "School and Home." For certain times, she lived in Vienna and Berlin.

Professor Meyer Waxman

Born in Slutsk in 1882, studied in famous *yeshivas*, and by 18 obtained [Orthodox] rabbinic ordination. Coming to America, he graduated with highest honors as [Reform] rabbi. He worked diligently to achieve two more university diplomas, both from the world-famous Columbia University. In 1912 – a Master of Arts degree, and in 1916 – Doctor of Philosophy (PhD).

Dr. Meyer Waxman was professor at the House of Torah Study [Hebrew Theological College] in Chicago, where he taught *tanakh* [the Hebrew bible], Jewish history and philosophy. In 1958 he retired and settled in New York.

Dr. Meyer Waxman is one of the most honored scholars, writers and thinkers that American Jewry has produced. He is the author of fifteen varied works, is mainly famous in both the Jewish and general world for his huge four [read: six]-volume history of Jewish literature, written in English. Dr. Meyer Waxman's *A History of Jewish Literature* in English consists of six volumes that contain 5,000 (five thousand) pages. The six volumes describe in detail the spiritual creations of the Jewish people since the *tanakh* was completed: from the Talmud and its commentaries, rabbinic literature, *kabala*, proverbs, Hasidism, the Enlightenment, [modern] Hebrew literature, literature in Yiddish up to the present day.

Among Dr. Meyer Waxman's works can also be found "A Handbook of Judaism" [?]; Jewish exegesis; a translation [with introduction] of "Rome and Jerusalem" by Moses Hess; his "*ketuvim nevkharim*" [selected works] in several volumes and his most recent collection of essays, "On the Roads of Jewish Literature and Thought," which appeared in Tel Aviv and for which Dr. Waxman was awarded the Lamed [Scholar] prize.

Dr. Meyer Waxman also wrote a great deal in Yiddish and published extensive series of articles. He also wrote for "*ha'olam*," [The World], "*hatkufah*" [The Era] and contributes to "*hadoar*" [The Post], and "*batziron*" [?] as well a number of English publications and a number of important encyclopedias.

Sh. I. Naumov

Born in Kapulye into a well-pedigreed family. Obtained a good Jewish and secular education. Emigrated to America around 1905. Participated in [Yiddish] "*yidisher kemfer*" [Jewish Fighter] in "*forshteyer*" [Representative] and mainly in "*kalifornyer yidishe shtime*" [California Jewish Voice], in "*progres*" [Progress], Los Angeles, in the Pacific "*folks-tsaytung*" [People's Newspaper]. Also wrote articles and feuilletons under the pen names Ben Nokhem, Ish Nemi, Itshke Kapulyer, Moyshe.

Dr. Faytl Lifshits *(Private docent in a Swiss university)*

Born – 1876 in Slutsk. Published the following important articles:

1. "What is Political Economy?", "*haolam*" [The World], Vol. 1, 1912, nr. 32.

2. Political Economy in Accordance With Its Systems and Trends.

   o First chapter: The Mercantile System ("*hashiluakh*" [The Release] 5663-64) [1902-3].

   o Second chapter: The Physiocratic System.

   o Third chapter: Adam Smith (5664-65) [1903-4].

   o Fourth chapter: Robert Thomas Malthus, 5665 [1904].

Dr. A. Damnitsh

Born 20 Tevet, 5644 (1884) in Romanova. His education in Talmud and Enlightenment literature was at the hands of his father, R' Osher, an erudite Jew [religiously] and an Enlightener, besides. Studied in the *yeshivas* of Slutsk and Minsk. In Minsk he headed up the society "Zion and Its Language," devoted to having its members speak Hebrew.

[Page 392]

On his arrival in America in 1906 he continued his Hebrew and Zionist activism. Was the first secretary of the "*histadrut ivrit*" [Hebrew League] in America, founded in 1908. Since 1919, settled in Baltimore and practices his dental profession. Publishes poems and stories in various newspapers and journals.

I. D. Berkovitsh

Born 1885 in Slutsk. Received a traditional Jewish education; studied Talmud, but unhappy with its dry laws, sought to still his fantasies in its stories and in the stories and legends of post-Talmudic literature. Later, as a teacher of Hebrew, he began to devote himself to auto-didacticism and became acquainted with European literature. Settled in Lodz, he debuted in "*eyn ha'tsofe*" [No Outlook?] with the stories "Yom Kippur Eve" and "Flogging." In that same year he was awarded first prize in the literary contest of "*ha'tsofe*" for his story, "My Swinish Liquor" [?] which made his name in Hebrew literature and he then devoted himself entirely to literary activity.

In 1905, invited to Vilna to edit the belletristic section of *"ha'zman."* Following the pogroms of 1905 he emigrated to New York, where his parents had previously settled. He was unable, however, to fit into Jewish life in America and returned to Europe with his father-in-law, Sholem Aleichem and thereafter lived with the family of the great Yiddish humorist in Nervi (Italy), Switzerland, Germany, etc., publishing from time to time in Hebrew and Yiddish journals and translating Sholom Aleichem's works into Hebrew.

After the outbreak of the World War, returned with Sh. A's family to N. Y. In 1919-20 edited the monthly *"miklet"* [Place of Refuge] (from Shtibl publishers), contributes *inter alia* in *"tsukunft"* [Future], where he published some stories, (the last of them "From Both Worlds," 1924, Vol. VIII) and the dramas *"landslayt"* – Town Folk (one-act play, 1921, vol. II) and *"untern tseylem"* – "Beneath The Cross" (three act drama, 1925, vols. III-V).

B[erkovitsh] is among the most important representatives of the realistic school in Yiddish and Hebrew literature. He is most interested in the experiences of people who cannot fit into their environments, or who find themselves in unusual circumstances; he has a sharp eye for the minor details of lifestyles and demonstrates profundity of psychological analysis in describing the pains of his weak, grey heroes, mostly – ordinary people who are often comical in their pitiful helplessness. His style of writing and his tendency toward humor reflect a certain influence of Sh. A., whom he so masterfully translated into Hebrew. In his pogrom-story, "Among The Sick," one of his best works, B. portrays the entire tragedy of pogrom-terror, raising the comic occurrences in the hospital to symbolic meaning. He also dealt with pogrom-psychology in his drama "Beneath The Cross," which was produced under the title "Moshkele Hog"[12] to great success in 1923 by Maurice Schwartz's "Art Theatre" and was also played in the Yiddish theater in Warsaw. *"landslayt"* was also successfully produced in N.Y.

His books: the novella *"ugerkes"* [Cucumbers] (Resnick & Kaplan, N.Y., 1909, 53 pp.); Collected Works (The Dawn publishers, Warsaw, 5670, 269 pp.); some of those stories and several others are included in his B[erkovitsh] Stories (5670, 199 pp.) of which "Fra Adam" was recently published under the title "From The Impoverished Nest" (*tsukunft* 1923, vol. XII). The Hebrew publishing house Small Texts, N.Y. also put out a series of two-folio booklets of B's, such as "Purim Play," ["?"], "David's God in America," [? a series of other titles too confused to permit accurate translation, including an apparent translation from Anton Chekov]. Some of his stories were translated into Russian, Polish, German, English (by Helena Frank), French (by L. Blumenfeld), and Spanish. He settled in the Land of Israel in 1928. In 1929 co-edited with F. Lakhaver the [?]. Five volumes of his collected works (*"sipurim umakhzot"*) [Stories and Plays] were awarded the Bialek Prize, 5712 – 1952, Israel Prize 5718. For translating Sholem Aleichem's works (vols. 1-10), awarded the Tshernikhovski Prize 5704.

He received the same prize in 5796 [!*sic*] for his translation of Sholem Aleichem's *"Yosele Solovey"* [Little Joseph the Nightingale] and *"a maynse bli sof"* [Story Without End]. Among B 's works in Israel are: "In Messiah's Time" and "Menakhem Mendl in The Land of Israel."[13]

Yefroyim [Ephraim] A. Lisitski

Born in Minsk on the 15th [t"u] of Shvat, 5645, 1885. His mother died when he was seven years old and after his father's re-marriage they moved to Slutsk. His father left from there to America, but he and his stepmother remained in Slutsk for nine more years. Here he obtained his education in *kheyder* and *yeshiva*. He came to America at the age of 15-1/2, studied at the *yeshiva* of Reb Itskhak Elkhonen and began to teach Hebrew.

[Page 393]

He spent three years in a remote village in Canada as a *melamed* [elementary religious teacher] and then went to Milwaukee. Entered the university there and studied pharmacy and chemistry. But he was more interested in teaching.

Since then he has taught in Buffalo and Milwaukee until he settled in New Orleans.

He has published seven books of Hebrew poetry and a very interesting biographical book, "*toldot adam*" – The Story of a Man.

His lyrics reflect pessimism and disappointment.

On the one hand, he demands justice, as an individual, for his stolen life in the world at large; on the other, he demands the rights of the Jewish totality from its oppressors.

R' Yehuda Leyb Davidson

Born in Kapulye. His father, R' Ber Kapulyer, excelled in learning and researching philosophy and mathematics. At the age of 12, Yehuda Davidson left the Mir *yeshiva* for Karelitsh, Minsk. His first article, "*lekadem pney haroah*" [?On The Ancient Face of Evil] was published in four installments in "*hakol*" [The Call]. Then he moved to Warsaw. Supported himself teaching Hebrew.

Studied medicine. At the suggestion of the Polish writer Klemens Yunasha, he translated into Polish "*mesoes benyomin hashlishi*".[14]

The books were quickly sold out. Dr. Davidson was well-known in Warsaw.

Mikhal Frenkl

Poet and Jewish-American critic. Died at the age of 62.

He was a grandchild of Mendele. Born in Kapulye, emigrated to America at the dawn of the current [20th] century. He traveled the world and settled temporarily in Paris in 1926. There he advised and encouraged Henry Miller to devote himself to literature. Together with Miller he published a book on philosophical treatises about Hamlet.

After World War II he moved to London.

His wife was the well-known French artist Daphne Mouchoux [?].

Zalman Ratner

Born May 15, 1885 in Starobin, as the son of a dry goods retailer. Studied in *kheyder* to the age of twelve, then attended a [secular] beginners' school in Slutsk. From the age of ten [*sic*] on, worked at various jobs in Minsk. 1918-23, managed the Yiddish book depository in Moscow. Since 1924 – employed by the State trading office in Moscow. He put together the bibliography of Yiddish books produced in the Soviet Union during the years 1917-1923 (a list of 1,500 books and brochures).

In the anthology "On The Roads to The New School," 1928, he published a list of all the Yiddish books that appeared in the Soviet Union in the year 1927

Zelig Ratner

Born in Slutsk in 1885, wrote Yiddish poems and also was editor in New York of the newspaper "*Ruski Golos*" (Russian Voice).

Yitzhak Epstein

Graduated Lausanne University in 1905; Doctorate in Literature in 1915; a writer, a linguist, pedagogue-psychologist. One of the first teachers in the new *yishuv* [pre-state Jewish settlement in Palestine]; teacher in the Teachers Seminary; a frequent lecturer on the Hebrew language on Israel radio. Brother of Zalman Epstein, born in Lyuban.

Studied in a *kheyder*, in the Odessa modern school, at Lausanne University, 1902-05.

In the Land of Israel since 1886 (one of the six sent by the Lovers of Zion [pre- Zionist settler movement] to study agriculture). 1891-1902, teacher in Safat; in Rosh Pineh and Metullah he introduced the system of [learning] "Hebrew in Hebrew."

In 1915-19, director of a school in Salonika; 1919-1923 – director of a teacher's seminary in Tel Aviv for teachers and Froebelists [kindergarten teachers]. One of the first to emphasize the importance of considering the question of relations with the Arabs and becoming close to them. One of the founders of "*brit shalom*" [Peace Alliance]. Lecturer and instructor in various theatre studios in Israel. Published research papers on various topics: education, Hebrew language, pedagogy and psychology; published the book "Hebrew in Hebrew." Died in 1963.

[Page 394]

Rokhl Faygenberg (Amri)

Born in 1885 in Lyuban. In the Land of Israel since 1924. A folk-story teller in Yiddish and Hebrew. She provided much help to the defense of [Samuel] Schwarzbard with her voluminous material on the pogroms in Ukraine.[15] She wrote stories about actual Jewish life in Poland. Her first book, "Childhood Years," made a strong impression. In "*megiles dubova*" [Scroll of Dubova] she described the destruction of Dubova in Ukraine; published [Yiddish] "On Foreign Roads," [in Hebrew] "Not Here Nor There," "In Days of Rage," "On The Shores of the Dniester," "Through The Years," "[?] Without Love" (about life in the Land of Israel). "The Last Stage" (about Jewish life in Poland).

Wrote and writes articles from time to time about current matters: the youth, the Jewish woman, building the Land.

Edited: "The People In Its Land" (1948-49). Translated into Yiddish the writings of the Russian-Jewish writer Semyon Yushkevitsh.

Maurice Hindus

Born near Slutsk [in Bolshoye Bikovo]. Well-known English journalist. Staff writer for "New York Herald Tribune."

His book in English, "House Without a Roof," appeared in 1961, published by Doubleday.

Rabbi Professor Simkhe Asaf [Osovski)

Born in Lyuban, 9 Tamuz 5649 (1889). Studied in *kheyder* and in the *yeshivas* of Slutsk and Telz (5665 – 5668) and received ordination. During the years (5670-71) served as rabbi in Lyuban.

During 5674-79 he headed the Odessa *yeshiva*, founded by Rabbi r' Chaim Tshernovitsh (young rabbi).

He began his scientific-literary work in Odessa and published his first articles in "*hashiluakh*" [?The Dismissal] and "*rishumot*" [The Records].

He had been an active Zionist in the Telz *yeshiva* and, in Odessa, he joined the activists in the Zionist movement and was elected a member of the Zionist City Committee.

He arrived in the Land of Israel in 1921 and was appointed as a teacher of Talmud in the "Mizrachi" [religious Zionist] teachers' seminary in Jerusalem. He published many research articles and books about the sects in Israel, educational methods, religious courts, relations between Torah-centers in the Land of Israel and those abroad.

Upon the founding of the Hebrew University in 5685 (1925), he was appointed as a lecturer and later a professor of Gaonic and Rabbinic Literature.

Was active in Mizrachi and its representative on the [pre-State] Government Council. Member of the governing board of the Mizrachi schools; member of the honor-courts of the World Zionist Organization and of the Mizrachi organization; vice-chair of the Historical-Ethnographic Society in the Land of Israel; member of the Language Academy and executive committee of Hebrew University. Vice-chair of the "B'nai Brith" order, etc.

Upon the creation of the Jewish State he was elected to the Supreme Court and rector of Hebrew University.

He published many important books.

Died at the age of 64, 9 Heshvan, 5714 (1953).

Mordkhe Lipe-Gorin

Born in 1890 in Slutsk. Resident of New York. In 1935 published [in Yiddish] "Songs of the Road," as well as poetry in English.

Nokhem Khinitsh

Born in 1895 in the village "Rizitse" near Slutsk. Studied at *yeshivas* in Slutsk and Lide. Graduated from the pedagogical school in Grodne. Wrote in [Yiddish journals] "California Voice," "Chicago," "Literary Pages," [and] in the Canadian Yiddish press. [Here follows a list of of 10 Hebrew journals.] Published an anthology "*khayi avoda*" [My Life's Work], edited the *yisker* books for Luninetse and Kobrin; collected material for the *yisker* books of Brisk, Minsk.

Elye Shulman

Born in Slutsk. Graduated from City University of New York.

Author of "History of Yiddish Literature in America, 1879-1905," "*yung vilna*" [young poets' group in pre-war Vilna], and of various monographs and reminiscences about Yiddish literature.

Avrom Regelson

Poet and critic. Born in Hlusk 1896. Came to America with his family at the age of 11. Was a teacher. His first

[Page 395]

poems were published in "*miklet*" [Refuge], New York. Published articles and reviews in American and Land of Israel newspapers.

His poem "Cain and Abel" was published in 5692.

While in Israel he was on the staff of "*Davar*" and "*Davar liyeladim*" [respectively, The Word and The Children's Word].

He returned to America in 1936. Upon returning to Israel in 1949 he worked at the book publisher "*am oved*" [Working People] and then on the staff of "*al hamishmar*" [On Guard].

Regelson is rooted in American literature in English. Many of his books of poems, translations, reviews and commentary were published in New York and Tel Aviv.

Borekh Katsenelson

Born – 12/21/1900 in Slutsk. Studied in *kheyder* and in the *yeshiva* but became acquainted with [modern] Hebrew literature early on, began to write poetry. Under the influence of the [Russian] revolution, went over to writing poems in Yiddish, published in the Minsk "*shtern*" [Star], 1919, and "*farn folk*" [For the People], 1920.

Came to America in late 1921 and was employed as a Hebrew teacher. Published poems in [Yiddish journals] "The American," "Yiddish Daily Newspaper," Winnipeg "Yiddish Word," "Free Voice of Labor," "The Big Stick" [humor journal], "Arising," "The Pen" and others. Also a series of critical articles (in "The Pen"). In the Land of Israel since 1934, three of his volumes of poetry were published there.

I. D. Abramski

Son of the famous Rabbi r' Yekheskl [Ezekiel] Abramski. Spent a short time studying in Slutsk, lives in Jerusalem. Wrote for almost all the daily newspapers in Israel, as well as three literary journals.

Chaim Lif

Born in Starobin. Studied at the Slutsk *yeshiva*. Published articles in various Hebrew newspapers, co-editor of two journals.

Arn Nisenzon

Born 1897 in the little village of Tshipeli, near Slutsk, to poor [but] self-employed parents. His father was a miller and a leaseholder of a field. Emigrated to America in 1911.

Published poems in [Yiddish journals] "The Jewish People," "Free Voice of Labor," "Future," "The Pen," "The Time," "Truth." Also wrote essays. Was coeditor of the [Yiddish] journal "The Beginning."

A volume of his poetry, "Hundreds of Songs," was released ("Our Journal" publishers, N.Y. 1920.) A collection of his poems, titled "Meters," was published in 1925. His work is distinguished mainly by the maturity of its form and style.

Ruvn Valenrad

Hebrew writer, born in Vizne. Studied in *kheyder*, *yeshiva*, and then in the Slutsk [government] middle-school. Came to the Land of Israel in 1920. Worked on the roads of Tiberia and Kfar-Ezekiel. Left the Land of Israel for France and then on to America. Worked in factories while studying at New York University and Columbia.

Teacher of Hebrew literature at Brooklyn college.

His stories are dedicated to the lives of Eastern European immigrants who become rooted in their new home. Six of his books in Hebrew have appeared to date by publishers in New York and Israel.

Authors, Translators, and Editorial Staffers

Yisroyl Levin

Born 1876, in a village near Romanova. Hebrew teacher in Boston. Wrote for New York [Yiddish] "Daily Newspaper." Translated Tshernikhovski's poems into Yiddish, as well as "Psalms" and "Song of Songs."

Sh. Nakhmani [Nakhmanovitsh])

Born in Hrazova in 1884. Studied in *yeshivas* of Slutsk and Minsk. One of the founders of "*kheyder mesukn*" [modern *kheyder*] in Slutsk. Teacher in Israel since 1913. Translated some 20 books from Russian into Hebrew, issued by three publishing houses. Wrote for "Kuntrus," "Hadavar".

[Page 396]

Zvi Asaf

Born in Lyuban 1902. Studied in *yeshivas* of Slutsk and Odessa. Secretary of the printers' union in Israel. One of the editors of "Echoes of the Presses," "World of the Presses."

Shimon Maharshak

Born 1904 in in Slutsk. Graduated from Hebrew University in Jerusalem. Teacher in the Tel Aviv commercial school "*geulah*" [redemption]. Published "Algebra," a three-part text book.

Rabbi Nisn Waxman

Born 1905 in Starobin. Studied in the Slutsk, Mir and Slobodka *yeshivas*, as well as in the *yeshiva* of R' Isaac Elkhonen. In the course of 12 years was a rabbi in Lakewood [N.J.] near New York. Wrote for [Hebrew] "Forts," [Yiddish] "The Jewish Light," New York, "The Word," Vilna. Published various works, such as "Good Aspects of the Torah," "Deborah's Palm Tree" with interpretations and historical commentaries, and still others.

Avrom Asaf

Born in Lyuban 1906. Studied in *kheyder*, graduated from the Mizrachi teachers' seminary in Israel. Director of the [secular Jewish] Dubnow Folk-school. Edited "Sabbath Book," "Days of Awe." Also published texts for various classes.

Sh. Bet-Zvi (Baskin)

Born 1906 in Slutsk. Engineer, teacher at the Tel Aviv "Max Fine" high school. Wrote for [Hebrew] "Not Yet," "The Generation," "Seasons."

Shmarye Barhan

Son of Nokhem Dan the *yeshiva* head. Born in Slutsk 1896. Member of the collective Degania A. Studied in the Slutsk *yeshiva*, at the Odessa [secular Jewish] teachers' seminary. Edited the [Hebrew] books "In Battle," "The Path of Degania A."

Zvi Hagbati (Khazanovitsh)

Born 1907 in Slutsk. Member of the collective "Fountain." Edited some 30 compilation-pamphlets published by the collective. Wrote for "On Ascent," "Young Worker."

Shmuel Damnitsh

Born in Romanova. Wrote for [Yiddish] "California Voice," "Chicago" and other publications. (*This list is ordered chronologically, assembled according to Zalman Reyzin's* Lexicon [of Yiddish Literature] *and other sources.*)

Translator's footnotes:

1. Beyond the six-year discrepancy noted here, Mendele averred that he may have been born even earlier, in the late 1820s. Unlike strictly recorded dates of death for purposes of *yortsayt* – memorial observance, birthdays were insignificant in Jewish tradition.
2. Avreml is a diminutive of Avrom or Abram, hence Abramovitish: son of Abram.
3. Actually, a collector of taxes on meat, candles and other necessities. One of Mendele's novels, *di takse* (The Tax), is a virulent attack on the practice.

4. Genius of Vilna, Elijah ben Solomon (1720-97), a determined opponent of Hasidism, whose efforts prevented that movement from engulfing Lithuanian Jewry.
5. The Announcer, weekly Hebrew journal of the Enlightenment, published 1856-1892.
6. "The Judgement of Peace;" it can also mean "The Judgement of Sholem," i.e., of Sholem Ya'akov Abramovitsh – Mendele.
7. Enlightenment, which brought modern scientific and cultural ideas into the Pale of Settlement.
8. Usually given as I. L. Peretz (1852-1915). See *The Three Great Classic Writers of Modern Yiddish Literature, Vol. III, I. L. Peretz*, Pangloss Press, 1996.
9. Friedrich Froebel (1782-1852) developed the concept of and coined the word, "kindergarten."
10. The Bund – General Jewish Workers' Alliance (*bund*) of Russia, Poland and Lithuania – was a major revolutionary movement. Zubatov headed the Czar's secret police.
11. Based on *Pirkei Avot* 4:5, which exhorts one to not make one's learning into a source of livelihood.
12. "Moshkele" is a diminutive of the insulting general name, Moshke, referring to all Jewish males by Russian anti-Semites.
13. Manakhem Mendl is a Sholem Aleichem character (Tevye the Dairyman's brother-in-law) who fails at all his schemes to earn a living.
14. The Travels of Benjamin the Third, perhaps the most famous work of Mendele Moykher Sforim, patterned after Cervantes' Don Quixote and Sancho Panza.
15. Schwarzbard was a young Ukrainian Jew whose family was among the estimated 200,000 Jews wiped out by pogromist bands, including those of General Petlura, during the post-revolution civil war. He traveled in 1927 to Paris where Petlura had taken refuge, tracked him down and shot him dead. His trial was a worldwide sensation and ended in acquittal by a jury that took only minutes to decide the case.

[Page 397]

Slutsk in Yiddish Literature

Excerpts from "Shloyme Reb Chaim's"

by Mendele Mokher Seforim

Translated by Hershl Hartman

A

In the Slutsk Yeshiva

…Shloymele, whose good fortune brought him days and nights of places to eat and sleep, also in time achieved charm and grace in the eyes of all the *yeshiva*[1] boys. Even the senior students there were won over and allowed him into the group. "Khart,"[2] a scamp who delighted in throwing wet rags around, letting out farts, a unique fellow, became Shloyme's companion – studying with him as a comrade, it was called. "Khart," as it turned out, was by nature a gem, a golden character with warm, deeply internalized feelings of compassion, of love that often burst forth in pearly, trembling tears in his eyes and a quietly sorrowful sigh on his lips – quite a fine little fellow but, alas, poor and lonely. Shloymele's great good fortunes, eating and drinking in companionship, did not aid his studies. He was led astray from the learning that he had wanted and needed to achieve. In truth, such fortunes were more ill than good, to be wished on all one's enemies; yet "days,"[3] even when eaten in the kitchen, exiled under an angry cook, were still better than *pas bimelekh*,[4] bread and salt; thin, watery *krupnik*, groat-soup, better than *mayim b'mshure*, water in small measure; sleeping on a warm "*lezhanke*" [warming-oven cot] much better than *le'al ha'erets tishn*, sleeping on the bare earth, and sometimes suffering that thing that a sated, sinning person desires – all of this is better than the bitter life of one who hungers, who suffers need.

Mendele Mokher Seforim

As for Shloymele's life in Slutsk – which lasted about two years including an interruption mid-way – it is worth pausing just a bit on certain aspects…

Shloymele remembers those wintery evenings in the *yeshiva*. The sun, after its mournful, short pass, would set on an array of the colorfully-playing, thickly outstretched clouds. Its last rays penetrate inside the *yeshiva* through its thick, frosted windows, and flutter on the opposite wall with all the impressed reflections of the semi- and somehow variously frost-embellished, decorated panes. Outdoors the cold rages, smolders. Indoors it is cold – dim. The scattered boys have just started to re-gather, each of them rubbing his hands, saying "Ah, ah." The warming-oven is alight. Two boys – among those who'd remained: one of them luckless, lacking a "day," and the other who had one, had brought along a few potatoes for supper – they kneel at the open door [of the oven] facing the fire, each paying attention to his sinful bowl where a single groat races angrily, up and down, drumming: *tyokh, tyokh, tyokh*! The fire crackles, illuminating their faces and of those around them. A brightly-burning log sticks out of the oven, sending out flaming tongues, erupting haughtily near

[Page 398]

the door with gleaming embers, blaring out, at the end, "pip-pip-fff," like the long blast of the *shoyfer* [shofar]![5] It grows warm, the crowd is happy. They pass time with stories, with sayings, with jests. The boys who have bowls take to eating – "Arise, Jews, in a momentous hour!" The 'priests' go off to eat 'the offering' – to slurp their groat-soup!…And the boys slurp, working diligently, accompanying every spoonful from the bowl to their mouths with a song of their lips, giving the onlookers wolfish appetites. Those scratch themselves; they lick their lips in great desire. On Wednesdays, Sholymele sits here, too, in the midst of them, eating 'the offering' of the little bread loaf that Yente the market-wife would give him that day. He eats it very seriously, piously, in a sort of *"leshem yikhud"* [cabbalistic invocation of deity's name], being as careful as a ritual guard that not a single crumb fall, heaven forbid.

That little loaf is truly dear, it must be treated like "an offering baked on a griddle," like a pancake fried in butter, dearer than the best "day," considering with what flaming love for God and his Torah the loaf was given. A pair of doves, the [Temple] sacrifice of a poor man, is considered by God equal to the fat bull of Bashan – the last possession of a poor man, alas!

…The first evil hour befell Shloymele on his "day" at a well-to-do householder's, there in the kitchen where he entered, as was the habit of a *yeshiva*-boy come to eat supper.

In a corner of the kitchen a grease candle sputtered. A woman with a red, twisted nose, with fat lips, a wide mouth, missing two front teeth, puttered around the stove, humming, murmuring angrily, for no special reason, avoiding looking at Shloymele's corner, as if he weren't there. Shloymele sits as though on needles, his soul expiring as he waits. The kitchen door squeaks, opens constantly. Any moment, he thinks, the redemption, the supper, will arrive – but nothing; the servants go to and fro. He sits and is almost consumed by his waiting. It is late, time to go to his rest in the place where he spends the night. They're awaiting him with yesterday's still-not-completed stories, and also with newly-fresh ones. He is noticeable by his *yeshiva*-boy movements – rising up once in a while, a scratch, a sigh, a cough, a sniff of the nose – and she: nothing! She keeps on murmuring as though she were arguing with someone, wishing Pharoah's plagues upon his head. Just then, as though sprung from the earth, there appeared before Shloymele's eyes a bright-colored picture of his life, past and present. And right in the midst of that he heard simultaneously a woman's voice, sounding like the cook's, calling and saying: "Go, little boy, go wash up. Little boy!" Shloymele washes his hands in his tears, raising his hands angrily, resentfully with "raise your hands," not, God forbid, against God, but against his dark fate and the woman with the red nose.

He manages a bite of bread, a sip of groat-soup, says the blessing, cutting it short, says goodnight to the four walls and leaves quickly, muddled, not kissing the *mezuze*,[6] extremely upset, sad, unhappy with himself or anyone; oh-and-woe – he thinks angrily in his thoughts – to him, to his luck, to what he has experienced! A ward, a *yeshiva*-boy, "eating days," unfortunately…Oh-and woe to his standing with his fellow-*yeshiva* boys, poor lads. Oh-and-woe to his privilege of going from door to door with the rabbi, poor-gathering alms in the little sack, as well as to the privilege of wandering about, sleeping on the warm *lezhanke*…great gifts…prospects – great prospects…

B

Reb Yoyne [Jonah]

…Among all its wonders, the wealthy Slutsker, *reb* Yoyne, rightly occupies a handsome spot. See him all at once: his house, his activities; regard him and imagine him! A single-story wooden house with a small porch a few steps high at the entrance, and a row of medium-high windows, glass eyes lining both sides, looking out on a large, fenced-in yard. And by that name, *"reb* Yoyne's yard," his home is known in the town. At one side of the yard there stands a tall, very attractive synagogue; that is, a house of study. A large crowd prays there – both family members and other Jews. There, too, both young and old sit and study day and night. Thus it was during his lifetime and later, in his son's time – a quorum of learnéd Jews, agéd and young men, would be paid wages to study constantly. Wages were also paid to a *yeshiva*-head to teach a portion of the Talmud with commentaries to the learnéd audience there, every morning after prayers.

Friday evenings the yard takes on a sort of new appearance: a holiday-like face, a pillar-of-fire of many burning candles in the synagogue, in the house, streaming through the windows and illuminating, spreading across the yard in every little corner. It feels as though, somehow, the good angels – servants of Him Above, sent from heaven by the Holy-One-blesséd-be-He – hover above there, awaiting the rich man and his children at their departure from the synagogue, to accompany them home. There in the house, in a bright, large salon, displayed before the residents and for scores of guests, poor people, affluent Jews, are *shabes* [Sabbath]-laden tables with everything wonderful – with blessing-candles in trios, in seven-branched silver candelabras, on expensively veneered credenzas. Wine

[Page 399]

sparkles, pearly in hand-cut, big-bellied, long-necked flagons, reflecting rainbow-colors into crystal *kidush*[7] cups. At each diner's place, the snow-white tablecloth is set with a pair of newly-baked rolls, looking like new-born chicks. Seeing all this it seems to one that a new soul is born, the *neshome yiseyre* [second soul of the Sabbath]. One feels that here is the Sabbath, here comes the belovéd bride, now we go to greet her, having welcomed her in the synagogue with *boyi b'sholem* [Come in Peace], singing *lekho dodi* [Come, Belovéd], loudly, passionately.

In such a manner did the rich man serve God and His Torah. However, as a resident and as a Jew, a son of his people, he also served the town and All Israel. He had partners in this. Certainly, a large share came from him. Nevertheless, he did not allow his general charity to displace specifics, like those among us who limit themselves to making the blessing over wine, and so forth. That is, his charity for the mass did not exclude needy individuals. Each of them individually obtained coins from him: wandering paupers of all sorts; beggars of this and that type, carrying alms-sacks; those lacking alms-sacks: fire-victims, abandoned wives, ne'er-do-wells with rabbinic notes and without them – no matter, everyone received his farthing. To say nothing of local folk: the town's unknown poor; quiet, "secret recipients," that is, who received food and drink hospitably, in the manner of our father Abraham.

There is the picture, dear Jews, an old-fashioned picture! A rarity, these days…Look at this, if you will: there, in the yard, directly across from the rich man's house – you see it? – a significant structure, long, windowless, with a pair of large, wide-open gates, like someone belted, sleeves rolled up, arms akimbo, hands outstretched, taking something from inside and handing it over to a pushing crowd outside, men, women loaded with packages, candles and bottles; this is – do you hear, dear Jews? – this is a storehouse of foodstuffs and other needful things from which the rich man's "person" in charge of this, distributes goods every Thursday to certain poor folk for their Sabbath. And those pitifully, badly fallen into poverty, ashamed to put out their hands, are sent aid to their homes in secret and honorably.

Keep looking, Jews, a bit farther!

At a side of the yard, a separate wing occupies a large area. Its chimneys emit pillars of smoke; servants, women, girls in white aprons, their heads covered in clean white cloths, rush about very busily, carrying pots, tableware, back and forth. A tall man, strong – look at him – a large-boned fellow, stands at the door. He issues commands and admits people who come and go one after the other – just listen to what an old-time rich man can do: establishing a kitchen for cooking and baking to feed, every day, hungry people, along with lonely prayer-house habitués, impoverished, weakened, alas! Yes, this is Slutsk's rich man's open kitchen for the poor and hungry! Not expecting, God forbid, honors for himself, nor any reward: Not even thinking that someday a portrait will be drawn of him – this very portrait!

And that one doing the commanding over there – he is the neighbor's husband, of that woman who lives in the second room in the house of the *minyan* [prayer-quorum]. Her husband, unable to tear himself from the kitchen as so much work there constantly depends on him, is able to come home only once a week for a few hours, bringing all sorts of good things. His basket overflows with good, tasty things, toward which, the more he tastes of them, Shloyme's heart and eyes are drawn ever more strongly. And the Evil Spirit, the guardian, sits hidden here in the basket among the goodies, encouraging Shloyme to be where a houseful of people are praying, keeping him from studying for the time being…

Translator's footnotes*:*

1. Schools for advanced studies in Bible, Talmud and rabbinic commentaries. Graduates could obtain rabbinic ordination or certification for other religious roles. Students were traditionally though minimally supported by local communities.

2. Possibly, an engraver.
3. "Eating days," as described herein, involved *yeshiva* students taking supper at a different home each evening. Rarely did the student have seven homes on which to rely.
4. Here and below, Mendele uses the Hebrew or Aramaic word/phrase from, respectively, the Bible or Talmud, or the Russian term, then provides the Yiddish translation. When he fails to do so, the translator has provided the meaning in brackets.
5. Ceremonial ram's horn.
6. Lit., doorpost. A case containing parchment on which are written verses from Deuteronomy, affixed to doorways.
7. Cups reserved to hold wine used in making the blessing (kiddish) over wine.

"Memoirs of a Jewish Revolutionary"
(In the Slutsk Prison)

by Beynish Mikhalevitsh

Translated by Hershl Hartman

– I, along with a group of some 15 people, was sent to the Slutsk prison.

[Page 400]

The prison there was considered to be one of the strictest, where those guilty of the most serious sins were confined. Criminals would shudder at the mention of the word "Slutsk," as its conditions were so rigid. In Kopyl we had encountered a Bundist[1] organization. Its representatives approached us during the convoy, presented us with an earthenware pot of tea and consulted with us about their party matters. We spent a day there at rest.

And after a week's time, spent in open fields and freshly-flowering woods, we [the convoy] approached the town of Slutsk.

The sun in our hearts is extinguished, the source of words is stopped-up: silently, lost in thought, with dragging feet and terrible tiredness, we approached our new housing – the famous Slutsk prison.

We stand in a tense mood in the office of the Slutsk prison. Some guards and a clerk regard us with angry curiosity. They're awaiting the *natshalnik* [warden]. The door opens. Breathing hard, a short-chubby little man with oxen eyes, bearded and with thick, hairy hands, comes running in. He regards us angrily from toes to top, emits an incomprehensible sound and hastily seizes ourpapers.

Meanwhile, somewhere in a far-off corner, a soldier drops his rifle. The nervous little creature in an official uniform shudders in great cowardice. This gave him a comic appearance and one of our women laughed out loud. The warden's eyes turn red with anger, he comes running up quickly to our corner and begins to shout, addressing us in the familiar form and cursing coarsely. As soon as he's finished, he receives a polite response from all of us. This seems to confuse him, he regards us all with widened eyes and addresses the chief guard of the convoy:

"What kind of people are these?" "Politicals," the other replies. The warden flips quickly through our papers. "Under control of the Justice Minister," "Under the Interior Minister," "At the Police Department." Apparently, all these institutions evoked great respect in this Slutsk satrap who had never seen prisoners who had not been convicted by order of an investigative judge or a district judge. He now speaks not a word to us. He quietly instructs the chief guard where to take us.

We find ourselves in a separate corridor. There are no criminals here. Everything is freshly-painted, white and clean. However, we are each locked into a separate cell and we are not permitted to communicate with each other.

We decide to strike the iron while it is still hot and to immediately put pressure on the warden before he has properly oriented himself as to who we are. We start the familiar music of banging on doors and shouting. The warden comes running in confusion and asks what we demand. He has no idea what to do with us and asks us to wait a few hours.

In a short time, our cell is filled with the town's power structure. The bailiff; a young prosecutor fresh from the university; a military man, and even the head of the Slutsk nobility. Their spokesman is the young assistant prosecutor. We put forward our demands: we want to be able to communicate with each other; we want our own kitchen, books, yard and other privileges. He asks about the regime we were under in Minsk and we tell him about it without embellishments. He assures us that things will not be worse here, he agrees to all our demands and adds that this is all temporary: he will correspond about all this with the gendarmerie. After this conversation the warden was completely lost. He actually turned the entire upper floor over to us. We were completely autonomous there and arranged things to our own hearts' content. When the criminals were not there, we would spend all day in the prison yard, strolling, amusing ourselves and organizing various sports. We ordered a complete croquet set and played with it for hours at a time. We would horse around, laugh and shout as though we were somewhere on an open field outside of town.

More than once the warden would call me out to his home (I remained in the role of *staroste* [village chief] here, too) and would plead with me to keep down the noise. "I've given you," he pleaded, "the yard, the office. At least let me sleep at night." He lived next door to the prison. It was only at night that we were locked into cells, though each of us could choose which room he wanted.

Then, some few weeks later, the warden called me in and told me confidentially that orders had been received from Minsk to rein us in somewhat and to institute a stricter regime over us. He, however, does not want to come in conflict with us and asks therefore that we be careful and not expose him. His submissiveness to us is explained not only by his cowardice, though he had a great dose of that. There was another reason here. We had brought with us a large sum of cash, which was deposited in the main office. The warden quickly spent it. It reached the point that we often did not get the most needed foodstuffs. When I would complain about this to the chief guard, he would whisper the secret that the warden does not give him any money and that the butchers, bakers and grocers no longer will extend him credit.

I recall this episode: That day, a dentist had extracted one of my teeth. That night, drinking hot tea caused a vein in my mouth to open and blood began to flow. I did not want to awaken any of my comrades and waited for it to subside. The flow, however, did not cease and I almost died of blood-loss. The awakening comrades began banging on the door and demanding a doctor. He came in the morning; afterwards, I had to stay in bed for several days. It was impossible for me to eat anything. I could drink tea. One of the women comrades who attended to me (our women were allowed to come into our section) sent the chief guard

[Page 401]

for a lemon. He returns and reports that the grocer will not sell it without cash payment. This is too much and my "warmhearted sister" sends for the warden. She [verbally] assaults him in great anger. He stands there, lost, begs her not to shout and runs off himself to the store and brings back a lemon…

His entire family was dysfunctional, made up of degenerates. He would play cards with anyone, his wife would have attacks of drunkenness and would keep drinking for days on end, and his son, a young high-schooler, would steal into the prison before dawn and sell the prisoners used decks of cards and liquor.

Though the warden waved us off and left us entirely on our own, he was brutally despotic toward the criminal inmates. He would call them by no other name than "animal" and often kicked them. Most of the inmates were small, weak little people, village peasants, horse thieves and accidental law-breakers. They did not have the spirit to stand up to the strict regime of the sick despot. When, sometimes, some serious criminals were brought there from elsewhere, he would keep them in solitary confinement and would torture them so badly that they would lose any ability to protest. A good life there was limited to some richer thieves and officials who had misappropriated government funds and who had larger amounts of cash deposited with the warden.

A short time after our arrival in Slutsk a great, very important event took place in the nation's political life – the Russo-Japanese War [1904-05]. We learned about it soon after the outbreak through the criminal inmates, to whom had been read, right after Sunday prayers, the official condemnation of the treacherous enemy. We recognized intuitively that this would have gigantic significance for revolutionary developments in Russia and we began to take a feverish interest in all its details. We could no longer live without a newspaper. We therefore called in the local prosecutor and demanded from him that he allow us to receive a newspaper, because of the unusual developments in the country. The prosecutor saw in this clear evidence of our patriotism and promised to send us the Petersburg newspaper published by Lord Ukhtomski. He would not permit any more "left" newspaper.

But no sooner had we legalized the reading of a newspaper in prison than the guards, for a pittance, were not afraid to bring us other newspapers. After a year of newspaper-hunger, I would devour two-three newspapers daily. Every new report on the course of the war would shake us up and cause intense discussion among us. Behind the thick walls of the Slutsk prison we seemed to hear directly the strong blows suffered by Czarism as a result of its defeats onthe battlefields of Manchuria and [of its Baltic fleet] in the deep seas of Tsushima [May 27, 1905]. Impatiently, we awaited every dawn to learn of some new upheavals.

On a bleak winter morning the Slutsk prosecutor and an elderly Justice official from Minsk appeared and invited us into a large room for a conversation. They began about the treacherous Japanese, talked about the great struggle awaiting the country, and, at the end, simply proposed that we enlist in the army as volunteers. They assured us that we would not be sent to the front, that this would be simply an act of peacemaking between the government and those groups who sought the well-being of Russia in their own way. All of us unanimously and categorically rejected the proposal.

As we later learned, this was an attempt by the then-dictator [W. K. von] Plehve[2] to entice all the "politicals" into the patriotic mainstream and the same proposal that was made to us had been made to all the [political] prisoners and exiles in all of Russia. But it is noteworthy that of all the thousands of "politicals," there was only a single exiled person who agreed to volunteer for the army. All the others turned away, despising the bloody hand that the all-Russian despot offered them.

Translator's footnotes:

1. Installed after the March, 1917, overthrow of the Czar, supplanted by the Bolsheviks in the October (November 7, current calendar) Revolution.
2. Czarist Interior Minister, responsible for the Kishinev pogrom of 1903, with whom Theodor Herzl a few months later negotiated support for Zionism as a means of reducing the Jewish population in Russia. See Laquer, Walter, *A History of Zionism*, Schocken Books, 1976.

[Page 402]

Homey Images

by Abraham Epstein

Translated by Jerrold Landau[1]

At last, dear friend and brother
I take up the pen again
After a long, long silence,
When my tongue was taken away.
But you know from a long time
My faults, my way:
Laziness overcame me – –
You have done nothing with me,
You have not seen me in a long time
Despite a pen dipped [in ink].
Until the good times come
When I will be renewed as ever before,
I will be free from my illness
And I write – on the table and bench!
Now I am completely prepared
To chatter, to speak long and wide,
About oneself and about people,
Everyone soaps up the sides,
Here a stich and here a pinch
Here a smear over the lip.
Here a kiss, a caress over the head.
Then they stir in a pot,
Everything which still lies upon the lung –
If only it would grind the tongue.
The shtetl of Slutsk is not futile,
Where everything is on the note,
Where no secrets are possible,
All ears are moving,
Where walls and stones listen,
Where one counts all your bones:
What you do and what you make,
What you say and what you think…
Also, dear friend and guest
I am again in my nest,
Among people I know well –
And you see – indeed "alright!"
I have left the big city
With the empty blowing of soap,
With its noise, with its bustle,
With its grey, smoky sky;
Courtyards – cages, houses – cellars,

Without a sun, a ray of light,
Heat in the house and a fuss,
It is not a life – pure poison.
It is crowded in the breast –
For me, it is a lost home.
Back to home, back to home,
Where every tree is known,
Where every leaf is alive –
Back to my fiercely loved shtetl!

———

I have come home,
I immediately made a reckoning:
"Does it make sense, I was in the big city,
I have heard everything and seen everything!"
I have two or three small girls
Very charming, one and the other,
And I spin around with them
On the left side of the highway,
For them, I am a wise man:
I crawl in high places,
I speak about art and life,
About love, about striving –
And in the meantime, the sun sets
In a sea of golden-red,
And the last golden rays
Fall upon the girls' eyes.
O, how do I love the girls
With the empty, sweet talk!
Light and naughty, like children,
They bother the old sinners,
And like flowers beneath the dew
The woman looks at them…

———

All the streets are measured
I go about leisurely
To the well-known S-Miyak[2]
With the pale, spongy cheeks,
With the wide – wide smile –
At last, under the acorn [tree].
There one eats a mikado[3]
And certainly morozhszene[3],
There, beer is poured,
One meets people there,
Jokes and words are formed,
And sometimes one plays cards.
And when S-Miyak gets bored,
And there is something left over,
One takes a raisin straight-away,

And there is something left over
One takes a raisin straight-away,
And one goes to the river.
Behind the city there is an alleyway
It is always frothing like a kettle:
Lads, girls, men, women,
In a grey, clouded house,

[Page 403]

With the clothes changed
They go in rows to bathe.
And the bathing suits tinkle
Some laugh, and some sing;
And a young poet's hand
Posts verses on the walls

— — — — — — —

And one prepares to go to sleep,
And one sleeps… in good health!
Only the young, hot blood
Does not sleep and does not rest.
And one goes, one sits and moves
Among the dark alleyways…
O, the magically sweet hours!
They virtually disappear.
Everything remains in a dream.
Beneath every bush and tree
Couples sit firmly bound together;
O, a kiss, sha, do not make a commotion,
Now is not the time to bargain
Let the night devour the secret.

— — — — — — —

(From Slutsker Sheigetz, 1911)

Translator's footnotes*:*

1. This is a very difficult poem to translate. The translation is not perfect.
2. I am unsure of this word. Probably a place name or the name of a person.
3. These words seem to be types of foods.

Slutsk My Little Hamlet [*shtetele*]
(A folk song)

by Abraham Epstein

Translated by Hershl Hartman

1.

I remember the little *shtetele*,
Where I first saw the light of day,
Where, as a child, I went to *kheyder*.
Where I was born, where I was brought up.

Refrain:

Slutsk, oh Slutsk, my *shtetele*, how I yearn for you,
Deep in my heart, you home of mine, you lie there.
A cradle hanging from a string, and a broken little bed;
And yet you are so dear to me, Slutsk, oh Slutsk, my *shtetele*.

2.

Everyday, carrying *beygl* [bagels], our mother went into the market –
So the children might have bread to eat;
And our father would flog us with his leather whip
So that we children would study well.

(*Refrain*)

3.

On Friday nights our mother would bless the candles,
And our father would go off to the House of Prayer.
From there he'd bring home strangers for the Sabbath-meal
And lovely *zmires* [Sabbath-songs] would be sung.

(*Refrain*)

[Page 404]

Cucumbers
(Excerpts of a story by that name)

by I. D. Berkovitsh [Berkowitz][1]

Translated by Hershl Hartman

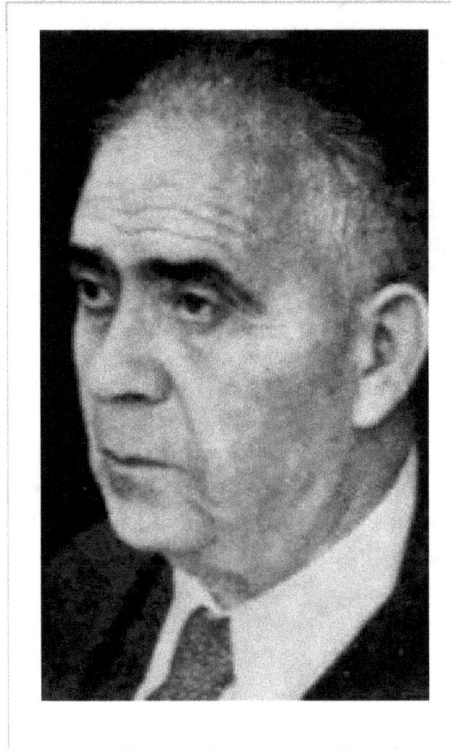

Uncaptioned. I. D. Berkowitz

The key time of the cucumber harvest had arrived. These were days during which, from the earliest morning until late at night, a strange, uneasy tumult ruled the house, a strange commotion, a dashing-about, a running of starving, distraught people who had suddenly seen a light. Mother was more distraught than all the others. During those days it was as if she were being steamed and roasted. She did not eat nor drink, neither rested nor slept, and paid no attention to housekeeping. All she knew was: cucumbers.

When Rifke awakes from sleep before dawn, she finds Mother already on her feet. Barefoot, with unruly hair and a naked bosom, Mother appears out of the dark sleeping area quietly, as unremarked as a shadow; she stands in the half-light thinking to herself and puts both hands into her tousled hair and starts to scratch vigorously, using her nails. Then she goes quietly into the kitchen, stands at the little window and thinks again, sighs over something, and it seems to Rifke that Mother hadn't slept at all. She had stood all night in some dark corner, loaded with worries, thinking her thoughts there, waiting and waiting for daylight to appear.

Mother doesn't stand at the window for long. A splash into the slop-bucket is heard. Mother quickly pours out nail-water[2], returns again to the dark sleeping area and begins to wake Father, quietly at first, then more and more loudly.

"Elye, wake up! Elye, you've slept enough. Elye, do you hear me? It's time to get up. Elye, you'll have time to sleep-in on *shabes* [Sabbath]. Elye, why do you pretend not to hear me? Elye, what sort of sleepy-headedness has he taken on all of a sudden, as if he hasn't slept for five days?…Lord of the Universe! There are a couple of loads of cucumbers out in the garden since yesterday, and he doesn't so much as care a hair about them…El-i-ye!"

"Ha? What?" Father awakens with a sleepy, hoarse voice.

"Ha? What?" Mother mimics him, angry now. "It's as though he's not from here…Have you forgotten yesterday's three loads of cucumbers?"

"Cucumbers – shmucumbers! It's still the middle of the night outside!"

"He's turning cucumbers into shmucumbers! There you go! Have you got anything better, my fine breadwinner? Have you ever seen such a habit: just a sleep-addict?…He's slept, I guess, all night long. Enough! How long is a person supposed to sleep? Do you have to bathe in sleep?"

For a while, Mother falls silent. Then her voice is heard, suddenly changed, softer, as though she is speaking to herself in the dark, quietly, heartfelt, thoughtfully:

"As for me, bless His Name, I haven't slept all night long. I know that we're, I believe, supposedly preoccupied, but sleep doesn't come, after all. Such strange thoughts creep into my head, some dreams…A dream isn't more, it's correct to say, than a thought-up thing, but still…There I lay about an hour ago, I think, not sleeping at all: but then the door opens and my father, peace to him, appears, wearing his *yarmulke* [skullcap] and white stockings, as he always did…Elye! You're back to sleep! What is one to do with him? No! Whatever will be, will be! I am not ever going back to the garden! Let them drag off whatever is there, let the pigs come in, let all the hard work be ruined, let three loads of cucumbers turn rotten…

[Page 405]

Three loads of cucumbers! I am leaving, it's not my thing, let him and his children beat their heads against the wall! Elye!"

Finally, Father appears out of the sleeping area, dressed all in white, barefoot, tall, angry. He comes into the room where Rifke sleeps, where the shutters are closed, coughing and sighing and mumbling something, puttering around in the dark until he finds the tobacco and begins to roll a cigar. He leans up against the commode, stretched up, not moving, and is silent, thinks of something, smokes the cigar and at every puff the lit end glows in the dark, illuminating his sleepy, angry face and his long, tousled beard.

Mother meanwhile is busy in the fore-house, opening wide the doors, dragging some loaded sacks, not resting. Through the open doors a cool fresh breeze blows in from the street and under the blanket; a beam of light shines and trembles on the wall in the dark little room – and Rifke tosses from one side to the other in her bed, buries her face in the pillow, wanting to drive off angry thoughts, but she can't.

Mother's voice is heard from the fore-house:

"Elye, d'you hear? You've already grabbed your pipe? Ay, ay, that pipe! I'm going to the garden. Finish your pipe there and come along. Don't forget that there are three loads of cucumbers lying there!"

"Well, and tea? Who will make my tea?" asks Father in a hoarse voice and inhales the cigar, lighting up his tall white figure and his hurt, darkened face.

"Now here's something new: tea…he lacks nothing more than tea! I tell him 'cucumbers' – so he answers 'tea'…I seem to have awoken him, my lord, so that he might sit down and have tea! This one doesn't even have any shame at all: in a time like this, tea…just a little nothing – tea? Someone might think he was born in tea…get dressed there and come out here! When the children awake, they will make both tea for you and pain for my enemies – oh, heavens, what will ever become of him?"

When Rifke arrives in the garden under her parasol she finds Father and Mother standing near a small open gate alongside a large pile of cucumbers. Avromtsi, reddened with sunburn, stands in a large wagon, and a peasant with a goat-like beard and a linen shirt hanging over his trousers carries over to him heavy sacks full of cucumbers and loudly empties them into the wagon.

Rifke is crestfallen and stands there, not knowing what to do. She looks around at the large, broad garden, at its long growing beds, covered in foliage drying and baking under the sun; at the peasant women, seen from afar in groups with their hoes, and her earlier bright thoughts disperse like smoke under the skies. Heat and quiet pervade the surroundings, as far as the eye can see. At times, a song issues forth from a group of peasant women, quickly caught up by the other groups. The peasant women pause in their labors for a moment, lean on their hoes in the growing beds and throw their heads back. Strong village voices pour, lamenting, across the urban fields, over the long, green growing beds, under the light blue skies. Suddenly the song is cut off mid-course: some young peasant woman lets out a strange shriek, there's resounding laughter, echoing from the far-off fields, and all becomes quiet again, while the burning sun rules over the stillness…Father stands, holding his cane near the pile of cucumbers, somehow lost in thought. Heavy beads of sweat roll off his forehead. His bearded, embittered face stares off into the void, as though he were listening to something.

But Mother won't allow him to stand there.

"Elye, you're lost in thought again?…And who will go to the marketplace?"

Rifke approaches her mother.

"Mama, I came to do something."

Mother stands there, worried, and does not reply.

"Five loads of cucumbers have been sent off. This will be the sixth."

The time of cucumbers had passed and a cold, wet winter arrived with its frigid winds and with fine, cold rains. In the little street, under the low, foggy sky, lay a loose mud puddle; around the fruit gardens, in small, glittering little ponds, withered, orphaned, fallen little leaves skittered about. Men appeared wearing warm fur coats, carrying huge umbrellas, and women, bent over, in raggedy head-shawls, chased after gangs of wet, honking geese, pursued and driven by the wind and rain. Householders in checked cotton caftans ventured out with their tools to survey their houses, adding earth to the protective piles around the foundations, smearing clay around the windows; near them, in the courtyards, stand the cows: lost, morose, like useless wives, stretching

[Page 406]

their necks, raising their cow-heads to the fogged-in sky and emitting a fearful, long "me-e-eh," mourning the fine, warm summer and its bright sun, its green fields, that have disappeared like smoke…

And the gardens had not yet been harvested. The earth had nursed-up the cold, wintery rain and borne rotten carrots and beets; on the beaten heads of cabbages, every morning heavy, cold drops of water were driven by the wind.

Translator's footnotes:

1. Known best as Sholem Aleichem's son-in-law who chronicled his more-famous relative and translated his works into Hebrew, Berkovitsh was also a prominent Yiddish writer in his own right.
2. *negl-vaser*: the perfunctory fulfillment of the morning hand-washing required by Jewish custom.

The Last
(A chapter of the story of that name)

by I. D. Berkovitsh [Berkowitz]

Translated by Hershl Hartman

Introduction:

I wrote the story "The Last" in 1908, while visiting my parents in Brownsville [Brooklyn], New York. My father, peace to him, told me an ancient story about rabbis in Slutsk that he had heard as a youngster while studying at a *yeshiva* in Slutsk, or perhaps Starobin. He dearly wanted me to convert the story into a "description." I fulfilled his wish and before returning to Europe I wrote it in my own style, naming it as "An Old Story From An Old *pinkes* [Civic Record]." I did not refer to the city by its real name, Slutsk, but as "Muravanka," (after The Muravankes [ant hills], the tiny synagogues that clustered about the large Cold Synagogue in Slutsk). The story was printed then in the New York "Amerikaner," and in the Peterburg "Fraynd," as well as in a volume of my "Collected Works." Later, when I adapted it into Hebrew as "*ha'akhron*" [The Last], I left out the first chapter – so that it appears here as an unknown fragment, because my "Collected Works" in Yiddish are now forgotten, a literary rarity.

I. D. B.

For generations upon generations, they were rabbis in the old, poor, covered-in-grey-honors of the Jewish community of Muravanka, lost in deep, dark woods. For generations they were famous all over, far and near, wherever a Yiddish word might reach, wherever the voice of the Torah resounds loudly in the old, warm Houses of Prayer.[1]

They were talked about everywhere, as one would talk about wonders at a time when wonders no longer occur, as one would talk of consolation at a time when hopes have been lost long, long ago. They also spoke of them as great-grandchildren would of their great-grandfather's riches that no longer exist in this world, and of the great old-fashioned, seven-branched candelabra that he had left them from the good old times.

Because they illuminated their surroundings just as an old-fashioned seven-branched candelabra, burning in the darkness – this old family of the famous Muravanka rabbis. This was back in ancient, far-off times. Then, Muravanka still lay sunken in the midst of the huge, dark Lithuanian forests. The old, low, moss-covered houses still stood amidst broad, green gardens; the gardens then still yielded beets and onions, thick hops still twirled and aged on the fences. In those times, fine Jewish householders still walked about in linen coats and smoked pipes filled with dried cabbage-leaves. The forest provided sustenance, yielding resin during the week. Jewish homes dined on corn bread and barley soup. When a family added a new infant – there was no need to worry. They merely praised God and took up the pail, went to the well and drew up water, added another quart to the barley-soup vessel – and the newborn creature of God's creation was assured of his own provender.

And when a Jew's daughter reached maturity, and there was no dowry available to bring her forth – he would take up a walking stick, put on a white shirt with a broad, starched and pressed collar, say the "prayers for the road" and go off on foot to Volin [Wolin], to that blessed wonderland where the speech spoken uses *i* [instead of *u*] and the food eaten even on a midweek Wednesday is *khale* [eggbread] with saffron, if not with honey.

There, in Volin, on a Friday night, strolling about his brightly-lit halls, is the rich Voliner proprietor, a heavy-set, meaty Jew, hairy, with a broad yellow beard, with a creased silken sash across his broad, solid loins – strolling in his self-conscious wealth and proclaiming *sholem aleykhem* [peace be with you] in his clipped, *i*-accented speech, joyous, lively, in a sing-song

[Page 407]

and with a snap of his fingers. The Lithuanian guest – whether a teacher or a preacher – the emaciated, dry, Jewish stranger with his black, piercing stranger's eyes, would sit in a far-off corner, only moving his lips slowly, looking only at the ground. Perhaps this was because he felt very crestfallen in this bright, decorated hall, and perhaps it was because he remembered his far-off home and his wife and children and his grown daughter, and because his remote home had suddenly become strangely dear to him, with its dark, hard-working Jews who pump resin from the forest all week long, with its old, warmly-heated Houses of Prayer, with its famous giants of the Torah who bend, holding candles in their hands, over the large, heavy books of the *gemora* [Talmud].

And here at the table, among the aromatic *gefilte* [stuffed] fish and the chicken soup with its thick "eyes" [fat globules], the angry silent guest would break his silence and speak in detail about his own corner in Lithuania.

"But we have us our own rabbis here! Nnu!..."

He would reply with fire and with profound pride, sharply and clearly, with love and deep yearning. His piercing dark eyes would ignite and glow, throwing off sparks. The guest would tell of those old giants and their brilliant minds, with iron-fast patience, who do not leave off studying either by day nor by night, who take only a half-hour nap during a full night-and-day, who fall like tired lions on their fists, with their wave-like beards on the open Talmud volumes, while the large lamp burns quietly as a guard over their heads and wakes them again to study. At dawn, when the congregation arrives, it walks about within its own confines, fearing to cast a glance at their corner, because their gazes then are sharp and burning.

"That's how studying is done among us, in Lithuania!"

The thick, hairy Volin proprietor, sweaty, good-humored, a believer, would listen intently to those wonderful stories, meanwhile slowly undoing the sash around his Sabbath-cloak, unbuttoning the waistcoat on his rich belly and puff up his cheeks, shaking his head back and forth, because one could believe anything about *Litvakes* [Lithuanian Jews].

Later, when the rich Volin Jew, through a once-in-a-blue moon miracle, found himself in Lithuania, he had to satisfy his curiosity by gazing upon the Lithuanian giant of learning. However, he stood before in him in fear and with wonder in his heart, as one sometimes stands before a tall, hard stone wall, barely seeing its top. Somehow, he feared the thick, dark eyebrows, the sharp, penetrating glances, the strict, deeply furrowed forehead, seemingly carved in stone. He was somehow confused by the hard, cold persistence of their words, that drill holes [into one's consciousness] and bore deep and know of no mercy.

Because in those deeply creased foreheads and under those dark, thick eyebrows shone the eternally-burning *shkhine* [Divine Presence].

Those were the famous Muravanker rabbis.

* * *

The Muravanker were an old dynasty of rabbis, a long chain of deeply learned men that continued from generation unto generation. They were all tall, strong, broad-boned Jews, all of advanced age, with thick curly beards. It was only infrequently that a hair of their beards would become silvered. They were all of them, stern and silent who heard all and saw all, but who spoke more with their thick eyebrows and with the deeply-etched creases in their foreheads than with their mouths. When a Muravanker rabbi issued forth the word "*nu*," [well…] – that sufficed.

Their rabbinic status was passed down by inheritance, from father to child, and in addition to the rabbinic chair and the 18 *gilden* per week salary, the son would inherit from his father a tall, old, candle-charred prayer-lectern in the old House of Prayer, at the edge of the Holy Ark; a thick, heavy, pitted, carved cane and an old Sabbath-robe of glossy material which, when worn on a bright summer's day, shines in the sun and "shouts" aloud.

They had arrived in Muravanka generations ago, when the town was still ruled by the old, wild *haydamaks* [Cossack tribal leaders] with fearfully grey mustaches and with large, angry dogs.

Translator's footnote*:*

1. *bote-midroshim*; sing., *besmedrish*; lit: houses where commentaries on the Bible and biblical stories were taught. Variously rendered as House(s) of Prayer, or of Study. Not to be confused with *shul* (pl. *shuln*) – in Southern Yiddish: *shil, shiln* – generally rendered in English with the Greek-origin word, synagogue. A *besmedrish* served a relatively small group of less-learned men; its limited space allowed for easy heating by a warming-stove.

[Page 408]

Y. L. Perets in Slutsk

by Nokhem Khinitsh

Translated by Hershl Hartman

At the end of summer, 1913, a rumor spread in Slutsk that Y. L. Perets and Ya'akov Dinezon[1] would be coming to visit. Impatiently, their arrival from Starave, a nearby village (35 *vyorst* [Russian mile] from town) was awaited; they had been staying there at the summer home of B. A. Kletskin, an owner of the large local glass factory. Kletskin, the well-known publisher, was known among the Jews of the surrounding villages as a non-believer [*apikoyres*, Epicurean].

Y. L. Perets and Ya'akov Dinezon did arrive one sunny morning. Their names were beloved among Jews.

Attempts to organize a public lecture by Perets were not successful. The police had received a report that the lecturer was not kosher – a Socialist.[2] Nevertheless, a banquet to welcome the honorable guests was arranged at the home of the richest Jew in town, Leybush Gutsayt. There were around 50 guests from among the "elite." Leybush Gutsayt, a Zionist and a lover of Hebrew, personally invited me to attend.

The hall was overflowing; there was no room to be seated. Russian was heard from all directions and the atmosphere was foreign, isolated. The guests were welcomed in both Russian and Yiddish. Slowly, a more festive mood developed. Everyone's eyes were on the cheerful, energetic Perets, and on the goodhumored, silent Dinezon. The final greeting in Hebrew by the local teacher Ruven'ke Altman somewhat confused minds and vexed spirits. He briefly and clearly recalled and referred to the Talmudic legend that "in the times to come" the synagogues would be torn out from their places and be transferred physically to the Land of Israel. The Talmudic legend could not abide the idea that the dead would roll through [underground] caves to the Land, but that the synagogues, the spiritual centers, would remain in

Exile [the Diaspora]. He, the speaker, believes that Perets's works must find their rightful place in Hebrew translation in the land of Jewish hopes – the Land of Israel.

The audience grew bored, not understanding a single word. But Perets's eyes twinkled. He felt that he was under a sharp attack.

Pale, with a tremulous voice, he began (I wrote down his words at the time): "I thank you all for the expected honor and attention that you have given me here. But I must note to the last greeter that I am not among those who disparage life in the Diaspora. In addition, I cannot agree that my creative works must be ripped from Yiddish and translated specifically into Hebrew, as eternal works that will find their true place in the Land of Israel. I want to be sure that you do not misunderstand me: I am not an opponent of Hebrew, which is still dear to me. And here is the evidence: I have written in Hebrew and I still do from time to time. But, what then? I am not a chauvinist who says that eternity and the rightful place is only in Hebrew and in the Land of Israel…Permit me to say that the struggle and the constant irritations between the "ists"[3] upsets me and causes me great pain and sorrow. Is Yiddish, then, a slave to slaughtered? I protest most strongly against such an attitude. The time has now come for us to proclaim publicly: Enough of playing with minor matters and empty phrases. Let each go his own way to seek his own truth! Let the forces grow, the spirits soar of those who create and produce. I must again stress that Jewish literature is in the folk-language [Yiddish]. I have no objection to my works being translated into Hebrew. But without hidden objectives, incantations, signs that create bad blood over what is prime and what is secondary…

"Honored guests! I hope you will forgive me for these words that I find necessary to say openly and clearly: Read in Yiddish, in Hebrew, but do read, become acquainted with our treasures and values of great range; then you will see how rich we are, but that we do not know how to use those riches and the folk-treasure. So we follow the instruction of King Solomon: cut it in half! And we cut halves, thirds, and quarters of our living body."

Pale and tired, he sat down next to his friend Dinezon. When they tried to get Dinezon to speak, he smilingly said: "I have nothing to add and nothing new to say. I am in fullest agreement with my friend, Perets."

(Published in *undzer folk* [Our People, Yiddish], number 5, October 14, 1931, New York; *ha'olam* [The World, Hebrew], number 13, March, 1933, London.

Translator's footnotes:

1. Y(itzhok) L(eybush) Perets, also known as I(saac) L(oeb) Peretz and Jacob Dinezon. The former is considered to be one of the triumvirate of classic modern Yiddish writers, known for his stories, poems and essays in the Yiddish press and for mentoring many outstanding Yiddish novelists, playwrights and poets. Dinezon, a vastly popular (in the 1880s) author of sentimental novels, campaigned for modern educational methods in religious elementary schools; those that followed his urgings were often dubbed "Dinezon schools."
2. Perets was, indeed, disbarred from practicing his legal profession on that charge. He actually maintained a sympathetic but critical view of Jewish Socialist advocates.
3. i.e., Hebraists and Yiddishists – advocates of one language over the other. Perets participated in the Czernowitz (now Chernivtsi) Conference in 1908 that, after much debate, declared Yiddish to be "*a* language of the Jewish people" rather than "*the* language…"

[Page 409]

Slutskers in America

by Israel Shwaidelson, New York

Translated by Hershl Hartman

The writer of this review was born in Hrozova in 1889, studied in Slutsk in 1901, and came to New York in 1904. He joined the Slutsker *landsmanshaftn* [hometown associations] in 1907 and was elected recording secretary in 1909. Since then he has been continually active in all group endeavors and positions, up to the present day. He was also among the main initiators and organizers of all the [war] relief efforts among Slutskers in America.

With his help the *"Beit Slutsk"* [Slutsk House] was built in Israel near the Migdial colony.

Editorial Board

The United Slutsker Relief Committee

The beginning of the relief campaign

Organized relief work by Slutskers in America for the Jews in their home town of Slutsk began in 1905, following the Russo-Japanese war, with the onset of the pogroms [anti-Jewish riots] in Russia. Fear that Slutsk might suffer the same hooligan outbreaks as in other towns electrified Slutskers in New York, where *landslayt* [fellow townsmen] were concentrated. An attempt was made to gather funds for the purchase of arms for self-defense.[1] No significant success was achieved at that time, because the economic level of Slutskers in America was not high. The majority were recent immigrants, each of whom had to struggle for his own existence and send money home to his family. There were as yet no well-established immigrants, with only a few exceptions.

The Slutsker organizations then in existence were quite young: The Slutsker *shul* [synagogue] — about five years old; "Independent Slutskers" — three years; and the "Progressive Slutskers" — all of one year old.

Only a few hundred dollars were gathered then, and it is not known whether the money was even sent. Fortunately, Slutsk by then had active youth groups and parties, such as Zionists, the [Socialist] *Bund*, Labor Zionists, Territorialists, and some others. Though as party members they disputed, fought against each other, quite often leading to bloody confrontations, they were nevertheless united when it came to facing the common foe. It is a known fact that Slutsk was protected thanks to the young men and women of the self-defense. The police severely oppressed the revolutionary activism of the proletarian parties. To assist them the police brought in Kulak, the constable of Hrozova, well-known as a bloody murderer and die-hard anti-Semite. The [Jewish self-defense] bunch didn't "keep him waiting" and the next day they "finished him off."

Somewhat more was accomplished after the First World War, when there were more Slutskers in America, since a large stream of more educated youth had arrived in the wake of the unsuccessful Russian revolution [of 1905] and the pogroms. The early arrivals brought over their families and became settled.

The economic situation improved after 1910, when the Jewish trade unions were established, bringing a spiritual and moral uplift to the Jewish masses. At the outbreak of the First World War there were three Slutsker organizations in existence that were of help to their members and to other charitable Jewish institutions. The Slutsker *shul* had acquired its own building for religious services, and there older *landslayt* found an atmosphere reminiscent of the old country.

The "Progressive Slutsker Young Men," around which the younger and more secularized elements

[Page 410]

from Slutsk and its surroundings were concentrated, had grown very large. Their clubrooms had, since 1906, become the gathering center for anyone who wanted to spend his free time in a friendly atmosphere. "The Independent Slutskers," which consisted of middle-aged *landslayt*, had also grown, and devoted itself mostly to aiding its members and the families of recently-arrived *landslayt*.

The Relief Committee sends collected clothing to Slutsk (summer, 1946). Israel Shwaidelson hands a sack of clothing to Mrs. Sarah Lefrak. Her husband Harry stands alongside.

During that time another Slutsker organization came on the scene. In 1913 a branch of the large fraternal organization, the *Arbeter Ring* [Workmen's Circle], known as "Slutsk Branch 500, A. R." was formed, around which were grouped mostly the young people who had been members of the *Bund* back home.

When the war broke out in the summer of 1914, the Jewish masses in America were thunderstruck. Many Slutskers still had their wives and children, parents and relatives, in the old country, to whom they would regularly send money. Suddenly, everything was interrupted. The Slutsker *landslayt* were even more affected, since the familiar "Max Cabra [?] Bank," with which they were financially connected, went into bankruptcy.

To the Slutsk *landslayt*, this bank had been more than a financial institution for savings and fund transfers, or for buying steamship tickets on behalf of relatives. For most, it was the address at which they received letters from home. It was also the place to which they came for advice on bringing over their families and relatives, and on various other matters.

Our Slutsker *landslayt* felt very much at home there, because they had a great friend in the person of

[Page 411]

the late Slutsker *landsman* Isaac Nayburg, a longtime major employee in whom the *landslayt* had the greatest trust and respect. The bank was also the gathering place where every Saturday evening people would assemble to exchange news from home, and to meet new arrivals who had brought greetings from relatives.

The closure of the "Max Cabra Bank" and several other banks left many *landslayt* in dire poverty. They lost their meager hard-earned savings as well as paid-up steamer tickets and transfer funds. Many had lost relatives. It was a disaster, yet the habit of coming to the bank remained. They would come and stare at the locked doors, like children visiting their forebears' graves.

At the end of the war the four organizations joined forces in an aid committee to help war victims in Slutsk. The chairman was Morris Osofsky; treasurer, the late Moyshe Kulak; secretary, Harry Marcus.

Several meetings were held at the Slutsker *shul* with the participation of the then-rabbi, *ha-rav* Yakov Eskolsky, and the famous Slutsk *landsman*, the preacher Tsvi Hirsh Maslansky, of blessed memory. A significant sum of money was raised. When it came to transmitting the aid, it became apparent that this would be practically impossible due to the chaos in Russia—first with the collapse of the Czarist regime, and later with the establishment of the Bolshevik government—so that aid from America was lost.

This was how things proceeded for a number of years. Representatives who had been sent to the various towns and villages [from the U.S.] with funds were unable to accomplish anything since the exchange rate was in constant flux and American dollars became almost worthless.

Around 1918 the noted Slutsker *landslayt* Max Tsurkof and Isaac Nayburg decided to travel to Slutsk to visit their relatives. Many Slutskers gave them money for their own families. The Aid Committee gave them the funds it had collected and named them its representatives. They were instructed to establish a committee in Slutsk that would distribute the funds in an honorable manner.

Upon their arrival in Slutsk they found an already-existing committee, of which Dr. Shildkroyt was the chairman. After only two days there was another overthrow of government[2] and they had to flee in great haste. They had to leave the earmarked money in the hands of Dr. Shildkroyt, relying on the committee's sense of judgment to deal with it as best they understood.

Following the final victory of the Bolsheviks it was totally impossible to have any communication with the committee in Slutsk because its members were oppressed both by the government and by their own *Yevsekes* [Jewish Section of the Bolshevik party]. A short time later the committee in America fell apart.

The renewed aid effort

The current committee, known as "United Slutsker Relief," was formed in November, 1944, before the Nazi armies had retreated. The chairman of the "Progressive Slutskers" conferred with the leaders of the other Slutsker associations about the formation of an aid committee for the survivors of the *khurbn* [Holocaust] in Slutsk and its environs.

On Thursday, November 20, the first meeting was held under the chairmanship of Israel Shwaidelson, chairman of the Progressive Slutskers. The following organizations participated: the Slutsker *shul*, "Independent Slutskers," "Progressive Slutskers," Slutsker Branch of the Arbeter Ring [Workmen's Circle] and "Progressive Slutsker Women's Club," (founded in 1930). All were prepared to do whatever might be necessary to help the survivors. At that time, no one was aware of the depth of the *khurbn*.

The second meeting was held December 16, 1944, for the election of officers.

But the meeting was gripped by the mourning spirit of *Tishe b'ov*[3]. That same day, the New York Herald-Tribune had published a report by the famous Slutsk *landsman* Maurice Hindus on his visit to Slutsk. It became clear that the *khurbn* was more horrible than had been imagined. Slutsk had been simply erased. Of its thousands of Jews, he found only 29.

Officers were then elected: as chairman, the honorable *landsman* Rabbi Dr. Tsadok Kapner, of blessed memory; treasurer—the noted businessman Harry Lefrak; financial secretary—Louis Temtshin; recording secretary—Sylvia Berg; vice-chairmen—Morris Osofsky of the Slutsker *shul*, Louis Bassin of the Independent Slutskers, Sam Cahn of the Slutsk Branch of Arbeter Ring, Sarah Lefrak of the Women's Club. Israel Shwaidelson of the Progressive Slutskers was chosen as executive vice-chairman.

Meanwhile, Maurice Hindus returned to New York. His verbal report was even more horrible. He promised to speak at an open meeting.

[Page 412]

At the signing of the contract between the Relief Committee and the Histadrut [Israel Labor Federation] for the construction of a "Beit Slutsk" [Slutsk House] in Migdial, Israel

From right to left, seated: Morris Osofsky, Israel Shwaidelson, Isaac Hemlin, Harry Lefrak, Dr. Abraham L. Bunin, and Gershon Levinson of Israel
Standing: Cohen, Sylvia Berg, Sam Travin, Sarah Lefrak, Sam Tshesnin—and Mordechai Tshoyna

Sunday, February 11, 1945. The chairman then was Morris Osofsky; the main speakers—Rabbi Dr. Tsadok Kapner and Professor Natan Klotz. The [fund-raising] appeal brought in about five thousand dollars. Regrettably,Maurice Hindus was unable to attend, but his telegraphic report devastated everyone.

In personal conversations, Maurice Hindus reported that while in Slutsk he had spoken with the chief commissar of the town, who informed him that the town needed most of all medications and surgical instruments because the Nazis had looted all the hospitals. Many were returning from hiding sick, broken, wounded, and medical aid was lacking. Maurice Hindus believed that priority must be given to sending this medical assistance, and that everyone should be helped without exception, Jews and non-Jews.

At the second mass gathering, April 2, 1945, the speakers were Prof. Natan Klotz, Rabbi Tsadok Kapner, Morris Osofsky, Israel Shwaidelson and Maurice Hindus. The appeal raised over eight thousand dollars.

The Committee, under the chairmanship of the noted *landsman* Dr. Abraham Bunin, proceeded to obtain the needed medicines. A sum of over two thousand dollars was expended. By mid-summer [the supplies] were sent to Slutsk, addressed to "Russian War Relief."

Early in 1946, a letter from Slutsk informed us that the final slaughter of Jews in Slutsk had occurred on February 8, 1943, [Hebrew calendar date] Adar 3, 5703. On that day the German murderers drove the remaining Jews into the *shul* courtyard, some eight thousand men, women and children, and burned them alive.

The Committee immediately called a *yortsayt* [commemoration of death] assembly. The devastation was marked by tears and sorrow and outcries of pain. That date has remained our *yortsayt* for an annual remembrance gathering.

When Rabbi Dr. Tsadok Kapner, of blessed memory, retired as chairman, Israel Shwaidelson became his replacement, inasmuch as Shwaidelson had actually been already directing all activities along with Dr. Abraham Bunin as vice-chairman.

A request was received from the Russian relief agency for used clothing and shoes for the Slutsk population. The Committee quickly

[Page 413]

a campaign and within a few months it had gathered some five thousand pounds of clothes and shoes of all kinds which were turned over to the Russian aid committee for transport to Slutsk.

After a year had passed we had still not received acknowledgment of the medicines that had been shipped.

During that time, letters were being received from Jews returning to Slutsk from their evacuation to distant areas [of Russia], by their American relatives. The returnees had no inkling about what had been shipped there.

The Committee chair corresponded with a surviving relative in Slutsk and proposed that a committee be formed in Slutsk to remain in contact with the American Committee. The response was that this was absolutely impossible, and furthermore the letter did not contain a single word about the aid that had been shipped. Subsequent letters from America received no replies.

At the advice of Maurice Hindus, a telegram was sent to the Slutsk commissar whom he had interviewed, inquiring about the shipped materials and asking what else he might need. No reply was ever received. The Committee decided that, lacking a response, nothing else was to be sent.

In contrast, letters arrived from *landslayt* in refugee camps. They requested aid and help in locating relatives in America. The Committee immediately responded with money and food packages and sought out local relatives. Over 100 letters arrived from various countries: Denmark, Sweden, Italy, Austria, France, Germany. We responded to all with letters, food packages, clothes and money.

We helped some *landslayt* to come to America. A certain number were helped in making *aliyah* [emigrating] to the [pre-State] Land of Israel. Among the letters [from there] the chairman received one from a fellow-townsman from Hrozova, Shimshon Nachmani, about locating a relative.

The Slutsker Relief assigned five thousand dollars for the "United Appeal," "HIAS," Histadrut campaign. The winter that the U.N. approved the creation of the State of Israel [on Nov. 29, 1947], a special meeting was called by the Progressive Slutskers. Various opinions were expressed: several held that the funds raised and held in the treasury should be donated for general relief purposes and the Committee be disbanded. However, the majority of the Committee held that its activities should be continued and devoted to helping the Jews in Israel in their battle with the Arabs. When, in late 1948, Dr. Abraham Bunin traveled to Israel, he was authorized to meet with the above-named Sh. Nachmani and other Slutsk *landslayt* in Israel, to determine how best to honor the memory of the martyrs of Slutsk and its surrounding communities.

Mr. and Mrs. Lefrak present the first check to Slutsker Relief
to Mr. Israel Shwaidelson (Feb. 1945)

At one meeting of Slutsker *landslayt* with Dr. Abraham Bunin in Tel Aviv, there was discussion on the question of building a children's home or a hospital wing in Israel as a monument to Slutsk. A committee was elected to remain in contact with the Slutsker Relief in New York. Upon Dr. Bunin's return, it was decided to endorse the plan the Israel committee had developed.

In May, 1949, the Relief Committee celebrated this writer's 60th birthday. In honor of his activities, it announced the "Campaign" project. Two months later, the largest contributors to the Relief, its treasurer Harry Lefrak and his wife, Sarah, traveled to Israel. In conjunction with the committee there, they closely examined several projects and focused on the proposal of the *kupat kholim* [National Health Care Service] to build a facility to be named Beit Slutsk at the Beit Levinstein Tuberculosis Hospital. Upon their return the plan was adopted.

[Page 414]

A contract was signed with the representative of *kupat kholim* and the first installment of ten thousand dollars was paid. The cornerstone of Beit Slutsk was laid on March 21, 1950. Many Slutsker *landslayt* living in Israel were present, as well as some from America, who just happened to be in Israel at the time

At the placement of the cornerstone of Beit Slutsk in Israel

Seated from right to left: Ben Eliyahu,(unknown), Pesye Shapiro, Bukhbinder, Bunin, Rabbi Tsvi Yehuda Meltzer, Sh. Nachmani, Dr. I. Kot, Sholem Shpilkin, Eliyahu Dagani
Standing from right to left: Sonia Nachmani, Nekhame Biler, Mrs. Epstein and Leybl Epstein, Yehuda Mayzl, Shmuel Toker, Mutye Melamed, Abraham Tshernikhov, Y. L. Grozovski, Nachum Chinitz, A. Shapiro

The project in Israel produced great enthusiasm among the *landslayt* in America. The Slutsk Relief was the first *landsmanshaft* [hometown association] to undertake memorializing its martyrs.

Harry and Sarah Lefrak supported the project very generously; Dr. Bunin and his wife, Marusha, were very active in the project. The required sum of money was raised in the course of 18 months.

The committee in Israel proposed that the chairman of the Relief Committee, under whose aegis the project was successfully completed, should come to Israel and participate in the dedication. After much negotiation, Israel Shwaidelson was invited to Israel for the dedication.

Harry and Sarah Lefrak made another trip to Israel, both to participate in the dedication of Beit Slutsk and simultaneously to deal with their own project of establishing a building in memory of their tragically deceased son-in-law.

A movement began in 1954 in the Committee to undertake another project in Israel. David Levin, a personal friend and longtime comrade of the chairman and an activist in the Relief Committee, visited Israel around Passover of 1955. He was authorized to consider the proposed projects, to confer with the Israeli committee and, upon his return, to express his opinion.

In April, 1956, the Committee made an agreement with the Histadrut for a project to build a children's home in Givat Chaim. This was an idea that David Levin, of blessed memory, conveyed in his letters from Israel to the chairman. Again, thanks to these two active groupings

[Page 415]

in the Relief Committee, the "Progressive Slutskers" and especially, the "Progressive Slutsker Women's Club," which devoted virtually their entire energies toward raising the required funds, the goal was achieved.

A clinic named for W. B. Lampert in Israel

Standing from right to left: Nachum Chinitz, Esther Chinitz, Mrs. Toker and Shmuel Toker, Sonia Nachmani, Sh. Nachmani, Ariye Shapiro, Pesye Shapiro
Back row, center: Harry and Sarah Lefrak

"Progressive Slutsker Young Men's Benevolent Association"

The "Progressive Slutsker Y.M.B.A." was formed in 1904 by about a dozen Slutsker fellows who felt uncomfortable in the Slutsker *shul* and among the "Independent Slutskers." Their world view was influenced by the Socialist enlightenment. In their first year they already numbered more than 100 members, and by the end of 1905 they opened the clubrooms that they maintain until the present day.

The members wanted to retain the youthful character of the organization, so it was determined that membership would be restricted to individuals under 30 and unmarried. In time the "Progressive Slutskers" grew so popular that many people joined who had originated from other regions and countries, such as Galicia, Romania, and so on.

[Page 416]

Slutskers were in the front ranks in the organization of the Jewish labor unions.

The clubrooms boiled over with all kinds of activity, entertainment, lectures and concerts. Classes in English were held in the reading room. The Slutsker balls, held four times each year, were famous.

With the outbreak of World War I and America's entry into it, more than a hundred members were drafted into the army. But the group's activity did not cease. After the war they were the first to help in establishing the "Slutsker Relief."

The Bolshevik revolution in Russia, which caused splits among Jewish workers and general progressive organizations, did not affect the "Progressive Slutskers." There were actually some Communists in its ranks, but that did not get out of hand. The organization's unity was maintained.

In time the "Progressive Slutskers" reached a membership of almost 500 members, and it grew financially strong. It maintained its Socialist tradition yet became more Jewish than it had been before.

Upon the entry of America into World War II, the "P. S." became active in the sale of War Bonds among its members: over a million dollars' worth was sold by them. The government gave them various awards and, in their honor—a warplane was named "Spirit of Slutsk." The "P. S." became the "breath of life" of the "United Slutsker Relief." Its headquarters were in the P.S. clubrooms. Their main officers held the same posts in the Relief. Upon the establishment of the State of Israel, the P. S. led the action by the Relief to honor the memory of the Slutsk martyrs with a monument in Israel. They also continued their activities on behalf of general relief agencies and Jewish charitable institutions in American Jewish life.

Now, when the "Progressive Slutskers" is over fifty-five years old, it still numbers around 400 members, though without the caché of its past. Yet it is still the largest and most active organization of Slutsk *landslayt* in America.

Progressive Slutsker Women's Club"

The "Progressive Women's Club" was founded in January, 1930, with the goal of creating closer comradeship among the women. It did not take long before they became involved in the general social activity of American Jewish life. At the beginning the women aided the P. S. in all its undertakings as well as in other communal activities, especially in the financial crisis of the nineteen-thirties, when unusual aid was required for members and charitable institutions.

The women were very active in the United Slutsker Relief in raising funds for Slutsk survivors. Upon the creation of the State of Israel, the small Slutsker women's organization did much to preserve the memory of Slutsk.

Through the years of their existence they proved that their group was a vibrant one, possessed of an intelligent membership. The "Progressive Slutsker Women's Club" is the pride of the Slutsk *landsmanshaftn* in America.

Slutsker visit Beit Slutsk in Israel

From right to left: Mutye Melamed, Ruven Gross, Eliyahu Degani of the *kupat kholim*, Ariye Shapiro, Israel Shwaidelson, Sarah Lefrak, Harry Lefrak, Sh. Nachmani, N. Chinitz, Sh. Toker

Translator's footnotes:

1. Led by Jewish revolutionaries, the self-defense movement during the 1905 pogrom wave was a previously unheard of form of resistance. Often, the mere rumor that Jews were armed dissuaded government- and church-inspired rioters.
2. During the years-long post-revolutionary civil war, many areas of Russia, Ukraine, Poland and Belarus changed hands between the pro-Czarist White and the Bolshevik Red Armies.
3. 9th of Av: Traditional commemoration of the destruction of the Jerusalem Temples.

[Page 417]

Slutskers in America 54 Years Ago [1908]

by Ch. Zaides

Translated by Hershl Hartman

The Family of I. D. Berkovitsh[1], Brownsville, N.Y., 1908

My father, Ezriel Zelig (5620-5694) [1860-1934], was known in Slutsk, especially on Vigoda Street, as "Zelig Tshipelayer," because his family came from the village of Tshipelay, near Starobin. His grandfather, Eliezer Lipe, who supplied dairy products to the landowner of Tshipelay village, had been expelled from the Starobin region in the wake of decrees by [Czar] Nicholai I against village Jews. Ezriel Zelig was also called "Tall Zelig" because of his stature. In addition, he acquired the nickname "Zelig The Orphans" (not "The Orphan," in the singular, but specifically "The Orphan<u>s</u>"), because while he was still young, after the early death of his father, Berl Tshipelayer, he remained the sole provider for his younger siblings. (His eldest brother, Avrom-Itsi, a *melamed* [religious teacher of young children] in the nearby *shtetl* Lyuban, was unable to fulfill the role.)

As a young man he left for America, learned a craft, returned, then later emigrated once again to America, this time with his entire family (except for his eldest son, I. D. B. [the author of this article], who remained in Europe. He settled in Brownsville [part of Brooklyn, N.Y.] where he opened a small business for washing, dying and ironing clothes. In his later years, he bought himself a house in Bensonhurst, Brooklyn, where he conducted a *kheyder* [elementary religious school], teaching American children Bible along with Rashi's commentaries, and preparing them for bar mitzvah.

Ezriel Zelig was a hearty prayer-leader. At the pulpit of the Vigoder *Shul* he led the *Musaf* [supplementary] prayers on the mornings of Sabbath and holy days, and led the [main] morning prayers on Yom Kippur.

Seated from right to left: Isser; my father Ezriel Zelig; Borekh; my mother Dvosye; Elkhonen
Standing from right to left: Basye; Yitskhok Dov; Reuven Leyb; Feygl
Descriptions follow below.

[Page 418]

In Brownsville, together with compatriots from Slutsk and Pogost, he founded a congregation, "Adas Isroel", which went on to build itself a *shul*, and he organized a Talmud study group where the Slutsker rabbi, Tomashov, would teach.

My mother, Dvosye (5619-5698) [1859-1938]—was known on Vigoda as a rare homemaker—tidy, wise and honest—who supported her husband in a variety of occupations, so as to provide their children with a good education, and who planted gardens on Vigoda as well as in her home-village of Bikoy.

Basye (5643-5698) [1883-1938]—wrote stories and poems, including descriptions of Slutsk, published (under the pen-name "Basye Lvovitsh") in the New York weekly, *Di Fraye Arbeter Shtime* [Voice of Free Labor], and in the daily, *Di Tsayt* [The Time], edited by Dovid Pinski[2]

Yitzkhok Dov (I. D. Berkovitsh) [see Footnote 1] —at the time [of this family portrait] was visiting from Switzerland.

Feygl (now lives with her husband and the Dorinson family in Chicago)—as a young girl she was active with the Zionist youth in Slutsk.

Reuven Leyb—came to America with his parents after having completed Jewish studies at the religious schools in Slutsk, as well as studies at the Russian government school there. He mastered Hebrew and English. Was a Hebrew teacher his entire life. Now in Philadelphia.

Elkhonen (5654-5705) [1894-1945]—studied in Slutsk until the age of 14, in elementary and advanced religious schools [*yeshiva*s]; grew up with Hebrew literature. In America, by virtue of his diligence and sharp mind, he became an outstanding scholar, graduating Cornell University, where he became an assistant professor. In 1924 he was appointed professor of Spanish literature at University of Wisconsin, Madison, where he taught for over 20 years as one of the best, most beloved, teachers. Received the Pulitzer and Guggenheim awards for literary works. Visited Spain twice (during the period of the Republic), where he was invited to lecture at the University of Madrid. Among other works, published a treatise on the Hebrew translation by Kh. N. Bialik[3] of *Don Quixote,* comparing Bialik's Hebrew text with the Spanish original (see Bialik's letter to him in *Collected Works of Kh. N. Bialik*, Vol. Three, Col. 204). The University of Wisconsin posthumously published his substantial book (in 1948) on the classic Spanish author, Pérez Gald?s[4]

Israel Isser [or simply, *Isser*]—graduated City College of New York, was a public school teacher for a short period, went into business, lives in New York.

Borukh—brought to America as a child, studied at New York University. Works in business. Lives in New York.

Slutskers in New York

by Ch. Zaides

Jews began to emigrate from Slutsk to America approximately 75 years ago [mid-1880s]. In those days, it was the poorest people who came. There were no Jewish organizations or unions at the time. Those who had skills managed to earn whatever they could in the sweatshops, where the workday was 14-15 hours. Those who lacked skills suffered terribly for a long time until they were able to find a shop that would take them in. Though everyone lived from hand to mouth, they still needed to send as much money as possible to their wives and children, and to pay back those who had helped them buy ocean passage to the Golden Land.

But every Jew is blessed with the quality of stubbornness — regardless of how hard and bitter it may be for them. And so, a handful of Slutsk Jews got together and established a *shul,* "Anshey Slutsk" [Men of Slutsk, or Congregation of Slutsk]. Each of the immigrants from Slutsk and its outskirts appealed to their ["more established"] *landslayt* [compatriots], even though the earlier arrivals were themselves in dire straits. Everyone was worried about their uncertain income. Yet, despite the fact that he himself might lack the money to pay his own rent, every ["experienced"] *landsman* would encourage the newcomers, and do what he could to find them jobs in a shop, or advise them on where to seek help. Before long a second Slutsk *shul* was opened, with a large number of congregants. A few years before the Russo-Japanese war [of 1905], the Slutsk religious judge, Rabbi Naymark, visited his children in New York. He was given a warm reception by the [community of former] Slutskers.

Reb Leybe Naymark was a giant of Torah knowledge and a scholar among scholars, as well as an imposing speaker. His address served to unite the two congregations into one large *shul* that existed for about half a century on Pike Street in New York. If anyone wanted to locate a Slutsk *landsman* he would get accurate information at the *shul.*

The *shul* eventually purchased land for a cemetery. Much good work was done by Morris Osofsky and his parents. The onetime Slutsk rabbi, *Reb* Yankef Dovid [Yaakov Dovid Willowsky, 1845-1913], known as "The Ridvaz" [or "The Ridbaz"; acronym of his full Hebrew name], who was known [throughout the Jewish world], passed away in *Erets Yisroyl* [Land of Israel, then Palestine]. Eulogies were delivered by prominent rabbis at the Pike Street *shul*.

[Page 419]

On the advice of Rabbi Yehuda Leyb Lazerov a proposal was put forth to establish a *talmud-toyre* [supplemental afternoon religious school] in New York, named for The Ridvaz. The proposal was adopted and the Ridvaz Talmud-Toyre was established in honor of their much beloved rabbi of Slutsk.

The Ridvaz Talmud-Toyre is a child of the Slutsk *shul*, and in recent years Slutskers have lived to see a grandchild: a *yeshiva* [school of advanced religious studies] has been established, named for Rabbi Yosef Kanovits, son-in-law of the *gaon* [rabbinical sage] *Reb* Yankef Dovid, rabbi of Slutsk.

Rabbi Dov Yehuda Daina

Rabbi Daina was born in Slutsk, where his grandfather *Reb* Zundl Salant was chief judge over religious matters [for the local Jewish community]. Zundl Salant was a cousin of *Reb* Yosif Zundl Salant of Jerusalem, who was in turn the teacher of [the famous] *Reb* Yisroyl Salanter[5] When his grandfather passed away, Dov Yehuda Daina replaced him as judge and religious authority. He was raised in Slutsk during the first eleven years of his life and in fact began studying at the Slutsk *yeshiva* [unusual for a boy so young].

In 1917 this judge and religious authority of Slutsk left for Harbin, Manchuria, where he remained until 1925. From his arrival in America until his death in 1945 he lived in Canarsie [Brooklyn, N.Y.]. Rabbi Daina also brought his young son Mordkhe to Harbin, where the latter learned the Russian language fluently, at a *gimnazye* [government high school]. In 1925 he and his father came to America, where the son entered Yeshivat Rabbeinu Yitzchak Elchanan [rabbinical seminary now part of Yeshiva University].

The young Rabbi Daina, upon ordination, became a rabbi in Syracuse, later in Brooklyn, until becoming a military chaplain in 1944.

Due to his knowledge of the Russian language, he was sent to Shanghai [a city of refuge for escapees from the Nazi invasion of Russia and of Eastern Europe in general]. There he was among the first American Jews to meet survivors from the European yeshivas.

Rabbi Leyb Naymark
(Slutsk religious judge and famous preacher)

Rabbi Mordkhe Daina

Rabbi Dov Yehuda,
Slutsk religious judge

(Credit for the official photos of Rabbi Mordkhe Daina and his father belongs legally to the U.S. Army.)

Translator's footnotes:

1. I. D. Berkovitsh is famous as the son-in-law and chronicler of Sholem Aleichem, translator of the latter's works into Hebrew, as well as a writer in his own right.
2. Dovid Pinski, famous Yiddish playwright, novelist, writer and editor, disciple of I. L. Peretz. His play *The Treasure* was staged by Max Reinhardt in Berlin in 1910 even before reaching Yiddish audiences.
3. Chaim Nakhman Bialik (1873-1934) is regarded as the founding poet of modern Hebrew literature. He also wrote in Yiddish.
4. Benito Pérez Gald?s (1843-1920), a radical, anti-clerical realist novelist, is considered second only to Cervantes in Spanish literature.
5. From Wikipedia: Rabbi Yisroel Lipkin, better known as "Yisroel Salanter" or "Israel Salanter" (November 3, 1810, Zhagory – February 2, 1883, Königsberg), was the father of the Musar Movement [non-Hassidic movement of ethical/spiritual life-goals] in Orthodox Judaism…The epithet *Salanter* was added to his name since most of his schooling took place in Salant (now the Lithuanian town of Salantai), where he came under the influence of Rabbi Yosef Zundel of Salant.

[Page 420]

Slutsk Shtetls/Towns

Uretshe
(Urechcha, Belarus)
52°57' 27°53'

Uretshe

by Nakhmen

Translated by Hershl Hartman

Uretshe was a distance of 25 *verst* (or *vyorst*) from Slutsk (1 verst = 2/3 mile). The *shtetl* spread across both sides of the old highway – a dirt road that led from Slutsk to Bobruisk by way of Uretshe and Hlusk. The houses were mostly wooden and many were also roofed with thatch. There were about 200 families. Most of the residents were shopkeepers, laborers or peddlers who would travel among the surrounding peasant villages, dealing in whatever came to hand: flour, hides, flax, kerosene, herring, etc. Transportation between Slutsk and Bobruisk was sustained by coachmen, both local and from Slutsk, who also delivered everything needed by the *shtetl* and its environs, even letters, newspapers and any requirements of the religious leadership.

Uretshe had an old, modest rabbi, a great scholar by the name of Avrohom Aaron Peshin, along with a large house of study [synagogue], plus a few *minyonim* [prayer groups] for Sabbath and holy days, *khadorim* [elementary religious schools] where *melamdim* [teachers] of the old style held forth and taught Torah to Jewish children. There were also intellectual Jews, Zionists like Avrom Borekh Epshteyn [Abraham Barukh Epstein]. Epshteyn was a flour merchant – known as the teacher Lvovitsh [Lev's son] from Bobruisk – and from time to time he would dash over to his hometown for vacation or simply to visit.

With the extension of the railroad line from Verkhutin to Uretshe during the time of the First World War, Uretshe blossomed. A post office opened. The former house of study, which had been destroyed by fire, was replaced with a new large and spacious synagogue. Starting from the train station, in the shade of tree-lined avenues, two rows of magnificent homes were built, comprising a new street over a kilometer in length. A branch of a kerosene firm from Baku was established, with a large kerosene reservoir. The tanks could be seen distinctly from far-off in the distance. The yard was filled with customers and wagons from the entire surrounding area. The branch was managed by Shmuel Resnik, a Jew and an ardent Zionist.

With the noise and whistles of the locomotive, a new and intense life was ushered into the *shtetl*. New faces appeared from time to time, trade blossomed and grew stronger day by day. Yiddish, Hebrew and Russian newspapers could be obtained by anyone who wanted them in the town's new bookstore.

A great dispute arose in the *shtetl* following the death of the old rabbi. The *shtetl* divided into two camps: *amkho* – the common folk – along with the workers, wanted the young Rabbi Apelman, who entranced them with his folk-sermons, whereas the intelligentsia and the businessmen wanted the Hresk rabbi, Ben-Tsiyon Tsvik, an erudite Jew with an imposing presence. The dispute lasted some time, during which the coachmen and their followers poured kerosene into the flour sacks of Epshteyn the flour-merchant (one of rabbi Tsvik's admirers).

Eventually the dispute calmed down, and the *shtetl* merited the honor of having *two* rabbis, each one earning a paltry sum.

A new spirit swept into the *shtetl* with the modernized "*Kheyder*," which opened in 1915. It was established by the talented teacher, Glinik, who had come from the [pre-state] Land of Israel. He earned the support of Uretshe proprietors, and the *Kheyder's* two classes, where the method of instruction was to teach "Hebrew *in* Hebrew" [Hebrew immersion – "*Ivrit b'Ivrit*"], became filled with pupils. Alta Asaf, sister of the late Rabbi Professor Asaf, also taught Hebrew in Uretshe for a short time.

The richest man in the *shtetl*, Dobrobarski, opened a private Hebrew school for his children and those of the other elite. He brought in a young teacher, Gurevits. With his help, and the aid and leadership of Mikhl Reznik, a passionate Zionist and talented Hebraist, a Zionist organization was founded. From time to time a variety of lectures would be presented, as well as Zionist sermons from the pulpit in the house of study.

The propaganda of the Bundists and other opponents [of these Zionist trends] had no effect at all. Collection plates would be placed in the synagogue and in the facilities of the smaller prayer-groups on Yom Kippur Eve, for cash contributions to the *Yishuv* [Jewish community] in the Land of Israel. *Shekels* [fund-raising coins] and Zionist stamps were sold, and public Zionist meetings were held quite often – especially on the 20th of Tammuz[1] and on the anniversary of the Balfour Declaration[2]. A [secular] literary circle existed as well, which held lectures on various themes.

[Page 421]

Zionism was banned and every cultural activity dissolved at the time of the Russian Revolution, and whenever governments [ruling Uretshe] changed, whether during occupation by the Germans [in World War One], Poles, or Bolsheviks.

Uretshe was set on fire by Polish soldiers before retreating [ca. 1920] and almost the entire *shtetl* was burned down.

Lastly, the hand of the Nazis wiped out the Jewish community of Uretshe, with only a very few managing to escape the murderers.

Rabbi Avrohom Aaron Peshin

The rabbi of Uretshe, Avrohom Aaron Peshin, was born in that town, of poor parents, and died in 1912 at the age of 75. Besides being a great religious scholar, he was also a great mathematician. As a young man he once stayed briefly at a Minsk inn and noticed that everyone there was upset over a resident who was a candidate for graduation from the *gymnazia* [high school]. The landlady of the inn told her husband that she feared the student-candidate might take his own life. The rabbi found out the reason for the distress. Two young Jewish men were about to take their final exam at the Minsk *gymnasia*, an exam involving a very difficult mathematical problem. If they failed to solve the problem they would not receive their diplomas and their efforts of long years would be for naught. The rabbi asked to see the problem and within half an hour he had solved it. Some months later the rabbi received 10 rubles with a copy of a letter written to the previously-depressed Minsk student by the Ministry of Education in Petersburg. The student had received the letter along with a prize of 50 rubles. It turned out that the teacher who had assigned the problem was an antisemite who had wanted the two Jewish candidates to fail their final examination. He himself was unable to solve it and considered the solution to be impossible.

Thick forests surrounded Uretshe. Two merchants, a Jew and a Christian, bought a forest in partnership. Unable to come to an agreement, they turned to the courts. The issue was very complex and the judge was unable to make a ruling. He then told them that he knows the *staroste* [Polish: mayor, reeve] of the *shtetl*, a wise person whose father was the rabbi of the *shtetl*. Rabbis could also pass judgments, so he advised them to turn to him. He gave them a written document of permission to use the rabbi. The rabbi succeeded in reaching a decision that pleased both the partners. Later he received a letter of thanks from a higher court.

In another case, the rabbi failed at first. He once replied as follows to two Zionists who sought to recruit him to their cause: "It is fortunate for you that you cannot add. If you could, you would see that the calculation is simple: The entire collective wealth of Jews around the world is insufficient to buy the Land of Israel. Even if we assumed that the Turk [i.e., the Turkish Sultan, then-ruler of Palestine] would turn the Land over to us free of charge, our total funds would still not be enough to transport all the world's Jews there. Not to mention that the Land is small and a wasteland. Therefore, we must wait until the Supreme One will send his Holy Redeemer [i.e., the Messiah] at which time all the promised wonders and miracles will occur. The desert will bloom and there will be a total redemption." The two Zionists were the ritual slaughterer, Alter Marshak, and his brother-in-law, Mordkhe Finkelshteyn [Mordechai Finkelstein].

Rabbi Peshin himself taught his only daughter the Hebrew Bible and told her: "You must learn *Torah* for two purposes. First, a Jewish daughter should know the *mitsves* [commandments] and Jewish history; second, I hope that you will one day come to know the Holy Tongue of Hebrew. When I studied at the *yeshiva* a great scholar told me that I would live to see 'the Messianic Times.' If he guessed correctly, I will see the Messianic Pangs and you will live to see the Redemption. Consequently, there is no doubt that you will have need to know Hebrew." That daughter now lives in the State of Israel. His prophecy has come to pass. Several of his grandchildren by his other children are also here. Others are in America and in Russia, even in Uretshe.

Uretshe *landslayt* [compatriots] in New York founded a synagogue which they named in his honor: *Beys Haknesses Anshei Bnei Avrohom* – Children of Abraham Synagogue.

Translator's footnotes:

1. Just prior to a midsummer Sabbath during which the Prophetic reading in the synagogue is Jeremiah 1:1-2:3, describing God's judgment of the nations at the gates of Jerusalem.
2. Statement of Nov. 2, 1917, by British Foreign Secretary Arthur James Balfour, affirming that "His Majesty's government view with favor the establishment in Palestine of a national home for the Jewish people..." The date was subsequently celebrated by pro-Zionist Jews in the Diaspora and in Israel.

[Page 422]

Horki
(Gorki, Belarus)
53°02' 28°02'

Horki and its Environs

By Joseph Nozick

Translated by Sandra Herzog and Phyllis G. Schulberg

Reb Mordechai Joseph,
Father of Sender Tumoshov

There were actually two Horkis: the little town and the village Horki. The little town was near a highway. Two times a day the carts would travel (from Slutsk to Staryye Dorogi, Bobruisk, and back) harnessed to four horses which carried passengers and a small amount of goods. I remember when the autobus appeared for the first time in 1910 in our little town. All the people, small and big, old and young, came out of their houses staring in wonder. In the little town of Horki there were around 30 Jewish families—tailors, cobblers, blacksmiths, carpenters and several coachmen and also a few shopkeepers.

The village of Horki had a few hundred Christian families and fifteen Jewish families. In the fall when it rained, and in the spring, the mud would be up to your knees.

During the war, the district and its chief extended into the small town of Horki where one always found the one who rents out the land (duke/count) and a pair of security guards.

Reb Herzl Reznick

Several intellectuals and rich Jews, a few scholars, lived in the town. We didn't have a rabbi. Reb Leib Freinkman, from Novosholk, a Jewish teacher ordained as a rabbi, was the owner of a steam engine and a sawmill where we sawed blocks on board and boards and took them to the railroad station at Staryye Dorogi. Reb Leib had five sons, Yeshiva students. From Novosholk to Horki there was a *Tihum Shabbas* (a limit to the distance one was permitted to walk on the Sabbath); Reb Leib would come to *shul* with his sons. We afforded him a great honor.

I remember an accident as a child before a holiday. Itshe the butcher had slaughtered a cow and Reb Noach Alihi, the *shochet,* found an adhesion and declared the meat non-kosher. Itshe, the butcher, a poor Jew, got confused. He was a worthy, poor man. And the Jews remained without meat for the holiday. He went to Reb Leib of Novosholk and with tears in his eyes told him the story. Reb Leib consulted the holy books and told the butcher to go home and sell the meat. He decided this way for two reasons. First, the butcher was a poor Jew. Secondly, it was a holiday and Jews were not to be without meat on a holiday.

[Page 423]

Reb Zev and Gitl Nozick, Joseph Nozick's parents

Gitl Kaplan,
Reb Dovid of Rozhishche's daughter

Another important Jew in Horki was Shmuel Shaul Reznick and his wife Rachel, an employee of an automobile company. Shmuel would deliver the mail from Slutsk, Staryye Dorogi, and Horki by horse and wagon. Velvl Tomoshov was a shopkeeper from the town, a learned Jew, a trustee of the synagogue and reader of the Torah in the *shul*. He took care of the books for the *shul*.[1] On the eve of Yom Kippur, people would pay for the Torah honors and donations. He and his wife, Chosheh, would give charity anonymously. The second shopkeeper was Yisrael and his wife Chaya Deborah. Reb Herzl Reznick from the village of Horki, an observant, intelligent Jew, a scholar, the *mohel* (circumciser) for the whole surrounding community, was also a good reader of prayers (i.e. cantor). There was a *minyan* in Herzl's house all year. But for Rosh Hashanah and Yom Kippur, all of the village Jews came to the shtetl. Reb Herzl would pray *Musof* (the additional holiday prayer) on Rosh Hashanah and recite *Kol Nidre* on Yom Kippur. He davened *Maariv* (evening prayer) and the next day *Musof* and *Ne'ilah*. Shimon, the wagon driver had a claim on the honor of opening the Holy Ark for *Ne'ilah* (the last prayer on Yom Kippur). No matter how much he was asked, he outbid others and paid the most for the *mitzvoh* (honor) of opening the ark.

There were a number of other important Jews, for example: Reb Shloyme the Cohen (from the priestly family, descendants of Aaron), a god-fearing person who loved people; a poor man, he supported himself by working the land. His wife Ese was known as the *bubbeh* (grandmother) of the neighborhood. Also of mention were Reb Dovid Leib Ostrover and his son Nachum; Yidl Seigalovich; Beril the miller; and Reb Michael.

Reb Fayvl, the wagon driver, was once in America and returned. He was no great scholar. He was a good prayer reader (cantor) and an even better Torah reader. His claim was leading the *shacharit* (morning prayer) on Rosh Hashanah and Yom Kippur (starting from the prayer) *Hamelech* (The King).[2] On Tisha B'Av when he read the Lamentation prayers, tears poured from his eyes. It was said that the walls of the *shul* cried with him. Boys would take aim from all sides and throw thistles straight into his beard.

Itshe the coachman had a good voice. On the Sabbath when the blessing was said for the new month, when he would come to the words, "May it be Thy will that the new month be blessed…," one would feel great passion, for his heart and soul were in the prayer.

Near Horki lived Reb Moishe Gezel of Rozhishche, an intelligent, well-to-do, earnest man. He had a big business and was a distinguished Jew. Rozhishche was six to seven viorst[3] from Horki. Reb Moishe Gezel would not come to Horki very often. Shabbas and Yom Tov there were *minyans* in his house with the nearby residents, for example: Mote Lazar and his son Beril from Kuchin, Itshe Leib from Kasarichi with his sons. And from a neighboring village, Starevo,[4] the Jews would come on *Shabbas* and on the holidays to the *minyans*.

Reb Dovid Margolin from Rozhishche was known through the whole community as a rich countryman and hospitable Jew—the tablecloth was never taken off the table. Everyone could sit and eat as much as the heart desired. He was a great charity giver and beloved even by the Christians in the village. He sponsored his sons-in-law, students in whom he took pride, such as Reb Zelig Chinitz and Reb Mendl Kaplan from Bobruisk. At a *Shabbas minyan* they convened in the inn of Reb Dovid from Rozhishche. Also there were Reb Moishe Gezel and Reb Shmerl with their grandchildren. Also many nearby residents, visitors and transients. During refreshment time, they would joke that it was as if they were at the table of the king.

Reb Noach Elia, the Horki *shochet*, had a handsome beard in addition to being fanatically religious. While he prepared the ritual knife, no one dared be in the room in order not to disturb him.

[Page 424]

Mones Gelfand and his wife Raynele

The Jews from both Horkis were poor. Each one, with great difficulty, earned a little bit of bread, but when a poor man or a guest came to the shtetl on a special *Shabbas*, he was treated with honor.

We would start to prepare for Passover right after Purim. At my parents' house almost each year we would have the *puhdroch*[5] during which we would bake matzoh. Everyone would bring their own meal (i.e. ingredients) to bake the matzohs. My father and mother, two or three weeks before the puhdroch, labored very hard day and night in order to earn rubles to make a wonderful holiday. The day before Passover, we would bake Shmurah matzohs[6] in our house. All the Jews from the shtetl and from the village would come to fulfill the *mitzvoh* (fulfilling the commandment) (of baking the shmurah matzohs). One would knead the dough; another would bring and pour the water; another would roll it; a fourth would put the matzohs in the oven. In general, each one was involved in the *mitzvoh* and at the same time we said and sang the holiday prayer, 'Hallel.'

At the Passover Seder in my parents' house voices were very high. Holiness prevailed.

At one corner of the table, I remember, stood six candlesticks. Sparkling, burning lights. A fourteen-branched lamp lit up the house. My father, may he rest in peace, was not educated, but a very honest, observant Jew. He sat reclining on two pillows at the table prepared with matzohs, *choroses*, horseradish, etc. And with a cheerful singing voice he would conduct the seder. My mother wasn't as religious as my father but she had pleasure when we were all around her. There were times when her face showed a melancholy from misery and hardship, worrying about us all. My father, always a great believer, would always say, "God will help."

Mones, the coachman, was considered a rich man in the shtetl. He owned four horses with harnesses. He and his wife, Riva Leah, had three sons and a daughter. The two older sons, Nachum Beril and Malkiel, worked with him when they grew up and also hired a Christian. It was said that they saved a good few hundred rubles and it could be noticed since they lived better and they dressed nicer. When Shmuel Shaul Reznick moved to Staryye Dorogi, Mones bought his beautiful house. His *chazaka* (entitlement) was to lead services on Rosh Hashanah and Yom Kippur beginning with the morning prayers up until 'Hamelech' (the name of a prayer). Their son, Malkiel, emigrated to America, and lives in Cleveland, Ohio.

Sholem's son, Ruven, a coachman, was a strong (heroic) Jew. His manner of praying was marked by many mistakes. I remember that for Passover, Ruven and I would go collecting alms for the poor.

There were more coachmen, for instance Meshl and his son Melakh, and Yerukham. They lived a virtuous, difficult life.

In the shtetl there were three blacksmiths: Bentsha, Mendl and Shaul, the mute. Shaul's wife, Malka, was surely not a mute. She possessed an abusive tongue. We trembled from her mouth. In 1923, their son, Isaac, married one of my sisters. According to the latest information, they are now in Slutsk. I remember Itshe, the tailor, Elchanan, the cobbler, and his brother Sholem. Also, Khatshe, the tailor from the village.

In 1920, when there wasn't any white flour, my father would on Friday night make *kiddish* over a loaf of black bread. Or over a glass of cold tea and make the proper blessing. In those days, a little salt, sugar and white flour were among the most expensive and hardest to obtain.

All of the coachmen, whom I had earlier mentioned, would draw their livelihood from Boris Kletzkin, from Vilna, the proprietor of the publishing house 'Kletzkin.' He had a glassworks factory in Starevo, ten viorsts from Horki. The coachmen would travel to Starevo, unload the wagons—special flat wagons with crates of glass—and take them to the Starevo village to the railroad. Sometimes they would also take goods from Starevo village to Slutsk.

Most of the workers in the glassworks were Poles and a few Germans. But there were white-collar workers who were mechanics, bookkeepers, overseers, barbers. The shopkeepers were Jews; the majority not orthodox.

After Hitler's invasion, everything in those regions was washed away. No more shtetl! No bright images! Honor their memories!

[Page 425]

Reb Yitzkhok Tomoshov with his wife, Horki residents

Reb Shmuel Tomoshov with his wife Libe and their son

Horki people: Chaim Zedes

Reb Shmuel Shaul Reznick with his wife Rachel, were well known in Horki, and also over the whole Slutsker region. Apart from their good works in charity and acts of kindness, hospitality to guests, Reb Reznick was very accomplished in a variety of languages.

All brokers from Slutsk-Bobruisk knew that Shmuel Shaul sought the best Jewish teachers for his four sons and price was no deterrent.

When a Horker Jew was in trouble, Shmuel Shaul was the person who helped him out of trouble. When a Jew needed to send his son or son-in-law to America, and needed money, Shmuel Shaul's funds were available for the needy. When the Horker bathhouse was burned, Shmuel Shaul was one of the first to come up with a great amount of money. Many Jewish teachers exulted in that they were worthy to be teachers for Shmuel Shaul.

Reb Shmuel Shaul played an important role everywhere. He was held in high esteem by everyone. Since he was a rich man, he had an open hand for everyone. Every holiday he hired Noach Elyu, the slaughterer to slaughter several calves, and sometimes a cow too, and distributed the meat to poor families. His wife, Rachel, helped to distribute charity to all. He was held in great esteem in the eyes of Horki landowners and also the regional officials. Everyone respected him. In the days when Nicholas ruled, Jews weren't allowed to have their own fields. But as Shmuel Shaul held the government contracts, he occupied many fields. He produced oats for the postal service horses. And in those days Shmuel Shaul had a mill to thresh oats.[7]

Shmuel Shaul treated all his farmhands and servants very well. Everyone was bound to him heart and soul. They called him master (*balehbus*) and his wife mistress (*balebusteh*). The peasants didn't want to leave them.

After the World War I, everything went to the Bolsheviks. The rich Shmuel Shaul with his wife Rachel were driven from their beautiful residence. Everything was taken from them.

The proud, rich Shmuel Shaul Reznick died from heartache. All of his children scattered. The once rich wife, Rachel Reznick, remained living in Staryye Dorogi lonely and poor.

As quickly as her countrymen in America learned of her difficult situation, many people offered their help.

Translator's footnotes:

1. It is not clear if this meant he did the accounting, or that he physically maintained the prayer books.
2. Synagogue honors: The honors of opening the Ark, being called to the Torah, and leading certain parts of the service were very important, and they traditionally went to the same men year after year. The men clung tenaciously to these honors, and it is not clear if anyone knows on what basis they were assigned.
3. A viorst is 3500 English feet.
4. The translation of this town from the original Yiddish document would be "Sareve;" we believe this was a typographical error and that the town should be Starevo as shown.
5. An event at which the entire town came together to bake matzohs for Passover.
6. Shmurah matzoh is traditionally eaten at the Seder. The Shmurah matzoh is watched even more carefully than ordinary matzoh during every phase of its production, to be sure that no leavening has taken place.
7. Remove from chaff.

[Page 426]

Hlusk
(Hlusk, Belarus)
52°54' 28°41'

Self-Defense in Hlusk

by Shmuel Lief (Miami Beach, Florida)

Translated from the Yiddish by Sol Krongelb and Jerrold Landau

Translator's note: This translation essentially follows the author's original style and structure. Some Russian and Yiddish words have been carried over without translation to help convey the flavor of the original. In many cases, the original text provides the definition; when deemed necessary, a translation has been added in brackets. Where I was able to, I have added explanatory footnotes for some of the customs which may not be familiar to the contemporary English reader.

Katonah, New York
March 11, 2001

The Jewish community of Hlusk numbered 3,148 individuals according to the census of 1847.

At one time, the name of the town was Hlusk-Dabrowicki, near the Ptich River.

There were two Pravoslavic churches, one Catholic church, a large synagogue, and five places of Jewish prayer, a folk's school, a Yiddish school, a and a seminary for girls.

There were two factories in town in which hides were processed, and 22 shops.

Hlusk was mentioned in documents from the 15th century. It is said that in the year 1580, Prince Michael Glinski conducted negotiations with various delegations there.

(From the Brockhaus-Efron Encyclopedia)

Hlusk[1] was a small shtetl in the province of Minsk. Jews constituted about three quarters of the general population.[2] The 25 per cent Christians (*meshchanes*)[3] spoke Yiddish mixed with Hebrew words and lived on good, neighborly terms with the Jews, except for Sunday or a holiday, when they got themselves drunk and broke their Jewish neighbors' windows and not infrequently beat them, but not by any means because of anti-Semitism but just to pass the time.

Hlusk was no different from the other surrounding *shtetlach* [plural of shtetl] – mostly poor people (except for a few wealthy individuals); crooked houses; dirty, unpaved streets. The principal livelihood was derived from the market, for which the poor peasant-farmers came to town 2 or 3 times during the week.

At the market there were 120 stores arranged one opposite the other in 4 rows, besides some ten or so stores in the side streets near the market. The remaining Jews engaged themselves in shoemaking, tailoring and other small trades. There were also many wagon drivers who would transport *parshoinen* (that's how they called their passengers) to and from the railroad. The nearest railroad was in Bobruisk, 50 *viorst*[4] away.

There was great competition in all aspects of earning a living. The shopkeepers would drag the peasants by their garments into their own shops. Even the *kheder*[5] teachers competed in the tuition fee and in their flattery of the *balebatim*[6]. Only one person in the shtetl had no competition – Reb Noah Itche Khloneh's[7]. He was the only candle maker in the shtetl and surrounding region, and therefore he was also called Reb Noah Lichtmacher [Candle maker].

Reb Noah was one of the most pious and respected *balebatim* in Hlusk. True, he was not wealthy. In winter, when a lot of slaughtering was done and there was enough tallow to make candles with an excess to send to the soap factories in Bobruisk, there was an income. But when the summer arrived, it was not so good because practically no slaughtering was done, and Reb Noah, along with the *shochtim*[8] and butchers, had no livelihood. So in the summer, Reb Noah became a *sodovnik*, that is, he rented a fruit-orchard from a *poritz* [land owner] and, if G-d helped, and the trees were not overrun with worms, and there was not too much rain and hail, they got by until winter.

Hlusk had a yeshiva where some ten or so young men studied. The head of the yeshiva was the renowned gaon Baruch Ber Lebowitz, z"l.

Because of the yeshiva there were a lot of *aidyms af kest*[9] which the wealthier *balebatim* took [as husbands] for their daughters. Many of the Hlusker yeshiva students are now prominent rabbis in America.

In 1905-1906 after the revolution there appeared in Hlusk, as in many other cities, groups of ruffians [known as] the Black Hundreds who incited the *meshchanes* and peasants in the surrounding hamlets against the Jews. The Hlusker Poali Zion formed a self-defense [movement] against pogroms.

One of the principal leaders of the self-defense [movement] was Nosson, Reb Noah Lichtmacher's son. Nosson was a real *ben Noach*[10], a young man, 17 years old, tall, strong, bold and energetic. He was assigned to manage the entire self-defense arsenal. Nosson hid all the arms somewhere in his father's house, but when the police began to make *"obysken"*[11] in Jewish houses, he transferred the arms to the rabbi's synagogue and stashed it in the attic under some old, torn holy books. And it happened one day that the chimney sweep was in the synagogue attic cleaning the chimney and found

[Page 427]

the whole arsenal. This occurred in the summer in the time between the afternoon and evening prayers.[12]

Reb Noah was studying a page of *gemorah* with the other Jews. The chimney-sweep told of the treasure he found. After a short deliberation among the synagogue Jews and Reb Noah, it was decided that all the arms which were discovered should be thrown into Bobe Penyeh Liebe's well. (For decades, she [Penyeh Liebe] was the only Jewish midwife, and everyone called her Bobe.) Said and done! After *maariv* [the evening prayer] the entire arsenal was submerged in the well.

The arms could not be retrieved from the well unless all the water was drawn out, so the [self-defense] group came up with an idea. They spread the word that a dead cat was found in the well, and the well had to be cleansed.

They found a time when Reb Noah was away, performed the "cleansing" of the well and rescued the arsenal of the Hlusker self-defense.

Translator's footnotes:

1. The current name is Glussk.
2. According to the 1897 Russian census, Hlusk had a total population of 5,328 people, of which 3,801 were Jews.
3. Jews, as well as all other Russian subjects, were classified as being a member of one of the following legally defined classes: guild merchants, townspeople or middle class (*meshchane*), artisans or agriculturists. (The two additional classifications, nobility and clergy, were not relevant to Jews.) Boonin (Harry D. Boonin, AVOTAYNU Vol. IX, No. 1, pp 18-25.) points out that "the words Middle Class may not correctly convey the poverty connected with the shtetl" and that almost all Jews appear to have been classed as *meshchanes*. The use of the word *meshchanes* in the present context appears to be an explicit reference to those Christians in Hlusk whose economic status was comparable to their Jewish neighbors.
4. A *viorst* is a Russian measure of distance equal to about 3500 feet (about a kilometer).
5. *Kheder* is the traditional Jewish elementary school. *Kheder* is the Hebrew word for room, and indeed, the *kheder* in the *shtetl* was often a one-room school.
6. The word *balebatim* is derived from the Hebrew and literally means "masters of the house." The term connotes reputable, responsible persons who were the community leaders.
7. Reb is a title of respect usually reserved for learned or otherwise respected individuals. It does not mean rabbi. Names of an individual associated with the person (e.g. a parent or spouse) would often be added to distinguish the person from others with the same name. Thus, Reb Noah could have been the son of Itche Kloneh's. As noted in the next sentence of the text, a person's occupation could also be added to his name as an identifier.
8. The plural form of *shochet*, a person who slaughtered animals in accord with Jewish ritual requirements.
9. An *aydim* is a son-in-law; *kest* means board (as in room and board). Study of the holy texts was highly regarded in the Jewish community, and it was a source of particular pride for a father to have his daughter married to a scholar. A father, if he had the means, might go so far as to provide financial support so that his son-in-law could devote himself to the study of Torah, in which case the son-in-law would be referred to as *an aydim af kest*.
10. *Ben Noach* literally means son of Noah and is a term used to refer to non-Jews or gentiles. Gentiles, like all people, were bound by the covenant G-d made with Noah after the flood as described in Genesis, but only Jews were required to follow the laws of the Torah, which they later received at Sinai. In the context of the present article, the author is making a play on the fact that Nosson's father is named Noah while also suggesting that Nosson was the sort of person who took direct action to deal with a situation without much regard to how the Torah and Jewish tradition might teach us to act under those circumstances.
11. Yiddishized plural of the Russian word *obysk*, which means a search of the premises.
12. An observant Jew says the morning, afternoon and evening prayers daily within prescribed time periods which vary with the season. In order to accomplish the afternoon and evening prayers with only one trip to the synagogue, worshippers, especially during the short days of winter, would say the afternoon prayers as late in the afternoon as was permissible and then wait a brief while till it was time to say the evening prayer. The summer months, with their many hours of daylight, allowed considerable leeway as to when the afternoon prayers could be said. This fact, combined with the late sunset, gave rise to the summertime practice of saying the afternoon prayers somewhat before sundown and then engaging in study till it was time for the evening prayer. Against this background, the author's description of the time makes it perfectly natural for Reb Noah to have been in the synagogue studying with other Jews as described in the next paragraph.

[Page 427]

The *Gaon* Borekh-Ber Leybovitsh

by Kheyn

Translated by Hershl Hartman

"Reb [a term of respect] Borekh-Ber" – words that were uttered with trepidation.

This was a name that had great weight in the rabbinic world – he was a *gaon* [Torah genius], a sage, a man of outstanding ethics. Among his students he was known as Rabbi "Borekh-Berl" – the meaning of his name implying a bear that does not frighten, does not scare a person off[1] . His loving glance was full of warmth, it drew hundreds of students close to him. In him they found encouragement, help and hope. His modest gaze reflected the pain and sorrow of those learnèd in the holy writings.

When he taught a lesson in Talmud in his unique manner, and a student would pose a question, he would struggle with it, to demonstrate that the question was truly a difficult matter. He would pause in thought for a couple of minutes, then reply earnestly and joyously, "My son, that's a good question! You truly deserve congratulations!" The students would look at each other in wonder. After the lesson they would ask, "Rabbi! You surely know that his question was not a solid question, so why waste time struggling with it?" To which he would reply, "You must show the learner that you are interested in him. He must be encouraged, strengthened. If you were to turn away a student's question contemptuously, he would be crestfallen and would not raise a question again."

Once there was a rabbi who came to him and presented a bit of his own original Torah insight. Reb Borekh-Ber listened, nodded his head in agreement and said, "These are new ideas you have formulated, and they are quite good." When the rabbi departed, the students said to him: "Rabbi! Who better than you would know that these Torah 'insights' of his are not original, that he took them from Reb Akiva Eger?"

Reb Borekh-Ber answered innocently, "If the rabbi had known that Reb Akiva Eger had already come up with these ideas, he would no doubt have given him the credit, [for he surely knows the aphorism] 'Whoever quotes something in the name of the one who said it [first], brings redemption to the world.' Obviously he had not been aware of Reb Akiva Eger's insights. Yet fortuitously, he reached the same conclusions as the sage. If so, he, too, deserves blessing."

Rabbi Shloyme Polyatshek, of blessèd memory (the
Maytshiter Prodigy)

The Maytshiter Prodigy – a title given the *Gaon* Shloyme Polyatshek – head of the yeshiva in Lida and one in New York, spent his last years at Yitzhok Elkhonen Yeshiva [Rabbi Isaac Elchanan Theological Seminary, at Yeshiva University]. When he was in Vilna [Vilnius] he attended the Knesses Beys-Yitzhok Yeshiva. [When the Maytshiter Prodigy visited one time,] Reb Borekh-Ber did not want to teach any lessons in Torah [in his presence], declaring that he

and the Maytshiter Prodigy had both been students of Reb Chaim Brisker, but that Reb Shloyme had continued studying with Reb Chaim [after Borekh-Ber had stopped]. How then could he, Borekh-Ber, permit himself to teach Torah in the presence of the Maytshiter Prodigy, whose insights and lessons would surely be superior? Consequently, Reb Borekh-Ber did not teach

[Page 428]

a Torah lesson that day, but instead spent time with the Maytshiter Prodigy, taking pleasure in hearing Reb Chaim Brisker's last Torah insights and in reminiscing together about this great *gaon*.

Rabbi Borekh-Ber Leybovitsh

Both of these rabbis, Reb Borekh-Ber and the Maytshiter Prodigy – counted among the most revered of their generation – had many hand-written manuscripts [of their teachings]. Naturally they were asked why they held back from publishing this original work, which would surely be of interest to the rabbinic and scholarly world. They replied as follows: "Wonderful manuscripts were left by our rabbi, the great Reb Chaim Brisker, that are languishing and waiting for redemption. How can we think of publishing our own writings as long as our rabbi's holy words are themselves not in print?"

Both men were known as fierce admirers of their rabbi's teachings. The Maytshiter Prodigy, together with the head of the Yeshiva of Mir, his friend Rabbi Eliezer Finkel, were deeply involved in helping ultimately to publish Rabbi Chaim Brisker's writings.

In the end, the works of all three – Reb Chaim, Reb Shloyme, and Reb Borekh-Ber – were published, over a number of years: *Insights of Reb Chaim Halevi* was published in Brisk in the year 5696 [1936-37], and *Insights of Reb Shloyme Polyatshek,* in New York, in 5710 [1950-51]. Reb Borekh-Ber's works on the Talmud were published collectively under the title *The Blessing of Samuel*[3]. They are very popular among students of Torah in yeshivas everywhere. Reb Borekh-Ber, of blessèd memory, is considered to have been one of the greatest heads of yeshiva of the last generation and almost all the great heads of yeshiva across the world are his former students.

Translator's footnotes:

1. "Ber" means bear; the diminutive form, "Berl," implies a cuddly cub.
2. Descriptions of Polyatshek were written by his students, N. Chinitz [Khinitsh] in "HaTsfirah," January 6, 1928, Warsaw; and Rabbi Nissen Waxman in "Talpiyos [Holy Towers]," Vol. 6, No. 1-2, New York. [This footnote was written by the author of this article.]
3. The book title was in honor of Borekh-Ber's father, Shmuel Leibovich (Leybovitsh).

[Page 429]

Hrozowa
(Grozovo, Belarus)
53°10' 27°20'

Grozow (Hrozowa) – a town, 211 inhabitants. The town was given privilege [official status] in 1693; two monasteries, Nikolski and Jan Boguslawski; two Greek Orthodox churches; a Catholic church; two Jewish Houses of Prayer; one synagogue; eleven stores, and one beer factory.

(According to the Encyclopedia of Brockhaus-Efron)

Hrozowa

by Sh. Frumkin

Translated from the Yiddish by Pamela Russ

They said that a Polish magnate from the Grozowok estate distributed a large area of his land and established a town by the name of Grozow.

This town was to serve as a center for the surrounding counties and for the farmers of the densely populated villages.

The town spread out with its four streets between tall, wooded mountains on one side, and a deep swamp on the other side. A narrow river ran nearby and met with the flow higher up from the Njeman.

The population comprised mainly of Jews who settled there from the surrounding villages. And that is actually what they were called: Bolewiczer, Boslawyczer, Khrynower, and so on. The majority of the families carried their lineage [names] from their grandmothers, such as: Rivas, Chayos'es, Rashes. There were also those who carried their lineage [names] from their grandfathers: the Aryehs, the Khunes, and the Borukhs.

Of the more respected families it is important to mention the Rivas, from whom there was Avremel Rivas Wygodski, the great host, and his brothers Shimon Rivas (Segolowycz), Dovid Rivas Segolowycz, their sisters, sons, and daughters. They were wholesale merchants and traded with the neighboring farmers and the Jewish merchants.

From the Chayos'es there was her son-in-law, the great merchant Reb Mikhel Epstajn and his daughter Golde, the founder of a large manufacturing business. Her husband was Reb Pesach Grinwald who was brought over actually from Lithuania, a great scholar and a handsome man. He died very young of consumption, leaving behind no children.

Also Leybe Szwarcbard, the village chief, was of the Chayos'es. He mastered with the Russian language to a degree, and therefore they would choose him as the head. He did not keep the position for long for certain reasons, and in his place there was the elderly, poor Khaim Zusel Krigstajn (the grandfather of Duvid Uzdan).

Leybe Szwarcbard's younger son Khaikel, from childhood, demonstrated a great talent for painting and sculpture. As a ten-year-old boy, he painted large landscape pictures and portraits, of which I remember the picture of his uncle Reb Pesach Grinwald, whose portrait hung for many years in Reb Mikhel Epstajn's room. He also etched and sculpted all kinds of figures from soft stone. They said in town that his mother came from Vilna, was a sister to the famous Antokolsky [famous Russian-Jewish sculptor, 1843-1902]. The family, whose lineage was from the grandmother Khashe, was not a wealthy one, and from here there were sextons, *melamdim*[religious teachers of young children], and small village merchants. The grandmother Rashe, as is said, was a capable woman with a strong character. Her sons, Itche Rashes and his brothers Duvid and Shaul had several fingers of their right hand chopped off. The grandmother Rashe did this with her own hands when the children were still very young so they would not be taken as conscripts. The wealthy would be reprieved by other means.

The well-known family Grozowski or Rozowski (according to Mendele Mokher Seforim) comes from a certain Reb Feivel Hrozower, a Jew, a great scholar, a *yeshiva* principal. From that family come all the Grozowskis and Rozowskis across the world. From them comes the famous writer and linguist Yehuda Leyb Grozowski, the author of the Hebrew dictionary.

[Page 430]

From the Shulman family, the first residents in town, it is important to mention the Hrozower *dayan* [judge in rabbinical court] and *gabbai* [beadle], who was Reb Shmerl Shulman – a Jew, a righteous man, and who received rabbinic ordination from the Slutsker Rav, Reb Yoshe Ber Soloveitchik. He lived and sustained himself from his toil, and never agreed to take on the position of rabbi. The Shulman family had many offshoots and its members are spread out, particularly across America, as *shochtim* [ritual slaughterers] and rabbis. The well-known Hrozower Rav, Reb Shmuelke, was a son-in-law of the Arkowyczes. The family name of the Aryeh's was Szklyar. They were builders, butchers, smithies, were physically strong, capable people, with healthy muscles, and if a scandal broke out about a Jewish resident, or a fight between Jews and drunken peasants, it was enough that Aryeh's should appear in the marketplace and then the drunken peasants and the gypsy horse traders would run off as mice into their holes. It's worth mentioning the name Oreh [Ora] the Saloon keeper, or Oreh Khrynower, also a host for the second class, as opposed to Reb Avrohom Wygodski's respectable inn. There, in Oreh's cellar, friends could share a good whisky and a bite to eat.

The cellar was filled with kegs of wine and Oreh himself was an expert at making raisin wine for the city's working men. His son, Meyer Oreh's, was known for his physical strength, and put the fear of him across the entire settlement. Later, as a soldier in the Russian army, for badly beating an officer, he was arrested and sent to a disciplinary battalion. From there he escaped to America.

The *Beis Medrash* stood neighboring Oreh [Ora] the Saloon keeper's inn. Once there also was a cold synagogue nearby, but in one of the frequent fires, the cold synagogue burned down and was never rebuilt. It was generally not crowded in the *Beis Medrash,* first because the people prayed in the *shtiebel* [informal house of prayer] of Folish, and second because at that time many people of the city immigrated to America. But during the Days of Awe, the *Beis Medrash* was overly filled because all the surrounding residents and their large families filled up the town and also the synagogue. At the Eastern Wall of the *Beis Medrash* [place reserved for the prominent], other than the Rav and the leaser of the Hrozower courtyard Reb Shloime Neikrug, a scholarly Jew, the major faces of the town who stood there were those of better lineage, wealthier ones, such as the Arkowyczes, Mikhel Chiyes's and his sons, the Rivas – Reb Avrohom Wygodski, his brother Shimon Segalowycz (the different name – Wygodski – was as a protection of freeing himself from military service), and his son the wealthy merchant Leybel Shimon's – still, the Eastern Wall was also democratic. Among the prominent people were Nakhum the shoemaker, and Moishke the smithy.

The former had a *chazaka* [more than three times give ownership] for the Torah reading on Shabbath during the afternoon prayers, and on Mondays and Thursdays. The latter, a hardworking Jew, who worked with his sons in Kuznie, but he was a refined and humble businessman in town, and he took a teacher as his son-in-law for his daughter. There was also Shaye Khana's Greisukh and some time ago he was a village leader and for all kinds of reasons he ran off to America. When he returned, he was a successful butcher in town, and his set time was at twilight when he would recite the verses of "*Ashrei temimei derech*" ["happy are those whose way is perfect"; Psalm 119, prayer of someone who delights in and lives by Torah], and "*Shir hamaalos*" ["Song of Ascents"], with a strong and sweet voice. His son Khone, a hide merchant, was a *maskil* [an enlightened person], wrote flowery correspondence in the Hebrew newspapers. There was another *maskil* in town, a secret one, Khatzkel Hurwyc, also a hide merchant, brother-in-law to the famous Y.L. Grozowski. In my childhood years I discovered in his house a treasure of Hebrew literature – "*Khur Oni*" (Robinson Crusoe),

Reb Khaim Zusel Krigstajn
(Reb Duvid Juzdan's grandfather)

"*Ahavas Tzion*" ["Lovers of Zion"], until the next issue of "*Hashakhar*" ["The Morning"] (Smolenski's). From there, the Enlightenment spread across town. In a corner at the pulpit, there sat an old Jew, Reb Khaim Zusel Krigstajn, a rare type. He used to be a resident, but later he moved to Hrozowa with his daughters. The sons remained residents in the village. Reb Khaim Zusel mastered the Russian language. Boys and girls used to come to his small house to learn to read and write Russian. He remained a poor man all his life, even after he was elected as village head.

The more important teacher in town was Reb Shmerl Shulman, who did not agree to sit at the Eastern Wall and always sat on a side bench in the *Beis Medrash*.

[Page 431]

At the large wall clock in the synagogue, there sat Reb Avrohom Shaye, a Jew over 100 years old, Reb Avrohom Wigodski's first father-in-law. Even though he was practically completely blind, he still sat in the *Beis Medrash* the entire day and studied everything by heart. The *yeshiva* students, who came home during their period of vacation time, would go into the *Beis Medrash* to study a page of the *Gemara* [Talmud]. When they encountered difficult concepts, they would turn to Reb Reb Avrohom

Shaye and he, the "blind one," answered all their questions. Shmuel the tailor, although I do not remember him as a tailor that's what they called him, was an excellent *baal tefila* [leader of prayers] on Shabbath and on the holidays, and had fixed ownership of leading the morning prayers during the Days of Awe.

The first rabbi that I remember was Reb Shmuelke Epstajn. They say that in his younger years he was a merchant. Much is said about his wisdom, scholarship, and sharpness. For many years, he held the rabbinic seat in town. In his older years, he immigrated to Israel and gave the rabbinic seat over to his son-in-law – Reb Shimon Tzvi Skokolski (also a former merchant), a smart, worldly individual. For certain reasons, he gave up the rabbinic seat, and in his place there was HaRav Reb Khaim Fishel Epstajn, an enlightened person, a Zionist, who published Hebrew Zionist songs in the newspaper "*Hapisga*" ["The Summit"]. The city's learned ones were his opponents (because of his Zionism, but he was beloved by the people until a confrontation broke out and his earnings, which until now was tight, became even less. Because of that he was forced to find a rabbinic position elsewhere, and he was taken on as a Rav in the Lithuanian city of Sajni.

They say that when Reb Khaim Fishel and his family left Hrozowa, many important men escorted him way beyond the city.

One of the escorts said: "But, Rebbe, Hrozowa is still a fine city!"

The sharp-witted Reb Khaim Fishel responded: "Yes, now that the important people are here and not there in the city, Hrozowa is really a fine town."

The Rav that took the position after him was Reb Nakhman Yosef. He took great interest in the economic situation of the town. Through his efforts a loan-and-save fund was founded.

One of the Hrozowa families traced their lineage from their grandfather Borukh: Mikhel Borukh's, Meyer Borukh's, Moishe Aron Borukh's, and their sisters.

In Hrozowa they used to say that the grandfather Borukh would go to trade at the fairs but would always be too late.

From there, they took the expression: He is taking his time like Borukh at the fair.

There were many *cheders* [religious children's schools]. Avremel the *chasid* [pious man] was a teacher of young children and Beryl Khaim Grozowski was the *Gemara* teacher. Until *bar-mitzva* age, the young boys would study in the *cheders*, and after that, some went off to study in the Slutzker *yeshivos*, and the rest helped with their parents' work and stayed in the city until their conscription, and then they left to America. The more refined girls remained at home waiting for their betrothed. Daughters of the poorer class became seamstresses or helped their parents in the bakery, and so on. Some of them left to the nearby or even faraway places and served as domestics in wealthy homes, restaurants. When they came back to the city a little better dressed, made up, hair done, the religious women in town would give them dirty looks.

In the year 1888, there was a terrible fire in town and the entire marketplace burned down along with all the stores and Minsk Street. Slowly, the town recovered, and prettier houses and shops were built. As they say: "After a fire, you get rich." I don't remember any other great fires.

In 1903, I left my home town. According to the information that I received during my wanderings, the town served as the "country house" for the area. Hrozowa was renowned for its forests, and summertime the city was filled with country homes. From Hrozowa, community activists and businessmen came to America, such as: Yisroel Szweidelson, the chairman of Slutsker Relief in New York; Shmuel Borowski, one of the founders of *Histadrut Ivrit* [organization for spreading Hebrew language] in New York and former principal of the renowned "*Makhzikei Talmud Torah*" in Borough Park [promoting religious Jewish education]; Duvid Udman, a prominent businessman in New York who was very instrumental in publishing the book "Slutsk and Its Surrounding Areas."

Also, Sh. Nakhmani [Nakhmanowycz], one of the founders of *"Kheder Metukan"* [the "improved *kheder"*] in Slutsk, teacher in many other schools such as in Kieve and in Israel, editorial board member of this book and translator of the new Russian literature into Hebrew, is also originally from Hrozowa.

The terrible fate of the destruction also reached the Hrozowa Jewish population. As one of the *olim* [immigrants] to Israel relates, he passed through Hrozowa in 1946 looking for Jews, and found just one woman by the family name Wendorf. I think that she came from the above-mentioned Shmuel Schneider's family. After that, the entire Jewish population was killed by the Nazi murderers.

May these lines of mine serve as a memory and tombstone for my beloved city of birth.

[Page 432]

Sixty Years Ago

by B. Epstajn (Bashe Greisukh)

Translated from the Yiddish by Pamela Russ

(According to a Letter from New York to Sh. Nakhmani)

In your letter you ask that I describe my memories of our home town. I thank you very much, but unfortunately I am a small writer, and secondly, I left Hrozowa fifty-five years ago and forgot almost everything. But still, I will try to push my memory and write something, maybe it will be worth something for the Yizkor Book.

About Zionism:

I remember how one Shabbath or Jewish holiday my parents were coming home from the synagogue and were speaking about a curious thing: After the Torah reading, Fruma Laya's young son went to the podium and delivered a speech about Israel. He encouraged people to donate money to settling in the Land of Israel, and he encouraged the listeners to actually leave the exile [that they were in].

As they [my parents] were talking, my uncle Reb Shaya Khana's came over, and they asked him how he felt about the Zionist speech in the synagogue. This is what he said: "What are you talking about? The things that today's children can think of and accomplish!" My mother mixed in and added: "What is there to talk about. If we will merit it, and repent, then the Messiah will come and take us all to the Holy Land."

About Your Mother:

I remember your mother Fruma Laya. She was the midwife in town, but not one who had trained in this. In general, in the small towns, there were no trained midwives yet.

Both the rich and the poor would summon her. Other than the woman who had the baby, the homes were filled with small children, and she would have to take care of all of them. She worked very hard and not everyone had the means to pay her, but she was never angry about this. "A *mitzvah* [good deed] is better than money," she used to say.

Reb Yakov Greisukh and His Brother Shaye Khana's (Reb Shaye Greisukh)

My father was a deputy in the city's administration. The elder official was Leybe Khiyotes (Leyb Szwarcbord). The twelve deputies would meet in the city office. If they would bring a Jew to the station to be arrested – without a passport, and he would say he was a Hrozower, my father would sign and confirm that he knew this Jew and his father, doing anything to remove the Jew from non-Jewish hands.

My uncle, Shaya Khana's, as the elder official, was once caught with this type of false signature, and a heavy punishment was to come, so then he ran away from Russia. But in a short time they gave him amnesty and he returned to Hrozowa and led a beautiful life.

* * *

My old grandmother Soroh was a righteous woman. She would take care of the old and sick. She was also devoted to the poor children and orphans who studied in the *Talmud Torah* [religious schools for children].

She would wash their laundry for free, taking care that they were clean and fed.

My Father

by Beinish Epstajn (New York)

Translated from the Yiddish by Pamela Russ

My father's first rabbinic post was in Hrozowa. My father, HaRav Reb Khaim Fishel Epstajn, of blessed memory, born in Tawrig, was one of the youngest students in Wolozhyn, when the *yeshiva* was closed in the year 5652 [1892] by the Czarist government. At the age of 22, he was already the Rav in Hrozowa in about the year 1897.

The town was far from Tawrig, not only in distance, but it also far in civilization and life status.

I was a young child when my parents came to Hrozowa. So my memories are really as I remember them – piecemeal.

As a young rabbi, full of ideals, my father quickly pushed against the resistance of old powers in town who were not supportive of the Rav's pressures to do good for the population. My father's first project was to rebuild the baths and the *mikvah* [ritual baths]. He found it broken down, presenting a danger to the people, in winter it was badly heated and offered a cold ritual bath. So he decided to reconstruct the building

[Page 433]

HaRav Reb Khaim Fishel Epstajn

and brought a boiler ["steamer"] that heated the water with steam and even whistled to notify the people when it was time to light the Shabbath candles. This required money, so my father took upon himself the debt of hundreds of ruble. Finally, he had to pay the debt for years from his earnings. Years later, the community repaid the debt to him.

A second issue was fodder for the animals. Almost every Jew in town had livestock for dairy, so there was an agreement between the community and the owner of the courtyard that a certain area of the baths belonged to the city so that the livestock could feed there. When this elderly owner died, his daughter, the "princess," wanted to nullify this arrangement.

With time, as the city officials saw that the Rav was a true leader, they came to the Rav so that he could take care of the issue of the "fodder."

My father went to Minsk and gave over the issue to the well-known lawyer Shimshon Rozenboim (later to be a minister in Lithuania), whom my father knew from the Zionist gatherings in Minsk.

The dealings with the "courtyard" were handled by my father in Hrozowa and a decision was made that was agreeable for both sides. In the city, there was a constable, a "bribe taker," who settled himself in the Jewish shops and on the two market days, Sunday and Thursday, he told the Jews to keep their shops closed.

My father went to see the Slutsker district official, and the constable lost his job.

I also remember, as a young boy, that there was a police officer sitting in the house, and he was looking through my father's religious books and letters. Someone had informed the district officials that the Hrozower Rav was "preaching revolution" and that he was conducting illegal Zionist activities. They took my father away for an interrogation and searched through his papers and religious books. All his correspondence was given over to a censor. In a few months' time, everything was given back with an apology.

The youth in town looked upon the Rav with great respect and would even comfortably accept the Rav's speeches of rebuke that they were roaming around in outside fields [areas].

Hrozowa was also the only town where the "socialists" did not dare come to the *Beis Medrash* to give their speeches as they did in other towns under the printed name "*Pistolets*." I remember how my father eulogized the Lebedower Rav whom the revolutionaries shot during an attack.

My father's influence in the town grew every year. Thanks to him, many young Hrozower boys left to study in *yeshivos*. With the young students in town, my father would "speak and talk." A significant portion of the response in his book "*Teshuva Sheleima*" ["Complete Responsa"] comes from that time. They would come to him from the surrounding areas for legal courts [conducted according to Jewish law].

For the town, the Rav's house was a place that connected with the outside world. My father and two other colleagues subscribed to the Peterburg Russian newspaper "*Birzhevaya Vedomost*" ["Trade Bulletin"] and "*Hatzefira*" ["The Siren"].

In 1905, when the news came about the pogroms of the Jews in Bialystok, Siedliec, my father went around worn out and broken. In town, people were afraid of the fairs, concerned that the peasants should not make any pogroms. Some young students came from Slutsk with "*bashlyks*" [cone-shaped headdress hood, especially worn by the Russian military] on their backs, and

[Page 434]

strolled among the peasants. A rumor spread that the Jewish "*Samooborona*" ["self defense"] had electric wires with them to burn down villages. The peasants disappeared and very quickly ran home.

Peasants used to come to the Rav if they had issues with the Jews.

In town they said: "The Rav won't last long with us. They're going to grab him away from us." But it was fated for my father to hold the rabbinic seat in Hrozowa for ten years. Many times, he was a candidate for larger communities, but his love for Zion blocked his way: Older rabbis looked at him crookedly because of his Zionism. Only when he became Rav in Sajni and published his book "*Teshuva Sheleimah*" did they forgive him.

Taking the rabbinic position in Sajni happened in Hrozowa in a dramatic way. One autumn evening, two Jews came to town and asked about the Rav. The people asked about the two Jews, who confessed that they came from Sajni, from the Subalko region, an old respected community, and that they wanted to take on the Hrozowa Rav as religious leader of their own community. They politely tried to dissuade these two Jews and even threatened to beat them off to make them leave as quickly as possible. But in a few weeks' time, my father assumed rabbinic position in Sajni.

On a cold winter day, the entire city escorted the Rav and his family on the Kopulyer road to say goodbye. We, the children, sat wrapped up on the post office sleds of Reuvke Pulman, that took us to

Horodaj to the train. In the open field, my father gave his farewell speech and the crowd broke out in cries. My father wiped his eyes and we frightened children cried along with him.

My father was the Rav in Sajni until the First World War. Then he was in a German prison as a guarantor, was a fugitive in Slutsk, and then was taken on as Rav in Libui (Libowa).

He came to America in 1923 and then became the head of the *kollel* [Torah study center for married men] in St. Louis, where he died in 5702 [1941] at the age of 68.

Other than "*She'eilos U'Teshuvos*" ["Questions and Answers"] on the four sections of the *Shulkahn Arukh* ["Code of Jewish Law"], he also published a book "*Medrash Hakhaim*" ["Explanations for Life"], about deeper explanations.

Reb Nakhum Hrozower

by Mendele Mokher Sforim

Translated from the Yiddish by Pamela Russ

(excerpt from "Shlomo Reb Khaim's")

When Reb Nakhum from the town of Roizew [Rzeszow] married off his last daughter, he remained a widower in his old age. He promised himself that he would die in Israel. But since a person needs with what to live before he dies – and a Jewish person also needs to get married, that means one needs money, so what does one do? Well, Reb Nakuhm did what other Jews in the same situation would do – For several years, he went around among Jewish children, from one city to the next, to say good bye – that means, to collect nice donations and make appointments, if possible, for the next time as well, God willing. This type of livelihood, "saying goodbye," is considered by Jews to be conducted possibly by someone who is going to die and is more respected than other collectors, idlers; and it is also the manner of someone who survived a fire. He already smelled of graveyard leaves – in Israel, he was already a candidate to be a Jerusalmite … Reb Nakhum went around like this for a few years and did not, Heaven forbid, lose any money because of the Jews. He was invited, to one for a supper, to another for something warm, and when he went to say goodbye, they also slipped some money into his hand. From his side, Reb Nakhum made many promises to them. This one for this, and that one for that – to pray for one person at the gravesite of Reb Meir Baal Haness [Jewish sage, 139-163 AD, "miracle worker"], and for another to bring earth from the Holy Land … Reb Nakuhm did not forget the town of Kopulye where he had acquaintances and a few distant relatives, and one fine summer day he went there to say his goodbyes.

Generally, during the summer, they used to eat their suppers by the light of the moon, if there was one. And if not, by the light of a small candle worth a *groshen* [penny]. They made it quick, and then – good night, or very soon [it was goodnight], after they had aired themselves out a little. One summer night, however, a very bright one, you could even grab some pearls [moonbeams], there was a change in Reb Khaim's house: The table was set beautifully, candles were burning in a brass candelabra, it seemed festive. Reb Khaim had invited Rebbe Nokhum Roizewer for supper. There was a long, extended conversation at the table about the Western Wall and the Cave of the Patriarchs; about the Mount of Olives, and the matriarch Rachel's tomb; about destruction and gravesites, and they enjoyed a bite of figs during the discussion, dates, pomegranates, and carob. Everyone enjoyed the food, their eyes

[Page 435]

were flaming, sparkling with great pleasure. Reb Nokhum was very talkative, speaking and speaking, as if he were already there, having already seen everything with his eyes, and everyone was staring at him, looking with love, with great reverence, and they were very envious of him that he was destined to be there [in Israel]. It is said so easily: Israel, Jerusalem! Imagining themselves in the airplane – a country, a city – a city, houses, earth, dust, waste, mud, but no! Something is different, and how is it different? You couldn't even imagine. There is no coarseness, only spirituality. You have to feel it. Today's names – in Hebrew. Cities, places that are named in the Torah!

Later, the discussion went to more mundane things. Reb Nakhum really traveled a lot, bid farewell to many Jews, may there be no evil eye, and saw and heard an ocean of things! In this discussion, Vilna played the main role. They were more interested in Vilna than in any other city. Reb Nakhum told fascinating thing about [Vilna's] very well-known rabbis, about its extreme magnates, and very prominent men, about *chassidic* courts, *yeshivos*, and poor young students. Ay Ay! Leaving out about half the monarchy, somewhere on a small street where it was dangerous and where one dared not go at night – [that was discussed] in a quiet, frightened tone. And at the end, he came out very heavy [on a discussion] of Berlin. – These Jews, from those schools of Lilienthal's gang [he introduced Reform practices and modernity 1840s], he said, turning up his nose, and he began to tell stories and make fun of them, saying that they were wild characters, sitting, when no one saw them, with their heads uncovered, and were eating without having washed their hands! Their Torah was in their language, in short lines with figures of speech. All of it. Ay! Ay! Woe! … One the oldest of them, they said, was eating snuff [of a candle] with bread. They said, he poked around a wax candle into the *kasha* [grains, cereal] and ate it … Beautiful creatures, as it were… Reb Nakhum says with a sigh … Oy! Oy! Oy!

Well, half the monarchy, ya! This is what Shloimeleh thought about this. The half-kingdom were probably the evil forces, those "good" women, such as Lilith and Rusalkas [female water spirit in Slavic mythology], about which he had heard many terrible stories, how they misguided people with their motions, and that they are hundreds of times worse than the devil, even worse than Ashmedai [Asmodeus, king of demons] himself. Therefore, it was right that the Vilner did not dare go out at night into those empty streets. But Berliners, not clowns, intellectual Jews, Jews with their hands and feet, Jews without head covering, without washing hands [before eating bread], these types, it is impossible to understand! That means, how is this possible, a Jew – and without a hat! That means, that means, a Jew! – and he doesn't wash before eating! They are crazy, or are they missing some brains? Do they not know what type of judgment goes on there because of that? Tar, sulphur, iron knights! … And even without all these things, how does it look to be a Jew without a head covering? But only these kinds of things Reb Nakhum said, a Jew who was leaving, who was going to Israel. You had to believe these kinds of Jews. There was no choice. These kinds of things were probably in Shloime'le's mind also, and the title Berliner, since then, already meant the following in his mind: a Jew without a hat, who does not wash his hands before eating bread with snuff.

[Page 436]

Hresk
(Gresk, Belarus)
53°10' 27°29'

Hresk

by M. L. G.

Translated from the Yiddish by Pamela Russ

Hresk was around 20 viorst from Slutsk. The Jewish population comprised sixty families among a larger number of Christians. Around the town were Jewish settlements who leased dairy farms and estates from the landowners. For example, in the village of Holcyc the well-known enlightened person and great scholar Reb Elezer Zeldowycz leased the estate and the brewery. The dairy farm was leased by Borukh and his children. The tavern and the inn were also in Jewish hands. In Holcyc there was a large Jewish population with their own *minyan* [set quorum for prayers] every Shabbath and on all Jewish holidays.

Along with the surrounding Jewish settlements, Hrest totalled 120 Jewish families. The "leasing" in Hresk itself was kept for the Radziwills [Crown of Kingdom, Poland family] by the well-known family Fulman, that was in ruins.

It is also worth mentioning that the daughter of the Slutsker Rav, Reb Meyerke Fajmer, ran away from home and married one of the Fulmans, against the wishes of her father.

There was a *Beis Medrash* in town, two *shokhtim* [ritual slaughterers], and rabbis often changed there. Once, even the rabbinic seat in Hresk was held by Reb Mordekhai Meyer Zilberman. He wasn't always in town, but more often he went to deliver sermons in near and far places. Following him were the rabbis Reb Yoshiye and Reb Khaim. In the later years 5670-5673 (1910-1913), through the Wolozhyner *Rosh Yeshiva* [head of the yeshiva] Reb Refoel Shapiro, a young Torah scholar was sent over, Reb Ben-Tzion Cwik. He became beloved by the Hresker Jewish population and took great interest in the difficult economic situation in town. Primarily, the Jews were artisans, small merchants, who would go to the surrounding villages and landowners' courts. A few were storeowners, such as Mikhel the Yellow, and Mikhel the Black.

Yitzkhok Berkowycz first was a teacher in Fulman's court, but when the Fulmans became impoverished, Yitzkhok Berkowycz became a butcher in town.

Income for the rabbis was according to the folk-humor of *"GeZeiLoH"* [robbery] – *Gaza* [gas], *Zalts* [salt], *Likht* [light], *Haiven* [yeast]. Reb Yosef Shulman, one of the merchants in Hresk, had the rights to sell yeast and give a certain percent of his earnings to the Rav. When they came to pick up the Rav's money, he used to put his right hand into the money box, take a handful of silver coins, not count, and give it over in good humor. The reason for the poverty in Hresk was that there were no fairs in town and no markets. The peasants in Hresk and in the surrounding villages would bypass Hresk and go to Hrozowa and Kopulye on the market days and did not stop [in Hresk], so the Rav, Reb Ben Tzion Cwik, decided to go to Minsk to the governor Girs and requested that there should be markets and fairs in town near the church on the Christian holidays. Since he was able to speak Russian well, he was successful with the governor who promised to fulfil his request, and that's exactly how it was. After that, the economic situation did improve.

About eight viorst from Hresk, in the dense forests, there was a large village called Werebiowa, far from a main road and a train station, in which there lived a pitch burner, the well-known Hirshel Werebiower (Tzvi Wiener), a *mohel* [one who performs circumcisions] purely for the *mitvzah,* who was prepared to come for no fee [and perform the circumcision] at every invitation in the entire area.

He was not a *chassidic* Rebbe with *shamashim* [sextons] and *gabaim* [beadles]. In his simplicity, wisdom, and his religious behavior, he made a strong impression on everyone.

Sick and broken people, bodily and spiritually, women *agunos* [title for women whose husbands' whereabouts are unknown, or whose husbands refuse to grant a divorce, thus creating a problematic status of "*agunah*" for the woman] would come to him pleading for advice and a solution to their problems. He would listen to everyone compassionately. Many asserted that they were helped and saved by him. The people's belief in him was so great that even peasants from distant villages would come to see him in Werebiowa.

This is how Hirshel Werebiower, the honest village Jew, the sorcerer, the healer of people in pain, became a legendary person. His large size, his strong figure, his beautiful face and snow-white beard, had a hypnotic effect on all those who came to him. His compassion touched everyone who came to see him. To those who needed, he would give cures, all kinds of herbs, and sometimes use words or amulets.

His name was known far and wide. He lived a long life, over one hundred years. In the era of the Soviet government, when Werebiowo was already connected to a train line, someone informed on him that he conducts himself like a doctor, but still they would come secretly for a cure, and even government personnel would come.

[Page 437]

Vizna
(Chyrvonaya Slabada, Belarus)
52°51' 27°10'

Vizna

Translated by Hershl Hartman

Edited by Paul Pascal

The region of Vizna belonged to Countess Pfaffenlola. It spread over some 5,000 *desyatina* [13,500 acres, using Russia's pre-Revolution system of measurement], and had 958 residents, two synagogues, a hospital, and five retail stores.

(Excerpt from Brockhaus-Efron's Encyclopedia)
[A turn-of-the-20th century Russian equivalent of Encyclopaedia Brittanica]

Vizna, a small *shtetl* of 150 Jewish families, two synagogues, one rabbi and one ritual slaughterer. Pious Jews, well-versed in the holy books, where even the "free-thinkers" followed the holy commandments and Jewish tradition.

The synagogue included study groups devoted to Talmud and Mishna, as well as an interest-free benevolent society that provided loans to those in need.

The *shtetl* residents earned their living as storekeepers, peddlers, employees of lumber merchants, and so on. Children [i.e., boys] were sent to study at yeshivas in Slutsk, Mir, Volozhin, and a few to government-run high schools. Vizna natives became rabbis in other towns; for example, Menakhem Mendl and Moyshe Yankif Mendelevitsh.

The first rabbi in Vizna was Shabsi Oyzer [Sabbatai Ozer] from Vilna [Vilnius]. The second rabbi, Yekhiel Mikhl Yazgur, was famous and popular throughout the whole region. The last rabbi was Moyshe-Meyshl Vayner.

Vizna Jews are to be found in Israel and in America, among them the writer Dr. Ruvn [Reuben] Wallenrod.[1]

Vizna Jews suffered greatly at the hands of the hooligan gangs commanded by General Bulak-Balakhovitsh (Bułak-Bałachowicz) in 1921.[2] The *shtetl* was almost totally destroyed in 1940, and its Jewish population slaughtered, by the Nazi beasts.

(Preface by D. M.)

My Shtetele Vizna

by Yisroyl Kantor (New York)

Translated by Hershl Hartman

Edited by Paul Pascal

The sun has still not arisen in the sky, but there's already a gentle warmth in the air. The Jewish cattle crawl out of their stalls and arrange themselves at the marketplace in a herd. The sound of their mooing mixes with the crack of the cowherd's whip. A young gentile lad with a blond, wind-tossed forelock gazes into the distance with small, keen eyes. My mother drives our cow along with a stick. It joins the others heading toward the pasture.

I look through the window at the booths in the marketplace. You can hear the sound of hammering on iron. Our neighbor, Kopl, hacks off a chunk from a large piece of iron. A peasant with unkempt hair and shoes of woven birchbark, in white linen pants and a loose, white, unbuttoned shirt, regards the chunk of iron, pays, shakes his head at the high price, and disappears.

Jews dash to the synagogue, their long *kapotes* [caftans] spattered with mud.

Meyshke the butcher, a Jew with a cheerful face, a long beard and lively dark eyes, carries his folded *talis un tfiln* [prayer shawl and phylacteries] under his arm as he returns from *shul*. In his other hand he holds the lungs and liver of a calf he had just slaughtered. A dog chases after him as he strides hastily toward home.

Mina Kasriel's stands in the market from morning to evening with a basket of white rolls which she calls "pierogis." Peasants from the surrounding villages who have come to buy white bread break open the "pierogis" with dirty hands, stuff their mouths and chew with great pleasure. Mina continues shouting "Pierogi!"[3] in a thick voice that grates on your ears. Some wagons appear in the marketplace. They have things to sell: a pair of fowl, five dozen eggs, a live calf lying in the wagon with its little hooves bound, and mooing pitifully as if mourning its bitter fate. Soon more wagons arrive. The horses are unhitched and their heads outfitted with feed-sacks filled with oats. With their heads buried in the sacks, the horses chew away with great enjoyment. Dealers appear, as well as livestock workers, and butchers with red faces and high boots, striding slowly. They stop at a wagon, feel the calf, and ask the peasant in Russian, "How much?" The peasant scratches the back of his neck and stammers a few words, because he is certain that he will be cheated. Here come the hostlers–"the Leyzerkes and Yashinkes" [these are nicknames]–to test out a horse. The horse

[Page 438]

Shmuel Mendelevitsh (the [accomplished] author) and his wife, Dina

Vizna ritual slaughterer, Moyshe Kantor

is tethered by a rope. A stableman runs ahead, followed by the horse, running at such speed that may God protect you if you were to get in the way.

Slowly the marketplace fills up. It becomes one big swirl of horses, people, and wagons with their hitching shafts pointed skyward. The sun rises higher in the sky. It is hot but the traders are preoccupied. Windows are open. The heads of young girls with dark hair poke out and they chat among themselves.

I have a clear memory of a fire in the *shtetl*. The bell in the crooked steeple of the church rings out scarily. I remember my mother's frightened eyes, her wringing of hands, her trembling cry: "What is on fire?" A huge wall of fire and smoke hovers over the roofs of the *shtetl* and throws fear into everyone. The fire brigade runs out, neighing horses draw barrels of water, and the fire-hose pumps as hard as it can. When the fire is put out and night approaches, we hear the cries of the victims, women and children, mixed with quiet breezes and night-time dreams.

So pass the weekdays of my *shtetele* Vizna, until the arrival of Sabbath eve.

My mother rushes to heat the oven and, instead of black bread we eat rolls that appear to be made of white flour, and a serving of fish-potato without the fish. When there is a festivity [like the Sabbath], we go to *kheyder* [elementary religious school] only half the day. Aaron the *melamed* [teacher], with a ragged beard and deep black eyes, drills us in chanting the week's Torah portion, and sings the concluding prophetic reading with an especially uplifting melody that carries through the window off into the distance.

The *kheyder* consists of a wide room with two long tables pushed up against each other. We sit on benches with our open Bibles and sing along with the teacher. At a corner near the stove sits his wife, Reyzele Zavil's, focused on the pot of potatoes on her lap. She eats, and tosses a cheerful glance of her blue eyes at the teacher and at us. On the wall above her hang photos of sons, daughters, grandchildren in America, all resembling her.

We go home at noon. There's a bustle in the house. My mother and a neighbor woman are busy at the oven. I run off to the river and undress on the bank. The earth is damp; my clothes get wet. I jump into the river. The water is dirty. I cannot swim, so I must bathe alongside the horse that Artshik the wagon-driver brought there, to make it happy. The horse stamps its hooves, splashes me and neighs. A group of boys take off swimming to "Sobitseve" [possibly an island or different section of the riverbank], lie down on the grass and stare at the girls who are also bathing.

I return home before the time [at sundown] when my mother should bless the candles to usher in the Sabbath. She is busy cleaning the house and keeps worrying that she will miss the designated moment for the blessing. The sun sets on the western horizon in blood-red flames. Dark shadows invade the house and bring with them the feeling that the holy Sabbath has indeed arrived, together with its serenity.

My mother is angry with me. "Do something and get out from under my feet." I clean off the ash from the lantern-glass, and get myself as filthy as a devil. I wash myself in cold water and go along with my brothers to *shul*. The old *shul* building is packed with Jewish men neatly dressed in their Sabbath *kapotes*, swaying sweetly at their prayer-lecterns.

[Page 439]

The large lamps are lit, making the *shul* bright. From my seat, I study the people. The first to draw my attention is the rabbi. A long, black beard, innocent eyes. He is dressed in a long satin *kapote* with a handsome sash.

Words flow from his mouth, pearls. Velvl the *shames* [rabbi's aide], an old Jew with a curved back and small eyes below a furrowed brow, enveloped in a *talis*, sings out from the Torah platform, "Come, let us sing [the opening words of the opening psalm]!" The entire congregation brings each section of prayer to a crescendo with rapt fervor. The moment strikes me as if the walls, the windows, the ceiling, the roof – everything and everybody–are melding together into a single worshipping whole.

We return home from *shul* and find a transformed house, clean and bright. The candles are lit and their light floods together with the light of the house-lamp and of my mother's shining and pious eyes. She sits over a *tkhine*[4], her face reflecting the calm of the Sabbath. In response to our wish of *"Gut shabes* [Have a good Sabbath]," she adds, "Have a good year," and then intones clearly and with piety, "I thank you, God, for the Sabbath." Late in the evening, following the heavy dinner that includes soup and compote, I lie down in bed. My younger brother shares my bed. He is already dreaming. My poor brother, may he at least have good dreams. The moon and twinkling stars peer in through the window. The words of the *krishme*[5] are heard from my mother's room. To me, it feels as if heaven is gathering the words up into its bosom.

Sabbath morning when I enter the *shul* the heat hits me in the face. Bearded Jews look at me indignantly for arriving so late. I sit down in "our spot" and add my voice to the prayers of the congregation. After lunch we stroll past the ritual bath, to the woods. We talk, swing on the trees and I hear words in the swaying of the branches. I touch a leaf and feel a pulse in my body. I lie down in the grass. My gaze wanders toward the tops of the tall trees. On the way home, fields with stalks of corn spread before us, swaying, bowing, falling to their knees; they are speaking to us.

At late-afternoon prayers I arrive at *shul* as the congregation is reciting "You are One and Your Name is One" [i.e., well on in the prayer service]. [Rather than leaving when the service is over and returning later for evening prayers,] I don't go home but remain seated in "our spot," awaiting dusk. A half hour later Jews return to the *shul*. Elye-Leyb the butcher stands at the Ark and from his mouth flow the words of Psalm 119 [the longest psalm in the Bible], which he sings by heart. The *shul* grows dim [as the sun sets and the lamps stay unlit]. Jews stroll about the *shul*, singing their prayers with utter sweetness. It is a holy atmosphere. People are transformed into shadows. The prayer-leader is also a shadow, and all are bound up into one prayerful choir. I feel as if the roof is opening, the words floating up, up, becoming luminous, and turning into fiery arrows, shimmering and flashing like lightning-bolts. In turn, the heavens open, angels with fiery wings are singing praises to the Throne of Glory. Elye-Leyb is standing, humbly, next to Him.

Moyshe Naymark

Translator's footnotes:

1. Reuben Wallenrod became a highly regarded professor of Hebrew language and literature at Brooklyn College. A novel he first published in 1946 was translated from Hebrew into English as *Dusk in the Catskills* (1957). Other books include a survey of Israeli literature, and textbooks on modern Hebrew grammar.
2. During the civil war which followed the Russian Revolution, the White Guard (armies opposed to the Bolsheviks) barbarously attacked Jewish communities throughout the region.
3. Pierogis: Normally, a pierogi is a stuffed dumpling made of unleavened dough.
4. Prayerbook specifically for women, written in Yiddish.
5. *Krishme*, or *Kries Shema* – prayer said before sleep (and at other times), beginning with the words *Shema yisroyl*, Hear O Israel...

[Page 440]

Verkhutin
(Verkhutina, Belarus)
52°58' 28°03'

Verkhutin

by Chanan

Translated by Hershl Hartman

Among thick forests, thickly gnarled trees, and in clear, clean, refreshing air, there was a Jewish settlement that came to life in 1905. Tucked away there in a secluded corner, surrounded by green grass and magnificent trees, the Countess Gagin-Logi had a haven, an imposing house, built on a broad hill. From time to time, especially in the summer, she would come to visit the place to rest in nature's embrace. It was sustained by the countess's fulltime estate manager and a number of workers who lived near the house.

Without warning, circumstances shifted and changed. A German company, "Fritz Schultz" of Leipzig, bought up the forest. It built a sawmill to produce lumber and veneer. The railroad line was extended from Starye-Dorogi to Verkhutin. With the first whistle of the locomotive and the first roar of the factory whistles, new life entered the area. Quarters and dwellings were built for the loggers, who worked in shifts around the clock. It was actually painful to see the gigantic trees sawn down and hacked up, falling with a horrible crash. The forest was filled with noise and chaos as fallen logs were browbeaten along to the sawmill to be cut into boards.

The small settlement came alive and new faces suddenly were appearing. Merchants, traveling salesmen, and trading-agents came to buy lumber, wood products and veneers. A large area was enclosed by a tall fence and that became the storage place for all sorts of wood products. Jews from Pinsk, Vilna, Warsaw, Koenigsberg and Berlin could be heard in the streets, with their variety of accents and unique forms of speech[1].

Verkhutin also had a tiny factory that belonged to Zelig Khinitsh [Chinitz] and Dovid Dobroborski, which converted tree roots – dug up and dried out – into turpentine, tar, and charcoal.

In addition to the company-owned townhouses, private homes were built by scores of Jewish families that settled in Verkhutin and drew their livelihood from the 800 employees [of the lumber operation] and the visiting sales personnel. The small Jewish settlement also included shopkeepers, employees, commission agents, hoteliers and craftsmen. Consequently, a small community developed; it even had two separate congregations, one for Hasidim and one for Misnagdim [skeptics, opposed to Hasidim]. In addition, there was a modern [i.e., secular] Hebrew "*kheyder*" [one-room school] for youngsters. A small-scale intelligentsia developed in the place. In the summer, vacationers of all kinds would travel to Verkhutin to enjoy the copious shade of the trees and the wonderful, dry air. Days were sunny, and the nighttime was flooded with electric lights, both in the houses and on the streets. This was thanks to the veneer factory and the sawmill that were operating day and night and provided electricity at almost no cost. Parents sent their older children [i.e., sons] to study at the yeshiva in Lida or the Slutsk yeshiva, "*Eyts Chaim*" [Tree of Life], while others went to the *gymnasias* [government high schools] and commercial schools.

Where are you, dear Jews, who served as such role models, with your education, your intelligence, and your friendliness? What has become of men like Ezriel Zelig Khinitsh [Chinitz], not so long ago a ritual slaughterer who then became a commission agent – a learnèd Jew, an intellect, a committed Zionist, a Hebraist? His house was a place of both religious learning and the enlightenment of secular learning. Another, Levi-Yitskhok Halpern – a congregational prayer leader, a committed Jew – who studied without stop, day and night. Yet another, Dovid Katzenelson, who was a Hebraist, a Zionist in heart and in soul, a person of culture. The Fish brothers – intellectuals, whose houses were immersed in culture. Goldman – a fat, broad-chested Jew, almost a giant – a man of the woods, employed in the lumber industry; his daughters were well-known for their secular and Hebrew education. Noyekh Vaynshteyn [Weinstein], a devotee of Torah and a bookkeeper. The brothers Dobroborski – the elder became rich and the younger remained a simple Jew.

Leybe the tailor – who didn't know him? He had a long beard and was laiden with children. "God be blessed for every day and for what He sends us," he would say – a man completely overflowing with children, just as he was with humor, with faith, and with belief.

Eliyohu Bodnitsh was a former baker who later ran a hotel. He had extraordinarily pretty daughters, and a house full of life and song, right across from the rail station and the post office. And there were the brothers, Binyomin and Efrayim Vinik, sons of Pinye Rasayer – one a storekeeper and the other a commissionnaire – simple, honest Jews.

Binyomin Shinderman was one who came all the way from Volhyn [Ukraine]. A down-to-earth, honest Jew, a storekeeper whose kind, unassuming family drew everyone's notice. And lastly, the Glinik family – the father, a Hebrew teacher, mainly in America, and the house itself, a place of Torah learning and worldly enlightenment. The family sustained itself by means of a grocery store.

Translator's footnote:

1. The difference in Yiddish pronunciation and idioms between, for example, Vilna Jews vs. those of Warsaw, was as great as between the English spoken by Americans of the Deep South or of Appalachia vs. that spoken in Boston.

[Page 441]

Tymkowicz
(Timkovichi, Belarus)

53°04' 26°59'

The governor visited our town Tymkowicz.

He was greeted with bread and salt. In the church, he spoke to the crowd saying that they should not do any bad to Jews, for this is against the regime.

Shmuel Gronem Rabinovich
(*Hameilitz* 31, 1882)

*

The police chief [*pristov*] called together all the elders from the nearby villages and announced that unrest must be avoided. At the fair, all means were utilized and everything passed in peace.

(*Waschod*, number 23, 1882)

*

Fires

We know the following about Tymkowicz from the *Navesti* newspaper: A fire broke out in the town on April 23 at noon (the cause is unknown) and spread from a woodshed in which also contained straw. To our misfortune, a strong wind blew the burning straw to the nearby houses. The fire spread to a third of the town within a short time.

The small houses caught fire like a candle and quickly burnt down. For the most part, there were two or three families in each house, who now remain naked and hungry.

There were no firefighters in the town. Therefore, when the fire broke out, the nearby residents dragged their baggage to a field far from the town.

To the good fortune of the unfortunates, a torrential rain fell and extinguished the fire.

Fifty-two houses burnt down. Forty poor Jewish families and twenty-four Christian families remain without anything.

Cattle and many horses were burnt.

The pharmacy burnt down. It was not insured.

The unfortunates require help.

Donations can be sent in the name of the town governing council.

(*Hameilitz*, number 97, 10 Iyar 5656, 1897)

*

A large fire broke out in the town on 20 Tammuz 5664 (1904), Dr. Herzl's yahrzeit.

Almost the entire town was burnt down, and only a few houses at the edge of the town remain.

Tymkowicz

by Sonja Kazhdan-Nachmani

Translated by Pamela Russ

Tymkowicz, my home town, ten viorst [measurement slightly longer than a kilometer] from Kopulie. The majority of the population was Christian. There were about 400 Jewish families. Among them were big merchants, such as, for example, the Dworecki brothers, who conducted a lot of trade: exported eggs to the entire Russia and outside of that; the Pjolka brothers, great forest merchants; the *Dayan* [rabbinic judge] Reb Avrohom Moishe Perlin, an ordained scholar, and also big wholesale merchant of dried fruit. The same was Areh Gershon Meyer's Rockewycz, a Jew, a scholar. These two sat and studied Torah day and night, and their businesses were managed by their wives Yudis Perlin and Soroh Rochel. Mordechai Mockewycz managed the Tymkowiczer estate of big manufacturing merchandise – Grunem and his wife Esther Rabinowycz, Polye Sodowski, Meyer Goldberg and others; grain merchant – Velvel and Nachman Kiewicki, Leybel Michol's and from the Sodowskis.

The Tymkowiczer Jews did business with oxen trade, herding them to the train in Gorodaj (Zomiria), and from there exported them to foreign countries. There were many shops in the marketplace, packed with all kinds of goods, especially for the village population, who, twice a week, on Sundays and Tuesdays, would bring their products to the town's small merchants, and then buy for their own needs: land working tools, kerosene, tar, herring, handmade ornaments, sugar, manufactured goods. There were large fairs twice a year. There was lots of noise and activity

[Page 442]

with a busy animal trade of horses, flax, linseed, hoar hair. Many merchants from distant regions would come to the fairs, gypsies with their fast, trained horses (sometimes even stolen ones). Through Tymkowicz, four times a week, the famous Slutsker "Oriol" would travel back and forth to Zamiriya to the train, and onwards. These were large wagons covered with canvas, packed with merchandise from the blessed Slutsker and returned with products from distant places. The drivers of the "Oriol" were exclusively Slutsk Jews. Other than that, the Tymkowicz wagon drivers, such as the well-known Pulka, rode daily to Slutsk with passengers and goods.

Yitzchok and Taibel Kazhdan (after their wedding) 71 years ago

In Tymkowicz there were Jewish people who worked the soil – plowing, sowing, reaping, harvesting. They lived from work in the field. The best known of these workers was Volf Yelin, who took care of the horses in the estate. There were inns in the town, for those who were passing through, and "clinics" for the peasants who came to town for trade and wanted medical help from health care providers or doctors in town. Among the inn owners were Areh Tzernogubowski, Shifrin, Fraide Chaya Leibes, Fruma Tolyes-Kulakowski, Sodowski.

In Tymkowicz there was a provincial hospital with a Christian doctor, and as I remember, there was always a private doctor in the town, that changed from time to time. The names of some were: Gersonowycz, Levinson, Roginski. For consultations, they would bring over doctors Slepian or Katzenelenboigen from Neswyzh.

In the provincial hospital, there was a Christian health care provider by the name of Grynyok, but the largest practice for the peasants and aristocrats in the surrounding areas was with my father, Itche Kazhdan, of blessed memory (his father Leizer Kazhdan was the doctor's assistant in Tymkowicz). He was a steady guest by the Cekhoike prince Domanski and in the courtyard of the Tymkowiczer prince (he was from the Radziwills).

During the great market days and fairs, our yard and home was filled with peasants' wagons. My father, may he rest in peace, did not rest, rode around day and night, even on Shabbath and on the Jewish holidays. He distributed necessary medicines for free, even leaving behind a bottle of wine to strengthen a poor, sick peasant. During the time of the Soviet government, he worked in the provincial hospital. (He died on the second of Shevat in the year 5695 [*January 18, 1934*] at the age of 70). That same year, on Lag b'Omer, my mother Taibe died as well.

A noteworthy story with the Tymkowiczer pharmacist. The pharmacist's family name was Cernomordik. In Chekhov's famous story "At the Pharmacy," the name of the main character was Cernomordik. So there was a rumor in town that since he was a military doctor, Chekhov passed through Tymkowicz and stopped in the pharmacy, and this served as the central theme for his story.

In the Tymkowicz estates, there was a brewery for alcohol, a water mill, and a windmill.

In every estate, there was a Jewish lease holder who would produce Dutch cheese: in Sowycz, Tymkowicz, Cekhoike, and others. There were all kinds of artisans in the town: famous coppersmiths, smithies, carpenters, tailors, shoemakers, furriers. All these worked for the neighboring princes, for the peasants, and for the local Jews.

A unique, interesting type was Reb Elye Yessil's Gowiznianski, a businessman, a community activist. He always made sure there was enough wood for heating and warming the *Beis Medrash* [Study Hall] during the winter. He also made sure that the bathhouse was in order. With all his capacity, he helped orphans, the poor, needy mothers of newborns. He collected money for new brides, and who could compare to him when he found a bride that he could help. His face shone and his eyes lit up. When Reb Elye Yessil's went to America for a year, they said in town that during that year there were no

[Page 443]

funerals or brides. Simply said, there was no one to escort the dead, nor anyone to celebrate with the bride and groom.

Reb Elye Yessil's Gowiznianski

Of the teachers in town, I remember Reb Yosef Yudel, Reb Leizer, Reb Nochum Bruks, and Reb Shloime Perles. Reb Shlomo was an exceptional Talmud teacher, and when he eulogized a deceased, he would have the entire town in tears.

At the beginning of the Zionist movement, these were well known: Zelig Zelikowski, an enlightened intellect and a Talmudist; Yakov Moishe Kozak, Velvel Sodowski (Dr. Herzl's picture hung in his home). In the later times, Sonja Kogan and Tzemach, the assistant pharmacist, were outstanding in their Zionist activities. In town, Nisel Kontor established a library of Hebrew, Yiddish, and Russian books.

The teacher Mandel opened a modern *cheder* [religious school for young children], where they studied Hebrew (not Hebrew in Hebrew). After that, a certain Grinberg from Kopulie, and his wife (the daughter of the Nieswiezer Rav Szerszewski) opened a school for Russian and other subjects, and also for Hebrew – Hebrew in Hebrew.

There were many Bundists [secular Jewish socialists], social democrats such as the Bundist Yehoshua, Yelena Rabinowycz, Moishe Rabinowycz. His brother Shimon was locked in the Slutsk prison. Tymkowiczer girls studied courses in the Slutsk gymnasium to be health care providers in Vitebsk, in schools for dentists, and so on.

A well-known person in Tymkowicz was the Jewish elder official Feitel Kozak, and before him, his father Chaim Leyb. One of Sonja Kogan's brothers, Moishke Kogan, was known for his participation in Captain Smith's expedition to the North Pole.

* * *

In Tymkowicz there was a *misnagdishe shul* [synagogue that opposed *chassidic* philosophy], a *chassidic shtiebel*, [small, informal synagogue], and a cold *shul*, and, to differentiate, a Greek Orthodox church and a Catholic church.

The *chassidic shtiebel* in town was an infrequently used place because in the entire area there was no *chassidic minyan* [quorum]. At the head of the small *chassidic* court in Tymkowicz were the businessman Pole Sodowski and my father.

Summer 1914, before World War One, my husband Shimshon Nachmani and I, left Tymkowicz and went to Israel.

A youth group in Tymkowicz

Sitting from right to left: Dolgin, Rosa Kazhdan (died in Tzfat), Soroh Yelin, Moishe Yelin
Standing: Meyer Kazhdan, Ida Yelin, Dr. Leizer Kazhdan (died in Sklow), Moishe Yelin's wife...

May my memories serve as a memorial for my deceased family, comrades, friends, and for the Jewish population in my home town, which was erased by Nazi murderers' hands.

[Pages 444]

Timkovichi

by Mendele Moykher Sforim

Translated by Hershl Hartman

(A fragment of [Mendele's novel,] "Shloyme Reb Chaim's: A Picture of Jewish Life in Lithuania")

On a flat, open field, only nine or ten *verst* from Kopyl [about 6 miles], your eyes suddenly become aware of some sort of hamlet off in the distance. As soon as you get there, you immediately recognize this to be a Jewish *shtetl*. The clear signs of this are the marketplace with its booths, the grounds of the *shul* with its little sanctuary and tiny house of study, and – not to be compared, of course – the bath-house with its ritual bath. The market, the shul, and the bath-house are three institutions that are set up as soon as a handful of Jews gather together, share life together. It is as impossible to live without them as it would be for fish to live without water.

The name of the shtetl is Timkovichi! There are several *minyanim* [prayer groups] there, and at the beginning of a particular summer one more soul joins them – a young boy, a stranger, who sits all day in the house of study, poring over the holy texts.

Is Timkovichi a center of Torah-learning, then? Is there a yeshiva there? No – by no means, no! The Jews who live there are struggling just to earn a living. The minute that prayers are finished, the house of study is suddenly empty. The grounds of the shul become totally bare, not a single foot treading there, not one person to be seen, as if all were dead. The crowd has scattered. This one – home. Another – to the marketplace. Everyone has his affairs to attend to.

And so it wasn't for love of Torah that the young boy came here from afar – he came, quite simply, for food. That is to say, to take meals on specified days of the week, on a rotation basis, at the homes of the shtetl's well-to-do. Neither did he come here of his own free will, but was driven here by need. His mother, Sarah, a widow with little children, lacked any means of support. She, alas, had to acquiesce and send her dearest child, the eldest of her youngsters, to the shtetl, and to count on the cordiality of acquaintances there.

Swaying over the *gemore* [part of the Talmud] with religious intensity, humming bits of a lonely melody, Shloymele spends his time in the deserted house of study alone. When he tires of swaying, he just sits there, frozen on a bench, staring blankly, not moving a hair. Or he wanders into the yard outside the shul where there is no one but himself, stands, yawns, gazes fixedly to one side, not knowing who or where he is.

Prayer – that was the one bright sunbeam that could tear through his clouds of melancholy, that shone into his darkened, orphaned soul. In Timkovichi he clearly could not advance his Torah learning, but somehow the sweet taste of prayer moved him. This was a *hasidic* form of prayer, a prayer with a burning fervor. It was here in Timkovichi that he first laid eyes on *hasidim*, on the hasidic world, of which there was not a trace in Kopyl. In Kopyl, hasidim were the occasion only for brusque epithets, nasty stories that were spread by vitriolic *misnagdim* [opponents of Hasidism], as if against enemies of the Jewish people – wild creatures, no better than cattle.

The householder with whom he would stay overnight and dine on *shabbes* [Sabbath], a good friend of his father's, may he rest in peace, was a *hasid,* but still a Jew. And, moreover, a passionate Jew, a fine person – a Jew in the best sense of the word! Shloymele prayed where his host did, in a hasidic *shtibl* [small gathering-place for prayer], and both the overall conduct there and the manner of their praying were to his liking. Shloymele was indebted to little Timkovichi, because it gave him his first push toward a deeper understanding in the whole matter of Jewishness, which in later years advanced further and further. For Shloymele, Timkovichi was a new discovery – like, for example, a newly-discovered island in the world's vast oceans. Hasidim are really Jews, too! But still there is a difference between them and the *misnagdim*, among whom he had grown up in his shtetl up until this point. A *misnagid* has a frozen soul. All that matters to him is reason; his heart – ice-cold. His Torah learning and his prayer life are carried out only according to the letter of the law, they do not extend any further than what is written down in the texts. The misnagid is like an honest debtor who pays off what he owes exactly on time, because those are the rules. "Well," he thinks, "I paid off my debt and I'm done." His God is an angry one: as soon as something is askew, He feels insulted, He grows angry, He gets red-hot, and He inflicts punishment. The hasid, on the other hand, as Shloymele now could see, is passionate. The main thing for a hasid lies in service to the Creator – joyfulness: "Let Israel rejoice in its Maker" [as the Psalms urge us], in *that* kind of God – the good, merciful Father that He is.

"While praying you should have nothing weighing on your mind, not even concern for the sins that you have committed." So said the holy Ar"i[1]. Here in the shtibl, the praying is enthusiastic.

However, the [luminosity of the] praying – that bright sunbeam – shone only temporarily in Shloymele's soul, which was so sad. The rest of the time Shloymele felt defeated, vacuous, less than conscious, almost like some sort of *golem* [creature of clay]. Soon he was in a reverie, imagining a fat red cheek under a closed, blind eye, floating in the air in front of him. [But the eye was real, and it] belonged to the daughter of the household where he was lodging – a strong, beefy, corpulent, and broad-boned young woman. Shloymele would normally not have been concerned at all with the young woman as such. Well, so she is blind in one eye, so what? The problem, though, was this: they wanted, so he learned, to make her his bride,

[Pages 445]

and this concerned him greatly. He would picture her [in his mind's eye] and a great resentment would begin seething inside him: "As if all your troubles aren't enough, all you need now is to get married! And to whom? To a blind spinster!"

And, too, Shloyme would be gripped at times by a deep yearning for home, for his shtetl, for everything that existed there in the good years.

But once, during *slikhes* time[2], is yearning became overwhelming and fantasies haunted him. Fantasy overcame reality. She carried him on her eagle's wings and brought him to his home, to his mother, sweating, panting, and in a single breath. Mother and child looked at one another, and bathed in each other's tears.

Translator's footnotes:

1. Acronym of Adoneinu [our Master] Rabbi Isaac – Rabbi Isaac Luria of Safed, leading Cabbalist (1534-1572).
2. *Slikhes*, or *slikhot*, is a period of penitential prayers, said during the last days of the Jewish year, and through Yom Kippur.

Under the Soviet Regime

(According to Moshe Kahanovich)

Translated by Jerrold Landau

Lipa Goren tells: In 1928, when I visited Slutsk as an American tourist, I traveled to Tymkowicz and stayed with my blessed sister Malka and her family. I saw her daughter and son-in-law. Her husband Reb Chaim Hirsch Pialka was a fine Jew. By trade he was a cantor, *shochet* [ritual slaughterer], *sandek* [godfather at circumcisions], and mohel [ritual circumcisor]. He was also a Torah reader for the lovely town of Tymkewicz, about 40 *vierst* from Slutsk. While in their house, I felt the growing need and pressure in their lives. Ritual slaughter and kashruth were not completely forbidden. The regime, which collectivized the meat business, killed animals in a non-kosher [*treif*] fashion, through which means they pushed aside the "declassified" Jewish elements.

"Woe!" – my brother-in-law complained to me We are going under. The regime, with its great cruelty, has pushed aside our people. They do not want to have us anymore. Do you remember, Lipa, the good times from previous times. We lived peaceful, home lives with a house, a garden, our own animal. Now," he sighed, "our lives hang by a hair."

Bashke Kazhdan, murdered in the Minsk
Ghetto with her husband David Lifschitz and
their children

Partisans

At that time, Tsyganov's group filled its role successfully. They destroyed six Nazi echelons between Baranovich and Minsk. On their way back to their base, the burnt 200 tons of wheat and the large alcohol brewery near Tymkowicz.

[Page 446]

Lyuban
(Lyuban', Belarus)
52°48' 28°00'

Lyuban

The soil of our little village belongs to Duke Wittgenstein, and since time immemorial everyone has paid a particular yearly tax for the use of the land. Twenty years ago, an agent of the duke came and demanded that, from now on, we would have to pay twice the amount as before.

A few of us did not even want to hear what he had to say, but the majority of the villagers signed a document agreeing to the demand. Later they regretted it. Appeals were sent to every quarter, representatives traveled to Minsk and attorneys retained, but it was all for nothing. The government official didn't budge from his position: we had to pay.

In the meanwhile, twenty years have flown by.

A few days ago, the police commissioner of Hlusk came to us and declared that according to the legal verdict the debt amounts to over twenty thousand rubles.

"Ha-Melitz" No. 54, 1884*

---

* *"Ha-Melitz"*, or "The Advocate", was the first Hebrew newspaper in Russia, beginning as a weekly in Odessa in 1860, and becoming a daily by 1886 in St. Petersburg, until it closed in 1904.

Rabbi Reb Nehemia Yeruzalimsky

by Hana Assaf

Translated from the Yiddish by Paul Pascal

My father, may his memory be a blessing, was a rabbi in Lyuban. The citizens of Lyuban loved him and respected him. He was particularly treasured and popular among the young people.

My father was a specialist in rabbinic lawsuits. Even people from other towns – from Slutsk, Bobruisk, Hlusk, and other places – sought him out. Christians, too – the priest, the doctor and the postmaster, for example – were friends with him, and guided their behavior by his opinions.

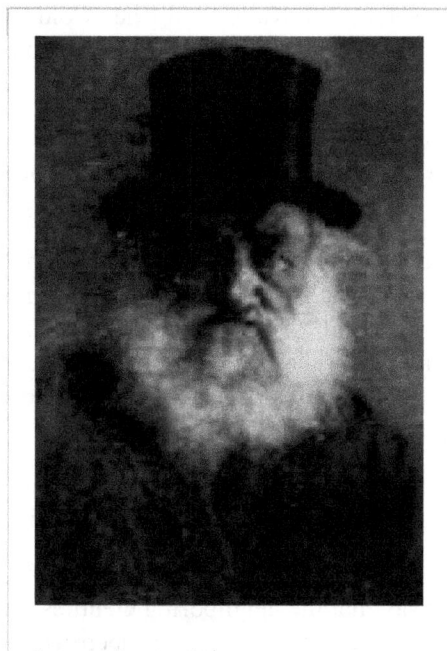

Rabbi Nehemia Yerushalmi
[Yeruzalimsk]

My father was very wise, possessing a strong character brimming with fine qualities. I recall how once – it was the Sabbath – arriving home from synagogue, he came upon his mother, dead. He made Kiddush, sang Sabbath hymns, and after the Sabbath meal, sat down to study Torah as always. Once the Sabbath was over, only then did he begin sitting shiva, and only then did he let himself mourn, crying bitter tears for his mother.

Each day he would wake up at 3:00 in the morning to sit and learn Torah. He set out the samovar, and holding a glass of boiling hot tea in his hands would warm himself as he learned his page of Gemora.

Prior to Lyuban, he was the rabbi of Shemezova.

His character was such that he looked on everyone as equals; he was very unassuming. But he was also by nature a joyful and fun-loving man. The festival of Purim at our house was a particularly happy time. The villagers would send the rabbi packets of delicacies, Purim presents, as is the custom, but with great generosity. We would dance and sing, people would drink wine and generally have a wonderful time. After just a sampling of liquor, my father would get tipsy, and then, full of mischievous, would tell joke after joke.

After some time, a second rabbi came to work in Lyuban, and that

[Page 447]

led to an on-going battle of the minds, a feud. The two rabbis would sit in the corners or on the edge of the easternmost pew, the bench closest to the Torah. My father's supporters settled themselves at the end of the pew precisely where the other rabbi sat. So my father scolded them. By the end of all this, my father emerged as the only rabbi in our shtetl. The community built him a house with seven rooms, a spacious home including one room that functioned as a court, and a meditation room.

Three synagogues existed in our shtetl: The Kalte Shul [the "Cold Synagogue," a nickname used also for a synagogue in Slutsk], the Tailors' Synagogue, and the Rich People's Synagogue [also known as the Great Synagogue].

Here are the names of some Lyuban streets: Broad Street (Breyta Gass), Narrow Street (Shmola Gass), Gypsy Street (Tsigaynersha Gass), Synagogue Street (Shul Gass), Rabbi's Lane (Dem Rovs Gessela). Trees graced Uretche and Tal Streets.

The market consisted of a variety of stores--Reb Zalmen-Borukh's dry-goods store, Basha-Malka's grocery store, and so forth. Along the market square lived the prominent people of the town: Zalmen-Borukh Dem Rov's ["The Rabbi's Son"], and Yoshiya Dem Rov's [also "The Rabbi's Son", Moishe-Velvl, Leyb-Volf (my husband's father, may he rest in peace), Sheyna-Leya the proprietor of the mill, Yankev Katzenelson, Streletz, Itsha the Doctor, Chaim-Berl, Faytl the Pharmacist, Mordkha-Ahron the dry-goods merchant, Ahron the Writer, as well as the Post Office.

Our mother was a woman of valor in the tradition of the Good Woman of Proverbs. Among other things, she spun her own thread, baked bread, and pastries, cooked every kind of food, milked the cow, made cheese and butter.

I remember the Great Fire. Some say that the neighboring Gentiles started it. The town burned down to the ground. All that remained of our home was the copper saucepans, the samovar, and a few metal pots. Our father got himself into a wagon, rode to the towns of Uretche and Tal, and picked up bread and supplies for the people of Lyuban.

My wise father early on took notice of the boy who later became my fiancé and husband, the rabbi Professor Simkha Assaf, of blessed memory. My father grew close to him after he came from the Telz Yeshiva

The funeral of Rabbi Simkha Assaf in Jerusalem — Cheshvan 5614 (1955)

[Page 448]

Chana Assaf

to be with his parents in Lyuban. Simkha Assaf would come to our home every day to study with my father. My father perceived and expressed that this young man Simkha would one day turn into an eminent sage among the Jewish people. One time, in the presence of both of us, he spoke out: "Simkha, are you agreeable to marrying my daughter Hana?" That's how the match was made and sealed, with a simple verbal assent, without even signing t'noyim [engagement contract], as was customary.

Our road was a long one before we ever reached the Land of Israel. We lived for a time in Odessa, neighbors with the great poet, Bialik, may he rest in peace. My brothers, meanwhile, had emigrated to America. When my father traveled to Omaha, Nebraska, to visit his children, it was proposed to him that he stay there as rabbi and in fact receive a rabbinic contract. He wrote our mother, asking her to come, and appealed to Simkha, my husband, to take over the rabbinate in Lyuban. But nothing ever came of all this, and finally, after all kinds of metamorphoses, he immigrated to Palestine. His children in the United States purchased a house for him in Jerusalem.

He passed away at a venerable age (76 years old), with a respected name in Jerusalem the Holy City.

Slaughter and Murder

by Binyomin Wolfson

Translated from the Yiddish by Paul Pascal

At the beginning of the year 5681 (1921), when Poland and Russia laid down their weapons, and delegates came together to resolve the conflicts and decide on borders, there remained between the two countries a neutral strip of land that had no government over it to establish order or provide protection. The Poles closed themselves off within their own territory, and the Soviet regime was not yet well organized. And so, that area came to be ruled by Balakhavitsh's Gangs, who robbed and murdered Jews in the countryside and in the villages.

On the 17th day of Kislev [mid-winter] of that year we began to hear of murders in the surrounding countryside. We responded by calling a religious fast. Before the prayers were said, our rabbi went up onto the pulpit and cried out, through bitter tears, "Brothers! Terrible news! In Kuzmitz they've killed the shoykhet [kosher-meat slaughterer], and Jews in other nearby hamlets have also been murdered!"

After prayers, a committee was appointed to assess our plight. Fear of traveling prevented us from bringing the murder victims into town for proper burial. As soon as Hanukah arrived [a week later] we tried persuading the Revolutionary Commissar to order the local Christians to bring us the corpses. And it was done. They brought in the bodies and we buried them quietly. After Hanukah they brought in more murder victims from the area. The same thing happened in other villages. In every cemetery you could see freshly dug plots for martyrs.

Our above-named committee ascertained that there was only one remedy: to ask the [Soviet] regime to send soldiers to our village. The Soviets had, in fact, already dispatched two squads of military police to catch bandits and deserters. The military had commandeered the little synagogue as their jailhouse. This only provoked the Christian population and increased their hatred toward Jews. As a result, the Jews needed to endure the soldiers' presence all the more.

An investigator arrived. He sucked our blood, exacting heavy payments from us Jews, while accepting bribes to free the criminals. He often arrested innocent people, which only turned the Christians' hatred into rage.

The soldiers left before Purim, but then Jews were not safe to travel outside of the village. If extreme circumstances forced a Jew to travel into the countryside, he would be robbed or murdered. The few Jews who lived in the country were frequently attacked and killed. In the days leading up to Passover, several Jews from outside of town were murdered, and those who survived took refuge in Lyuban. However, it wasn't necessarily safe in our village, either. During the Passover seder, Jewish sentries circulated in the streets. A small watch was organized on every block. Our young people quietly supplied themselves with some weapons. Life came to a standstill. After Passover, the wealthier Jews drove out on their wagons and left the shtetl. The poorer ones didn't even have a wagon.

Just before the holiday of Lag B'Oymer [springtime], alarming rumors spread about a

[Page 449]

Reb Binyamin Wolfson

possible attack on the village. We had already managed to rent a wagon so that the children could be spirited off somewhere safe. But the citizens' patrol we had set up did not permit travel outside of the shtetl. They tried to reassure us, saying that soldiers and weapons from Minsk and Bobruisk had been promised and would shore up their defense. But the writing was on the wall. The Revolutionary Commissar himself had left town. From the little town of Pohost came seven mounted soldiers. We were given to understand that 40 armed soldiers were on their way, and this calmed us for the moment.

Our calm was shattered by gunshots from the other side of the river. The seven soldiers returned fire. Panic followed, with people running in every direction, not knowing where they were heading, and leaving their homes unlocked and open. We began running in the direction of Uretche, 20 versts [about 13 miles] away. The citizens' patrol sent out riders to turn us back. They explained that the shooting by the seven soldiers was designed to give the attackers the impression that our shtetl was filled with military. We all decided to head back and at least stay overnight.

All of a sudden we heard machine-gun fire. There was me, my wife (may she rest in peace), our three children, our daughter with her ten-month old infant, and my in-laws, who had come for refuge to Lyuban from a nearby hamlet. Their children were at that time in Slutsk. The streets of Lyuban were filled with screaming and chaos. People were running in every direction, stopping only to take cover. Then suddenly, a booming voice shouted [in Russian]: "Stand where you are!" And we found ourselves surrounded by bandits. They took everything we had, then confined everyone to a house. Grief-stricken, we sat and waited for death. In the background, voices, bitter cries and wailing, mixed with the roar of gunfire.

In hushed voices, we each said our Vidui [Final Confession], and made our last goodbyes to each other. At this point, without warning, two bandits broke in, and like wild animals, broke dishes, the mirror, the clock. Whatever appealed to them they took, and the rest they destroyed. As for us, they lined us up and pressed the points of their blades against our hearts, yelling: "Bring out the gold you're hiding!" We begged them to understand that we had no gold and tried the best we could to prove it to them.

Bandits Rob and Murder

They didn't want to listen, and they assaulted us with the butts of their rifles. One of them took out a rope and passed it to one of the others to string up somewhere, saying he'd hang us if we didn't give them any gold. The other gangster said, "Why are we wasting our time here? Let's go find some place richer."

They left, threatening that they'd be back soon. We waited a bit, then crawled up into the attic. The poor children were shuddering and trembling from fear and from the cold. We wrapped them up in old winter things until they warmed up a little and were able to fall asleep. Meanwhile we heard the attackers breaking windows and doors, the terrified screams of victims, and the wild shrieks of the half-human criminals.

We stayed in the attic until about 10 a.m. Hearing quiet weeping, I dropped down from the attic and saw my sister-in-law, my wife's older sister. She told us: "In the synagogue the bandits carried out beatings, murder, rape. The thugs wanted to blow up the synagogue, but the church priest and other Christians prevailed upon them not to."

Not long after that, more victims appeared. Each one had his or her own story. One woman was grieving for her young son, whom they dragged from his sickbed to the synagogue, where they murdered him.

When we were sure the desperados had gone, I left the house and went out looking for our daughter and her child. As I passed by one hamlet, I saw the bodies of butchered Jews, one of whom I knew – my brother-in-law. In a garden I saw one girl with a foot shot off. Terrified people were beginning to crawl out from the barns and thickets.

I went about on foot like this for several hours, coming back home exhausted and drained. I found my wife again, and both of us went out looking for our daughter until around 5 p.m. We were too frightened to stay in the house, so we spent the night in the barn of a Christian we trusted. By then our younger children were already there with us.

Suddenly more people were fleeing from the shtetl. It seems the seven soldiers sent to protect us had links with the bandits.

Meanwhile we carried some of the dead bodies to their homes, carried others to the synagogue.

[Page 450]

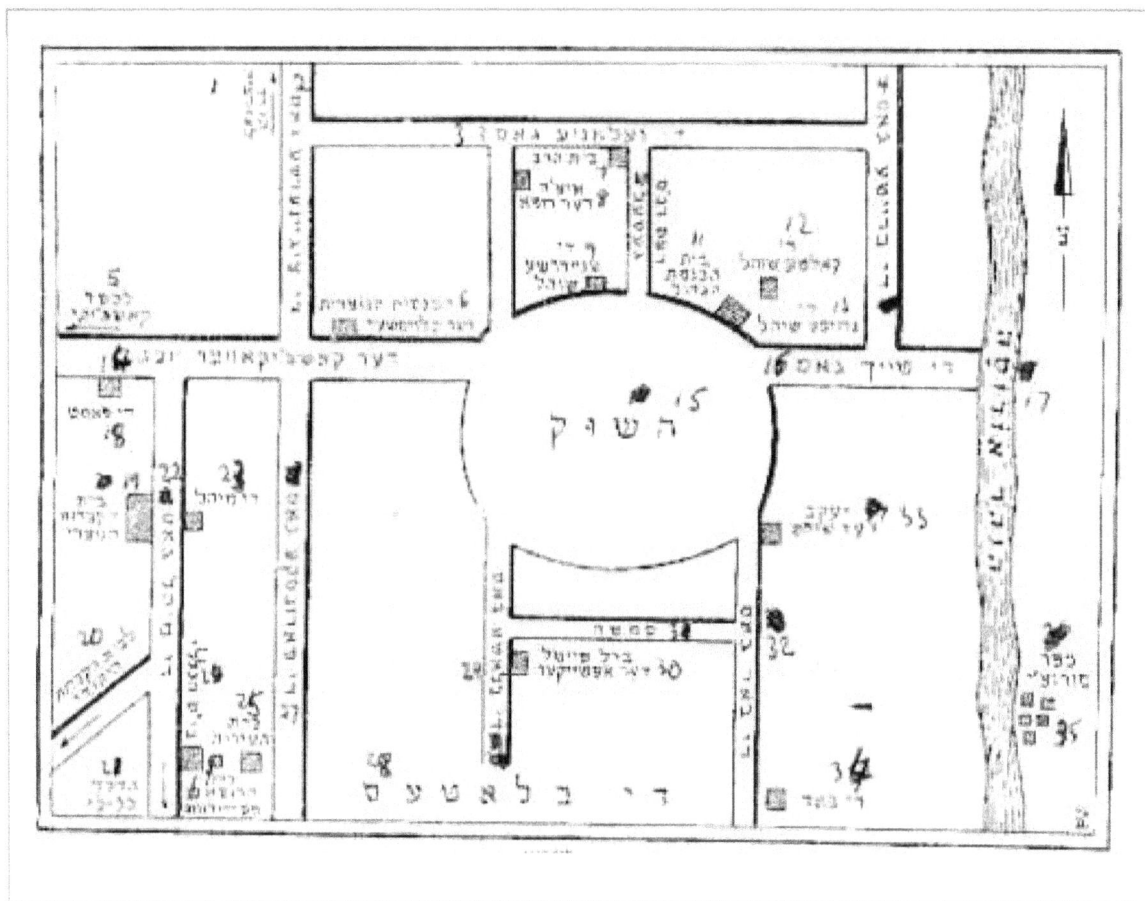

Note: The same map appears in the Hebrew section on page 217 with a translated legend

We helped the wounded get to various houses. Behind the village more families with small children were arriving, as well as frail elderly people. Every bush, every rustling in the woods, revealed yet another horror. As the hungry children burst into tears, it was decided: we had to hide overnight in the forest.

By luck, we found an abandoned, partly overgrown cabin in the forest. Everyone crowded in and lay down uncomfortably on the grass floor. I was worried about where we'd get water, in case we had emergency. There was no choice but for me to go to the village, about two versts away [one and one-third miles] by way of forest and field. Perhaps I would succeed in bringing back some water. A girl whose grandmother was still in the village came with me. As we emerged from the forest, we saw more people walking away from the village, others running. Whoever had their own horses, rode. For fear of the marauders, the Christians were not renting their wagons to the Jews.

When we heard that the criminals were returning, we turned back into the forest and told the others. Everyone got up and started running, a congregation of the damned and their little children. Along the way we found corpses strewn on the road. As we passed one hamlet, a Christian woman whom we knew came out and informed us that our daughter and her child had been through there that morning. She said they'd been walking in the direction of Uretche. Suspending our trek for the moment, we decided to stay overnight in the nearby hamlet of Tal.

To the Jewish Burial Ground

In the distance we could see a soldier with a rifle. One of the refugees in our group recognized him as a Jewish soldier who was once billeted at the refugee's home. Everyone began running toward the soldier. Upon hearing our story, he cried in sympathy with us, and tried to consoled us, saying that Soviet soldiers were on their way. But nonetheless, he did not advise us to go back to our shtetl.

Just then a regiment of soldiers did, in fact, appear, marching along the road that led to Lyuban. With them were many who had fled our shtetl at the same time as we had. They asked after the welfare of their friends and relatives. Some of them stayed in Tal to spend the night, while others continued on in the direction of Lyuban, together with the regiment. The Jewish householders in Tal did not let any Christians into their homes. But at the far side of town there were Jewish millers who were happy to take in everyone.

Come daybreak, we left the children in the care of our hosts and returned to Lyuban to see how conditions were. In the synagogue lay many corpses, not all recognizable.

[Page 451]

Dejected and depressed, we nevertheless knew the dead had to be buried. The organizing of this job fell to me, because I had been an official of our Burial Society. The dead in the synagogue numbered 15 men and eight women. We also went around to collect victims who had been murdered in their homes. A heart-rending scene took place in every house where we had to take away a body.

Suddenly – bedlam. The barbarians were back. A few soldiers had been stationed on watch, but most of the regiment had gone to the front. Many of us ran, but a number of us stayed behind. In the midst of this, our group managed to bring the eight women who were killed to the cemetery and bury them. Then part of our group rode back to get the murdered men. Some in our party did the job of carrying back the corpses, while others, including me, buried them. This continued through the day until 6 p.m. At that point we took our leave of the holy ground, and with embittered hearts headed home.

At home I found my sister-in-law, now a widow, with her orphans, who were sitting broken and crying. My hands were covered with blood from the corpses. Anguished, I went back to town to see what I could do for others who were suffering.

All this happened on the eve of the Sabbath. We conducted our Sabbath service in total darkness. The newly bereaved said kaddish [the prayer for the dead]. On all sides, new moans, new tears. Everyone attending wanted to know if the soldiers were still in the village. Sabbath morning at the synagogue felt like Tisha B'Ov [Jewish day of fasting and mourning for the destruction of Jerusalem and its Temple].

The following morning, Sunday, we got up and gathered a quorum for prayers with the mourners. I tried to record entries in the Burial Society register, including information as to where each new grave was located. I soaked the register with my tears, just as I had done to the graves themselves. I went out into the street. The devastation was overwhelming. Every window was broken, every family was left with only one or two members, after the rest had been killed or fled.

So I returned to my own home. There we tried to decide what to do, because the children, whom we'd left in the neighboring hamlet, had by now been taken to Uretche. They were terrified to come home. We concluded that it really was not yet necessary to bring them back to Lyuban. Instead, I got myself ready to go to them: I gathered together clean underwear, milk, and a few other things for them.

Then, several days later, yet another worry: the soldiers were leaving, and there was fear about remaining in Lyuban unprotected. Consequently, we decided all to go where everyone else was going. By then the children had come back from Uretche; there had been an attack on a family there, too, and many people had fled in fear. It was clear that the children were languishing and weak, yet now it seemed they were going to have to summon the energy and courage to run back with us to Uretche yet again.

After a great deal of difficulty, I managed to borrow a wagon from an acquaintance. I placed my children in it, and a few others placed their children in, too. Many of the old, the sick, and the blind were forced to struggle on foot. As for the very little ones, who were being carried, their small mouths so parched and cracked, I tried to moisten their tiny lips with a drop or two of milk.

By dusk we arrived in Uretche. Terrified Jews from Lyuban and elsewhere asked us anxiously for news from home. What's happening there? What are they doing now? For my part, I at last found my daughter and grandchild, lodging with a friend of mine along with some other unfortunates. The ad hoc Refugee Committee of Slutsk was providing bread and other necessities. The hands that were given bread trembled as they took it.

That night the children lay on hard floors, while the adults sat outside until morning. There was very little indoor space where you could sit; Uretche was ablaze. The Poles had set it on fire before retreating. We decided to head for Slutsk.

To Slutsk

The younger children and I rode off to Slutsk, but my wife and older daughter stayed for the moment in Uretshe, to see if they could still salvage something from Lyuban. Arriving in Slutsk, we were permitted to come into town [by the Soviet authorities, who were generally very restrictive]. We carried the small children in our arms. The local Council did not stop us (either because they weren't aware of us, or perhaps by choice). We made inquiries about a friend who had escaped Lyuban a few days before the pogrom. We found him and were received sympathetically.

On the streets I came across more refugees from our shtetl. A few found friends or acquaintances they could stay with, while others slept in the synagogue. Myself, I looked for a place to stay, too, but money was always demanded up front, and I had none. Later I tried places at the edge of town. There were many wagons there, carrying Jews from Lyuban. Christians from surrounding farms and hamlets had brought these vehicles to Lyuban, and the fugitive Jews gave their last savings to rent the wagons and escape to safety in Slutsk. From the people in the wagons I learned that my daughter had done what they had done, and had managed to bring a few supplies along with her, as well.

I found my daughter. She told me that Lyuban was now completely empty of Jews. She had grabbed whatever bedding and linen she could, had locked the door, and had given the key to a Christian neighbor. She had asked the neighbor to keep an eye on our house, our cow, and our chickens.

Some acquaintances had to be persuaded to look after the few things my daughter had retrieved, because space was tight for everyone. In the end, we found a place to stay, at the edge of town. The proprietor did not ask for the rent money ahead of time. He received us in a friendly way and gave us our own room. However, there was nothing to eat. Our landlord was himself a pauper. So together we all suffered, and together we kept silent.

In the meantime, escapees were streaming into Slutsk from all the surrounding villages and hamlets. We were advised to form a Refugee Committee and the government would provide support. At the home of the town rabbi a meeting was held of all the influential people in Slutsk. Money was collected, as well as bread, provisions, and linen. In addition to that, the refugees did form their Committee, and I was part of it. A representative came from the provincial government in Minsk

[Page 452]

and registered the homeless. The procedure took many days, and during that period no provisions were forthcoming from the government. They had promised five pounds of corn meal; for the smallest children, they had previously sent wheat flour, sugar, potatoes, and salt, which was then a rare commodity. When provisions did finally arrive, officials portioned out rations to two or three people, but after that it was only by scrambling and jostling that you got anything at all.

A shelter for orphans was organized, with a limit on the number admitted. As a result of this restriction, a great deal of effort had to be devoted to running around and determining which children needed to be given priority.

Since there wasn't room in the shelter for all the orphans, people had to be convinced to take some of them into their homes.

Myself, I made a habit of visiting the hospital where the pogrom's wounded lay. Each time I walked home from there, I was tormented by anxiety over where to get food. This is how I lived for almost a month, partly hungry, partly sick, and entirely consumed by heartache.

The Slaughter in Starova

For me there was a still worse personal tragedy in the making: a sister of mine had lived for many years in Starova (there used to be a glassworks there). Her family was made up of five souls – three children and the two parents. A daughter of theirs had managed to get to Poland and was preparing to emigrate to America. My sister and her family were imagining that in time they, too, would emigrate.

When the hooliganism started, they decided to move to Slutsk. They took a few things with them – this was a Wednesday – and returned to get more, intending to be back in Slutsk before Saturday. Friday went by, Saturday, Sunday, and still they hadn't come back. I was preparing to set out to urge them to come back when I felt someone's hand on my shoulder. It was a woman I knew who had relatives in Starova. She broke down in tears, saying, "Have you heard what has happened in Starova? The marauders were there tonight." To my question as to what exactly did happen, she answered that she didn't actually know the details. I felt she was keeping something from me. Later she did reveal that a nephew of mine had been brought from there to Slutsk, wounded.

I sought out my nephew, and when I found him I took him to the hospital. He was no more than 17 years old, horribly beaten up, his teeth knocked out. In anguish he told me his story: he had been staying overnight at a neighbor's. In the middle of the night the bandits fell upon the village, bludgeoning everyone, including himself, stealing everything from the houses. He said that when he had recovered enough from his assault to move, he made his way home. There he saw all the windows broken, his father sitting immobile with serious injuries, his mother and sister dead.

During my nephew's account, some Christians from Starova arrived and reported that there were 14 murdered people there, among them my sister and her daughter, and many, many wounded, including my brother-in-law.

Uncaptioned. A registration card from the Slutsk provisional committee for the homeless in Warsaw. The name on it is Nachum Gutzeit. It is signed by the chairman and secretary of the committee.

[Page 453]

Many of us wanted to go there, but we were intimidated. Instead we went to the authorities to beg for more soldiers who could bring us back the dead and the wounded.

This was on the 20th day of Sivan [late spring, early summer], a date infamous in our bloody history. Escorted by 10 soldiers, we entered Starova. The sun was almost setting, and the soldiers were pressing us to be quicker in gathering up the bodies. The windows had all been smashed with boards. My sister's house was locked. I went looking for the key and found the friend who had kept it hidden. I entered the house with him. In horror I saw my sister, lying in a pool of blood, my two-year old niece dead in a second room. I stood there like a man deranged – no sounds came from me, and no tears.

They led me out of the house, directing me to sit in a wagon where a body lay. When we set out, the wagon bore other bodies, and I understood that I was traveling with my saintly sister. The cart drivers brought the bodies to the grounds of the Old Folks' Home, unhitched the horses, and headed home. As for me, I stood frozen next to the wagons.

At dawn the watchman found me. He told me to come in and lie down, to get some rest. From somewhere behind him I could hear snatches of screaming and wailing by the victims' relatives. The wounded had been led away earlier for help elsewhere. In a few hours, the grounds of the Old Folks' Home were overflowing with people. The cries and screams were too much to bear.

Special arrangements for the funerals were decided on by Rabbi Meltzer [eminent head of the Great Yeshiva of Slutsk] and the community leaders. We would gather at the Shuleff [courtyard shared by the five main, adjacent, synagogues] and from there proceed as a cortege to all the major government departments to protest their complicity in the spilling of Jewish blood. They had given us no arms for self-defense and they knew we had none of our own. We would bring the dead bodies with us in the same carts with which we had retrieved them. All stores and businesses would be closed. We demonstrated at every government institution.

When we arrived later at the cemetery, there were eulogies, wailing, and screams.

The burials were done by family. In one Starova household, eight people had been murdered: father, mother, daughter, son-in-law, three grandchildren, and a tutor. The interments continued on until nightfall.

From the cemetery I went straight to the hospital. My nephew [must have been in shock, for he] was still inquiring about his mother and sister. I told him that they had been wounded and were in another hospital. My brother-in-law, meanwhile, lay unaware of his surroundings or himself. They did not permit water to be given to him. He didn't speak for two weeks and even after that he didn't recognize me. Every day after saying kaddish, I would go to visit the wounded in the hospital. In the end, my nephew, too, was liberated from his suffering. We brought him to where he would join his father, his mother, his grandfather, his grandmother, his sister and brother, though not in one grave.

Reb Manes Lvovitsh

During all this time, the hunger at our house was getting worse. When any of us would come across someone we knew, usually as afflicted as we were, the two would talk it out and quietly have a cry together.

To Poland

For the time being, no one was venturing back to Lyuban. If someone had to retrieve something, it was done quietly and stealthily, because we saw that those who had resigned themselves and remained in Lyuban had usually paid with their lives. The entire Jewish way of life, the entire Jewish presence in Lyuban, had stopped. Even the daily prayer services had come to a halt. All of the Torah scrolls and holy books had been transferred to Slutsk.

Some time later, I began to hear rumors that there might be a prayer service on the Sabbath in Lyuban. In my own family, there was no one I could travel there with. The children were too young, my wife too weak. As for myself, I was terribly apprehensive. All this notwithstanding, my wife and the children did risk going back to Lyuban for very brief visits, to obtain a little milk from our cow, vegetables from our garden. This food did not go very far. Consequently, I looked for my own ways to make ends meet, to improve our circumstances. The committees had by then terminated their support. Those individuals who had been lending money were now deferring their loans, saying, "Tomorrow," or, "Maybe later on," to the point where it was loathsome to go to them.

I felt I had no choice but to face the danger of crossing the border into Poland. From there I would seek help from relatives in America. It was painful separating from my family. But deprivation can crack iron, and what deprivation is greater than hunger? I didn't have a penny for the journey, however a friend lent me five banknotes of 500 rubles each, and I prepared myself to go.

On the 12th of Tamuz [mid-summer], I left Slutsk and made my way

[Page 454]

to a small town just inside the border, seeking a way to cross over into Poland. I attached myself to a group which was in the business of spiriting people across the border. Two days of hiding, then a full night of running – through forests, across fields, in and out of swamps and ditches. Despite all this, after what we'd lived through and what was yet needed, nothing seemed too difficult. At long last, on the 18th of Tamuz, we landed in a little Polish town – hungry, parched, and terrified. But safe. To the wretched, homeless souls who were already sojourning there, came a new crop of wretched and homeless, and among them, Binyomin Wolfson of Lyuban.

Lyuban in a Transitional Period

Translated from the Yiddish by Paul Pascal

Jewish Daily Forward ("Forverts"), October 13, 1921

In Lyuban there were around 600 Jewish families who were employed as farmers, shoemakers, tailors, blacksmiths, and a fair number of gardeners. The pogrom began on May 26 at 3 a.m., and lasted around five hours. Twenty-eight people were murdered, 10 wounded. Jewish property and goods were plundered and destroyed. The following account of the pogrom is taken from a report of an eyewitness, Eliyohu Kaptchitz, a teacher:

On the afternoon of May 25, a reconnaissance platoon of seven soldiers on horseback, from the 21st Frontier Brigade, rode into Lyuban. They were on their way to Pliusnya. In Lyuban they intended to meet up with an infantry detachment of 60 men, whose equipment included a machine gun. Evening fell and the detachment had still not arrived in Lyuban, so the cavalrymen had to spend the night there.

The peasants in the district were by then covertly passing the word on to Jews known to them that bandits were in the vicinity of Lyuban and that an attack was imminent. Obviously, we all wanted to believe and hope that help would arrive quickly. We dispatched a deputation to the battalion in Pustin, near Uretche, as well as one to the 21st Brigade in Slutsk. But no help came. The panic in our shtetl increased. A group organized for self-defense never slept, and every night they were on their watch from the Great Synagogue. The cavalrymen were quite pleased with this; they shared their password with us, then went off to sleep!

As soon as I ran out of the synagogue, I was immediately overwhelmed. What I saw was a horrifying attack; the gang was vicious. Thoughts began flying through my mind: I tried to think of something that would delay the marauders, so that all those who were fleeing would have time to escape. A few friends were also standing there with me. One of them had a rifle, but he wasn't able to shoot.

I grabbed the rifle from him and found a way to make it work. I fired five shots, but that was all the ammunition there was. In the market square there was shouting: "Ura, ura, sdavayesya!" ["Hey, you there! Give yourselves up!"] I ran behind the Tailors' Synagogue and through the Rabbi's Alley. I saw countless people running, as if they were a single body. At this point, a friend gave me another supply of bullets. I loaded the rifle and fired four more rounds. Then I heard, not far off: "Surrender!" Two of the hooligans had run into the alley. Still, they seemed fearful of trying to catch us [because of our rifle]. Their companions called out to them: "Hey, boys! Over here!" Three more bandits had appeared.

However, by then we were already on Gypsies' Street. Again we encountered a hail of bullets. The street was swarming with bandits. Through a yard we managed to escape to a field at the edge of the shtetl. A whole army of bandits was chasing after us. Heavy shooting persisted, while the sound of a single voice could be heard wailing inside our shtetl.

Bit by bit, through cultivated fields, forest, and muck, we emerged onto the road to Uretche. Even here a trace of gunfire followed us. But the danger was now not as intense. I came upon a large party of fugitives - old people, women, girls, small children. They were running in silence, and only sporadically did a few of them speak, to ask whether we'd seen their loved ones among those who had escaped.

One father was considering leaving his child in the rye field and continuing the flight on his own. But the child cried inconsolably. The father picked the child up again and carried him further, then decided to leave him in the field after all. He was tortured by bitter regrets.

At one point along the way there was an old man spread out, lying on the road. No wound was visible. It turned out that he had died running. A long red ribbon extended across the road [presumably to demarcate a respectful space for the deceased].

The sun was already high in the sky. We headed for a group of farmhouses. Milling around the gates of the houses were groups of peasant women, wringing their hands, evidently not knowing what to do. Their husbands stared at us anxiously and questioningly. Lying on the porch of one Jewish house there was a wounded man. He begged us to help him. One of the Christians who had accompanied us in our escape, the Red Army soldier Borodeyev, tried to procure a horse from the leader of the farm community, so as to take the wounded man away for help. The answer was: "We don't put ourselves out for those who are ahead, only for those who are underprivileged." We ran on.

By 7:30 in the morning we were in Uretche. I telegraphed Slutsk, Bobruisk and Minsk to notify them about the attack.

[Page 455]

Half of Lyuban was there in Uretche. Everyone was running up to me asking about a father, mother, sister, brother. Heart-rending cries filled the air. A few people kissed each other, others broke down in mournful weeping. Everyone was depleted, everyone was depressed. A large percentage of the refugees had no idea of the whereabouts of their parents or children. Great numbers of people were heading for Slutsk. Myself, I was feeling beaten down and deeply pained. Clumsily, I stumbled into a house and fell immediately into a deep sleep. On the morning of Friday the 28th, I went back to Lyuban.

In Lyuban very few people were left. The hooligans had driven some 200 Jews into the synagogue – men, women, and children. Then they picked out the prettier and younger girls, 17 and 18 year olds, dragged them to the women's section in the balcony of the synagogue, and in the most vicious manner raped them. The cries of the girls tore at us to get out of our confinement. Everyone in the sanctuary fought the bandits with sticks or carriage whips. When the "Captain" entered the synagogue it suddenly got quiet. He went up onto the Torah platform and demanded that we provide him, as ransom for the girls, the sum of 1,000,000 gold rubles in cash, twenty pounds of silver, 10 pounds of gold, 80 pairs of boots, and 500 pairs of undergarments – all by 10 o'clock in the morning. And with that, he picked out three older Jews and made them responsible for collecting this astronomic sum.

The ransom was obviously too steep, impossible to come up with. In the end, those who could, resorted to redeeming their daughters individually. Others borrowed up to several thousand rubles in cash from the Russian Orthodox priest and in this way were able to buy their daughters back.

They killed on the road one of those they had delegated to collect the ransom – an old man. After a while the "Captain" again came into the synagogue and said, "You can all thank your village's priest and his wife! If not for them we would have incinerated you and your synagogue together!" The viciousness and cruelty of these cutthroats cannot be described.

Another of the bandits got up on the Torah platform and gave orders for us all to be gone in half an hour. Then the bandits went back to the high school, where they spent time with the director, Yasenov, with the village doctor, and with other Gentiles. Above all they were especially kind to the priest. Before they left they burned down Volispolkom's house. And the "Captain" expeditiously dumped Volispolkom's briefcase on a table in the synagogue, with all its important documents.

By 11 a.m. they left, back through the hamlets of Shipilovitsh and Yurkovitsh, back to the forests and their farms.

A Partial List of Names of Those Murdered

1. Dovid Kustanovitsh of Retkevitsh
2. Yankev Elia Ayzentsohn of Abtsin
3. Shmaryohu Kaplan
4. Refoel Tirushkin of Zakalno
5. Matisyohu Podlipsky
6. Yeshaya of Kuzmitsh
7. Yeshaya's son
8. Tsvi Kustanovitsh
9. Zalmen Kaplan
10. Avrohom of Spilovitsh [Spilyava?]
11. Chaim Epshtein
12. The young man Avrohom Krik
13. Moishe Hofun [Hopun? Hafun?]
14. Shmuel of Tritshan [part of Slutsk]
15. Faytl Pakin, who died of wounds in Uretche the following day

[Page 456]

A Letter from Lyuban

by Fanya [Lvovitsh]

Translated from the Yiddish by Paul Pascal

It is impossible to imagine what we, hunted Jewish children, went through at the hands of the Germans. When the war began, Hana and I were in Minsk. For five days in a row 80 airplanes bombed the city. I would never have believed that we would survive. In Lyuban they had already mourned for us. During the time the Germans occupied Minsk there was a reign of terror such as is frightening even in the retelling. For several days I didn't dare leave the house out of fear of the venom I saw in their brutish faces. But hunger forced me to go looking for food: there was no choice.

Astonishingly, we were able to come and go without interference, to and from Lyuban, and to let everyone know we were not harmed. This included our dear father, our beloved mother, Chaim, Tsipoira, Hava and her two children, and our other relatives and friends, to whose names we must now add, "May they rest in peace." But the joy of our cherished parents was not to last long, for very soon the bloody agenda of the German murderers was set into motion, in collaboration with their dogs, the Russian police, who played a substantial role in the doom of Lyuban's Jews.

At the beginning of August, 1941, a German "Punitive Battalion" [of the Einsatzgruppen] captured over 200 Jewish men and murdered them in pits near [the village of] Kastiuki. Of those who had not been captured, no one believed that these men had been murdered. In fact, when the pits were exhumed the next morning, no one recognized any of the victims, and people assumed that our men had merely been taken away on work detail. It should be understood that none of the exhumed bodies were turned over.

The remaining men in Lyuban, including my dear father, Berl, stayed in hiding. They did not dare be seen by those evil eyes. Day after day, they would stay in deep holes in the ground where not a ray of sun could penetrate. Such an irony! In effect, they had buried themselves alive. They would barely hold on until nightfall when they could come out and catch their breath briefly, then seclude themselves again in their burrows like moles.

Obviously, hope and the will to live were great. The first day of this, in August, Yankev the shoykhet [ritual meat slaughterer], Heshl the Torah tutor, another shoykhet from Poland, and many others, did not survive. All of us in the village were convulsing in fear, because the Germans, and their Russian dogs, were endlessly making their "inventories," taking the last of our measly possessions and food, and beating us mercilessly. With a single word, each new day was made more unbearable than the last, in our short, accursed lives…

And the days passed, and those who survived lived to see the most obscene of the assassins' bloody acts. They forced all the Jews to gather in the ghetto, which was set up in the finest streets of our shtetl, behind the market square. Chaim and I moved in to the home of Hertzl, Yidl's son. (He, himself, had perished by then.) They caged us in with barbed wire, and no Jew had the right to walk out of the gates.

Oh, what dark clouds were then hanging over us! It felt as if the sun had forever abandoned us… and how right we were. For us, the damned, the sun never rose again. The severity of our living conditions intensified unabated, but Jews were nevertheless forced to go to work. A local Jewish merchant, Borukh Malin (you may remember him), had to take on all Jews as employees.

Under those circumstances, it was difficult to hide. But even this didn't last long.

On November 8, my beloved father and Uncle Yisroel perished, along with 50 other Jewish men and boys. Even now I can picture my father, completing his prayers, and with a morsel of bread in his mouth. His features at that moment are etched in my memory forever, for this was the last time I saw him.

Berl and Esther Rachel Lvovitsh (Fanya's parents)

November 8 was a Sabbath. The cries of "Shma Yisroel" [a key Jewish prayer; recited by observant Jews who know they are about to die] still ring in my ears today. I don't understand how you couldn't hear, or how Heaven could stay silent and not see, such merciless acts of savagery.

I find it very difficult to write about these things. Perhaps it is altogether too early to be telling about them. For one thing, I don't even know who will read these terrifying accounts. I want to believe that my dear grandmother, my uncles Yoisef and Lipa, along with my aunts and their children, and Motl, Chaim's son, with his wife and children, are alive and are waiting to hear a few words

[Page 457]

from us. I don't want to acquiesce to dark thoughts. We have been punished enough… And so, for their sakes, permit me to continue.

My dear ones! After the horrific tragedy, Lyuban was enveloped in depression. From one day to the next, people waited for death. There was no longer any possibility of bearing our grief, and to expect a swift deliverance we had no right. Every day that we survived only brought the anticipated death closer. Our life was so oppressive that death became that much dearer and more urgent. We thought of death as a remedy, thanks to which we could be liberated from our anguish. That was the attitude of most of us, consequently we bore every punishment, every inflicted tax and burden, every murderous assault, quietly and without protest.

Escaping from Lyuban was impossible. First, there was nowhere to run to. Jews had no safe haven. Secondly, for every Jew who escaped they murdered 100 others. With just a word from our torturers, we had to accept our "pay" duly. But I'll have to break off from writing now; it's too much.

* * *

My dearest ones! I fancied that all of our troubles, all of our torments until now, were no torments at all. Only in this way, despite terror and starvation (they did not allow us to keep more than a few days of food rations at a time), could we survive for almost a month following the death of my father. Chaim was then still alive. Thursday, December 4, at 11 o'clock in the morning, another "Punitive Battalion" of the criminals rode into Lyuban. Following that, not a single Jew was left…

Jews perished by the hundreds, suffering terrible deaths. Shot in their sickbeds, buried alive… Those who lay face up from their graves and watched, petrified, those whose eyes waited for the murderers to cover them with earth – their last breaths were of air that was humid with Jewish and non-Jewish blood.

[After the war] I returned again to Lyuban. I was told with even greater detail what had happened there, and I went to the ground where over 1,000 people lay. The place was filled in with grass, but here and there you could still see a tattered rag. The field is behind the shtetl as you go toward the valley, by the path, along the Gromica [River?].

It seems that after the barbarous pogrom, a few Jews were saved, but they, too, died during two and a half years of homelessness and wandering. My beloved mother, Hava, and I all clung together in the same locality, deep in the swamps (of Zahalia). The Germans seldom went there. Partisans dwelled there, leading an oppressive, a terrible, existence.

Among the partisans there were a few Jews left. The horrible times had taken their toll on them. Their last shred of hope had gone, though obviously, when the Red Army launched a counter-offensive in the summer of 1943, hopes rose again and spirits were more buoyant. But the front came to a standstill in January of 1944 near Mozyr, that is, not far from Lyuban, and then our situation grew even worse. With the front close to us, Germans and their police [accomplices] were rife in every hamlet and throughout the forest. We had to leave the farmhouse we'd been using and live in the mud. You have to realize that from February 1944 until the arrival of the Red Army on June 30, we did not see a single house. We survived in the open air, pelted by the snow and rain. Even this would have been tolerable, if the Germans had left the bog alone. Picture 2,300 dogs surrounding the Zahalia swamp, with every farmhouse and every bush held by the enemy.

And it was here I experienced my worst moment. We lost our devoted mother forever. A German sentry post had noticed us and opened fire. As we found out later, our mother did not have time to extract her foot from a twisted root. There were so many calamities that we obviously had not protected our mother from, but it was to our everlasting sorrow that on that Wednesday, April 12, she was not right by us. Later, however much we searched for her, it was useless.

And so we were left orphans. Our mother had written and sent you a letter when we were still at the farmhouse [in the swampland]. Airplanes came and went, but they never brought a response. Many times she would say that if you had known where we were, you would have dispatched a special airplane for her. I know she wasn't wrong about you.

We had no news of Uncle Chaim and his family until we got to Lyuban, because Chaim had by then determined to hide out with a peasant he knew in Shipilovitsh. To join him would have added too much of a burden. As a result, on Saturday night, the 6th of December, we parted ways with him, forever. Last I heard, Chaim had died in a cellar from coal fumes. Tsipoira and Hava perished separately later. Exact details as to how and where, I don't know. The whole time that we lived in Lyuban, before the invasion, they had lived in our house with us, because the area around their house was always swarming with Germans.

That's all for now. I can only add that we have had letters from our Leya, from Haya Feygl, and Simkha. Leya has had no news from Motl after 1942. For the time being, there's also nothing from Hirshl. Feygl and Simkha don't mention anything about him.

Taken all together, I don't know. How does one bear it? How does one keep from going mad? How can I prevent my heart from breaking?

I have found work. For now I'm a bookkeeper at the school division in Lyuban. Our homes, ours and Chaim's, have been torn down. When I'm by myself I feel depressed

[Page 458]

and lonely. There have been no additional Jews arriving back, from among the one-time residents. Besides a few evacuated families, 14 people were left. Not including Hava and me, there's Alta, daughter of Yankl the Blind, Haya Dvoira, niece of Nekha Mashegua, and the rest you don't know: Dvoira, daughter of Chaim Rukhover, Alter Mannes, Yankl Berkovits, and a few other families. Please understand that at this point we are, as it were, bare naked, barefoot, without hope of getting dressed up sometime.

It has been raining for three days non-stop. The mail is not yet functioning properly. I must close now. Forgive me for writing so much. Perhaps it seems to you that what I've written is exaggerated. I swear to you that the whole truth is more bitter still.

I can't let you go. You are now the only friends with whom we have any hope, yet the distance between us only grows more removed.

Warmest regards from Hava and the remnant of Jews here. I await a detailed letter from you.

* * *

Reb [1] Chaim Katzenelson (Rukhover)[2]

Reb Chaim (Rukhover) Katzenelson with his wife Haya-Lea

Reb Chaim was an influential proprietor in Lyuban. The Zionist group [3] met in his house. He raised his children in the spirit of Jewish nationalism. His oldest son, Akiva, is currently in Vancouver, Canada, where he is active in the Jewish National Fund (JNF), in the Zionist Committee, and in other Jewish community institutions. Reb Chaim's four daughters live in Israel.

Dovid Katzenelson

by P. K. [or F. K.]

Translated from the Yiddish by Paul Pascal

Dovid Katzenelson combined within himself the qualities of a Torah scholar who studies day and night, and a community activist. Born on the eve of Passover, 5647 (1887), in Lyuban, his early education took place in Lyuban heders [4]. Later he fulfilled the Hebrew dictum, "Locate yourself in a place where Torah is studied," by turning to studies at the famous Yeshiva of Mir, where he became known for his sharp intellect and prodigious memory.

The head of his yeshiva predicted a great future in Torah for Katzenelson. However, this was the era of Dr. [Theodor] Herzl's trail-blazing treatises and of the First Zionist Congress, which shot through Jewish towns and villages like a meteor. Katzenelson felt that Talmud alone would not satisfy him. Among his friends he started to become an agitator for Zionism.

The supervisors of the yeshiva were opponents of the new movement. But out of respect and love for this young man, they turned a blind eye to his activities. When news of Herzl's death reached the yeshiva, however, the head of the yeshiva received the report by publicly reciting the Biblical verse, "At the loss of the wicked – joy." That rebuke prompted Katzenelson to leave the Mir Yeshiva and begin studies at the Yeshiva of Lida with Rabbi [Isaac Jacob] Reines, the famous Talmudic genius, Zionist, and founder of Mizrachi [Religious Zionism].

Dovid Katzenelson

Katzenelson studied diligently and with great success for several years at the Lida Yeshiva. But when he learned that Rabbi Chaim Tshernovitsh (also known as "Rav Tsayir", i.e., "Young Rabbi") was founding a modern, outward-looking yeshiva in Odessa, and that its teachers included Dr. Yosef Klausner [the renowned historian] and Chaim Nachman Bialik [the legendary Hebrew and Yiddish poet], Katzenelson lost no time in becoming a student there. He stayed several years, and he left his mark there.

With his completion of the "Odessa Yeshiva," Katzenelson ended his formal schooling. His plans to continue his studies were temporarily interrupted due to his

[Page 459]

marriage and a year-long trip to Palestine in 1911. With the onset of World War I three years later, his education plans were permanently shelved. On the other hand, his self-taught, "unofficial" learning continued constantly. Study from a holy book was a daily need of his. He found time for that, regardless of how busy he was with other things. His private library of over 10,000 volumes covered the walls of his home.

After the war, Katzenelson settled in Baranovitsh [west of Slutsk] (which was under Polish jurisdiction until World War II), and worked as a teacher of humanities at high school there for 20 years. He educated thousands of students, and many of them remember their captivating and devoted teacher with honor and respect. In the standards he set for his students regarding the Hebrew language, Katzenelson did not brook any compromises. His two children heard no other language spoken in the home outside of Hebrew, and were the only children in the entire Minsk Guberniya [present-day Belarus] whose only mother tongue was Hebrew. Even the Byelorussian nursemaid had to stutter her way through taking care of his children using only the few dozen Hebrew words she had managed to learn.

As for Zionism, Katzenelson devoted himself to it with all the fire in his soul. For many, many years he was chairman of the local branch of the General Zionist Organization, and was also a member of the wider General Zionist Organization ("Et Livnot" – "A Time to Build" – a middle-class faction of the G.Z.O.; chief delegate of the Jewish National Fund; member of the Jewish community council; president of the "Oneg Shabbat" Society. In the town's Zionist-leaning synagogue, hundreds of people would gather on the Sabbath as well as during the week to hear Dovid Katzenelson deliver Torah commentary, views on issues of the day, or perspectives on Jewish history. He was almost always head speaker at any mass meeting of the town's Jewish community. As a speaker, he would communicate in a popular style, wittily injecting a familiar passage from the Talmud, or, offhandedly, something from the ancient sources which applied to the theme, in this way creating a tight, intimate connection between himself and his audience. To this day, Jews of Baranovitsh tell how Dovid Katzenelson inspired them with his discourses.

The onset of World War II found Dovid Katzenelson a broken man, due to the tragic death of his older son in Palestine. By then he was no longer a young man, and trying himself to establish residence in Palestine was a very difficult undertaking. After a great deal of struggle and grief, he finally secured part-time work at a Tel Aviv high school. He lived austerely, but did not complain about his fate.

As it happens, he was among the first to get a letter from Lyuban even before the end of the world war. His sister, running from Lyuban with a band of partisans, was notifying him about the death of their mother and another sister and her family.

Dovid Katzenelson did not live a long life. He wrestled with death for five days following a heart attack, but died on February 7, 1948 (25 Shvat 5708).

Translator's footnotes:

1. " Reb" is a title of respect, like "Mr." It does not necessarily denote a rabbi.
2. This nickname may indicate that Katzenelson or an ancestor of his originally came from Rukhov or Rokhov.
3. The term "minyan" was used here, in the original text. It may have been figurative, meaning simply "group," or it may have been literal, meaning "religious quorum." If it was the latter, it was unusual to find it in combination with its adjective, "Zionist." In those days Zionists were mostly secular, and the Jewish religious world was antagonistic to the idea of a modern Jewish homeland.
4. One-room religious schools.

[Page 460]

Starobin
(Belarus)
52°44' 27°28'

Starobin – 3213 souls, a church, a school, a post office, large stretches of swamp.

Other than business, the city Jews were occupied with vegetation and cultivating large stretches of straw and grass.

My Town Starobin

by Rabbi Nissen Waxman

Translated by Pamela Russ

Many years have already passed since I have said goodbye to you, my place of birth. I have experienced much over time, and traveled through many countries, lived through many events. I have seen many larger and even more beautiful cities than you. But still, you stand before my eyes, with all your faults and merits, with all your forests and fields, with your mud and swamps, with your simpletons and your bright, refined, deep Jews who will never be erased from my memory.

HaRav Nissen Waxsman and his mother Shayna Laya
(Photo Yukhnin, Slutsk 1908)

Starobin was a town of about 300 Jewish families, and is located in the Minsk province, 35 viorst from the prestigious city of Slutsk. In addition to the general Jewish vocations such as shoemaker, tailor, and shopkeeper, Starobin had its own industry from which the majority of Jews drew their income. In Starobin, Jews used to have large gardens in which they grew cucumbers. In the summertime, they guarded the cucumbers like an eye in the head, and at the end of the summer, they picked them in the fields, and with their hands, they cut them in half lengthwise, removed the seeds, then washed and dried them in the sun. Then merchants would come from deep in Russia and buy the seeds for planting and then grow the cucumbers in their own place, and they would pay twenty or thirty ruble a pood, a high price, but you can imagine how much work went into this until there was a pood (40 pounds) of dried "seeds." One can also imagine how much profit you could make with this.

Because of this, Starobin was rich with prominent Jewish souls, with rare Jewish types of which it could be very proud.

Starobin was actually divided into three parts. Slutsker Street, that was called "edge of town," the marketplace, that was called the "upper class neighborhood," and Israel Street (yes, that was what the street was called). Each of these three had its own *Beis Medrash* [Study Hall], with its own charm.

In the *Beis Medrash* of the "edge of town," there were really no great scholars, but they studied diligently. Pesakh the teacher prayed there. He was the *Gemara* teacher of the town. He would take 10-15 children and "work" with them from the morning until late at night, with all his energies. He worked like that, with young Jewish boys, for 25 years, until he became hoarse, and would speak with the voice of a duck. In fact, a gang of jokers called him "Pesach the quacker." And if this Jew wasn't already exhausted from his teaching, every day, between *mincha* [afternoon prayer] and

[Page 461]

maariv [evening prayer] he would recite a chapter of *mishnayos* in front of the congregants – not for money, Heaven forbid, and during the Shabbath day, he would recite *Chumash*.

In the "upper class" *Beis Medrash,* the more intellectual crowd prayed – those who were more educated in the worldly and Jewish sense.

Reb Zelig Velvel's (Khinitz)

A *Gemara* teacher in the "edge of town" and a beadle of that synagogue in Starobin. He was the grandfather of HaRav Avrohom Khnitz and of the writer Chaim Liff and his brothers in New York.

The city's *Maskilim* ["enlightened ones"] and half-modern teachers prayed there. They argued that a Jew must know *Tanach* [acronym for *Torah*: Five Books of Moses, *Neviim*: Prophets, and *Kesuvim*: Writings] actually with its grammar. Each Shabbath, they would study a page of *Gemara* there, and in attendance were about 20-30 fine Jews. The Rebbi was Reb Shlomo Landau, a great Torah scholar, who earned his livelihood from the post office that his father-in-law Yankel Itche Chaim's had in the lease of "Kozno," and he gave this over to him as an eternal dowry when he took him as a son-in-law for his only daughter. So Reb Shlomo sat and learned and was involved with community work, and the father-in-law took care of the horses and coaches along with all the tools that were required to provide the area with postal services, and for this he was very proud of his son-in-law. In that *Beis Medrash* there was someone who was called Hirshke the shoemaker. He had an outstanding voice and would lead the prayers during the Days of Awe [High Holidays, Rosh Hashanah and Yom Kippur]. The *maskilim* would shrug their shoulders a bit, complaining about why it was just in their synagogue that such a simple Jew was leading the prayers, a former shoemaker; but no one had the audacity to say a word to him, because they knew that no one could compare to Hirshke's *Yaaleh* [significant part of the Yom Kippur prayer] and his Yom Kippur *mussaf* [afternoon prayers].

Hirshke's wife, Chasha Merke's, was a real pious woman. She worked as for ten women. Wherever there was a poor person, wherever there was an orphan boy or girl that needed to get married, or a poor person's funeral to be arranged, Chasha Merke's was the first to arrange everything discreetly so that no one would realize that they "got lucky," so she was very careful that even the person in question for whom she was working, did not know how or through whom he or she was helped.

In 1915, when almost all the Russian armies went through White Russia, a nation of Cossaks arrived in Starobin right on Yom Kippur in the middle of the day. When they saw a few Jews in the street, they began to taunt them. The Jews ran to the *Beis Medrash* and began to scream that Cossaks were beating Jews. Chaos erupted and the majority of the Jewish men and women ran to their homes. The beadles ran over to Hirshke, who was standing at the podium leading the *mussaf* prayers, and pleaded with him to end the prayers because there was a life threatening situation and the congregants must go home.

Reb Osher Domnycz (renowned as a teacher, an enlightened individual, and a Zionist, with his wife and son Zev)

But Hirshke waved them away with his hands and shouted in surprise, "*Avodah*!" That means how can one allow himself to interrupt while reciting the *Avodah* [highpoint of prayers] where no interruption is permitted. He did not budge from his place and continued his *mussaf* as if nothing had happened.

Seeing his determination, many Jews remained in the synagogue, and in a short while, a group of Don Cossaks with their long sabres entered into the synagogue, but

[Page 462]

when they saw Hirshke with his *kittel* [white robe] and *talis* [prayer shawl] standing at the podium and saying "*Ve'hakohanim…*" [the opening words of the priests's blessings for the congregation], and then all the men dropping down to the ground for *Kor'im* [the word at which the men bow and drop to the ground in reverence during the priestly prayer], they became unsettled and left quietly.

HaRav Reb Yosef Rozowsky studied in Starobin, Poltawa, Mir. He died in Russia.

The third section of the town was concentrated around the large *Beis Medrash,* that was the main synagogue. The Rav and all those who held positions in the religious field, prayed there, and that was the "kingdom" of Moishe Nomi's. This was a rare type of Jew that you don't find already for many years. Actually, he was only the beadle of the great synagogue, but in truth, he was the manager of religious life in town. First, he was a genius in the Talmud and responsa, with a touch of *Kabbalah* [mysticism] as an addition. There was no limit to his religiousness. He would literally sit day and night in the *Beis Medrash* and study. Elderly Jews used to say that in fifty years it never happened that someone would come into the synagogue, either by day or at night, and not find Moishe. Even though in Starobin there were always great rabbis of world renown, it was Moishe who would be the one to be learning a page of Gemara in the great synagogue and the great rabbi would be one of the listeners. As the city beadle, he would go through the city every Thursday and collect money for those poor who needed bread.

Starobin, as good as the entire Slutsker Jewish area was, did not have *chassidim* with the whole "*rebbe*" [*chassidic* leader] atmosphere. But they would come to Moishe as to a good Jew even from other cities in the area to receive a blessing. Not only Jews, but often non-Jews would also come to him with requests, and the only payment that he would take from them was candles and towels for the *Beis Medrash*, when their wishes were fulfilled.

In Starobin, there was also a *yeshiva* for a few years before World War One, and it was run by HaRav Reb Zelig Fortman. I too studied there. It happened once that he had to leave town for a few weeks, so he asked Moishe to conduct the classes for the *yeshiva*, and on one day, in the middle of his conducting a class, a peasant entered with a large package of towels and wanted to see him. Moishe excused himself from us, and conversed for a while with the peasant, and took the towels from him. When he came back to us, he noticed that the incident had made an impression on us, the young men, so he said to us with a divine smile:

"Two cows ran away from this peasant, so he came to me a week ago so that I would "charm them" [remove any "charm" or evil eye from the peasant so that this would not happen again]. Why would it bother me if a peasant believes in such things? He now brought towels that will provide for the *Beis Medrash* for a year! When peasants believe, then it's good. You can't laugh at them because when they stop believing, then it becomes terrible!" …

In the large synagogue, sitting in a corner was Reb Avrohom Reuven Hinde's (Rubnitz) reciting *Alshich* [a Midrashic commentator]. He was the eldest of his brothers, son of Pesach the teacher and Elye Hinde's. In town they were called the "sons of Reuven," likely because of their grandfather after whom they were named – Rubnitz. Along with the Khinitzes, they were the largest family in town. According to my memory, Avrohom Reuven was already in his high eighties and he had already long before given up his business. He used to be a merchant of fur and boar hair, of which he considered himself to be the consummate expert. But all this "foolishness" was only with things. His main interest in life was something else. For over sixty consecutive years, he recited *Alshich*. That means, he studied with a group of Jews every day between *minchah* [afternoon prayers] and *maariv* [evening prayers] the Torah portion of the week along with the commentaries of *Alshich*. Among his listeners were those who had been there from when he began this learning – those such as Moteh Yankel the wagon driver and Moishe Berl the glazier, who themselves were also elderly Jews. For all his students who were from the working class elements of town, Avrohom Reuven was the symbol of Torah and intellect. His word was a piece of wisdom, even though he considered himself to be a simpleton, and would often make unnecessary comments.

One of his comments circulated around the town, that he did not believe that "in this world" there were such places as Moscow and Petersburg. "Well, at least places like Vilna and Warsaw"

[Page 463]

he used to say – "you can't deny because you see the names in black and white – on the Talmud." From Minsk and Smolensk he himself saw merchants who came to buy his furs and boar hair, but the others – created falsehoods and deceits, a made-up story with which those who were idle used to drive you crazy, because they were too lazy to attend the class on *Alshich* and preferred to discuss nonsense!

Who can deny this? Maybe he was right after all!

As was mentioned earlier, there were always famous rabbis in Starobin. In the last tens of years, the Rav there was Reb Dovid Feinstein, of blessed memory, who was a renowned name in the rabbinic world, known for his genius and extraordinary behavior. He was a brother-in-law to Reb Elye Pruzhiner, who was also a Rav in Starobin.

In general, Starobin was a city filled with Torah. In all the great *yeshivos*, they knew that Starobin was a reservoir of yeshiva students in comparison to the population. They would joke in town that the name of the town, in fact, was "*sto rabin*" which in Russian means – one hundred rabbis.

The last we heard from there before the Nazis invaded was that the Bolsheviks dried out the swamps there and lit everything up with electricity, but at the same time, they dried out the minds of Jewish life and left not even a spark of light of the glory and richly spiritual town Starobin.

Editor's remarks*:*

The attached letter was the last one that was received from HaRav Reb Yosef Leyb Kaplan from his father Reb Moishe Nomi's in Starobin. For certain reasons, the letter was delayed and it could not be entered into the Hebrew section. So, we are printing this letter in the Starobiner Yiddish section, because this letter mirrors the life of the great Torah scholar, Reb Moishe Nomi's, as well as the life of Starobiner Jews, in the twenties of this century.

Am'I As'v[1]

Translated by Jerrold Landau

Wednesday of the Torah Portion of *Binsoa Haaron*, 5686 [1926][2]

Much blessing, success and peace to my dear son, the sharp, expert, G-d fearing, honor to his name, Rabbi Yosef Leib with all his family. All shall be blessed, and you shall see much contentment from them.

After issuing the proper greeting, I inform you that I received your pleasant letter last week, and the writing from my pleasant grandchildren. Much thanks to all of you.

What can I say to you, my son, for you have revived my soul with your letter. I cannot describe to you the joy that I had when I read your letter, for my soul greatly desires to see you and to hear about your wellbeing. May the Master of Giving [i.e. G-d] repay you in accordance with your good desires.

It should not be a wonder to you why I was so afraid. I will tell you my words, and give a report to you: What remains for me from all my toil that I have toiled throughout all the days of my life in the world. – – – My son B., it has been several years since I have heard from him, even though I have heard from others that he has wealth and property. I will tell you that I have no contentment from his riches. Thank G-d I do not need to support him and sustain him. From my son D., due to my great sins, I have a full measure of dismay in my soul, for he has been sent to a foreign land and he cannot come to his home. There he is naked and lacking everything. From my son Eli' I have had agony up to this point. His wife been ill, it should not befall you, for three years already, and they are in great debt, to the point where they had to sell their cow and their fine clothes. Finally, he went to jail. They sealed his store along with all its machines and work implements. He has remained idle and has earned nothing until I made efforts and gathered a hundred rubles. I gave it to him, and he purchased a machine to do his work, but he still is in great debt. Who knows when he will discharge his debts, for his expenditures are greater than his small income. The householders in our city have all declined in their fortunes. Eli' is not the only one in the city. There are three other quilters.

After this report, nothing is left for me from all the toil that I have toiled in the world. It is only when I receive your letter that I have satisfaction. Therefore, I ask that you, and my pleasant grandchildren, may they live, that you do not withhold your good gift of treating me with letters. Explain to me well about your studies and good behavior. May the Blessed G-d give you energy to study and to do His will with a full heart.

Know, my dear son, that up to now, I have been hoping every day that I may perhaps be able to travel to the Holy Land or at least to America, so that it would be fulfilled for me: "And Joseph shall place his hand on your eyes." [Genesis 46:4]. But now I see that my hopes have been dashed, and I am forced to remain in the "impure" land without any support. One must play 300 rubles for a pass. My energy weakens every day, and my eyes have become dim. I traveled to an eye doctor in Slutsk after Passover. He tested me with several tests and told me that I do not need glasses. He gave me medicinal drops. I have been using them daily for four weeks, and I see no benefit from them. My power of speaking has become affected, and my voice has become weak. I read the Torah before the congregation with great effort, and there is nobody to take my place. They do not know the day... if Heaven forbid the difficult days of judgment will pass before the news reaches you and there will be nobody to intercede on my behalf [3]. Therefore, I place my request before you that from this time, you study at least a chapter of Mishnah every day, and serve as the prayer leader at least once a day, without pushing aside the mourners, if it is possible[3].

Your father who blesses you with all good. – – –

Moshe Chaim Koptzitz

[Page 464]

Reb Moshe went to his eternal world exactly four years after he wrote that letter. He was buried in the city cemetery. The following appropriate words, which were sent by his son Rabbi Yosef Leib Kaplan sent from Pittsburgh, United States, were written on his grave.

<table>
<tr><td style="text-align:center">Here is buried
Reb Moshe Chaim the son of Reb Yehuda Leib</td><td style="text-align:center">Here is buried
His wife Mrs. Sara Rivka</td></tr>
</table>

Died 16 Sivan 5690 [1930]	Died four years after him
He toiled in Torah, and was great in deeds	
He was diligent, observant, a doer, an establisher	A woman of valor, modest and proper
He taught the elderly and lads in public	Sarah was her name, and proper she was
He was pious, modest, and a performer of	She performed many good and benevolent deeds
benevolent deeds	Holiness, fear of G-d, and love of Torah
He shall be eulogized in the gates	Were her desires throughout all the days of her
His dispersed sons will continue to mourn for	life
The dear one of our eyes and the crown of our	The number of her years was eighty-three
heads	Sarah Rivka the daughter of Reb Moshe Dov
He was the elderly one, our teacher and guide.	She passed away on Wednesday 9 Tevet 5694
	[1934]
	May her soul be bound in the bonds of eternal life

A group of Yeshiva lands in Mir in 1924 with several natives of our city among them

First row sitting from right to left: Chaim Wysoker of Kobrin, Zushe Terushkin of Starobin, Yisrael Senderovski of Zhetel, Yosef Weiss of Khomsk, Gershon of Zhetel, Yosef of Kobrin, Leib Gurevitch of Maltsh
Second row: Reuven Rosin of Lyuban, David of Cherkas, Yaakov Yankelevitch of Zhetl, Shlomo Genochovitch of Baranovich, Shlomo Pintchuk of Khomsk
Third row: Hertzl Domnitsh and Yitzchak Chaim Krasnich of Starobin, Shlomo of Volozhin, Berl of Rumshishak, Moshe Shoshkes of Tiktin, Tzvi-Hirsch Zirin of Starobin, and Mordechai Karpenshprung of Kobrin

Translator's footnotes:

1. The acronym for *Ezri Me'et Hashem Oseh Shamayim Vaaretz* [My help is from G-d, the Maker of Heaven and Earth]. Psalms 121:2.
2. Binsoa Haaron [as the ark traveled] is a quote from the Torah portion of *Naso*. Return
3. In this obscure sentence, he seems to be worried that he might die, and the news would reach his son much later, so the son would be able to say Kaddish in a timely fashion. In the next line, he requests that his son fulfil on a regular basis some of the customs that are performed by a mourner during the year of mourning for a parent.

[Page 465]

The Destruction of Starobin

(as related by the Starobiner partisan Chaim-Simcha Rubnitz, written by R. Rivin)

Translated by Pamela Russ

Seven days after the Germans attacked the Soviet Union, the Hitlerist mobs entered Starobin. The first victim to fall was Yosel Isser's, the second Yankel Dovid's grandson who tried to protect himself from them and beat up one of their soldiers. First they herded all the Jews from the market to a designated area where the Bojana was, and there they were murdered. After that, they herded together a large number of city Jews on the road to Slutsk into the Koziharer forest and they murdered them there. Some remained in the city, and at night, in the dark, many fled to Slutsk, Pahost, and to other surrounding towns. Of those remaining, the Germans selected twenty skilled workers: such as Grojnem the tailor, Herzel the butcher, and others like that, in order that they teach their skills to the Christian residents. The active helpers of the Germans were the former chief Valadya and Oxenke Karpowyczes. They were the main instigators and evictors of the Jewish population. The old chief, who considered himself of the most prominent people of the Christian population, and the medical assistant's son Karpowycz, who earned his entire living from the Jews, showed themselves to be the worst enemies and murderers. They helped expel all the Jews except for 20 skilled workers that the Germans left alone. These 20 skilled workers were allowed to live for a whole year, and after that they too were murdered.

Among those who fled into the forest and survived were: Shmulik Pisarewytz, Boruch Kalman Stubke's grandson, Hirshel Swercinuwski, Yankel Elye's son, Yankel Lipzyc, Zelig the tailor's grandson, and my sister Surke's son, Sender Menke, Shaya Avremel's grandson, Aharel Khinitz, Yisroel Mekhnewicer's son, Avremel Priwiszjer and his two children, Yisrolek Kaplan, Artze the wagon driver's son.

We organized ourselves into partisan groups together with the non-Jews in the forests of the village Dominowyc, in Polesia. In the beginning we did not have enough ammunition. There were few guns for one hundred people. We acquired food and clothing from those times that we attacked the villages at night. Later, when the number of partisans increased, it became easier for us. Our first organized attack on the Germans was on the road to Pahost on the Tczew "estate." The Tczew village was exceptional in helping the Germans capture Jews, so we had to first attack Pahost, and kill the commandant and his staff. Then we burned down the courtyard. During this attack, the Starobin partisan Shmulik Pisarewyc was extraordinary. Also, the first of the Starobin partisans was killed, Yedidya Rapaport, son of Yerachmiel the carpenter, who earlier had lived in a village near Starobin. After this attack, we had more ammunition and increased our units. When we acquired more weapons we were able to decrease the number of Jewish victims that were killed by Christian hands, that hurried to receive a large reward for each Jewish head.

Other than Shmulik, another Starobin partisan that was exceptional was Aharel Khinitz. Because of the effective advice that he gave to the general of the partisans, thanks to his instruction, our units were enlarged and strengthened. One of his smartest suggestions was that after our attack on the villages we should take people from the villages with us so that the families could unite with the partisans. This is how we maintained ourselves until 1942, and when the partisan units grew, we began to deal with the Germans. That's how we conducted partisan slaughters until 1944. That was when I came back to Starobin, but I did not find any Jews there. Also, the town was almost completely destroyed. Slutsker Street, the marketplace, Poworcicer, Kropilanka streets, were all wiped out. On the long Slutsker Street, I found two houses – Sender Khinitz's and Zameh the shoemaker's. There was nothing left of the cemeteries. The Bolsheviks even took down the tombstones of the old cemetery, and in the new cemetery, the Germans burned and destroyed the tombstones. Here and there a broken tombstone was still standing.

That's how the destruction was in all the surrounding towns, and the same destruction was in Slutsk. The main thing that the Germans destroyed was – the center. There was nothing left of the large synagogue courtyard. Before that, the ghetto was located there. Of Slutsk, all that remained was Wigoda Street, and some small side streets around Kolonya. Parts of the Slutsk houses and of the houses in the surrounding areas were taken by the Christians to their villages. I found my father's house in the village of Paworcic. The Starobin partisans returned to the town, and then later those few

[Page 466]

who remained alive in White Russia came as well. About 300 Jews gathered in Slutsk. At first, we would drag ourselves from Starobin to Slutsk and back. On one of my Slutsker visits with Yisroel Artzig, who was usually a little drunk, in order to drown out his problems, while walking on Khaposzker Street, Yisrolik suddenly met his daughter, a young child. She fell on him with hysterical cries: "Father! Father!" How did she survive, and how did she get here? She related the following…

When the Germans took over Slutsk, there were fugitives in Slutsk from many different towns. From Slutsk, the Germans would chase out camps of Jews, and on the roads the Germans would murder them all. Once, when the Germans assembled a camp of 500 children, and chased them out to the Starodoroger highway to kill them on the road, a peasant family from a nearby village snuck her [Yisrolik's daughter] out of the camp and took her to their home, and hid her as their child. They kept her like that until the time that she met up with her father. But she did not want to leave those who had saved her. They had no children of their own and kept her as their own child. She became as close to them as to her own parents. In the end, Yisrolek also went to their home to be together with his daughter and with her rescuers.

That's how I wandered in loneliness and sadness, lost my entire family, my wife and children, until I left Starobin, and as a former Polish citizen before the war, I continued wandering and then finally arrived in Israel.

Translated by Jerrold Landau

Rabbi Yisrael Tanchum HaKohen Portman, may G-d avenge his blood, was born in Starobin. He was first the Shveksner Rabbi and then the Zezmerer Rabbi. He was popular in Lithuania as a great and fine orator. He displayed oratory talent already from his youth. He became known in the Yeshiva world as an unusual artist who entertained the crowd with poetic verses and witty speeches. For many years, he would travel from Yeshiva to Yeshiva.

Here we include one of his interesting, sarcastic lectures. He would chant it with a wonderful, preacher's melody, blended with a joyous festive voice, then sad, and then again joyous, to the point where the crowd broke out in a dance.

This humorous lecture became known throughout all the Lithuanian Yeshivot, and became perpetuated as folklore. The interpretation of the words were Russian or close to "Russian."

N. V.

A Wise Lesson Regarding Shtetls

Translated by Pamela Russ

There is a town called Szwerzna, and there is a town Nieswizh; a town Krinok and a Nowy-Krinok. There is also a town Starobin and two other towns – one Wysoka and the other Gluboka. There is a difficult question: Why is one town called this way, and the other the exact opposite?

The answer is this:

The Creator created the entire world for the Jews, as it is written in the verse: "In the beginning, G-d created," so Rashi [famous Biblical commentary] says: "It was created for Israel," "first, – Israel is chosen of His produce." And He created the Jews that they go in His ways and they should be good and pious, as it states in the verse: "It is only in the merit of Torah study that G-d keeps the world running." Therefore, every Jew must know that the whole dance [of the world] keeps spinning only because of him, and he must spin and spin for the Creator and always be fresh in Torah studies and in keeping the *mitzvos* [positive commandments]. As it states in the verse: "Every day there should be novelties in your eyes."

This is the translation of the name "*czwerzne*," which means "fresh," lively, enthusiastic before the Creator.

But how is it that the Creator takes a look and sees that it is "not so fresh"? A Jew is a little lazy to do a *mitzvah*, but he runs sharply, like an arrow in a bow, to commit a sin.

The Creator says: Dear little Jew, I have a little town for you, "Krinak," I'll bring you a "*krenk*" [play on word for "sickness"], then you'll consider why you are here in this world.

If the dear Jew repents, then it is good. But if not, then the Creator says: "*Nowy Krinak*" [new sickness], I will bring upon you a new *krenk* [sickness], a stronger one that will awaken you from your sleep.

If the Jew catches himself in time, then it is good. But if not, the Creator says: "Dear Jew, it won't help. I have a town for you, Starobin, and you have to do the "*starb*" (in the Slutsk region, the "sh" sound is pronounced like an "s", therefore it really sounds like "*shtarb*," to die), and there they will see what they can do with you."

And even if he is close to dying, if he awakens himself

[Page 467]

and turns to the "Father in Heaven," the Creator says: "Fine! I'll accept you and send you to "Wysoka," up high [Polish: *wysoka* means "high"]. Your body will be burned and roasted but your soul will be washed and polished until it becomes like crystal – pure, and then it will be sent to the glorious Garden of Eden."

But if the person is stubborn and says: "No, I don't want to repent!" then the Creator says: "I have a town Gluboka – first you will be killed by a nasty death and then you will go deep, deep [Russian: *gluboka*: "deep"] into the ground and sink ten fathoms deep in the earth!"

Folklore

by Raphael Rivin

Translated by Pamela Russ

I

Every town had its nickname, such as:

Kopulier *naronim* [fools], Hrozower *ladishkes* [milk pots], Lekhewyczer *peltzlekh* [animal skins], Kletzker *ganovim* [thieves], Nieswyzher *lasunes* [fancy people], Starobiner *dekhtzarnikes* [?], and so on.

A story was told: Kopulier Jews, for whom the mountain obstructed a vision of the world, decided to push away the mountain. So they pushed and they pushed, and did not know whether the mountain had moved from its spot. What to do? So they went and took Lekhewyczer *peltzlekh* [animal skins], placed them beneath the mountain, and once again took to pushing the mountain.

They sent a messenger, and he heard that the skins had disappeared. But the truth was that the Kletzker had taken away the skins. Meanwhile, however, the Kopulier became exhausted from the grueling job of pushing, so they brought a *krupnik* [barley vegetable soup] filled up in Hrozower *ladishkes* [milk pots], so that they could enjoy this. In between all that, when the Kopulier went to wash their hands after using the bathroom before reciting *"Asher Yatzar"* [blessing recited after bathroom use], the Nieswyzher *lasunes* [fancy people] came and gobbled up the entire *krupnik*. And that's how the Kopulier remained. With the mountain and with the milk cans they really did earn their nickname.

II

If you grease the wheel – it goes smoothly.

Starobiner Jews were primarily transporters. The drivers [haulers] transported wood chopped down from the surrounding forests and took them to designated places. Many would drive through the villages to sell their own products.

Wagon drivers were busy with their surroundings and since painting the wheels with grease was a good way to maintain the standard of wheels, horse collars, bags, and leather straps, it was easy to sell this in the immediate areas.

sWith the abundance of grease, the Starobiner Jews also used this to polish their shoes and tall boots that shone, and you could smell the sharp odor of grease from a distance.

So the Starobiner really deserved the nickname *"dekhtzarnikes* [?]."

Starobiner Heretics

I

Reuve Mote-Yankel's, as a young man, was the one who introduced the Bund [secular Jewish socialist movement] to Starobin. Always busy, he would come home late at night, and finding the windows and doors locked, he would bang on the door and call out: "There is no G-d, no Kaiser, no father or mother, Mote-Yankel, open the door!"

II

Artze the teacher, a religious and a naïve man, could not in any way understand how it was possible that a Jew could be a heretic and not believe in G-d. It states explicitly in the Torah: "And G-d spoke to Moses and He said, I am your G-d." And with a victorious tune, he would sing out loud, "So, what do you say about that!"

III

A debate between a wagon driver and a Komsomol member [Communist youth of the Communist Party of the Soviet Union].

Alter Taker suddenly became a heretic and stopped praying. And he also laughed at the Jews who were going to pray. Since Alter was almost a genius in black dots [mathematical/multiplication calculations], Artshik the Wagon Driver asked him: "Tell me, Alter, on the spot, how much is six times thirteen?" For Taker this was too difficult and he could not answer the question. So, Artchik sang a "*kal ve'khomer*" ["how much more so"] in his face: "Thickhead, you, such an exception and so outstanding, and yet, you can't even answer such an easy question. So with your simpleton common sense, how can you talk against the prayers?"

* * *

Mendele tells about Starobin that they caught a tailor in town committing a terrible robbery. One morning, he was called up twice to the reading of the Torah. The first time was in the tailors' small *shtiebel* [small, informal synagogue], and the second time was in the large *Beis Medrash*.

[Page 468]

Starie-Dorogoi
(Staryya Darohi, Belarus)
53°02' 28°16'

Starie-Dorogoi

by Khen

Translated by Pamela Russ

In the really old forests, out in the wild, there was a remote village with the name Nowo-Dorogoi. When the train was introduced by Osifovitch, the Starie-Dorogoi station was built and a new settlement was created on the old, empty, abandoned roads.

The Minsker Jew Polyak-Weisbrem built a factory for veneer workings and sawing machines. A fresh, busy life took hold in this new settlement. On both sides of the train station there grew a lively settlement of 200 Jewish families. Jews came, built houses, opened stores, inns. This is how a small community of *chassidim* and *misnagdim* [opponents of *chassidim*] was set up, with two synagogues – a *chassidic* one and a *misnagdic* one. Reb Hertzel Horker used to recite the "*Kol Nidrei*" [central evening prayer for Yom Kippur] and recite *maariv* [the evening prayers] at the *misnagdic* synagogue, and *mussaf* [the late morning prayer] at the *Chassidic* synagogue. There was a rabbi and a ritual slaughterer in the town. It's worth mentioning that the rabbi sold coal and wood. Even though the rabbi, Reb Khaim Faisakhowycz, was known as a fine lecturer, the jokers in town would say that he could not warm the crowd with his speeches but could do so with this coal and wood.

Later he came to Jerusalem, and then died there. (One of his lectures was printed in Segalowycz's "*Maasif Drushei*" ["A Collection of Lectures," Section 1, page 98, Vilna 5672 (1912)].

A group of wagon drivers would ride along the highway of Starie-Dorogoi to Slutsk and back, driving loaded wagons with merchandise and all kinds of products. Their hard work drew everyone's attention to the highway, and later – the two leveled passenger car on the route of Starie-Dorogoi – Slutsk. The town buzzed and bristled with merchants, workers, shopkeepers, brokers. There were also Jewish students, intellectuals, such as Reb Yeshaye Khaim Khinitz, Reb Ber Moishe Wajnstajn, his son-in-law Yitzchok Kapilowycz, Freed, Reznik, and other Zionists and Hebraists. As forest merchants the well-known ones were Freed Rabkin, Hertzel Garacikow. Starie-Dorogoi had three hotels: Rabinowycz's, Berezina, and Rabkin's hotel. Of the stores, there were mainly distributors: Levin's wholesale store (Soroh Kazakewycz's husband), Lipa Wecerebin's store, and Nekrice's large wholesale store. In the town, a prominent place was given to: Sender Reznik, Kopel Simkhowyc, Itzele Reznik, very respected was Dubrowski, a prominent Jew, with a large income.

The city Jews subscribed to Hebrew-Yiddish-Russian newspapers that came by mail.

The Hebrew teacher M. Khazanowyc, first taught Hebrew to the children of the community activist Leyb Berger in Starie-Dorogoi, and from there he went over to Slutsk and became one of the founders of the "*Cheder Metukan*" ["Improved School," or reformed school, still with Torah learning but incorporating progressive ideas]. Khurgin was one of the first Hebrew teachers in town and also a bookkeeper of the loan-and-save fund. Starie-Dorogoi merited running a Hebrew "*Cheder Metukan*" opened by Khaim Rabinowycz. The school became beloved in the town. Khaim Rabinowycz participated in the famous children's journal "*Haprachim*" ["The Flowers"] and in other publications. He came to Israel in 1925, worked in a primary school in Ramat Gan, and died in 1931. His blessed work was presented by the teacher Maron.

This city was different than all the surrounding cities with the intelligence of its residents, and with their relationships and reactions to all kinds of experiences in life. If a guest came to town, whether he wanted to or not, he had to express his enthusiasm for the small, blessed, lively island. Jews lived in the old ways – Starie-Dorogoi with a new content for a happy, joyous life. But new times and new melodies came, the happy tunes disappeared. The town remained orphaned. Zionism was forbidden, the *Cheder Metukan* crossed off, fear befell everyone.

The Nazi powers brought the end, everything fell apart and was destroyed by the vicious beast. The old roads became emptied – also Starie-Dorogoi was once again nothingness and void, with emptiness at each tread and step.

[Page 469]

Pohost
(Pogost, Belarus)
52°51' 27°40'

Pohost is near the Slutsch River, and is mentioned in the history of the 15th Century: 500 residents. There is an Orthodox Church, 1 synagogue and 2 fairs.

(According to the Bruckhaus-Ephrons Encyclopedia)

Pohost

By Chaim Kuntser

Translated by David Goldman

Donated by Jeffrey Mark Lackner

I was born in Pohost in 1916 and studied in kheder and community school from 1920-21. My father Zvi was a shoemaker and a hard-working honest Jew. There were approximately 200 Jewish families and about 50-60 Christian families in town. Most of the residents were artisans and agricultural worker. Wagon-drivers from Pohost used to travel to Slutsk, Starobin, Vizna, Timkovitch, Uretcha, and transported travelers and merchandise. There were also small merchants, storekeepers and shipbuilders.

Market fairs were held twice a year in Pohost, and large markets on Sundays. From time to time rafts would float by on the nearby Slutsch River. There were two synagogues in town – a House of Study [Beit Midrash] and a "Cold Synagogue" [sometimes a euphemism for a non-chassidic synagogue]. At first there was only one ritual slaughterer, R. Yaakov Leizer the Ritual Slaughterer, who was later joined by a second, R. Alter Marshak. There was one rabbi, and Arka Aronovitch, in addition to being the caretaker [it is unclear whether he was the caretaker (shamesh) of one or the other synagogue, or served as an assistant to the rabbi], was also responsible for the Jewish cemetery. In Pohost there was a Christian country doctor named Rakovetz. There were two pharmacists, one of whom, I recall, was named Tchiptchin.

Until 1920 there were kheders [religious elementary schools] in Pohost, and two government-run Russian schools: one went up to the 4th grade, and the second to the 7th.

In the Jewish school (that had 4 grades) students studied in Yiddish and Russian, and White Russian [Belarussian] was a school subject. The kheders were closed in 1926-1927. The teachers were arrested, and then later two teachers – Itshe Ba'al Haturim and Hillel the Teacher – were released. Jews had to make heavy payments to prevent their stores from being closes. The property of the landowners/nobles was expropriated and their land was distributed to poor peasants and day laborers.

In 1932 the synagogues were closed, as were the churches. The synagogues were taken apart and rebuilt elsewhere as a theater and garage for the fire trucks. The church was turned into a grain elevator.

Collective farms [kolkhozes] and cooperatives were set up in town and cities to put stores and private enterprises out of business. Many of them [unclear who or what this refers to] were sent off to various locations, and tailoring, shoemaking and blacksmithing and wagon-driving workshops were set up. Both Jewish and Christian young people aspired to leave the towns and move to the cities. Those with an education got settled in their own profession, and the unskilled looked for any job they could find. Some Jewish young people studied to become technicians, engineers, doctor; others studied foreign languages such as English, French and German in education institutions in Minsk.

I worked in Minsk, and in 1941 I returned to Pohost for a visit. A couple of weeks later the war broke out, and the Germans invaded Russia and bombed all the airports in Minsk and Slutsk. I traveled to Slutsk by foot, was drafted into the army there, and then sent to Minsk. Fifty airplanes bombed Minsk, which was now on fire. I experienced many things in various places, fought as a soldier in the Red Army in a number of battles, and remained alive. In June 1946 I was sent on a mission from Gomel to Minsk. The city was in ruins, and I arrived in Slutsk in the morning by train. Everything was burned down on Zaretsa Street; only the bathhouse remained standing. The streets were destroyed, and everything was in piles of bricks and ash. The old market was totally unrecognizable. I wanted to sell some of my possessions, and ran into a couple of Jews. They told me that they had returned from deep within Russia, and that another couple of people survived as partisans. They tearfully told me that everything was lost, and wondered about the fate of their loved ones. I noticed small boards, booths and a couple of Jewish stores with half-empty shelves, and a couple of restaurants.

[Page 470]

First row, bottom, seated from right to left: Father, Zvi David Kuntser, son Chaim, Mother Roiza
Second row, above, standing from right: Children Leible, Ethel, Michel and Sarah

They asked me whether I had found anyone of my family still alive, a survivor or refugee. The city was really a huge Jewish cemetery. I met Keila, the daughter of Nachum Koppel, the dyer (she was our neighbor in Pohost). She told me that her entire family was killed, and she was saved by virtue of her Aryan appearance and documents, and remained with Christians. She was only 12 years old then, and once the Germans withdrew she went to live in an orphanage in Slutsk. I wandered through the ruined streets of Slutsk in a daze. This is Slutsk? There was death and destruction every step of the way, and I finally let for Pohost in a truck. The driver looked at me as if I were crazy. Why was I traveling to Pohost? Everybody there was killed. My heart was thumping and I didn't ask him anything else.

I kept looking forward, trying to find Pohost. At the entry to Pohost I found the Christian homes still standing, and the center of town empty like a desert. My heart started throbbing and my eyes turned dark. I only saw the stones of the sidewalk and went into the house of our Christian neighbor Roman, a friend of

Jews and an elderly good-hearted Christian. He got himself together and told me that the wicked ones arrived here, murdering and pillaging, burning and slaughtering. They had no fear of G-d, and those dogs only sought to kill Jews. Avramtsha Reingold of Pievesha and his two sons remained alive because they had joined the partisans. His wife and daughters, however, perished. The murderers shot his mezinik in one eye, and he was left with only one eye. In town I met my aunt's daughter, Sarah Shapiro, who told me that her husband and 9 year-old daughter perished, but that she didn't know what they did to them.

When the murderers were taking a group of Jews to the slaughter, the automobile stopped for a moment, and Sarah found the strength and will to jump out of the car and into a ditch. The Germans shot at her but didn't get her. They didn't stop, and when she realized that she had lost her husband and daughter, she started running after the automobile in order to share their fate. There was no trace of the people taken to the slaughter, and in depression she made her way to the partisans and worked for them. She cooked, baked, etc. When she returned to town she married Alter Epstein. I met Yankel Gorodnitsky in town, who had survived as a partisan; his son served as a captain in the Red Army.

The two brothers Yosef and Moshe Damnitch survived as well. Yosef escaped with his wife, jumped into the river and tried swimming to the other side. The Germans shot at them but didn't get them. When they got across they ran into the forest where they hid and then joined the partisans. Unfortunately, the German police arrested them in the village of Sliv, and confined them to a grain warehouse, where they were kept under guard. At night they picked up a couple of boards and were able to bribe the guard and escape.

[Page 471]

Jews from town fell in battle as partisans in battle against the Germans. One of them was Yosef Zalmans.

According to reports, there was a gentile in town named Belka Riher who spoke excellent Yiddish. When the Germans arrived in town, he offered to work as a translator. He was appointed as an employee. Through his efforts the Jews were concentrated into a special ghetto in the priests' residences near the church on Priests Alley. The Germans confined them there with barbed wire. There was almost not a single young person among those Jews, because they had fled to the partisans.

The gentile offered to kill the Jews so that no epidemic would break out. Eighty Jews, plus a four gentiles and a Christian woman were killed near the Nevolosch Forest.

The Christians were killed out of revenge. Three partisans were dressed as Nazi officers and went to the church, and by chance the gentile woman was standing there. They told her to call out the priest; as soon as he appeared they pushed him into a closed car and fled. The priest was found a week later hanging on a tree around Zolzevitz.

The partisans held a trial because the priest was collaborating with the Germans, and persecuted and informed on Jews and partisans. The Germans suspected that the gentile woman and four other gentiles were implicated in the priest's death, and killed them in revenge together with the 80 Jews.

A couple of weeks later, the remaining women and children in the ghetto were shot on orders from the traitor Belka.

I spent 3 days in Pohost, and what I heard and saw shook me up. No Jews were there, and their property had been taken over by gentiles without any legal proceedings at all. I noticed my mother's cow at one gentile's house, and our stable at the house of another. Since I was still a soldier and owned a revolver, I drew it and warned the gentile to pay me for the stable. We worked out a payment: part of the money was in cash and the rest would be paid to me when I returned after being discharged from the army. I repossessed the cow, and no one dared confront me. I left the animal with an acquaintance on the condition he return it to me. Two months later I returned to Pohost after my discharge from the army and took the cow away to

Luban, where I sold it to a Jewish woman. I also met my brother's brother-in-law, Yankel Kavalerchik, and Baruch [un Bruchen]. Luban wasn't as destroyed as Pohost, and was able to financially help out a Jewish woman in Luban who had to prepare her papers to travel to her brother abroad.

The survivors of Pohost moved to western Belarus – to Pinsk-Luninetz. I started weeping about my own situation, and decided to go wherever my eyes took me. I arrived in Baranovich. The rest is a long story: from there to Lodz, Czechoslovakia, Austria, Germany, France; then I went through a lot with the ship, Exodus, and battles with the English; I returned to France and then went back to Germany. I spent a year in camps, and then on May 1, 1948, just before the creation of Israel, I finally arrived in Israel, where I participated in the War of Independence, serving seven and a half months as a Jewish soldier in Israel.

I still feel as if it were all a dream: from the little town of Pohost in the Red Army, destruction and chaos in the Diaspora to creating a new life in our own independent State.

[Page 472]

Shmuel Mehrshak

by Miriam Mehrshak

Translated by David Goldman

Donated by Jeffrey Mark Lackner

Shmuel Dov Mehrshak, of blessed memory, was born in Pohost and study ritual slaughtering. At 16 years old his father passed away, leaving behind a widow with five children without any means of livelihood. Since he was a ritual slaughterer, Shmuel Dov was hired for that position and was thereby able to support the family. He was a Zionist, and immediately became an activist on behalf of Jewish settlements in Palestine; he was especially devoted to the Jewish National Fund – Keren Kayemet, and in synagogue promoted the idea of each person sending mail using a kopek stamp of the JNF. Not everyone agreed that a mailed letter should cost an additional kopek, so Shmuel went to the post office that sent mail from Pohost to Slutsk, and asked that the postal official return any mail that did not include a JNF stamp, with a note saying that it required that stamp. This was how he made sure that everyone would send mail using the JNF stamps. Later, he spoke with the synagogue's Torah reader who was a Zionist, and they decided that anyone called up to the Torah would have to promise to make a contribution to the JNF. Anyone who didn't want to promise to contribute was not given an aliyah during the Torah reading. This is how he gradually made all the Jews of Pohost Zionists.

In 1912, the community of Slutsk was looking for a new ritual slaughterer, and my husband got the position. He did very well on the examination, but the rabbi, R. Isser Zalman Meltzer was against him. "It is true," he said, "that everyone likes you. However, we cannot take you as ritual slaughterer."

Shmuel asked the reason, and the rabbi responded, "It's because people say you are a Zionist." "Yes, rabbi, I won't lie. I am a Zionist," Shmuel said. The rabbi then told him that as soon as he gave up Zionism he would be hired." Shmuel responded, "You'll become a Zionist before I ever give up Zionism." Nevertheless, he obtained the position, and we moved to Slutsk.

As soon as he arrived in Slutsk Shmuel again began working on behalf of Zionism, and encountered open territory for his activities. He visited the kheders and told them to teach Hebrew to the children. He and Leibush Gutzeit brought a kindergarten teacher from Vilna and opened a Hebrew-speaking kindergarten. They also established a community Zionist organization, and Shmuel planted the seeds of Zionism in the hearts of his own children. His work continued until World War I.

In 1914 food and clothing became scarce for some of the Jews. Together with Leibush Gutzeit and Dr. Shilderkraut, Shmuel became active in assisting them. Meat, white flour, rice, oil, canned products and old clothes were sent from the United States. The local committee met for four hours a day, distributing assistance to needy people. There was also a charity fund.

When the Bolsheviks arrived in Slutsk, our children were arrested – first a son, and then a daughter. When Jewish slaughtering was prohibited, we contacted my sister, who brought us to the United States. My husband found a position as a ritual slaughterer in Rochester, where he looked for a Zionist organization. He also found a Mizrachi women's organization for me. However, he didn't want to join the General Zionists or Poalei Zion, so he joined the Mizrachi association.

In addition to his activities for the JNF, he devoted a great deal of time to the Talmud Torah school, with the purpose of strengthening Jewish education through teaching children in Hebrew and through the spirit of Zionism.

[Page 473]

Kopyl
(Kapyl', Belarus)
53°09' 27°05'

Kopyl – a shtetl near the Komenka River. It was settled hundreds of years ago.

Utensils made from stone and bones were found. Kopyl became a city in the 14th century.

Together with Slutsk, Kopyl was made a special principality during the era of Lithuanian rule. At the beginning of the 17th century, the land was given to Prince Radziwill.

Three hundred thirty eight inhabitants, forty one courts, a Russian Orthodox Church, a Catholic Church,a Reform Church, two Jewish prayer houses, a public school and two *botei medrashim* [plural of *besmedresh*, synagogue, study house], a brewery, two waters mills and two stores.

(According to Brockhaus-Efrons Encyclopedia)

A community, a type of city, stood in the center of the Kopyl area.

Twelve kilometers from the railroad station at Timikhovichi (in the net Osipovitch-Baranovitch), one hundred eight six kilometers from Bobruisk.

There is one dairy in Kopyl that produces butter and cheese, two middle schools (a Russian and a White Russian), a library, and movie theater.

The surrounding fields are planted with various vegetables and potatoes. There are three garages for machines and tractors, coal burning factories, a brick factory, seven electrical stations.

(According to the Soviet Encyclopedia)

Occupations in Kopyl

by Mendele Mocher Sforim

(Extracts from Shlomo, Reb Chaim's)

Translated by Judie Ostroff Goldstein

One of the main occupations that made Kapulie different from all the other towns in Lithuania was "astrohonke" and especially "woven articles." "Astrohonke" – this was a sort of linen, dyed dark green, and laid together in pieces from a certain number of *arshin* [a measure of length formerly used in Russia, equal to 28 inches] that would be used mainly as linings and also for caftans for the poor.

Why was this linen called "astrohonke?" This was never explained in the history of the shtetl. A bleached piece of linen, long and narrow like a towel was called a veil, also made by the shtetl weavers. With the look of a towel, the women wound them around their heads, over their bonnets, tying them behind at the nape, leaving two large corners hanging in the shape of a windmill and two smaller ones on the sides that were called "fans." The veiled head was like a hoop wrapped in a folded shawl, twisted, with a knot on the forehead and the corners of the shawl tucked in or pinned, one on each side of the head. Old, pious women and those of the middle-class wore the knot in the front of the head, like a " *shel rosh*" [phylactery worn on the head by men] on the forehead. Young, modern women, shoved the knot a little to the side. On the Sabbath and holidays they wore silk, cashmere or Turkish shawls and during the week, woolen ones with large flowers – apple shawls. Both these types of shawls were given to brides as wedding gifts from the groom's parents. The bride's parents gave the groom a *shtreimel* [fur edged hat worn by Orthodox Jews on Sabbaths and holidays].

Map showing the area around Slutsk
Includes Bobruisk, Minks and Mogilev

[Page 474]

This is what our grandmothers looked liked in a veil. The veil had to be white as snow, starched and rolled. Rolling the veil flat was a job for two women and one held the corners with both hands at one end and at the other end the other woman did the same. In this way the veil stayed stretched out between the women like a long, narrow gutter in which a large, round, smooth glass or iron ball was placed. One of the women raised her hands a little and the ball ran in the veil from her side to the other. The woman on the other end raised her hands a little and the ball ran back. The ball ran back and forth until the veil was smooth as a turner's lathe. To look at the women, they seem so earnest. They stand far apart, raising their hands with a shake of the shoulder, pushing out their bellies, laying their heads on the side as if to bend, twisting their noses, watching with their eyes and sending from one to other sweet, poisonous smiles, good conversation with stinging barbs. To see this, one would think there is nothing more beautiful in the world. To hell with today's theater.

This veil as well as the "*astrokhonke*" gave work to gentile weavers in the shtetl. Several had their own workrooms at home. The Jews took away the merchandise they had paid for. Each one dealt with his own weavers. Those involved in this trade were children after *kest* [room and board provided to a son-in-law so he could continue his Torah studies], or just finishing *kest*, or who still had dowry money. Reb Chaim's children already given in marriage were also involved and made a living from this trade. The merchandise was bought up by large merchants and sent to all the Lithuanian cities where it always sold well.

Everyone praised Kopyl veils. This was the profession in the shtetl and a lot of Jews made their living from this trade.

And suddenly an evil decree was issued. The evil decree concerned clothing – women were not allowed to shave their heads and Jews had to dress like everyone else! No more veils, no more commerce, no more income! It was as if the town had been killed. Everyone felt the blow, the weavers and spinners, small and large buyers. The tavern keepers also felt it as the weavers did not have money to even buy bread and certainly were not drinking. These were sorrowful times for the storekeepers. The artisans and everybody was touched. As fate would have it, more bad luck was in the offing. Suddenly one beautiful summer day, the season when fires break out in Jewish towns, there was a fire, a hellish fire in Kopyl. More than half the houses were lost. Among those lost to the fire was Fradel's parents' house. There were hills of ash where once there were houses. Naked chimneys stuck up from the ash heaps like gravestones in a cemetery. Hungry, displaced, scrawny, pale people, really living corpses, wandered in the streets. Some rummaged and searched in the handful of garbage that was their homes. They searched, as is said, for the horseshoes from a dead horse. They were searching for a trace of their household goods. And what joy when somebody found these valuable things under the ashes, such as a nail, a pot or several roasted potatoes.

The Kopyl Market Place

The shtetl Kopyl, as some know, lies in a corner on the side. Far from the beaten path, there is no mail, no bells are heard, aside from one; the ringing of the assessor's bell on his carriage.

But still it is not a foolish town. It is quiet, calm and law-abiding, concerned mainly with studying *Torah* [Five Books of Moses, the Bible], praying and important work. The *Torah* students labor in the *kloyiz* [house of study] in the *besmedresh* [synagogue, house of study, meeting hall] spending time, giving their hearts to studying and discussions.

Important work refers to the work of small taverns, small shops, small stores-these are called businesses. Not racing, not making a great uproar, or hoo-ha, not cracking the whip in far off places like Moscow, Leipzig, Krakow or Lemberg [Lvov], God forbid! Only small taverns, small stores for their own people or for townsmen or peasants from the surrounding villages. The peasant usually comes to town on Sundays riding on oxen with sacks of potatoes, beets, cabbage heads, also with a game rooster, an already smoked old fool. During the autumn, around Chanukah, this fellow brings geese, sheepskins and the like. He gets a drink of liquor at the tavern, one drink, several drinks, snacks on an old baked bagel and leaves to roam, a little tipsy, among the shops, to buy salt, matches, cheap

[Page 475]

tobacco; one man buys a red shawl with large flowers for his wife and the other a crimson ribbon to tie his daughter's braids – short and sweet. A shtetl it is called, and it conducts its trade, alone, between its inhabitants, quietly, slowly, and so smoothly, nothing for a rooster to crow about!... That is with the exception of several summer fairs where trade is a little broader and tumultuous.

There one truly sees all sorts of new faces: Here is the small town simpleton, with his head to side, a crazy, backward hat, caps, clothes of strange, wild styles. And there one sees hands, tapping something in the wagon, beady little eyes and twisted noses, that thing pretends to be doing nothing; also lots of hair, new fur caps. Squeaking bast shoes, smelly, thickly smeared heavy shoes of the village peasants with ugly wives, a string of beads hung around naked necks, and coarse linen embroidered shirts. The majority of folks are sitting, not touching.

Among spring onions and small baskets of eggs, is a recently born calf with all four legs tied up, yearning for the breast. The calf is strong, languishing in a loaded wagon, to which a cow stands tied by its horns. The cow is the mother, poor thing, and she is led out to sell, her milk to go elsewhere. This child of hers – this calf – is to be slaughtered.

Suddenly a hound runs from under the mountain of animals and humanity, lifting its wagging tail, kicking its hind legs and raising its back end. Now the drove of horses scream, an uproar, and hooligans crack their whips, lashing their sides. The horses will be exhibited at the horse market. Contractors (horse dealers) are the big experts. They look at the horses' teeth, treasures, and haggle and wrangle, all the while as they slap each horse on the flank. There walking about very excited is Grishka, the gypsy with his horse which is tall with a fat round belly, glossy brown hide and fiery eyes.

Leyzer-Ber, the towns water carrier, upon discovering this merchandise, this lovely horse, is trembling, almost epileptic. But he laughs – a horse yet, a horse! Oy, pauper, pauper! Leyzer-Ber pauper, this you should not desire. This is not for your pocket. Well, as the *gemore* says, one must try. No – no, and maybe yes? Hey, Grishka! Tell me brother! How much?

A word here, a word there, the point is – a good man, Grishka, the gypsy! Grishka sits on the horse, travels quickly here and there. The horse runs, kicks with his feet, stands upright. Grishka and Leyzer-Ber bargain, plead with each other, swear a death oath and smack their hands. They stick close to each, nose to nose in a corner of the floor – here, another ruble! To make it even one more ruble! Also, a stubborn man! A final price! Now they nail down the agreement, saying, "Agreed! You should have good fortune!"

They drink to it, Leyzer-Ber takes the bargain, and goes home drunk with joy.

Meanwhile the summer sun bakes and overheated faces run with sweat. The men go off for a drink. Not a drop of water in the pails. The noise from the tumult is everywhere, Over there a group flocks something amazing. A show booth exposes wild crazies, among them a man-eater, horrible winged animals, witches, and devils. A comedian stands in trousers with spangles of all different colors. He blows a trumpet, calls people inside to see the show – a marionette show. He does somersaults, rolls, he talks to the crowd that stands gaping and stupefied. They are splitting their sides laughing at this antics. Then a scream is heard from the corner of the market – a fight! A gypsy is being beaten and slapped!

Listen to this story: Leyzer-Ber goes to see the horse in a couple of hours and he does not recognize it. Where is the horse? What horse, only a ghost – the ghost should only infect that gypsy!

Where is the stomach? This horse is old, scrawny, skin and bones. See what a gypsy is capable of! He blew up the horse under its skin. He also filed the teeth and gave him some herbs – sneeze-wort in liquor. These herbs warmed up the horse enabling it to stand upright, start its fee – a fire burning!

Now a circle of people forms around a newly arrived person with an accordion, an important person, a musician, who gives a concert! He moves the accordion and it plays, songs. A small monkey all dressed up in human clothes dances on its hind legs, a small girl in pants jumps through a hoop, and a pale, mute young boy walks around on his hands with his feet in the air. The crowd quivers, mad about this amazing display – they have never seen or heard such artistry!

Meanwhile time does not stand still. Hour after hour is passing until, little by little, afternoon shadows are spreading. The market place says a song of praise! Somewhere in a wagon, a tied pig squeals. He is hungry, tired of lying the entire day without food. From a distance his is answered by the cow, tied by the horns, who is also weary of standing such a long time. Fettered roosters wait in the wagons, crowing in anger – such a long time to be separated from their wives!

Now all the animals start complaining. A chorus of calves lying stretched out, with a bleat, coarse and rough

[Page 476]

voices, chimes in. The sun is going down to rest. And the people begin to leave – no more fair!

Hens are walking about the market place searching only for a morsel to put in their mouths. Village cows, voracious eaters, constantly hungry, while walking, grab a handful of straw, a small bit of hay.

And young boys with sticks, sent from home expressly to find bargains, poke in the garbage. Just in case something good was thrown out, they will take it. At home a fire burns in the fireplace. Supper is being cooked. The men are in the synagogue at evening prayers. Night falls – hush, peace and quiet!

Kopyl

by Abraham Jacob Papirna

Translated by Judie Ostroff Goldstein

I do not know if any of my readers have seen my dear hometown Kopyl or if anyone has heard of its existence. But those who have seen it found it impossible to believe that this small, poor shtetl possessed a very special past. In the seventeenth century it was the capitol of Lithuanian princes – the house of Lelevitch-Algerdov.

It is historical fact. You can still see in a cone shape on the mountain, surrounded below by rampart – "the castle" ruins which are still visible, silent witnesses to its past richness and glory.

It is a sad fact that the princely residence in Kopyl became the jail for Slutsk District, Minsk Province. The castle mountain that had once been so lively, full of passion and richness has now become a playground for schoolboys on Saturdays.

It was in this condition that I found Kopyl in 1840, where I was lucky to enter the world.

I met this shtetl of wooden buildings covered with straw or shingles and overgrown with moss. The first time I really looked at it, I was left me with an oppressive feeling, but with time I became used to it and also came to love the beautiful area, the mountain, fruitful fields, meadows and hilly forests.

Kopylites in general were great optimists; even fires rarely broke out there. During my childhood, around 1845, I was a witness to a fire that destroyed half the shtetl, and in 1865 there was another fire that burned down almost the entire shtetl.

What the Kopylites were most proud of was their struggle and defense against Hasidism that spread a "*shulkhan arukh*" way of life.

In this struggle they were the victors. When the Hasidim gathered in their "*shtibl*" to pray or talk together and tell about the great wonders of their sage, the Kopylites immediately took out their drums and beat them loudly with venom so the Hasidim could not pray or talk. That is how the Kopylites stopped them and the *shtibl* remained closed forever.

At that time there were about 3,000 people in Kopyl from three different populations, beliefs and groups: Jews, White Russians and Tatars. The three groups were different from each other in language, customs and beliefs. Even their history represented three different worlds, and still they lived a peaceful, quiet life together.

They were inevitably united as neighbors and in their economic interests. There was no enmity between them because they had no reason to be jealous of one another. It was difficult for all them to make a living, and because their businesses were different, there was no competition between them. The groups communicated by fulfilling the needs of each other and paying for these services.

The Jews, who made of up the majority of the population, were storekeepers, selling bread, wood, flax, and various other products that they would buy in the fall from the peasants at the market.

During the winter they traveled by sled to Stoybts on the Nieman to sell their products to the rich merchants who would then send them on to Konigsberg and Memel. All the storekeepers and bread sellers dealt in

[Page 477]

small sums of money because there was not a large source of money in Kopyl. Thus, there were a lot of traders, and the competition between them was fierce.

Others were busy selling beverages and tavern fare. Some were wagon drivers, teachers, and artisans. There were a large number of artisans. Many of them could not find work in the shtetl so they traveled to the villages and worked there.

There were about fifteen Tatar families in the shtetl. They were gardeners. They peacefully did their work, were by nature clean, and stuck close to the Jews. The White Russians worked in the fields and as weavers.

The shtetl and surrounding area then belonged to Count Wittgenstein, Prince Radziwill's heir, and all the houses stood on royal land. So, as the income from working the fields was not sufficient to live on, the Christians took jobs during the winter weaving white linen that was needed and used by Jewish women. Jewish merchants ordered the goods, furnished the raw material, paid the workers weekly, and sold it at the fair in Zelva. Kopyl linen and especially "Kopyl veil" were famous and renown in the Lithuanian market places.

The above-mentioned groups settled separately from each other:

Christians and Muslims were on the side streets on and behind the mountain. The Jews took the best part of the shtetl on the highest part of the mountain where the marketplace was located. This included the street where the synagogue courtyard was located. All the special Jewish religious and community institutions were there. Occupying such a respected place with its large Jewish population who carried on such lively commerce, Kopyl gave the impression of a clean Jewish community.

Religious and Community Institutions

The marketplace and the synagogue courtyard-the two Kopyl main centers-were complete opposites in their activities. In the synagogue courtyard a Kopylite felt a heavy sense of religious obligation.

Leywik Feker and his wife Roza

There spirits were calmed. At the marketplace that same Kopylite looked for work and food for the family. Many Jewish institutions were located in the Synagogue courtyard, too many for such a small, poor community. The Christians had one church, but the Jews had four synagogues in the courtyard: the *groyse shul* [the Great Synagogue], a *besmedresh* [house of study, synagogue, meeting hall], the Kloyz [prayer house] and a Tailor's *shul*.

The Synagogue courtyard was in the old style. The walls were fantastically painted with symbolic figures taken from the chapters of the *Tanakh* [Old Testament, Five Books of Moses]. The cemetery was located right at the *shul*. In the *shul* one would find the highly esteemed Ber'ke *Chazan* [Cantor], tall, handsome, with a black beard, black eyes, and a sweet, sonorous voice. As his salary did not provide a living wage, he worked as a *shochet* [ritual slaughterer]. He also had a distinctive calligrapher's handwriting and was knowledgeable in Jewish religious and State law. Thus he also served as a "writer." People would turn to him to have written various *proshenyes* [petitions], contracts and wills. He was responsible for writing about people and events in Kopyl's *Pinkus* [Jewish community record book of important events].

The *besmedresh* was used for prayer, mainly by the middle class. The *besmedresh* was also used as a general meeting hall, as the *Talmud Torah* [a school, free of charge, for orphans] and "*kootoozke*" [jail], with iron doors and iron bars on the windows. In this building "recruits" were held under guard until they were sent to provincial capitals as soldiers.

Not far from the *besmedresh*, in the shul courtyard was the rabbi's house, always open to everybody. Men and women would come here to have questions about rituals clarified. Others came for advice or with accusations. As Kopyl did not have a courthouse, the Christians took care of their own differences

[Page 478]

with fistfights or made peace in the tavern over a drink. But all Jewish money and family conflicts, as well as other business, was taken care of through the rabbi's court of justice. Everyone had full confidence in the rabbi's court, even Christians in their conflicts with Jews. The rabbi heard the accuser and sent his beadle to call the accused. This person would come immediately (nobody refused to come). Both sides sat down at the table and gave their accounts. A short time later the decision was given, and it was carried out without the help of the police. The rabbi's authority was that strong.

The *kloyz* was the only stone building in the shtetl and served also as a prayer house for Kopyl's scholars, Orthodox Jews, and philanthropists. These were honest Jews, with strong principles who kept their word and were respected by the townspeople. Dressed in black satin *kapotes* [long, black coats worn by Orthodox Jews in Poland] with collars and *shtreimels* [round fur hats worn by Orthodox Jews] on their heads, they made a great impression on everyone. They were known as the "handsome, silk men."

The *kloyz* was used as a sort of reading room, or a school for grown young men, where they, leaving all business and worries to their wives, were busy after morning prayers or after evening services. Each one was busy either with a page of *gemore* [the part of the Talmud that comments on the *Mishnah*] with a chapter of *mishnayes*[six volume set of the Mishnah which is post biblical laws and rabbinic discussions of the 2nd century B.C. and forms part of the Talmud], or with an *Ein Yankev* [well-known collection of stories from the Talmud]. The *kloyz* also served as a sort of club: The men would gather around the oven to discuss everything: religion, world affairs, politics and personal questions.

The Men of the Kloyz

I can still see them. Reb Chaim'ke is standing right there and with him are his four brothers – men of property, bosses in the marketplace and aristocrats, relatives of the Iventsiskes – rich men. First among them is Reb Chaim'ke, a man whose appearance does not make much of an impression. But he is a G-d-fearing man, a man of prayer. He prayed quietly, but cried, moaned and shed tears. He was called "the Great Weeper." Thanks to his qualities and crying he was selected as one of the community leaders.

At first the Kopylites were afraid that, because of his good-heartedness, Reb Chaim'ke would not be able to lead a government that demanded strength and, in certain cases, ruthlessness. But their fears were unfounded. Reb Chaim'ke took the government in hand, and, when necessary he set aside his politeness and became stronger and more heartless.

Also standing there at the eastern wall is a tall man with a lined face and silver hair. He is my uncle, *Reb* Layzer'ke the son of my late grandfather, Rabbi Ziskind who had been a rabbi in Kopyl. My uncle inherited his father's *shtreimel*, fox coat, orthodoxy, and his great knowledge of *Talmud*. At earning a living, he was good for nothing. He served as a judge in the rabbinic court, was a teacher, and in certain circumstances also a marriage broker. But from all these professions, he did not see many blessings. He appeared skinny and pale, but held his head high, and his eyes shone with pride with the knowledge that he fulfilled his religious duties honestly. But he grieved and his voice was full of tension, so tormented was he by "Jewish pain" – in a word his troubles poured out while he prayed.

He prayed, screamed, and clapped his hands making the bitter sound of protest. In his prayers I always heard: "Truthfully, My G-d, what do you do in your world? You offered your Torah to the seventy peoples of the world and none of them wanted to take on such a burden; but we willingly agreed and carry out the sacred six hundred thirteen laws and thousands of other oral commandments – where's the reward for all this? Like sheep we are led to the slaughter – where is justice?"

My poor uncle! He never made peace with the Diaspora.

Reb Leyb'ke *ha-Kodesh* [the holy man], a man of medium height, with a blond beard, a yellow complexion and a high forehead, at the top of which was a knob. He specialty was Kabbalah [a Jewish mystical philosophy] and his favorite book was the *Zokhar* [holiest, mystical book of *Kabbalah*] in which he was always searching to learn the hidden secrets of the Torah and raise the level of his wonderful riches.

About anxiety, Reb Leyb'ke knew nothing. He owned his own house on the market place and his wife was a wonderful, capable woman: she discovered a drink of an indefinite color and the taste-not quite beer, not quite kvass [a fermented drink]. The Kopylites called it *"unter beer"* [under beer]. The Kopylites knew him as a generous man. On *Shabes*, after a salty, satisfying lunch, long lines of men, women and children went to Leybke's house to refresh themselves with this famous drink.

[Page 479]

Leybke's wife did not work on *Shabes*, but allowed everyone to ladle from the barrel without measuring how much each one had taken. The price was well known: a *groschen* [penny] for each portion-no money changed hands. Everyone was known and was given credit. Everybody paid. This is why Leybke was able to give his time to *Kabbalah*. Kopylites did not think his undertaking was important and many laughed at him.

The keen minded Nach Hasles gave him the name *"ha-Kodesh"* and Leybke waited for an event when everyone would be convinced of his wonderful, sacred, secret craft. It came about in 1853 during the war with Turkey and the Crimea, a difficult, bitter time. Taxes were demanded with merciless strictness. Military divisions passing through the shtetl would throw people out of their houses and take it over. Men were often drafted into the army. In truth, they were captured. Then Leybke put his heart into searching for the *"ketz"* [the end of time, messiah's coming]. And he found it in Psalms 4th verse chapter 126, "Like streams [returning] to the Negev desert"-according to the first letters: after the death of Alexander Pavlowitz, Constantine will reign several days. During the days of Nicholas redemption will come.

Leybke's discovery spread throughout Lithuania and people waited with joy for redemption. But the joy did not last long. That year Nicholas I died and Leybke's *"ketz"* came to naught. Beaten, embittered and disappointed with himself, he died shortly thereafter.

Close by is Reb Leyzor Yankel, a tall man with long hands, who nature insulted by not giving him a beard. He would nibble, tear and pinch his chin, in vain. Despite his efforts there was no sign of a beard. Therefore he had long, thick ear-locks that he would put in his mouth and chew especially when he was thinking or studying. A sagacious man, he knew how to move mountains, turn white into black and black into white. His brain worked well. He knew that his accomplishments had no real significance. It was art for the sake of art. Reb Leyzor Yankel was an artist, a painter who lived in the Talmudic sea and built castles in the sky.

The *"Kloyz"* Youngsters

The *Kloyz* also served as the high school where the best students from the shtetl's grade schools received a thorough education in Talmud and Rabbinic literature. At the start of the 50th year, two young boys, Sholem and Shlomo, drew attention. They gave themselves full time to studying *Tanach* [Five Books of Moses] with commentaries. Studying a book such as the *Tanach* turned out to be a waste of time. One of the "lovers" of *Tanach*, Sholem, a tall young boy, was fated to become one of the best representatives of modern Hebrew and Yiddish literature, known by the pseudonym "Mendele Mocher Sforim".

Unmarried young men and those living away from their wives in order to study also studied in the *Kloyz*. When a young man appeared with a bundle on his shoulder, he would be surrounded, made welcome and provided with "days." [Students from other towns would eat in private homes, one day here, one day there, but generally only a few days a week.] When a young man had a place to eat, enough candles and books, a place to sleep in the *kloyz* on a hard bench, what else could he want?

They studied aloud and diligently, with great success.

The young men lived peaceably together and helped each other.

When a dispute broke out, a sort of fight about the meaning of something, or a course of debate in Talmud and in commentaries; it would start quietly and then became a tumult. Every debater had to show his brilliance, quickness, dialectic, logic, even sophism. Others joined the dispute, taking one side or the other. In one word: it was transformed into a war between two sides. It became noisy and tumultuous; seeing the chance of victory, people quickly changed from one side to the other, until one of the debaters gave in and were beaten by his opponent's arguments.

The yeshiva young men who were not Kopyl residents sooner or later married Kopyl daughters, and became sons-in-law for Kopylites. They served as the nucleus of the scholars. These young men, furnished with "kest" [room and board provided by the father-in-law so that the son-in-law could continue studying] at their father in-law's home, would often have to search for a position as a rabbi, a Hebrew teacher, or other religious profession in distant regions (in Podolia, Volyn, Novorosaysk region) where the knowledge of Talmud was not wide spread.

Community and Private Libraries

In order to meet the needs of so many keen minds and various tastes, there was a large, rich library in the Kopyl *kloyz*. Along with the *Talmud*, with the codex and rabbinic books, there were also books on *Kabbala*, philosophy (*Moyra Nevuhim* [Guidebook for the Perplexed] by Maimonides (Rambam), "*Kuzani*" [an important philosophical book by Reb Yehuda HaLevi], "*Ikorim*" ["Principles"], "*Shalsheles Ha-kobolla*" ["Chain of the Received Wisdom"], and "Paths of the Upright." Books concerning History were also there, such as: "*Seyder Hadoros*" [The Order of Generations], "Josephus," "*Shalsheles Hakabballah*" and others.

[Page 480]

But the library did not have modern literature such as the "Berliner" which originated in the 18th century in Berlin, and continued after in Galicia and in Russia. This was considered a forbidden book, but it soon arrived in Kopyl secretly smuggled in.

In Kopyl there were a lot of small, private libraries. Everyone had procured books according to their tastes. A bookcase with a full set of Shas [six books that make up a set of *Talmud*], bound in red leather beautified every Jewish house like diamonds and earrings for a wife. In case of need, it could be sold, or pawned. If worse came to worst, it could be used as a daughter's dowry.

The women had their own libraries for spiritual development and their particular needs. These were mainly Yiddish books, as women were not taught Hebrew. Mostly, these were books of a religious nature such as the "*Tzenerene*", the Five Books of Moses with legends [translated into Yiddish], "Menoyres Hamoer" [Bright Candlesticks], instructive stories from *Agadah* [ethical part of the Talmud] and *Midrash* [body of post-Talmudic literature of Biblical exegesis]. There were also books of a historical nature such as "*Gdules Yosef.*"

There were also secular books, translated from other languages, such as "*Bobe Mayse*" (Bava Karalevitz), "Thousand and One Nights" etc. In forty years there were from time to time various biographies and humorous stories by talented writers such as the father of the new Jewish literature A. A. Dick, a strong supporter of Hebrew literature. Thanks to Dick, this literature was available to a lot of readers. At the beginning the readers were simple Jews and women, earnest Jews, with a smile they would think of their wives and daughters who pursued "funny stories", but the youngsters soon understood that the writer did not mean to be only funny and read them with interest.

Erudite Kopylites were not friendly with the poor-the artisans, coachmen, etc. A learned Kopylite would not arrange a marriage with an artisan for such a thing would have brought shame to the family.

I would often hear my mother say, "Thank God there aren't any rogues or artisans in our family."

The aristocrats had all the respected positions and places in the synagogue, leaving the bank bench near the door for the common folk. The artisans left and built a separate building and felt exactly like the aristocrats: they bought *Torah* scrolls, had their own trustees and their own "rabbi" who explained and taught them. Unfortunately the richer aristocratic tailors took over the management of the *shul* and insulted their fellow tradesmen and gave them lesser seats. This brought about quarrels and even fights. So the latter had to search for another place to pray.

The *Shul-Klapper*, the Bathhouse, and Finke the Bath Attendant

Yudel the "*Shul-klapper* called everyone to *shul* for prayers in the morning. He would go around with hammer in hand and knock twice at every Jewish house. This was the sign that it was time to pray. Whenever, God forbid, somebody died, he would let everyone know by knocking three times. On *Shabes* he would go around the shtetl and call out with a ringing voice: "Jews, go to *shul*!" Friday at noon he would call out with the same voice "Jews, to the bath!" For penitential prayers it was his custom to knock and pull the shutters until he was convinced that somebody was up.

Yudel was a shoemaker and lived from his labor; he did not receive a salary from the community. Even the hammer that was usually used to hammer nails into boots belonged to him. The only use and right Yudel had was to take part in weddings, betrothals, circumcisions and to gather donations for tasteful purposes. They made allowances for Yudel because of his sedateness, his strong hands and feet, and his pleasant voice.

Having the same person call the men to pray and bathe gave the bathhouse status. It was located in the same place as the *mikvah* [ritual bath used by women], which gave the place a religious character. Also for the men it was customary to take a steam bath and wash every Friday in preparation for welcoming the Sabbath Queen.

The Kopyl bathhouse was the property of the community and was rented for ten Polish zlotys (one ruble and 50 kopecks). This money paid the rabbi's salary. It was an old, blackened, bent building, with many posts and supports and always looked as if it was about to collapse. As it wanted to draw importance from its existence, it continued, during my twenty years in Kopyl, aside from Fridays and *Shabes*, to serve as a

[Page 481]

candle factory, where Finke the bath attendant made cheap candles. It also served as the "almshouse" for the poor, old, and sick, and also as a place to sleep for poor travelers. The price for a bath was set at two Polish groschen per person, a high price, but Kopylites were not stingy and as soon as they heard the *klapper's* voice shouting "Jews, to the bathhouse!" they all left their businesses and went to bathe.

On Friday Kopyl wives did not feed their husband until sundown. This was done, first of all, so that the husbands would have a proper appetite at dinner *shabes* evening. Secondly and mainly, the wives did not have the time. From Thursday on, with the daughters, the women toiled, without sleeping the entire night. Not by choice, but from fear that they would not have finished preparing by sundown. The women were nervous and edgy, so the men thought it would be smarter and better to be somewhere else and not underfoot. And the best place for them to be was the bathhouse. And they stayed there until dusk, steamed, washed, whipped themselves and each other with brooms and at intervals sat on the benches - aristocrats in front and the common people behind, just as in shul. They talked about politics, the news of the day, and tried to be witty and smart. My uncle, Reb Layzer'ke, after washing would go to the barber-surgeon's space where he had his head shaved and had cut, cupping glasses put on his head and back. Although Reb Layzer'ke was white as a sheet, he was convinced that one of the causes of his illness (there were seven in all) was in his blood. In any case he liked to have his blood let. Twice a month he would go through this. According to his custom, not only was water poured at the bathhouse, but also blood.

Finke the bath attendant was a versatile, distinguished man. Besides being the bath attendant he was the manager of the candle factory, the gravedigger and a *badkhn* [entertainer at a wedding, specializing in humorous and sentimental semi-improvised rhymes]. He was an excellent *badkhn*. Before a young couple was led to the *chuppah* [wedding canopy] he told them about ethics and indicated the important significance of their new life. He also told them that they must not devote themselves to joy and comfort because life is a temporary matter. When the young couples were orphans, he did not forget to remind them about their dead parents, indicating that a person is like a flower in the field. Today it grows, blooms and tomorrow-see, it is withered!. He said this with feeling and everyone was in tears.

But when the couple and the guests sat down at the table full of food and drink, Finke changed and became a joker and a juggler. He sought to bring joy, to amuse everyone, and drinking one glass after another, he was in ecstasy, sang folk songs, told happy stories, anecdotes, jokes, epigrams, and puns. He cracked jokes about the "silk men," the rich, and the rabbis, and all this was expressed in verse. With his hands he divided his face in two. One side laughed, the other cried; showing his two professions as *badkhn* and gravedigger.

The Administration

All management functions were in the hands of the Police Commissioner, Sheriff Zdroyevsky, who ruled over Kopyl and surrounding area for more than ten years.

There was no other authority in Kopyl, which was far from the beaten path, other than the Police Commissioner. The higher authorities did not look into anything there. The character of the ruler was independent. Under this kind of authority it was not possible to differentiate "the saddened population," especially for the Jews. Expressed by the noted A.M. Dik: "Every Jew can go the hospital, put on a gown, lie in bed-and the doctor will examine him and certainly find something wrong with him. In the same way a policeman can collar him and drag him to the District, and they will find out that the Jew had committed some offense." In Russia there were many laws and for Jews many more.

These were not good times-the era of Nicholai's evil decrees, one after the other, terrifying and unbearable.

Zdroyevsky, the Police Commissioner, was tall, and had broad shoulders. He spoke Polish and bad Russian, and he would scold mainly in Russian and only in a correct manner. The Kopylites were convinced that the devil was not as terrible as men made him out to be. One morning a drum was heard at the market place, which meant a new evil decree. The Police Commissioner arrived and announced that Jews must dress in ordinary clothing. They must not wear beards and ear-locks. The women are not allowed to shave their head and wear wigs.

[Page 482]

The Jews claimed that these were conversion decrees. They prayed, decreed a fast, but, alas, without success. The rural police would catch prominent Jews, drag them to the district police and without ceremony would cut up their *kapotes*, shave their beards, and cut their ear-locks to the root. Bonnets and wigs were torn off respectable women in the street.

A delegation presented itself to the Police Commissioner and he put a stop to this business.

The rural police ceased to rage. For those who had their *kapotes* cut up, they had new ones made and the beards, ear-locks grew with time, and everything was as it was before. The Police Commissioner lived in harmony with the Jews. On *Shabes* he would go to someone's house to drink a couple of glasses of wine or *schnapps*, snack on fish, and never said no to a Jewish cholent [casserole of meat, potatoes and vegetables served on the Sabbath, kept warm overnight in the baker's oven].

He did not pay particular attention to the business of hygiene and building plans. People built as they wished and where they desired. The slaughterhouse was located in the center of the market place. Terrible bellowing was heard from the animals being slaughtered. Blood flowed and terrible odors spread and remained in the air until it rained and the smells were carried away with the storm water.

The road from Kopyl to Slutsk was a difficult one when coming down the mountain. On rainy days there were terrible obstacles. The drivers had to keep their heads when going to the city with wagons. In order to descend, men had to be very careful and courageous. The peasants would often break their wagons and injure the horses. This hazard was accepted as a natural thing, just like thunder and lightening or an earthquake. There was nothing they could do-they were helpless.

The investigator is coming to the shtetl. His visit brings fear to everyone. Only the Police Commissioner is advised of his arrival. A storekeeper says: "Why are you terrified, what are you afraid of? We do not deal in contraband. A big deal-an investigator!" Reb Chaim'ke looks at him, grabs him by the beard and yells: "And this is not contraband?"

In the meantime Zdroyevsky tries to restore calm. The investigator is a good friend, even a distant relative. He will go easy and it will not be expensive. He advises them not to look him in the eyes.

On the day the investigator arrived, there were only young women in the stores and streets. The older Jews were sitting at home, and the young children were not allowed out from school. The investigator, accompanied by the Police Commissioner, visited the stores. He ate a good lunch at the Police Commissioner's in the company of the priest and clergy. The Jewish representative was Reb Chaim'ke. On the second day the investigator left and the storm was over.

"Six Hebrew Words".
Kahal, Tributes, Monopoly, Excommunication

The duty of the Kahal [Jewish Community Council] was to take care of religious affairs and be the go-between for the community with the government. During my time, the affairs of the first part were carried out without any help from the community, according to long standing customs. They were in charge of registration and especially the books of the population, collecting taxes, giving them to the government, and furnishing recruits.

The Jewish population in Kopyl was very poor. Artisans and peddlers worked with a capitol of 50 to 100 rubles and barely made a living. Many residents left for other places to search for work and left behind the family at the mercy of God and help from goodhearted people. Forty or fifty lucky people (those who were counted among Kopyl's bosses, storekeepers, who worked with 500 to 1000 rubles) had to carry not only the expenses for all the community institutions but also had to help the poor. In all the Lithuanian Jewish communities around 20% of the population were poverty stricken. They had to pay all the taxes for the religious and community institutions. There were many more taxes than just those for the general government. Provincial and state taxes were levied, especially for Jews, on items like candles and boilers. The military recruits ate up a lot of money. It was necessary to support the secret agents and guards and feed the recruits until they were turned over to the military. The *Kahal* was always in need of money. Community and religious expenses were covered by the meat tax on kosher meat, but it was never sufficient, so the *Kahal* had a monopoly on various products such as candles or yeast and this brought in a certain yearly income.

In order to enforce local buying, if people got their products from other villages it meant excommunication.

The text of the excommunication was terrifying. The offender was cursed in this world and in every world, separated from the community and the synagogue. The excommunication was strong and terrible.

[Page 483]

It was forbidden to have any contact with an excommunicated person, and he could not receive help. The ban on a certain person was announced in the synagogue with extraordinary ardor. The rabbi, surrounded by his helpers, would make the announcement near the Holy Ark from which the Torah scrolls had been brought out. Black wax candles were burned and the *shofar* [ram's horn] was blown.

The Rabbis of Kopyl

Kopyl's rabbis were respected in Lithuania and renowned throughout the region, thanks to the great rabbi Yom-Tov Lipman (the last quarter of the 18th century), the grandson of the famous commentator Yom Tov.

A grandson printed Rabbi Lipman's remarks on the Talmud with the title "Holy Commentaries" or "Holy Yom Tov." It was very popular in the rabbinic world.

During his life Reb Yom Tov did not publish his interpretations and did not care to compete for a rabbinate in one of the better, first class communities in Lithuania. He spent his entire life serving the poor community of Kopyl.

He gave his entire being over to the study of Torah, far from worldly pleasures. He would be home only on *Shabes* and holidays. The rest of the time he spent in the *kloyz* in a corner behind the oven (that remained "holy and historic" from that time on). He ate, slept, studied, took care of religious and community affairs and wrote his interpretations there.

According to his grandson and the Kapulier Pinkus:

After the death of "the last" Vilna Rabbi, Rabbi Shmuel, the Vilna *Kehilla* [Jewish Community Council] selected Reb Yom Tov as the next Vilna rabbi. A group of well-known Vilners came to Kopyl with the news that he had been chosen as the Vilna rabbi. Arriving in Kopyl, the delegation did not meet him in the rabbi's house. The rabbi's wife did not want to call him in order not to disturb his studies. The messengers had to wait until *Shabes* when *Reb* Yom Tov would be at home.

Having found out what the Vilners wanted, Rabbi Yom Tov called a meeting after *Shabes* with the Kopylites and let them know that his salary of 35 groschen a week was not enough. In order to stay he would need a small raise or he would have to go to Vilna. This information grieved the Kopylites. On one hand, it would hurt them to be separated from their great rabbi, and on the other hand, where would they find the money to give the rabbi a raise?

As both sides were dear to each other, they found a solution. The rabbi was given an increase of one and a half groschen and he stayed in Kopyl.

Not long after his death-as written in the Pinkas-Reb Yosele Peimer was invited to be a Rabbi in Slutsk. He was known as Rabbi Yosele Slutsker.

On the way to Slutsk, he spent a *Shabes* in Kopyl where he heard about one of Rabbi Yom Tov Lipman's pronouncements. He was astonished by Rabbi Yom Tov's profound knowledge and wisdom. Rabbi Yosele said that if in Kopyl, almost a suburb of Slutsk, there is such a prominent learned man, he would not dare be a rabbi in Slutsk. When he was told that Rabbi Yom Tov was already dead, Reb Yosele remarked: "In that case I will go to Slutsk. I am not afraid of the dead."

The rabbinical chair, after Rabbi Yom Tov Lipman's death was taken over by Rabbi Ber, who was greatly esteemed by the Kopylites for his ideas and his holy way of living. He was taken with the *Rambam* and led his life according to that codex, not taking any notice of the recent rabbinic authorities. Something amazing happened after his death. Mendelssohn's writings were found in his library and so a mystery remained for the Kopyl Jews.

During his youth, Rabbi Ber was a private teacher of the well-known Ivanitsker, the rich man Shmuel Eliasberg, a fervent follower of Rabbi Moshe Ben Poress, known by the name Menashe Ilier (his book "Elpi Menashe" was burnt in the Vilna synagogue courtyeard).

In Eliasberg's home Rabbi Ber was absorbed in the Torah by the Reformers. On becoming the Kopyl rabbi, he held strongly to the morals of Rabbi Menashe in his personal life and endeavored to alleviate the "yoke of the law." As for his own perspective about many areas of religious life, he discussed this only with his young students.

Reb Ber's students, who later were employed throughout Lithuania as rabbis, Hebrew teachers, etc., spread his teachings everywhere. Kopylites were suspicious of them, calling them Rabbi Ber's "society."

After his death my grandfather, Rabbi Ziskind, took over the rabbinate. As if he were still alive, I see this old, wise man standing in front of me. The entire time he struggled to throw off the appearance of the Kopyl rabbi and lived the poor life of an ordinary Kopylite.

In his youth my grandfather was a businessman and gave most of his time to studying Torah. The community paid attention to him and he was greatly esteemed. After Rabbi Ber died, he was invited to take over the rabbinate

[Page 484]

and did not change his lifestyle. He was friendly with everyone, did not lecture anyone, and sought only the good in everyone. He was very tolerant when it came to beliefs.

Rabbi Ziskind's oldest son-in-law, Rabbi Elia Goldberg (later the Bobruisk rabbi), distinguished himself with his ideas. For several years he lived in Vilna, without his wife in order to study, and studied with the *Gaon's* students. When he returned to Kopyl, everyone remarked that he had changed. First of all he had given a lot of time to studying "*musar*" and secondly he had brought an atlas written in German from Vilna, which he loved to look at. It seemed strange, but there was nothing suspicious about his religiosity. However, a scandal quickly broke out.

Yom Kippur, when Kopyl Jews sat in the synagogue and prayed, Reb Elia left the *kloyz* and did not return. The young men went looking for him. They searched a long time and finally found him at the "poor house" (where the sick lived).

There stood Reb Elienke. He chopped wood and put it in the oven and cooked soup for the sick. One can imagine the how surprised these people were. They called him an apostate, left quickly to go back to the *kloyz* and told what they had seen. The last person to hear about it said: "It is a shame that the young people know better than their elders about how to spend a holy day!" Rabbi Ziskind's authority worked and calmed everybody down. They did not talk about and discuss this for long.

(Translated from Russian to Yiddish by Nach)

[Page 484]

From Kapulie to Slutsk

by Joseph Morgenshtern, Cleveland

Translated by Judie Ostroff Goldstein

For a young Jewish boy who had to eat at strangers' tables in his own hometown because his hard stepfather did not want to feed his wife's children, going to the nearby city Slutsk with its yeshivas was very attractive.

There would be "*essen teg*" [eating days, free board by days in several houses] at strangers' tables, only they would not be in Kopyl where everyone knew me, but in Slutsk where all the young boys who came to study from far off towns were doing the same.

Besides, Slutsk was famous for its yeshivas. I hoped that in Slutsk my studies would open possibilities for me.

I traveled the forty *versts* [former Russian measure of distance, about .66 of a mile] from Kopyl to Slutsk with my friend Noach, a boy my age. We traveled by wagon, crushed in with other passengers who were traveling to Slutsk on business. The scenery over the forty *versts* was beautiful but it is not necessary for me to describe it because our great "*zayde*" [grandfather], Mendele has already described it so masterfully in his book. I will immediately continue with the Slutsk situation and my personal survival there.

My friend Nach and I reached the *kloyz* [study house] together.

The *kloyz* was renown. It was not only a yeshiva where young men rocked over an open *gemore* [Hebrew gemore, part of the Talmud that comments on the *Mishnah* (post-biblical laws and rabbinical discussions of the 2nd century B.C.E.)] night and day. It was also a sort of reserve station for all those who needed a place to lay their heads.

In order to be provided with "days" people had to come to Reb Israel who was in charge of the accounts for all the householders who had given certain days to the yeshiva boys from other towns. The yeshiva boys did not get "days" from *Reb* Israel just like that – without any reason.

For every "day" that Reb Israel granted, for the "semester" the yeshiva boy had to pay him fifty kopecks in cash. In order for a student to be given all seven days of the week for the semester, he had to pay Reb Israel a ruble and five kopecks. And when a boy did not possess such a sum, nothing good came of it.

Therefore a boy that had a little cash was able to buy more than seven days.

So, the story was that not every day was an eating day. There were also some that we, the young boys, called "*mezumene*" [cash, money].

The latter were at women's stores who did not have the time to prepare a meal at home for the yeshiva boys, so they received the boys in the store and gave them several kopecks with which to buy their food.

With these "days" Reb Israel had a good business. I was able to get nine "days". Seven "eating" and two cash. The latter two that cost thirty kopecks gave us better value for the money.

[Page 485]

Once in a while there was a little trouble. This would happen when a storekeeper decided to go home and cook a meal for the family and for the yeshiva boy. In such a case the student ate two meals and consoled himself by praying twice that day, for which he would obtain double merit in the world to come.

Sleeping in the *kloyz* was not bad when there were no nuisances with the crazies.

There were a lot of crazies in Slutsk who would get together there from the entire area. They could be seen in the streets, heard in the market place cursing the bosses, and at night at least one of them found a resting place in the *kloyz*.

It was a difficult semester for me in Slutsk. I was drowning in the dark, so before the term finished I returned to Kopyl.

At that time I became a Bar Mitzvah boy and suddenly felt a sense of shame towards eating "days." Is this what one is supposed to do with one's time? So I put an end to it. I went to my Uncle Shimon, who had an iron store at the market place and who could use my help. The main thing was that I began to earn my daily bread by working every day in my uncle's iron store, but I hadn't counted on my Aunt Brayna:

During the week you work for your food, but on *Shabes* you do not work so why should I feed you? So, Aunt Brayna was right and I celebrated Sabbaths in hunger.

In the evening hours I studied in the *besmedresh* [house of study, synagogue, meeting hall] under the supervision of Reb Shlomo Shvitzitzer.

Reb Shlomo Shvitzitzer was a modern Jew. When he studied a page of *gemore* with us poor boys his voice was loud, but as soon as he finished the lesson, nobody heard a sound from him, as if he was a mute.

And not only did he lose his voice, but he carried himself with a great sorrow as one who has been left defeated. He was tall and thin and wandered around alone like a stranger. For some time I was unable to understand what the reason was and felt bad for him.

People called him Shvitzitzer because he came to Kopyl from the nearby village of Shvizit where he had lived for a long time with his wife, four sons and an only daughter. He was a tenant farmer in the villages.

Being a Jewish scholar he taught his children *Yiddishkeit* [Judaism] and was happy when a Jew strayed to him and he was able to perform a good deed by giving him a place to stay. On holidays he came to the shtetl just like all the tenant farmers in the area. He hoped, God willing, to arrange marriages for his children as God commanded. But suddenly a great misfortune struck, and it broke him entirely.

His only daughter, who was the apple of his eye, fell in love with a neighboring peasant's son and there was no saving her. He left Shvizit with the family and settled in the Kopyl *besmedresh* when a priest married his daughter to the man she loved in church. To this day I cannot forget Reb Shlomo Shvitzitzer.

Kopyl Gets Other Faces

One began to see young men wearing Russian shirts and hats in the streets of Kopyl. Their language was a juicy Yiddish – also entirely different.

These young men had been brought from other places, mostly from Bialystok, for Fayvel Riplis's tannery that at that time grew to be a large enterprise.

The air in Kopyl was full of words like "Socialism", "strike", "bourgeois" and others. There were songs like *"Shvester un Brider"* ["Sisters and Brothers"], *" Az es falt, falt der Bester "* [It so happens, the best fall] and *" Baruch Shulman Der Groyser Held "* [Baruch Shulman the Great Hero]. In short, Kopyl had suddenly and unnoticed been given a good shaking.

I felt a strong pull towards Zionist ideals.

At the same time with the new speeches and songs from the young men who were brought to Kopyl, one also heard speeches and songs about Israel.

The main speaker was the Jewish apothecary in Kopyl who wrote for the daily Hebrew newspaper from Vilna "HaZman." Every day I ran to him to see leaving for Israel was possible.

The subject of Israel for Jews who would return there from Kopyl, from Slutsk and from other towns and villages captured my young heart. So I jointed a youth group that collected money for Zionism.

We said that they should know that we, poor Jews, also stood with them.

At that time we heard the news that there would be a Zionist meeting in Minsk. The city of Minsk grew in my eyes greatly and mightily and it was my dream to go there.

A small matter, Minsk! Minsk began to seem like the greatest center in the world.

[Page 486]

All the ideals of Zionism and also Socialism were bubbling up there.

It was said that in Minsk, Jewish sons and daughters refused riches that their rich parents possessed. They went off to fight for the people and for a better and freer world in the form of glory and purity that for me was embodied in the form of the famous revolutionary Gershony.

I was drawn to the large Minsk library where books were free for everybody. It was what had drawn me to Minsk and I began to make plans to reach Minsk.

[Page 486]

Folklore

Translated by Judie Ostroff Goldstein

In Kopyl there was a rich Jew, Reb Isser. He was the respectable man in the shtetl and a very powerful.

Once the shtetl had a difference of opinion with the rabbi. *Reb* Isser said to the rabbi: You are lucky rabbi, that for us you have no face, otherwise I would slap it…

* * *

Reb Meshel, who worked at the Kopyl school, translated a chapter of Joshua which in Hebrew says: "Cry with full throat, without restraint; raise your voice like a ram's horn! Declare to My people their transgression, To the House of Jacob their sin." His translation read: "Call in the barn, you should not be dark like a *shofar* [ram's horn], Warn My people unexpectedly-their transgression."

He does not want Jews, God forbid, To Tell Lies

When Rabbi Yudelevitch was rabbi in Kopyl, things were not always peaceful between him and the city bosses. He had no respect for wrongdoers and was not afraid to tell them off. The bosses did not keep silent and they tried to find fault with him and once they made a serious allegation about the rabbi.

Once, before Passover, the rabbi, with the alms collector, went out to collect "wheat money" [contributions for providing the poor with Passover *matzah* and cakes]. They went from house to house and from business to business. The Jews gave what they could and from the heart. They gave whatever amount they wanted to and whatever they could afford to give up to a half ruble. The alms collector held a red handkerchief in his hand and whatever amount one had to give, he put into the handkerchief.

They came to a tobacco store in the market place. They went in and the rabbi asked for a package *titun* [an inferior brand of tobacco]. He filled his pipe and told the alms collector to take money from the handkerchief and pay. The alms collector looked at him and did not understand.

"Rabbi, the wheat money?!" "This is for the Kopyl poor Jews who need *matzah* for Passover".

The rabbi gave him a look and said:

"I am ordering you to pay from the charity money. I know the Kopyl bosses. Several of them wish that every week they could earn as many rubles as the rabbi takes from them for "wheat money." So I am ordering you to use this money to pay for my tobacco. I do not want the Kopyl Jews to, God forbid, tell lies. The community sees they are telling the truth. And they should, with the help of the Most High, earn every week a thousand times as much".

As told by Chaim Zaydes

Partisans

Translated by Pamela Russ

Before the war, the Jew Gilczyk was on staff at "*Zagockot*" (government contracting trade company for meat) in Kopulye. After the Germans arrived, he soon ran away into the Rojowska forest and joined a small Russian partisan group of communist activists. Later he became the commander of the Jewish unit "*Zhukow*."

In a very short time there were about 200 men in the unit – 130 Jews and 70 Christians.

In January 1943, his unit already had 11 cannons, 23 automatics, and 136 guns.

Other than the commander Gilczyk, the others who belonged were the Russian Martinov – commissar [Communist political officer]; the head of individual matters – Weiner (Kopulye); chief of staff – a Jewish teacher from the town of Kopulye; commander of the first council – Moishe Fish, a former under–officer in the Polish army; the organizer of the uprising in the Kletzk ghetto; company staff – Maze Ozer.

The Jewish unit *"Zhukow"* (Kopulye region) organized the escape of 170 men from the Swierzhen labor camp into the local forest of the partisans...

(According to "The War of the Jewish Partisans")

Kopulyer Resistance

Right after the Germans chased the Jews into the ghetto, the feeling of rage against the bloody murderers arose. There were about 2,500 Jews imprisoned in the ghetto

[Page 487]

among them a few hundred from the surrounding small towns – Pesocna, Boboyna, and others. The regime was intolerable, and not a single day would pass without murder victims, without the pouring of blood, and terrible screams of pain. Quietly, we began to rejoice when we acquired some weapons and prepared for an armed uprising. It is easy to say – acquiring weapons – as we could have no contact with the outside world! With great personal risk, some weapons managed to be obtained. Elye Peker made a cannon ready. We acquired guns, revolvers, hand grenades. Underground hideouts and tunnels were prepared in many houses. "Double walls" were made wherever possible, such as in chests, where people could hide in moments of danger...

In the ghetto, things were boiling as in a kettle. Scouts from the town already began looking into the forest. The Germans already instinctively sensed something.... In March 1942, suddenly, storm troopers invaded. They selected 1,200 people and locked them into the so–called "cold *Beis Medrash*" [Study Hall]. Here, in the court of the *Beis Medrash*, the first terrible slaughter took place. The wild orgy lasted for three days, and almost all of the 1,200 people were shot. Only eleven young people were able to escape successfully. The fugitives ran through the forest and joined a small partisan unit. They armed themselves and sought to make contact with the remaining Jews in the ghetto. It was decided that when the armed uprising would begin in the ghetto (they had not yet discussed the exact hour and day of the uprising), the partisans would be there to help.

The Jewish partisan detachment meanwhile grew in number and strengthened itself. Who are they, the first eleven Kopulyer partisans? Sosin – a student; Godel Zhurawicki – a lecturer in the Minsk university; Hozberg – a railway worker; Meyer Weiner a shoemaker; Khaim Menaker – an electrical technician; Lyovo Gilczyk – chief of provisions for the Kantor region; and others.

The forest came to life. The Germans began to feel that the brush was burning underfoot. Slowly, the partisans began to remove people from the ghetto.

Very soon, the partisan detachment, under the direction of Gilczyk (the chief of staff was the Kopulyer teacher Itcze Berkowycz), totaled hundreds of armed people, among them many from the surrounding towns and settlements. In the Zhwolker, Lawer, and Starecer forests, there came new partisan detachments. When they united, the detachments strongly beat the German murderers – blew up trains, bridges, arms and provision warehouses, and killed many policemen and other traitors. The German punishment units, in confusion, flew from one forest to another, searching for the partisans who, in real earnest, frightened the fascist command.

In the ghetto, the German vandals instilled a horrifying terror. They did not permit anyone to leave their houses, and every day they took the security men and shot them. In the place of Menashe, whom the Germans madly searched for but could not find (as it later became known, this partisan was a Jewish young man from Poland), they shot 40 Jews from the ghetto.

One day, a special German military detail came into town, armed with cannons and automatics, and with terrible cruelty, they began to liquidate the ghetto, as this was already done in other places. But the Germans encountered what was for them the unexpected – from the attics, the cellars, and ditches, they were met with a hailstorm of bullets. For a long time, they could not get close to many of the Jewish homes.

The courageous and brazen Elye Peker died a heroic death. He barricaded himself in his house, with his wife and mother–in–law, planted a cannon on the roof, and from there, continuously threw fireballs onto the German thugs and police. Wildly enraged, the Germans poured benzene onto Elye Peker's house and set fire to it. By the time the house was engulfed in flames, Elye Peker's family died heroically, and around that house lay 48 dead Germans.

The household of the tailor Zekhariah Kahan met the Germans with a volley of gunshots, and the same for Golder Monus, Moshe Kahan, and others. The Germans moved in barrels of benzene, poured the benzene over the houses, and many heroes of the ghetto were burned to death along with their wives and children. Of the more than 700 houses in Kopulye, more than 500 were burned down.

More than 70 Jews were able to flee into the forests, and to join up with the partisans.

(As told by the partisan Avrohom Ber Szloimowycz, retold by Izak Kahan, *Einkeit* ["Unity"], New York, February 1947.)

In Kopulye, the Jews were shooting at the Germans from their houses. The Kopulyer *shochet* [ritual slaughterer] Meyer Weiner hid in the slaughter–house and later escaped to the partisans, and fought with gun in hand. He died in one of the mass slaughters.

(According to P. Novek, *Morgen Freiheit* ["Tomorrow's Liberty"], March 2, 1947.)

[Page 488]

Romanova
(Lenino, Belarus)
53°03' 27°14'

Translated by Judie Ostroff Goldstein

From Romanova Slutsk is a distance of twenty kilometers in all. There were about two hundred families in the shtetl, mainly peasants, of which about 30 families were Jewish.

Twenty years had already passed since twenty Jewish families had arrived to cultivate Prince Vitenshtein's property.

He rented each Jewish family ten acres of fertile land for a term of six years.

The Jews went out to work in the morning and returned late in the evening, the same as the Christians. Besides properly fertilizing the fields, they saturated the land with their sweat and toil.

The Jews were happy when they had the possibility of buying the fields as private property because the high cost of the yearly rent exhausted them.

A lot of Jews in the surrounding towns were willing to stop peddling in order to feed themselves by farming.

It was necessary to call the rabbis of the small towns together, as well as the town elders. They had to take charge and help thousands of unfortunates while they prepared to farm for their living with the hope of happiness in a new life.

Ish Yehuda Sfra
(*"HaZfira"* number 31, 1880)

Romanova

by Chaim Zeides

Translated by Judie Ostroff Goldstein

As usual, a Jew in Romanova building his *suke* [sukkah, tabernacle erected in celebration of Sukkoth, in which meals are eaten] for the holiday, was already worrying about how he would make it through the winter. Although everyone had a full measure of potatoes, a barrel of sauerkraut, a tub of pickles and a large amount of dried onion. The well to do would also have a couple of bags of white flour to make *challah* [braided egg bread eaten on the Sabbath] and several cords of wood for the winter. Every household, rich and poor, had bread which they baked themselves during the entire week. As usual, families generally ate meat only on *shabes* [the Sabbath]. During the week they were satisfied with a meal called fish potatoes, which meant potatoes without fish.

Romanova was a long way from the railroad. Berl the wagon driver who drove passengers and cargo to Slutsk and back told about marvels, from when he was a soldier and saw a train – wagons traveling without horses…

And then the village policeman came with a government order that Berl must put a bell on the harness. And the village gained pleasure from it; hearing the bell everyone knew that Berl was arriving from Slutsk with various goods.

Chaim the shoemaker lived at the gateway to the shtetl. He was a poor man in every way because the well-to-do Romanova Jews ordered new boots from the surrounding villages. The gentiles wore bast shoes, and only on Sunday to go to church did a gentile put on a pair of boots, so they would last years and years. So, Chaim the shoemaker did not have a lot work and not enough bread to eat his fill. But his wife, Hinda, presented him with a child every year. The sexton of the synagogue would say: *Reb* [Mr.] Chaim, you know, in view of our allotted time on earth, you will have your own *minion* [quorum of ten men required for certain prayers] at home. Chaim would answer: But meanwhile all of them want to eat…

All week long Chaim's family ate more potatoes than bread and buying flour for *Shabes* was as difficult as parting the Red Sea. Hinda worked hard in the gardens and walked to the villages to buy hens and eggs, and still there was not enough to make *shabes*.

One beautiful morning Chaim received a ship's ticket from one of his brothers-in-law. Hinda pawned her bedding and candlesticks so that Chaim could leave.

A short while later Hinda was able to redeem her pawned goods and blessed the candles in her own candlesticks and bought white flour in honor of *Shabes*.

Hinda no long worked and did not walk to the villages. The *melamdim* [plural of *melamed*, teachers in boys' elementary school] charged her tuition each month. She hoped that her Chaim would come home with a fortune. Later she received a letter telling her to sell everything and to come with the children to him. She was not expecting such a problem: Does it mean she must go

[Page 489]

to America, a country without Judaism? Better that Chaim comes back to Romanova. Chaim wrote that she must come and she answered that she could not leave the family and the graves in the cemetery. She received a letter from Chaim saying he would be moving from New York to Brooklyn and she would have difficulty getting his address. This scared Hinda. She could, G-d forbid, become a deserted wife. She went to the Romanova rabbi, Reb Abraham Pinkhus Goldberg, the famous "good Jew". The Romanova rabbi sat day and night studying. All questions were screened by the *rebetzin* [rabbi's wife] so his Torah studies would not be disturbed.

Hinda arrived with swollen eyes and pleaded: she must see the rabbi personally to pour out her troubles to him. Her Chaim writes that he is going to leave New York over the Williamsburg Bridge. She will be a deserted wife! Also she will not go to a country where people work on *shabes* and eat *treif* [non-kosher food].

The rabbi listened to hear and then said: Romanova is very far from New York, so if your husband is traveling further it is then of course a very distant place. According to the law a wife must follow her husband. Secondly, rather than become a deserted wife, it is better that you travel with the children to him. G-d, blessed is he, will light your road. With a broken heart she took leave of her family, acquaintances, and friends and went to the cemetery and had a good cry

Reb Itsche Gites, the *Gemore-melamed* [teacher of the part of the
Talmud commenting on the mishnah] in Romanova.
The picture is from the reign of Nicholas I as teachers had to have
photograph without a hat for their teacher's certificate.

Arriving in America she found out that traveling from New York to Williamsburg cost only two cents. Hinda would often say: I would not have gone to America, if not for advice of the Romanove rabbi.

The grandchildren would joke: If *bobe* [grandmother] Hinda had known how close Williamsburg was to New York, she would not have come here.

How lucky it was that she was afraid of being a deserted wife.

Shmuel Domnitz

Translated by Judie Ostroff Goldstein

A long, crooked street, muddy,
Frogs croak in the ditches,
Jews wander together from afar
To see a healer, not an unusual thing.
A tattered sloping thatched roof.
Walls of knotty logs,
Windowpanes all colors of the rainbow:
Pine splinters stuffed into open spaces.
Damps walls growing moss,
The floor of yellow clay,
Mother is spinning flax
And the spindle sings a slow melody.
With a *yarmulke* [skull cap] and a *talis-koton* [ritual four cornered garment]

Father sits and teaches children,
Over the walls their shadows flicker,
From his students he draws pleasure and beams with joy.

[Page 490]

Shemezeve
(Semezhevo, Belarus)
52°57' 27°00'

Shemezeve

by Sonia Kazhdan-Eisenson (Los Angeles)

Translated by Ronni Kern

In my village of Shemezeve, there was a population of 2,000 peasants who worked the land, while the Jewish population was extremely small in number. Though I left the *shtetl* of my birth when I was not yet 17 years old, I can still remember 25 Jewish families, and the little *shul* by the market square across from the church, which was topped with a gilded dome, proud and bold. Our tiny *shul* would be packed on holidays and [remembering it] leaves my heart filled with a deep longing for those days and years.

My father, Yekhiel Kazhdan, the *feldsher* (barber-surgeon), shared himself with everyone, in poverty, joy, and suffering.

As in all *shtetl*s, the way of life was in every respect primitive. Occasionally, merchants would visit with dry-goods to sell, and this would lend a festive atmosphere to our village.

During the grey, frozen, winter days, which seemed to stretch out endlessly, my village did not falter nor flag. Children went to school in the *kheyder*s [to study Jewish subjects] and also learned Russian.

Among Jews you would see no ignorant people. Most of them knew how to write a Yiddish letter. There were no divisions among us there. And so the years shuffled along, at times better, at times worse.

At a celebration – a wedding, or a *bris* [ritual circumcision] – the entire village rejoiced and participated. We would parade the bride and groom into the street with music, heading down to the market square, where next to the *shul* the wedding canopy would be set up and ready. The klezmer musicians played, the new parents-in-law danced with each other joyfully, and you could feel the Divine Presence permeating the village.

After such festivities, the grey, stolid, cheerless days would return, especially in the summer, when the days were long. True, nature did give us the gift of her splendor: green poplars, beautiful flowers; but these could not dispel the despondency of the young, who had the notion that somewhere else there was a more interesting world.

Little by little, emigration's appeal reached even our far-flung little corner. People began leaving for the new world. We hadn't experienced much that was exciting [in our little village]. However, I do remember an incident that we suffered through one time, on a particular Sabbath evening: As in all small *shtetl*s, where no newspapers were accessible, we made do with getting our news by word of mouth, including a little gossip and stories blown out of proportion that possibly never even happened.[1] [On this occasion,] a rumor had spread that a *pogrom* [organized massacre] would break out in our *shtetl* after *shaloshudess* [the third meal of the Sabbath, eaten before dusk]; the Gentiles of the village, apparently, had definitely made up their minds. No one wanted to believe it, because we had always felt comfortable with them. Nevertheless, wild imagination took possession of everyone. I will never forget this. It was a hot day. At twilight, thick black clouds began to close in, as if conspiring with the evil rumors. This only increased the panic. Even now I can picture Pesha Berls, wringing her hands. She gathered all her children together and came running into *Kapulyer* Street. Oh, how she implored the black clouds: "God, have mercy on us!" And so, all of us sure of what was coming, we gobbled down our *shaloshudess* and prepared to face the pogrom straight on. [Of course,] the Gentiles of the village had known nothing of all this, poor things, and the whole episode ended happily. But I will never forget the terror.

In the summer months, fires would break out because of lightning, which would ignite the thatched roofs.

We don't have many Shemezeve compatriots in America. My brother Lazer died in the First World War. My father-in-law, Reb Elyeh Eisenson, from Optsin, died in the Lyuban pogrom. I was married to his son, Aaron Eisenson, who endured a great deal in France during the First World War as an American soldier.

Uniformed soldier: Lazer Kazhdan

Translator's footnote:

1. It never even happened: Lit.: "never arose, and never flew up." This colorful Yiddish phrase indicating incredulity is a metaphor drawn from Jewish skepticism regarding the central story of Christianity. The phrase avers (without naming names) that Jesus never emerged out of the grave, and never ascended into Heaven.

[Page 491]

Appendage Material

On the Threshold of Life
(Fragments)

by Zalman Wendroff*

Translated by Pamela Russ

At the "Large *samovar*" [hot water urn]

In front of the yellowed page of the leather bound book "*Moreh Nevukhim*" ["Guide for the Perplexed"; written by Maimonides, published in 1204], my father would mark off the most important dates of the family chronicles; birthdays on one side of the page, *yahrzeits* [date of death] – on the other side.

My birth was recorded by the family historian on the ninth line of the empty side of the page.

It is easy to figure that they could very much have gone on without me.

For the circumcision ceremony, as I later heard many times, my father tried to be very proud, as is appropriate for the host of the festivity. But my mother did not demonstrate much joy. She knew – another child, another worry on her head.

My father, a scholar, a *maskil* ["intellectual" person], "a thinker," – was more of an enhancer of the family rather than a provider. The main provider, the active one, was my mother.

My mother greatly respected my father, just as if he was the head of the household. But I knew, and everyone else knew, that the house was being completely upheld by her, by my mother.

I loved my father very much, but did not fear him in the least. My love for my mother was more like awe of G–d, mixed with real fear. This G–d–fearing sense was like a stone wall between us and did not permit any warmth between my mother and me, even though I longed for her warmth with all my limbs.

In my childish mind, I always imagined my mother with her hand stretched out straight, as if she would be saying: "Not so close!"

My mother never raised her voice, was never angry – never with her own family, not with others.

When she did not like something, she furrowed her thick, entangled eyebrows, and quietly but strongly she said:

"This is not good."

In worse situations:

"*Feh*! This can make you faint! This is not what you do!"

This is how she behaved with strangers, and this is what she did with her own children.

And these few words were a lot more effective than my father's, "You can go out of your mind."

People held my mother in great esteem.

– Zelda, so smart!

– A wise woman! A knowledgeable woman!

– A man's head! A person with a clear head!

– Such an active person, Zelda!

These are the things I constantly heard about my mother even before I could figure out what they meant.

A stately woman, proud, authoritative, always calm and controlled, it was only with me that her outward appearance evoked fear of her.

In her dress with the velvet collar at the throat, and with the velvet design at the bottom, and with a black satin burnous [hooded cloak] in the winter, and in a black satin pelerine [short cape] in the summer, with proud, measured steps – prouder and more measured than during the week – she went on Shabbath across the street looking as if the entire city belonged to her.

According to the rich "Good Shabbath" that everyone – even important

[Page 492]

businessmen – would greet her with, I felt that "my mother was not just anyone," and even I began to feel myself a prestigious person.

But with all her "G–dly" grandeur, my vision of her is on Friday night at the "large *samovar*."

We owned two *samovars*. One for twenty glasses, which was simply called – the *samovar*, and a second one, for sixty glasses, that was called "the large *samovar*."

This *samovar* was "large" not only in size, but in the role it played in the house.

The *samovar*, the simple *samovar*, we set up every morning and every evening. Drinking tea from this simple *samovar* is a weekday concept, just like eating, or having supper. The simple *samovar* stands on the table from five a.m., when my mother and father wake up, until midday, when the middle sister, the "*monitzipatzya*" ["emancipated one"] who read until the late hours of the night and slept until late in the day, often drinks tea. Several times during the morning, they pour water into the simple *samovar* and pour hot coals underneath. Everyone drinks tea from there, when he wants and as often as he wants. In the early morning, neighbors come in to boil up some candy for their child, "If you don't mind." And once in a while a neighbor comes in to "rinse off the sleep from his heart" with a lively cup of tea, "If you have one."

But the large *samovar* is put up only during festive nights – on Shabbath [Friday] nights.

My mother says that these Shabbath nights are the only evenings when she feels that she is still alive on this earth. All week long, she is "not alive." On those Shabbath evenings, lying on my bed in the second room, I hear how my mother is complaining to my father that she is suffocating, that she does not know how to manage for herself, that the finances are consuming her, that the Friday night "large *samovar*" was one of the means of maintaining the reputation of an "open house."

For the Shabbath night "large *samovar*" event, neighbors, acquaintances, important people, scholars, and *maskilim* ["enlightened" people"] gather together, to hear or recite a good word, discuss worldly topics, and simply to spend an evening in a "refined environment."

Our neighbor Shmuel–Yosef Rabinowycz comes, an intellectual thinker, who is studying the *Tanakh* [Bible] with Mendelsohn's *Be'ur* ["Explanation" 1780–1783, written with commentaries in German by Moses Mendelsohn, "Father of the Enlightenment"], and is wearing a black shirt with a black ribbon instead of a tie; the old man Salanter comes, a *maskil* who writes critiques in "Hamelitz" ["The Judge," first Hebrew newspaper in Russian Empire]; Zisel "*Ertszemikhoset*," ["hear me out"] a Jew with many ideas in his head and who cuts into everyone's talk with his "hear me out!" A regular guest at the Shabbath evening "large *samovar*" is Uncle Hessel – a little bit of crude person, but a happy Jew, who always has a story to tell, that happened to him "the other day." Some refined young people come, who are not really there for the refined talk and refined setting, as much as for spending some time with my sisters, particularly with the "emancipated" one who is preparing to go study and is a lovely girl on top of that.

In the dining room, the large lamp burns brightly; the "large *samovar*" on the table is giving off an impressive amount of steam and rumbles comfortably underneath like a good humored head of the household after his Shabbath afternoon nap. My father is telling of his insights on the "kempernem" of the day's Torah portion, and recites by heart pieces of the "*Moreh Nevukhim*." Smart words are spoken, and "intelligent thoughts" are expressed; Alter Salanter tells of the latest news from *Hamelitz*, and a discussion ensues of high politics … It's festive, homey, and cozy. And over everything and everyone, my mother reigns. – – –

Golden Hands

My mother ran a soap factory with a worker load of one, and only one person, the soap maker.

My mother said that he "owns golden hands, but that he is like the "white of an egg." You cannot leave him alone for a minute.

Certainly, we wanted to see a person with golden hands, especially if he himself was like the white of an egg. This must be as curious as a magical elf, a disguised person, as something that sees but cannot be seen (sees but cannot be seen: Hebrew)… The factory itself, where there are people with golden hands, must be a magical palace where wondrous things happen.

With difficulty, I pleaded with my older sister to at least once allow me to take some hot food for my mother to the factory.

But instead of a magical palace I found a half darkened house with smoky walls and with a wet, slippery floor. It smelled like carcasses, with rancid fat, and the air was filled with moist humidity, as in a bath.

Even mother herself, in my eyes, lost a lot of her royalty in the factory. This was not the same proud, poised, refined mother that I knew from home, the queen of the "large *samovar*."

Nervous, anxious, and sweaty, every once in a whole, she would urge the soap–maker:

"Watch the barrel … Look at it, questioning

[Page 493]

if the fat is ready… if the corrosive chemicals are weighed properly? … Don't pour in so much soda… You are pouring in so many materials that this will soon turn into vinegar…. Don't forget the colophony [rosin] and salt…"

"Am I cooking soap for the first time, do you think?" the Jew with the yellow beard bristled. My mother hardly noticed me.

"So, are you bringing me something warm? Where is love?" she remarked jokingly. She took my hands off the cup, put it on the windowsill, and immediately forgot about me and about the warm things.

Choosing a job

– Nothing else, but that he became crazy.

– So, suddenly you are a skilled worker! Did you have to blind your eyes for many nights with those books?

– You can be a tailor or a shoemaker without history or geography!

It was with that type of talk that my family countered the news that I wanted to be a skilled worker.

Only my older brother, the one who "hated the Kaiser," and therefore chose to leave for America as soon as he would get a ship's travel ticket from his bride – agreed that maybe "it is not as bad an idea as you think."

Sooner or later – he'll have to go to America, so he may as well learn a skill. It will be very useful for him there. In America, it is not an embarrassment to have a skill.

But when he heard that I was going to become a bookbinder, he also shrugged his shoulders.

"Why specifically a bookbinder? Why not a watchmaker or a goldsmith? It's also a fine skill."

"I prefer bookbinding."

"If you can't read Pushkin or Gogol, at least you can bind their books, right?" my brother the focused one teased.

"One can read Pushkin and Gogol, and even bind their books."

"Ridiculous!"

"What is it that you don't understand here? He wants to be reassured with poverty for the rest of his life, so he'll become a bookbinder." I heard this and smiled to myself. If they would only know the truth about my "craziness"!

Having selected bookbinding from all other trades, and of all the bookbinders – having selected Hirshel the yellow one, from whom to learn the trade, I had in mind: Shprintzel. Next door to Hirshel the yellow one, lived the first desired love of my heart. This alone was enough to make bookbinding the most interesting thing for me in the entire world, and Hirshel the yellow – the "greatest artist in his field." To always be next door to Shprintzel, to see her and speak to her every day, a few times in the day, whenever I wanted, every minute these opportunities showed her my commitment to her, my love – this is what chose a profession for me! – – –

The First Strike

Taller than the average height, broad shoulders, with a "Russian" beard around full, red cheeks, with a wide and confident stride of a person who is happy both with himself and with the world – was Polye Kravitz, who with not even one hair was similar to our familiar Jewish tailor – the hungry but happy beggar.

Polye Kravitz was not just any tailor – he was a princely tailor, "for men or women, for the civilian or the military" – which was broadly described in words and in pictures at the entrance to his workshop.

On one of the posters, there was a young man with red cheeks looking down, wearing a morning coat with lapels, in striped pants and a cylinder hat on his head. Opposite that, on the second poster, a no less elegant woman smiled, wearing a green dress with a long train and with a deep décolleté, that even for a woman in a poster was a little too deep. On one hand of the blond beauty was a raincoat, and in the other hand she was carrying a rider's whip that said anything could be sewn here – from a ball dress to a raincoat. From the third poster, a brave military personnel in a "Nikolayevski" cloak with a cape over his arm, and with a big beaver–skin collar, looked out severely with a hard look. "Here, here," he says with a shout, "Silence!" or "Calm down!" … A military uniform, completely covered in medals, and a vice–uniform with silver buttons, both of them with strong male chests, were in the same manner set up on the fourth poster. – – –

Polye Kravitz did not need any advertisements. Everyone in the city and in the district also knew that from Polye Kravitz you can order – from your own or from the tailor's material – "local or foreign" – whatever your heart desires: from the casual to the uniform, from the working pants to the military uniform, from a wedding dress to a female fighter's dress, in which the marshall's various daughters were dressed when they went riding. The notices, that covered the entire front wall

[Page 494]

of his fine house on the main street of the city, were only a small part of the decorations on his home, where there were for example carved ledges, colored chips in the glazed balcony, a colored weather vane on the top of the roof.

Polye Kravitz was by nature a great lover and patron of art. His home, like a museum, was filled with works of art: with clay, red–faced, smiling, and capped Germans holding foaming beer mugs in their hands, and with long tobacco pipes in their mouths; with plaster Italian young boys in patched up pants, in hats with their brims turned to the side, and with cigarettes in their mouths; with porcelain dogs; with stone elephants; with pictures and engravings, for example: "Moses Montefiore Goes to Visit Queen Victoria," "Three Generations," "Cash and Credit," – a picture of ethical instruction for merchants, and other such works of art slowly bought up during his travels for merchandise in Lodz, Bialystok, and Tomaszew.

When a few itinerant actors were lost in town – leftovers from a splintered, traveling Jewish theater – Polye was the first to take them into his house, give them food and drink, negotiated with the chief official of the town for permission for a few performances of the "Jewish–German" troupe, sponsoring them with Jabrow for the printing of the posters, getting the fire station for free for performances, standing himself at the door and watching that more than half the crowd without tickets should not enter the theater. In short, he put forth his life to help the "troupe" not leave the city as they came in – on foot.

Cantors went to his house first, before going to their own. The entire cantorial world – from Lithuania to Wolhyn – knew that food and lodging, both for the cantor and for the choir members, was taken care of by Polye. On the contrary, if someone dared not go to Polye, he would earn an enemy for his entire life.

A minor rabbi who would carry his obligation from house to house [collect charity], a lost preacher, a poor bride, a rider from a traveling circus, a drunken official who was languishing for another drop to revive himself after a full day of drinking, the Talmud Torah, and the "Wolne–official–commando," the *yeshiva*, the city baths and the courtyard – for everything and for everyone, there was a ruble at Polye's.

Polye Kravitz could afford to be a patron and a philanthropist; other than sewing for all the foremen in town and for the aristocrats for about twenty miles around the town, he also took orders for clothing the policemen, the prison guards, the city firemen, the couriers, those from the "Vojenske Presence," from the gymnasium, and from the police.

Polye had work all year round. He managed, you can say, an entire factory with ten or twelve associates and a few apprentices, other than the simpler work that he gave to the "peasants," to the poor tailors in their homes.

Polye was an entrance to the aristocrats, his own person with the authorities, a trusted person with the officials. Small bureaucrats, teachers in the gymnasium, and impoverished princes, who had tailoring done by him on loan and badly repaid debts, came to visit him showing respect on Shabbath, for some Jewish *gefilte* fish [special cooked ground fish eaten on Shabbath] and Russian whisky.

If a Jew had to "register" a child in gymnasium, "remove" himself from the false accusation of a suspicious fire, "crush" a protocol, do a favor in conscription issues, or get a contract from the city – he would ask Polye to throw in a good word, and Polye did "whatever he could."

Polye never took any money for these things. He did this, he said, because it was a mitzvah [religious mandate] and because he naturally loved to do a favor for another Jew.

"They" don't believe in mitzvos, they believe in the ruble. And in each of these cases, Polye figured out about how much this would cost.

"I will do for them as I would do for myself. A Jewish kopek is very dear to me. But better to give a few ruble more, and it will straighten out… If you grease the wheel, things move better."

And even though prestigious Jews, wealthy businessmen, belittled the nouveau riche contemptible tailor, nonetheless, they called him "Reb Refoel" and sat with him at one table at all community events.

If you wish, he is not really a tailor, but more of a contractor than a tailor. – – – He probably had not held a needle in his hands for ten years. People work for him, and still he has an open hand.

Only the workers did not look for any privileges from him nor heed his honor, not in his own eyes or under his eyes. Polye Kravitz was the first and only one in town who had organized piece work in his workshop.

"In piece work, everyone is his own boss," Polye convinced his associates. "If you wish, you can work an hour longer and earn more gilden. If you don't want, you can make Shabbath on time. It won't bother you, you'll see that piece work is more worth your while."

But soon workers saw that they

[Page 495]

were very wronged. The earnings were even smaller, some by a quarter, and some by even a third. Polye demanded work of "the first quality sort." But somehow, the knife slid through the knot, there was unstitching from top to bottom, a rip on a lapel, and then he would throw it in the face of the worker: "Do it again! Like this you'll end up sewing for village weddings." – – –

Understandably, he did not pay for redoing the work.

"It doesn't bother him if I have to redo this three times. It doesn't cost him anything, right?"

"His daily earnings are taken care of."

"Even for boasting about himself with nice donations."

"A philanthropist with someone else's pocket…"

"He is bragging about himself, he does, may the evil spirit enter the belly of his fat father!" That's how the workers cooled their hearts.

* * *

Shloimke turned to the tables where all the people were still sitting with their feet still under them and the pieces of work on their knees, and he, with a ringing voice, said: "Fellow workers, if you have respect for yourselves, if you want that the Polish woman, Polish women exploiters should not become fat from your blood and sweat – – –, then show that you are skilled workers –, put away the work, and let the Polish woman see who lives from whom: we from them, or them from us.

"Call a strike! Nothing else, but a strike!" the young workers declared.

With hesitation, the older workers also put aside their work, some unwillingly, and they slid away from the work tables…

* * *

The strikers put the following demands to Polye:

1.   Abolish piece work and reinstate weekly wages.

2.   Establish a 10–hour work day.

3.   Abolish work on the winter Friday nights when work has ended —— on the winter Fridays.

4.   No beating and taunting the young men apprentices. Do not use them for housework. Teach them the skills from the very first term. From the third year on, no less than one ruble a week as wages.

5.   All strikers will be rehired for work.

* * *

Polye used all his connections with the city officials to break the strike. – – –

Each striker sat in his own home and did not bother anyone. It was only in the evenings that they would gather together in the tailors' synagogue.

The Rav [main rabbi] also intervened in a conflict between Polye and the people.

Editor's comments:

*   The famous writer Z. Wendroff is, as is known, a Slutsker. Until now, we did not have the opportunity to publish some of his literary works in the Slutsk *Pinkus* [chronicles, history book]. Recently, when completing the book, we by chance received several issues of "*Morgen Freiheit*" ["Morning Freedom," New York based newspaper, established in 1922, as a self–described "Communistic fighting newspaper" in the Yiddish language; folded in 1988.] with the first chapters of his autobiography, "On the Threshold of Life," in which Slutsker daily life of 81 years ago is reflected. We are pleased to publish several excerpts of these chapters which are in our possession.

[Page 495]

Setting Out from Romanova

by Meyshe Yehude Mayzl (Staten Island)

Translated by Sheldon Clare, Paul Pascal and Judie Ostroff Goldstein
(Last version: Sh. Tsivion)

The Rabbi

Long ago in Romanova there lived a rabbi, a good, honest, holy, and pious man. Possibly one of the world's legendary "thirty-six saintly souls." His name was revered far and wide. Bursting into this man's life of sanctity, there came a desperate woman, as beautiful as she was alien – the landowner's wife. "Save me, rabbi! I am about to lose my estate, all of my property!"

The rabbi had been sitting alone, poring over his religious books. "What does this hussy want from me?" He was frightened to the point of fainting. Everyone in the house, large and small, ran to the study, trying to help, to revive their cherished and beloved father, so badly shaken. He managed to stand now, and was peering sternly out through the window. From outside, the landowner's wife studied him and wondered, "What is the pale man whispering? I've heard that this is how he makes a blessing. So will his blessing be fulfilled? Is my happiness then assured?"

[Page 496]

Itshe Gittes the Hebrew Teacher

Let me tell you about my Hebrew teacher, Itshe Gittes, the Torah tutor of Romanova. He would instruct a class of nine or ten students, tackling *gemora* [Talmud] using the simplest of approaches. He didn't delve into the subtleties or the knotty conundrums. When a difficult passage in an obtuse chapter would present itself, he would go for the easy, literal meaning, the interpretation most common-sensical and logical. But when it came to Hebrew grammar – whether the accent on a word was on the last syllable or the second-last, whether a vowel was unstressed or a consonant doubled – for this he had a distinct gusto. "You rascal!" he would scold a pupil good-naturedly, "this is Hebrew, our holy language! Don't forget, if you are careless with it, you'll really catch it from me!"

Earning a wage? Getting paid for his teaching? It was the last thing on his mind. One boy, a lad named Chaimke, had an aptitude for Biblical Hebrew. Chaimke's clothing was tattered, one patch on top of another, His father long since dead, his mother a widow who survived on alms, the boy had found, however, a permanent place in the rabbi's heart – he was treasured. Certainly far more than the boy who came to *heder* dressed in a brand-new suit, his father a magnate, always offered the place of honor, a boy who peered at a holy book with no more understanding than a rooster would have, looking into the same book.

My Zeyde

The mayor of Romanova was a feeble, old Jew – my *zeyde* [grandfather], Reb Yankl, may he rest in peace. His face was stern, his expression cold. (This is how I still often see him in my dreams.) But in his heart he was as gentle and sweet as a child. He would regularly take in boys, strangers, to his home, clandestinely, so that they could study Torah rather than be caught by the authorities to serve in the Czar's army. He did this, even though in *gemore* he himself wasn't that well versed.

One particular Sabbath, my *zeyde* was standing before the congregation, taking his turn leading the morning prayers. The synagogue was festive, and full of people. Suddenly, pandemonium! What's going on? What happened? Soldiers, pointing rifles, were rushing into the synagogue, going in after a particular young man, a brilliant Torah scholar, who had been hiding there to escape military service. They even brought a rope to tie him up and take him. But he "got lucky." He was able to disappear. How did he do it? My *zeyde* had figured out what was happening, and in the middle of the *kedusha* prayer, started coughing and hacking, with increasing intensity, then fell down. There was such a turmoil, even the soldiers got swept up in it. But thanks to that turmoil, the young victim was able to save his skin. And my *zeyde* ? My *zeyde* had died on the spot!

My father, who then had to *sit Shiva* [ritual mourning], but who neither cried nor lamented, later explained, "My child, your *zeyde's* death was a holy sacrifice. But now, in heaven, he is without doubt very happy; for his death liberated a learned Jew from the clutches of heathens."

The Ritual Slaughterer

My uncle Leybke was a *shoykhet* [community ritual slaughterer] in Romanova, as well as being a judge, an ordained rabbi, and a cantor. A person of stately appearance, he had a glorious beard and a sunny countenance. His clothing was inevitably spick and span, always neat and tidy. He was ready and willing, at a moment's notice, to help settle disputes between a husband and a wife, any kind of quarrels between people. On the go non-stop, he constantly tried to fulfill the holy obligation of peacemaking, like Aaron *ha-Kohen* [Moses' brother, renowned as a peacemaker *par excellence*].

In his role as *shoykhet,* do you think he would take home his own portion of the slaughtered meat, as was his right? God forbid! On the way home from the slaughterhouse, butchering knife still in hand, he would divide up his share to give to this person or that in the street. And to whom? Anyone he felt needed it, a pauper, a widow...

On top of all this, my uncle was highly knowledgeable in worldly matters, too, political issues, and he would read newspapers and journals in various foreign languages. If a war broke out, his left hand would delineate the battle fronts as well as any map hanging on the wall, as he named all the mountains and valleys, rivers and oceans.

Today, the Sabbath morning prayers he customarily led were not up to the usual standard. As it happened, my uncle the rabbi was away today, solving religious queries for the community. His life looked at as a whole, my uncle was accomplished in all things that mattered. He had it all.

Reb Itshe the Preacher

Reb Itshe of Muravka was the inn-keeper's son-in-law, and was from Muravka. However, as it happened, this tragic story took place in Romanova, where his bad luck and his feet had brought him. He had gotten advice on how he could earn a living. Blessed with a talent for oratory, he threw his pack of things over his shoulder and took a gnarled walking stick in his hand, transforming himself into an itinerant preacher. The process itself accorded him confidence. Traveling only on foot, this tall and athletic figure never accepted a seat on a wagon. In this manner, he wandered from village to village, town to town, teaching the world how to live an ethical life, as our forebears had done, to be pious, to be honest, and to keep God's commandments.

A talented preacher was our Reb Itshe, and an advocate of the common folk. His voice flickered with fire and flame, his eyes blazed like rays of the sun, and his words resounded and roared like waves of the sea. Subsisting on bread and salt, and a ladleful of water, he never knew the taste of meat or fish. Yet despite all this, he was always cheerful, with healthy color in his cheeks and all his limbs fit and hardy.

*

One frosty day he came to Romanova and went directly to his lodgings. And where was it? The synagogue, where he finally laid his pack down, on one of the benches. This was his "hotel" throughout Lithuania, Belorussia, and Poland.

Mikhl the baker invited him for dinner. Mikhl was a pious Jew who had no truck with hypocrisy or falsehood. Sitting there at this unpretentious Sabbath meal, he began reflecting on the day's Torah reading, the last chapters of the Book of Exodus. He went up the two or three steps to the curtain that covered the synagogue's Holy Ark and kissed it, evidencing a particular physical and spiritual exertion. He stood by the Holy Ark enveloped in his *talis* [prayer shawl]. Here he was at ease. He knew the village well; he knew everyone and everything here. He began his presentation low-key, with some simple scriptural problem, answering it straightaway with a solution from [the famous interpreter of Holy Writ] Rashi. Then suddenly and forcefully, out poured a mystical, esoteric insight, which was quickly absorbed into his discourse like a spark consumed by its fire.

[Page 497]

"In the desert our forefathers built a holy tabernacle. They were celebrating its dedication when presently the news spread that Nadav and Avihu [sons of Aaron the High Priest] had been struck dead...The festivities were thrown into chaos, the entire pageant ground to a halt. We learned from this, and it's well-known to everyone now, that the two had presumed to bring "strange fire" to the sacrificial altar. And why was the sentence of the court so severe? Why was consumption by fire the decision to be meted out upon these priests, the two older sons of Aaron? Strange fire, my friends, strange fire!"

His voice, now full of pathos, seemed almost to be singing. "For strange fire, one pays dearly!" His tone was laced with urgency. "Our own fire, my friends, our own fire, fire that is authorized and sanctioned, such fire is holy. Our own fire is from the divine World-to-Come. Strange fire, alien fire, is from "That Other Place," that world where Satan has dominion, from man's Evil Side, which tempts him into doing that which is forbidden.

"Strange fire! This is a world in which no one takes responsibility! On today's equivalent of Mount Sinai there stands, shamelessly, the god of money. Everyone is trying to get to it. They go on their hands and knees, they fall, they get up and crawl some more. They contort themselves with their crawling, along their crooked, narrow, alien paths. Drained of all decency, all their spiritual resources are dammed up. Our precious inheritance, God's 613 commandments to us, are left to rot."

The preacher would heap guilt upon guilt on the congregation, like slaps in the face. He would lose all sense of rationality, all sense of composure. He was more a wild tempest than a human preacher – savage, thunderous – searing the assembly with lightning. He would throw the congregation into the numbing cold, then into the agony of conflagration. Sins, transgressions of all kinds, in That World – you'll pay for them all, this was his message.

Sinners, sinners! Boys, girls, men, women, all are guilty! Before long, a screeching wail would break out from the women's section of the synagogue. And all of the preacher's harangues would be backed up with solid quotes from the Torah, biblical exegeses, Talmudic references. Yes, it's on account of our unspeakable sins that the Exile – our dispersion and banishment – has been brought upon us, with all its evil consequences and pain.

Where is it he is referring to? Obviously, he means Hell, where the Angels of Torture, all seven categories of them, are howling savagely, screaming and shrieking, lashing at their victims with red-hot pokers. "Burn them! Roast them!" they cackle. "Tear strips from their skin!" Let evil-doers never forget: there is judgment in this universe and there is a Judge!"

With screams, roaring, and stirred up colors he described heaven and earth, life and death with fearsome, terrible images; as if he had just now come from there – not from Lazava, not from Romanova.

Everyone was upset, excited and consciences were aroused. Itshe, Itshe, you such and such, do not place such heavy stones on people's hearts...understand your people whom you teach. They are not so difficult, not so bad. Restrain yourself, come to your senses. Give them a smile for once.

Ingeniously he changed his manner of speech to one of gentleness and refinement. He would start with a tasty melody, like a *yiddeshe mama* rocking her tiny child in the cradle and singing a song about the little white goat.

Now I will tell you story from Hell: Once, during a short Sabbath the synagogue sexton yelled: "Repent you sinners in Hell. It is already late!" They turned to him with a plea: Wait a while, have pity. In Yaneva it is not yet time for *Havdalah* [blessing at the end of Sabbath], also in Romanova. That is indeed right! Soon I will know. Sometimes a passionate preacher talks and talks and cannot be interrupted. You should benefit from his merit. What be done with him? He is a man inclined to anger! Once again, "Repent you sinners in Hell!"

A certain merchant, Reb Detz, headed the delegation and stood and argued. "It is still before *Maariv* [evening prayers] in my *Hotzeplotz*! [town proverbial for its remoteness]."

"*Pani* [Polish title for gentry] Detz! You respectable man, you have lost your memory entirely. You know very well that in *Hotzeplotz* men play cards now, they drink liquor and snack on cakes. Aha! You forgot…Repent you sinners in Hell! Too many already remain unmarried."

He continued singing an amazing story about two pious men who separately knocked on the gates of paradise. Understandably, both were accepted with great honor. But the pious men found no joy there. Why? We will see together. Now listen, gentlemen! This is what happened: those two made an alliance and ran away from paradise. One of them was a *lamedvav* [one of the thirty-six hidden saintly men without whom the world could not exist], a pious man, "one who is hidden." The second one was a very poor Hasid, a simple man, a "wise man from Chelm." But do you know where they ran? There, to the sinners in Hell…the devils. The Angels of Torture screamed at them with terrible, savage voices and with raised fists drove the two out. But the two strange men were stubborn and did not want to go back to paradise. They stayed in the middle of the road, neither here nor there. This is a deep subject…one must understand this.

This was not like him, was not his style. The uninspired congregation listened calmly and quietly. The clock struck half past nine and people were thinking: it is already late, time to finish. He has understood the message. And if in passing the road takes us to paradise, we will talk about them a little. He paints various pictures, compares each tenderly and gently, gives his evidence taken from judgements, Midrash [a body of post-Talmudic literature of Biblical exegesis] and Shas [the Talmud]. But the images were watery and pale, the similes, the examples, dry, cold, thrashed out and old. There sit pious men everywhere, good, religious men before G-d, prophets, angels, rishoynim, akhroynim, tanayim, amorim and *gaonim* [sages] from every generation until now. Their names shine forth from both Torahs, Babylonian and Jerusalem. Among the tanayim, the famous Chanina, who made a measure of carob last an entire

[Page 498]

week and there are more pious men, and more and more. They sit crowned by the shade of the canopy of the divine presence. The fathers and the mothers are in the seats of honor. If I am not mistaken, there are the benevolent from "the nations of the world," the gentiles who saved Jews from murderers and even men. With crossed hands they listen to the song, the songs of praise of the angels/choir…without good deeds, without sins, without drink, without food. They sat like that constantly and so will they eternally sit. Their task? To defend and protect the people of Israel.

In the middle he considered throwing in a subtle hint to ignite that what was dear to him. Perhaps it will kindle a spark, a little fire – but no fire was lit. For a short time he was silent, then he sang a sweet melody. When Messiah comes I wish for you all, brothers, good and religious, that while still being in good health, you should enjoy the ox and fish that is prepared for the pious at the time of the Messiah. Me? He who does not already know, shall know: I belong to a society, an association, spread over the Russian and Romanian Diaspora, who observe a new commandment; no meat and no fish, no G-d fearing man should talk about it at our table. Therefore this is my desire: leave me a small bottle of wine, reserved for the righteous at the time of the Messiah, he declared with good, courageous humor. As it is stated in scriptures: a glass of wine puts joy in people's hearts, illuminating faces embittered and dark from pain and suffering. Even the end of the sermon left the congregation with a cold smile. Because time is short, I will stop here for today about the world to come and about paradise in the other world. We will with G-d's help begin the month of Nissan. Herewith I conclude the lecture. Praised is the Master of the Universe, praised be his name, and come to Zion, Redeemer, and we say amen."

Reb Michl sat at the table. The silver and copper coins clinked in the plate. Young *heder* boys ran to eat supper. As Reb Itshe spoke, the young boys frolicked and ran through the snow and in my memory I am one of them.

On a beautiful morning the synagogue sexton, Borach Rosh's and a middle-class man went to collect money in the shtetl to pay the preacher for his lectures. "He has, may the evil eye not harm them, a large family that needs to be supported. The Muravaker has legitimately earned the right to be healthy and alive, for he leaves to the mercy of the Almighty the task of planting justice and faith in human hearts." The sexton took some of the collection for his trouble, but there still remained a large sum. The main thing was that that these pious, middle class men opened the knots of their pouches. The heavy, filled handkerchief is soon carried off to *Reb* Mikhl, the baker.

Wednesday evening after a rare sermon, the preacher was again invited to Reb Michl's. The religious, honest man showed his respect by serving a dairy supper with a glass of liquor and a cake. The preacher exchanged the coin for bank notes and thought: It will be sufficient for the holidays, for wine, matzah [unleavened bread], prayer books, hats, shoes and clothes for the boys and girls. Also there is enough for a gift for Tema, a warm shawl like the one on the shoulders of Reb Michl's wife. The balance will go to support me and for tuition fees. After Passover, if I will still be left in this world with G-d's help and without any holy promise, I will go on foot, without a horse and wagon, to another district for the entire summer. Do I have then a choice? What can one do? It is indeed wrong to leave children with only a mother. Parents are obliged to protect their children together like young saplings before they bloom.

Thinking about this, he took his leave: "Go in good health – be healthy, thank you!" He left and went to his place on his bench. Under his head there was a folded towel for a pillow. He lay down near the heated stove and covered himself with a fur coat that had lost most of its fur, (the father-in-law's gift – the former fur coat). He soon slept and dreams came, dream after dream:

He is at home…Shalom Aleichem! [Peace unto you, a greeting] Aleichem Shalom! [unto you peace, a greeting]. The children are happy, there is the furniture. Tema's bright face…tears from her eyes that laugh…in the dream as in reality, everything distinct, substantial and clear…

That week a beggar was staying at the synagogue, a lame wretch, an idiotic short man. Reb Itshe thought him curious. "Mister, what do people call you?"

The beggar kept silent and looked the preacher right in the eye. The preacher asked again, this time properly. "What are you called, my friend?"

In response the beggar was silent and shook his head.

"Why are you silent? What is your name? You are not a mute. I heard you say amen after a blessing and you pray as a pious Jews. I do not mean you, G-d forbid, any harm."

The beggar let out a groan, spoke a couple of words with a sniffling reprove. "What do you want? I am called Leyzer."

"Leyzer? Good!"

Reb Itshe thinks, even though the man's an idiot, he is still a pious Jew. Who damaged him? This god fearing, poor, punished soul; it will be a good deed to speak to him more often.

After going from house to house, Leyzer arrived at the synagogue ready for his feast. He took his sack off his shoulder, put it down next to his prayer shawl, took out two half challahs [twisted egg loaf], washed and made the blessings over the bread. Laid out on the bench were pieces of cheese and a hard boiled egg. A housewife gave him a sour pickle from the pot and two onions. He also had a bottle of kvass [drink made from fermented bread]. He ate with great gusto, gulped, swallowed, and guzzled

[Page 499]

from the kvass bottle that a storekeeper had given him in the street.

Reb Itshe sat on the side contemplating and thinking about deep mysteries. He noticed that Leyzer smiled while reciting the Grace after Meals. What is the condition of such a Jew? A cripple, an idiot, who eats and is happy. A thought chases a thought, a supposition that Leyzer, his short-term neighbor, this beggar is one who relies on G_d. Suddenly he lifts his head from the *gemore*. He has made made a decision:

"Reb Leyzer, let us talk a little. It will be nicer and pleasanter for both of us."

But Leyzer is a hard nut. "I do not want to, leave me alone. What do we have to say to each other? You are a teacher and I am a beggar with a thick skull. I do not want to and you cannot make me." Not another word, neither good nor bad, did he utter.

And that is how four days and four nights passed. Itshe sat or lay on one bench and the beggar remained opposite him on another. This Layzer was a criminal, one who could make himself seem crooked when he needed to, or blind. He crept around in chinks and peepholes and came out to make quick swindles. He was, as it is said, like the wind in a field. This Leyzer only made himself seem idiotic. He knew that the preacher slept deeply. He had seen the bulging wallet. This was his trade and he was a master. With nimble fingers he took the pouch from Reb Itshe and quietly, carried it away. Noiselessly he opened the door, did not close it, and disappeared into the snowy night.

All morning men came to pray in the synagogue and they noticed that the preacher was still lying on his bench. What is wrong, Reb Itshe? Are you sick?

He was silent. They lit a candle and brought it near to light his face. When they turned to look at him his mouth was contorted from pain and troubles. Why are you silent, Reb Itshe? Speak to us. Where is your tongue? From his open eyes, tears ran – their fire, their ardor extinguished.

My Father

by Rabbi Dr. Raphael Gold of New York

Translated by Jerrold Landau

When the elders of the city of Izabelin near Wolkowisk came to the head of the Yeshiva of Volozhin, the Netzi'v of blessed memory, to request a fitting rabbi, they turned to him and said, "Despite the small size of our community, it has a special merit, for the Gaon Rabbi Yitzchak Elchanan Spektor began his rabbinical service there."

The Netzi'v listened to their words and recommended to them his dear student, who was known as the "Ilui [Genius] of Grajewo," my late father Rabbi Yaakov Meir Krawczynski.

By nature, my father was very diligent from his youth. He used to have an adage, "A Torah personality must study for at least eight hours per day, for Torah is his profession, and his law is like that of an employee." On the other hand, he did not consider the study of foreign languages as a waste of time, and he found a free hour to read secular literature. This behavior, and his splendid countenance endeared him to all the residents of Kapoly [Kapyl]. Almost all of them, including the Christians, appreciated him, through the influence of the local priest Sawicz, who honored Father and spread his name amongst the farmers.

In Father's praise, I will tell an interesting story here: An important Jew of the family of the author of Afikei Yehuda lived in Kapoly. His family name was Edel. Once, the Jews of Hamburg imprisoned him due to some libel. My father of blessed memory travelled to Hamburg, appeared before the Parliament-Freistadt, and vouched for the innocence of Mr. Edel. Thanks to his intervention, the man was set free.

The well-known battle between the *Gaonim the Ridba'z* and Rabbi Meier Feimer of blessed memory broke out during the time that Father served as the rabbi of Kapoly. They both urged Father to stand at their side. He stood afar since his soul was disgusted when he heard the details of the dispute. However, when the Ridba'z brought the Gaon Rabbi Isser Zalman Meltzer with his Yeshiva from Slobodka to Slutsk, Father decided to send me to that splendid Yeshiva. I was eleven years old then, and this was my first journey from Kapoly to Slutsk in the company of my father of blessed memory. When I was still young, I entered under the wings of Rabbi Shachna, who taught in the *Beis Midrash* on Hapaszker Street. Rabbi Isser Zalman promised Father to keep an eye on me and test me from time to time.

However, it was not my fate to benefit from that wonderful atmosphere for a long time. My older brother, Rabbi Zeev, who already served as a rabbi in Chicago, urged Father to send me to him. It was very hard for my parents to part from me and remain alone. The difficulties of the situation in Russia at that time caused my parents to finally agree to let me go. I returned to Kapoly, and my parents accompanied me to Baranovich.

When the train started moving, I heard the voice of Father full of trembling and love: "My dear son, be a faithful Jew even in the far-off land."

[Page 500]

The Rabbi from Kapoly

by Rabbi Yaakov Meir of blessed memory

Translated by Jerrold Landau

Rabbi Yaakov Meir Krawczynski

Rabbi Yaakov Meir Krawczynski, who was renowned as the rabbi from Kapoly, was born around 5627 [1867] in the city of Grajewo to his father Rabbi Avraham Mordechai, a friend of the Gaon Rabbi Shmuel Mohilewer.

The aforementioned Rabbi Yaakov Meir studied in the Yeshiva of Volozhin under the supervision of Rabbi Naftali Tzvi Yehuda Berlin, along with the following family Gaonim: Rabbi Avraham Yitzchak HaKohen Kook, the rabbi of the Land of Israel; Rabbi Avraham Dov Shapira, the rabbi of Kovno; Rabbi Isser Zalman Meltzer, the rabbi of Slutsk who served as the head of the Eitz Chaim Yeshiva in Jerusalem at the end of his days. His father-in-law was Rabbi Yehoshua Menachem Goldwasser of *Szczuczyn*, a wealthy merchant, a wise man, a scribe, and an activist of the Chovevei Zion movement.

Rabbi Yaakov Meir continued to study in the Yeshiva of Volozhin with a group of excellent young men, who were supported by the well-known manufacturer and merchant Brodsky, and were called "Avreichei Brodsky." He also studied in the *Beis Midrashes* of the cities of Eishishok [Eišiškės] and Sislovich [Svislach]. About ten years after his marriage, in the year 5657 [1897], he was accepted as rabbi in the city of Izabelin near Wolkowisk, the place of the first rabbinical tenure of Rabbi Yitzchak Elchanan Spektor. He occupied the rabbinical seat of Kapoly from the year 5660 [1900], where the famous Rabbi Yom Tov Lipman, the author of the books *Kedushat Yom Tov* and *Melechet Yom Tov* on the Talmud, had previously served.

Rabbi Yaakov Meir earned a good name as one of the great rabbis of the vicinity. He was a great scholar, a splendid orator, wise in the ways of the world, with a noble personality. His son Rabbi Zeev Gold of blessed memory expresses his memories in the following words, "There was no rabbi as handsome and with such a fine appearance as him in the entire country. He was tall, with a noble countenance and large, bright eyes, whose mouth exuded pearls."

He also excelled in his traits and his fine relations with his fellow.

Rabbi Gold gave over a characteristic fact from which we can learn a great deal about the character and behavior of his father of blessed memory.

A certain householder, great in Torah lived in Kapoly. He could trace his lineage to the Rema. He was very wealthy. He behaved in a high manner due to his greatness, and his relations with the local rabbis were always haughty. Rabbi Yaakov also suffered from him, for he impinged on his honor from time to time. Nevertheless, due to his great wisdom, he knew how to manage with him.

One day, that wealthy man sat with a group of studiers in the *Beis Midrash*, and talked in a denigrating fashion about the rabbi. Suddenly, he suffered a stroke and died on the spot. The residents of the town, who knew about his relations with the rabbi, were surprised that the rabbi burst out in bitter weeping, and eulogized him with warm words, emanating from the heart.

Around the time of the First World War, Rabbi Yaakov Meir was accepted as the rabbi of Mariupol. The city was conquered by the Germans at the outbreak of the war. When it was conquered by the Russians, the Christians slandered the rabbi, that they saw him signaling to the Germans. The Russian commander sentenced him to death within 24 hours. However, a miracle occurred, and the commanders changed at that time. The new commander had mercy on him and ordered him to leave the place immediately. This event affected his health badly.

He died suddenly of a heart attack on the train to Minsk. He was taken off the train in the town of Gorodi, and buried there on 20 Kislev, 5674 [1913][1].

His wife, Rebbetzin Freda-Dvora, who was an intelligent woman with a wise heat, wandered to cities in Russia, and from there traveled to her children in the United States. After the war, she made *aliya* to the

Land of Israel and settled in Tel Aviv. She was honored for her intelligence and her activities in communal institutions. She died in 5701 [1941].

Rabb Yaakov Meir left behind two sons of renown. One was Rabbi Zeev Gold of blessed memory, who served as rabbi in various communities of the United States, and was one of the heads of worldwide Mizrachi and a member of the leadership of the Jewish agency. He died in 5716 [1956].

His second son is Rabbi Dr. Rafael Tzvi Gold, who also served as rabbi in different communities of the United States. He currently serves as a professor of psychiatry in a university in New York, and heads various institutions of Mizrachi.

The wife and children of the writer of these lines, currently in Israel, are among the grandchildren and great-grandchildren of Rabbi Yaakov Meir.

In the estate of Rabbi Yaakov Meir, there were compositions on *halachic* novellae on the four sections of the Code of Jewish Law, but they were lost during his time of wandering during the time of war.

Translator's footnote:

1. The Hebrew date given here precedes the First World War, and therefore may be in error.

[Page 501]

Rabbi Zeev Gold of Blessed Memory

Translated by Jerrold Landau

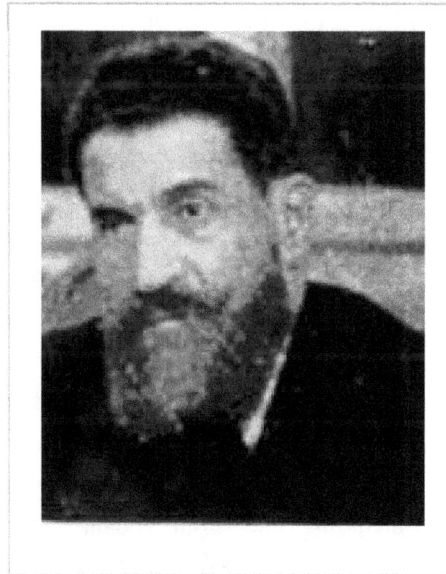

Rabbi Zeev Gold

Among the people of renown who originate from Kapoly, we should note Rabbi Zeev Gold, the son of the rabbi of Kapoly, Rabbi Yaakov Meir Krawczynski.

Rabbi Zeev Gold was born in the year 5649 [1889] in the city of Szczuczyn. He came to Kapoly with his father's family at the age of ten. There, he studied Torah from the *melamdim* Reb Shlomo Szwyzycer and Reb Shmuel Zaricki, and later in the group of lads who heard Torah from his father.

He spent a brief period in the nearby Mir Yeshiva. At the age of 18, his father decided to remove him from the bounds of Russia out of concern for being drafted in the army.

Equipped with letters of ordination from his father and the rabbi of Minsk, Rabbi Eliezer Rabinowitz, the young Zeev arrived in the United States. When he arrived in America, he found himself in dire straits and literally suffered from hunger. However, thanks to his wonderful rhetorical talents, he found favor in the eyes of those who heard him, and they supported him. In the interim, he gained experience in teaching and also in the English language, and began to travel from city to city, preaching to the masses.

Thus, did he arrive in Utica, where he met his wife Yocheved Reichler, the daughter of the local rabbi, who had died a few years previously.

From that time, he had great success, and moved from one rabbinical position to the next in various cities until he arrived in San Francisco. In all the places, he endeared himself to the community as one of the most talented rabbis. He perfected the American art of public speaking and communal mannerisms. He gained worldly wisdom and life wisdom. He was graced with a penetrating voice and a clear style. He also stood out in his fine appearance. He enthused the hearts and aroused the spirits.

He set times for Torah study, and broadened his knowledge in *halacha*. He specialized in *Aggadaic midrashim*. He gained competence in various subject, especially ancient and modern philosophy. He read and studied a great deal, and became a basket full of books [i.e., a man full of learning]. Due to this, his sermons were full of content, built on the foundations of our sages of blessed memory, and constructed with values of thought, philosophy, and knowledge, in the form of old wine in a new bottle. He was enthusiastic about every mitzvah. He had a wide heart and an open hand for charity and benevolence.

Since he was enthusiastic about Chibat Tzion already from his youth, he joined the Mizrachi movement, and then dedicated himself to it with all his energy, devoting his life to it. He wandered from city to city setting up branches of that movement and disseminating it broadly.

When Rabbi Meir Berlin came to the United States, he stood at his right side. Through their efforts, they turned Mizrachi into an all-encompassing national movement. From that time, he participated in all the Mizrachi conventions in the United States and throughout the world, and took a leading position. He served as a delegate from the 13th to the 23rd Zionist Congresses, and was one of the illustrious leaders. He also participated in the Zionist convention in London in the year 5679 [1919], after the Balfour Declaration, which led to the foundations of the national homeland in the Land of Israel.

After the First World War, when the Yeshiva heads of Europe began to visit the United States to conduct fundraising campaigns for their institutions, Rabbi Gold became their first address. He would host them in his home and work a great deal for their benefit.

He also dedicated himself to Torah educational activity in the United States, and was among the founders of various educational institutions, including the Torah Vodaath Yeshiva of New York. Rabbi Gold made *aliya* to the Land with some of his family and settled in Tel Aviv around the year 5684 [1924]. After he made several journeys in the world for the benefit of Mizrachi and the national funds, he was invited by the Chief Rabbi of Israel, the Gaon Rabbi A. Y. Kook, to make the rounds to the various settlements of the Land as an itinerant rabbi, to strengthen the Jewish spirit in them. He then worked a great deal to firm up the spiritual and religious situation in the various settlements in the Land. Rabbi Gold noted that this role was the most precious role he fulfilled during his lifetime.

For various reasons, he returned to the United States and was accepted as a rabbi in Brooklyn, where he continued his work for strengthening Judaism and building the Land. At times, he served as the president of the Mizrachi organization of the United States, and stood at the helm of various Zionist institutions. Some of his family remained in the Land. Rabbi Gold would visit the Land every year and spend some time there. In the meantime, two of his daughters got married and set up their families in Israel.

After several years, he settled again in the Land, and was chosen as the chairman of the world Mizrachi center. In this role as well, he not only had to travel through the Land, but also to all the countries of the world to work for the benefit of Mizrachi and the upbuilding of the Land.

At the outbreak of the Second World War, he was summoned to return to the United States to work there for the benefit of the settlement of the Land, both in the economic and political realms. He was appointed to the Jewish delegation on behalf of the Jewish Agency in Lake Success[1], and played an active role in the declaration of the State of Israel as the Jewish State. With the declaration of the State in 5708 [1948], he was chosen as the vice president of the provisional council of the state.

In the year 5707 [1947], he was chosen as a member of the leadership of the Jewish Agency, where he was given the role of heading the division for the development of Jerusalem. From that time, he settled in Israel and dedicated himself to that task. Much of the development of that city after it was emptied of part of its residents during the time of the battle of independence can be attributed to him. In his time, he was one of the initiators of the idea

[Page 502]

of Binyanei Hauma [The Jerusalem International Convention Center], and he placed great effort in setting it up. In the year 5712 [1952], the Zionist Congress gave him the role of setting up the division for Torah culture and education in the Diaspora, and to stand at it head. He dedicated himself to this task with his entire soul, in order to save the youth from defilement and foreign influences. He once again took up the wandering staff and traveled to many countries to set up Torah educational institutions and to encourage the Jewish residents to make *aliya* to the Land. The Jews of North Africa (Morocco, Tunis, and other places) revered and appreciated him. He founded a rabbinical and teachers seminary in Ramsgate, England for students who came from South Africa. He also came up with the idea of bringing talented students as well as teachers from the lands of the Diaspora to Israel to complete their Torah education, so that they can return and fulfil their tasks as teachers, educators, and counselors.

He did a great deal of activity a head of the Mizrachi organization in the Land and as a member of the world center, as well as in various Torah endeavors.

Despite the fact that he suffered from a heart ailment in the latter years, he continued with energy and great activity in many endeavors. He participated in all the issues of the country. He made appearances with stormy speeches, and read and wrote a great deal.

In the year 5709 [1949], he published the first volume of his book *Nivei Zahav*. In the last year of his life, he also began to lecture on the philosophy of Judaism at Bar Ilan University.

At the age of 67, when he was still full of spiritual energy, he fell under the burden of his important, heavy work. On 27 Nissan 5657 [1957] his large heart stopped, and the orator, Zionist leader, and veteran Torah personality was gathered unto his people.

Translator's footnote:

1.   Where the U. N. resolution in favor of the founding of the State of Israel was passed in 1947.

Chaim Kriwicki

by Rafael Rivin

Translated by Jerrold Landau

Chaim Kriwicki

He was born in 1896 in Starobin. He was the son of a working family. He received a traditional education in the *cheder* and yeshiva. He was drafted to the army in 1916, sent to the war front, and volunteered for the Red Army at the end of the war.

He was attracted to the Zionist movement already at a young age. At the beginning of the First World War, when Zionist activity was prohibited, people would gather in his house in the village outside the town. The small Zionist library, *shekalim* [tokens of membership in the Zionist movement], Keren Kayemet stamps, and other such items were transferred there. He returned to Zionist and communal activities when he was freed from the army. He was a member of the committee of the Zionist chapter in the town, and one of the heads of the military Hechalutz that began to organize in Russia in 1917. He was also among the founders of the defense of the town, which suffered at that time from regime changes as well as lack of government. He founded the first group that was organized for *aliya* to the Land before the final conquest of the town by the Red Army in 1920. When he was living in Poland, his family members in America sent him money and papers to come to them, but he forewent this and distributed the money to his friends who did not have the means to make *aliya* to the Land.

He worked on the Neve-Shaanan - Haifa Road for about half a year. From there, his group was transferred to Atlit to work in the salt company there. He was among the first workers in that company, where he worked until his last day. While he was still working on the road, he stood at the head of the guard. When he moved to work in Atlit, he was among the organizers of the Haganah [defense] in the district, and stood at its head until the outbreak of the War of Independence.

He was beloved by his friends, and helped his fellow already from his youth. He saw his purpose in the Land as a life of labor, and in renewing the society on the foundations of labor and social justice.

He died on 5 Cheshvan 5622 [1961].

[Page 503]

Among Our *Landsleit* [Compatriots] Who Contributed to the Publication of the Slutsk Chronicles

N. W.

(According to the "Alef–Beis")

The *landsleit* [compatriots] of Slutsk and the surrounding areas hold a very respected place among the professional and commercial fields in America. To write about each person individually and in detail would fill many books, and this would certainly be interesting. But here we will limit ourselves with a few lines about several individuals who held important positions in American Jewish life and who were very instrumental in effecting this project of the Yizkor Book. Their extensive aid inspired all the friends of the New York committee to follow through with this difficult work, despite many difficulties and challenges. The following people, being pioneers in their very nature, did not consider the current circumstances, and this helped them to develop their personal projects. Therefore, they also had the strength to support this critical work of the Yizkor Book, ignoring the many others who ignored or mocked this entire issue. Because of the commitment of these persons, it is worthwhile to relate their life stories.

Eliyahu and Sarah Altman

Eliyahu Altman, son of Yehuda Leyb and Rivka, was born in Slutsk. Their home was in the synagogue courtyard. Their oldest son, Reuvke [Reuven] Altman, was a "prominent" person in Slutsk. After having learned in the Slutsk and Slabodka yeshivos, he returned to Slutsk, became a *maskil* ["enlightened" intellectual] , and threw himself into the Hebrew–Zionist movement, and together with the teacher Yitzkhok Katzenelson, they established a "*Kheder Metukan*" ["improved school"], where, together with others, they spread the Hebrew culture among the Slutsker youth.

His younger brother Eliyahu, also studied in the Slutsker "*Mekhina*" ["Preparatory" program] with Reb Nekhemiah, and in the "great *yeshiva*." After that, he went to study in the half–modern Lieder yeshiva. When he came back to Slutsk, he completed the course in the "Real–School." He and his brother were very active in all areas of national thought and education. He was also active in founding the "*Tzeirei–Tzion*"

["Youth of Zion"] party, and also the local "*Hekhalutz*" group ["The Pioneer," preparing youth for agricultural work in Israel]. Many of these people are now in Israel.

In 1920, Eliyahu, along with a group of "pioneers," began their journey to Israel. For a short time, Eliyahu stayed in Poland, where he worked energetically for the *Tzeirei–Tzion* and *Hekhalutz* movements. He went from city to city, recruiting pioneers for Israel, and finally, he himself arrived in Israel.

Here he became active in "*Hapoel Hatzair*" ["The Young Labourer," Labour Party] and "*Histadrut*" ["General Organization of Workers"] and participated as a member in the refugee committee of the "*Moetzes Hapoalim*" ["Workers' Council"] in Yaffa – Tel–Aviv.

Sarah and Eliyahu Altman

In 1923, when Eliyahu came to New York, he also gave much of his time for nationalist and cultural projects.

In the first years, he devoted himself to teaching and at the same time, he proceeded with his own personal studies of jurisprudence and law. Eventually, in 1931, he received his diploma from the Department of Law in New York University. And from then on he practiced as a lawyer with great devotion. During that time, Eliyahu married Sarah Klajnman, the daughter of Khaim and Tzippe.

[Page 504]

Her father, from the small town of Pogrebyscz near Kiev, was a passionate nationalist Jew, and already as a successful merchant, at the beginning of century, left all his business activities and went to settle in Israel. He even succeeded to buy baths near Khedera, but unfortunately he was unable to settle himself and returned, and tried his fortune in Turkey. There, in Constantinople, a group of Russian *Khovevei Tzion* ["Lovers of Zion" promoted immigration to Israel] created a colony by the name of "*Mesila Khadasha*" ["New Path" in Istanbul] where they hoped to prepare themselves for immigration to Israel. The father of Sarah Klajnman also settled in that same colony. Within a few years, the plan fell through, and the Klajnmans were forced to immigrate to America and once again wait for the right moment to go to Israel.

Eliyahu Altman was one of the first to warmly come forward and offer to work on the Yizkor Book, and served as secretary for the entire time on the New York committee. His wife Sarah helps him alongside in this work.

Dovid and Sarah Bezborodka

Dovid Bezborodka is a Slusker for many generations back, and despite the fact that his grandfather Reb Hershel Hillel had already left Slutsk in 1866 to go to Peterburg, fate always brought the family back to Slutsk and they never really went far from there.

His grandfather, Reb Hershel Hillel, was a learned and good–hearted man. He was of the first Jews in Russia, and he ran a glass factory very successfully.

His name is remembered among the esteemed people of Slutsk as part of the committee of the great fire in the year 1868 (see page 30).

As was mentioned, he moved his business in the year 1866 to Sestroreck near Peterburg, and within several years, he moved to Moscow. At the same time, he did not want to totally remove himself from his birthplace, and so he opened a second glass factory also in Hancewycz, which he visited several times a year.

His major projects and businesses did not distance him from Jews and Judaism, which he also infused into his children. He sent his son Yosef, after completing his gymnasium course, to study in the Mirer yeshiva for several years.

In 1890, when Hershel Hillel was elderly but still active in his business, a Jewish soldier from Slutsk visited him in Moscow and told him that there was a severe penalty on his head because someone had informed on him. His wife and children remained "lost" in Slutsk. Reb Hershel Hillel's heart was so moved by this that he left his business "helter skelter" and went to Slutsk to deal with the dangers that faced this soldier. In fact, he succeeded in freeing the soldier, but this affected him so strongly, that he became very ill. The Rav of Slutsk of that time, Reb Yakov Dovid, visited the "Moscovite" Hershel Hillel and gave him a blessing that because of what he had done [for the soldier] he would merit that his own children would not fall into the hands of the Czarist powers. But this blessing did not save him from the Angel of Death, and he was buried near his parents in the Slutsk cemetery.

Several years later, his wife came to visit his gravesite, and also 'by chance' died in Slutsk.

Reb Yosef and his wife Mashe Laya Bezborodka (second generation)

Reb Tzvi Hillel and his wife Perl Bexborodka, a well—known businessman [community leader], at the beginning of the 19th century

[Page 505]

In 1891, during the "Moscow expulsion," the son, Yosef Bezborodka, who was conducting business alongside his father, left everything behind, and at the age of 24, packed up and went to Orsza, into the "Jewish quarter" [so–called Jewish area in Czarist Russia], and there opened a new glass and mirror factory, but was not successful.

In 1901, Reb Yosef and his wife visited the factory in Hancewycz, and to "make the trip" [enrich the trip], they went to the cemetery in Slutsk. While in Slutsk, the wife Bezborodka gave birth to their son – Dovid (July 26, 1901).

In 1907, Yosef moved his factory to Czestochow. He, the Litvak [from Lithuania], the *misnaged* [anti– *Chassidic* philosophies] from generations back, in a new world with all kinds of *Chassidic* circles, still evoked great respect from all sides of the population. He infused into his children a love for Torah and a nationalistic interest, particularly for Israel. In 1919, there was a pogrom in Czestochow. His Polish workers protected him and his family with their lives, and did not allow any harm at all to befall them.

Yosef died in 1922 at the age of 55, and the Czestochower Jewish community honored him, this very Slutsker *misnaged*, with a cemetery plot near the prominent gravesite of their beloved Pilczer Rebbe!

Dovid Bezborodka (third generation)

With time, Dovid grew up, studied and perfected the mirror and glass production. His business often demanded his visits to all different countries. In this way, while traveling, he settled in Paris and there opened two factories of glass and mirrors – one in Saverne and one in Paris.

In Paris he also met Miss Sarah Cuker, daughter of a very prominent Polish–Jewish family,

Yosef Aron Bezborodka (fourth generation)

who he married (1930). His factories in France grew greatly.

When the Nazis occupied France, Dovid Bezborodka left behind his entire fortune, and with just his soul and with his household, and with the help of the French League for Human Rights," in which he was active, he arrived in New York.

As a dedicated branch of the family that was fated to keep moving, always building and start over with even more energy, Dovid B. also threw himself into this in New York, with his particular family rhythm, in order to set up a mirror factory. This was even more difficult for him than his father in Orsza and in Czestokhow. According to the New York manufacturing regulations, and the large amount of capital that is required for this, the project seemed impossible for someone who brought with him his name only. But here, Dovid's inborn Slutsker intelligence came to use – in that it ignited people with its enthusiasm and won over their loyalty. Until today, the "Mechanical Mirror Company": is a prominent factory which employs tens of Jews. As a fiery nationalist and devoted friend of *Hapoel Hamizrachi* [pioneering labor movement in Israel], Dovid had all kinds of other ideas about his family's future. His father, the Slutsker born glass manufacturer, once told him that the best raw material for the glass industry was found

[Page 506]

in Israel, because in the Biblical verse *"sefunei temunei chol"* ["hidden treasures of the sand" Deuteronomy 33:19], Rashi [principal Biblical commentary] explains: *"Toris ve'khilozon u'zekhukhis levanah ha'yotzim minhayam u'min ha'khol"* ["The *taris*" (type of fish, in the tuna family) and the *khilozon* (type of fish) and white glass which came out of the sea and are in the sand], and would translate: "Taris" a type of fish, "*Khilozon*" and another type of snail which produces [purple] dye, "*u'zekhukhis levanah*" and sand for white glass.

This explanation of Rashi, Dovid Bezborodka carried with him in his long traveling years, and he realized this with a factory that is being built in Acco, and he hopes to employ hundreds of Jewish workers in the "mirror and glass industry."

Moshe and Aidel Himelstayn [Gimelstayn]

Moishe Himelstayn – born in Slutsk. His parents – Pesakh son of Moishe HaKohen [the priest] and Rokhel daughter of Reb Yakov (Gersowycz).

His father Pesakh studied Torah and was also a *Maskil* [enlightened person]. On his Hebrew letters he would sign his name as "Pesakh *Even–Shamayim* (Himel–Stayn). [*Even*, Hebrew–stone, Yiddish– *stayn*; *Shamayim*, Hebrew–sky, Yiddish– *himel*].

Pesakh earned a living from cheese production in a cellar on the main road, and from upstairs in a shop of dairy products. He did business with Dutch cheese which he exported even to Siberia.

When the Polish legions receded from White Russia in 1920, the young Moishe Pesakh's decided to go along with them to Poland and not remain in Red Slutsk. He remained in Poland for three years. In 1923, Moishe went to Cuba. As all new immigrants, he struggled hard in the beginning, but slowly good fortune smiled upon him, and he bought stretches of land and built up many projects, and they brought him a fine annual income. He figured that if his father could manage a dairy business in Slutsk, then why could he not manage a factory in Havana? While he was in Poland, for a short time he worked in a perfume store and "infused" himself with some knowledge about this type of work. He really did prove his good fortune, and opened a factory of cosmetic products.

Meanwhile, he married Aidel Skolnik, a real Slutsker, daughter of Zelig the teacher. She became not only his lifelong companion, but also

Reb Pesakh Himelstayn with his wife Rokhel and their daughter

... the main salesperson of his cosmetic products. That's how the two Slutskers developed quite a nice business in Havana. Their income grew from year to year. But one fine day, Fidel Castro arrived, and he nationalized all the privatized businesses in Cuba, and among them also Himelstayn's. Fortunately, he was lucky to pre-empt some of this and he invested some of his capital in Florida. Now the Himelstayns and some other Jews and non–Jews are sitting in Florida, having run from Cuba, and as they sit at the shore of the Atlantic Ocean, under the rays of the burning sun, they are thinking about all their migrations, from the Slutsker mud pools to the rich Miami ocean shore. But in spite of all these experiences, Moishe Himlestayn is fresh and upbeat, and he still hopes to build new worlds in his adopted Havana, Cuba, larger and more beautiful ones than in his hometown of Slutsk. The more that this sweet dream poured out in the present, the stronger was the feeling and the longing for Slutsk, his childhood home. At the beginning of the activity for the Yizkor Book project, Moishe Himelstayn came right to work and since then gave a hand, and helped compile the memories.

Beryl Skolnik (Aidel Himelstayn's brother)

[Page 507]

Louis Chinitz

Original English article typed up by Genia Hollander

Louis (Hebrew name: Arie Leib) Chinitz, was born to David and Chaya Rachel in Starobin on June 15, 1899.

In 1912, he arrived together with his parents to the U.S.A. and settled in Brooklyn, New York. He attended elementary schools at P.S. N°2 and N°62 and De Witt Clinton High School. He also endeavoured to continue his education at college but was regretfully stopped because of financial difficulties. On Dec. 17, 1923, he married Leah Finkel, daughter of Abraham Finkel.

Mr. Finkel, blessed be his memory, was a native of Court of Rudobelka near Slutsk, and upon his arrival to the U.S., he occupied himself in the building line. He was well-known as a profound scholarly and truly G-d fearing person. Regardless of circumstantial financial difficulties, he never swerved as to his strict observance of the Sabbath and in his adherence to all Jewish orthodox requirements.

On February 13, 1926, Mr. Chinitz, together with Mr. Louis Litt, started a clothing manufacturing business at 833 Broadway, New York City. The business grew considerably and they later moved to their present location at 85 Fifth Ave. New York City and opened branches at 1122 Kings Highway Brooklyn, N.Y. and 327 E. Fordham Rd. Bronx, N.Y.

The firm of Litt-Chinitz, Inc., is well-known in the metropolitan clothing industry and is one of the most reputable in this trade for its quality and dealings with its workers and its customers. Mr. Chinitz is also well known in the New York real estate circles where he occupies a prominent position.

With all his financial progress, Mr. Chinitz did not lose his simplicity and modesty which he brought along from his native town of Starobin. His warm heart and human touch to his fellowmen and their needs are highly praised in his own community of Great Neck, New York, as well as among the national American and Jewish welfare organizations.

Mr. & Mrs. Chinitz have three daughters. Sydelle, Rosaline and Florence; of whom Sydelle is married to Mr. Benjamin Prince, and active member of the Litt-Chinitz firm; Rosaline to the prominent surgeon, Dr. Arthur Tessler of Great Neck, and Florence to Mr. Morton Blanck who conducts a finance organization in Baltimore, Maryland. All these three families are truly following in the footsteps of their lovely parents, participating in all religious and communal affairs. They are highly respected in their communities, and among the broader circles of their professions.

[Page 508]

Dovid Juzdon

Dovid Juzdon was born to his parents Nasanel Tzvi and Dvoire–Bashe Juzdon, on June 19, 1893, in Hrozewie (Shabbath eve, 25 Sivan, 5653).

His father, whom they used to call Sanye Dodzhe's (Nasanel Dovid's), was a respected merchant in Hrozewie. They used to call this son Dovid Dodzhe Sanye's. His first *Rebbi* [religious teacher] in Hrozewe was the well–known teacher Burstayn, Yehuda Leyb Grozowski's brother–in–law from Pohost.

When Dovid got older, his parents sent him to Slutsk, where he studied for two years with Reb Yoshe Triconer.

In 1910, Dovid went to America and worked in a gross–paper store that was run by a German Jew by the name of Heller.

Even though Dovid was just then a mere eighteen years old, he demonstrated a great business acuity, and in a short time, Heller invited Dodzhe Sanye's to become a partner in the company. So they gave it a name "Heller and Judzon Paper Store" and the company proudly bears this same name until today.

In 1917, when America entered World War One, David volunteered as a matross [type of gunner] in the American navy. The entire time during the war, he participated in many clashes.

Once, when a warship was in the middle of the ocean in great danger, Dovid swore that if God would help him survive the war and come home safely, he would go to Hrozewie and bring over his entire family to America. After the war, he really fulfilled his promise and in the year 1920, he brought over seventeen souls from Hrozewie to New York and helped each of them settle in.

In 1923, Dovid married Miriam Yaffa, daughter of a prominent Lithuanian family of great refinement and lineage.

In time, his company grew bigger, and today "Heller and Juzdon" is one of the most respected companies in the paper industry in New York.

During all this time, Dovid Juzdon was active in all the Jewish welfare organizations and institutions, locally and nationally. For many years he was chairman of the "Hebrew Institute in Long Island" and Far Rockway, New York, one of the largest and most beautiful traditional high schools in the New York area. Also, for many years he was president of the large "*Beth Shalom*" synagogue in Lawrence, Long Island, that is also one of the richest and intellectual traditional schools in that area. For a long time, Dovid Juzdon was director of the "Jewish War Veterans," former soldiers of the American army.

Other than in local activities, Mr. Juzdon was also very devoted to working for Israel, such as for the UJA [United Jewish Appeal], and Israel Bonds, where he was exemplary, and also for regular Jewish cultural institutions such as for *yeshivos* [religious schools], and so on, and everything that he does, is always with humility, refinement, and discretion.

Mr. and Mrs. Juzdon succeeded in raising a beautiful generation, and their children, who worked along with them in the business, are also devoted to Jewish tradition and activity.

When we began to think about the Slutsker Yizkor Book, Juzdon was the first to provide all the paper for the entire book. His great support largely inspired all the friends and compatriots, and helped realize the idea.

Generally, one can say that the Hrozowier teacher Burstayn, together with Reb Yoshe Triconer can be proud with what they implanted into their student Dodzhe Sanye's from Hrozowie.

[Page 509]

Harry and Sarah Lefrak

Harry Lefrak is one of the most popular Slutsker compatriots in New York, both because of his great participation in all the welfare interests and also because of his phenomenal growth in the business world, that sounds like a legend.

His Jewish name is Hershel Meilekh, and he was born to his parents – Aron, Moishe Beryl the glazier's son from Slutsk and his wife Dvoire Henye from Kozlowyc, a village near Urecze. The parents lived in Bobruysk at the time that Hershel was born on the first *seder* night of Passover, year 5645 (March 30, 1885). Right after that, they moved back to Slutsk, which remained as the home for the family for many years.

It seems that Moishe Beryl at that time already had relatives in Israel with whom he was closely connected, and he tried to figure out how to get there.

When he was already there for a few years, Aron Lefrak learned of his father's death, and because of an heir's dispute, he and his family returned to Slutsk.

In 1897, once again he wanted to try his luck, and again went with his family to Israel. They remained there until after Hershel Meilekh's *bar mitzvah*, that took place in Jerusalem in the year 5658 [1898].

Unfortunately, once again they had to return to Slutsk through the Black Sea to Odessa. But instead of going along with his entire family, Hershel Meilekh convinced his father to allow him to stay over in Odessa. The father relented, even though Hershel Meilekh was still young, but since he came from a family of glaziers, and knowing the details of the work, he immediately got a job in the field and demonstrated great skill. It did not take long, and he soon began earning about four ruble a week, a great sum in those days.

Hershel Meilekh spent about two years in Odessa and he saved a great amount of money. So in 1901, he returned to Slutsk.

Since he had already "seen the world," and since he was independent, it was now difficult for him to fit in with the small–town life of his father's house and lifestyle. Therefore, conflicts arose between the two of them. Hershel Meilekh hardly made it through three years, and one day, after Passover 1904, he ran away from home to steal across the German border at Lomzo. Unfortunately, the Russian police caught him and brought him back "hotly" to Slutsk. Eventually, he convinced his father to allow him to go to America, and on January 5, 1905, Arel the glazier arrived in New York together with Hershel Meilekh and with another younger son, leaving behind the wife and daughters in Slutsk. When the immigration officials asked Arele how he thought he was going to make a living, he took out 150 ruble from his pocket and pointing at his two sons, he replied: "With this in hand and with my two sons, I hope that the Creator will not abandon me."

In the beginning, they, as the other immigrants of those years, struggled very hard and did all kinds of heavy work, and even shoveled snow in the New York streets, but their main business was as glaziers – their call for generations.

In 1906, they began to build the

[Page 510]

large tenements in New York, on 28th Street between First and Second Avenues, and the young Hershel Meilekh talked to the builders and told them how to save money with the glass [for windows, etc.]. For this, he immediately received a position and in one year he saved more than $3,000 and met Sarah Schwartz, a Slutsker girl, and she became his bride. At the time, in 1907, there was a crisis in America, and Hershel Meilekh lost his few dollars and had to start all over again.

Finally, he married on June 7, 1907, and right away he taught his wife the glass business and they worked together. In 1910, in the electricity station of the train center, there was an explosion. When they were rebuilding the station, Hershel Meilekh took on the job of glazier, and demonstrated great skill in this vocation. He acquired a wide knowledge and began to work for seven insurance companies with a balance of $80,000 a month.

In 1914, the glass business fell significantly, and Lefrak lost his entire capital, a sum of $35,000. But in about several years, glass once again became valuable, and in 1920, he worked himself up to having a fortune of $300,000. Then he threw himself into the building industry and rose higher and higher. 1930 was the time of the great crisis in America, and Harry Lefrak lost around $650,000 and remained with barely $100,000. A few years later, he once again began to rise in the construction industry, until today. Now about 134 buildings carry his name. All of them in large New York, the value of about $100,000,000, and this brings in about $15,000,000 of rent per year.

Harry Lefrak is very active in all kinds of community matters, and particularly in the United Slutsker Relief Committee, where he was treasurer for many years and greatly supported and aided the work. Also, he was a great contributor with a generous hand to *yeshivos* and all other national–cultural organizations.

In 1950, there was a great tragedy in his family, when his son–in–law, Mr. William (Zev) Lampert died in an airplane tragedy. Harry Lefrak decided to perpetuate his name in Israel and, in a hospital in Ramat Gan, he opened a room in his name, and also, in *Yad Eliyahu*, there is a clinic of *Kupat Kholim* [provides health plan] specially built by the Lefraks in his memory.

Their son Shmuel is also a follower of his father's ways. He participates in all important community matters with a generous hand and great finesse.

When the Yizkor Book committee was organized, Harry Lefrak was one of the first supporters who enabled the printing of this book and encouraged others to participate as well in this project.

Avrohom and Khaike Maizel at a family gathering for the Slutsker Pinkus [book of records] in Los Angeles

Seated from right to left: Shmuel Kohen, Akiva Aizenstat, and Avrohom Maizel
Standing: Rawycz, his sisters: Zelda Kohen, Faigel Aizenstat, Khaike Maizel, and her niece Lila with her husband Dr. Eliyahu Epstayn.

[Page 511]

Avrohom and Khaike Maizel

If they would distribute medals for good work in the New York committee for the benefit of the Yizkor Book, then Avrohom and Khaike would certainly earn them.

They [the Maizels] were of the first to whom the idea of publishing such a book had such appeal. Right after my first appearance at a memorial gathering of the United Slutsker Aide Committee, that took place on February 27, 1955, in room 504 of the Forwards building, Avrohom and Khaike approached me and greeted me warmly for speaking about this, and they really helped from the beginning until the end of the project. The first meeting was held in their home…

Moishe Maizel (Avrohom Maizel's father)

… where the first $500 were collected for this objective, and upon which the foundation was placed for continued work.

Avrohom Maizel was born in Slutsk, on Shabbath of the Torah portion "*Vayeitzei*" ["And he went out" Book of Exodus], 13th of Kislev (November 30, 1895), to his parents Moishe Leyb and Khava Maizel. His father was known as Moishe the smithy on Ostrower Street. Avrohom studied in *kheder* until he was twelve years old, under the teacher Avremel the yellow one [blond], and after that in the "Hebrew School." When he was sixteen, he began to work for this father in Koznie. But his heart pulled him into the big world.

In 1916, he left for Yekaterinoslav, and worked in a government metal factory.

In 1918, in the heat of the Russian civil war, he returned to Slutsk and became one of the main directors of the *Poalei Tzion* party in Slutsk.

His dear wife Khaike, is also a Slutsker from birth, born to her parents Meyer Velvel and Alte Rawycz. Her father was a "talented" Jew with "golden hands." A carpenter by trade, everyone knew that whatever Meyer Velvel would make would be a piece of art. He made a few arks for Torah scrolls which everyone ran to see, and his name was reputed everywhere.

But from a holy ark to earning a living is a long distance, so he had an idea to try and "blow the *shofar* [ram's horn blown in synagogues on Rosh Hashanah] for the Christians." So he left and became a contractor for construction, to differentiate, for churches for the Christians, in which he also excelled. His skill in this district acquired a great reputation, and many churches in the Slutsker area actually rang with Velvel Rawycz's work.

They lived far away in Wygoda, and since the entire family had an intellectual curiosity of the free national wing, there would be many Zionist gatherings secretly held in their home, when it was still forbidden in Slutsk.

Avrohom and Khaike married in Slutsk in 1918, and three years later they came to New York, where a part of their family had already come earlier.

Even in New York, the Maizels belonged to the intellectual workers' circles, and in their house there were always all kinds of meetings for cultural and benevolent activities.

The Maizels have a son Moishe Leyb and a daughter Etel. Both married children are raising intellectual, Jewish families in the footsteps of their beloved parents.

[Page 512]

Yitzkhok and Rokhel Mishelow

Yitzkhok Mishelow was born in Wyzne. When he was a child, Yitzkhok's father Nisen, a cousin of the known Mishelows (owner of the Slutsker mill), went out to Slutsk. Later, Yitzkhok studied with the well–known teacher Reb Lipe Szinjowker.

Yitzkhok received a sound Hebrew education from Reb Lipe, as well as a love for the Land of Israel.

From Lipe, Yitzkhok went to study with Beryl, the *Rosh Yeshiva* [head of the religious school].

In 1921, Yitzkhok came to New York. After several years of hard work and simultaneously perfecting himself in world knowledge, Yitzkhok went to Jerusalem, and there he married Rokhel Segal, who was also a Wiezner. Very soon, Yitzkhok and his wife Rokhel returned to Brooklyn and quickly settled in.

Yitzkhok Mishelow – specialized in the construction industry, and when the opportunity presented itself, he threw himself into his work with great energy and success. Now he is tied to large building projects that take up a significant place in the Brooklyn area. For this entire time, Yitzkhok and Rokhel Mishelow remained close to all the national–culture circles. Both daughters, Elke, the wife of Mr. Sam Gordon, and the younger daughter Gitel, received a worldly and Jewish education.

As active friends of the *Poalei Tzion* association, the Mishelows own a summer house in the association colony of "Rannana" in New York, where intellectual and cultural friends gather, and there they plan and create all types of projects for benevolent activities.

[Page 513]

R. Moshe Reuben and Shimka Pissetski (Poses-Perry)

Prepared for online presentation by Genia Hollander

Moshe Reuben was born to his parents, Gershon and Shifra Pissetski in Slutsk. Like other Jewish boys in those days, he obtained his elementary and higher education in strictly religious schools which were chiefly devoted to the study of the Bible, its Commentaries and the Talmud.

The young Moshe Reuben greatly excelled in these studies and became famous as a young scholar. It must be remembered that the Jewish community of Slutsk was known for centuries as profusely filled with

Torah-learning and Lithuanian-Jewish wisdom. Indeed, there were no ignorant Jews in Slutsk. Even the small shopkeepers and the poor craftsmen were well versed in Jewish studies. All the groups of artisans according to their professions had their own Beth Midrash where they gathered daily and pored over their Mishnayoth and big volumes of the Babylonian Talmud from dusk to midnight. Hence, to achieve a reputation of scholarship, there was quite an accomplishment.

His fame and standing among the scholars of the community gained for him the love of the beautiful and energetic Shimka Rivin, a daughter of a prominent and scholarly family from the nearby town of Starobin. In order to provide for their material needs, the newly-married Pissetskis entered into a partnership with the reputable Isaac Feinberg in his established windmill which ground flour for the entire vicinity. As was customary in those days, the wife, in addition to bearing children and keeping house, was also the main provider of the family. So Shimka too managed the business while her husband spent there only a few hours daily, devoting the rest of the day to furthering his Talmudic studies.

Though he was never officially ordained for the Rabbinate, he was recognized as one of the leading scholars of the community. R. Maier Pehmer, a renowned Gaon who was the Rabbi of the city, visited him almost daily and together they spent hours in Talmudic discourse. Whenever the Rabbi had to be absent from the city, he advised his congregants to turn to Reb. Moshe Reuben for Rabbinic decisions. His word and opinion were highly regarded by Jew and Gentile alike. Even the local White Russia peasants, who had to grind their flour at the Feinberg mill, would always manage to come during those hours that he was there. They were wont to say: "Whatever Pan Pissetski says is as holy as the word of the Bible".

At the turn of the century when Chaim Michel Goodside opened the first steam-driven mill, the Feinberg establishment was completely ruined. This put the Pissetskis, who were by this time quite a large family, in a most difficult situation. They then took over the management of the Hotel Europa which was the largest hotel in the city. This venture did not last very long because of the demise of Moshe Reuben.

By this time, the older children had gone to the United States. Because of the instability of the political atmosphere in Russia and the ever-increasing limitations imposed upon the Jewish population, Shimka took her family and migrated to America. Despite the many hardships encountered in establishing themselves, their traits of love for learning and intellectual faculties inherited from their father and the warm encouragement and wise guidance given them by their devoted mother, enabled them to pursue their education and attain a fine position in society.

[Page 514]

Shimka Poses lived to a ripe old age and was greatly loved and respected by all members of her family. In August 1945, she passed away with a feeling of satisfaction of the place her family occupied in New York circles. The descendants of Moshe Reuben and Shimka continue their traditional family prominence of intellectuality and benevolence. They are well represented among many educational and philanthropic organizations in American Jewry.

Smelkinson Brothers – Baltimore, M.D.

The Smelkinson brothers, well known for their communal activities in Baltimore, Md., stem from a family which originated in Starobin-Slutsk in the beginning of the 19th century. Aaron Smelkinson, later known as "Areh Der Desyatnik" (Aaron the police officer), was a Slutsk youngster who was drafted into the Russian army during the reign of Czar Nicholas I and, as was customary in those days, served for a period of twenty-five years, from 1840 to 1865. Throughout that long period of service he did not lose his Jewish identity nor did he forsake his religious principles.

Aaron Smelkinson

Upon his release from military service and after he was given by the Government an acreage on which to build a home, a pension for life and an appointment as local police officer, Aaron Smelkinson married a girl by the name of Chincka. They raised a family of ten children: Mordecai Leib, Asher Yoel, Chananya, Yitzchak Isaac, Gitel, Chashka, Nissel, Michael, Peretz and Esther, of whom five migrated to the United States at the turn of the present century. Chananya returned to Slutsk in 1903 and died there shortly thereafter. Chashka and Esther settled in Philadelphia. Peretz took up residence in New York and Michael established himself in Baltimore and raised his family there.

Of those who remained in Slutsk, Yitzchak Isaac married Rebeca Epstein and they bore nine children. Six of them: Morris, Henie, Teibel, Shifra, Joseph and Benjamin came to the United States shortly after the Russo-Japanese War of 1904 and joined their relatives in Baltimore. Although they came to the American shores with very meagre material means, they brought along with them a strong and rich spiritual heritage.

The portrait of their ancestor, Aaron Smelkinson, as he appears above with his beautiful white beard and a traditional Yarmulke, together with the adornments of the Czarist army medals upon his breast, signifying his steadfastness and strong adherence to his tradition despite the great hardship that he encountered in his life, always stood before the eyes of his descendants and his memory was like a beacon to them throughout the years. The Smelkinson brothers, Benjamin in particular, are highly prominent in the business world and Jewish cultural and social circles of Baltimore. They have also succeeded to transmit the same spirit to their own children who were born and raised in the United States.

Upon the departure of Morris Smelkinson in 1948, all the Smelkinson descendants formed a Family Circle in his honour, of which his son, Ralph is the president. Through their occasional meetings, the entire family is trying to preserve the tradition and spirit which they brought along from Slutsk and which is so precious to all of them.

[Page 515]

Zalman and Fania Parton

Uncaptioned. Zalman and Fania Praton.

Having a younger brother at home, Zalman had to take care of him as well. So, he gave up his law school plans and enrolled in a commerce school which he completed in three months, and immediately found work with a salary of $10 per week.

At the end of 1910, Zalman took on a new position in a factory that produced paper production wheels in the city of Lowell, near Boston.

This business appealed to him, and for the nine years that he worked there he learned all the details of the business, through and through. And in 1919, he opened his own factory of the same type.

The business was very successful and grew greatly, with factory units in other cities, along with the production of many other products that were developed over time. Today, the "Middlesex Paper Tube Company" in Lowell, Massachusetts, with all its branches, is one of the largest in the country, and Zalman Itche Gittes is the president.

On Tuesday, Adar 23, 5672 (March 12, 1912), Zalman married Fania Ricz, daughter of Yakov Ricz of Portland, who was also a Romanower, his father "Leybke the *shokhet* [ritual slaughterer]" was a prominent name in Romanowa. In Romanowa he was the *shokhet* and the *chazzan* [cantor] and when the *Rav* [city's rabbi] would leave the city he would say that if anyone had any questions involving decisions to be made according to Jewish law, then he should go to Leybke, even though they always used to pair up and "argue when they learned together."

Leybke also possessed a beautiful voice that used to shake the walls of the *Beis Medrash* [Study Hall] when he prayed *musaf* [the late morning prayers] there, and his *"neilah"* [closing prayer on Yom Kippur] and his musical undertones would elicit such emotion, which Romanower Jews would remember all year.

Zalman Itche Gittes and Fania, the grandson of Leybke the *shokhet*, have a son and two daughters who are of the prominent families in their region.

Since 1920, Zalman is the annual treasurer of the "United Jewish Appeal" in Lowell and is greatly loved by young and old. Even though the Jewish community in Lowell is only around 400 Jewish families, thanks to the energetic activities of Zalman Parton, in time he raised more than a million dollars for Israel causes.

The love of Torah that Zalman inherited from his father the *Gemara* [Talmud] teacher in Romanow, did not

[Page 516]

disappear with him. When you come to the Lowell "Jewish Center," which Zalman greatly helped build in 1955 for a sum of $600,000 (six hundred thousand dollars), you see the names of Zalman and Fania Parton displayed in the library, which was dedicated to them.

But his Romanower *"Yetzer Harah"* ["deep desire"] does not leave him even in his old age, and his *khazaka* ["fixed deed" after doing it several times] is *"maftir Yonah"* [the final portion read after reading the Book of Jonah during the Yom Kippur evening services, very prestigious position for reader], a task that everyone in Lowell knew belonged to Zalman Parton, and for him this is as important as his factory of paper – tubes, and maybe even more…

Shmuel and Sonia Rokhlyn

About the great Tanna [knowledgeable, wise teacher during Midrashic times, 10–22 CE], his Rebbi Reb Yokhanan ben Zakkai said: "Praised is the one who gave birth to him" (Ethics of Our Fathers chapter 2, Mishna]. Rashi [commentary], according to the Jerusalem Talmud, explains: that the mother of Reb Yehoshua held his cradle in the *Beis Medrash* so that his childish ears, right from the start, could hear only words of Torah and wisdom, and this would have an effect on his whole life.

In a certain sense, the same can be said of Shmuel Rokhlyn. From his fresh youth, his mother, may she rest in peace, brought him into the warmth of the *Beis Medrash* and implanted in him a love for Torah and Torah scholars. This love accompanied him his entire life, despite his many travels and spiritual fluctuations that obscured his vision in various camps and streams [ebbs and flows]. The person who came a little closer to him, a little deeper, a little more fundamentally, would soon recognize the warmth that flows out of his boiling soul that is always searching for a rectification for his errors.

Shmuel Rokhlyn was born in 1897 in Slutsk. His father, Hirshel the furrier died at the age of 38, leaving behind a wife and six tiny children, among whom was Shmuel, three years old, and a sister of three months. There was only one route left for this woman – to gird her loins and search for a livelihood to provide for her children.

Khaya Rokhlyn began to bake bread and the people were very sympathetic to her, so "Khaike the baker" with time became a well–known name, an institution in Slutsk, someone everyone knew and respected. Since she lived and managed her business in the synagogue courtyard, her bakery became almost like a part of the community Jewish life that centered around the Slutsker synagogue courtyard. During World War One, many of the first refugees arrived, they were Jewish families that fled warzones in Poland and Galicia. Khaike's bakery was always filled with people who got their daily bread ration regardless whether they had payment for this or not. Khaike was also the official seller of bread to the *yeshiva* and all the *yeshiva* students felt at home with her just as they did in their own homes.

A special closeness was felt between Khaike's family and the house of Reb Isser Zalman. First because they were neighbors, and also because of her constant business dealings of bread for the *yeshiva*. So her children were always in the Rav's house. Especially when her son Shmuel and his brother Dovid had grown up, studied in the *yeshiva*, and became well–known as being very talented [smart], then the Rav's home became their spiritual home, and the Rav, understanding how difficult it was for the mother to raise them, would give them special attention and paternal closeness.

At the outbreak of World War One, Shmuel Rokhlyn obeyed Rav Meltzer, and left to Radzyn because of the conscription, and went to the Khofetz Khaim's *yeshiva*. [*trans. note: Israel Meir Kagan (1838–1933), Talmudic and rabbinic scholar, ethical and religious teacher, authority in Jewish law, universally known by the title of his first book "*Khofetz Chaim*"]. But as soon as the war's front reached closer there, the *yeshiva* had to move more deeply into Russia, and Shmuel left to Vilna and after that to Kovno that was already occupied by the Germans. There, he studied for three years in the Slabodka *yeshiva*, and at the same time delivered lectures in "*Ein Yakov*" ["The Eye of Yakov," compilation of ethical and inspiration teaching of the Talmud] in the Slabodka "great Beis Medrash" where the elite of the city prayed.

In Kovno, Shmuel also became acquainted with the other streams of thought that conflicted with their worldliness and Jewish lifestyles.

After several reincarnations [deep soul changes], Shmuel returned from Russia. His cousin Sonia Seperowyc later became his life's companion.

Sonia also came from a prominent family in Slutsk. Her father was a Torah scholar whose skill was writing Torah scrolls and scrolls for *tefillin* [phylacteries]. Everyone in Slutsk knew him as Khaim the *Sofer* [scribe]. His wife Itel Wieder was well known in her own right because they lived on the main road near Ostrag. Itel took to helping the Jewish arrestees or their families with their needs.

Other than having a sound Jewish education, Sonia also completed the Slutsker gymnasium [high school] and studied for two years in the medical faculty of the university in the distant Woroniez. But because of the Russian Civil War and its aftereffects, she had to

[Page 517]

end her studies and came to Vilna. In Vilna, the famous Rav Yitzkhok Rubenstayn, a great personal friend of theirs, performed the marriage ceremony for Shmuel and Sonia Rokhlyn, and a short while later, they left for America, in 1923.

In America, Shmuel tried to conduct his life in Torah and study circles, but the former Slutsker–Radziner and Slabodker Torah scholar did not to fit in with the modifying and watering down that these professions required according to the circumstances in America. He was too serious and spent too many years at the wells of Torah to be able to follow the compromising of religious life in Jewish America. So, he threw himself into the business world. His skills served him well here too, and he was successful economically as well. At the same time, he helped out greatly in the New York Jewish school situation, where he holds a very esteemed place, as well as in other cultural circles. For that, he is blessed with a healthy logic, and with an exceptional analytical skill.

Sonia Rokhlyn is also active in her own circles, and by nature is very refined and compassionate. Her father, Khaim the scribe, in the year 1932, was sent to Siberia and died there. Her mother Itel was killed by the Nazis in Slutsk.

The Rokhlyns have a son Hirshel and a daughter Laya, both educated, married, and run a cultured Jewish life.

Alex and Enny Rajkhman

Eliyahu (Alex) was born in Slutsk to his parents Feitel and Matla Rajkhman. His father Feitel, as a young intelligent boy, already tasted discussions and novels, in the province of Poltowa. After the wedding, he began a business of mushrooms and skins, and was actually very successful. His business grew and brought him in contact even with Germany, to which place he would export his products. His wife Matla would be his assistant.

As a child, Eliyahu studied with Slutsker teachers such as Reb Itche Note's and others, but when his father died at the age of 41, he had to take on the responsibility of helping his mother to support the family.

Despite all this, that Matle Rajkhman (Osowski) became a young widow with small children, she maintained the standards in her home as before. She would invite several *yeshiva* boys and a guest to her home each Shabbath.

In 1915, in the heat of World War One, Eliyahu left Slutsk, and after great difficulties and long wanderings in Siberia, Croatia, and Japan, he finally worked his way to Chicago in 1916, and later came to New York and married Khana Perel (Enny Orman), a Bialystoker.

Khaim Rajkhman

[Page 518]

Over the years, Alex Rajkhman brought over his brother Khaim from Tel Aviv to America. Khaim died in New York (19 Nisan, 5702 – 1942).

Alex and Khana Perel are very active and support many benevolent institutions. Recently, they have become active in selling Israel bonds, and Mrs. Rajkhman directs the activities of the Pioneer Women of the Labor Union campaign.

A few years ago, when the Rajkhmans returned from a trip to Israel, they were the first to join the book committee and have helped realize this project.

Aron and Yentel Rolnik

Aron Rolnik, son of Lipman and Slova, born in Slutsk. Studied in the schools of Reb Lipe Szinjowker and with the scholar of the Tanakh, Sh. A. Rabinowyc, later with Reb Beryl Grybenstik and for a few years at the great *yeshiva*.

From his young years, he was caught up in national thinking and was very active in the groups of "*Tzeirei Tzion*"["Youth of Zion"]. He was also in the administration of the Slutsker library.

In 1921, he and a group of Slutsker went to Israel. There he worked along with all the other *khalutzim* [pioneers], built houses, pounded rocks, planted orchards for seven years straight. But sadly, for all kinds of reasons, he had to leave the country and go back to America.

Here too, he did not give up his idealistic past but he remained loyal to his former ideals. His wife is Yentel Epstajn, a Slutsker friend from youth. Their children are Avrohom Tzvi and Esther. Aron was of the first to register in the Slutsker committee for the Yizkor Book and served all the time as the recording secretary.

At a committee meeting in New York From right to left: **Eliyahu Altman, Rav Nisen Waksman, Dovid Juzdon (standing), and Avrohom Maizel**

[Page 519]

Protocol

From the First meeting of the Slutsker "Yizkor Book Committee" in New York, October 14, 1956

Sunday, October 14, 1956, in the home of Avrohom and Khaike Maizel, in New York, there was a meeting held with a group of compatriots from Slutsk and the surrounding area, about publishing a Yizkor Book to perpetuate the memory and the name of the martyrs who were killed by the Nazis, may their name be erased.

The following people participated: Avrohom and Khaike Maizel, HaRav Nisen Waksman, Eliyahu and Sarah Altman, Shmuel and Sonia Rokhlyn, Alexander Rajkhman and his wife, Sam Goldberg and his wife, Dovid Post and his wife, Aron Rolnik and his wife, Meyer Badkhan and his wife, Meyer Grinwald and his wife, Mina Klotz, and, Lewis Goren.

The meeting was opened by Lewis Goren, discussion was of the goals and the tasks involved with the job.

The chairman, Avrohom Maizel, said that he had just been in Israel where he met Nakhum Khinic and other compatriots who expressed their support for the need to publish a Yizkor Book. They gave him a lot of material that they had and they are awaiting a sponsor. They asked for help and asked to create a fund for this.

With heartfelt, warm words, HaRav Nisen Waksman explained the importance that Slutsk and the surrounding towns played in Jewish life and in Jewish history for the last hundred years, and how important it is for the future to eternalize their memory in the form of a book. It is a great merit for us to assist in and to realize this project.

With his request, a sum of $350 was raised immediately, to which all those who were present contributed, and promised to provide further assistance.

A discussion followed, with the participation of A. Altman, L. Goren, Mrs. Post, Khaike Maizel, A. Rolnik, and Shmuel Rokhlyn. All those present were all excited about the project, and are sure that the work will be very worthwhile. Shmuel Rokhlyn explained in a short, informative speech the enormity of the project and how the Jewish world will be so grateful for this.

At a suggestion made by HaRav Waksman, the issue of electing officials for a committee is postponed until later. Instead, he suggests that all those present who belong to different *landsleit* [compatriot] organizations, should talk about this project at their meetings and ask

At a meeting of the New York Book Committee, in Eliyahu Altman's house, February 1958 Seated from right to left: Shmuel Rokhlyn, Sarah and Nisen Waksman, Avrohom Maizel Standing from right to left: Mishelow, Khaike Maizel, Mr. and Mrs. Alex Rajkhman, Mr. and Mrs. Eliyahu Altman, Mr. and Mrs. Aron Rolnik

[Page 520]

that they select representatives for our organization and help with the work. Only after that will we elect officials with the participation of all the organizations.

But for now, a temporary executive of six people is formed: Avrohom Maizel, HaRav Waksman, A. Altman, Shmuel Rokhlyn, Alexander Rajkhman, and Mrs. Mina Klotz, to take care of the work in the interim. It was decided that the committee meet in the office of Friend Altman for future discussions, and that the next large meeting should be held in the Hotel Martinique.

With that, the business part of the meeting is closed.

Mrs. Khaike Maizel invited all those present into another room to a lovely, filled table, Everyone spent a wonderful time and recounted memories of childhood years in Slutsk and the surrounding town.

At the end, Eliyahu Altman expressed heartfelt thanks to Avrohom and Khaike Maizel, in the name of all those present, for their wonderful welcome.

Told by Aron Rolnik

The Closing of the Yizkor Book

At the end of December 1954, when I received a letter from our dear friend Nakhum Khinic, in which he asked that I participate in the publishing of a book about our region, the idea that I had been carrying with me for several years came to life.

In the early forties, in the middle of the fire of World War Two, when the first tragic news of the destruction and devastation reached us, I thought about doing something in writing for the memory of my hometown. Finally, no one has found a better means to preserve the past then with the written word.

As a beginning, I printed in the New York "*Morgen Zhurnal*" ["Morning Journal" Yiddish newspaper, founded 1901] a short summary about my place of birth, for which I won a literary prize. But this was not my point. I was not looking for any prizes from this destruction. But I felt, or better said that I was taken over by a voice that often rang in my ears: Good brother, give a helping hand

Seated from right to left: HaRav N. Waksman, the pedagogue Y.N. Adler, Dr. Meyer Waksman, and the Hebrew author Dr. Aron Domnyc

[Page 521]

and assist, so that a short 500 years of active Jewish life and creation should not be forgotten. Help at least to set up a gravestone, good brother, help!

This feeling flowed together with the words of about 60 letters (read 60!) that I received over the last six years from the same Reb Nokhum Khinyc, and each time I read one of his letters I thought this was from the "Other World." Through him, all those "fortunate ones" who died one generation after the other, spoke to me – those who were buried in the Jewish cemeteries of our cities and towns, but "only" their graves and tombstones were wiped out and no memory of them is left, and also the tens of thousands of recent martyrs who wanted only to be buried in Jewish cemeteries, but tragically, did not have this privilege.

The cries of the tens of funerals that I attended in my youth were refreshed in my mind, when a person's life still had value, and these funerals evoked a sadness. But the deadened voices of the deceased themselves cried louder than the others and pressed and ate away even more strongly and deeply. Oh how terribly do these unheard voices cry out!

These sounds awoke me and hurried me to the work of this book. With their echo I gave many speeches about the importance of this book, to all kinds of *landsleit* gatherings, even though at the time those who listened received this coldly, and even sometimes hotly attacked the speaker and his ideas.

These voices inspired me to write and speak to individual people, both to receive their financial help that now reached a nice few thousand dollars to print the book, but also to receive the appropriate printing material from competent people. This second objective was not easier to receive than the first. The majority of the writers had to be spoken to personally and then afterwards I had to call them tens of times within a few months, and in some cases, even for years, with great tact and patience, until they agreed to discuss memories and feelings that were hidden and dormant inside for many years and were waiting to be awoken and uncovered. The same was to get the many pictures that were to be put into the book. For all these years, I was busy as a bee, running from one to the other searching for and collecting whatever little piece there was for the book, to realize and to enhance it, to complete and improve the gravestone for all the destroyed gravestones and for those who were left without.

But it should be mentioned here that the best intentions and efforts these goals would never have been realized without the devoted help of several other idealistic, persistent people who did not pay attention to the apathy of the official naysayers, but actually paid heed to the unheard calls of the souls of those who died and disappeared, and to the moans of the few ordinary people who raised themselves over the heads of their leaders and presented themselves warmly for the situations.

Just as in Israel where only a few "fanatics" came forward to this, and did not anticipate the ground rules of the "big shots" and the great challenges that stood in their way, similarly, in New York the few people on the committee worked for the goal with a devotion, not considering any challenges, but went on with the work until the last few years, until the book was completed.

To the closing of our work and for the book itself, I feel it is appropriate to express a heartfelt thanks to the few rare individual compatriots and friends who made it possible to realize this book. For everyone, first the friends in Israel: Friend Nakhum Khynic, Sh. Nakhmani, my relative Tzvi Assaf, Aryeh Shapiro, Tzvi Hagivati, who, other than doing unlimited personal work, after that awoke and inspired others to the task. After that, to our compatriot, well–known writer Y.D. Berkowycz, thank you to him for his assistance.

Great recognition must be given to our friends on the New York committee: the president Avrohom Maizel and his dear wife Khaike, the secretary Eliyahu Altman and his wife, the treasurer Shmuel Rokhlyn and his wife, the vice–president Alex Rajkhman and his wife, and the recording secretary Aron Rolnik and his wife.

Of the larger financial supporters, it is important to mention the very esteemed Mr. Dovid Juzdon, who with great amicability, contributed the paper for this book, and we should also mention, for good things, the beautiful and warm assistance of my brother–in–law Dr. Yehoshua Yosef Szwarc, the famous director of Joint, of the United Appeal, and of Israel Bonds in New York, and also the Israel finance minister, Sr. Levi Eshkol, for his wonderful actions toward the book. We must also not forget the great financial help that the compatriot and philanthropist Mr. Harry Lefrak and his wife and son Shmule contributed – may all these be blessed and be eternally remembered for the good, for their assistance and support to perpetuate the holy memory of Slutsk and the region.

Nisen Waksman
Brooklyn, New York

[Page 522]

For Eternal Memory
(Yahrzeit list of departed Landsleit)
Translated by Judy Petersen

Family name	First name(s)	Father	Remarks	Yarzheit
UZDENSKI	Nesoniel Tsvi	Dovid		26 Iyar 5686
UZDENSKI	Dveyra Basha	Chaim		15 Tamuz 5707
ALTMAN	Yehuda Leyb	Reuven		12 Shvat 5677
ALTMAN	Rivka	Yeshayahu		
BADCHAN	Simkha Leyb			
BADCHAN	Elke Dveyra			
BUNIN	Lipman	Chaim		
BUNIN	Chaya	Avrohom		
BUNIN	Sora	Lipman		19 Tevet 5718
BUSSEL	Yitzhok	Lipman		25 Iyar 5681
BUSSEL	Rokhl	Binyomin		18 Tevet 5694
GALLINSON	Yakov		and Sora	
GOLDBLUM	Feivel	Elkana		1 Shevat 5719
GWOSDOFF	Shmuel Yosef	Aryey Zev		10 Menachem Av 5720
GWOSDOFF	Rishe Henye	Tsvi Hirsch		12 Iyar 5688
GOREN	Meir	Pesach	Rabbi	15 Adar 5657
GOREN	Tzeshe	Zev Wolf		18 Cheshvan 5671

GREENWALD	Yosef	Leizer Mordekhai		26 Adar 5705
GREENWALD	Svetla	Moshe Zalmen		23 Elul
DOMNITZ	Asher	Chaim		26 Tishrei 5712
DOMNITZ	Chaya	Yirmiyahu		23 MarCheshvan 5696
HOLLAND	Borukh	Yitzhok	haKohen	7 Sivan 5696
HOLLAND	Fale	Reuven		7 Elul 5719
WAXMAN	Reuven	Tsvi Hirsch		15 Shevat 5720
WEINSTOCK	Tsvi Hirsch		and Gitel	
ZEIDES	Shimon Leyb	Chaim		9 Tishrei 5704
ZEIDES	Leah	Shlomo		25 Shevat 5663
CHINITZ	Feivel	Isser		7 Nisan 5684
CHIPCHIN	Dov Ber	Menahem Mendl	haKohen	
CHIPCHIN	Mordekhai	Menahem Mendl	haKohen	
MILKOWITZ	Zelig	Yeheyshua		29 Adar 5688
MILKOWITZ	Golde	Mendil		15 Marcheshvan 5691

[Page 523]

Family name	First name(s)	Father	Remarks	Yarzheit
MECHANIK	Blume	Chaim		15 Nisan 5720
MECHANIK	Yosef	Tuvia		Erev Sukkot 5692
MAIZES	Chaim-Dov	Mordekhai Eliezer		6 Nisan 5672

MAIZES	Rivka Rokhl	Yakov		25 Elul 5695
NOZICK	Dveyra	Moshe Getzel		7 Adar 5717
SIROTOWITZ	Ahron	Yoyna		1 Kislev 5708
SIROTOWITZ	Shlomo	Ahron		9 Tishrei 5718
SAGALOWITZ	Chaya Braina	Mendl		27 Tevet
SAGALOWITZ	Eliezer	Yitzhok		1 Nisan
SEGAL	Yerukham		and Rivka	12 Shevat
FEIVISHOWITZ	Moshe	Yomtov Leyb	haLevi	2 Adar 5668
FEIVISHOWITZ	Elka	Binyomin		2 Marcheshvan 5693
POSTOW	Borukh	Eliyohu		unknown
POSTOW	Golde	Eliyohu		21 Kislev
FIALKO	Chaim Hertz	Avrohom		Killed in the war
FIALKO	Etil Itke	Meir		Killed in the war
FEISS	Boris			Killed in the war
FEISS	Hinde			Killed in the war
FORTMAN	Shimshon Zelig	Shimon	Rabbi	27 Shevat 5711
FORTMAN	Khvale	Moshe Getzel		2 Tamuz 5721
ZIRKEL	Rokhl			19 Adar I 5719
KASBERG	Alte Leah	Shlomo Yosef		21 Tamuz 5694
KASBERG	Tsvi Yoyna	Yakov Dov		28 Adar 5720
KAMINSKY	Chaim	Yakov		
KAMINSKY	Hana	Menashe		

KAMINSKY	Yakov			10 Nisan 5672
KANTOR	Moshe Yitzhok	Yehuda Leyb		12 Cheshvan 5676
KANTOR	Malka	Mordekhai		5691
KANTOR	Shlomo	Shmuel Shimon		3 Nisan 5696
KANTOR	Riva Leah	Yeheyshua		7 Nisan 5677
KANTOR	Yosef	Moshe Yitzhok		27 Tamuz 5721
KANTOROWITZ	Lipa	Mendel		20 Tamuz 5720
KATCHENENOVSKY	Lipa	Gershon		27 Shevat 5683
KATCHENENOVSKY	Batsheva	Menahem Mendl		27 Tevet 5684
KAPCHITZ	Moshe Chaim	Yehuda Leyb	Rabbi	15 Sivan 5690
KAPCHITZ	Sora Rivka	Moshe Dovid		9 Tevet 5694
KAPLAN	Yosef Leyb	Moshe Chaim	Rabbi; father a Rabbi	1 Elul 5712
KAPLAN	Chaya Miriam	Chaim		21 Nisan 5685
KRANITZ	Heschil	Tsvi Hirsch		8 Tishrei 5691
KRANITZ	Chaike	Yehuda		5 Shevat 5677
KUSTANOWITZ	Yakov Moshe	Pesach	haKohen	10 Menachem Av 5701
KUSTANOWITZ	Rivka	Aharon		8 Tamuz 5696
KUSTANOWITZ	Mordekhai	Yakov		unknown
KOOSMAN	Yehuda		his wife Sora Leah	

[Page 524]

Family name	First name(s)	Father	Remarks	Yarzheit
KRIVITZKY	Chaim	Avrohom		5 Cheshvan 5722
RAVITCH	Meir Zev	Zelig		12 Marcheshvan 5705
RAVITCH	Alte	Mordekhai		27 Iyar 5701
RAVITCH	Etke	Meir Zev		Erev Sukkot 5680
RAVITCH	Simkha	Meir Zev		17 Tishrei 5680
RAVITCH	Nisan	Meir Zev		Purim 5681
RAVITCH	Eliahu	Meir Zev		Yom Kippur 5718
RAVITCH	Yekhiel	Meir Zev		9 Elul 5717
RESNICK	Avrohom Ahron	Yakov		12 Tevet
RESNICK	Henye	Yeheyshua		10 Iyar
ROLNICK	Yomtov Lipman	Mordekhai		3 Adar
ROLNICK	Esther Slawe	Moshe		23 Elul
RUBINSTEIN	Moshe			8 Menachem Av 5686
RUBNITZ	Henye	Tsvi		27 Tishrei 5699
RUBINSTEIN	Yitzhok	Avrohom Reuven		8 Cheshvan 5702
RIVIN	Avrohom Ahron	Dov Ber		2 Tamuz 5715
RIVIN	Golya	Aryey Leyb		3 Av 5714
SHIFFMAN (WIZNE)	Yakov Shlomo	Moshe Ahron		28 Cheshvan 5664

SHIFFMAN (WIZNE)	Shulye	Avrohom		10 Kislev 5664
SHWARTZ	Rafael	Tsvi	haLevi	1 Tamuz 5710
SHWARTZ	Rakhel	Moshe	haLevi	26 Iyar 5708
SHWARTZ	Elke	Yisrael		14 Tevet 5693
SHWAIDELSON	Sora	Tzadok		3 Adar 5703
SHWAIDELSON	Chaim	Yakov		29 Adar 5677
SCHWEDOCK	Shayne Dveyra	Yosef Mendl		26 Nisan 5688
SCHWEDOCK	Yitzhok	Chaim		22 Cheshvan
SHKOLNICK	Zelig	Nete		12 Shevat
SHKOLNICK	Zlate	Dov		Shushan Purim

Natan Nota
the son of Reb Tzvi Yoel, 15 Iyar 5671 – 25 Kislev 5704

NORMAN EPSTEIN

University of Louisville, Kentucky, School of Medicine 1938. Interned at the Jewish Hospital in St. Louis, Missouri and a resident in the Jewish Hospital, Brooklyn, N.Y. Commissioned a first Lieutenant in the Medical Corps. Army of the United States, June 9, 1942 and later promoted to Captain. Killed in action in New Britain, Southwest Pacific, Dec. 2, 1943.

[Page 525]

For Eternal Memory

Sholom Family Circle of the Meisel Family

Family name	First name(s)	Remarks
DOROSHINSKY	Borukh	Died 4 Aug 1931
DOROSHINSKY	Leah	Died 4 Jul 1927
DORIS	Beni	Died 4 Feb 1958
TABACHNICK	Reuven	Died 4 Jan 1941
TABACHNICK	Rokhl	Died 19 Jul 1954
TABACHNICK	Silya	Died 7 Apr 1958
FINKELSTEIN	Mordekhai	Died 23 Av
FINKELSTEIN	Zelig	Died 1 Adar
GIVENTER	Itka	7 Tevet
NESHIN	Tzira	
NEWMAN	Hillel	Died 7 Apr 1947
NEWMAN	Beile	Died 10 Aug 1936
NEWMAN	Dov	Died 7 May 1956
GRAUER	Sadie	Died 9 May 1947
SKLAR	Shmuel	Died 31 May 1948
TIKTINSKY	Yosef	Died 26 Dec 1920
FEINBERG	Feygel	Died 8 Sep 1959
MAISEL	Shalom	Died 1936

MAISEL	Sora Rivka	Died 1901
MAISEL	Moshe Leyb	Died 21 Feb 1920
MAISEL	Chava	Died 24 Nisan
MAISEL	Michel	Died 5 Nov 1953
MAISEL	Shmuel Chaim	Died Jan 1937
MAISEL	Shmuel and Eidle	Died 8 Tevet
MAISEL	Fridman	Died in Russia, 1941
MAISEL	Shalom	Killed in WWII
MAISEL	Shmuel	Died 20 Jul 1954
MAISEL	Sofia	Died 5 May 1952
MAISEL	Hertzil	Died 13 Sep 1932
MAISEL	Chaim	Died 4 Nov 1955
MLOTOK	Liowa and Grisha	Twins; killed in WWII
GRANOFF	Dov	Died 9 Apr 1952
RAPPAPORT	Yitzhok	Died 22 Jun 1933
RAPPAPORT	Yehudit	Died 1940
RAPPAPORT	Reuven	Died April 1942
RAPPAPORT	Beile	Died Jun 1932
WEINBERG	Eliahu	Died 28 Jun 1959

[Page 526]

Captions translated by Jerrold Landau

Left: Chasia Zeides, burnt alive in Slutsk. Her
daughter Musia – died of hunger.
Right: Her son Yitzchak, fell in the war.
Left: Yisrael, a partisan, remains an invalid.

The Mendelevich family (Reb Rafael-   Yosel's
grandchildren) From right to left: the mother Dina
Tzipa,   the   father   Reb   Leib.
Standing from right to left: Rivka, Gershon, Eidele.
Murdered in the ghetto.

Leibel Riklin and his wife Riva-Dina, from among
The active members of the Slutsk Bund. Murdered
in the ghetto

Reb Yaakov Meir Poliak

[Page527]

Rabbi Hershel Malinski with his
wife. (He was the son of
Reb Berl the Yeshiva head).
Murdered in the ghetto.

Esther Kazberg

Right: The mother Chaya Rivka Meizel. The daughter Golka (Standing),
Neske (sitting), the father Mordechai (left).

Reb Pesach Rubnich with his family (the Gemara teacher in Starobin)

Sitting from right to left: his son Reb Aharyon Yaakov with his wife, Reb Pesach with his wife, his son-in-law and daughter Itka.
Standing: Moshe Baruch with his wife, Yosef Elya with his wife, Noach with his wife. All the sons with their families perished in Russia,
except for the family of his eldest son Reb Aharon Yaakov and Sheinka, and their children in New York.

[Blank]

Index of Names, Listed Alphabetically

Slutsk Yizkor Book

Transcribed into English by Paul Micheikin Pascal

Transcriber's preface:

The Index of Names in the Slutsk Yizkor Book integrated Yiddish spellings and Hebrew spellings, with no obvious criterion as to which spelling to use where. Included were names which the transcriber found frankly difficult to transcribe, because vowels, considered to be understood by the reader of Hebrew, were omitted from the index, and often from the body of the text as well. There were no other contextual clues for the names, as there are with ordinary words within sentences, except where a name spelled in Hebrew in the index was spelled in Yiddish in the body of the book (Yiddish *does* use vowels).

At times, the same name occurring more than once in the text was spelled differently in each case, and different again in its spelling in the index. (Ironically, this sometimes helped to decode the pronunciation.)

In this transcription, the system used was a YIVO model, modified to conform with the local Yiddish dialect. Thus *Meysha = Moyshe = Moshe*, and *Yeysef = Yoysef = Yosef*. (In these examples, the first spelling represents local pronunciation; the second, YIVO standard Yiddish pronunciation, and the third, modern Hebrew pronunciation).

The *Meysha* example above alludes to a second modification the transcriber made on the YIVO system, on the advice of Yiddish linguist, Prof. Dovid Katz (of Oxford, Yale, and in the Yiddish seat at the University of Vilnius), namely: words ending with a short E sound were usually rendered with the letter A. This sacrifice of absolute accuracy was a lesser of two evils, for the YIVO practice of rendering the short E *sound* with the *letter* E often creates confusion in English-speakers who are accustomed to English rules of spelling.

In English a final E usually has a much different function than YIVO has given it. (In any case, this use of A is not original with the transcriber; note, for example, these familiar Yiddish names: "Golda" instead of "Golde", "Dina" instead of "Dine", etc. The last vowel in each of these names is properly pronounced as a short E.) Other anomolies: the common name normally rendered in English as Jacob and in modern Hebrew as Yaakov, was pronounced in Jewish Eastern Europe as *Yanke* v, the "N" deriving originally from a nasalization. The name appears frequently in this index. Another common name known otherwise as Mordecai, Mordechai, or Mordekhai, is rendered here as Mordkha, according to its folk pronunciation. Itshe, Ayzl, and Ayzik were popular variants of Yitzhok or Isaac.

Transcription of the gutteral sounds was of necessity inconsistent, i.e., it depended on context and on popular familiarity with the name in question. Surnames, indeed all names, of Hebrew origin were rendered in their Ashkenazi, or Eastern European, pronunciation, not in modern Israeli pronunciation (e.g., Efros not Efrat), unless it was clear that the name in question was acquired after arriving in Israel.

Inasmuch as the transcriber tried to remain faithful in his spelling to how the individuals of the index would themselves have pronounced their names, he also departed from this custom if the name appeared in English somewhere in the Yizkor Book. The same is true if the individual was so well known that his/her name was commonly spelled a certain way in other authoritative texts (usually Encyclopedia Judaica).

In most cases, once this was discovered, it was applied to all instances of the same name.

Readers should be aware of other conventions in this transcription. If a comma is not present after a surname, it indicates that it is *not* in fact a surname. Several entries were first (given) names, often followed by a parent's first name and/or title (in the possessive), e.g., Itshe Nota's, or Rivka Reb Isserka's. Please also note that, where possible alternate spellings or pronunciations are suggested by the transcriber – in square brackets – after a name, they are usually only provided once; if the same name occurs repeatedly in that column, the spelling or pronunciation aid is not repeated.

The same is true if the transcriber is suggesting that the reader check out another entry related to the one the reader is currently studying (e.g., "Razovsky: See also Grazovsky" is stated only after the *first* occurrence of Razovsky.) Round parentheses ( ), incidently, are simply transcribed from the original index; square brackets [ ] always indicate an insertion by the transcriber. Where the transcriber found errors in the index, whether typographical or factual, he tried to correct them using corroborative evidence from the text or outside sources, and indicated the correction.

Hopefully, the transcriber has not made too many errors of his own. He takes full responsibility for that possibility.

Finally, please note that while the names listed here are supposedly "alphabetical", this is not a straightforward matter. To start with, as alluded to earlier the list seems to include many individuals who are placed alphabetically in the list by their *first* (given) names, not their surnames (sometimes there was no surname at all, in fact). This was retained in the transcription for the sake of faithfulness to the book.

Secondly, adjectives – which can at times be an integral part of the name beyond merely modifying it – usually take a different word order in English, Yiddish, and Hebrew.

Thirdly, the Yizkor Book's alphabetical listing follows the Hebrew/Yiddish alphabet, not the English/Roman one, and this order was retained in the transcription.

These three facts have profound consequences on potential name searches. For example, because the letter "Alef" is itself silent, it depends for a sound on the vowel-symbol beneath it or the letter following it. This means, for example, that a name listed under "Alef" could begin with any of the following possible sounds: short or long A, short or long E, long I, long O, long U, and so on. It means also, that a Hebrew spelling of a name will place it in a different position from the Yiddish spelling of the same name. "Rabinovitsh", for example, is found in two completely different places in the index; this is "correct", ironically, given that one spelling is in Yiddish and the other in Hebrew.

Researchers who are seeking a particular name, but who are unfamiliar with the rules and pronunciation of Hebrew and/or Yiddish, would be best to look at every name under a given initial letter heading. If the name sought after begins with a vowel, they should look under "Alef" and "Ayin" as well as under the expected initial letter. In any case, readers of this transcription should be wary of using transcription spelling for other than pronunciation purposes.

The transcriber has discovered a number of names within the body of the text which did not appear in the Yizkor Book index. Where this was noticed, the missing names were inserted into the transcribed index below, inside square brackets. Unfortunately, one suspects that there may be more such omissions, and the inevitable inference is that, as thorough as the original index was, it was not 100% complete. – PP

Alef	א	Bet	ב	Gimel	ג	Dalet	ד	Hey	ה
<=""" a=""">									
Vav	ו	Zayin	ז	Het	ח	Tet	ט	Yod	י
Khaf	כ	Lamed	ל	Mem	מ	Nun	נ	Samekh	ס
Ayin	ע	Pey	פ	Tsadek	צ	Kuf	ק	Reysh	ר
Shin	ש					Tav	ת		

[Page 529]

Name	Pages [numbers refer to original book]
Alef א	529
Abarsky	217
Avigdor Reb	349, 351
Avaclidus (Classical author)	138
Avrohom the Rabbi	358
Avrohom Borukh the Rabbi	133
Old Avrohom the Rabbi	237
Avrohom Yitzhok (The Nezvizher Preacher)	358

Avrohom Yankev (the Hunchback)	65
Avrom Noyekh [Noah] the Shoemaker	215
Avrohom (from Sfilovitsh)	455
Avrohom Shaya	431
Avrohom (The *Shammes* of the Burial Society)	80
Avrem'l the Hosid (hasid)	192, 431
Avrem'l the Lame	388
Avrem'l (The Tax Collector [on Kosher Meat])	129
Avrem'l of Frivish (or Privish)	465
Avrem'l the Rabbi	134
Abramovits, Binyomin	23
Abramovitsh (of the Zionist Youth Orgn.)	24
Abramsky, I. D.	92, 395
Abramsky, Yekhezkl the Rabbi	12, 40, 84, 117, 272, 274, 308, 313, 314, 317, 395
Abramtsi [Avramtsi, Avromtse]	405
Aginsky [Eginsky]	276
Agranoff, (Khinitsh) Yokheved	181
Agranoff, Gershon	181
Adler, Dr.	151
Adler, I. N.	171, 235, 520

[Page 530]

Beyz (Bet) ב

Berg, Sylvia	411, 412
Bargin [Bregin, Bergin]	74
Bergman [Bregman], Rokha'le	
Berger	119, 240, 242
Berger (the Teacher)	77, 92, 300
Berger (the Teacher's Son)	287
Berger, Yitzhok (from Minsk)	48
Berger, Yitzhok (from Kopulya)	246
Berger, Leyb	91, 240, 468
Berditshevsky, Mikha Yeysef	77
Barhon, Itsik Mikhoel [Mikhl]	281
Barhon, Alter	287
Barhon, Yeysef	278, 280
Barhon, Isroel	44, 276, 280, 281, 288
Barhon, Meysha	59, 287
Barhon, Nokhum Dan (The Head of the Yeshiva)	
Barhon, Riva	280
Barhon, Shaya Yova	280
Barhon, Shmaryohu	59, 60, 78, 282, 300, 396
Brodotsky, Yitzhok Tsvi	139
Brodesky	132, 500

Galician Hebrew writer, social critic, and Zionist]	
Barenfeld, Shimon	153
Barents [Brents? Brenetz?], H.	235
Barents, Mordkha	239
Brener	14
Berenshteyn	256
Berenshteyn, Yankev Naftoli Hertz	103
Berenshteyn, Isroel	152
Berenshteyn, Leyzer	243
Berenshteyn, Shoel [Shaul]	241, 244
Berenshteyn (Shapiro), Shimon	233
Barsky, Akiva	14
Brevde	375
Berkovitsh, Avrohom-Itshe	417
Berkovitsh, Itshe	487
Berkovitsh, Isser	417, 418
Berkovitsh, Elkhonon	417
Berkovitsh, Borukh	417, 418
Berkovitsh, Basya	417, 418
Berkovitsh (Tshipeleyer), Berl [from the village of Tshipeley]	417
Berkovitsh, Dvossi	417, 418

Gimel ג

[Page 531]

Gold, Rabbi Zev	247, 500, 501
Gold, Rabbi Dr. Refoel Tsvi	247, 499, 500
Goldos, Peretz	418
Goldblum, Fayvl	522
Goldberg, Rabbi Meysha-Issakhar	46, 76, 110, 140, 199, 366
Goldberg, Eyli	484
Goldberg, B.	23
Goldberg, Rabbi Chaim Zev-Volf	113
Goldberg, Yeysef	48, 91
Goldberg, Yankev	373
Goldberg, Isroel Noyekh	60, 282, 300
Goldberg, Meir	441
Goldberg, Sam	519
Goldberg, Reb Pinkhes	252
Goldvasser, Reb Yeheyshua Menahem	500
Goldman,	196, 440
Golda	429
Goldshteyn, Dr. Alexander	60
Gonta [Cossack General]	141
Gur ([Grozovsky], Yehuda	11, 131, 134, 178, 189, 245, 274, 293, 389
Gorovitsh [Gurvitsh? Gorvitsh? Gorovitz? Gurovitsh? Gurovitz?]" [Gurvitsh? Gorvitsh?	185, 420

Dalet ד

Dukhovitsh, Ahron	239
Dukhovitsh, Yankev	270
Dukhovitsh, Yerakhmiel	239
Dovidovitsh, Yankev	270
Dovidovitsh, Yitzhok	247
Dovidovitsh, Yitzhok Ha-Levy	230
Davidzon, Ber	393
Davidzon, Yehuda Leyb	247, 393
Davidzon, Issakhar	247
Davidzon, Dr. Yehuda	247
Dolgin	443
Dolgin, Hertzl	239
Dolgin, Haya	239
Dolgin, Fruma	235
Dolgin, Keyla	239
Dolitsky	75
Domnitz, Avrohom	239
Domnitz, Dr. Ahron	58, 105, 135, 233, 251, 252, 391, 520
Domnitz, Reb Asher (Teacher of Religious School)	135, 233, 251, 391, 461, 522
Domnitz, Borukh	115, 132, 172, 251, 253, 254, 262
Domnitz, Hadassa	251
Domnitz, Hertzl	233, 464

Dickens	389
Demburg, Reb Shleyma	312, 313
Danin [Dinin, Dnin]; store in pre-state Israel]	134
Danikin [Dnikin]; pogrom perpetrator]	141
Danielka	72
Droyanov [Darvianov, Dravionov]	177
Dorinson	418
Deretshin	42, 334
Deretshin, Yeshayohu Mendl	113, 117
Deretshin, Feygela	117

Hey ה

Hozberg	487
Holland, Borukh	522
Holland, Folla	522
Halber, Fayvl	169
Hafun [Hofun], Meysha	455
Hafka [Hopko, Hapka; chief state prosecutor]	146

[Page 533]

Name	Pages
Zhukov	386, 387, 486
Zhurovitsky, Godl	487
Zhizmer	302
Zheligovski [General]	348
Hes (Het) ח	
Hadash	345, 346
Hovanski [Duke]	270
Hatsha (The Tailor)	424
Hana	430
Hasla's, Neyekh	479
Hart	397
Charach [Harakh], Ahron	312
Charach, Ester Fruma	312
Charach, Hava	312
Charach, Fayvl	312
Havulson [Hvulson? Hevulson?], Daniel	153
Hava (The Bean Porter)	305, 368
Hurgin	240, 242, 468
Hurgin, Yishayohu	23, 26

Hefetz, Naftoli Tsvi	27, 37
Hefetz, Rabbi Tsvi Hirsh	36, 37
Khrushchov	345
Harif, Rabbi Aryeh Leyb	81
Tes (Tet)	
Tambak, Nota	293
"Tatelakh" ["Daddies"]	45
Tabachnick, Celia	525
Tabachnick, Reuven	525
Tabachnick, Rokhl	525
Twain, Mark	389
Toybela, Reb Shmuel's	349, 350
Tulman, Meysha	47, 301
Tumanik, Ayzik [Isaac]	360, 361
Tomashov, Alexander Yeheyshua	81
Tomashov, Basha	81
Tomashov (The Printer)	285
Tomashov, Velvl	423
Tomashov, Hasha [Chasya]	423
Tomashov, Yitskhok	425
Tomashov, Liba	425

Yud (Yod) ׳

Yankev (The Synagogue Sexton)	70, 28

[Page 534]

Name	Pages
Yankev Leyzer (The Ritual Slaughterer)	469
Yakobi, Yisroel	219
Yakobovitsh, Eliyosha	169
Yaffe, Yisroel	187
Yaffe, Mordkha Leyb	37
Yaffe, Miriam	508
Yafin [Yefin, Yapin], Yisroel Shoel	231
Yitzhok Ayzik	126
Yitzhok Ayzik (son of Avigdor)	19
Yitzhok Elkhanan [Spector], Rabbi	82, 108, 205, 230, 316, 353, 392, 396, 419, 427, 499, 500
Yitzhok Yekhiel [incorrectly entered as Yitzhok Yisroel. Grandfather and namesake of poet Yitzhak Katzenelson]	247
Yitzhok Meyir, son of Yeyna, head of the Rabbinical Court	19
Yitzhok, Rabbi of Volozhin	36, 152
Yerukham	424
Yerushalmi [Yerusalimsky], Rabbi Nehemya	205, 206, 209, 210, 211, 216, 219, 317, 446
Yerikho, Gitl	122
Yerikho, Meysha	45, 122

Lamed ל

Name	Pages
Liota (The Synagogue Sexton)	312, 318
Lieder, Chaim Yeysef	247
Lieder, Yisroel Yankev	247
Litt, Louis	507
Litvak [Litwak], A.	302
Litvin [Litwin]	348
Leyb [Yisroel, son of...] (The [late 18 C.] Preacher to Poland)	350
Leyb-Volf	447
Leybovitsh (The Teacher)	375
Leybovitsh, Lipa	276
Leybovitsh	185
Leybovitsh, Rabbi Borukh Ber	54, 81, 82, 83, 426, 427, 428
Leybovitsh, Shmuel	106, 112, 113
Leybl Mikhl's	441
Leyba Uzder [The Famous Cantor]	275
Leyba (The Saintly Man)	296
Leyba (The Tailor)	196, 440
Leybe Yoikh the blacksmith [Leyba "Soup", the Blacksmith]	117, 307, 364, 365, 366, 367
Leybka	496
Leybka (The Ritual Slaughterer)	515
Leybka (The Holy)	478, 479

Mem מ

[Page 535]

MaHaRSHaK (Baskin), Krayna	64, 65, 67, 69, 300
MaHaRSHaK, Reuven	32
MaHaRSHaK, Rabbi Reuven	139
MaHaRSHaK, Shmuel Dov (Alter the Ritual Slaughterer)	35, 45, 59, 62, 63, 115, 139, 191, 258, 300, 421, 469, 472
MaHaRSHaK, Shimon	63, 64, 67, 241, 242, 259, 262, 375, 396
MaHaRSHaK, Shimon Yitzhok	139
Mohilover, Rabbi Shmuel	500
Mozeszon, Rabbi Yoyl Dovid	84
Mozeski, Jan [18 C. Armenian or Hungarian designer of famed Slutsk woven belts]	17
Mozeski, Leon [son of the above]	17
Mokhov	42
Mukhin [Brothers]	278
Monomakh Vladimir [Kiev Grand Duke]	16
Montefiore, Moses	151, 494
Moshos, Dafna [French educator]	247, 393
Moshelov, Meysha	30
[Mikheikin [Micheikin]. Maiden name of Gruna Iskolsky]]	224
Meyzus [Mayzus? Mayzos?] Reb Shmuel Yitzhok	199
Maisel [Mayzl]	310

Mendele (Head of Yeshiva)	9, 81, 96, 106, 128, 352
Mendele Moykher Sforim (Abramovitsh, Sh. Y.)	11, 14, 133, 136, 147, 154, 159, 189, 192, 199, 242, 247, 248, 274, 278, 291, 361, 388, 393, 397, 429, 434, 444, 467, 473, 479, 484
Mendelson, Yitzhok Yankev	233
Mendelson, Simkha (Felix)	233
Menahem Ari	124
Menahem Mendl, The Rabbi	28, 193, 272, 392, 437
Menahem, Sh.	47, 57, 299
Menaker	295
Menashe	487
Mas, Yehuda	182
Mstislav	16
Mechanik, Bluma	523
Mechanik, Dvosha	296
Mechanik, Hana Haya	296, 297
Mechanik, Tevya (Tevya the Carpenter)	296, 297
Mechanik, Yeysef	47, 297, 523
Mechanik, Malka	296
Mechanik, Feygl	296
Mechanik-Shapiro [Shapira?], Pesya	60, 296
Melnik	145
Melnik	380
Menaker, Chaim	487, 488

Mendl	364
Mendl (The Blacksmith)	424
Mendelson	492
Menka Sender	465
Messl	424
Meshl	486
Margolin, Avrohom	239
Margolin, Dovid	423
Margolin (The Rabbi's Wife)	117
Margolin, Yankele	235
Margolin, Mordkha	235, 236, 238
Mordkha [Mordechai ben Neyakh] (of Lachowicze) [Reb Mordkha Lachovitsher, Hasidic master involved in conflict with local *Misnagdi* m, ideological opponents]	351
Mordkha Ahron	447
Mordkha The Mute	296
Mordkha The Butcher	196
Mordkha Yeyna [Yona]	364
Mordkha Yankev (Scribe of Torah Scrolls and Mezuzahs)	191, 341, 359
Mordkha-Nisn	370
Mordkha son of Pinkhes (from Kletsk)	31
Mordkhe'la (Oshmener [from Oshmyany])	353

Marmur, Yankev	239
Marmur, Nisn	225, 226
Marmur, Rokhl	239
Moishe [Reb Meysha], Rabbi (from Radom)	34
Meysha son of Peysakh, Rabbi	33, 372
Meysha Ahron Barukh's	431
Meysha Berl (The Glazier)	462
Meysha Getsl, Reb, Rizhitser	423

[Page 536]

Name	Pages
Meysha Dov, Reb	464
Meysha Dovid The Cantor	222
Meysha Velvl	447
"Meysha Yidaber" (Shusterman)	46, 131, 283, 359, 360
Meysha of Lyakhovichi [Lachowicze], Reb	111
Meysha (Masha) Naomi's, Reb	236, 238, 462, 463
Meysha Nesha's [Nisia's?]	202
Moshka The Ritual Slaughterer	437
Moshka The Blacksmith	430
Moshke'la Pig	392
Nun **נ**	

Skakolsky, Rabbi Shimon Tsvi	190, 431
Sakovitsh [Sakovits? Skovitsh?], Avrohom	132
Sklar [Shklyar] Shmuel	525
Ayin ע	
Ebin [Evin?]	281
Ebin, Asher	241
Ebin, Binyomin	12, 13, 97
Eberl, Meysha Yekhiel [reference not found on this page]	29
Edel	499
Eyzer [Oyzer]]Reb Shabsa [Shabtai], Rabbi [See Shabsa]	437
Ezriyel	382
Etya	423
Elyotka [The Thief]	294, 295
Elyasberg, Shmuel	483
Elyashberg [Elyasberg]	26
Eleys [Alace?], Herbert	515
Enzil, Rabbi Asher	272
Enzil, Rabbi Yehuda Leyb	34, 272
Eplboim [Applebaum], B.	388
Efron	267, 295, 357

[Page 537]

Epshteyn, Mikhl	429
Epshteyn, Nosn Nota	524
Epshteyn, Sasha	300
Epshteyn, Rabbi Menahem Mendl	81
Epshteyn (The Firefighter)	276
Epshteyn (The Dentist)	281
Epshteyn, Sholem	26
Epshteyn, Shmuel'ka	431
[Eshman, Rabbi]	276
Pey and Fey 𝔭	
Fogelman, Dr. Eliyezer L.	331
Podlipsky [See also entries following [Pevzner]	296
Podlipsky, Shmariyahu	455
Pavlovitsh, Alexandr	479
Patt, Yankev	319, 322
Polyatshek [Folyatshek?], Rabbi Shleyma	427, 428
Polyak [Folyak?]	190, 240, 241, 468
Polyak, Yankl	117
Polyak, Yankev Meyir	258, 526
Polyak, M.	30
Paleyev [Foleyev?], Hana	197

Pietkevitsh [Gentile lawyer]	68
Fialko	441
Fialko, Chaim Hirsh	445
Fialko, Chaim Herts	523
Fialko, Malka	445
Fialko, Etl Itka	523
Feygl Stisha's	97, 100
Faygenberg [Feygenberg], Ber	220
Faygenberg, Yeheyshua	220
Faygenberg, Yankev	220
Faygenberg, Yitzhok	220
Feygenberg, Rokhl (Imri) [writer]	11, 220, 221, 224, 274, 394
Faygenberg (Epshteyn), Sora	220, 223
Feyga's, Yeysef	214
Feivishowitz [Fayvishovitsh], Meysha	523
Feivishowitz, Elka	523
Fayvl	423
Fayvl (The Synagogue Sexton)	277
Fayvl (Hrozover [from Hrozov])	189, 429
Faytl	447
Faytlson	279

Chipchin, Sh.	60
Tsirin, Chaim	235
Tsirin, Meysha Ahron	238
Tsirin, Tsvi Hirsh	233, 234, 236, 464
Tsira Barker	368
Zirkel [Tsirkl]	50
Zirkel, Rokhl	523
Tsemakh	140, 153, 443
Chesnin [Tshesnin. Tsesnin?], Sam	412
Tsernogubovsky, Ora [Timkovitsh innkeeper]	442
Tsernomordik [Timkovitsh pharmacist]	442
Tsernovits, Rabbi Chaim (The Young Rabbi)	394, 458
Tshernikhov	337
Tshernikhov, Avrohom	60, 300, 414
Tshernikhov, Yehuda Leyb	21, 122
Tshernikhov, Yeysef	42, 122, 300
Tshernin, Sheyna	239
Kuf ק	
Kabrin	286

Name	Pages
Kagan (Teacher of the *Heder M'sukn* ["Modernized Hebrew School"]	
Kagan, Chaim	78
Kagan, Moshka [Mishka?]	443
Kagan, Sonia	443
Kahan, Ayzik	487
Kahan, Zakharia	487
[Kahan, Meysha 487]	50
Kahan, Refoyl	274
Kahanovitsh, M.	387
Cohen, Sam	411, 412
Cohen, Zelda	510
Cohen, Shmuel	510
Cavaliertshik, Borukh	471

[Page 538]

Name	Pages
Cavaliertshik, Yankl	471
Cava [Kaveh; nickname? lit. "Coffee"], Eliyohu Borukh	282
Kovelin [Kavelin?]	30
Kozatsinski [Kozitsinski], Mikhail [18 C. Superior of Russian Orthodox Monastery]	271, 272
Kozak, Chaim Leyb	443
Kozak, Yankev Meysha	443

[Page 539]

Karasik, Mikhl	176
Karasik, Nehemya	176
Karasl [Krasl? Karosel? Krosl? Kerasl?], G [writer]	12
Krasnitsh, Yitzhok Chaim	233, 234, 236, 459, 464
Krepkh, Fanya	60, 115, 300
Kremer, Sora [Kremer: See also seven entries above]	331
Krakovsky, Menahem [Krakovsky: See also eleventh entry in this column]	198
Kszivicki [Kshivitski], [Prof.] Ludwig [Polish sociologist]	347

Reysh ר

Rabinovitsh, Ester [Rabinovitsh: See also first entries of Column 3 on this page, and last entry of Column 2.]	441
Rabinovitsh, Berl	301
Rabinovitsh, Grunem	44155
Rabinovitsh, Yelena	443
Rabinovitsh, Shleyma	390
Rabinovitsh, Shleyma Yeysef	492
Rabinovitsh, Shimon	443
Rabinovitsh, Sh. A.	518
Rabkin	240, 468
Roginsky, Dr.	442

Rozin [Razin? This entry refers to a document signature "N. Rozin" shown on the page cited]	452
Rozental [Rosenthal]	330
Rozentsvayg [Rosenzweig]	290
Ratshkevitsh, Ahron	198, 199
Ratshkevitsh, Ora Gershon	441
Ratshkevitsh, Yisroel Dovid	199
Ratshkevitsh, Sora Rokhl	441
Rakhlin, Dovid	516
Rakhlin, Hirshl	516
Rakhlin, Haya	516
Rakhlin, Leya	51756
Rakhlin, Sonia	387, 516, 517, 519, 521
Rakhlin, Shmuel	516, 517, 519, 520, 521
Rakhmielevitsh, Itsha	295
Rakhmielevitsh, Leya	295
Rolnick [Rolnik], Avrohom Tsvi	518
Rolnick, Ahron	75, 262, 280, 518, 519, 520, 521
Rolnick, Ester	518, 524
Rolnick, Ester-Slava	518, 524
Rolnick (The *Bun* dist)	304
Rolnick, Yon-Teff [Yom-Tov] Lipman	518, 524

Rubnitz, Reuven	239
Rodgin [Rod-ghin], Yankev	239
Ruderman, Feygl (The Rabbi's Wife)	318
Rozovsky, Rabbi Yeysef [Rozovsky: Grozovsky	459, 462
Rozovsky, Shimon	247
Rozin, Yeysef [See also in previous column]	81
Rozenboym [Rosenbaum], Ephrayim	122
Rothschild [Rotshild]	132, 361
Romanov [See also previous column]	102
Rumshishok, Berl [Probable error. In text, Rumshishok refers to a location [it is in Lithuania, known also as Rumsiskes], but not as a surname for this resident, Berl]	464
Rusak, Avrohom Yitzhok	146
Rusomkha [Rosumkha? Rosomekha?], Sora	244
Razran, Tsvi [Gregory Razran: later, professor in New York]	60, 95, 269, 300
Rokhl Shimon's	365
Rakhmielovitsh, Yehuda Leyb [See Rakhmielevitsh], Column 2 of this page]	233
Rakhmielovitsh, Dr. Nahmen	233
Ratner	115, 259
Ratner, Avremela	115

renown [this is an understatement]	
RaSHaL, Rabbi Yehiyel	33
Shin שׁ	
Shakhravitsh ['Sakharovitsh?], Reuven	341
Shaklyuta [Error: name not found on this page]	281
Shor (The Teacher) [See also this page, column 2]	375
Shashkess [Possible nickname = "Sabers"; alt.: Shoshkess? Shoshka's = child of Shoshka, assuming Shoshka is itself a pet name, e.g., for Shoshana], Meysha	464
Shevaliyov [Shebaliyov? Shvaliyov? Shaveliyov?], Avreml	154
Shevaliyov, Avrohom Meysha Ha-Levy	138
Shevaliyov, Menahem	138
Shabsa [Shabtai] Baal Ha-SHaKH [Shabsa ben Meyir Ha-Koheyn, 17 C. Torah scholar]	79
Shabsa Eyzer [Oyzer] [See Eyzer]	193
Shabsa-Tsvi [Shabbetai-Tsvi, the notorious 17 C. "False Messiah"]	11
ShaDaL [Rabbi Shmuel David Luzzatto, renowned exegete] [See also Luzzatto]	104

Tof (Tav) ת	
[All surname entries under this letter are the same: "T'eymim", *teomi* m, meaning "twins" in Hebrew. In each case, it is a conventional surname, not a description.]	
T'eymim, Yeyna	20
T'eymim, Rabbi Yitzhok Yeysef	35, 272
T'eymim, Yitzhok Meyir	34, 272
T'eymim, Meyir	20

English Section

SLUTSK AND VICINITY
MEMORIAL BOOK

**Hlusk, Horki, Hresk, Hrozova, Kapule, Luban,
Pohost, Romanova, Shemezera, Stari-Dorogi,
Starobin, Timkowitz, Uretehe, Verchatin, Vizna**

Edited by
N. CUINITZ and SH. NACHMANI

Members of the Board
NISSAN WAXMAN
ZV1 HAGIVATI ·
ZVI ASSAF

**Published by the Yizkor Book Commitee
New-York—Tel-Aviv 5722—1962**

[Page II]

This book may be obtained in the U.S.A. from:
Mr. Eli L. Altman 113 W. 42 St. New York, 36, N.Y.

OR

Rabbi N. Waxman 1644 52 St. Brooklyn, 4, N.Y.

PRINTED IN ISRAEL

"Achduth" Corp. Press Ltd, Tel-Aviv, Israel

[Pages III-VII]

[Page VIII]

[Blank]

[Page IX]

Slutsk: Its Glory and its Destruction

By Nissan Waxman

The city of Slutsk in White Russia was one of the foremost Jewish centers in Eastern Europe. Though not large in size and population, it occupied at many important moments in the history of Russian Jewry a more prominent place, and was better known, than the state capital city of Minsk. The Jews of Slutsk were noted for their excessive pride in their city, for which they were often taunted. Considering, in retrospect the history of the community and its merits, they seem to have had full justification for their attitude, and even a cursory perusal of this volume will engender a similar pride within the hearts of all those whose lives were once touched by Slutsk.

Over four hundred years ago there was already in Slutsk a fully organized Jewish community, distinguished in its conduct and unique in its mores. The echo of her love for scholarship and her pursuance of charity and kindness resounded in distant lands and attracted many outstanding families to come and settle there.

Despite the general poverty that prevailed in White Russia due to its lack of natural resources, and more so in Slutsk because of its distance from a railroad connection (until 1914), the Jewish population was quite well established and contented in Slutsk. For their lack of material riches they were compensated by their spiritual opulence, and they exerted a great influence among their brethren throughout Russia. The Rabbis of Slutsk had also always been renowned for their scholarship and were acclaimed as the spiritual leaders of their generation. Their opinions were highly esteemed in the Torah world and their services were often sought by many large Jewish communities. Throughout the years, Slutsk retained an enviable reputation as a center of Torah and true Jewish wisdom unequalled by many larger Jewish communities.

Slutsk Jewry was always in the forefront of Jewish life and action in Russia, and all other communities looked to her for guidance and leadership. Whatever ideologies and movements appeared on the Jewish horizon, their propagators endeavored to obtain a foothold in Slutsk, whence the doctrines would spread far and wide. The Jews of Slutsk, however, steeped in their traditional culture and possessing a natural skepticism, were extremely cautious towards untested ideologies and viewed new movements with grave suspicion. They were highly reluctant to accept them and at times fought vigorously against them.

During the seventeenth century, when the cult of the false messiah, Sabbatai Zevi (1626-1676) was rampant throughout the Jewish world and many great leaders fell prey to it, Slutsk Jewry was not swayed whatsoever, despite the special emissaries that were sent to influence the population there.

[Page X]

In the eighteenth century, when the movement of Hassidism was on the march and its leaders attempted strenuously to make inroads in Slutsk, the people remained steadfast to their tradition and all efforts of persuasion did not produce any recruits for that movement (see Lubavicher Rabbi's Memories, Volume 11, pp. 143-153 and 164-165, New York 1960).

By its strong resistance Slutsk became synonymous with opposition to Hassidism and was so labeled in the Jewish lore. A "cold Mithnagged of Slutsk" is a well-known appellation in the Jewish vernacular. This was later expanded to the wider term of "a cold Litvak", in contrast to "a hot Hassid". In the courtyard of the Slutsk central synagogue there was a gigantic flintstone upon which, according to a legend, Rabbi Israel of Mezbizh, known as the "Besht" (1700-1760) had been put for a spanking when he appeared there to preach his ideas. As a result of this offensive act, Rabbi Israel is said to have uttered in anger that no Hassidic congregation shall ever arise in Slutsk. This imprecation was obviously fulfilled and the Jewish population there was rather amused and proud of it.

Towards the end of the nineteenth century East European Jewry was overwhelmed by the Haskalah, the so-called "enlightenment" movement. For the first time in many generations Slutsk, too, was greatly influenced and affected. The spirit of the new trend shook the very foundation of this ancient citadel and produced there a host of leaders who distinguished themselves in various modern intellectual activities throughout the Jewish world. At the same time, however, it maintained its former tradition as a reservoir of Torah through its great Yeshivah, headed by the renowned Gaon R. Issar Zalman Meltzer, to which students flocked from everywhere. Though the general spirit of the city was by then greatly changed, the Yeshivah preserved somewhat the pristine reputation and fame of the community.

In addition to the city of Slutsk, its Province consisted of about 15 smaller Jewish municipalities. They were: Hlusk, Hresk, Hrozova, Kapulie, Liuban, Pohost, Romanove, Starobin, Timkovitz, Uretche, Verkhutin, Vizne and others. Each one of these was a fully organized community, possessing a wealth of traditional Jewish culture and contributing greatly in its own way to the general spiritual panorama of the vicinity.

All this came to an end with the October Revolution in 1917. The Bolshevik Government suppressed every vestige of religious, national and spiritual life there. The historic and beautiful synagogues of Slutsk were confiscated and, one by one, their leaders were forced to flee the city to avoid deportation to Siberia where they would perish by famine and torture in the labor camps. Rabbi Meltzer attempted to remain in Slutsk with his Yeshivah, enduring great hardship, deprivation and oppression by the local government and party officials. In 1923 he succeeded in escaping and found refuge outside of the Russian borders. The Jewish community of Slutsk thus lingered on in the last two decades of its existence impoverished in spirit and despoiled of its former glory.

A description of the physical annihilation of Slutsk Jewry by the Hitler battalions in 1941 is given in the following report of the Nazi district commissioner to his superior in Minsk. This secret document was presented at the Nuremberg International Military Trial and is included in the United States Government report of those proceedings published under the name of Nazi Conspiracy and Aggression Volume 111, page 785 (United States Government Printing Office, Washington, D. C. 1946). Parts of this document also appear in the book GESTAPO by Edward Crankshaw (Viking Press, 1956 and Pyramid Books, 1959).

[Page XI]

DOCUMENT 1104-PS
Copy/T of the copy

The commissioner of the Territory of Slutsk

Slutsk, 30 October 1941

SECRET

To the Commissioner General Minsk

SUBJECT: Action against Jews

Referring to the report made by phone on 27 October 1941 I now beg to inform you in writing of the following

On 27 October in the morning at about 8 o'clock a first lieutenant of the police battalion No. 11 from Kauen (Lithuania) appeared and introduced himself as the adjutant of the battalion commander of the security police. The first lieutenant explained that the police battalion had received the assignment to effect the liquidation of all Jews here in the town of Slutsk, within two days. The battalion commander with his battalion in strength of four companies, two of which were made up of Lithuanian partisans, was on the march here and the action would have to begin instantly. I replied to the first lieutenant that I had to discuss the action in any case first with the commander. About half an hour later the police battalion arrived in Slutsk. Immediately after the arrival the conference with the battalion commander took place according to my request. I first explained to the commander that it would not very well be possible to effect the action without previous preparation, because everybody had been sent to work and that it would lead to terrible confusion. At least it would have been his duty to inform me a day ahead of time. Then I requested him to postpone the action one day. However, he rejected this with the remark that he had to carry out this action everywhere and in all towns and that only two days were allotted for Slutsk. Within these two days, the town of Slutzk had to be cleared of Jews by all means. I immediately protested violently against it, pointing out that a liquidation of Jews must not be allowed to take place in an arbitrary manner. I explained that a large part of the Jews still living in the towns were tradesmen and families of tradesmen respectively. But these Jewish tradesmen were not simply expendable because they were indispensable for maintaining the economic life. Furthermore, I pointed out that White Ruthenian tradesmen are so to say non-existent, that therefore all vital plants had to be shut down all at once, if all Jews would be liquidated. At the end of our conference, I mentioned that all tradesmen and specialists, inasmuch as they were indispensable, had papers of identification and that these should not be pulled out of the factories. Furthermore, it was agreed that all Jews still living in the town should first be brought into the ghetto in order to segregate them, especially with regard to the families of tradesmen which I did not want to have liquidated either. Two of my officials should be assigned to segregate them.

[Page XII]

The commander did not in any way contradict my idea and I had therefore the firm belief that the action would be carried out accordingly. However, a few hours after the beginning of the action the greatest difficulties already developed. I noticed that the commander had not at all abided by our agreement. All Jews without exception were taken out of the factories and shops and deported in spite of our agreement. It is true that part of the Jews was moved by way of the ghetto where many of them were processed and still segregated by me, but a large part was loaded directly on trucks and liquidated without further delay outside of the town. Shortly after noon complaints came already from all sides that the factories could not function any more because all Jewish tradesmen had been removed. As the commander had proceeded on his way to Baranowitschi I got in touch with the deputy commander, a captain, after searching a long time, and demanded to stop the action immediately because my instructions had been disregarded and the damage done so far with respect to the economic life could not be repaired anymore. The captain was greatly surprised at my idea and stated that he had received orders from the commander to clear the whole town of Jews without exception in the same manner as they had done in other towns. This mopping up had to be executed on political considerations and economic reasons had never played a role anywhere. However, due to my energetic intervention, he finally halted the action toward evening.

For the rest, as regards the execution of the action, I must point out to my deepest regret that the latter bordered already on sadism. The town itself offered a picture of horror during the action. With indescribable brutality on the part of both the German police officers and particularly the Lithuanian partisans, the Jewish people, but also among them White Ruthenians, were taken out of their dwellings and herded together. Everywhere in the town shots were to be heard and in different streets the corpses of shot Jews accumulated. The White Ruthenians were in greatest distress to free themselves from the encirclement. Regardless of the fact that the Jewish people, among whom were also tradesmen, were mistreated in a terribly barbarous way in the face of the White Ruthenian people, the White Ruthenians themselves were also worked over with rubber clubs and rifle butts. There was no question of an action against the Jews any more. It rather looked like a revolution. I myself with all my officials have been in it without interruption all day long in order to save what could yet be saved. In several instances I literally had to expel with drawn pistol the German police officials as well as the Lithuanian partisans from the shops. My own police was employed for the same mission but had often to leave the streets on account of the wild shooting in order to avoid being shot themselves. The whole picture was generally more than ghastly. In the afternoon a great number of abandoned Panje carriages with horses were standing in the streets so that I had to instruct the municipal administration to take care of the vehicles immediately. Afterwards it was ascertained that they were Jewish vehicles ordered by the armed forces to move ammunition. The drivers had simply been taken off the carriages and led away, and nobody had worried in the least about the vehicles.

I was not present at the shooting before the town. Therefore I cannot make a statement on its brutality. But it should suffice, if I point out that persons shot have worked themselves out of their graves some time after they had been covered. Regarding the economic damage I want to state that the tanner has been affected worst of all. 26 experts worked there. Of them, fifteen of the best specialists alone have been shot. Four more jumped from the truck during the transport and escaped, while seven others were not apprehended after they fled. The plant barely continues

[Page XIII]

to operate today. Five wheelwrights worked in the wheelwright shop. Four of them have been shot and the shop has to keep going now with one wheelwright. Additional tradesmen such as carpenters, blacksmiths, etc. are still missing. Up till now it was impossible for me to obtain an exact survey. I have mentioned already in the beginning, that the families of tradesmen should be spared too. But now it seems that almost in all families some persons are missing. Reports come in from all over, making it clear that in one family the tradesman himself, in another family the wife and in the next one again the children are missing. In that way, almost all families have been broken up. It seems to be very doubtful whether under these circumstances the remaining tradesmen will show any interest in their work and produce accordingly, particularly as even today they are running around with bloody and bruised faces due to the brutality. The White Ruthenian people who had full confidence in us, are dumbfounded. Though they are intimidated and don't dare to utter their free opinion, one has already heard that they take the viewpoint that this day does not add to the glory of Germany and that it will not be forgotten. I am of the opinion that much has been destroyed through this action which we have achieved during the last months and that it will take a long time until we shall regain the confidence of the population which we have lost.

In conclusion I find myself obliged to point out that the police battalion has looted in an unheard of manner during the action, and that not only in Jewish houses but just the same in those of the White Ruthenians. Anything of use such as boots, leather, cloth, gold and other valuables, has been taken away. On the basis of statements of members of the armed forces, watches were torn off the arms of Jews in public, on the street, and rings were pulled off the fingers in the most brutal manner. A major of the finance department reported that a Jewish girl was asked by the police to obtain immediately 5,000 rubles to have her father released. This girl is said to have actually gone everywhere in order to obtain the money.

Also within the ghetto, the different barracks which had been nailed up by the civil administration and were furnished with Jewish furniture, have been broken open and robbed. Even from the barracks in which the unit was quartered, window frames and doors have been forcibly removed and used for campfires. Although I had a discussion with the adjutant of the commander on Tuesday morning concerning the looting and he promised in the course of the discussion that none of the policemen would enter the town anymore. yet I was forced several hours later to arrest two fully armed Lithuanian partisans because they were apprehended looting. During the night from Tuesday to Wednesday the battalion left the town in the direction of Baranowitschi. Evidently, the people were only too glad when this report circulated in the town.

So far the report. I shall come to Minsk in the immediate future in order to discuss the affair personally once again. At the present time, I am not in a position to continue with the action against the Jews. First, order has to be established again. I hope that I shall be able to restore order as soon as possible and also to revive the economic life despite the difficulties. Only, I beg you to grant me one request: "In the future, keep this police battalion away from me by all means."

signed: *Carl*

[Page XIV]

Upon receiving this descriptive report of the truculent and atrocious action committed in Slutzk, the Commissioner General, himself a trained and hardened Nazi, was so moved that he immediately dispatched this report to his superior in occupied Riga, Latvia with his own following comments.

* * *

Minsk, November 1, 1941

SECRET

To the Reich Commissioner for Eastern territories, Gauleiter Hinrich Lohse, Riga.

Enclosed, I submit a report of the commissioner for the territory of Slutzk, Party member Carl, with the request not to let this matter rest.

For about the last three weeks I have discussed the Slutzk action against the Jews with the responsible SS Brigadier General Zenner, member of the Reichstag. I request to grant my motion to prosecute the entire staff of officers of the police battalion 11.

I am submitting this report in duplicate so that one copy may be submitted to the Reich Minister. Peace and order cannot be maintained in White Ruthenia with methods of that sort. To have buried alive seriously wounded people, who then worked their way out of their graves again, is such extreme beastliness that this incident as such must be reported to the Fuehrer and the Reich Marshal.

* * *

Commissioner General for White Ruthenia
signed: *Wilhelm Kube*

The office in Riga followed up the matter and transmitted these reports directly to the Minister in Berlin with the following note:

Riga, November 11, 1941

To the Reich Minister for occupied Eastern Territories, Berlin:

Original with two enclosures with the request for consideration. It is deemed necessary that higher authority take immediate steps.

The noted British historian and commentator of the London Observer, Edward Crankshaw, after quoting some excerpts from the above in his book "Gestapo" remarks: "This was the impression made on a German official, who had already in the nature of his job seen many dreadful things, who has prepared to see the Jews of Slutzk completely liquidated provided be had a day's warning to organize the affairs in an orderly manner, but who, nevertheless, was so shocked and affronted by the reality that, after brooding about it for three days, he still could not overcome his indignation and, taking courage in both hands, laid bare his heart to his Fuehrer, via Goering. He was an innocent, of course. The Fuehrer had ordered that these people should be killed, and did not care how."

By order of the Reich Commissioner
for the Eastern Territories
Signed: *Wichman*

[Page XV]

Slutsk After World War II
(As seen by an eye witness)

By Maurice Hindus

The writer of this article is a world-renowned author and Journalist. In 1944 he was probably the first American Jew, who was privileged as a Journalist, to travel together with the Red Army and enter with them the city of Slutzk upon its re-occupation from the collapsed German armies. At that time, he related his observations in a series of articles in the New York Herald Tribune. The following article has recently been written by Mr. Hindus especially for this publication.

In mid-November, 1944, 1 made a journey in a dilapidated Ford from Minsk to Slutsk. Several Officials from Minsk who knew Slutzk accompanied me on the trip. We travelled over country that was laid waste by war. Again and again, now on one side of the chaussee, rural roads, now on the other, I saw clusters of blackened and battered chimney stacks, all that was left of once thriving villages and towns. In their retreat the Germans had burned and blasted every- thing in their way.

We drove for hours and hours and still saw no Slutzk. My companions kept telling we would get there soon; we could not possibly miss it. Slutzk was a big town and, though road signs had not yet been restored, they were confident that we would see it sprawling along the chausse. But we didn't see it. We drove past it without knowing we had done so. Only when we inquired of an old peasant woman bent under a load of firewood how far we were from Slutsk, did we learn that we had driven about ten kilometers beyond it.

I am mentioning this incident because driving along the chaussee, we could not identify the town, and the reason we could not, was because Slutzk was one of the bleakest and flattest ruins I had seen in war-torn Russia, and I had seen Stalingrad.

We drove into Slutzk from the direction of the old Gutzeit flour-mill. All the way to the bazaar I saw few buildings. The bazaar itself which, as you remember, boomed with trade in autumn was practically deserted. It seemed strange not to hear cackling geese, squawking hens, grunting pigs in November in the Slutzk bazaar; and not to see a single peasant with sacks or baskets of the late autumn apples and pears for which Slutzk and the surrounding countryside were famous.

I shall always remember the shock I experienced when I walked along Broad Street. I could not recognize the loveliest street in the city. The boulevard was gone. Out of spite the Germans had cut down the trees and I saw nothing but stumps overgrown with weeds and grass. The houses, the finest in town, were nearly all demolished. The Lutheran Church with its Gothic tower and old clock, one of the architectural landmarks of Slutzk, was cracked and wobbly and about to collapse. So the once beautiful playground of Slutzk was now a wild and dreary waste.

Kapuler Street should be renamed Shekhita Street. Actually there was no street any more – nearly all the buildings were levelled to the ground. But it was on this street, behind barbed wires, that Jews were herded and slaughtered. Nobody could tell me how many Jews fell victim to German machine guns. All I learned was that out of a population of 23,000 about one-third were gentiles, and that not many had escaped the slaughter. The tangled and rusty barbed wires that had not yet been cleared away were the only silent witnesses of the Great Pogrom.

Slutzk was occupied three days after the war broke out. Some Jews fled the moment they heard German planes flying high over the city, which was in the morning of the first day of the war. Since trains, trucks, and all other

[Page XVI]

forms of transportation were either paralyzed or mobilized by the army, walking was the only mode of escape. Three of my nephews, Refoel, Gershon, Shlomo Gendeliovitch just picked up their families and left on foot for the interior of Russia. Gershon finally reached a village on the Volga and settled there. Refoel and Shlomo, who were members of the Slutzk kolhoz, managed to get to a village in the province of Kostroma and joined a kolhoz there. By fleeing from Slutzk before the Germans had arrived, they saved themselves from death.

From the information I gathered from party and Soviet officials, no more than about one hundred Jewish families walked out of the city and succeeded in making their way deep into the interior. Who they were and where they finally settled, nobody could tell me.

The other Jews stayed in Slutzk. They didn't believe the Germans were as wicked as they had been depicted. They thought that they could somehow come to terms with them and work and live. They could not imagine Germans killing men and women, let alone children, in cold blood. This was the grimmest mistake our brethren made, not only in Slutzk but all over Europe.

Nor did the Germans show any particular hostility to Jews when they first occupied the city. They told the Jewish community to choose a representative who would speak for them in their dealings with the German commandant. Chipchin, the lawyer, was chosen for the position and for several weeks he seemed to get along well with the new masters of Slutzk. But when repressions began, he again and again raised his voice in protest. Then one day German authorities summoned an outdoor-mass-meeting of Jews, presumably to give them an opportunity to air their grievances in the open. Chipchin was the first speaker and he had no more than said a few words when the German officer whipped out his revolver and shot him. This was the first shooting of Jews in Slutzk.

The Jewish community was terrorized. For the first time they realized the devil was even blacker than he was painted. They felt hopelessly trapped. Yet a few of them, only a few, managed to escape. A women named Mishalova braved the terror of the Nazis and walked out of the city with her two children. She had procured a false passport and her light hair and blue eyes protected her from the close scrutiny of the Nazi guards. Three other men, the Neumark brothers, likewise made their way to the Russian rear. There were several others who were equally plucky and lucky, though nobody could give me their names.

Slutzk was surrounded by a powerful partisan army, and the Germans were so afraid of the partisans that they rarely dared to travel of the main highways. I was in villages outside of Slutzk where not even the geese were molested. These villages lay off the main highways and the Germans left them alone. They wouldn't even risk going after the geese, and goose as you surely know is a favorite German food. Several young Jews in Slutzk joined the partisans and saved themselves. At the time I was in Slutzk they had already been mobilized by the Red army and were at the front so I didn't see them.

But why didn't other Jews, especially the young people, run off to the partisans? Once with the partisans they would have been safe unless they perished in battle or fell victim to a partisan's anti-Semite bullet. That there were anti-Semites among the partisans, nobody in Slutzk denied. But the mayor of the city, who had been commander-in-chief of the partisan garrisons, assured me that Jews under his charge rarely suffered from anti-Semitism, and that he dealt harshly with partisans who offended their Jewish fellow-fighters. Besides, as partisans, Jews were as well armed as non-Jews and could protect themselves against attacks on their person. The fact is that not only in Slutzk but in all Byelorussia, comparatively few Jews joined the partisans. Meyer S. Handler, a fellow correspondent who was in Moscow for the New York United Press, made a journey to Pinsk about the same time that I went to Slutzk. On his return to Moscow he and I compared notes. He brought back from Pinsk the same sorrowful tale that I did from Slutzk, from Minsk, from Pohost and from a few other communities in Byelorussia – very few Jews threw in their lot with the partisans. Why didn't they?

In Slutzk I met a carpenter by the name of Popoff. He told me that one evening during the occupation, the wife of a Jewish barber, named Melnick, rushed into his house and begged him to save her children. Popoff went with her to her house, picked up her three children and brought them to his house. He kept them for a week. As it was dangerous for him to keep them any longer, the mother came and said she would take them back home. Popoff pleaded with her to run off with the children to the partisans. He was one of their secret agents in Slutzk and offered to help her make her way to partisan territory. The mother refused. "If I were alone", she said, I might try. But with the children I'll never make it, and I won't go without them." Despite Popoff's entreaties and expostulations, she refused to follow his advice. Soon afterwards she and her children were murdered.

There were many other instances when mothers, fathers, sons, daughters could have saved themselves by

[Page XVII]

running away to the partisans. But they would not leave without one another. So fathers and mothers stayed with their children and sons and daughters stayed with their parents. The terror of the Germans had firmly solidified the Jewish families. If they couldn't live together, they would die together. They ended up behind the barbed wire fences on Kapuler Street.

New York City,
January 1958

Addenda

In a personal conversation with Mr. Hindus, after receiving from him the preceding article, I asked him to recall whether he saw any relic of the many Slutzker Synagogues and particularly the Great Synagogue known as the "Kalte Shul" which stood in the center of the Synagogue Courtyard and known as an ancient landmark throughout White Russia, around which there has prevailed many legends, and also concerning the Jewish cemetery on Zaretzer Gasse, where some of internationally famous Jewish saints and scholars have found their resting place.

Mr. Hindus replied that he did see the cemetery and its fence in a state of extreme neglect and devastation but not completely destroyed. As to the Synagogues, he did not recollect of having seen or heard anything about them in the one day that he spent there, a matter which indeed provoked Mr. Hindus himself at the time of writing this article.

In a later conversation with Mrs. Rachel Pickoltz, a native of Slutsk, who was there during the Nazi occupation of Slutsk in June 1941 till July 1942, when she succeeded in leaving the city and joining the Partisans, the Synagogue matter was fully clarified to me. Mrs. Pickoltz told me that all the Synagogues of Slutsk have long been occupied by the Soviet government for secular purposes and the "Kalte Shul" has been used for a bakery since the middle twenties, to the extent that the younger generation has completely forgotten to identify these buildings as Houses of Worship. Furthermore, in June 1941 when the Nazi planes bombarded the city of Slutsk, the Synagogues were among the first buildings to be destroyed. Hence, when Mr. Maurice Hindus visited Slutsk after the Russians re-occupied it, he really could not have seen a trace of any synagogue nor heard any thing about them.

Rabbi Nissan Waxman

[Page XVIII]

Some Early History and Recent Memories of Slutsk

By Gregory Razran

The city of Slutsk, originally known as Sluchesk, is one of Russia's oldest cities, founded by the Dregovichi tribe, and mentioned first in 1116 in a "Lavrenty Letopia'." The Letopia' says that: "Gleb of Minesk (Minsk) fought with the Dregovichi and burned Sluchesk" and that "Volodimer (Vladimir Monomakh, famous Kiev Grand Duke) sacked in turn Gleb's Minesk." Slutsk was then a part of the Kiev Grand Duchy. In 1148, it was transferred to the Chernigov principality (knyazhestvo), in 1662 returned to Kiev, and soon after it became a part of the principality of Turov-Pinsk, remaining so for more than 200 years.

Slutsk attained the status of a separate principality in 1395, with Olel'ko Vladimiroch, a direct Rurik descendant, as its first prince. However, by that time the entire region had fallen under the general sovereignty of Lithuania-Poland, and the Olel'kovichy princes were apparently only semi-independent. Their dynasty lasted for more than 200 years – until, at the beginning of the 17th century, a last daughter of the Olel'knivichy, Princess Sophia, married Prince Januez Radziwill and Slutsk became Radziwill-governed.

In 1579, one of the Olel'kovichi princes divided Slutsk into three separate parts, Old Slutsk, New Slutsk (Troychan), and Ostrov, bequeathing each part to one of his three sons. The Crimean Tartars besieged the city in 1503-1504, but could not take it. Likewise, Slutsk successfully beat off a Russian attack in 1655 during the Russo-Polish War when such cities as Minsk, Wilno, Kovno, Grodno, and Mogilev originally fell to the Russians (later retaken). As is known, Slutsk returned to Russia in 1793, after the second partition of Poland in the last years of the reign of Catherine the Second.

A curious fact about Slutsk is that in the last half of the 17th and first half of the 18th century, it was a world center for the manufacture of a special kind of oriental (Persian) belt[s] made of silk, gold, and silver and known then as the Slutsk belts (Slucki Pasi or Slutzkyiye Poyasy). The Slutsk design of the belts was imitated by manufacturers in Polish, Russian, and even German, French, and Italian cities.

The manufacturing was begun in 1758 under the direct supervision of the Radziwill estate and for a long time business apparently flourished. When, however, in 1832, "the business began to decline, it was leased for three years and then for another three years to the Jewess Bluma Liberman, the daughter of the merchant Kantorowicz."

The "Yevreyskaya Entsyklopediya" states that the existence of Jews in Slutsk is first mentioned in documents of 1583, that Slutsk became a part of the Vaad D'Artsoth Lita in 1695 and that the Vaad met in Slutsk in 1761 (its last meeting), and also that the Russian Census of 1897 counted in the city a little more than 10,000 Jews and a little more than 2,000 non-Jews (the exact number of the Census, I now note, was 10,264 Jews and 2,285 non-Jews).

Still, I was very much fascinated when I examined the texts themselves of the Slutsk documents in the *Regesty i Nadpisy* (vol. i published in 1899 by the St. Petersburg Mefitze Haskalah; vols. 2 and 3 published in 1910 and 1913 by the Yevreiskoye Istoriko-Etnograficheskoye Obshchestvo). The first document, the 1583 one, merely

[Page XIX]

Slutsk - Turov - Pinsk in the 10th and 13th century

[Page XX]

These figures indicate the right and left of a belt with Slutsk marking.
Item 12544, People's Museum, Warsaw

[Page XXI]

mentions that "Il'ya Lipstitz and Merkel Novakhovich of Slutsk paid toll in Brest for transporting various goods to Lyublin." The second, third, and fourth documents, of the year 1622., relate how "Avram Aronovich, a Slutsk Jew, complained that a Slutsk 'meshchanka' Yaroshevitseva hid her son Karp who stole goods from Aronovich." Later, Karp was jailed, and "Yaroshevitseva, on the advice of her son Stephan, a known Jew-hater, complained that Aron willfully arrested Karp who was innocent and that Aron himself robbed her house."

A 1645 document describ[e]s a complaint of the priest Voskresensky against Itska Abramovich, a lessee of an inn on the Oressa River. Itska's "bakhur-servant" ("bakhur" in Russian text) was drowned in the river and the priest's servants, Ivashko Rachkovets and Sapon Astapkevich, found the drowned and hid a knife and three "osmaks" that were in his possession. As a result, "the Jew tortured the priest's servants in the

manner of an enemy of Christian people, brought them to his 'Pan' and incarcerated them in the Slutsk jail."
At the trial, the court released Rachkovets when he swore that he

The figure shows a belt with the Slutsk marking
(Collection of the Radziwill Foundation Nieswizh, Poland)

had not killed the "Bakhur" but also excused Itska from any monetary fine (nothing is said about the trial of Astapkevich).

Again, a 1659 document tells of a letter from the Slutsk Protopope Yoann Bokachich to the Lithuanian Prince Boguslav Radivil (Radziwill) in which the protopope informs that "a Jew from the village of Doktorovich, who adopted Christianity and was a Christian for ten years, came to Slutsk after his wife died, remarried, and at the instigation of Slutsk rabbis returned to Judaism with his second wife and children who had been born Christian." The document continues that "Bokachich, seeing in this an insult to the Church, complains to the Prince in the name of the clergy, reminding thereat that "a Christian child killed by them in Doktorovici ten years ago still remains unburied."

Then came five letters of complaint against Slutsk Jews from the Slutsk Archimandrite Theodosius Vasilevich to the Lithuanian Prince Boguslaw Radivil (Radziwill) - one written in 1666, two in 1668, and two in 1669. Some of the Archimandrite's complaints are: that the Slutsk Jew, Yakub Davidovich, insulted him and the Glory of the Lord and even threw himself upon him with a knife and that the court freed the accused, not because of legal considerations, but because of special respect for Jews; that while Christians had more than once been sentenced to death on account of Jews, not once had Jews paid such penalty for insults to the Lord, His House, His Holy Objects or His Clergy; and that in Slutsk there were many Jews and Jewesses who were first converted to Christianity and then returned to Judaism.

So far for the early history of the city. As for the Slutsk of my own days, all I need do is to close my eyes, and it all comes back to me. I remember, of course, the two years that I spent in Slutsker Yeshivah, Reb Zundel Meltzer's brilliant Talmudic Expositions and Reb Sheftel Kramer's melancholic Mussar talks in the Sabbath eve twilights. During the day Reb Sheftel's presence was revealed to us, as a rule, only from above, watching us from a high balcony window; a pair of eyes peering and a black beard swaying. But he never managed, however, to detect the "prohibited" books which I avidly read in the Yeshivah outhouse. It is there in the outhouse where, believe it or not, my first serious secular education began, where I first became acquainted with Mapoh, Smolenskin, Byalik etc.

The books had their effect. I soon converted into a full-fledged Haskalah Searcher, left the Yeshivah at 14 and plunged into a world of opposite values and opposing concerns. Brenner, Berdichevsky and Borokhov, Hess and

[Page XXII]

Hertzl, Pinsker and Peretz, and a little later the vast and varied Russian luminaries became my guides and mentors. I joined the Zeire-Zion party and also had a strong sympathy for the Poale-Zion. (I was therefore, happy some years afterwards, when I was already in the United States, that a union between Zeire-Zion and Poale-Zion was affected).

After that the first image that I get is usually that of Solomyak's Cafe with its blend of delicious rum cakes and abstract sociopolitical and philosophical debates; the bald and learned "kazyonny ravvin" and orthodox Marxist and menshevik-internationalist Bronstein; the cynical and quizzically perceptive socialist-Zionist Charney; secular and sympathetic gray-haired "askon" and "Folkist" Feinberg; and worldly Zeire-Zionist Landau; dedicated and oratorical and much-popular-with-the-girls Gabai; pedantic yet highly gifted Mlinsky; bespectacled and studious Solomon Chipchin and the charming and altogether lovely "Bundist" Malke Boruchovich.

My second image is that of the "kalte shul" and the birds hovering and soaring in and out under the lofty ceiling during the prayers on Shevuoth.

My third… well, the clubs of Zeire-Zion: first, the suburban and greenery-covered one on Yuryevsky Street; second, the stuffy and crowded one in the market place; and third, the spacious and modern one, supplied with two electric bulbs, on the *chaussee*, the property of Mrs. Feinberg. My third really runs to romance. I remember most vividly and with considerable nostalgia the benches of the Broad Street boulevard strewn with chestnut-blossoms on which we teenagers sat and loved and recited to each other Nadson and Shneur and David Einhorn and some of us even Heinrich Heine.

The aforementioned Charney was fond of saying that Slutsk was governed by "Four Lions" Lev Grigorevich, Lev Mikhailovich, Lev Isakovich, and Lev Mironovich. As secretary of the Slutsk Kehilah after the Revolution, and for a number of years secretary, and also president of the Slutsk Zeire-Zion, I knew them all. Lev Grigorevich is of course the almost-legendary Dr. Shildkret, a giant of mind and heart, revered and loved by Jew and non-Jew, poor and rich, old and young. Shildkret was by all tokens the foremost intellect in the entire "uyezd", even if he lost somewhat in popularity after the revolution because of his political conservatism. Lev Mikhailovich is the town "Gvir" and Zionist Leibush Gutzeit. The image created by his material success and alleged industrial and commercial toughness had always puzzled me, contrasting as it did with my impressions of him as a soft and gentle, somewhat blundering, and probably henpecked man much concerned with spiritual values, with self-improvement, and with the acquisition of abstract knowledge in Judaic and general lore. I remember Mrs. Gutzeit, once at a dinner in their home, offering a toast to her daughter studying in Italy - a strange and awesome and far-away land to me, at that time - and of course, the gifted and most democratic Gutzeit's son Yasha.

Lev Isakovich is the name of the "nice" bundist Myshkovsky, and Lev Mironovich of the "Zealot" Bunin. Myshkovsky was married to Clara Mironovna who was not only a very ardent and active Zionist but also one of very strong right-wing tendencies. We thus did not have to argue with Myshkovsky – Clara Mironovna could do it better – but we had to argue a lot with "Leibele" Bunin. In the course of the arguments, our opposition to his sociopolitical position carried over to his personality. Yet in retrospect Bunin appears to me to have been a fine representative of the Bundist and Jewish working-class masses of Slutsk, a highly efficient organizer and leader of integrity and high ideals and principles.

I cannot leave this epitaph without revealing some personal feelings about the charming girls of our Zeire-Zion Organization: Fanya Kreph, a subtle blond of level-headed intellect and deeply felt emotions; Basya Barnak, full of whims, intuitive perceptions, and striking originalities; Mutya Peimer and Besya Chozik with whom I was secretly in love but who never knew it; and others. Where are they all and what has become of them? – -

* * *

It was a hot day, June 30, 1941. My wife and I and two friends had left New York a few days before on an automobile trip to Mexico. Hitler had invaded Russia, and the day before the war was raging, according to the communique we read in a newspaper bought in Nashville, Tennessee, in the direction of Baranovichi and Luck (Lutzk). We had been motoring all day and stopped late in the evening, strangely, in a city named Palestine in the state of Texas. We had seen no newspaper all day and could find none in Palestine. The next day, however, we bought a New York Times in San Antonio, Texas, and there I read that "the battle is now in the direction of Bobruisk and Borisov". Slutsk was obviously already in Hitler's inferno. Later, I heard that the remainder of my family in Chaplitsy near Slutsk was drowned in a Polesie river trying to escape. I heard no more.

Queens College, Long Island, N.Y.

[Page XXIII]

A Grandson's Reflections on Slutsk

By Emanuel Rackman

Slutsk I have never seen. Yet her mood and her commitment appear to be as much a part of my personal experience as if I had walked her streets and breathed her air and sat at the feet of her wise men. Though I was born in Albany, New York, to a mother who was also born there, I was reared and nourished from early childhood upon the beautiful tales and legends of Slutsk. My distinguished father is from Slutsk; my first Rebbe at Yeshivah University also from Slutsk. The Spiritual Prince of American Jewry, the philosopher and Talmudic scholar of our generation, Rabbi Joseph Dov Soloweichick is named after his great-grandfather who was the Rabbi of Slutsk. He is also the exponent of a method in Halacha which his grandfather began to develop under the guidance of a savant of Slutsk (See page 81). 1 feel, therefore, much of a spiritual native of Slutsk and I am indeed grateful for the invitation to participate in this memorial volume.

It is difficult enough, if not impossible, to defend the thesis that there are racial or national characteristics. How does one then dare go further and posit characteristics also for a city! The objection is well taken. Slutsk was very much like other cities – it had its poor and its rich, its saints and its scoundrels, its scholars and its morons – everything that other cities had. But a city also has aspirations – and Slutsk seemed to aspire to some particular greatness. The aspiration made her people proud, and 1, too, always craved to share that pride. When in 1956 I was privileged to be a member of the first group of Rabbis to visit in the Soviet Union, I tried to obtain permission to visit Slutsk. I wanted to see what remained of one of Jewry's great centers of learning. Many of her exiled scholars I knew. I had met them in America and in Israel. Her Yeshiva in exile I also knew, and her Yeshiva in Israel – now known as Yetshivat Hadorom in Rehovot – I, as an officer of the Rabbinical Council of America, had helped to found. But Slutsk herself I could not see. She remains only an aspiration to her widely scattered grand children who were born to her children in other lands.

In Slutsk it seems the gift of life meant the opportunity to study Torah. He who studied Torah was alive and free; he who did not study, alas, was in chains. The Rabbis there so contended on questions of Jewish law, that they often caused the community bitterly to divide into two camps in support of the contending positions. As it is so well known, in Slutsk the war was waged against Hasidism and against the teaching of Mussar in Yeshivot; also Socialism and Zionism were hotly debated there.

However, the scholars there were also aware of their own limitation and with the cultivation of the most exacting standards of Jewish scholarship they also cultivated a sense of humor about their own inadequacies, a skepticism with regard to their own mastery of the truth, and an eye which impishly and devilishly could unmask the hypocrite who pretended to be a saint, and that which presumed to be scholarship but was not truly so. Slutsk was so committed to the loftiest standards of intellectual excellence that her leaders viewed with suspicion any new course or movement lest it be mere camouflage for mediocrity.

Thus, alas, I have no vision of Slutsk as a citadel of peace, nor even as a bastion of toleration. On the contrary, it was rather a city of intolerance – she was intolerant of sham, hypocrisy and pretentiousness, of progressives whose visions were mirages, and of conservatives whose obstreperousness reeked of omniscience.

That did not mean that the people there knew no happiness. They may have lived in intellectual heights but they never froze in the ratified atmosphere as an incident of their icy intellectualism. Indeed, their capacity for happiness was greater because of their exacting standards. Their happiness had depth. It was not Hasidic singing and dancing to induce a hypnotic spell which stimulates a moment of communion with G-d. It was rather the kind of happiness that overcome them as from the innermost recesses of their being, they became aware of personal fulfillment in their knowledge of G-d and His word.

Slutsk had been known as a center of Torah for

[Page XXIV]

many generations. When for a short period there was not a big Yeshivah there, the immortal Gaon known as Ridbaz went to the Yeshivah of Slobodka and imported from there the most revered and beloved of all teachers of Talmud of that era – Rabbi Issar Zalman Meltzer together with a score of young men. With this nucleus, the Yeshiva of Slutsk was founded and thus Slutsk again became a center of higher Jewish learning. The town was transformed. The Yeshiva students in their highly modern external appearance but imbued with Torah and true Jewish ethics induced a sense of awe and respect in all the inhabitants. My father told me of the joy of the Ridbaz when he used to enter the Beth-Midrash to visit with the students. He would stand in the doorway virtually unseen and simply listen. Tears would well up in his eyes. He had resanctified a city by a simple relocation of fifteen men!

Not without a quarrel, however, was this achieved, The other Rabbi of the city, the Gaon R. Mair Pehmer, attacked the new Yeshiva, especially because the study of Mussar was taught there. This attack precipitated a violent controversy all over the land with regard to the propriety of teaching Mussar as a special subject. Needless to say, none would deny the importance of training in ethics, which has been the practice of all

Rabbis ever since. However, should this training be assumed to be the subtle, indirect *consequence* of regular Torah study, or are some special hours and indoctrination required for it? It is hard to believe that so much bitterness and personal vilification would ensue because of so seemingly simple and innocuous a problem of curriculum. However, in Slutsk Torah-study was one's life and, therefore any issue with regard to it was taken so seriously that any new approach to curriculum had to be challenged. just as Slutsk had been a historic battleground between "Mitnagdim" and "Hasidim", because Hasidism was regarded as a threat to the primacy of study in the Jewish hierarchy of values, so the Mussar movement represented an indirect insult to the efficacy of Torah scholarship by itself to produce men of excellent moral character and profound religious commitment.

Wars, however, move men's hearts – especially when they are purely verbal and ideological. My grandfather was a Melamed in Slutsk and he favored the Ridbas. On one occasion he had an opportunity to demonstrate in the home of a champion of the opposing Rabbi Mair Pehmer the great learning of the Ridbaz. The incident occurred in the Sukkah of one of the community's most prominent laymen whose son was my grandfather's pupil. The follower of R. Pehmer had erroneously ruled on a matter of Jewish law. The ruling was contrary to that of the Ridbaz. The host complained about the Ridbaz and my grandfather was able to prove that the Ridbaz was right and evoke the concurrence of the host who, theretofore, had been hostile to the great scholar. That my grandfather was able to add to the prestige of the Ridbaz so delighted him that he proudly communicated this achievement to his children. How different were the trophies which men sought in that atmosphere than those we crave today!

This closing note of my epitaph was written by one of the great Rabbis of Slutsk who for years was supported by an affluent father-in-law and was therefore, able to write great scholarly works. When the wheel of fortune turned, and this father-in-law lost everything, the son-in-law was forced to take a Rabbinic post to earn a livelihood. His first work published thereafter, bore the following inscription after his name as author, "Presently enslaved; but in the past a free man".

Slutsk is now in chains. But her spirit is free. Wherever her children are, her spirit endures and inspires.

Far Rockaway, N. Y.

[Page XXV]

The Heritage of Slutsk

By Mordecai Waxman

Of the physical Slutsk, I know next to nothing. I have a mental image of huddled houses, of frequently mired streets, of a square girdled by synagogues, and houses of Study, and of "der kalte schul" – a big – and in the winter months – often deserted house of worship, which was just too large to heat properly. I know that it had its students, and its laborers, its saints and its sinners, its genteel ladies and its harridans, its societies and its charities, and its study groups. I know that most of the people who sauntered or scurried through its streets were Jews, that Yiddish was the language in which voices were raised, endearments uttered and debates conducted. In short, I know what facts can tell me. And yet, of course, I know nothing. Never having been to Slutsk nor seen its counterpart on the landscape of Eastern Europe, I find my imagination unable to bridge the gap and visualize that historic place which is so much remembered and cherished by all its descendants.

That Slutsk is dead with almost all its latter day inhabitants. I can never hope to know it. But there is a Slutsk that I do know. It is the spiritual Slutsk. I know it because I have met some of the people who carried it abroad with them when they left native home to seek other parts of the world. I know it because I met it in Chicago and in New York and in casual conversation on a bus in Tel Aviv. I have seen it glowing from printed pages and have heard its overtones in the spoken word; and I know it most of all because it resided in my parental home and because, insofar as I know myself, it is a part of me, who am a second generation of the expatriates of Slutsk.

If I, then write about it, it is out of the deepest knowledge, out of a journey into a personal interior, and I deal with what is more characteristic of Slutsk than its stones and its houses and its streets; more characteristic and more enduring. Because I write of the spirit it sent forth abroad and that planted itself in other landscapes and yielded new fruits.

What then is the spiritual Slutsk and what are its values which I have observed, which I have inherited, which I cherish, which I would transmit?

The Slutsk I have encountered was a Jewish world at peace with itself. The product of long centuries of Jewish thought and experience; it had achieved a maturity about its Jewish values. Its descendants, whom I have met abroad, have been notably free of rejections and extremism, of narrowness of affirmation and negation which are, regretfully, so prevalent in our midst. It was suffused with religion – it took it seriously; it observed it devoutly. But it was devoid of the fanaticism which was so rampant elsewhere. It produced people who spoke, read and wrote Yiddish, but did not confuse it with the totality of Jewish life and culture. Zion struck a responsive chord in its heart, but it was not prepared to set the totality of Jewish experience aside and to say that nothing save Zionism was important. Hebrew was a cause dear to its heart and it sent abroad men who spoke and wrote in Hebrew and enriched Hebrew letters. But they did not make the mistake of regarding the language as an end rather than a means. Always, there abided with them the notion that Hebrew was not merely a "lashon", but rather a *lasbon ha-kodesh*.

In short, the spirit of Slutsk abroad has been a spirit of wholeness and of balance. Nothing Jewish has been alien to it. But it has insisted on harmony, on a golden mean, on the recognition and cultivation of many values, each in proper balance with the other.

This mature harmony of the spirit was the natural outgrowth of certain well-recognized and cultivated values.

There was first of all, a sheer love of Jewishness. Slutsk did not feel that Jewishness was a burden to be borne, a state to be regretted. It might have laughed at the dictum of Heinrich Heine that: "Judaism is not a religion, but a misfortune." It is a sentiment which has been shared by many Jews plummeted into the modern

[Page XXVI]

world. Slutsk might have laughed at the witticism, but it certainly would have rejected the sentiment. It had been nurtured in the feeling that it is a privilege to be a Jew. It was a tenet of the prayer book which came easily to its life; it was the underlying sentiment of the traditional literature in which it was at home; it was the theme of the Sabbath and the festivals in which it found both joy and awe.

Hand in hand with this love of Jewishness and fundamental to it went the love of Torah and study. If not everyone in Slutsk was a scholar, everyone at least appreciated scholarship. The familiar "techinah" of the Jewish woman as she kindled her candles on Friday evening that: "even as the candles glow, so, I pray, may the eyes of my children glow with the light of the Torah" was the most natural prayer in Slutsk.

Study was both work and avocation in Slutsk. It had its workers and its businessmen who competed in knowledge and recognition of recondite texts. It had its students who studied diligently through the livelong day and were the living exemplars of Bialik's HaMatmid. It was at home in the Talmud, the Midrash and in their commentaries. It took them seriously. But it could also appreciate a scholarly jest. It could relish sharpness of intellect, seriously intended, and equally enjoy a cynical employment of the same faculties.

Slutsk above all strove for clarity and lucidity. While it valued sheer knowledge, it also demanded that knowledge be combined with common sense, or with that more elusive and broader quality which is called "sechel". It sought the application of knowledge to life, but insisted that the result should not be merely an absurd triumph of intellect and text, but rather a practical illumination of life and experience. If it believed wholeheartedly in the pursuit of knowledge, as it saw it realized in its own Jewish literature, it demanded that knowledge be the companion of reason. Pilpul, studying the Torah, may have been a favorite sport, but the real preoccupation of Slutsk was meaningful living.

The chief achievement of Slutsk was that it combined these attributes with a sense for the demands made upon Jews by the modern spirit which was burgeoning in many parts of the world. There were many Jewish communities which sent their residents forth into the world of the West unequipped to deal with the intellectual and sociological demands of the twentieth century. Slutsk, by contrast, was a community which both sensed and responded to the currents in the world and sent its expatriates able to cope with new situations with a spirit and a temper of mind equal to the challenge.

The Haskalah movement which represented the response of a segment of Jewry to a world coming into being found a hospitable home in Slutsk. Mendele Mocher Sfarim had studied for some time in Slutsk. The memory of the later Mendele was treasured in his temporary abode. In Slutsk there were many who spoke and cherished modern Hebrew, who followed the Hebrew press, who responded to the play of new ideas. Zionism was at home in Slutsk, even as the Talmud was at home there. The Jewish philosophers of the middle ages, dead and forgotten in many other communities, were part of the intellectual fare of many in Slutsk. In brief, Slutsk was a community in which the modern spirit of the new era was fully alive side by side with ancient ideas and practices. This all-embracing spirit was carried by those who departed from Slutsk into other lands.

Perhaps the outstanding quality of that spirit is the right of free thought and dissent which it carries, combined with an abiding and unquestioning love of Judaism. The ability to disagree and yet remain within the same universe of discourse is a quality to be cherished. It is the quintessence of the harmony and maturity which Slutsk achieved. It is more than tolerance. It is tolerance without a diminution of concern and it implies that behind the disagreement and dissent there are values so deeply imbedded and so deeply accepted that no disagreement may affect them. This is the spirit which I have seen in many whom Slutsk sent abroad and this is the quality which I value most.

All these qualities of Slutsk which I cherish – its love of Torah and learning, its cultivation of knowledge applied to life, its intellectual lucidity and clarity, its code of Jewish living and behavior, its free spirit and its recognition of the right to dissent, are, perhaps caught up in a story of the last Slutzker Rav R. Issar Zalmon Meltzer. A question arose in a Slutsk synagogue during the Sabbath services whether the prayer of "Av HaRachamim" should be recited on a "Shabbos M'Vorchim" preceding the month of Sivan. Usually that somber prayer is not recited on a Sabbath when the new Hebrew month is welcomed. The Sabbath before the month of Sivan, however, falls during the time of Sefira which is a period of mourning, and the cantor therefore chanted the prayer. But many worshippers in the congregation did not agree with the cantor's decision and began to bang upon the benches in protest When someone of the congregation turned to the rabbi for his opinion in the matter, Rabbi Meltzer is credited to have replied: "that is exactly the right custom. The cantor recites the 'Av HaRachamim' prayer and some of the worshippers bang the benches in protest!".

[Page XXVII]

This decision came fittingly from the Rav of Slutsk and he spoke the spirit of a community which was well versed, which encompassed a variety of theories and opinions but still worshipped in the same manner and out of the same prayer book.

The Jewish life of our generation has been benefited by this spirit of Slutsk. It has been enlightened and uplifted by some of the men whom Slutsk produced, who have written and preached and lectured in many tongues and lived their conceptions in many lands. It is a spirit to be cherished and to be developed in the community of tomorrow.

It has been reported by many – including Slutzkites themselves – that the residents of Slutsk went about with a bent index finger. Apparently, they took pride in their native town and were not backward about mentioning their distinctions. However, when challenged to enumerate their virtues and to count them off on their fingers, they were often reduced to bending the index finger and saying: "in the first place, I come from Slutsk." Many remained with only one bent finger, unable to adduce further and personal virtues. But one finger might well have been enough, for no Slutzker could readily escape the spirit and the virtues which Slutsk bequeathed to all its children.

Great Neck, N.Y

[Page XXVIII]

Acknowledgement to Benefactors

Prepared for online presentation by Genia Hollander

The American "Slutsk Yizkor Book Committee" wishes to express its sincere appreciation to the following organizations and individuals for their assistance in making possible this publication. May their generosity be a source of inspiration to others and an everlasting pride to their descendants.

The Lefrak Foundation (Harry and Sarah Lefrak)
Slutzker Shul (Morris Asofsky)
United Slutzker Relief (Israel Schwaidelson)
Hlusker Benevolent Ass'n. (Ellix Richman)
Sholom Family Circle Soc. (Abraham Maisel)
Ablon Finishers, Inc. (Abraham Maisel)
Progressive Slutzker Young Men's Benev. Ass'n. (Samuel Travin)

Family name	First name(s)
A	
ABRAMSON	Ida
ALTMAN	Mr. & Mrs. Eli
APPLEBAUM	Mr. & Mrs. Sam
ARONOWITZ	Mrs
B	
BABKOW	Sam
BADEHAN	Mr. & Mrs. Meyer
BECKER	Mr. & Mrs. William
BERKOWITZ	Mr. & Mrs. Kalman
BERKOWITZ	Mr. & Mrs. Reuben
BEZBORODKO	Mr. & Mrs. David
BLECHER	Libby
BUNIN	Dr. & Mrs. Abraham
BUSSEL	Mr. & Mrs. Eli
BUSSEL	Mr. & Mrs. Max
C	
CANTOR	Mr. & Mrs. Joseph
CANTOR	Mr. & Mrs. Saul

CHARNEY	Mr. & Mrs. Alex
CHASEN	Mr. & Mrs. H.
CHASIN	Mr. & Mrs. Sam
CHINITZ	Rabbi Abraham & Mrs.
CHINITZ	Mr. & Mrs. Louis
CHINITZ	E. Ch.
COHEN	Mr. & Mrs. Isaak
COHEN	Mr. & Mrs. Max
COHEN	Minie
COHEN	Sam
COHEN	Mr. & Mrs. S.&.T.
COHEN	Mrs. Z.
D	
DEREVENSKY	Mr. & Mrs. Morris
DIAMONT	Mr. & Mrs. L.
DOMALTZ	Dr. & Mrs. Aaron
DOMNITZ	Mr. & Mrs.Samuel
DUBOWSKY	Mr. & Mrs. Z.
E	
EISEN	Charles & Fannie

EISENSTADT	Mrs. R.
EPSTEIN	Mr. & Mrs. Harry
EPSTEIN	Mr. S. & Mrs.
EIKIND	Mr. & Mrs. Nathan

F

FAYNBERG	Mr. Meyer & Mrs.
FRIEDLAND	Gertrude

G

GARFINKEL	Mrs. Emerson
GIMELSTEIN	Mr. & Mrs. Morris
GOLDBERG	Mr. & Mrs. Sam
GOLDBLUM	Mrs. Anna
GALLINSON	Ben
GOLDSTEIN	Chasha & Mendel
GOREN	Mr. & Mrs. Jacob
GOREN	Louis
GOREN	Mr. & Mrs. William
GREENWALD	Mr. & Mrs. M.
GWASDOFF	Mr. & Mrs. Sam

H	
HELFLAND	Mr. & Mrs. George
HELFLAND	Mr. & Mrs. Victor
HERMAN	Mr. &a Mrs. L
HOLES	Louise & Son, Inc.
HOLLAND	Dr. & Mrs. Reuben J.
HOROWITZ	Mr. & Mrs. Sam

J	
JACOBS	Mr. & Mrs. Isadore

K	
KAMINSKY	Mr. & Mrs. Max
KAPLAN	Mr. & Mrs. Ariall
KAPLAN	Mr. & Mrs. Bernard
KATCHEN	Mr. & Mrs. George
KATTEF	Mr. & Mrs. David
KATZ	Rabbi & Mrs. Nehemiah
KENT	Mr. & Mrs. H.
KLOTZ	Mrs. Minnie
KOSBERG	Miss L.
KRONITZ	Ruby

KULICK	Mr. & Mrs. Hyman
KULOCK	Mr. & Mrs. Morris
KOOSMAN	Morris
L	
LEVINE	Mr. & Mrs. Julius
LEVOVITZ	Rabbi & Mrs. M.L.
LIFF	Mr. & Mrs. Samuel
LIFSHITZ	Mr. & Mrs. Jacob
LUBKIN	Mr. Samuel
M	
MAISEL	Abraham & Chaika
MAISEL	Mr. & Mrs. Charles
MAISES	Mr. & Mrs. Isidore
MASLAN	Mr. & Mrs. Philip
MEISEL	Mr. & Mrs. Morris
MILKOWITZ	Mr. & Mrs. Harry
MILKOWITZ	Mr. & Mrs. Max
MILLER	Mr. & Mrs. I.
MISHELOV	Mr. & Mrs. Isidore
MONES	Yale (formerly Rubinstein)

N	
NELSON	Mr. & Mrs. J
NISSENSON	Mr. & Mrs. Harry
O	
OCKO	Mr. & Mrs. Ely
ORNSTRAT	Edith
P	
PEIMER	Mr. & Mrs. Chaim
PICKHOLTZ	Rachelle
PORTON	Mr. & Mrs. Samuel
POSES	Samuel & family
POST	Mr. & Mrs. David
R	
RACKMAN	Rabbi and Mrs. David
RACHLIN	Mr. & Mrs. S
REZNICK	Mr. & Mrs. Paul
RICH	Mr. & Mrs. A.
RICHMAN	Mr. & Mrs. Ellix

RIVIN	Moe and Louis
ROCKMAN	Rabbi & Mrs. David
ROLNICK	Mr. & Mrs. A
ROSENTHAL	Mr. & Mrs Hyman
ROTHOLZ	Esther
RUBIN	Mr. & Mrs. Max
RUBINSTEIN	Mr. & Mrs. Nathan
RUBNITZ	Solomon

S

SARKIND	Mr. & Mrs. R.
SCHILDKRET	Rev. & Mrs. S.
SCHWALDELSON	Mr. & Mrs. Israel
SCHWARTZ	Ira and Mrs.
SCHWARTZ	Mr. & Mrs. Isaac
SIEGAL	Hyman
SCHWARTZ	Mr. & Mrs. Louis
SEROTOWITZ	Mrs. Mollie
SHAPIRO	Mrs.
SHEIN	Mrs. E.R.
SHELB	Benjamin P
SHIFFMAN	Mr. & Mrs. Benjamin

SHIFFMAN	Mr. & Mrs. I.
SHIFFMAN	Mr. & Mrs. Jerome
SHUB	Mr. & Mrs. Harry
S.N.A.Stationary Co. (Maisel)	
SMELKINSON Bros	
T	
TRAVIN	Mr. & Mrs. S.&.T.
TULMAN	Mr. & Mrs. Morris
U	
USDAN	Mr. & Mrs. David
W	
WALLENRAD	Dr. & Mrs. Reuben
WASSERMAN	Mr. & Mrs. Samuel
WAXMAN	Rabbi & Mrs. Nissan
WAXMAN	Mr. & Mrs. Reuben
WEINER	Miss. R.
WEINSTOCK	Joseph

Z	
ZEIDES	Rev. & Mrs. H.
ZIRKEL	Mr. & Mrs. Samuel

[Page XXIX]

Index of Names in English Section

In English Section

Prepared for online presentation by Genia Hollander

BERDICHEVSKY		XXI
BERKOWITZ	David & Mrs.	XXVIII
BERKOWITZ	Kalman & Mrs.	XXVIII
BERKOWITZ	Reuben & Mrs.	XXVIII
BEZBORODKO	David & Mrs.	XXVIII
BECKER	Libby	XXVIII
BOKACHICH	Yoan	XXI
BOROHOV		XXI
BORUCHOVICH	Malke	XXII
BRENNER		XXI
BRONSTEIN		XXII
BUNIN	Dr. Abraham & Mrs.	XVIII
BUNIN	Lev	XXII
BUSSEL	Eli & Mrs.	XXVIII
BUSSEL	Max & Mrs.	XXVIII
BYALIK		XXI
C		
CANTOR	Joseph & Mrs.	XXVIII
CANTOR	Mr. Saul & Mrs.	XXVIII
CARL		XIII
CHARNEY	Alex & Mrs.	XXVIII

CHARNEY	Eli	XXII
CHASEN	H & Mrs.	XXVIII
CHASIN	Sam & Mrs.	XXVIII
CHINITZ	Abraham Rabbi & Mrs	XXVIII
CHINITZ	E. Ch. & Mrs.	XXVIII
CHINITZ	Louis & Mrs.	XXVIII
CHIPCHIN	the lawyer	XVI
CHIPCHIN	Solomon	XXII
COHEN	Max & Mrs.	XXVIII
COHEN	Minie	XXVIII
COHEN	Sam	XXVIII
COHEN	S.T. & Mrs.	XXVIII
COHEN	Z and Mrs.	XXVIII

D

DAVIDOVICH	Yakub	XXI
DEREVENSKY	Morris & Mrs.	XXVIII
DIAMONT	L. & Mrs.	XXVIII
DOMNITZ	Aaron Dr. & Mrs.	XXVIII
DOMINITZ	Samuel & Mrs.	XXVIII
DUBOWSKY	Z & Mrs.	XXVIII

E		
EINHORN	David	XXII
EISEN	Charles & Fannie	XXVIII
EPSTEIN	Harry & Mrs.	XXVIII
EPSTEIN	S. & Mrs.	XXVIII
ETKIND	Mr. & Mrs.	XXVIII
F		
FAYNBERG	Meyer & Mrs.	XXVIII
FEINBERG		XXII
FRIEDLAND	Gertrude	XXVIII
G		
GABAI		XXII
GARFINKEL	Emerson & Mrs.	XXVIII
GENDELIOVITCH	Refoel, Shlomo, Gershon	XVI
GIMELSTEIN	Morris & Mrs.	XXVIII
GLEB	of Minsk	X
GOERING		XIV
GOLDBERG	Sam & Mrs.	XXVIII
GOLDBERG	Anna, Mrs.	XXVIII

GOLDSTEIN	Chasha & Mendel	XXVIII
GOREN	Jacob & Mrs.	XXVIII
GOREN	William & Mrs.	
GOREN	Louis & Mrs.	XXVIII
GRANKSHAW		X, XIV
GREENWALD	M & Mrs.	XXVIII
GUTZEIT	Mrs.	XXII
GUTZEIT	Leibush	XXII
GUTZEIT	Yasha	XXII
GWASDOFF	Sam & Mrs.	XXVIII
H		
HANDLER	Meyer S.	XVI
HEINE	Heinrich	XXII, XXV
HELFAND	George & Mrs.	XXVIII
HELFAND	Victor & Mrs.	XXVIII
HERMAN	L. & Mrs.	XXVIII
HERTZL		XXII
HESS		XXI
HINDUS	Morris & Mrs.	XV, XVII
HLUSKER	Benevolent Ass'n (Eleix Richman)	XXVIII

HOLES	Louis son inc.	XXVIII
HOLLAND	Reuben J. Dr. & Mrs.	XXVIII
HOROWITZ	Sam & Mrs.	XXVIII
I		
ISRAEL	of Mezbizh	X, XXI
J		
JACOB	Isador Mr. & Mrs.	XXVIII
K		
KAMINSKY	Max & Mrs.	XXVIII
KANTOROWICH	the merchant	XVIII
KAPLAN	Arial & Mrs.	XXVIII
KAPLAN	Bernard & Mrs.	XXVIII
KATCHEN	George & Mrs.	XXVIII
KATEFF	D. & Mrs.	XXVIII
KATZ	Nehemia, Rabbi & Mrs.	XXVIII
KENT	H. & Mrs.	XXVIII
KLOTZ	Minnie Mrs.	XXVIII
KOOSHMAN	Morris & Mrs.	XXVIII

KOSBERG	L. Miss.	XXVIII
KRAMER	Reb Sheftel	XXI
KREPEH	Fanya	XXII
KRONITZ	Buby	XXVIII
KUBE	Wilhelm	XIV
KULICK	Hyman & Mrs.	XXVIII
KULOK	Morris & Mrs.	XXVIII
L		
LEFRAK FOUNDATION	Harry & Sarah	XXVIII
LEVINE	Julius & Mrs.	XXVIII
LEVOVITZ	M.L. Rabbi & Mrs.	XXVIII
LIBERMAN	Bluma	XVIII
LIFF	Samuel & Mrs.	XXVIII
LIFSHITZ	Jacob & Mrs.	XXVIII
LIPSTITZ	Ilya	XXI
LOHSE	Heinrich	XIV
LUBAVICHER	Rabbi	X
LUBKIN	Samuel Mr.	XXVIII

MISKOSVSKY	Lev	XXII
N		
NADSON		XXII
NELSON	I & Mrs.	XXVIII
NEUMARK	brothers	XVI
NISSENSON	Harry & Mrs.	XXVIII
O		
OKO	Ely & Mrs.	XXVIII
OLELKO	Vladimiroch	XVIII
OLELKNIVICHI	Sophia	X, XVIII
ORNSTART	Edith	XXVIII
P		
PEIMER	Meir Rabbi	XXIV
PEIMER	Chaim & Mrs.	XXVIII
PEIMER	Mutya	XXII
PERETZ		XXII
PICKOLTZ	Mrs.	XVIII
PICKOLTZ	Rachele	XXVIII
PINSKER		XXII

POPOFF		XVI
PORTON	Samuel & Mrs.	XXVIII
POST	David & Mrs.	XXVIII
R		
RACHLIN	S. & Mrs.	XXVIII
RACKMAN	David Rabbi & Mrs.	XXVIII
RACKMAN	Emanuel	XXIII
RADZIWILL	Boguslav	XXI
RADZIWILL	Januez	XVIII
RAZRAN	Gregory & Mrs.	XVIII,XXVIII
RESNICK	Paul & Mrs.	XXVIII
RICH	A. & Mrs.	XXVIII
RICHMAN	Ellix & Mrs.	XXVIII
RIVIN	Moe & Louis	XXVIII
ROLNICK	A. & Mrs.	XXVIII
ROZENTHAL	Hyman & Mrs.	XXVIII
ROTHOLZ	Esther	XXVIII
RUBIN	Max & Mrs.	XXVIII
RUBINSTEIN	Nathan & Mrs.	XXVIII
RUBNITZ	Solomon	XXVIII

S		
SABBATAI	Zevo	IX
SARKING	R & Mrs.	XXVIII
SCHILDKRET	S. Rev. & Mrs	XXVIII
SCHWAIDELSON	Israel & Mrs.	XXVIII
SCHWARTZ	Ira & Mrs.	XXVIII
SCHWARTZ	Isaac & Mrs.	XXVIII
SCHWARTZ	Louis & Mrs.	XXVIII
SEGAL	Isaac & Mrs.	XXVIII
SEROTOWITZ	Molie Mrs.	XXVIII
SHAPIRO	Mrs.	XXVIII
SHEIB	Benjamin P.	XXVIII
SHEIN	E.R. Mrs.	XXVIII
SHIFMAN	Benjamin & Mrs.	XXVIII
SHIFMAN	I. & Mrs.	XXVIII
SHIFMAN	Jerome & Mrs.	XXVIII
SHILDKRET	Lev. Dr.	XXII
SHNEUR		XXII
SHOLOM	Family Circle Soc. (Abraham Maisel)	XXVIII
SHUB	Harry & Mrs.	XXVIII
SLUTZKER	Prog.Young Men's Benev.	XXVIII

	Ass'n (Samuel Travin)	
SLUTZKER	Shul (Morris Asofsky)	XXVIII
SLUTZKER	United Relief (Israel Schwaidelson)	XXVIII
SMELKINSON	Bros	XXVIII
SMOLENSKY		XXI
SOLOMYAK		XXII
SOLOWEICHICK	Dov. Rabbi	XXIII
T		
THEODOSIUS	Vasilevich	XXI
TRAVIN	S. & Mrs.	XXVIII
TULMAN	Morris & Mrs.	XXVIII
W		
WALLENROD	Reuben. Dr. & Mrs.	XXVIII
WASSERMAN	Samuel & Mrs.	XXVIII
WAXMAN	Mordecai	XXV
WAXMAN	Nissan. Rabbi & Mrs.	IX, XXVIII
WAXMAN	Reuben & Mrs.	XXVIII
WEINER	R. Mrs.	XXVIII

WEINSTOCK	Joseph & Mrs.	XXVIII
WICHMAN		XIV
Y		
YAROSHEVICH	Karp	XXI
YAROSHEVITZEVA	Meshchanka	XXI
YAROSHEVICH	Stephan	XXI
Z		
ZEIDES	H. Rev. & Mrs.	XXVIII
ZENNER	General	XIV
ZIRKEL	Samuel & Mrs.	XXVIII

NAME INDEX

A

Elyashberg [Elyasberg], 497
Elye-Leyb (the butcher), 273
Elyotka (The Thief), 497
Enzil, 15, 497
Eplboim [Applebaum], 497
Eplboym, 191
Epshtein, 301
Epshteyn, 15, 19, 193, 240, 427, 428, 498, 499, 502
Epshteyn (The Dentist), 499
Epshteyn (The Firefighter), 499
Epshteyn (The Flour Storekeeper), 498
Epshteyn [Epstein], 498
Epstajn, 257, 258, 260, 261, 262, 263, 401
Epstayn, 390
Epstein, 23, 32, 33, 34, 58, 59, 60, 62, 178, 199, 211, 214, 229, 240, 327, 395, 411, 565, 574
Eshkol, 405, 429
Eshman, 22, 429, 499
Eskolsky, 224
Ester (The Milkmaid), 426
Etinger, 422
Etkind, 574
Evin, 32
Eydlman, 423
Eyzer [Oyzer, 532
Eyzer [Oyzer], 441, 497

F

Fainberg, 27
Faisakhowycz, 323
Fajmer, 267
Faygenberg, 19, 199, 502
Faygenberg [Feygenberg], 502
Faymer, 16
Fayn [Fein, Fine], 503
Faynberg, 503, 565, 574
Faynberg [Feinberg, Fineberg], 503
Faytl (the Pharmacist), 288
Faytl [Paytl, Peytl], 433
Faytlson, 502
Fayvl (The Synagogue Sexton), 502
Fayvl (the Town Sexton), 81
Fayvl (the wagon driver), 246
Feder, 506
Feimer, 371
Fein, 122
Feinberg, 58, 60, 76, 120, 394, 412, 556, 574
Feinberg [Faynberg], 503

Feinstein, 314, 503, 504
Feinstein [Faynshteyn], 503
Feiss, 408, 504, 506
Feiss [Fayss], 504
Feitlson, 29
Feivishowitz, 408, 502
Feivishowitz [Fayvishovitsh], 502
Feker, 336
Feller, 86, 88, 89, 90, 507
Ferovskaya, 98
Feygenberg, 502
Feymer, 18
Fialko, 408, 502
Ficus [Picus?], 505
Finke the bath attendant, 341
Finkel, 256, 385, 504
Finkelshteyn [Finkelstein], 242
Finkelstein, 31, 412, 505
Finkelstein [Finkelshteyn], 504
Fish, 276, 348, 505
Fishel, 260, 505
Fishka (The Lame), 505
Fishke (the Lame), 191
Fishkin-Horn, 85, 505
Fishl, 505
Flayshtik, 163
Flayshtsik, 161
Fleysher [Fleischer, Flaysher], 506
Fleyshtshik, 506
Fleyshtshik [Fleyshtsik], 506
Fogelman, 111, 499
Folke (the tailor), 49
Fortman, 314, 408, 500, 501
Frank, 197, 507
Frankl, 508
Frankl [Frankel], 508
Frankman, 508
Freed, 323
Freinkman, 244
Frenkl, 198
Frid [Freed, Fried], 508
Fridland, 508
Fridman, 508
Frid-Rabkin, 508
Friedland, 565, 574
Froebel, 204
Frokovnik [Prokovnik?], 507
Frumkin, 257, 507

U

V

www.ingramcontent.com/pod-product-compliance
Lightning Source LLC
Chambersburg PA
CBHW062019090426

42811CB00005B/906